# WHERE TO EAT IN AMERICA

## New Edition

## EXECUTIVE EDITORS
William Rice and Burton Wolf

## SENIOR EDITOR
Kate Slate

## CONTRIBUTORS
Molly Abraham
Jane L. Baker
Virginia Bartlett
David Bauer
Myram Borders
Barbara Bratel
Sharon Cadwallader
Felicia Coates
Bill Collins
Carol DeMasters
John Dorsey
Nathalie Dupree
Tom Fitzmorris
Kathleen Lancaster Fliegel
Tom Gable
Ruth Gray
Carol Haddix
Paula Hamilton
Marge Hanley
Ellen Hawes
Richard W. Johnston
Lincoln Kaye
Richard and Carol Kreck
Carole Lalli
Karen K. Marshall
Elizabeth McIlhaney
Donna Morgan
Françoise Neill
Janice Okun
Eleanor Ostman
Stan Reed
Trish Rich
Monda Rosenberg
Yvonne Rothert
Marie Ryckman
Frederick W. Woolsey

## EDITORIAL STAFF
Melissa Davis and Mardee Haidin

# WHERE TO EAT IN AMERICA

## New Edition

An indispensable guide to finding *what* you want to eat *when* you want to eat it in 50 of North America's most-traveled cities

EDITED BY WILLIAM RICE
AND BURTON WOLF

Random House New York

To the memory of Duncan Hines and Silas Spitzer, who searched our country for the best in dining in earlier eras, and to Calvin Trillin, to whose *American Fried* we hope we have added poached, baked and flambéed

---

And, as always, to Carol, Emily, Stephen, Andrew and James

---

 Published in the United States by Random House, Inc., New York, and simultaneously in Canada by Random House of Canada Limited, Toronto.

Library of Congress Cataloging in Publication Data
Main entry under title:

Where to eat in America.
1. Restaurants, lunch rooms, etc.—United States—Directories. I. Rice, William, 1938– II. Wolf, Burton.
TX907.W48 1979 647'.9573 79-15073
ISBN 0-394-73728-8

Manufactured in the United States of America
98765432
First Edition

---

# CONTENTS

# Introduction

One day as we were talking about food equipment, the subject of restaurants popped up.

"I'm tired of traveling to a strange city, asking for directions to a good restaurant and ending up in a plastic palace or being told the best food in town comes from the assembly line at my hotel," one of us said.

"I'm tired of coming home after a trip, bumping into someone from the city I've just visited and being asked did I enjoy ——, it serves the greatest ribs in the world."

"Not only did I not enjoy ——, I didn't even know it existed."

We agreed that the traveler to whom good food is important is all too often in a no-win situation. The city guides he or she finds in the hotel offer no quality judgments: the restaurant that buys the biggest ad is given the biggest display. On the other hand, the well-meaning friend or acquaintance who lives in the city almost invariably directs or escorts the out-of-towner to some overdecorated, overpriced temple of Continental cuisine on the assumption that it would be an insult to take you to the hole-in-the-wall restaurant where his family goes for great pasta or to a noisy Middle Eastern place, even though it *does* serve the world's best *hummus*.

For once, griping wasn't enough. We decided to do something for ourselves and, to use a political phrase (we were in Washington), for our fellow Americans. We decided to compile a guide to major American cities for the person to whom eating well is a passion.

It could serve as a survival kit for the New Yorker in Seattle who needed a "fix" of lox and bagels. It could help the person who had time for only one fine feed in a city, or, with a few hours between planes, wondered if somewhere nearby there was a restaurant in which to find something more attractive and wholesome than the variations on Styrofoam cooked and served at the airport.

What about Guide X? Neither Guide X nor Guide Y, we decided, speaks to the person for whom food quality and kitchen originality is the primary concern when dining out. There was a void, we decided, to be filled.

The result is *Where to Eat in America,* a tour of fifty cities for the dedicated eater. This is not just another collection of "best restaurants": it is a guide keyed to special interests and needs, compiled through consultation with food experts who live in the cities listed. While we feel sure the chapter on your city will be valuable to you, we have not attempted to be comprehensive. Our chief aim is to aid the person or family who is traveling. Many restaurants that are famous in one way or another have not been included, either because reputation often outlives performance or because, whatever its other virtues, the restaurant fails in the narrow, but to us essential, point of view of distinctive cooking.

The focus of eating in America has changed a great deal in recent years. Once much of the great dining in this country was provided expressly for travelers. Hotel dining rooms and railroad dining cars were symbols of the best this country had to offer or had imported from Europe. These days the traveler is wooed instead by the fast-food franchises that line the nation's highways. Their purpose is obvious, their popularity undeniable, but from a culinary point of view the kindest word one can find for them is "boring."

Yet eating out in America these days is not so limited as the fast-food franchisers would have us believe, nor need it be boring.

More and more meals are eaten away from home, we are told by government statisticians. We learned in compiling this book that more and more effort and imagination is being spent on creating distinctive restaurants. From Philadelphia to Seattle, explosions of restaurant activity are being inspired and supported by a generation of young people with money to spend, with the sophistication to demand accurate reproduction of foreign cuisines, and the discernment to reject overdressed, overpriced frauds.

Taken together, the introductions to the various cities in this guide give encouraging answers to the question "Where to Eat in

America?" The country is not in danger of having no alternative to away-from-home dining except mass feeding at McDonald's. There is some wonderful eating to be done out there. Let's enjoy it together.

# Introduction to the New Edition

Since the first edition was compiled two years ago, the trend toward dining out has accelerated. More people than ever are eating in restaurants, though only one percent of all the meals Americans eat are in so-called full service or "tablecloth" restaurants. According to an industry survey, "menu variety and type of atmosphere" are very important to patrons of these restaurants, along with cleanliness, quality and preparation of food, and courtesy.

We took these factors into account as we reviewed our original recommendations. No restaurant was sacred. Many favorites survived and new choices were added. Deletions and additions were prompted, in no few instances, by the generous response of readers of the first edition who took time to fill in the evaluation form in the back of the book or to write letters.

We also looked farther afield this time, to several of this country's most exciting vacation cities and across the border to Canada. There are 20 additional cities in this new edition and a total of more than 2,100 restaurants are discussed. We have added a category to aid families traveling with children and another for those who arrive in a strange city on a Sunday evening.

Defenders of the restaurant industry criticized us for having written negatively about fast-food franchises while including a number of chain restaurants in our guide. To us, the management structure of a restaurant is immaterial so long as it inspires a concern for quality and respect for the customer. To our minds, the best restaurants are those that achieve what they set out to do, be it a faithful reproduction of classic French cuisine or a superb hamburger. We think the pages that follow contain a fascinating cross section of just such restaurants.

William Rice
Burton Wolf

New York City
June 1979

# How to Use This Guide

This book before you is intended for anyone away from home who is hungry or is about to be hungry.

It guides the reader through fifty North American cities often visited by travelers. For the dedicated gourmet it represents a map to survival; for the ordinary traveler it will point the way to unsuspected culinary pleasures.

We have compiled this guide for people whose primary desire is to find food prepared with imagination and distinction. Accordingly, we formed no preconceived parameters of price, atmosphere or degree of formality. In all cases, the primary reason for inclusion is the quality of the cooking. The listings for each city are not comprehensive. Instead, we take the visitor by the hand and reveal outstanding restaurants and shops within certain, defined categories that are likely to fill most needs. If we have missed any deserving restaurants, we encourage you to bring them to our attention. (A form for this purpose is provided at the back of the book. The hundreds of responses we received from readers of the first edition were helpful, encouraging and in some instances highly amusing.)

Each city is introduced with a description of its food history and customs. A list of restaurants and food sources follows. When those restaurants and food sources are referred to in the introduction, their names will appear in boldface type. However, other worthy restaurants not in the listings are often mentioned, for which reason the introduction should be read with some care.

The restaurants and food sources have been broken into the following categories: BIG DEAL is a major, first-class restaurant. In cities where a Big Deal restaurant's fame and price outweigh its performance, we have included a self-explanatory subcategory titled "Not Worth It." INTERNATIONAL shows the ethnic diversity of the city. SPECIALTY COOKING contains specific types or styles of food and cooking. FOR INDIVIDUAL NEEDS fills the gaps for those with special dining requirements. For example, the first listing in this category is called "If You Have Time for Only One Meal." This is our recommendation on where to eat if a visit allows only one gastronomic highlight. While the restaurant clearly is among the best in the city, it may also have been chosen because it offers local flavor, local food specialities or represents dining history. IN THE SUBURBS provides guidance for those outside the city's core. And MARKETS adds the dimension of food shopping to eating.

Although these major categories remain basically the same from city to city, the subcategories may differ, either as a reflection of different ethnic mixes (under the INTERNATIONAL category) or because we could not find a restaurant that satisfied our standards for that subcategory—in which case we suggest you shift your focus.

Each individual listing provides address and telephone number, as well as a description of the restaurant's atmosphere, food and—frequently—specific menu recommendations. In most cases, instead of offering an ambiguous guess at the cost of a meal (which may vary sharply depending on what and how much is eaten and drunk), we list lunch and dinner entrée prices at the low end of the scale. You may begin with this information and go wherever your fancy and pocketbook allow. Unless otherwise indicated, restaurants are open for luncheon and dinner service during "normal" hours (roughly 11:30 A.M. to 2:30 P.M., and 6 P.M. to 10:30 P.M.). Naturally, prices and hours of operation are subject to change. Those given were accurate at press time, as were the credit card listings. Nonetheless, it is a good idea to inquire by telephone and make reservations if possible, especially in a strange city.

We show major national credit cards where applicable. The symbols are AE (American Express), CB (Carte Blanche), DC (Diners' Club), MC (Master Charge) and V (Visa).

A final word: these recommendations and evaluations are entirely our own, gathered without solicitation or commercial sponsorship. No restaurant paid for a listing, nor was our work sponsored by any organization other than Random House. The editors and food experts who collaborated with us are sharing with you where they really *do* eat in America.

# The Other Side of the Coin

Draw a mental picture of the restaurant owner or manager: "Well-dressed, well-fed, wearing a welcoming smile and a gracious manner," you suggest.

Look a little closer. The paunch may be real enough, but there's a good chance the collar will be slightly frayed or the suit in need of pressing. The smile is straight from central casting, there is a slight tic in an eyelid—caused by fatigue or worry or both—and the gracious manner may just be an outward impression given by someone too preoccupied to concentrate.

It appears to be such a glamorous life that no one feels sorry for the restaurateur except himself. As he (or she) sees it, the "middle man" who operates a restaurant business isn't the one who buys low and sells high; instead he takes the heat for mercenary suppliers and inept cooks on one side, and rude, uncomprehending patrons on the other. These customers are oblivious to his best efforts and usually complain from ignorance rather than enlightened concern.

This is exaggeration, of course. There are restaurateurs who are happy in their work. But most of those who populate the world of restaurants do feel themselves misunderstood and often mistreated. Furthermore, for fear of offending a fickle public, few of them will speak out, even in the face of outrageous behavior.

One evening I encountered a maître d' of my acquaintance in some pain. He had just been kicked in the groin by an angry (and drunken) customer who had forgotten to have a parking ticket validated and had been forced to return to the restaurant.

That's not normal, but broken reservations are. So are people who ignore reservation times or dress codes at will, who steal china, silver, table appointments and even bits and pieces of the décor.

Pity the poor restaurateur. When he takes steps to improve quality, his customers argue about price. When he introduces something new to the menu—an exotic dish or a classy domestic wine, they ignore it until it disappears, then complain about being offered only "the same old things."

Also, although only the help complains about it, he, too, works lousy hours and sees home life suffer for it.

Sooner or later, he may become cynical and develop a severe case of contempt for the customer, a dangerous disease that some feel can be found in epidemic proportion among the French restaurant community.

It's not all one-sided, though. There are restaurant operators without talent, taste or any sense of public relations. There are restaurants, some of them financially successful, so flawed that Laurel and Hardy's best efforts could scarcely disrupt the dining room. There even are people in the business filled with malice and evil intent. The industry hasn't done much to curb its cheaters and frauds, but neither have the medical or legal professions.

At some point, perhaps, during the 200 years or so public eating places called restaurants have been urban institutions, there was peace and harmony. But I doubt it. There were, however, fixed hierarchies in the dining room and kitchen. Waiters were not too proud to serve attentively and skillfully; journeymen cooks knew their craft thoroughly.

Today, the owner or manager lives constantly with uncertainty. A restaurant is an expensive business to run and one that requires a consistent short-term cash flow. Only a few weeks of slack business can disrupt projections and cause serious problems.

"We have a difficult situation," François Haeringer, the widely respected owner of Auberge Chez François, once said. "You just shrug if the shoe or television repairman tells you it's not ready, to come back next week. But we must be ready twice a day, at 11:30 and 6, no matter what's happened. No excuses will do." On the other hand, I've yet to encounter a situation where a note on the menu announced, "50 Percent Off Today" because two cooks didn't show up, inferior cuts of meat were delivered, the air-conditioning failed and the maître d' was hung over.

There is constant concern with the cost of food, labor and rent, three of the four horsemen of what consumer specialist Sidney Margolius has called "the inflationary apocalypse." Net profits, according to several owners, aren't what they once were and the pot seems even smaller if it is shared among several partners or part of it goes to the chef or maître d'.

The restaurant operator may feel himself caught in a vise on several fronts.

• To save labor costs and keep prices down, he turns to prepared foods. Then the consumer demands fresh. Back come the extra cooks and close behind them is the health department, much more likely to find violations in restaurants where extensive "hands on" preparation is done. (A French chef once told me with irritation of a health inspector asking him what a cook was doing with a product he didn't recognize. "The cook was checking mussels to throw out any that were bad," the chef said. "And this guy is marking me down because there are cracks in my floor.")

• To the customer, the kitchen is a place apart where men in tall white hats perform culinary miracles. To the owner, it is a shadowy world filled with members of a medieval cult. In hiring them, recommendations and background are meaningless. Cooking is a craft, but there is no exam, no rating system. A skilled technician may prove to be a dreadful administrator—a cook but not a chef. There are personality conflicts within the kitchen, arguments about art vs. economy, and opportunities for loss, theft or inefficiency that can send food costs skyrocketing. Few survive in the restaurant business who don't know the back of the house or learn it.

• It is no wiser to feel secure about waiters and barmen. They, too, have opportunities to take advantage. Furthermore, being in direct contact with the public, they can hurt the restaurant's image with a bad attitude, by inattention to duty or by being untidy or unclean. They are not being paid much, so a fall-off in business or miserly tipping will drive them elsewhere.

• The public blames the restaurant, not its suppliers, for slippage in quality, for menu items that are not available and for sudden jumps in price. The need for careful supervision of deliveries and the need to do battle in the face of inadequate provisions are other strains that aren't supposed to show in the dining room.

• What of the menu? The old-line restaurant operator sees it as an advertising and sales tool for him, not as an information sheet for the consumer. After all, he pays to have them printed. So, if customers are used to such romantic notions as "spring" lamb or chicken, "Roquefort" instead of blue cheese or "homemade" pastry, what's the harm? Everybody does it, right?

Wrong, of course. Jack Cockrell, who heads the Restaurant

Association of Metropolitan Washington, prefers the term "accuracy-in-menu" to "truth-in-menu" and hastens to point out that his association supports it and has worked closely with local authorities to promote it.

But, in the language of a menu, all of the above are served with the main course. They are part of the pangs of a business that those who stick with find exciting, challenging and ever changing. After a static period of seeming decline, young people have been coming into the restaurant trade once again. Eating out has become a national way of life. Questions of quality and style are raised, as they always have been, but the industry's future is promising.

—William Rice

(This material appeared originally in the *Washington Post.*)

# Wine in Restaurants

It is a glorious era for those who are turned on or turning on to wine. Yet the restaurateur's view of wine is lagging badly behind public perceptions, and wine lists often betray three cardinal sins of a service industry: indifference, ignorance and cynicism. Restaurant owners say they are forced to mark up wines 300 percent or more to offset other operating expenses; they say they haven't time to keep a wine list up to date, nor the time or money to train the staff in wine tasting and service. As a result, restaurateurs lose out on many wine sales, and so they should.

On his side, the customer has every reason to respond with mistrust until he sees signs of knowledge and concern on the part of the wine waiter or management. (I write "he" and not "she" because in too many restaurants the woman attempting to order wine is a nonperson, tendered at best the condescending recommendation of a rosé.)

Since surprisingly few who approach your table with wine list in hand are experts, here are a few "dos and don'ts."

Don't be impressed by those tasting cups hung about the neck on fancy ribbons. If the man knows his cellar, he should know the taste of his wines. Only in aged wines, of which few are served, is the line between "good" and "bad" apt to be so subtle that a referee's judgment is necessary. If the wine is bad, it is usually apparent to the discerning nose long before a sip has been taken.

Don't pay much attention to the cork either, if it is placed before you. Smell the wet end, if you wish to be polite. A strong, harsh odor may or may not warn you of a bad wine to come, and a neutral or pleasant odor is no guarantee of quality.

Don't order top-of-the-list wines. The price represents too high a gamble on problematical pleasure. You have no guarantee the wine has been well treated. If it is an older red vintage, bad handling may well spread sediment through the bottle, clouding the wine. But don't order the very cheapest wine either, because low-priced wines often carry big markups and are no bargain. A possible solution is to count up three wines from the bottom (or cheap end) of the list and point.

If something more logical appeals to you, try the following: ask for the wine list as soon as you arrive. There is a trend toward replacing cocktails with wine, and if you wish to do so, the wine ordered early can carry over into the meal.

Examine the list. If the selections include the name of a shipper or producer and a date, there is hope. (But be sure the date on the bottle that comes to the table conforms with the date on the list.) Too often, unfortunately, the Bordeaux will be young and the Beaujolais will be old, when just the reverse should be the case.

When ordering, first consider how much you plan to drink. If you are alone or the only wine drinker in the party, ask for a glass. The price per ounce is astronomical, but the cost will be less than anything else. Carafe wine probably will be from an outsized bottle produced in California, Italy or France. There is seldom a choice, other than color, although a variety of "house" wines would make sense, as the difference in style (level of sweetness) among these wines is more pronounced than differences in quality. Only by tasting can you be sure the wine available suits you.

Since the publication of the first edition of this guide, prices for French wines have increased so sharply that the French selections, while still the largest category in most fine restaurants outside California, are no longer of more than vicarious interest. The excellent 1978 Beaujolais and 1976 Rhône wines may offer relative value for money, and wines from lesser regions are popping up here and there. Most of these last, however, have no track record in this country, so to order them is to take pot luck. The great Burgundies, red and white, are simply too expensive; so are most lesser Burgundies. Bordeaux's acclaimed 1975 reds are maturing slowly. The 1976s may drink agreeably sooner than the '75s, but at what price?

As a result, the number of California and Italian wines available is increasing. California presents a double puzzle because it turns out great quantities of generic and varietal wines. The generics—Chablis, Burgundy and the like—are sold by most producers. These wines bear no resemblance to the wines of the regions for which they are named. They are blends of several types of grapes, their style and quality altered to suit the supposed taste of a mass market. Almost all of them range from "mellow" or semi-dry toward sweet. Only a few are distinctive, but only a few others are truly awful.

Varietal wines are made from a specific grape (or at least a majority of the wine in the bottle comes from a specific grape). The best known of these among reds are Zinfandel and Cabernet Sauvignon; among whites, Chardonnay, Chenin Blanc, Johannisberg Riesling and Gewürz-Traminer. Producers who make small quantities and have large reputations are selling their wines at prices that march upward in near lock-step with the French. Large producers have been more cautious in raising prices.

In general, California varietals are fuller and more alcoholic than their European counterparts. Cabernets will mature more rapidly than Bordeaux reds. It is also argued, though the restaurant patron needn't worry, that they do not live as long. Zinfandel styles vary sharply. Some can substitute for Burgundies or be used in situations that might call for an Italian red. The heavy Zinfandels are expensive and may be served in place of a big Cabernet. California Chardonnay may be used in the same food situations as white Burgundy. Johannisberg Riesling lacks the fruit and lightness of German Riesling, however, and may be dry or sweet. California underwent severe drought in 1976 and 1977, but no recent vintage has been as unsatisfactory as was 1977 in France and Germany.

Italy has not been blessed with a great vintage of late. But it has benefited from the sharp rise in price of wines elsewhere and now accounts for more than half the imported wine sold in this country. In general, mass-circulation wines from Italy and Eastern Europe tend to be harmless and relatively cheap. Character is lacking, but as modern production methods are implemented, the quality of white wines such as Soáve and Verdicchio is improving.

Italian reds warrant more attention. Some small producers have been convinced to export, and their wines can be excellent. They are found only in restaurants where there is a passion for wine, and even there the supply is sporadic. Consider Bardolino or Valpolicella when seeking a light red. Most Chianti is medium-bodied, but it can be rough when young. Merlot, Dolcetto and Nebbiolo fall into the same category. The biggest Italian wines, Barolo, Gattinara, Ghemme and Barbaresco, can be magnificient if they have been allowed to age. Match them with beef and a rich sauce, or drink them with cheese.

Unless a restaurant specializes in them and the food is to be uniformly light, I reserve German white wine for home consumption.

Loire wines are worth trying in restaurants where the wines are chosen and vouched for by the management.

As for the endless debate on how to deal with orders for meat and fish within the same group, there are several alternatives, none involving rosé. (For me, rosé is best drunk without food or with cold plates or salads.) Consider wine by the glass, the demi-carafe, or half-bottle. A party of four might, for example, all drink from a bottle of white wine with the first course. Then two could move on to a half-bottle of red or a carafe while the other two continued with the white. Also, the white-with-fish, red-with-meat rule isn't carved in stone. Bend it to suit personal tastes and the meal being eaten.

A side thought: tiny wineglasses are an irritant to the consumer and a reflection on the ignorance (or parsimony) of the management. Don't suffer them. Ask for larger glasses. If there are none, ask for empty water glasses.

Most restaurants have their white wines already chilled. They may, however, be too cold and thus mask the flavor of the wine. It is quite proper to ask the waiter to leave a cold bottle on the table instead of placing it in an ice-filled wine bucket. Sauternes and champagne should be served well chilled, but among so-called dry white wines, the older and more costly the bottle, the less chilled it need be. Some light red wines, however, such as Beaujolais, Lambrusco or Bardolino, or some Zinfandels, may benefit from being lightly chilled, especially if the wine has been kept in a relatively warm place.

If the wine is poured correctly into the proper glasses, a bottle will serve six and the level of the wine will not climb more than halfway up the glass.

If the wine is red, it should benefit from "breathing," the period of time it is allowed to rest after the removal of the cork and the first sip. Due to the nature of things in restaurants, there may not be a great deal of time—if any—between delivery of the chosen wine and the food it is intended to accompany. It makes sense, therefore, to ask that it be poured directly into the glass once the wine has been sampled and approved. (Taste it before you nod your head for the pouring. If in doubt, taste it again. Let the man wait until you are sure.) Pouring the wine will let it breathe faster by exposing it to more air.

A final word of advice. The "bad" bottle of wine is often already bad—inferior or overaged, or a victim of mishandling—when it is delivered to the restaurant. Don't place all the blame for such a wine on the restaurateur. His supplier and the producer may deserve a share of the guilt. Nor can he be blamed if nature failed to cooperate and the wine of a certain vintage isn't up to standard, although he can—if he is knowledgeable—avoid placing such a wine on his list.

Following is a loose guide to recent vintages. There will be occasional good wines from bad years. Finding one by chance is unlikely, however, so unless you want to take a flyer on a lower-priced bottle of a famous vineyard (if, in fact, the price is lower), play the odds and look for a similar wine from another year.

—William Rice

# VINTAGES

P = Poor F = Fair G = Good E = Excellent

| | **California** | | **Bordeaux** | **Burgundy** | | **Rhône** | **German** | **Italian** |
|---|---|---|---|---|---|---|---|---|
| | **Red** | **White** | **Red** | **Red** | **White** | **Red** | **White** | **Red** |
| 1978 | E | G/E | F/E | E | G | E | F/G | G |
| 1977 | G | E | F | F | F | F/G | F | F |
| 1976 | E | F | G | G/E | E | E | E | G |
| 1975 | G | G | E | P | F | P | G | F |
| 1974 | E | E | G | F | G | F | F | F |
| 1973 | E | E | G | F | G | G | G | G |
| 1972 | F | G | P | G | F | G | P | P |
| 1971 | G | G | G | G | E | G | E | G |
| 1970 | E | — | E | G | — | E | — | E |
| 1969 | G | — | F | G | — | E | — | F |
| 1968 | E | — | P | P | — | P | — | P |

- Champagne vintages were declared in 1969, 1970, 1971, 1973, 1976.
- Years to look for in Sauternes are 1970, 1971, 1976.
- Years to look for in German dessert wines are 1971, 1973, 1975, 1976.

# Tipping

All too often difficult decisions that were made along the way—where to dine, at what hour, menu and wine choices—pale to insignificance when the check is presented and the diner has to calculate the tip. What's a proper percentage of the bill? Who gets it? Should it be one amount, or do various figures in the diningroom hierarchy get something just for being there?

To restaurateurs the ideological question of why customers should be expected to tip is moot. That's the way it is, they say. If the customer didn't pay a tip, he or she would have to pay through higher prices on the menu, which, they claim, nobody wants.

There have always been those who have questioned this venerable custom and refused to play the game, sometimes at their peril. (An acquaintance told us once of being chased down a San Francisco street by a Chinese waiter brandishing a knife.) The name of the economic Moses who fixed 15 percent as the standard tip has been lost to history. But the rate stuck and is referred to in various chapters of this book. Lately, however, there have been signs of change. The trade press has reported a move to have a fixed service charge added to the bill, replacing the free-form tip. At least one major credit company issues sales slips that suggest tipping the waiter and captain separately. There is a push in some parts to raise the "standard" tip to 20 percent.

The fixed service charge is common in Europe. Here it seems to offend diners as an infringement on their independence. Inflation has made its mark on menu prices, so—since the dollar amount of tips is higher—the rationale for increasing the percentage escapes us.

The "tip" earned its name a couple of centuries ago when coffee-houses emerged as "in" places in London. Customers in a hurry deposited a small amount of money on arrival "to insure promptness" of service. Thus TIP. While we are not about to upset the pastry cart and recommend tipping before the meal, we feel deeply that a tip should be earned. We generally respond to competent or even well-intended service with a 15 percent tip, but feel no pangs about reducing the percentage if the job is not done properly. Surly, inattentive service deserves no reward at all. If a waiter's performance is outstanding, a larger tip than normal may be in order.

When the meal has been served by a team, you may want to give more than 15 percent. It is proper to simply determine the amount (20 percent is fine—more if the service was extraordinary, and certainly less if it was lacking) and ask the captain to distribute it. Another hint: cities such as New York and Washington, D.C., place an 8-percent tax on food and beverages sold in restaurants. By doubling the amount of tax on the bill, you quickly arrive at a 16-percent tip.

# Atlanta

"Welcome to the land of grits and honey" would have been an appropriate greeting to Atlanta's visitors prior to 1965. Then as now, most natives ate grits with their breakfast eggs and ham, and entertaining was done in one's living room or perhaps at "the club." But in recent years, travel and exposure, increased affluence and an influx of new residents have prompted a spurt in restaurant activity. While there have been notable failures, the effort continues and the restaurant scene here is still very much in transition.

It wasn't always thus in these parts. Pre–Civil War history tells us a manor or plantation house would support a game cook, a meat cook and a pastry cook. While the owners dined in European style, the slaves produced a cuisine of their own. They were given the cast-off pieces of a hog (the primary source of meat in this region) such as ears, tails and feet, and would cook them with wild greens such as pokeweed and collard. The sweet potato or yam was a main ingredient in nearly every meal, and squirrel, rabbit and possum provided variety. Corn meal was made into corn bread and hush puppies. During the Civil War this food, called "soul food" these days, became the basis of everybody's diet.

After the war the best places to eat were boarding houses; later a revived economy gave rise to a number of fine hotels. Traditional Southern food was professionally prepared for the hotel dining rooms and inevitably became refined. Ice became commonplace; refrigeration permitted longer storage and allowed for the importation of seafood from the coast, and beef from the Midwest.

By the 1920's there were two restaurants of consequence, the Ship Ahoy and the Seven Seas. The former was operated by a Greek and the latter by a Chinese, although they did not feature ethnic cuisine. They were, however, dedicated to the workingman's taste and pocketbook. The great dining rooms continued to be located in the hotels.

Particularly notable were the Ansley Hotel and the Piedmont Hotel, both of which have been demolished. One old-timer recalls a meal for four at the Ansley during which "they brought out the biggest piece of sirloin steak I'd ever seen and served it off a piece of oak board." (The oak plank was seasoned, so during cooking it would flavor the meat.)

Ever present at even the finest dining tables was a large pitcher of iced tea, usually presweetened. Enormous quantities of tea were consumed with the meal, a practice that continues in Georgia today. As more restaurants sprang up, so did an unusual distinction: if it was run by a man, it was known as a restaurant; if run by a woman, it was called a "tearoom." Today a number of tearooms and boarding houses continue to provide "family-style" meals. Friends and strangers alike gather at large tables with a dozen or so chairs and help themselves from platters of vegetables and several kinds of meat. It usually takes no longer than thirty minutes for a group to fill a table, consume the food and depart. **Mary Mac's** is a good example.

Today's hotels are mostly new, big and chrome-plated, with restaurants to match. But the spectrum has broadened considerably; French and Chinese restaurants now compete with places featuring more traditional American or Continental menus. There are several dependable, old-time Italian restaurants as well, a smattering of other ethnic cuisines and some that defy description.

There have been several attempts to tie fine dining to the popular discotheque fad. So far none of them has become an established spot at which to dine. The latest innovation might be called "chic Western." Western gear decorates the walls, but the menus are conventional steaks, fried shrimp and the like. An example is Max in the Omni Complex, which is somewhat set apart from the other hotels and is a "you-have-to-see-it-to-believe-it" setup that includes offices, a hotel, a sports arena, shops, stores and a very long escalator.

The major hotels rise above downtown Atlanta like futuristic fortresses. They are showcases, and from the inevitable lounge and restaurant atop most of them, the view over the city is guaranteed. Whether culinary quality will match expectation or price is less certain. **Nicolai's Roof,** atop the Hilton, is small and boasts a local chef. It is not a chain operation, as is Trader Vic's—also in the Hilton—or **Hugo's** in the Hyatt Regency. There is an exciting ride in an exterior elevator to the Sundial atop Peachtree Plaza, and the menu shows considerable imagination.

Downtown dining is not nearly so exciting. Atlantans no longer go home for lunch, but neither do many return downtown in the evening. Apart from the hotels, the most active dining spots are **Herren's, Midnight Sun, Pittypat's Porch** and The Abbey. This last is a converted church in which the waiters wear monks' robes. It is popular, but service can be slow and the promise of one of the city's most ambitious menus is not always fulfilled.

Fresh seafood consistently well prepared is not available, but the New Orleans influence in Atlanta culinary circles is growing, and several Creole restaurants are popular choices for seafood lovers.

Those who seek distinctive dining with an emphasis on food preparation are advised to search out smaller owner-operated restaurants in neighborhoods that would be suburbs if Atlanta's city limits were not so far-flung. The prime target is the affluent Buckhead section, about twenty minutes north of downtown. In that general area are **Coach & Six, Brennan's, Rue de Paris, Bahou Container, La Grotta,** Patio Plaza and a number of others.

Between downtown and Buckhead in the vicinity of Route I-85 is another concentration that includes night spots and restaurants, among them **McKinnon's Louisiane, Alfredo's** and Peking. As a rule of thumb, many of the city's better dining spots are located on or quite near Peachtree. There are more than a dozen roads, streets, lanes, etc., bearing the name of Peachtree. The one we are referring to is the major north-south thoroughfare running from downtown to Buckhead. Beyond Midway it changes from Peachtree Street to Peachtree Road, so to most it is simply "Peachtree."

There are over 100 Chinese restaurants in Atlanta, plus the **Asian Trading Company,** one of the finest Chinese groceries anywhere. But the situation is very fluid and a good restaurant today may have a new owner, chef or headwaiter tomorrow.

As overnight accommodations are scattered around the city, geographical location should be a factor in determining where to dine.

One source of nourishment that should not be ignored is the private club. Invitations are necessary, and should certainly be accepted should one be proffered for lunch at any of a number of clubs, including the Commerce Club, the Capital City Club and the Piedmont Driving Club.

In recent years most good restaurants insisted on jackets and tie. Indeed, for several years city law required jacket and tie before entering a bar that served liquor. (Beer halls were excluded.) Attitudes have changed, but if you are a casual dresser, it is best to inquire about the need for a jacket when making a reservation. Pants suits for women are acceptable everywhere. Once in the restaurant, plan to tip 15 percent or upward, depending on service.

Consider taking home a slab of cured bacon or a Georgia smoked ham as a souvenir. The best known are Talmadge hams, sold in Winn-Dixie stores and in kiosks at the airport. Other possibilities are homemade jams, relishes and condiments.

While Atlantans are slow to break old habits (many still turn up their noses at vegetables cooked briefly and without bacon), there has been a change. There is a growing number of cooking schools, and the restaurants in the listing that follows prove it.

# Restaurants and Food Sources

(Area code: 404)

## BIG DEAL

### WORTH IT

***Nicolai's Roof,*** at the top of the Atlanta Hilton, 255 Courtland Street N.W. (659-2000). Many consider it Atlanta's outstanding restaurant. Small (it seats 70) and handsome, Nicolai's serves French food in a Russian atmosphere. Waiters in Cossack dress recite offerings that change every two weeks. You select an entrée, then discuss a soup, appetizer and dessert to match. Reservations essential. Dinner only. Open seven days a week. The fixed-price ($22) dinner consists of five courses, including salad. (Piroshki, borscht and hot dessert soufflé always on menu.) AE, CB, DC, MC, V.

### NOT WORTH IT

***The French Restaurant,*** Omni International Hotel, at Marietta and International Boulevard (659-0000). An elegantly designed restaurant that offers terrace-style dining within the Omni's controlled-atmosphere megastructure (one of the scenic wonders of downtown Atlanta). The menu is *haute cuisine,* but what comes from the kitchen lacks accent and flair. Serving personnel too often are guilty of arrogance. Even a new menu where the diner may choose à la carte or fixed price ($20.50 for five courses) hasn't improved the food or service. Saturday, dinner only. Closed Sunday. Entrées from $3.75 (L), $12.75 (D). AE, CB, DC, MC, V.

***Midnight Sun,*** 225 Peachtree Street N.E., in Peachtree Center (577-5050). The setting is Scandinavian contemporary, with a huge marble fountain as the centerpiece of the main dining room. Apathy abounds in the kitchen and is found among the serving personnel as well. A five-course private smörgåsbord is $18.50. Among the entrées, skip the reindeer. Open seven days a week. Entrées from $2.50 (L), $6.75 (D). AE, CB, DC, MC, V.

# INTERNATIONAL

## AMERICAN

***Aunt Fanny's Cabin,*** 375 Campbell Road, Smyrna (436-9026). (See description under IF YOU HAVE TIME FOR ONLY ONE MEAL.)

***Pittypat's Porch,*** 25 International Boulevard (525-8228). It's something of a put-on, but visitors line up to dine in this stylized version of life in the Old South. Drinks are served on the "porch" and you may even get to sip your mint julep in a rocking chair. You descend to a seven-course buffet of Southern specialties. The menu's written on a fan, the waitresses are in costume. Chaîne des Rotisseurs. Reservations recommended, but held only between 5-6 P.M. Dinner only. Closed Sunday. Complete meals from $8.95. Children's menu $3.50. AE, CB, DC, MC, V.

***The Pleasant Peasant,*** 555 Peachtree Road (874-3223). The neighborhood is somewhat seedy, but there's often a line outside the door of this cleverly designed, casual restaurant. Pâtés and other dishes show a French influence. The servings are large. Dinner only. Open until midnight Monday through Thursday and Sunday, until 1 A.M. Friday and Saturday. Entrées from $4.95. AE, MC, V.

***Thomas',*** 3442 Stewart Avenue (768-4101). (See description under RESTAURANT NEAR AIRPORT.)

## CHINESE

***Grand China,*** 2975 Peachtree Road, Buckhead (231-8690). Formerly a midtown hole in the wall, Grand China is in a new location with a spotlessly clean dining room and a gifted chef. Hostess/owner "Che Chee's" warm personality is another asset. Shrimp in fish sauce is especially good. Hunam and Szechuan dishes available. Saturday and Sunday, dinner only. Open seven days a week. Entrées from $2.25 (L), $3.85 (D). AE, DC, MC, V.

# FRENCH

***Rue de Paris,*** 315 E. Paces Ferry Road, Buckhead (261-9600). Owner Yves Durand, a Frenchman with a sunny disposition, is responsible for the warm ambience. The mood and menu are country French, with a cream of asparagus soup and mussels *poulette* (when available), both memorable dishes. Reservations recommended. Dinner only. Open seven days a week. Entrées from $6.50. AE, CB, MC, V.

***Petite Auberge,*** 2935 N. Druid Hills Road N.E., in Toco Hills Center (634-6268). The restaurant's name is French; the chef's name is Wolfgang. The result is an eclectic menu and large portions of dishes such as shepherd's *cassoulet,* a blend of veal, pork and beef served with homemade *Spaetzle.* Another outstanding choice is *le ragoût fin,* an appetizer of veal and mushroom pieces. Local patronage keeps the restaurant busy, but service is friendly and prompt. Chaîne des Rotisseurs. Saturday, dinner only. Closed Sunday. Entrées from $2.25 (L), $7.45 (D). AE, MC, V.

***Bernard's,*** 1193 Collier Road N.W. (352-2778). Atlanta's elite (attracted by the popular former maître d' of a private club) appreciate the special attention and competent kitchen. Bernard's can be a costly but cosy experience. Ask for a secluded booth. Try the rack of lamb or sole meunière, and mushroom salad. Chaîne des Rotisseurs. Saturday, dinner only. Closed Sunday. Entrées from $3 (L), $8 (D). AE, V.

***Sidney's "Just South,"*** 4225 Roswell Road N.E. (256-2339). Eclectic is the word for the menu. "Jewish Country French" are Sidney's own words—and sum it up nicely. Chicken liver pâté, sweet and sour cabbage, lukchen kugel and—just to confuse matters—"Phoenix chicken." Normally pleasant, service cordial and informal. Wine list thoughtful in selection and price. Be sure to try the fresh trout in dill sauce and one of his desserts. Sunday, dinner only. Open seven days a week. Entrées from $3.75 (L), $10 (D). AE, MC, V.

***Pano's and Paul's,*** 1232 West Paces Ferry Road at I-75 (261-4739). The French influence is obvious in the menu—smoked mountain trout, veal scallops in cognac sauce with morels, baby chicken breasts with Calvados, sweetbreads with chanterelles and walnuts. Both the co-owners cook. Their dining room is "Rumanian Victorian," tastefully done, and the young staff is alert and informed. It's new, but already popular with local *becs-fin.* Dinner only, until midnight Friday and Saturday. Closed Sunday. Entrées from $7.95. AE, MC, V.

## INDIAN

***Anarkali,*** 2115 N. Decatur Road at Clairmont, Decatur (321-0251). Just behind a filling station in a small shopping center. You can order off the menu here, but many Atlanta customers call owner Abu Faruque ahead of time and ask him to plan the meal—usually priced from $8 to $10—and come away blissfully content. Saturday and Sunday, dinner only. Closed Monday. Entrées from $3 (L), $4 (D). AE, MC, V.

## ITALIAN

***Bugatti,*** Omni International Hotel, at Marietta and International Boulevard (659-0000). Located one floor below The French Restaurant, Bugatti is another story. It's plush and expensive, featuring Northern Italian sophistication. Don't look for heavy doses of tomato sauce or garlic. Try either the veal scaloppini or Florentine (with fresh spinach). High-quality olive oil is used in the salad dressings. Service is polite and usually prompt. Open seven days a week. Entrées from $4.95 (L), $5.75 (pasta) (D). Italian Sunday brunch, $7.95 per person, 11:30 A.M. to 2:30 P.M. AE, CB, DC, MC, V.

***Alfredo's,*** 1989 Cheshire Bridge Road N.E. (876-1380). Chef-owner Alfredo reserves his talents for the kitchen; one tends to ignore the noise and the outdated vintage décor when enjoying his heady, garlicky, Italian cuisine. When available, choose the mussels. Dinner only. Closed Sunday. Entrées from $3.75 (pasta) and $5.50. AE, MC, V.

***Gene and Gabe's,*** 1578 Piedmont Avenue N.E. (874-6145). Jimmy Carter reserved the whole place for his family and the press one Sunday. The food here can be excellent, but it's unpredictable when the chef is in bad humor. Specials are often exceptional and sell out quickly. Dinner only. Open seven days a week. Entrées from $6.95. AE, MC, V.

***La Grotta,*** 2637 Peachtree Road, Buckhead (231-1368). The single dining room of this Buckhead restaurant in the basement of an apartment building is a visual treat. Sparkling crystal and crisp linens set the stage for Northern Italian cuisine. Try the Italian version of steak tartare—*carpaccio*—with an herb-flavored lemon vinaigrette, or the pasta dishes (ask the waiter which are made with fresh pasta and which not). The kitchen uses fresh herbs as well. The veal roast is good, but be sure to request that your scaloppini be pounded very thin. Thick pieces tend to overcook and be quite tough. Dinner only. Closed Sunday. Entrées from $6.75. AE, MC, V.

## JAPANESE

***Ginza Benkay,*** 231 Peachtree Street, in Peachtree Center Complex (659-5323). A large restaurant with stark, representative Japanese décor. The *sushi* bar, where you can watch a skilled craftsman carve raw fish, comes in view as you enter. There is a grill room for dining, a "shoes-off" room that is elevated so the diner's feet go into a pit under the low table, and a room with tables, chairs and table settings arranged in conventional Western style. The menu is typical and the dishes are well executed. There are multicourse full meals available at various prices up to $30 per person. Open seven days a week. Entrées from $3.50 (L), $7.50 (D). AE, DC, MC, V.

## MIDDLE EASTERN

***Bahou Container,*** in the rear of Lenox Square Shopping Center, Peachtree Road, north of Buckhead (262-7872). A favorite of Atlanta's more adventuresome diners, the Bahou Container features an imaginative menu of predominantly Middle Eastern cuisine. Beef, lamb and eggplant, listed separately and in various combinations, are highlighted, as are a number of tasty vegetarian dishes. Recently remodeled, the restaurant now has a spacious, multileveled dining area inside and a walled courtyard outside, complete with fountain, for dining or drinking. Sunday, brunch (kosher) and dinner only. Open seven days a week. Entrées from $2.95 (L), $11.95 (D). AE, CB, DC, MC, V.

# SPECIALTY COOKING

## BARBECUE

***Harold's,*** 171 McDonough Boulevard S.E., at Lakewood (627-9268). A working-people's restaurant in an industrial section that serves no alcohol and has religious slogans on the walls. Casual décor and service. Sliced pork barbecue and sauce are outstanding. Don't ignore the highly seasoned Brunswick stew. Closed Sunday. A sandwich is $1.25, a BBQ plate is $3. Entrées from $2.25 (L & D). No credit cards.

***Old Hickory House,*** (there are 11 locations, check Directory Assistance and call, as days of opening and hours are not standard). An Atlanta success story based on pork shoulders, beef roasts and ribs slow-cooked over a hickory-wood fire. There's not much atmosphere, but the sauce is enough to start a conversation. Entrées from $1.50 (L & D). No credit cards.

## CREOLE

***McKinnon's Louisiane,*** 2100 Cheshire Bridge Road N.E. (325-4141). Some of the best-known New Orleans dishes are re-created in this comfortable, smallish restaurant. Alert, tuxedoed waiters are helpful without being obsequious. Fresh fish, lump crab meat and oysters are the primary ingredients among the 30 entrées. Moderately priced. Chaîne des Rotisseurs. Dinner only. Closed Sunday. Entrées from $5.95. AE, MC, V.

***Joe Dale's Cajun House,*** 3209 Maple Drive N.E. (261-2741). Always crowded, always garlicky and spicy, you may just love the noise and camaraderie, the he-man portions and reasonable prices. Owner Dale has antique toys and oddities on display. No reservations. Saturday, dinner only. Closed Sunday. Entrées from $3.25 (L), $7.50 (D). AE, CB, DC, MC, V.

***Brennan's,*** 103 W. Paces Ferry Road, Buckhead (261-7913). Good management and innovative menus (developed for the Atlanta Brennan's by its sister restaurant, Commander's Palace in New Orleans). Try the filet of beef with "debris" sauce or soft-shelled crab. The Sunday brunch has new additions as well as the famous Brennan's special drinks and egg dishes. Chaîne des Rotisseurs. Reservations suggested. Open seven days a week. Entrées from $3.50 (B), $4.50 (L), $6.50 (D). AE, DC, MC, V.

***Joseph's,*** 3129 Piedmont Road N.E. (261-3232). A small, attractive Creole newcomer, expensive with some good entrées including crab. The wife cooks, her husband hosts. Skip the salad—its dressing might ruin the rest of your dinner. Dinner only. Closed Sunday and Monday. Entrées from $8.50. AE, MC, V.

## DELI

***D. B. Kaplan,*** Lenox Square (266-1111). A spin-off of a Chicago restaurant, they knish it out here in true deli form. Reading the zany copy on the two-foot-long menu will leave you bemused and the food will please you. Chocolate chip cheesecake is a memorable dessert. There are 152 sandwiches priced from $1.75 to $85 (for a six-footer that serves 40). Open seven days a week. No credit cards.

## HAMBURGER/HOT DOG

***The Varsity,*** North Avenue at the Expressway (Route I-75/85), adjacent to Georgia Tech (881-1706). This claims to be the world's largest drive-in and boasts a double-decker parking lot as evidence. Three assembly lines prepare thousands of pounds of hamburgers, hot dogs, onion rings and fried apple pie daily. Open until 2 A.M., seven days a week. Orders from 45 cents. No credit cards.

## SOUL

***Deacon Burton's Soul Food Café,*** at Edgewood and Hurt S.E. No telephone. Deacon Lendell Burton provides filling, well-prepared food doled out cafeteria-style. At lunch there is fried chicken, greens, ribs, maybe some pig's ears, superb corn bread and pound cake (while it lasts). In midafternoon the Deacon closes his door and goes around the corner to work in his TV repair shop. Open from 4 A.M. to 4 P.M. Closed Sunday. Lunch entrées from $1.25. No credit cards.

## STEAK

***Coach & Six,*** 1776 Peachtree Road (872-6666). A large, extremely popular restaurant that features prime cuts of steak and roast beef. You should be pleased with the triple-cut loin lamb chops. Black bean soup is a specialty; all baking is done on the premises. It's crowded and somewhat noisy, but the service is brisk. Make a reservation. Saturday and Sunday, dinner only. Open seven days a week. Entrées from $3.25 (L), $7.95 (D). AE, CB, DC, MC, V.

## VEGETARIAN

***Bahou Container,*** in the rear of Lenox Square Shopping Center, Peachtree Road north of Buckhead (262-7872). (See description under MIDDLE EASTERN.)

# FOR INDIVIDUAL NEEDS

## IF YOU HAVE TIME FOR ONLY ONE MEAL

***Aunt Fanny's Cabin,*** 375 Campbell Road, Smyrna (436-9026). It's not far, but the route to the one-time quarters of a household retainer is complex. Call for directions. Authentic Southern cooking, with the help decked out in plantation regalia. Of the four entrées, either fried chicken or country ham should be your choice. Food is served family style, so there will be plenty of vegetables, biscuits and corn bread; some musical entertainment, too. Dinner only except Sunday, when lunch is also served. Open seven days a week. Complete dinners from $7.45. AE, CB, DC, MC, V.

## BEST HOTEL MEAL

***Hugo's,*** Hyatt Regency Atlanta (577-1234). This Hugo's offers oysters, steaks and accompaniments—all well prepared and served with care. No surprises here, but a pleasant atmosphere, with music from a harp and a bandoneon. Dinner only. Open seven days a week. Entrées from $14.50. AE, CB, DC, MC, V.

## RESTAURANT NEAR AIRPORT

***Thomas',*** 3442 Steward Avenue (768-4101). This restaurant is for big eatin' Southern style—especially at breakfast. Standouts include homemade biscuits with cream gravy, country ham and fried eggs. Owner Thomas farms his own vegetables and cuts his own meats. Specials include chicken and dumplings ($2). He maintains a shuttle to and from the airport for pilots, but you can join the 4-minute ride by calling the restaurant. Open seven days a week, from 5 A.M. to 9 P.M. Entrées from $1.78 (L), $2.61 (D). AE, MC, V.

## BUSINESS BREAKFAST

***Brennan's,*** 103 W. Paces Ferry Road, Buckhead (261-7913). (See description under CREOLE.)

## BUSINESS LUNCH

***Pewter Mug,*** 38 Auburn Avenue (577-6161). The bar is to the right as you enter. Special, 3½-ounce martinis make for lively conversation and noisy dining. For quite, choose the dining room in the rear, where the waitress will probably call you "honey." Good roast beef and large "hambourgers." Closed Saturday and Sunday. Entrées from $2.50. AE, MC, V.

***Herren's,*** 84 Luckie Street (524-4709). This is a local institution with many tables filled by regular customers at luncheon. The menu is rather unimaginative, but does feature some very good dishes, such as mushrooms with crabmeat, planked seafood Herren, and freshly cooked lobster (selected from a tank). For dessert, the lemon icebox pie is a winner. Saturday, dinner only. Closed Sunday. Entrées from $2.95 (L), $8.25 (D). AE, MC, V.

## FAST, GOOD FOOD

***Mary Mac's Tea Room,*** 224 Ponce de Leon Avenue, N.E. (875-4337). A cross section of clients ranging from students to (during his term) Governor Lester Maddox. Entrées come with three vegetables; you sit at Formica-topped tables and write your own order. It's home-style cooking: chicken and dumplings, black-eyed peas, okra and other regional favorites, including a "Jimmy Carter custard." Closed weekends, and by 8 P.M. weekdays. Entrées from $1.75 (L), $2.05 (D). No credit cards.

***The Park,*** Colony Square (881-6449). Soup and tasty sandwiches. A half-sandwich for 95 cents, small soup $1.25. Also a bargain breakfast from 7:30 A.M. to 11 A.M. Closed Sunday. Two eggs are 55 cents. MC.

## BEST WINE LIST

***Dante's Down the Hatch,*** 84 Prior Street (577-1800). A most unusual setting for wine and music, both of which are featured here. Jazz is played inside a replica of a sailing ship, where cheese or fondue is served along with wines from an extensive list. The music in the other room, the "wharf," is folk and classical guitar. Reservations recommended. Dinner only. Open seven days a week. Entrées from $4. AE, CB, DC, MC, V.

## FOR DRINKS

***Billy's,*** 3130 Roswell Road, just off Peachtree (261-6100). A slick, popular bar/lounge that successfully caters to both the avant garde and yokels. Easygoing but upbeat. A deli-burger menu includes fried seafood and a raw bar. Open seven days a week, from 11 A.M. to 4 A.M. AE, MC, V.

***Clarence Foster's,*** 1915 Peachtree Road (351-0002). The drinks are fine, and various dishes on the ambitious menu can be well executed, though not consistently. Open seven days a week. Entrées from $2.25 (L), $7.50 (D). AE, CB, DC, MC, V.

***Harrison's,*** 2110 Peachtree Road N.W. (351-7596). The huge front bar was imported from Ireland. Lots of plants, live piano music. In the rear, a game room with pool table. If you want to eat, there are steaks, fried shrimp, roast beef. Closed Sunday. Entrées from $3.25 (L), $5.50 (D). AE, MC, V.

## RESTAURANT WITH MUSIC

***Club Atlantis,*** Hyatt Regency Atlanta (577-1234). Provides a trio for dinner-dancing until show time at 9 P.M. Headliner shows at 9 and 10:30. Cover and complete meal (with entrées such as lobster, tournedos, roast duck) $23.50. Cover without dinner $3 week nights, $5 Friday and Saturday. Closed Sunday. AE, CB, DC, MC, V.

***Dante's Down the Hatch,*** 84 Prior Street (577-1800). (See description under BEST WINE LIST.)

## ROMANTIC

***Bernard's,*** 1193 Collier Road N.W. (352-2778). (See description under FRENCH.)

## LATE-NIGHT SERVICE

***The Country Place,*** Colony Square (881-0144). This restaurant in the heart of Colony Square is a relative of The Pleasant Peasant. It has been decorated with all the flair of the other Peasant restaurants. Always full. Large helpings. The menu includes roast duckling with a bourbon-plum sauce and rack of lamb with an apple stuffing. The fried bread is a treat, as is the vegetable dish presented with each meal. Late supper starts at 11 and goes until midnight, Monday through Thursday; until 1:30 A.M. Friday and Saturday. Closed Sunday. Entrées from $2.75 (L), $4.75 (D), $1.25 (late supper). AE, DC, MC, V.

***The Pleasant Peasant,*** 555 Peachtree Road (874-3223). (See description under AMERICAN.)

***Billy's,*** 3130 Roswell Road, just off Peachtree (261-6100). (See description under FOR DRINKS.)

## SUNDAY BRUNCH

***Brennan's,*** 103 W. Paces Ferry Road, Buckhead (261-7913). (See description under CREOLE.)

***Bugatti,*** Omni International Hotel, at Marietta and International Boulevard (659-0000). (See description under ITALIAN.)

## SUNDAY-EVENING MEAL

***Coach & Six,*** 1776 Peachtree Road (872-6666). (See description under STEAK.)

***Brennan's,*** 103 W. Paces Ferry Road, Buckhead (261-7913). (See description under CREOLE.)

## FOR FAMILIES WITH CHILDREN

***Morrison's.*** This chain of eight cafeterias offers good country-style food, in clean and cheerful surroundings at moderate prices. Check telephone book for the Morrison's nearest you. No credit cards.

## COUNTRY INN

***Old Vinings Inn,*** 3020 Paces Mill Road, corner of Paces Ferry Road, Vinings (434-5270). Yvette Greune was Ambassador Ann Cox Chamber's private chef until she took over this old inn in Vinings. It's small (seats 55) and the continental cuisine is done creatively. Lovely décor and informal, cheerful service. Cocktails, beer and wine. Chaîne des Rotisseurs. Reservations necessary. Sunday, dinner only. Closed Monday. Entrées from $3.25 (L), $8.50 (D). No credit cards.

# MARKETS

***Atlanta's Municipal Market,*** 209 Edgewood Avenue S.E. A 15-minute walk from downtown Five Points is a soul-food paradise. Many stalls offer huge displays of pigs' ears, tails, feet. Also "medicinal" roots and herbs, "edible" clay, smoked hams and fish, mountains of collards, yams, bananas and homemade jams, jellies and sorghum by the pint, quart or half gallon. Closed Sunday.

***Asian Trading Company, Ltd.,*** Broadview Plaza, Piedmont (266-0362). Stumble through crowded aisles where almost every type of Asian food from homemade won ton skins and noodles to dozens of dried fish, fresh Chinese celery, kiwi and lotus roots will overwhelm you. Fresh fish is sold in the back, and some fascinating Chinese cooking equipment lines the floors as well. Open seven days a week. No credit cards.

***Flea Market,*** Piedmont at Lindberg. 352 stalls. A true flea market with nearly old antiques, nearly new clothes, old-timey kitchen gadgets, witches' brews, herbs, spices and some fresh produce. Open seven days a week.

# GIFT WINES

***McCall's Wine and Cheese,*** in Phipps Plaza (266-1316) beyond Buckhead; across Peachtree in Lenox Square; and at 320 Pharr Road, Buckhead. A wide selection of imported wines and knowledgeable personnel selling them. The Lenox Square store is open Sunday; the rest are closed. MC, V.

***Skinflint's,*** 1943 Peachtree Road N.E. (351-7012). They call themselves the South's largest fine-wine merchants and they may be right. Owner Frank Stone and manager Don Reddicks are usually available to provide advice. Closed Sunday. AE, DC, MC, V.

# Atlantic City

The world's most profitable casino (Resorts International) has turned what was a fading pearl of the Atlantic shore into a year-round city of fun and games—with the accent on the latter. With at least two more casino hotels on the drawing board, and a location within driving range of Philadelphia and New York, it is already one of the most-visited cities in the Middle Atlantic states and expects to get even busier.

According to most city fathers, Atlantic City itself was at stake when New Jersey voters approved a November 2, 1976 referendum to allow gambling here. From a swank summering place for the well-heeled through the first 40 years of this century, the town had lost much of its glitter and charm. Not the broad beaches, the famous Boardwalk, the elegant old hotels, not even the Miss America Pageant; nothing had been able to stop a general deterioration of the city's face, charms and main industry—tourism. Like the rest of its attractions, most of its once-grand restaurants faded into oblivion.

But as the city is reviving, so are its public dining facilities. While the Jersey Shore Dinner—a collage of deep-fried, heavily breaded seafood, most often made with creatures caught long ago and far away—is still the dominant staple on most big restaurant menus, there are several worthwhile new places, as well as some of the fine old landmarks that have survived Atlantic City's dark age.

Dress tends to be less formal here than in other eastern cities, but the better places usually request jackets for men at dinner. In most cases, a single 15-percent tip covers all gratuities other than coat checking and valet parking.

Parking, by the way, is a serious and often costly problem. Taxis or public transit are welcome alternatives to driving within the city, and because Atlantic City's restaurant district is only two blocks deep, bus service is simple and frequent.

A problem particular to shore resort restaurants is refusal to accept reservations, especially during the high season from June through August. Dining in and around Atlantic City can mean waiting literally hours in the bar, which is almost always bigger than the dining area and often staffed with aggressively sales-oriented barkeeps. The best approach is to sign up for a table, and if the wait is an hour or more, leave the place and spend the hour strolling, shopping or playing a round of mini-golf. Many of the best restaurants, however, do reserve tables.

The most popular street foods, like the most frequent visitors, come from Philadelphia, just 60 miles to the northwest. These are the steak sandwich, the hoagie sandwich (actually an Italian loaf, split and filled with cheese, bologna, salami, lettuce, onion, oil and oregano) and the soft pretzel. Most tourists take home boxes of Atlantic City fudge or salt-water taffy—which may be the stickiest, most tooth-destroying sweet on earth.

All in all, it looks like the Old Queen of the South Jersey seashore is beginning a new, long and joyous reign.

# Restaurants and Food Sources
(Area code: 609)

## BIG DEAL

### WORTH IT

***Knife and Fork Inn,*** Atlantic and Pacific Avenues (344-1133). One of the best restaurants of its kind. Top-quality, fresh seafood distinctively prepared, though prices are high and credit cards are not honored. Try the mussels marinière as an appetizer, or the meaty crab fingers on crushed ice with mustard dip. The bouillabaisse is big and excellent. The vegetables are sometimes the best part of the meal, especially the julienned, deep-fried zucchini and pancake-sized corn fritters. Service is generally top notch in one of the lasting culinary landmarks of the city. Reservations for groups of more than four only. Closed Monday. Entrées from $3.25 (L), $8.50 (D). No credit cards.

### NOT WORTH IT

***Le Palais,*** Resorts International Hotel, Boardwalk at North Carolina Avenue (340-6400). Big and ornate, but while Sinatra, Gleason, etc., are playing the supper club elsewhere in this big casino, the main dining room does not have its act together. The service can be—and often is—a tragicomedy. The kitchen tries, but doesn't quite come up to the price level. Portions of the French-Continental fare are small, only average in quality. If you're there, try the Dover sole in cream sauce with grapes as garnish. The best pasta is the fettuccine verte Le Palais, with smoked salmon and shards of truffle. Dinner only. Closed Monday. Entrées from $10. AE, CB, DC, MC, V.

# INTERNATIONAL

## AMERICAN

***Ram's Head Inn,*** White Horse Pike, Absecon (652-1700). Close enough to the Boardwalk to note here, even though it is not within the city limits. Generally fine seafood in an old renovated building. Beautiful grounds, polished, early-American décor. Try the oysters with caviar or shrimp in a fine mayonnaise curry. No reservations Saturday night. Sunday, dinner only. Open seven days a week. Entrées from $4.95 (L), $8.95 (D). AE, DC, MC, V.

## CONTINENTAL

***Casa del Sol,*** Holiday Inn, Missouri Avenue and the Boardwalk (348-4011). Ocean and Boardwalk view, elegant décor and surprisingly good food and service. Paella, French, Italian and American dishes in a Spanish décor. Good lobster, rack of lamb, prime rib. Music (sometimes classical guitar) most nights. Dinner only. Open seven days a week. Entrées from $8. AE, DC, MC, V.

## FRENCH

***The Palm Court,*** Howard Johnson's Regency Motor Lodge, Atlantic and Arkansas Avenues (348-4411). Large, well-appointed room, pale-green carpeting and velour walls. Good service, good food. Mildly curried veal with fruit chutney and bananas is recommended. So is crêpe Louise, with lump crab meat and sauce Nantua. Sweetbreads are well prepared, too. Fair wine list. Saturday and Sunday, dinner only. Entrées from $5 (L), $7.50 (D). AE, CB, DC, MC, V.

***Le Café de Paris,*** 2825 Atlantic Avenue (344-5553). A small, budding bistro that may be the precursor of things to come on the shore. *Canard à l'orange*, red snapper *du chef* and many other pleasant entrées. Informal, cozy. Dinner only. Open seven days a week. Entrées from $7. DC, MC, V.

## ITALIAN

***Ristorante Alberto,*** Pacific and Mississippi Avenues (344-7000). Northern Italian cuisine, cooked by Chef Albert Couf. Veal Florentine, a good fettuccine, strolling violinist Friday and Saturday evenings. Saturday and Sunday, dinner only. Open seven days a week. Entrées from $3.75 (L), $6 (D). AE, CB, DC, MC, V.

# SPECIALTY COOKING

## SEAFOOD

***Captain's Galley,*** 12 S. Douglas Avenue, Margate (822-6100). Informal setting adjoining a retail seafood store, with the fresh catch of the day: sea trout, fluke, flounder, bluefish, scallops, clams, plus fine if not local shrimp. Most dishes are cooked Italian style in red sauces and with cheese. Specialty is Sauce Daufuskie, a delicate mix of white wine, onion, mushroom and mayonnaise. Daily blackboard specials. Most seafood is poached in wine, then broiled. Open seven days a week. Entrées from $5.50 (L & D). No credit cards.

## STEAK/ROAST BEEF

***Casa del Sol,*** Holiday Inn, Boardwalk and Missouri Avenue (348-4011). (See description under CONTINENTAL).

# FOR INDIVIDUAL NEEDS

## IF YOU HAVE TIME FOR ONLY ONE MEAL

***Knife and Fork Inn,*** Atlantic and Pacific Avenues (344-1133). (See description under BIG DEAL/WORTH IT.)

## BEST HOTEL MEAL

***The Palm Court,*** Howard Johnson's Regency Motor Lodge, Atlantic and Arkansas Avenues (348-4411). (See description under FRENCH.)

## BUSINESS LUNCH

***Le Grand Fromage,*** 25 Gordon's Alley (347-2743). Quiches, cheese plates, salads, sandwiches, plus an attractive menu of French entrées in a pleasant country-French setting. *Coq au vin*, chicken and veal Cordon Bleu and sautéed crabs are among the features. Desserts include chocolate fondue ($2). Saturday, dinner only. Sunday, brunch and dinner only. Tuesday, lunch only. Open seven days a week. Fixed-price Sunday brunch $5.95; entrées from $4.75 (L), $6.50 (D). MC, V.

## FAST, GOOD FOOD

***Momma Tucci's,*** Pacific off N. Carolina Avenue. Hoagies and pizzas among the best in town, at the counter or at one of the tables in the back. Open 11 A.M. to midnight. Closed Sunday during the winter. No credit cards.

## ROMANTIC

***Front Porch,*** 132 S. New York Avenue (345-1917). This used to be the upstairs porch of the old Chester Inn Hotel. American food and French dishes (duck in orange sauce) are served in a setting of white wrought iron and greenery. Open seven days a week. Entrées from $3 (L), $6.50 (D). AE, DC, MC, V.

## LATE-NIGHT SERVICE

***Wedgewood Pavillon Buffet,*** Resorts International Hotel, N. Carolina Avenue and the Boardwalk (344-6000). All-day, all-night service with an ever-changing buffet of cold and some hot foods. Open seven days a week. Entrées from $2.50. AE, CB, DC, MC, V.

# Baltimore

There was a time, and it lasted a long time, when the food and wine to be had in Baltimore were almost without rival in America. When George Washington traveled from his plantation in Virginia to the capital at Philadelphia, he liked to stop in Baltimore and feast at the Fountain Inn, first of the city's famous hostelries (those were the days when inn was a name you gave to an inn, and not to every third-rate steak house with an electric fireplace and a ceiling beamed in Styrofoam).

In the ensuing century and a half the reputation of the Monumental City was kept alive for such visitors as Lafayette, Dickens and Henry James by the likes of Barnum's City Hotel, the Caswell and the Rennert, the last-named of which, as late as the second quarter of this century, served an oyster pie that drove H. L. Mencken to orgies of euphoric prose.

Those were the days when diamondback terrapin and canvasback ducks were as plentiful as oysters, and all three shared the menu of a typical Baltimore banquet. A winter banquet, of course, but thanks to the richness of Maryland's lands and waters every season brought its own delights: in the spring shad, asparagus and strawberries; in the summer the great blue crab accompanied by Anne Arundel cantaloupes, shoepeg corn and home-grown tomatoes; in the fall hams and scrapple, buckwheat cakes and sausage.

None of these foods ever went out of fashion (though terrapin, now enjoying a small comeback, priced itself out of the market for a time, and it is illegal to shoot canvasback ducks), nor did the traditions of Maryland eating, which continued to thrive as they always had in local homes and in a dwindling number of private clubs. But dining out in style was virtually killed in Baltimore as elsewhere by three successive plagues, namely Prohibition, the

Depression and World War II. It is scarcely surprising that since the combined life span of these assassins of gastronomy totaled a quarter of a century, their invidious influence should have lingered almost that much longer, and that as recently as a dozen years ago, Baltimore (like many another community across the country) was all but devoid of good restaurants.

The sixties, however, witnessed the generation of an increased interest in most of the arts—not the least of which was that of eating out and well. As a result, the number of acceptable to excellent restaurants on the scene has increased dramatically; and, perhaps most significantly, the variety has grown to include restaurants reflecting the cuisines of many nationalities. The city is still a long way, it must be added, from being a great restaurant center, such as New York, New Orleans, San Francisco or (a name recently added to that list) Washington, D.C. But it is improving, and the visitor to Baltimore, if he knows where to go, can dine out every night for a week or even for a month without either repeating a restaurant or growing bored with the sameness of the fare.

In truth, there are a large number of restaurants in Baltimore left over from the days when a shrimp cocktail, crabmeat imperial and an ice-cream sundae were considered the ultimate culinary adventure. Not that there's anything wrong with those, particularly for the newcomer to the city, but after you've lived in Baltimore for over thirty years they do pall. Fortunately, there is now a great deal more variety. But for all the new-found riches, there have been the inevitable losses, and not since Miller Brothers (famous up and down the East Coast) closed in the early sixties has there been a restaurant that did a significant number of seafood dishes well.

This has its advantages as well as its disadvantages. In the old days you went to one restaurant over and over again. Today, if you want the best steamed crabs in town you go to **Obrycki's;** the best soft-shelled crabs are to be had at **Marconi's;** the best crab cake changes spots almost monthly, and the best imperial seems to be looking for a spot; the best fried oysters come from what is almost literally a hole in the wall on Falls Road; but for steamed clams or clam chowder it's **The Chesapeake,** one of the most popular and expensive restaurants in town.

One of the problems of categorizing restaurants in Baltimore, in fact, stems from an abundance of seafood. Every restaurant has seafood of one kind or another, and the reason the "seafood" category that follows is so short and so misleading is that *all* the good restaurants could more or less be put under seafood without stretching the point too far. **Haussner's,** for instance, listed under German restaurants, has possibly the longest seafood menu in town. Similarly, Schellhase's (known also as a German restaurant and as a former Mencken haunt) has one great dish—crab au gratin. It is probably best, therefore, for the newcomer in town to take the ten minutes or so required to read the listings all the way through.

A few words to the wise: Baltimore is impossible to get around in by public transportation, and taxicabs are ridiculously perverse. You can't find an empty one on the street, and even if you call for one, you're likely to be told there's an hour's wait, and if it's raining, two hours'. Therefore, the best thing is to either go to restaurants within walking distance of your hotel or beg, borrow or rent a car. Either way, get a street map and study it for half an hour. It's the best way to learn any city.

If you do have a car and some time to spare, it is worth exploring Maryland's countryside and one of its country inns. North of Baltimore is **The Milton Inn;** south is **The King's Contrivance.** But don't simply drive out to them from midtown—the most direct way is not at all attractive. Get a map, find out where you're going, and map a route that takes you through country roads to get there. You can take the direct route back when it's dark.

More words to the wise: Baltimore's dining hour is generally around 8 P.M., and if you want a reservation in one of the popular restaurants between 8 P.M. and 9 P.M., it is wise to call the day before, if possible. Restaurants that do not accept reservations are noted in the listings.

Baltimore is a little less expensive than most other major East Coast cities, but only a little. As in most places, if you're going to a very inexpensive restaurant or a Chinese restaurant, you probably won't have a bottle of wine. And, in any restaurant, an appetizer and dessert can make the meal almost twice the cost of just an entrée and what goes with it. Tipping is such a personal thing that it's hard to give advice, but as in other cities the general rule is about 15 percent—more or less depending on so many variables. When the meal has been very inexpensive, a larger percentage is sometimes in order, and when it has been very expensive, a smaller percentage may be adequate, unless the service is outstanding.

Baltimore is a conservative city, and although they are growing rarer, there are still places where you will *not* be seated without a coat and tie. There are even a couple of places that won't seat women in pants.

# Restaurants and Food Sources

(Area code: 301)

## BIG DEAL

### WORTH IT

***Tio Pepe,*** 10 East Franklin Street (539-4675). A charming look, superb food (when they're trying in the kitchen) and punctilious if occasionally haughty service are combined in what many consider Baltimore's best. The shrimps in garlic sauce make a fine appetizer or a perfect light lunch with a spot of salad. Other specialties include black bean soup, sole with bananas, rack of lamb and tournedos. Everyone ought to try the rolled dessert cakes. The one with pine nuts is best, followed closely by chocolate. Reservations must be made several days to several weeks (for a Saturday) ahead, but if you happen to be in town for a couple of days, call anyway—you might get lucky, especially if you don't mind dining at the popular Spanish (but not Baltimore) hour of 10:30 P.M. Saturday and Sunday, dinner only. Open seven days a week. Entrées from $4.50 (L), $7.25 (D). AE, MC, V.

## NOT WORTH IT

***Shane's,*** 1924 York Road, Timonium (252-4100). Shane's isn't really a bad restaurant, but it is definitely a big deal, with its huge space, its garish décor, its hovering service and pseudo-sophisticated airs. With all that the food—prime rib, veal *française,* rock fish stuffed with crab meat—seems quite secondary. There's a cabaret theater downstairs four nights a week and Sunday afternoons. Open seven days a week. Entrées from $4.50 (L), $8.95 (D). AE, MC, V.

# INTERNATIONAL

## AMERICAN

***Prime Rib,*** Horizon House Apartments, 1101 North Calvert Street (539-1804). There is a sleek, mostly chic excitement here that Baltimoreans say gives them the feeling of New York. But it isn't all surface; the Prime Rib is also notable for its fine food and service. The menu is limited to a few dishes (steak, prime rib) that the restaurant does extremely well. They used to have the best imperial (crab and lobster) in Baltimore, but for some reason it's been changed, and not for the better. The Greenberg potato skins are still interesting, though, and the salads have improved recently. Dinner only. Open seven days a week. Entrées from $9.95. AE, CB, DC, MC, V.

***Pimlico Hotel,*** 5301 Park Heights Avenue (664-8014). No matter when you go, no matter whether you have made a reservation or not (but by all means do) you will have to wait. Despite its seemingly endless series of dining rooms, this popular restaurant (it isn't a hotel) is always crowded, and no wonder. The food is consistently on a high level and the portions are huge. The menu, too, is enormous. If you don't want lobster (fresh), a steak or veal Parmesan, try something from the Chinese menu, or a pizza. Eclectic, yes. The homemade desserts are not to be missed, but one piece of anything will sink a moderate-sized rowboat. One warning: despite all its virtues, the Pimlico has a noisy, rushed atmosphere about it. Open seven days a week. Entrées from $3.95 (L), $8.50 (D). AE, MC, V.

# CHINESE

***Bamboo House,*** Yorktowne Plaza at York and Cranbrook Roads, Cockeysville (666-9550). Don't be put off by the shopping-center entrance. Inside, it is small (too small for its popularity), attractive, rewarding. Northern Chinese (Mandarin and Szechuan cuisines), including Peking duck (order a day in advance), Ming shrimp Szechuan style and a "Friends of China Club" mystery dish that has proven less gimmicky than its name. They also have a suckling pig dinner for 10 to 15 people at $150. Good soups and appetizers. Saturday, dinner only. Entrées from $2.95 (L), $4.95 (D). AE, MC, V.

***Imperial Palace,*** 3541 Brenbrook Drive at Liberty Road (922-3300). Big and sometimes crowded and noisy, this is at its best midweek. At *their* best, the Peking and crisp duck, *moo shu* pork, shrimp with garlic or with walnuts, Mongolian barbeque and other specialities are quite remarkable. Hot-and-sour soup makes an excellent starter, as do boiled dumplings. The restaurant, on several days' notice, will serve a ten-course Chinese dinner to ten or more people for $12 plus tax a person. Open seven days a week. Entrées from $2.50 (L), $3.50 (D). AE, MC, V.

***Wong's,*** 5509 Reisterstown Road (358-2700). More modest than the other two mentioned here, Wong's is nevertheless a most attractive place. Cantonese food is the specialty, though some Szechuan dishes have been added recently. Try chicken wonton soup or the unusual shrimp toast for an appetizer, pork with snow peas, curried shrimp or duck with almonds for a main course. Open seven days a week. Sunday, dinner only, from 2 P.M. Entrées from $2.95 (L), $3.50 (D). AE, MC, V.

# FRENCH

***Café des Artistes,*** in the Morris Mechanic Theatre Building, 9 Hopkins Plaza (837-6600). From the time it opened in 1977, the Café had good food and attractive dining rooms. Now the service has caught up and its appeal is even greater. Duck pâté with hazelnuts, and mussels in herbed garlic butter have proven good appetizers; among the main courses, trout stuffed with salmon mousse and served with lobster sauce is excellent when available, as are tournedos Charlemagne with truffles and foie gras. Saturday, dinner only. Closed Sunday. Entrées from $4.75 (L), $7.25 (D). AE, MC, V.

***Country Fare,*** 100 Painters Mill Road (363-3131). No, it's not fried chicken and corn-on-the-cob, as the name might lead one to believe. It's an ambitious and successful Continental (mainly French) restaurant in a 1760 building. You enjoy being there, and you enjoy the *escargots dijonnaise, tournedos périgourdine, escalope de veau champignons,* sweetbreads Gismonde. Saturday and Sunday, dinner only. Open seven days a week. Entrées from $2 (L), $7 (D). MC.

## GERMAN

***Haussner's,*** 3244 Eastern Avenue (327-8365). With its huge art collection (the biggest outside of a museum in Baltimore) and the city's longest menu, Haussner's is as much a tourist attraction as a restaurant. The art ranges from the vaguely interesting to the totally laughable, but it's there in such profusion that it's fun. The food, half German and half Maryland seafood, ranges from the expectedly acceptable to the surprisingly good, considering that this place serves 2,000 people on a busy day. On such a day you will have to wait in line an hour outside to get in the door. It's worth it because Haussner's is a happy place. No reservations. Closed Sunday and Monday. Entrées from $2.95 (L), $5.95 (D). No credit cards.

## GREEK

***Ikaros,*** 4805 Eastern Avenue (633-9825). The city's oldest established Greek restaurant is still its best, though others have their moments. It used to be small, ugly, cheap and dependable; it expanded a few years ago and is now large, ugly, cheap and dependable. Among the specialties: stuffed grape leaves, spinach pies, cheese pies, lemon soup, lamb prepared several ways (try *kapama,* with tomatoes and rice), moussaka, sometimes fish (the squid, though, is better in Little Italy). There are Greek salads, and the homemade desserts include baklava. Reservations necessary for parties of more than five people. Closed Tuesday. Entrées from $3.50 (L & D). No credit cards.

## INDIAN

***Jai-Hind,*** 5511 York Road (323-8440). Baltimore's only Indian restaurant is as unprepossessing as anyone could want, sharing a building with an Indian food store. But there is more here than meets the eye. The specialties include chicken *tandoori* and any number of curries, which can be served mild to very hot, depending on your preference. Unless you know and like them, don't bother with the side dishes, except for the delightful *raitha,* a fresh, cool combination of yogurt, cucumbers and spices, and a perfect foil for the hot Indian food. Closed Monday. Entrées from $3.50 (L), $6.50 (D). AE, CB, MC, V.

## ITALIAN

***Capriccio,*** 242 South High Street (685-2710). One of the area's two Northern Italian restaurants of consequence (see also **Fiori** under IN THE SUBURBS/REISTERSTOWN), this relative newcomer also serves a few French dishes. The kitchen's accomplishments may not be uniformly excellent but are usually interesting. Among the better entrées are chicken and veal dishes, and the house's best creation is an appetizer called toast Capriccio, with mussels. There can be much flambéeing in the tiny dining room at dessert time. Dinner only. Open seven days a week. Entrées from $6.50. AE, DC, MC, V.

***Chiapparelli's,*** 237 South High Street (837-0309). Among the dozen or more restaurants in Little Italy that serve the well-known southern dishes, Chiapparelli's has been a favorite for some years, though performances vary and others (notably **Sabatino's**) give it a run for the money. Money is the operative word here, because Chiapparelli's has lately priced itself almost up there with the town's more expensive restaurants and it doesn't always live up to those prices. Still, the pesce Lauren, the lobster, clams and shrimp Pasquale, the veal Bryan are awfully good, and some of the salads are as good as any around. Saturday, dinner only. Open seven days a week. Entrées from $4.50 (L), $6.50 (D). AE, DC, MC, V.

## MEDITERRANEAN

***Café de Paris,*** 413 North Charles Street (685-1211). The name doesn't at all suggest the sort-of-Spanish, sort-of-Middle-Eastern, sort-of-North-African fare served late into the night (on weekends—other nights until 11 P.M.). By all means try it if you think you'd like a dish such as fish in a sauce combining tomatoes and lots of cumin. Closed Sunday and Monday. Entrées from $1.25 (L), $7 (D). MC, V.

## SPANISH

***Tio Pepe,*** 10 East Franklin Street (539-4675). (See description under BIG DEAL/WORTH IT.)

***Torremolinos,*** 101 West Monument Street (752-9305). After a change of ownership about two years ago, this once so-so restaurant has become a real contender. Anyone who needs convincing should try the mussels in green sauce or artichoke hearts with ham for an appetizer, followed by chicken with mushrooms and green olives or shrimp in a light tomato sauce with Pernod, or veal. It's plainer than Tio Pepe, the desserts aren't as fine and they put tuna in the salads; but then the prices are cheaper than Tio Pepe, too. Saturday and Sunday, dinner only. Open seven days a week. Entrées from $2.75 (L), $5.25 (D). AE, MC.

# SPECIALTY COOKING

## CRÊPES

***Sascha's,*** 80 North Charles Street (752-5228). This outdoor April-to-October café has a menu that includes anything you can put in a crêpe (and that's just about anything) to sandwiches, omelets and other relatively light fare. It's not great, but a casual sort of place, and fun. Closed Monday. Entrées from $1.65 (L & D). No credit cards.

## DELI

***Attman's,*** 1019 East Lombard Street (563-2666). In nearby East Baltimore there is a street of shops that have hung on from the days when this was the center of the Jewish community. It no longer is, and some of the stores have closed, but there is enough life left in "corned beef row" to make it an enjoyable sightseeing expedition, especially on Sundays. Attman's will feed you a good corned-beef sandwich, or roast beef, pastrami, blintzes, pickles, herring roll-mops or Mrs. Adler's matzo-ball soup—if you're willing to wait in line and shout out your order when it's your turn. Open seven days a week. Entrées from $1.50 (L & D). No credit cards.

## HAMBURGER

***Uncle Charlie's Bistro,*** 2 East Madison Street (539-1228). A charming, informal bar and dining room with the menu listed on slates on the walls. A very upbeat atmosphere and good, simple, semi-French food such as brie soup and filled crêpes. They also have a delicious hamburger, alias chopped sirloin. Open seven days a week. Entrées from $4.50 (L & D). AE, MC, V.

## HEALTH FOOD/VEGETARIAN

***The Green Earth Café,*** 823 North Charles Street (752-4465). At last there's a health food restaurant in Baltimore where the emphasis is on good food attractively prepared and served. There are vegetarian meals, but fish and even chicken are served. You can bring wine and, believe it or not, you are allowed to smoke. Sunday, dinner only. Open seven days a week. Entrées from $1.50 (L & D). No credit cards.

## OYSTERS

***Faidley's,*** in the Lexington Market, Eutaw and Lexington Streets (727-4898). That "great protein factory," as H. L. Mencken called the Chesapeake Bay, has been serving Marylanders oysters and crabs faithfully for hundreds of years. It used to be that every self-respecting restaurant had a raw bar that you could walk up to and order your oysters shucked right there, and eat as many as you liked with a beer or two. Those days are gone now, but a couple of raw bars still hang around. The best-known is Faidley's, because it's in the famous Lexington Market (a tourist must). Farther uptown, the **Lafayette Seafood Company** (in Corcoran's at 2118 North Charles Street) also will shuck your oysters as you watch. Prices go up every week, but a half dozen good-sized ones will probably cost about $1.50. Both places closed on Sunday. No credit cards.

## PIZZA

***DeNittis,*** 906 Trinity Street (685-5601). The closest thing in Little Italy to the old-time Italian restaurant where you used to go for filling, inexpensive, flavorful food in a neighborhood atmosphere, DeNittis has kept its character while many around it have gone the route of the trendy and chic. It has the best pizzas in town, thick and gooey with lots of cheese and tomato and anything else you want to order. Open seven days a week. Entrées from $3 (L & D). AE, DC, MC, V.

## SEAFOOD

***The Chesapeake,*** 1701 North Charles Street (837-7711). Somewhat less stuffy than it used to be, and not quite as good either, the Chesapeake is still the closest thing to an all-round seafood restaurant in Baltimore. From clam chowder and oysters Rockefeller through crab lumps in butter and Newburgs, the fare is generally satisfactory to very good. They have nice steaks, too. Saturday and Sunday, dinner only. Open seven days a week. Entrées from $5 (L), $8 (D). AE, CB, DC, MC, V.

***Obrycki's Olde Crab House,*** 1729 East Pratt Street (732-6399). Anyone who wants to become familiar with Maryland seafood should try oysters on the half shell and steamed crabs. Trouble is, to try both and be reasonably sure they're from local waters, you have to be here in September or October, since crabs are a summer and oysters a winter food. Some people think steamed crabs are not worth all the trouble to eat them, but they deserve a try under the best circumstances, and the best local circumstances are to be found at Obrycki's, open from April to October only. You *can* have a few hard crabs and go on to an entrée from Obrycki's menu, but the other seafood isn't any great shakes; besides local people don't do it that way. Here, you eat crabs and drink beer and that's it. Prices are by the crab, and nowadays the crab is $1 or more apiece. Dinner only. Closed Sunday and Monday. No credit cards.

## STEAK

***Danny's,*** Charles and Biddle Streets (539-1393). This pretentious restaurant is over-priced, ugly, and has lackadaisical service. Nevertheless, the raw materials are the best obtainable, and whether it's a plain steak you want or a filet Henri IV, the chances are you won't be disappointed. There are also other excellent choices on the menu, from fresh Scotch salmon to Dover sole, live Maine lobsters and beef Wellington. Saturday, dinner only. Closed Sunday. Entrées from $4 (L), $8 (D). AE, DC, MC, V.

# FOR INDIVIDUAL NEEDS

## IF YOU HAVE TIME FOR ONLY ONE MEAL

***Marconi's,*** 106 West Saratoga Street (752-9286). A lady who remembers this restaurant from its earliest days back in the immediate post–World War I period says that it is essentially the same today, and how many restaurants in America can make that claim? Located in a former row house, Marconi's is not at all the place to go for glamour, beauty, comfort or expensive dining. The wine list is a joke, the waiters have been there for a generation or more and are set in their (not your) ways, and if it is crowded (as it almost always is), you will have to stand and wait in the dingy hall for up to an hour. Why, then, is Marconi's popular? For the best of reasons, its food. Part French, part Italian, part American, part Maryland, the food is all-important at Marconi's. Have sole anything (a favorite is Marguery), lobster cardinal, sweetbreads *bordelaise,* the best soft-shelled crabs in town or excellent lamb chops. Vegetables are always fresh (where *do* they get the peas in January?), and the most popular are creamed spinach and fried eggplant. Have a chocolate sundae for dessert—no kidding. No reservations. Closed Sunday and Monday. Entrées from $3.25 (L), $3.50 (D). No credit cards.

## BEST HOTEL MEAL

***The Crossroads,*** Cross Keys Inn, Cross Keys (532-9090). The Cross Keys Inn is the best hotel in Baltimore, and its trendy-elegant restaurant manages a better than average hotel dining room dinner. Sunday, brunch only. Open seven days a week. Entrées from $3 (L), $8.95 (D). AE, CB, DC, MC, V.

## RESTAURANT NEAR AIRPORT

***The Bard's Tavern,*** Friendship Hotel, Baltimore-Washington International Airport (761-7700). Perfectly presentable if not really exciting, the restaurant pretends to English airs, but beneath all the palaver is a good piece of roast beef with a popover. Open seven days a week. Entrées from $3.75 (L), $9.95 (D). AE, DC, MC, V.

## BUSINESS LUNCH

***Café des Artistes,*** in the Morris Mechanic Theatre Building, 9 Hopkins Plaza (837-6600). (See description under FRENCH.) Also, for those who want just a snack while closing the deal, the same restaurant's **Brasserie.** (See description under FOR DRINKS.)

***Hollander's,*** 14 East 25th Street (467-1662). An old standby among the sporting crowd, Hollander's has had its ups and downs in recent years, but if you're in the northern part of town at lunchtime, it's a pleasant place for a crab cake and a chat. Closed Sunday. Entrées from $2 (L), $4.95 (D). AE, CB, DC, MC, V.

## FAST, GOOD FOOD

***The Woman's Industrial Exchange,*** 333 North Charles Street (685-4388). About one hundred years ago a small store was opened downtown where women in, as the phrase went then, "reduced circumstances" could take the product of their labor, be it bureau scarves or apple pies, and have it sold anonymously. The Woman's Exchange, believe it or not, still serves that function, but now is far better known for its lunchroom in back. You can't get a drink, but you can get chicken salad made with homemade mayonnaise, old-fashioned sandwiches, homemade rolls, and such daily specials as broiled tomatoes and bacon or, in the winter, buckwheat cakes and sausage. A real piece of Baltimore. No reservations. Lunch only. Closed Saturday and Sunday. Lunch from $1.50. No credit cards.

## BEST WINE LIST

***Danny's,*** Charles and Biddle Streets (539-1393). (See description under STEAK.)

## FOR DRINKS

***The Brasserie,*** in Café des Artistes, Morris Mechanic Theatre Building (837-6600). The tony bar of one of the city's best restaurants provides a bit of glitter that the downtown can well afford, a bit of food for those who want a crab cake or a piece of quiche after their martinis, and sometimes a bit of entertainment (piano and singer). Closed Sunday. Entrées from $2.95 (L & D). AE, MC, V.

***Owl Bar,*** in the Belvedere, Charles and Chase Streets (539-6000). Once the city's grandest hotel—Sarah Bernhardt and Fritz Kreisler slept here, Marie of Rumania stopped by and the Duchess of Windsor frequented the tea dances during World War I when she was just Wallis Warfield—the Belvedere has been renovated as an apartment house. Its magnificent barroom has been cleaned and polished but remains much the same otherwise. Currently as popular for a drink or an informal meal as it ever was in the good old days, but the food isn't much. Also try the Belvedere's recently opened 13th Floor Bar. Open seven days a week. Entrées from $5.95 (L & D). AE, MC, V.

## RESTAURANT WITH MUSIC

***Tom Jones,*** Glenmont Towers, Goucher Boulevard off Loch Raven Boulevard, Towson (828-1187). Those who like fifties dance music (with a vocalist), and who want lots of it and loud, will be happy at Tom Jones, where the food is passable, too. Prime rib, steak, beef-oriented menu. Dinner only. Open seven days a week. Entrées from $6.95. AE, DC, MC, V.

## LATE-NIGHT SERVICE

***Little Italy,*** near the center of town, has a dozen or so restaurants, and most of them stay open until 1 or 2 A.M. for either a full meal or just cannoli and coffee. (See listings under ITALIAN and PIZZA for some suggestions.)

***Café de Paris,*** 413 North Charles Street (685-1211). (See description under MEDITERRANEAN.) Often open until 4 A.M. on weekends. Call first to check.

***The Green Earth Café,*** 823 North Charles Street (752-4465). (See description under HEALTH FOOD/VEGETARIAN.) Open until 3 A.M. weekends, but you have to bring your own wine.

## SUNDAY BRUNCH

***Uncle Charlie's Bistro,*** 2 East Madison Street (539-1228). (See description under HAMBURGER.)

## SUNDAY-EVENING MEAL

***The Bard's Tavern,*** Friendship Hotel, Baltimore-Washington International Airport (761-7700). (See description under RESTAURANT NEAR AIRPORT.)

## FOR FAMILIES WITH CHILDREN

***Haussner's,*** 3244 Eastern Avenue (327-8365). (See description under GERMAN.)

## COUNTRY INN

***The King's Contrivance,*** Route 32 at Route 29, Columbia (995-0500). Sheltered from the roads and buildings around it by a grove of old trees, The King's Contrivance is at its best in the summer, when it is possible to sit on the enclosed porch and watch the sun go down across the lawn. In any season the Continental dishes are interesting, among them shrimps *rémoulade en coquille,* baked stuffed cherrystone clams, exquisite crab-and-lobster bisque, followed by Dover sole, steak with green peppercorns, frogs' legs, crabmeat Dewey, fine salads and a superior chocolate mousse. Saturday and Sunday, dinner only. Open seven days a week. Entrées from $2.50 (L), $7.50 (D). MC.

***The Milton Inn,*** York Road at Sparks, north of Cockeysville (771-4366). An eighteenth-century house where one sits by the fire in a dark-paneled room for cocktails, then proceeds to an elegant formal dining room for dinner, this restaurant is more dependable for atmosphere than for food or service. The last two are *usually* fine, but on occasion there can be a disaster. It is as well to know one is taking a bit, if only a bit, of a chance. The menu is French and Italian. Try red snapper *marseillaise, saltimbocca alla romana,* tournedos Rossini, rack of lamb. Although not overwhelming, the food is reliable; the dinner is almost always worth the check. At its best The Milton Inn is a lovely experience. Saturday and Sunday, dinner only. Open seven days a week. Entrées from $3 (L), $9 (D). AE, MC, V.

# IN THE SUBURBS

## LOCH RAVEN

***Peerce's Plantation,*** Dulaney Valley Road, seven miles north of Towson (252-3100). In the old days it was an open-porched chicken and corn-on-the-cob emporium. But lately the porch has been closed in and a new Continental menu with a few twists (Bermuda fish chowder, filet Stephanie, veal in ample portions) combine with good service to produce a very pleasant evening. Open seven days a week. Entrées from $4 (L), $7 (D). AE, MC, V.

## OWINGS MILLS

***Country Fare,*** 100 Painters Mill Road (363-3131). (See description under FRENCH.)

## REISTERSTOWN

***Fiori,*** Route 140, just west of Reisterstown (833-6300). Formerly this was the home of the Country Fare. When Country Fare moved closer to Baltimore, it left behind this very charming Northern Italian restaurant where the prices are reasonable and the service is spirited and dedicated. Saturday and Sunday, dinner only. Open seven days a week. Entrées from $2.25 (L), $5.50 (D). MC.

# MARKETS

***Lexington Market,*** Eutaw and Lexington Streets (685-6169). It bills itself as "world famous" and maybe so. Certainly anyone with an interest in food and markets who comes to Baltimore goes there, for the atmosphere as much as the food. This is a real old-fashioned market, complete with stalls and sawdust on the floor and rabbit carcasses hanging up. It is for shopping, of course, but there are a remarkable number of items to be bought and consumed on the premises, from yogurt to raw oysters to crab cakes to deli sandwiches, Polish sausages, fried chicken, salads, pastries and doughnuts. The Lexington Market ought to be seen by anyone spending time in Baltimore, because it's as much a part of the city as Fort McHenry, and a lot more fun. Open from 7:30 A.M. to 6 P.M. Closed Sunday.

## GIFT WINES

***Harry's Liquors,*** 3113 Greenmount Avenue (235-4883). Good selection of French, some German and Italian wines. They are less interested in American wines, but have some. Closed Sunday. DC, MC, V.

# Boston

Once the early colonists had managed to establish a secure toehold on the edge of the New World, they found themselves surrounded by a gustatory banquet of unbelievable richness and variety. There were rivers virtually teeming with fish, rocky shores encrusted with mollusks, and forests alive with deer, quail, wild turkey and other game. By all accounts the local fauna, running around as it did in the wild, feeding on sweet berries, leaves, roots, and each other, was extraordinarily tasty, if a bit chewy from overexertion.

The only trouble was, the colonists were Englishpersons. They applied to all this *richesse* the culinary techniques of their homeland, which is to say they either left it whole and roasted it (plain), or hacked it into chops and fried it (plain), or threw it into a pot and boiled it (still plain) to a watery death. Being Puritans as well as Englishpersons, they just didn't hold with much fancying-up of their food.

Mercifully for us, corrupting influences crept in almost from the beginning. Long before the enlightening contributions of our own Julia Child, the brilliant Madeleine Kamman, or even Fannie Farmer, New England fishermen learned from French fishermen how to make *chaudré,* which the Yankees spelled chowder.

In those days chowder was a hearty soup of fish or seafood poached in its own tasty broth, fragrant with salt pork and onion. They threw in little cubes of potato, to keep the seafood company, and toward the end they thickened the broth with crushed dry crackers from the barrel, and enriched it with heavy, creamy milk. Today you'll find chowder on almost every menu in Boston. Some of it is still pretty good, though a lot of it comes from cans and might be put to better use as library paste. What you will *never* find in these parts, by the way, is that thin, reddish concoction known as "Manhattan chowder," which all proper Bostonians consider a contradiction in terms and an abomination.

Like chowder, codfish still plays a featured role in local cuisine in the form of scrod: delicate white filets cut from young cod or haddock, delicious either broiled or deep-fried. And Indian pudding, a sweet, creamy dessert of corn meal and molasses, survives at a few local eateries, notably **Durgin Park** and **Locke-Ober.**

But don't come questing after Boston baked beans, because they don't exist, except in sugary versions the Puritans wouldn't have recognized. You probably won't run into the New England boiled dinner that was once so unavoidable at boarding schools, either; and the mutton chop, still a favorite fifty years ago, is now virtually extinct.

Contemporary Bostonians enjoy as varied and sophisticated a diet as citizens of most much larger towns. You can still dine grandly here in the opulent dining rooms of such venerable landmarks as the **Ritz Carlton Hotel,** the **Parker House,** and **Locke-Ober;** and you can feast for very little on amazingly exotic fare in dozens of simple family-run storefronts.

One of the great delights of Boston is that its vital center remains a patchwork quilt of clearly defined ethnic neighborhoods, each with its cluster of restaurants, groceries and shops, and all within a few blocks of the Boston Common. In the old North End, for example, almost thirty homey Italian restaurants perfume the narrow streets with spicy aromas of garlic, basil and sweet peppers frying in oil. You can eat very cheaply here, at places like **The European** and Piccolo Venezia; or you can eat extremely well, at **Francesca's, Felicia's,** Ristorante Lucia and others. After dinner you might want to sample the extra-special cappuccino at the Caffe Paradiso; and for a take-out dessert or a snack, the *cannoli* at Etna Pastry on Prince Street may be one of the crispiest, most luscious pastries in the world.

A few blocks away is the waterfront, with its handsome brand-new parks and newly developed wharves. Here you'll find a lot of elegant boutiques and contemporary restaurants. The best-known seafood restaurants are a short taxi-ride away. Just two blocks in from the waterfront is the newly renovated Faneuil Hall Marketplace complex: three long warehouse buildings full of super-chic shops and eateries. The central building, also known as **Quincy Market,** is a bustling open mall devoted entirely to food and drink, from raw meat (Mort Berenson's The Prime Shoppe sells the finest cuts in town) to fast foods of all ethnic persuasions. Come here for a quick sandwich, a culinary souvenir of hard-to-find herbs or health foods, or a gustatory orgy. If you happen to be in town on a Friday or Saturday, be sure to take in the frenetic activity of Haymarket, Boston's open-air produce market, where pushcart vendors still offer great bargains. It's next door to Quincy Market.

On the other side of the Boston Common, tucked behind the Washington Street theater district, Boston's compact little Chinatown boasts a whole new crop of Hong Kong-trained Cantonese chefs. For exceptional Oriental fare, try steamed whole fish or clams at **King Wah,** Fung Won, or Carl's Pagoda. For cheap family-style meals, still authentic but folksier, you can't beat Henry's at 52 Beach; noodle-lovers shouldn't miss his fat, hand-cut *chow foon.*

And then there are Copley Square and Back Bay, bastions of Boston's blue-blooded aristocracy. Today their descendants and neighbors are energetic young working people who like to meet for drinks at **Friday's** or the **Ritz Bar** and for dinner wherever the food is good and the crowd lively.

Across the Charles River in Cambridge, the well-traveled and well-fed academic communities of Harvard and M.I.T. support a colorful jumble of international cuisines. Within four blocks of Harvard Square (which is only eight minutes from downtown Boston by subway) you can choose among restaurants offering French, German, Chinese, Vietnamese, Italian, Mexican, Spanish, Swiss, Brazilian, and Moroccan cooking, not to mention American, soup-and-salad, International Eclectic, etc. Here and elsewhere in Cambridge, restaurants of the latter category are often staffed by disaffected graduates of the local universities, whose adventurous palates and enthusiastic-if-untrained cooking can lead to some memorable meals; **Voyagers,** Peasant Stock, and the Turtle Café are good examples.

Serious cooks from all over New England come to Harvard Square to shop at **Cardullo's** for exotic ingredients; and a block away, in the Garage complex, **Formaggio** offers the city's finest array of imported cheeses, excellent charcuterie, and much-lauded sandwiches.

# Restaurants and Food Sources
(Area code: 617)

## BIG DEAL

### WORTH IT

***The Ritz Dining Room,*** Ritz-Carlton Hotel, 15 Arlington Street, Back Bay (536-5700). Classic French cuisine and impeccable service in a splendidly elegant high-ceilinged room overlooking the Public Garden. The Ritz prides itself on its sautéed Maine lobster in whiskey sauce, but most dishes are strictly traditional, and the real features here are the ambience, the excellent wine list, and the feeling of pampered luxury. Reservations are a good idea. Chaîne des Rotisseurs. Open seven days a week. Entrées from $8 (L), $9.50 (D). AE, MC, V.

***Locke-Ober,*** 3 Winter Place, downtown Boston (542-1340). The downstairs Men's Grill, which is now sexually integrated, is done up gorgeously in polished dark wood and gleaming silver; upstairs is drab by comparison, though the food is the same. Squads of deft white-haired waiters deliver superb fresh seafood prepared in various continental ways, as well as a wide variety of traditional meats and vegetables. Reservations recommended. Closed Sunday. Entrées from $3.25 (L), $6 (D). AE, MC, V.

### NOT WORTH IT

***Lechner's Gourmet Restaurant,*** 21 Broad Street (523-1016). Someone here evidently labors under the belief that pompous presentation is more important than thoughtful service. The place is off-putting—from the patronizing lectures printed on the German-Continental menu, to the slightly seedy pseudo-Baroque décor, to the elaborate pyrotechnical flourishes with which far too many dishes are served forth. The food varies from passable to mediocre, but portions are generous, and some people like this place. Saturday, dinner only. Closed Sunday. Entrées from $4.75 (L), $9.25 (D). AE, DC, MC, V.

# INTERNATIONAL

## AMERICAN

***Durgin Park,*** 30 North Market Street, Haymarket area (227-2038). This is an ancient and honorable establishment where several generations of pushcart vendors from the produce market have sat down at long communal tables, with several generations of upper-crust Bostonians, to stuff themselves on gigantic portions of simple home cooking. Best-known for its giant slabs of roast beef, Durgin Park also serves fine fresh seafood at very fair prices, and dozens of other entrées. Their Indian pudding is the real thing. No reservations, long lines at mealtimes, bare-boards atmosphere, and traditionally brusque waitresses. Open seven days a week. Entrées from $2 (L), $3.50 (D). AE.

***Chart House,*** 60 Long Wharf (227-1576). This is a nice old red brick warehouse, prettily refurbished with navigational charts as tabletops, captains' chairs, hanging plants, etc. The menu features a short list of steaks, prime ribs, and seafood, and it's all worth eating. Limited reservations accepted. Dinner only. Open seven days a week. Entrées from $6.25. AE, DC, MC, V.

## CHINESE

***King Wah,*** 25-29 Beach Street, Chinatown (426-2705, 426-2706). If you think Cantonese food is that gloppy stuff served as "Chinese-American cuisine" across the nation, King Wah's superb chefs will set you straight. This big, bright red-and-gold room is usually packed with Boston's most knowledgeable Sinophiles. Refuse the menu that starts with Family Dinners, and ask for the one that starts with a whole page of soups. Or don't use a menu at all: ask your waiter what kind of seafood is best today; if available, the stir-fried crabs will dazzle your tastebuds. Or try the very untraditional broiled sirloin steak, which arrives presliced, and is sensational. Reservations accepted. Open 365 days a year from 9 A.M. to 3:30 A.M.; bring your own beer or wine. Entrées from $3 (L & D). AE, MC.

## CONTINENTAL

***The Voyagers,*** 45½ Mt. Auburn Street, Harvard Square, Cambridge (354-1718). "Continental" is much too narrow a word for the innovative dishes that turn up on the menu here. Most are in the *nouvelle cuisine* tradition of light sauces, ultra-fresh ingredients, and vivid use of herbs and condiments. The menu changes daily, but the duck in any manifestation is superb, as is the rack of lamb. You will probably prefer the pretty new upstairs roof garden to the somewhat eclectic décor downstairs, but try to sit wherever the harpist/harpsichordist is playing. The best wine list in Boston offers some 250 well-chosen bottles at fair prices, some as low as $7. Reservations recommended. Dinner only. Closed Monday. Entrées from $9.50. AE, MC, V.

***Harvest,*** 44 Brattle Street, Harvard Square, Cambridge (492-1115). This restaurant-cum-café-cum-bar in the heart of the Design Research complex has become immensely popular with the Cambridge jet set. Décor consists of a lively mix of bold modern fabrics with cutesy antiques. The menu varies seasonally, but tends toward reliably good *nouvelle cuisine;* and there's a café menu (soups, pâtés, etc.) available before and after standard meal hours. Limited reservations accepted. Open seven days a week. Entrées from $5.50 (L), $8.75 (D). AE, MC, V.

***Café l'Ananas,*** 281a Newbury Street, Back Bay (353-0176). Small, comfortable, and pleasing to the eye, l'Ananas leans toward streamlined versions of modern French dishes, with occasional forays into exotica. They stir up the best *kir* in town, and then serve you (at dinnertime) a nice little pot of velvety fresh liver pâté to keep it company. Reservations recommended. Saturday and Sunday, dinner only. Open seven days a week. Entrées from $4.95 (L), $9.95 (D). AE, MC, V.

***Front Street,*** 260 Berkeley Street, Back Bay (247-0011). Front Street is a very appealing restaurant. There are two small rooms nicely done up in apricot and magenta, respectively, with assorted eye-pleasing art on the walls and pleasant mood music in the background. And there's good, competent service, a well-priced wine list, a fine house wine, and a sense of genuine good will toward the diner. Most of all, the food is lovely. Everything may change daily, but there are at least six entrées to choose from at both lunch and dinner, all vaguely international, imaginative, and beautifully balanced. Don't pass up a chance to try the seafood broth with *rouille;* or the meat loaf stuffed with wonderful surprises.

Reservations recommended. Saturday and Sunday, dinner only. Open seven days a week. Entrées from $3.75 (L), $8.50 (D). AE, MC, V.

## FRENCH

***The Modern Gourmet,*** 81R Union Street, in Newton Centre (969-1320). (See description under IN THE SUBURBS/NEWTON CENTRE.)

***Maison Robert,*** 45 School Street (227-3370). This is actually two restaurants: a large, graceful room upstairs, called Bonhomme Richard, and a series of smaller, warmer rooms downstairs, known collectively as Ben's Café. Both occupy the handsome old City Hall building, a few steps from the Parker House. On pleasant summer days, Ben's Café expands out onto the terrace, and lunchtime service, which is strained at best, becomes almost impossible. Upstairs, however, things are more serene, and you can get reliably good French food, done in the classic tradition, for just a few dollars more than you would spend downstairs. Featured items include rack of lamb, saddle of lamb, delicate veal, and duck with exotic fruits. A daily lunch special that includes soup, salad, and coffee goes for $7.25 upstairs, $6.25 in Ben's Café. Reservations recommended. Saturday and Sunday, dinner only. Open seven days a week. Entrées from $6.25 (L), $10 (D). AE, DC, MC, V.

## HUNGARIAN

***Café Budapest,*** 90 Exeter Street, Copley Square (734-3388). The Budapest provides an ornate Old World setting for continental and Hungarian dinners, carefully prepared and beautifully served. Begin with one of the appetizer mousses, either herring or chicken liver; and be sure to save room for the pastries, especially the strudel. The wine list, though brief, offers several delightful Hungarian choices at low prices. The coffees, both light and dark, are freshly ground several times a day. For some reason the Budapest is almost deserted at lunchtime; avoid it on Friday and Saturday nights, when it's mobbed. Reservations recommended. Open seven days a week. Entrées from $4.95 (L), $8.50 (D). AE, CB, DC, MC, V.

## ITALIAN

***Francesca's and Villa Francesca,*** 147 and 150 Richmond Street, in the North End (523-8826). For the past few years Boston's cognoscenti have been lining up outside Francesca's, sometimes waiting for hours in rain or snow, for a chance to eat the inspired work of owner/chef Bill Ramauro. The only problem in this tiny place has been lack of seats to accommodate its many admirers. This year, happily, Ramauro has expanded into additional space across the street. The old Francesca's still offers a well-balanced à la carte menu for both lunch and dinner, while Villa Francesca serves fixed-price multicourse dinners, by reservation only, at 6 and 9 P.M. The Villa is fancier, with mellow turn-of-the-century décor, including a 100-year-old oak bar in the room where customers wait to dine across the street. Specialties include homemade pasta (ask which dishes contain it), excellent vegetables, beautifully executed veal and seafood dishes, and flawless *cannoli,* filled at your table for maximum crispness. Both restaurants are closed Mondays. Francesca's entrées, with pasta or salad, from $5.25 (L), $5.50 (D). Villa Francesca dinners, including wine, cost $14.50 on weeknights, $18.50 on weekends. AE, DC.

***Felicia's,*** 145a Richmond Street, in the North End (523-9885). Right next door to Francesca's, and one flight up, Felicia's remains popular year after year. The room is large, high-ceilinged and handsome, with nice old paintings in heavy frames; the tuxedoed waiters are efficient, if sometimes brusque. Try the chicken Verdicchio, which marries boned chicken pieces with artichoke hearts and mushrooms in a well-seasoned white wine sauce. Beer and wine. Reservations accepted only for large groups. Dinner only. Open seven days a week. Entrées from $5.95. AE, DC.

# SPECIALTY COOKING

## DELI

***Ken's at Copley,*** 549-553 Boylston Street, Copley Square (266-6106). An endless list of hefty, super-cheap sandwiches, plus solid breakfasts, lunches and dinners priced proportionately. Big and bustling. Full liquor license. No reservations. Open seven days a week, from 7 A.M. to 3 A.M. Sandwiches from $1.35. No credit cards.

# HAMBURGER

***Mr. and Mrs. Bartley's Burger Cottage,*** 1246 Mass. Ave., Harvard Square, Cambridge (354-9830). Here you'll find 22 variations on "the Beethoven of burgers": 5½ ounces of prime beef, freshly ground daily, charcoal-broiled, and served up on various breads and rolls, with toppings both traditional and kinky. There are also soups, salads, sandwiches, chili, spaghetti, meat loaf, stew, etc. The fried onion rings are super-fine, crispy and sweet. No booze, and no décor either; generally packed with Harvard students. Closed Sunday. Hamburgers from $1.75. No credit cards.

***Charley's Eating and Drinking Saloon,*** 344 Newbury Street, Back Bay (266-3000). This is a jolly olde saloon with a cordial, well-trained staff. For $2.50 you get a terrific hamburger and a lot of conviviality. No reservations. Dinner until 1 A.M., drinking until 2 A.M. Open seven days a week. Entrées from $2.95 (L), $3.95 (D). AE, CB, DC.

# SEAFOOD

***Legal Sea Foods,*** 237 Hampshire Street, Cambridge (547-1410); and 43 Boylston Street, Chestnut Hill, Newton (277-7300). Unless you come in the middle of the afternoon, you're going to have to wait in line here; and unless you come with a big crowd of your own, you'll be seated (finally) at long communal tables, and served (*after* you've paid) on plastic plates. But the immense variety of fresh seafood makes it all worthwhile. Everything comes either broiled or deep-fried, with French fries or a baked potato, and cole slaw or salad. For more adventurous eaters, there's a handsome platter of sashimi, as well as succulent raw oysters and clams. Luncheon specials give you fish, a vegetable or salad, and all the coffee you can drink for $3.25. Full bar; no reservations. Open seven days a week. Most dinners cost between $5.50 and $8. AE.

***No-Name Restaurant,*** 15½ Fish Pier (338-7539). This place started out as a tiny lunchroom for fishermen and dock workers, and then was discovered by everyone else in town. It's bigger now, but still very plain and modest; and the fish, while less varied than at Legal, is fresh and well prepared. Where else can you get, for 95¢, a bowl of steaming-hot chowder that contains almost a pound of seafood? If you're very lucky, or patient, you may get a table overlooking the harbor. Bring your own wine or beer. No reservations. Closed Sunday. Entrées from $3.25 (L & D). No credit cards.

***Anthony's Pier 4,*** 140 Northern Avenue on the waterfront (423-6363). In a recent poll, readers of the *Boston Globe* voted Anthony's their favorite restaurant in Boston. This surprised no one, as Anthony's has always served up enormous portions of very good seafood, plus a lot of colorful ambience, for very reasonable prices. Don't come here for a tranquil evening, as the place is enormous and always very busy. But do come when you're in the mood for a little festivity. There are costumed waitresses and all sorts of ship gadgetry, and passing ships are described in some detail over the loudspeaker. Reservations accepted at lunch but not at dinner, which means waiting—sometimes for quite a while—for your table. Chaîne des Rotisseurs. Open seven days a week. Entrées from $4.50 (L), $6.95 (D). AE, CB, DC, MC, V.

## SOUL

***Bob the Chef,*** 604 Columbus Avenue, South End (536-6204). Negligible décor of the Formica variety, but the atmosphere is down-home funky and the spareribs and "Glorified Chicken" are worth the trip. Terrific vegetables, too, and a memorable sweet potato pie. No liquor. No reservations. Closed Sunday and Monday; open the rest of the week from 11 A.M. to 9 P.M. Entrées are in the $4 range, sandwiches even cheaper.

## STEAK

***The Colorado Public Library,*** Hearthstone Plaza, Brookline (734-6772). Décor here is wall-to-wall bookshelves. The service is good, and the steaks and prime rib are top quality. Full bar. Reservations accepted until 6:30. Dinner only. Open seven days a week. Dinners (including a fine salad and potato or rice pilaf) start at $5.95. AE, MC.

***Copley's,*** Copley Plaza Hotel, Copley Square, Back Bay (267-5300). Here's a pleasant old restaurant with the plush comfort of a British gentlemen's club. There's a magnificent bar here too, that does a thriving cocktail trade. The menu varies cyclically, but the carpetbagger steak is a perpetual favorite. Reservations accepted. Chaîne des Rotisseurs. Open seven days a week. Entrées from $3.75 (L), $5.95 (D). AE, CB, DC, MC, V.

***Chart House,*** 60 Long Wharf (227-1576). (See description under AMERICAN.)

# FOR INDIVIDUAL NEEDS

## IF YOU HAVE TIME FOR ONLY ONE MEAL

***The Modern Gourmet,*** 81R Union Street (969-1320). (See description under IN THE SUBURBS/NEWTON CENTRE.) Serious gourmets who have only one evening in town will find the commute to Newton Centre well worthwhile.

***The Ritz Dining Room,*** Ritz-Carlton Hotel, 15 Arlington Street, Back Bay (536-5700). (See description under BIG DEAL/WORTH IT.)

## BEST HOTEL MEAL

***The Ritz Dining Room,*** Ritz-Carlton Hotel, 15 Arlington Street, Back Bay (536-5700). (See description under BIG DEAL/WORTH IT.)

## BUSINESS BREAKFAST

***Café Plaza,*** Copley Plaza Hotel, Copley Square, Back Bay (267-5300). This is a lovely room in the old tradition of truly elegant hotels. If you come for lunch or dinner, have a drink beforehand in the soothing Library Cocktail Lounge adjoining the dining room. The kitchen specializes in French cuisine, preparing duck in orange sauce, sweetbreads Eugene and beef Wellington, among other entrées. At breakfast (served Monday through Saturday from 7 to 10, Sunday from 7 to noon), they offer omelets, pancakes, corned-beef hash, plus pastries straight out of the oven. And visitors who hanker after scrod can order it here for breakfast, lunch, or dinner. Reservations recommended. Sunday, breakfast only. Open seven days a week. Entrées from $3.25 (B), $4.25 (L), $7.95 (D). AE, CB, DC, MC, V.

## BUSINESS LUNCH

***Locke-Ober,*** 3 Winter Place, downtown Boston (542-1340). (See description under BIG DEAL/WORTH IT.)

***Copley's,*** Copley Plaza Hotel, Copley Square, Back Bay (267-5300). (See description under STEAK.)

## BEST WINE LIST

***The Voyagers,*** 45½ Mt. Auburn Street, Harvard Square, Cambridge (354-1718). (See description under CONTINENTAL.)

## FOR DRINKS

***The Ritz Bar,*** Ritz-Carlton Hotel, 15 Arlington Street, Back Bay (536-5700). Small, dimly lit, and deeply comfortable. The service is swift and unobtrusive, the music subdued, and the drinks reliably big and tasty. Tables tucked behind the bar are less desirable than those between the bar and the windows. In the food department, there are light lunches at noon, salted peanuts all day long, and a tray of exquisite hors d'oeuvre is passed—once only, alas—between 5 and 6 P.M. Wine drinkers will appreciate the excellent house wines, available by the glass. Open seven days a week from lunchtime until 2 A.M. AE, MC, V.

***Friday's,*** 26 Exeter Street, Back Bay (266-9040). A hip young crowd keeps Friday's packed and jumping from noon till midnight every day. Come for the décor, an eye-catching mélange of gleaming dark wood, bright brass, stained glass, and all sorts of eclectic period pieces; or come for the good big drinks and, between 4:30 and 6:30 on weekdays, the tasty free hors d'oeuvre. There's also a very long menu of good sandwiches as well as full lunches and dinners that range from vegetarian to hefty steaks. You don't have to be young and unattached to have a good time here; but if you are, this is where the action is. No reservations accepted. Open seven days a week. Entrées from $3.50 (L & D). AE, MC, V.

## RESTAURANT WITH MUSIC

***Lulu's,*** 3 Appleton Street, between Berkeley and Tremont Streets, South End (423-3652). In a warm red setting faithful to the memory of the original Lulu White, who ran the best-known house of ill repute in New Orleans, you can dine handsomely on various Continental meat or seafood dishes, including Creole specialties such as jambalaya and shrimp Creole. At 9:30 on Tuesday, Wednesday, and Thursday nights there are concerts by mainstream jazz headliners, and on Friday and Saturday there's dancing to a Dixieland jazz band. On Sunday nights there's music, but only snacks are served, not full dinners. Reservations recommended for dinner, not accepted for music only. Closed Monday. Entrées from $5 (D). AE, CB, DC.

## ROMANTIC

***The Rendezvous,*** 24 Holyoke Street, Harvard Square, Cambridge (547-5005). Don't be misled by the bright lights and Formica of the street-level fast-foods place: the restaurant itself, one flight down, is a quiet little underground *cave.* Soft lights and gentle classical music, thoughtful service, a full bar with tropical mixed drinks and good, inexpensive wines. Best of all, the menu features both Vietnamese and French dishes. Be sure to try the delicate spring rolls, made with tissue-thin wrappers; beef with lemon grass, and chicken with lemon grass are also very popular. Reservations accepted, and recommended on weekends. Monday, Tuesday, Wednesday and Saturday, dinner only. Closed Sunday. Entrées from $2.50 (L), $3.50 (D). MC, V.

## LATE-NIGHT SERVICE

***King Wah,*** 25–29 Beach Street, Chinatown (426-2705, 426-2706). (See description under CHINESE.)

***Ken's at Copley,*** 549–553 Boylston Street, Copley Square (266-6106). (See description under DELI.)

## SUNDAY BRUNCH

***Parker's,*** Parker House Hotel, 60 School Street, downtown Boston (227-8600). You can really treat yourself royally at Parker's Sunday brunch, helping yourself to endless servings from a buffet heaped bountifully with assorted salads, herring in sour cream, various seafood dishes, scrambled eggs, sausages, ham or bacon, liver pâté, ratatouille, quiche, and an all-too-seductive assortment of luscious desserts. Enjoy all this in a many-splendored setting of velvet banquettes, elaborate paneling, ornate mirrors and baroque statuary. The waiters wear tuxes, but you don't have to, though you must wear a jacket. The menu during the rest of the week is Continental and familiar. Chaîne des Rotisseurs. Reservations are required for brunch, for which there are two seatings, at 11:30 and 1:30. Reservations recommended at all other meals. Saturday and Sunday, dinner only. Open seven days a week. The brunch costs $9.50. Entrées from $5.50 (L), $10.50 (D). AE, CB, DC, MC, V.

## SUNDAY-EVENING MEAL

***Harvest,*** 44 Brattle Street, Harvard Square, Cambridge (492-1115). (See description under CONTINENTAL.)

## FOR FAMILIES WITH CHILDREN

***Durgin Park,*** 30 North Market Street, Haymarket area (227-2038). (See description under AMERICAN.) p. 61

***The European,*** 218 Hanover Street, in the North End (523-5694). This is an enormous place, with an equally enormous menu of popular Italian dishes, including pizza. The food isn't the most refined in town, but everything is tasty, portions are huge, service is very prompt, and the prices remain amazingly low. On weekdays there are lunch specials—soup, entrée, vegetable, potato and beverage—for just $2.65. Of the several rooms, the most attractive is the front room nearest the bar, with its rows of old wooden booths. Full liquor license. Reservations accepted on weekdays only. Open seven days a week. Entrées from $3.25 (L & D). AE, DC, MC, V.

## RESTAURANT NEAR AIRPORT

All restaurants in the Haymarket and North End districts are only ten minutes by car or taxi from the airport. (See descriptions under ITALIAN and AMERICAN.)

# IN THE SUBURBS

## NEWTON CENTRE

***The Modern Gourmet,*** 81R Union Street (969-1320). In Piccadilly Square, just across the street from the MBTA stop (and down a narrow flight of steps), a 20-minute ride from downtown Boston by car or train. Madeleine Kamman is a Frenchwoman whose brilliant and highly original cooking is inspired by the classical tradition and by the pragmatic and innovative cooking of the French housewife. Through her Modern Gourmet cooking school where she trains professional chefs, her several excellent cookbooks, and her restaurant, she has achieved an international reputation. In the modest but pretty little restaurant, you will have an opportunity to savor the excellent food created by her students under her strict supervision. On Friday and Saturday, dinners are à la carte and feature *nouvelle cuisine* as interpreted by Ms. Kamman. Sadly, Ms. Kamman is reportedly leaving the U.S. in mid-1980 to return to France. The restaurant is expected to remain open. A four-course dinner costs about $30, and reservations are required. On Tuesday, Wednesday, and Thursday the kitchen re-creates the much simpler but very tasty cooking of various regions of France (and other

European countries, occasionally), offering a fixed-price four-course dinner (with your choice of entrée) for $15; limited reservations accepted. Both menus change frequently. Excellent wine list. Dinner only. Closed Sunday and Monday. No credit cards.

# MARKETS

***Quincy Market,*** in the Faneuil Hall Marketplace, Market District, downtown Boston. A handsome old restored warehouse in which sixty different enterprises sell almost every conceivable kind of raw and prepared foodstuff, as well as pots to cook in and the dishes to serve on. Lots of fast-food stands and several chic restaurants, too. Fun to stroll, shop, and munch. Open Monday through Saturday from 10 A.M. to 9 P.M. (restaurants till 10 P.M., bars till 2 A.M.), Sunday from noon to 6 P.M.

## GIFT FOODS

***Formaggio,*** 81 Mount Auburn Street, in the Garage, Harvard Square, Cambridge (547-4795). The best selection of fine imported cheeses, oils, vinegars, teas, jams, and condiments, as well as excellent homemade pâtés and other charcuterie. Beautiful sandwiches and salads, too, mostly for take-out (a few tables are available for self-service). Open seven days a week. No credit cards.

***Cardullo Gourmet Shop,*** 6 Brattle Street in Harvard Square, Cambridge (491-8888). A wide range of imported ingredients and gift foods; also fresh delicatessen foods and sandwiches to take out. Closed Sunday. AE, DC, MC, V accepted for orders over $5.

## GIFT WINES

***The Harvard Wine and Liquor Co.,*** 288 Harvard Street, Brookline (277-9000). Excellent selection of foreign and domestic wines. Closed Sunday. CB, DC, MC, V.

***Cave Atlantique,*** 34 Boylston Street, Harvard Square, Cambridge (492-1780). A good selection of wines in all price categories. Closed Sunday. AE, DC, MC, V.

# Buffalo

Oh, the Er-i-ee is risin', and the gin is gettin' low
And I scarcely think
We'll get a drink
'Til we get to Buffalo.
—Erie Canal song, around 1850

The Niagara Frontier's reputation for lavish hospitality has a long history—a two-block stretch fronting the Canal terminus was known through most of the 19th century as the "Barbary Coast of the East." Ninety-three saloons, 15 "concert halls" and hundreds of dancing girls marked the area, and every day brought wilder brawls between the "canalers" and regular Great Lakes seamen. "These people," solid citizens complained, "are as interested in a good fight as in good food."

In the 1870's, Sheriff Grover Cleveland tried to clean things up, but he wasn't terribly successful. It took time and a changing world to do the job. Now, railroad tracks and the New York Thruway cover the filled-in Canal district land.

And the bar and restaurant scene? It's still pretty lively, although admittedly it's calmed down a bit. It covers a much wider geographical area, too, stretching from downtown Buffalo, through the suburbs to Niagara Falls, New York, 20 miles away.

Stretching even into Canada. Five minutes from the Buffalo City Hall, the Peace Bridge crosses the Niagara River to Fort Erie, Ontario. Once a strong defense point for the British during the War of 1812, Fort Erie now has a culinary distinction. There are eleven Chinese restaurants in this town of 23,000 souls.

If you want to look at the Falls from the Canadian side, cross the Rainbow Bridge from Niagara Falls, New York, to Niagara Falls,

Ontario. The views are outstanding. Plan a 30-minute drive from there to the charming town of Niagara-on-the-Lake, Ontario, scene of the Shaw Drama Festival. Picnic by the river. Or eat in The Oban Inn, The Buttery or the Prince of Wales Hotel.

The Frontier offers a versatile food line-up. As you cover the area you'll note laconic signs—"Wings"—in just about every tavern window. This is not a boost for the Air Force. The signs simply mean that deep-fried chicken wings are available inside.

Another local culinary contribution: "Beef-on-Weck." Translation: a layered roast-beef sandwich on a salt-encrusted hard roll.

Ethnic restaurants are plentiful in this area, as are sophisticated Continental restaurants—particularly in downtown Buffalo, near the Convention Center and the Theater District. You might try Valentine's (91 Niagara Street), St. George's Table (675 Delaware Avenue), **The Cloister, Manny's** or the new and still unproven Shubert Alley (333 Franklin Street). **The Park Lane Manor House,** a Buffalo landmark, is not far away.

Less expensive food, offered less formally, can be found on "The Elmwood Avenue Strip," about ten minutes from downtown. Try the No Name Bar (946 Elmwood) and Cole's (1104 Elmwood) for good salads, omelet lunches, and light suppers. By 10 P.M., they've become lively bars. After 10, The Tralfamadore Café (2610 Main Street) is also worth visiting for its top jazz and good snacks.

If it suits your fancy, you can even eat buffalo meat in Buffalo. The Scotch 'n Sirloin (3999 Maple Road, Amherst) is good for strip steak or porterhouse, starting at $13.

# Restaurants and Food Sources

**(Area code: 716)**

# BIG DEAL

## WORTH IT

***The Park Lane Manor House,*** Gates Circle (885-3250). This large restaurant is chock-a-block with fake and real Olde English artifacts, paneled staircases, suits of armor and some (very forlorn) fox heads. The wine steward wears a monk's habit complete with hood. And yet the food remains high quality. This is one of Western New York's most popular spots. Dinner includes Dover sole amandine, lobster Thermidor, beef Wellington, veal Oscar, as well as less fancy steaks and chops. The salads rely too much on iceberg lettuce, but there is an excellent dressing called "Peter Gust." Dinner until 10; a satisfying supper menu takes over until 1 A.M. Lunch is good here, too. Elaborate wine list and a fine bar. Valet parking. Reservations suggested. Chaîne des Rotisseurs. Sunday, brunch, dinner (and supper) only. Open seven days a week. Entrées from $2.50 (L), $5 (D). AE, CB, DC, MC, V.

## NOT WORTH IT

***Skylon Tower Dining Room,*** Skylon Tower, Niagara Falls, Ontario (direct line from Buffalo, 856-5788). It's unfortunate that few dining-rooms-with-view exist in Niagara Falls, but don't let that fact lure you into actually taking a meal in this admittedly handsome, revolving restaurant. One boards a bright-yellow scenic elevator to ascend some 500 feet. (The $2 transportation fee is *not* deducted from the price of your dinner.) The menu is standard hotel (the place is run by Canadian Pacific)—overdone meat and fish, undistinguished vegetables, and canned fruit for dessert. Nevertheless, there's a minimum of $5 for lunch, $9 at dinner. Open seven days a week. AE, CB, DC, MC, V.

# INTERNATIONAL

## CHINESE

***Ming Teh,*** 126 Niagara Boulevard, Fort Erie, Ontario, Canada (416/ 871-7971), five minutes from downtown Buffalo. Dishes from every province of China. Recommended are dumplings, chicken in lotus leaves, pork in sweet bean paste, *moo-shu* beef, steamed fish. Tiny place, understated décor, one table overlooks the Niagara River. Service inclined to be slow. Reservations recommended. If the place is full, there are 10 other Chinese restaurants in the immediate area. They are more conventional in menu, but most of them are good, especially the very informal **Parkview Restaurant** at 93 Niagara Boulevard. At Ming Teh: beer and wine only. Monday, dinner only. Open seven days a week. Entrées from $4.50 (L & D). MC.

## GREEK

***Yianni's,*** 581 Delaware Avenue (883-6033). This attractive restaurant, located in an old mansion, has a minimum of tourist artifacts and is very comfortable. Among the appetizers, note *melizanosalata* or puréed eggplant with plenty of garlic, and *saganaki,* a Greek rarebit, made from mild white cheese. Good moussaka and delicious baby lamb à la Grecque that is long-simmered with lots of vegetables. Fresh vegetable plates excellent. A small selection of Greek wines. Saturday and Sunday, dinner only. Open seven days a week. Entrées from $2.60 (L), $5 (D). MC, V.

## ITALIAN

***Chef's Restaurant,*** 291 Seneca Street, Buffalo (856-9188). A Buffalo favorite, especially of political types who remember this place when it was a two-by-four bar with a stove in the middle. This is now the first room you pass through. The menu is limited, the pasta is well cooked, with sauce thick and strong. Extraordinary Italian bread. On Fridays order the linguini with clam sauce. In summer, zucchini salad is featured. Reservations recommended. Closed Sunday. Entrées from $3.25 (L), $3.50 (D). AE, MC, V.

***Donna Felicia's,*** 490 Center Street, Lewiston, about five minutes from Niagara Falls, New York (754-7901). This is a family-run Northern Italian restaurant, tucked in an old white house in an historic village. Lots of veal, lots of cream sauces, adroit seasoning. The only drawback: several of the most interesting selections can only be ordered for two or more persons. Among them: filet of sole Florentine, manicotti *del mare* (filled with rock lobster, baked in cream sauce), veal cutlet *à la Nero* (stuffed with sweetbreads, mushrooms and wild rice cooked in rich gravy). Among the "single" offerings the fettuccine Alfredo is best—your choice of green or white pasta. Reservations necessary. Dinner only. Closed Monday and Tuesday. Entrées (for two) about $25. AE, MC, V.

## POLISH

***Polonia,*** 193 Lombard Street (892-4455). Buffalo is a city full of Polish-Americans, yet there are few Polish restaurants. But right across from the famed Broadway Market (see description under MARKETS) is the absolutely authentic Polonia. Tiny, complete with counter as well as tables, no wine or liquor served. Soups are extraordinary. Earthy mushroom, beet borscht, *szczaw* (sorrel) or sauerkraut. Goulash is good, as are the *nalesnik* (crêpes). Also stuffed cabbage, beef tongue in fruit and wine sauce, Polish tripe, fresh rye bread. Reservations recommended. Closed Monday through Wednesday. Entrées from $2.75 (L & D). No credit cards.

# SPECIALTY COOKING

## BEEF-ON-WECK

***Ace's Steak Pit,*** 166 Franklin Street (842-1549). For years, Western New York was renowned for these huge, thinly layered beef sandwiches on *kummelweck* rolls—hard rolls encrusted with caraway seeds and coarse salt. But today, a good beef-on-weck is hard to find. At decidedly unfancy, centrally located Ace's, the beef is sliced to order in front of you the way it is supposed to be and usually you can get it rare. Sit at the bar to eat it. Add horseradish. Wash it down with beer. A nifty, speedy lunch. Closed Sunday. Open until 1 A.M., but no roast beef after 8. The sandwich costs $1.90. No credit cards.

## CHICKEN WINGS

***Anchor Bar,*** 1047 Main Street (886-8920). Most out-of-town visitors fall in love with Western New York chicken wings. Just about every corner tavern or pizzeria makes them available, but the Anchor, a dark little Italian restaurant, claims to have been first in the area. The wings are halved to look like small drumsticks. Then they are deep-fried and mixed with butter and hot sauce. They come mild, medium or (very) hot; are always accompanied by celery sticks and blue-cheese dressing. Like pizza, they make a fine light meal or snack. Ten wings are $2.50; 20 wings are $3.50. You will eat many more than you expect to. Open seven days a week, until 1:30 A.M. No credit cards.

## HAMBURGER

***Mother's Bakery,*** 33 Virginia Place (881-4881). In an old coach house. Dark paneling, brick walls, big bar. Best bet is the Guidry Burger (the restaurant is owned by former Buffalo Bills players Paul Guidry and Edgar Chandler). It boasts bacon, American cheese and blue-cheese dressing on a good soft roll and will set you back $2.25. Also recommended, the English burger on a you-know-what muffin, topped with cheese. At dinner, there's a more elaborate menu, but the hamburgers are best. Singles love this place—also its suburban cousin, **Mother's Bakery Amherst** at 4575 Main Street, Snyder (839-5214). Reservations limited. Both restaurants: Sunday, dinner only. Open seven days a week; snacks until 2 A.M. No credit cards.

## HOT DOG

***Ted's,*** 2312 Sheridan Drive, Tonawanda; 2351 Niagara Falls Boulevard, Amherst; 7018 Transit Rd., Williamsville; and Porter Avenue near the Peace Bridge (no phones). Some locations have indoor dining. This frankfurter empire goes back to 1913 when Grandpa Spiro Liaros sold dogs from a horse and wagon. Order excellent, charcoal-broiled, Buffalo-made "Sahlen" sausages. Ask for the "regular" size. "Jumbo" (quarter-pounders) are too tightly packed. French fries are good here, and the onion rings are sensational—exquisitely greasy delights. Open seven days a week. Regular hot dog $.75. No credit cards.

## STEAK

***Manny's Supper Club,*** 471 Delaware Avenue (881-3727). Sophisticated little spot in the basement of a handsome town house. Your waitress will bring a tray with samples of meat to your table to help you order. An extravagant display of raw flesh, the prime steaks come in two sizes, and there are filets, double lamb chops and thick pork chops. Fine salad, excellent home-fried potatoes, fresh vegetables. On Friday only, filet of sole Rosemary (with cream sauce and vegetables) is a treat. Good bar. Reservations advised. Saturday and Sunday, dinner only. Open seven days a week. The smaller New York strip (the "senorita cut") with dinner is $8.95. AE, CB, DC, MC, V.

# FOR INDIVIDUAL NEEDS

## IF YOU HAVE TIME FOR ONLY ONE MEAL

***Mastrantonio's,*** 899 Niagara Falls Boulevard, Eggertsville, about 20 minutes from downtown Buffalo (836-3366). Attractive spot—ask to sit in the Round Room, if possible. Innovative menu featuring well-prepared Continental dishes with the accent of northern Italy. At lunch, spinach salad, tasty quiche. At dinner, the food is rich and highly seasoned: *pollo au poivre,* veal Tosca (in a brown vermouth sauce). For dessert, in season, strawberries Francesca with yogurt and honey. Good pastries. Service is highly professional. If you have strong feelings about garlic, be sure to mention that fact to the waiter when he prepares your pasta or salad at tableside. Reservations advised. Sunday, dinner only. Open seven days a week. Special early dinner from 4:30 to 6:30 P.M. Sunday brunch. Entrées from $3.95 (L), $6 (D). AE, CB, DC, MC, V.

## RESTAURANT NEAR AIRPORT

***Salvatore's Italian Gardens,*** 6461 Transit Road, Depew (683-7990). You will be stunned when you see the outdoor statuary, especially the draped ladies who line the driveway, each with a round light bulb on her head! Indoors, it's a choice of the Chariot Room or the Rome Room—both sport three-dimensional models of their themes. The food is good and there's a lot of it. Italian specialities, also lobster, steak or chops. The airport is about five minutes away. Dinner only. Open seven days a week. Entrées from $8.95. AE, CB, DC, MC, V.

## BUSINESS LUNCH

***Plaza Suite,*** 1 M & T Plaza, downtown Buffalo (842-5555). Twenty stories high, atop a handsome bank building, a series of rooms each decorated in a different style. Hearty meats at lunch, also omelets, eggs Benedict, sandwiches. Comfortable atmosphere, reasonably quiet and you won't be rushed. At dinner, park your car in the basement and take the elevator. Reservations advised. Saturday and Sunday, dinner only. Monday, lunch only. Open seven days a week. Entrées from $2.10 (L), $5.95 (D). AE, CB, DC, MC, V.

## FOR DRINKS

***The Cloister,*** 472 Delaware Avenue (886-0070). Romantic, dimly lit, full of memorabilia. Includes a piano bar (music after 9). Also an old popcorn machine, which is still functioning nicely. Hot hors d'oeuvre. While you're here take a look at the adjoining restaurant. It's spectacular. The Greenhouse room boasts an outdoor waterfall; the Crystal Garden room features Waterford chandeliers. If you decide to eat here (dinner only), stick to basics such as roast beef. Portions are huge. Dinner reservations recommended. Chaîne des Rotisseurs. Open seven days a week. The bar opens at 4 P.M. and stays open late. Dinner entrées from around $9. AE, CB, DC, MC, V.

## SUNDAY BRUNCH

***Mastrantonio's,*** 899 Niagara Falls Boulevard (836-3366). (See description under IF YOU HAVE TIME FOR ONLY ONE MEAL.) Sitdown champagne brunch from noon to 3 P.M. Starts at around $9.50.

## SUNDAY-EVENING MEAL

***The Park Lane Manor House,*** Gates Circle (885-3250). (See description under BIG DEAL/WORTH IT.)

## FOR FAMILIES WITH CHILDREN

***John's Flaming Hearth,*** 1965 Military Road (297-1414) ; or in the Motor Inn, 443 Main Street, closer to the Falls themselves (284-8801). (See description under NIAGARA FALLS.)

# NIAGARA FALLS

***Donna Felicia's,*** 490 Center Street, Lewiston (754-7901). (See description under ITALIAN.)

***John's Flaming Hearth,*** 1965 Military Road (297-1414); or in the Motor Inn, 443 Main Street, closer to the Falls themselves (284-8801). An utterly reliable, limited menu—steaks and seafood. The more attractive Military Road location, especially, is always jammed. For dessert, the Pumpkin Ice Cream Pie is a real treat. Sandwiches, omelets for lunch. Military Road: Sunday, dinner only. Open seven days a week. Motor Inn: open seven days a week. Entrées from $2.95 (L), small steak at dinner, all inclusive $7.45. (In Buffalo, there's a John's Flaming Hearth at 1830 Abbott Road, 822-2448.) AE, CB, DC, MC, V.

***J. P. Morgan's,*** Rainbow Mall (285-5555). Centrally located, reconverted bank building serving everything from reubens to *coquilles St.-Jacques.* Lively bar. Outdoor café in summer. Open seven days a week. Entrées from $2 (L), $5 (D). AE, CB, DC, MC, V.

***Schimschacks,*** 2943 Upper Mountain Road, Pekin, New York, 20 minutes from the Falls (731-4111). High on the escarpment overlooking Lake Ontario—on a clear day you can see Toronto. Tables on tiers so everyone can view. Legend has it that this is where Joe DiMaggio courted Marilyn Monroe (she was filming *Niagara*). Once a neighborhood hangout, it's now a handsome restaurant. Try the baby backribs and the peanut-butter pie. Late snack menu, too. Dinner only. Open seven days a week in the summer; closed Monday and Tuesday in the winter. Entrées from $5.95. AE, MC, V.

***Pepie's Plum,*** 102 LaSalle Arterial (beneath Envoy Motor Inn) (285-2000). Three minutes walk from the Falls, this very attractive restaurant features fine quality meat, seafood and salad. Particularly noteworthy: the Seafood Medley in a pastry crust. All entrées are garnished with a purple plum, the restaurant's signature, and the Plum Trifle dessert at dinner (pound cake, tapioca, plum sauce and whipped cream) is divine. Open seven days a week. Breakfast at 8, lunch at 11:30, and then the kitchen stays open until midnight. Entrées from $3 (L). $6.75 (D). AE, MC, V.

# MARKETS

***Broadway Market,*** 999 Broadway (office, 893-0705). An indoor market where more than 20 stalls provide meat, sausage, poultry, baked goods, cheese, and fruits and vegetables, many with a strong Polish-American flavor. At its best before Easter and Christmas. Buy your *kielbasa* (sausage) here and watch the lady grate fresh horseradish. Two lunch counters, too, dispensing such goodies as *czarnina* (duck's blood soup), a chocolate-colored staple in many Buffalo homes. Closed Wednesday and Sunday. No credit cards.

***Farmers' Markets.*** At least three in the area offering, outdoors and in season, Western New York strawberries, salad vegetables, magnificent apples and peaches. Bailey and Clinton streets in Buffalo open from about 4 A.M. until early afternoon. Closed Sunday. Payne Avenue and Robertson in North Tonawanda open Tuesday, Thursday and Saturday (also has beautiful, inexpensive flowers). And just off Pine Avenue in Niagara Falls, open Monday, Wednesday and Friday. No credit cards.

## GIFT FOODS/WINES

***Premier Liquor Corp.*** (873-6688), and ***Premier Cheese and Gourmet Foods, Inc.*** (877-3574), both at 2965 Delaware Avenue, Kenmore. Two wide-assortment stores under the same management and the same roof. If you look carefully, you'll find some high-quality New York wines. Ask to talk to the manager for special help—some of the staff are young and inexperienced. Closed Sunday, except for the cheese store, which is open until 2 P.M. Liquor store: no credit cards. Cheese store: MC, V.

# Chicago

Most native of American cities . . . big shot town, small shot town, jet propelled old fashioned town, by old world hands with new world tools built . . .

—Nelson Algren, *Chicago: City on the Make*

Chicago has always been a city of contrasts. It provides a backdrop for sleek skyscrapers and crumbling slums, a refuge that supports equally a world-famous symphony and funky low-down blues, a haven for corrupt politicians and courageous crusaders. The restaurants reflect this multifaceted personality. It's possible to dine one night at a streamlined space-age emporium and spend the next at a humble family-run storefront, where décor means a 7-Up sign, orange plastic flowers and perhaps a faded postcard or two.

Although Chicago does boast first-rate French restaurants and some excellent seafood spots, it is the neighborhood hideaway that gives the city its gastronomic vitality. While inroads have been made by fast-food emporiums and steakhouses that look like left-over sets from a Randolph Scott movie, the simple Mom-and-Pop storefronts survive. These are the places most likely to reward one with honest food and atmosphere, soothing to both the stomach and the spirit.

A cook's tour might begin with a mammoth lox-and-onion omelet at **The Bagel** in Albany Park, and lunch of Swedish fruit soup and a hot meatball sandwich on *limpa* bread at **Ann Sathers** on

Belmont Avenue. If the weather is good, there's no better snack than a juicy, sloppy Italian beef-and-sausage combo at Solly's on Taylor Street, washed down by a fresh, watermelon-studded Italian lemonade at Mario and Donna's tiny stand across the street. Dinner could be a multicourse Peruvian extravaganza at either El Piqueo or El Inca. Nor should one leave Chicago without savoring at least several bites of its most enticing edible invention—the deep-dish pizza at **Gino's East,** Uno's or Ghiordanos.

For those who prefer the trendy over the ethnic, there are R. J. Grunt's, Great Gritzbe's, Jasands and The Chicago Claim Company. Although their atmospheres rely heavily on gimmicks and the lines are long, food is plentiful, imaginative and reasonably priced. If one is after the chic rather than the cheap and doesn't mind the Art Deco à la carte, head for **Arnie's, Gordon's** or **Tango.** For truly artistic *haute* as well as *nouvelle cuisine,* there are the grand kitchens of **Le Perroquet** on Walton Street and **Le Français** in suburban Wheeling.

If New York is the Big Apple, then Chicago could aptly br called the Big Potato or better yet, the Big Piroshki. Dumplings are rolled from scratch in the morning, meat inevitably wears a mantle of gravy, and fresh vegetables are as rare as a non-machine mayor.

To find a complete soup-to-strudel spread for under $3, just take a trip down Milwaukee Avenue for a Polish version, Chicago Avenue for Ukrainian, Marquette Park or Bridgeport for Lithuanian, or follow Cermak Road out to the Bohemian dumpling domain of Berwyn. Even in the Loop (the downtown area), it is easy to dine economically and ethnically on such delights as **The Berghoff**'s Alpen ragout, Epicurean's stuffed peppers or cheese-filled *palacsintas,* and Old Polonia's potato pancakes.

The melting pot refuses to stop bubbling. Thais, Israelis, Koreans, Greeks, Filipinos, Colombians, East Indians and Arabs have arrived to join the already established Slavic, German, black, Italian, Irish, Puerto Rican and Chicano communities. They all brought native food traditions with them. It is possible to spend days eating one's way across the city without ever hitting the same nationality or neighborhood twice.

Although the stockyards are but a memory, the city still boasts a corral of top-quality beef, notably prepared at the **Blackhawk,** Gene and Georgetti, House of Bertini, and **Eli's The Place for Steaks.**

Chicago restaurants are generally casual. Guccis mix comfortably with sneakers. A few of the more refined establishments do require men to wear a coat and tie; so if in doubt, give a call first. Reservations are always a good idea, especially in the Loop and Near North areas. Tipping is a standard 15 percent, but 20 percent will garner a broader smile, especially if the service and price tag merit it.

# Restaurants and Food Sources

(Area code: 312)

## BIG DEAL

### WORTH IT

***Le Perroquet,*** 70 E. Walton (944-7990). Imaginative, exquisite French cuisine served in a gracious environment. Niceties include dainty hors d'oeuvre with cocktails. Menu rotates and is apt to include *mousseline* of salmon, *pavé* of beef with green peppercorn sauce, quails Perroquet and broiled breast of goose in Armagnac sauce. Delicate puréed vegetables; elegant desserts. Restrained, careful service. Coat and tie necessary. Reservations recommended. Closed Sunday. Fixed-price dinner, $25.75. Lunch entrées from $12.75. AE, DC.

### NOT WORTH IT

***The Ritz-Carlton Hotel Dining Room,*** Water Tower Place, Michigan Avenue at Pearson (266-1000). The menu is tantalizing, but the preparation doesn't deliver hoped-for magic. Prices are sinfully extravagant. Open seven days a week. Complete dinners average $25 to $30. AE, CB, DC, MC, V.

## INTERNATIONAL

### AMERICAN

***Genesee Depot,*** 3736 N. Broadway (528-6990). An unlikely location for a delightful plant-and-antique-filled storefront restaurant. Menu limited to three entrées. Brisket, sporting a horseradish sauce with a mild bite, is always reliable. Vegetables vinaigrette, choice of soup or salad and superb homemade bread offer fine support.

Desserts include firm, fudgy chocolate cheesecake, cranberry/orange cake and rhubarb custard tart. Service can sometimes be stiff. Otherwise, a certified charmer. Bring your own beer or wine. Dinner only. Closed Monday and Tuesday. Entrées from $5.75. No credit cards.

***Blackhawk,*** 139 N. Wabash (726-0100). Pure Chicago. Thick cuts of prime rib and outstanding steaks accompanied by the special Blackhawk salad, baked potato, creamed spinach and toasty garlic-buttered miniature rye. Lavish portions. Reliable service, with a bit of showmanship thrown in. Make a reservation. Chaîne des Rotisseurs. Full bar. Sunday, dinner only. Open seven days a week. Entrées from $3.50 (L), $7.25 (D). AE, CB, DC, MC, V.

## CHINESE

***Formosa,*** 7108 W. Higgins (763-3652). Tiny, convivial storefront restaurant not far from the airport offers wide selection of Mandarin, Cantonese and Taiwanese delicacies. For the spicy tastes, try the La Tse chicken with carrots, eggplant in garlic sauce, or shredded beef with peanuts. Sizzling steak, and *moo shu* pork are milder, but equally fine, and worth the out-of-the-way jaunt. Bring your own liquor. Open seven days a week. Entrées from $3 (L & D). No credit cards.

## FRENCH

***La Fontaine,*** 2440 N. Clark (525-1800). A fine meal more than worth the $14.50 fixed price, served in a comfortable refurbished brownstone. Begin with *la coquille deauvilloise* (hot seafood and mushrooms in a velvety champagne sauce). Recommended entrée: crisp duck glazed with orange sauce and peaches. The chef also displays a sure hand with seafood. Desserts aren't spectacular but crème caramel or chocolate mousse offers a smooth finale. Service attentive without being overbearing. Jackets preferred. Reservations recommended. Dinner only. Closed Sunday. AE, DC, MC, V.

## GERMAN

***Golden Ox,*** 1580 N. Clybourn (664-0781). Old World atmosphere and attentive service almost match the excellent food at this Near North Side institution. Favored by businessmen who come for the large portions, the Golden Ox features superb liver dumpling or oxtail barley soup, crispy roast duckling with red cabbage, smoked pork chops, and veal paprika with nutmeg-spiced *Spaetzle.* Assorted strudel and tortes for dessert. Fine imported beer and wine list. Open seven days a week. Entrées from $5 (L), $7 (D). AE, MC, V.

## GREEK

***Greek Islands,*** 766 W. Jackson (782-9855). Located a block off the main strip of old Greek Town, this is about everybody's favorite local Greek eatery. Exceptionally well prepared seafood: broiled snapper, sea bass, squid, smelts and shell-intact shrimp. Also, good *dolmades* (stuffed grape leaves) and lamb with artichoke hearts. For an opening flourish, don't miss *saganaki* (flaming cheese). Open seven days a week. Entrées from $2.50 (L & D). AE, CB.

## INDIAN

***Gateway to India,*** 1543 N. Wells (642-7755). Delicious, easy-to-take Indian food served in an ornate mansion in Old Town. Seductively spiced mulligatawny and cream of tomato soups. Delicate cauliflower curry, chicken *shaki korma* (laced with dried fruit and almonds), well-marinated *tandoori* chicken, and lamb *tikka.* Don't ignore the Indian breads. If in need, cool off with a frothy mango shake. Waiters are helpful, but please exercise patience, as the food is prepared to order. Full bar. Closed Monday. Entrées from $3 (L), $6 (D). AE, DC, MC, V.

## ITALIAN

***La Fontanella,*** 2414 S. Oakley (927-5249). The archetypal family-run, neighborhood Italian restaurant. The kitchen goes easy on oil and tomatoes, but not on garlic. Try the richly sauced green noodles, *saltimbocca* or chicken *alla Franca* (juicy fried chicken stuffed with butter, herbs, garlic and Parmesan). Don't miss the ambrosial medium-crust pizza (split one as an appetizer). *Cannoli* for dessert. Small wine list. Reservations recommended on weekends. Closed Monday. Complete, filling dinners average $5. No credit cards.

***Doro's,*** 871 N. Rush (266-1414). Fine Northern Italian cuisine in an ornate, yet relaxing dining room in the center of the busy Rush Street area. Homemade pasta is excellent—try the fettuccine Alfredo prepared tableside. Equally fresh-tasting are the scaloppini alla Sorrentina and *suprema di pollo* Gismonda with spinach and mushrooms. Zabaglione, a Marsala-flavored custard, is a treat for dessert. It, too, is prepared tableside. Reservations recommended. Closed Sunday. Entrées from $6 (L & D). AE, DC, MC, V.

## JAPANESE

***Kamehachi,*** 1617 N. Wells (664-3663). An adventure into the delights of *sushi* and *sashimi* await in this clean and brightly lit spot in the heart of Old Town. If the raw fish treats don't tempt you, then sample the excellent tempura or sukiyaki. Portions tend to be small, Japanese-style. Watch the chef's artistic knife magic at the sushi bar. Full bar. Closed Monday. Entrées from $3.50 (L & D). AE, MC, V.

## MEXICAN

***Ostioneria Playa Azul,*** 1514 W. 18th (no phone). Though you'll find a few of the tacos, enchiladas and such on the menu, this small storefront in the middle of a Spanish-speaking part of town is known for its excellent seafood. Seviche and red snapper are just two excellent choices—both spicy but not too hot. The Formica atmosphere is warmed by a Mexican jukebox and a selection of Mexican beers. Open seven days a week. Entrées from $3 (L & D). No credit cards.

## SWEDISH

***Ann Sathers,*** 925 W. Belmont (348-2378). Marvelous baking. Meals begin with three to four breads (thick, cakelike white; orange-studded *limpa;* banana; carrot) and end on a caloric high with fresh-baked pies, cobblers and puddings. In between, choose a superior soup, chicken or lamb potpie, Swedish meatballs or catfish. Tearoom setting, motherly waitresses. Open seven days a week until 8 P.M., 7 P.M. Sunday. Complete meals from $3.20 (L & D). No credit cards.

## THAI

***Thai Villa,*** 3811 N. Lincoln (472-9478). Small, but warmly decorated storefront that stands out among a handful of Thai restaurants. Food not as fiery as most. Try sautéed whole pompano with dried mushrooms and red-wine sauce, Thai-style barbecued chicken, fried beef in oyster oil, and hot-and-sour shrimp soup. Four varieties of egg rolls, including Vietnamese. Order several dishes and share the wealth. The owner willingly explains the menu. Bring your own liquor. Closed Monday. Entrées from $2.50 (L & D). DC.

# SPECIALTY COOKING

## DELI

***Manny's,*** 1139 S. Jefferson (939-2855). Serve yourself, steam-table style. Everything from roast veal breast to *kreplach* soup to *kishke.* Terrific mashed-potato knish stuffed with ground meat. Carved-to-order brisket and corned-beef sandwiches, some with potato pancakes and pickles. Loud, lively, colorful, mixed crowd. Closes at 5:30 P.M. weekdays. Closed Sunday. Entrées from $2.50, sandwiches from $1.50. No credit cards.

## HAMBURGER

***Acorn on Oak,*** 116 E. Oak (944-6835). Small dimly lit bar, in the midst of Oak Street boutiques, which serves the best hamburgers in town, juicy and spiced with onions and peppers, and served on fresh buns. Large, homemade fries are also the best around. Evening reservations usually necessary. Open seven days a week. Half-pound burger is $4. No credit cards.

## KOSHER

***The Bagel,*** 3000 W. Devon (764-3377). Hearty, stick-to-the-ribs dinners served in a busy but warm restaurant-bakery. Daily specials are usually good choices in addition to cabbage borscht, pickled whitefish, kishke, kugel, blintzes and potato pancakes. Good omelets, too. Closed Monday. Entrées from $3.25 (L & D). No credit cards.

## PIZZA

***Gino's East,*** 160 E. Superior (943-1127). In either the upper or lower level you'll find dim booths scratched with college-style graffiti and the best of all the Chicago-style deep-dish pizzas. Served from deep pans, it is loaded with layers of cheese, sausage or other ingredients of your choice, and topped with a just-right tomato sauce. Their Special pizza is a work of art, starting at $5.65 for a small (enough to feed four). Sunday, dinner only. Open seven days a week. AE.

## SEAFOOD

***Tango,*** 3170 N. Sheridan (935-0350). Beautifully decorated, sophisticated restaurant in the Hotel Belmont. Main dining room can be noisy. Ask for one of the semi-enclosed booths for more privacy. Menu is mostly seafood with a few steaks and poultry entrées. Try their daily specials like poached sea bass or walleye pike when available. Also great bouillabaisse, Lake Superior whitefish, and a long list of hot and cold appetizers. Complete wine list. Reservations necessary. Sunday and Monday, dinner only. Open seven days a week. Entrées from $4.25 (L), $6.75 (D). AE, MC, V.

## SOUL

***Glady's,*** 4527 S. Indiana (548-6848). Plump fried chicken, biscuits that could float, smothered pork chops, turkey wings and dressing, greens, scalloped corn, peach cobbler and sweet-potato pie. Not a street on which to loiter, but vibes inside are easygoing and warm. No liquor. Never closes. Entrées from $1.75. No credit cards.

## STEAK

***Eli's The Place for Steaks,*** 215 E. Chicago (642-1393). Dine with local politicos, columnists, and show-business celebrities in this subdued, rather small restaurant near Chicago's famed Water Tower. The steaks are among the best in town. Try the sirloin butt or the tournedos of prime beef tenderloin. Eli is also known for top-quality calves' liver, sautéed with onions, green pepper and mushrooms. Reservations necessary. Saturday and Sunday, dinner only. Open seven days a week. Steak prices range from $8.95 to $14.45. AE.

## VEGETARIAN

***Heartland Café,*** 7000 N. Glenwood (465-8005). Airy, plant-filled restaurant serving lunch, breakfast, and dinner vegetarian-style. Some fish and poultry items also available. Try roast chicken with bulgur wheat, stir-fry dinners with ginger sauce, or dinner salads served with homemade soup of the day and corn bread. Breakfast items such as whole-wheat French toast with butter and honey and *huevos rancheros* are excellent. Friendly, though sometimes slow service. Open seven days a week. Entrées from $3.50 (L), $5 (D). No credit cards.

# FOR INDIVIDUAL NEEDS

## IF YOU HAVE TIME FOR ONLY ONE MEAL

***Le Perroquet,*** 70 E. Walton (944-7990). (See description under BIG DEAL/WORTH IT.)

***Le Français,*** 269 S. Milwaukee, Wheeling (541-7470). (See description under IN THE SUBURBS/WHEELING.)

## BEST HOTEL MEAL

***Cape Cod Room,*** Drake Hotel, 140 E. Walton, at Michigan Avenue (787-2200). Cozy New England Inn-style dining room decorated with hanging copper pots, beamed ceiling, red-and-white checked tablecloths. Very reputable seafood. Try the Bookbinder soup, cherrystone clams on the half shell, Cape Cod scallops, sole amandine. Full bar. Reservations and jacket required. Open seven days a week. Entrées from $6.50 (L & D). AE, MC, V.

## RESTAURANT NEAR AIRPORT

***Formosa,*** 7108 W. Higgins (763-3652). (See description under CHINESE.)

## BUSINESS BREAKFAST

***The Café,*** the Ritz-Carlton Hotel, Water Tower Place (266-1000). Good for atmosphere and croissants, but only if you want to spend big money for them. Open seven days a week. AE, CB, DC, MC, V.

## BUSINESS LUNCH

***Crickets,*** in Tremont Hotel, 100 E. Chestnut (751-2400). A masculine, almost clublike atmosphere reigns here, with plenty of memorabilia to keep the eyes busy. But the food soon attracts attention with well-prepared lunch items like chicken hash mornay, mixed grill, sweetbreads in a sauce of wine, bacon, and green olives. Good selection of fish and beef, too. Excellent service. Full bar. Sunday, brunch only. Open seven days a week. Entrées average $8 (L), $12 (D). AE, CB, DC, MC, V.

## FAST, GOOD FOOD/BREAKFAST

***Lou Mitchell's,*** 565 W. Jackson (939-3111). A few blocks west of Sears Tower and Union Station. Great aromas; top quality. Try any omelet (served in a skillet) or the double-yolked fried eggs. Thick-cut Greek-style toast and fresh marmalade. Award-winning coffee. Closed Sunday. Entrées average $2.50. No credit cards.

---

## FAST, GOOD FOOD/LUNCH

***The Loophole,*** 59 E. Randolph (236-6243). Fast, serve-yourself food with flavor and flair. Go for the "soup-and-a-half"—chunky goulash soup (or a daily special) and either half a shrimp-studded egg-salad sandwich or corned beef on an onion roll. Try a late lunch—it's packed at noon. Closed Sunday. Soup-and-a-half is $2.45. No credit cards.

---

## FAST, GOOD FOOD/DINNER

***The Berghoff,*** 17 W. Adams (427-3170). Comfortable multiroomed setting for substantial, nicely priced German meals. Enormous menu varies each day and may include braised oxtails, Wiener schnitzel, ragout à la Deutsch, sauerbraten. Good seafood selection, soothing soups, wonderful desserts, German beer. Efficient, ultraprofessional service. Can be very crowded and reservations are not accepted for parties under four. Closed Sunday. Entrées from $2.50 (L), $3.95 (D). No credit cards.

---

## FOR DRINKS

***Arnie's,*** 1030 N. State (266-4800). Handsome, stylish atmosphere highlighted by view of plant-filled atrium. A fine place to see and be seen. Open seven days a week. AE, DC, MC, V.

***Harry's Café,*** 1035 N. Rush (266-0167). Join a younger crowd in this elaborately decorated café filled with plants, Tiffany lamps and stained glass galore. Open seven days a week. AE, MC, V.

---

## RESTAURANT WITH MUSIC

***Miomir's Serbian Club,*** 2255 W. Lawrence (784-2111). Any eating done here is purely coincidental to the entertainment, ranging from gypsy violinists to dancing Russian-style. The later it gets, the louder, with diners often joining in on the dancing and songs. Traditional Serbian dishes include *cevapcici* (a veal and beef sausage) and *muckalica* (veal and beef embellished with onion, tomato and green pepper). Full bar. Reservations suggested Dinner only. Closed Monday and Tuesday. Entrées from $6.95. MC, V.

## ROMANTIC

***Sayat Nova,*** 157 E. Ohio (644-9159). An intimate and shadowy little hideaway just off Michigan Avenue, featuring Armenian delicacies. Can be crowded during lunch. Open seven days a week. Lunch from $2.50. Dinners from $5. MC, V.

***Geja's Café,*** 340 W. Armitage (281-9101). Pleasant little bistro specializing in fondue dinners. For more privacy, request a booth. European cheese platters team well with a bottle from small but interesting wine list. Try the chocolate fondue for dessert. Classical guitarist plays nightly. Dinner only. Open seven days a week. Entrées from $5.50. AE, MC, V.

## LATE-NIGHT SERVICE

***Miller's Pub and Restaurant,*** 23 E. Adams (922-7446). American-style food, sprinkled with a touch of Greek and Italian, is found in this vinyl- and wood-decorated spot in the middle of the Loop. Try the baby back ribs in a hickory-flavored sauce, accompanied by thick fries. For other late-night snacks try the sirloin steak sandwich with onion rings, or a Greek burger. Open seven days a week until 4 A.M. Sandwiches from $3.50, ribs $8.50. AE, CB, DC, MC, V.

## SUNDAY BRUNCH

***Gordon's,*** 512 N. Clark (467-9780). Although the location is seedy, inside it's pure posh. A bountiful brunch features seafood (salmon mousse, fresh oysters, smoked trout topped with caviar and sour cream, etc.), choice of eggs (perhaps Mexican or Florentine). Desserts include fresh strawberry, blueberry and raspberry tarts, rich fudge-like chocolate torte, or cheesecake. Closed Monday. Brunch from 11:30 A.M. to 3 P.M. Total indulgence for $7 to $8. MC, V.

## SUNDAY-EVENING MEAL

***L'Epuisette,*** 21 W. Goethe (944-2288). Expertly prepared seafood in a subdued décor enhanced by generous portions and professional service. Try Rocky Mountain trout stuffed with crab meat, soft-shelled crabs amandine, turbot Véronique. Creamy clam chowder, Caesar salad and rich desserts. Full bar. Dinner only. Closed Monday. Complete dinners from $9 to $12. AE, CB, DC, MC, V.

# IN THE SUBURBS

## CALUMET CITY

***The Cottage,*** 525 Torrence (891-3900). An off-the-beaten-track location, but from pastry-covered pâté appetizer to inventive desserts the meal is superb. Try pork schnitzel as an entrée; delicious salads, lovely vegetables. Well-chosen wine list. Reservations recommended. Chaîne des Rotisseurs. Dinner only. Closed Sunday and Monday. $10 to $12 fixed price. No credit cards.

## EVANSTON

***Café Provençal,*** 1625 Hinman (475-2233). French-provincial setting that turns out some of the best country-French cooking in the area. Limited menu features seasonal specials such as *cassoulet,* chicken with morels in Madeira sauce, salmon with fresh-basil sauce. Desserts are special. Full bar. Reservations required weekends. Dinner only. Closed Sunday. Entrées from $7.50. MC.

## GLENVIEW

***Hackney's,*** Lake Avenue, east of Waukegan Road (724-7171), or Harms Road, south of Lake Avenue (724-5577). Juicy hamburgers on black bread, great fries and slaw, and what may be the best French-fried onions ever (they're served in a loaf). Always crowded. Full bar. Open seven days a week. Hamburger costs $2.95. AE, MC, V.

## HAMMOND, INDIANA

***Phil Smidt's,*** 1205 N. Calumet (212/659-0025). Big, family-style restaurant serving huge portions of perch, frogs' legs, pan-fried chicken. All-you-can-eat relishes. Attentive, concerned waitresses. Full bar. Closed Sunday. Entrées from $3 (L), $4.35 (D). AE.

## WHEELING

***Le Français,*** 269 S. Milwaukee (541-7470). A restaurant with a well-deserved national reputation. Expensive ingredients exquisitely and imaginatively prepared; much to choose from: partridge pâté, wild-duck pâté, fresh salmon *en croûte* filled with lobster mousse, boneless squab stuffed with squab mousse, pastry-wrapped lobster tail with champagne sauce. Beautiful vegetables; brilliant desserts. Extensive wine list. Personalized service. The chef is from Lyons, so he's come further than you will have to drive to get here. Worth the voyage. Reservations mandatory. Dinner only. Closed Monday. Be prepared to spend 2½ to 3 hours, and at least $40 per person. AE, MC, V.

# MARKETS

## GIFT FOODS

***Stop and Shop,*** 16 W. Washington (726-8500). Right in the heart of the Loop, a gourmet gallimaufry: goose, partridge, quail eggs, truffles, fancy glazed fruit, even chocolate-covered ants and much more. Closed Sunday. MC, V.

***Conte Di Savoia,*** 555 W. Roosevelt (666-3471). Barrels of dried herbs and spices, over forty types of pasta, tinned imports from all over the world, dried Polish and Italian mushrooms, delicious rum balls. Open seven days a week. MC, V.

***Kuhn's Delicatessen,*** 3063 N. Lincoln (525-9019). Cheeses, sausages, fresh-made salads, German imports, enormous beer and wine selection. Open seven days a week. No credit cards.

***Treasure Island,*** 1639 N. Wells (642-1105). There are mangoes, kiwi, ugli fruit, raspberries, artichokes, miniature eggplant, snow peas, etc. Organic foods, juice bar, Greek pastries inside this Old Town supermarket. Open seven days a week. MC.

***Ideal Candy Shop,*** 3311 N. Clark (327-2880). A charming old-fashioned shop that specializes in homemade chocolates: dark-chocolate-covered orange peel, cherry cordials, English toffee, plus nut brittle and hand-dipped caramel apples (autumn only). A small soda fountain, too. Closed Tuesday.

## GIFT WINES

***The Chalet,*** 405 W. Armitage (266-7155), 444 W. Fullerton (871-0300) and other locations. Wide range of U.S. and European wines. Fresh bread, croissants and cheeses sliced to order. Open seven days a week. MC, V.

# SPECIAL EVENTS

***Chicagofest,*** Navy Pier, on the lakefront. Music, drama, comedy and food combine to make this week-long summer festival a hit. Usually the last week in July, the event draws big-name talents and food offerings from Chicago restaurants including egg rolls, ribs, corn-on-the-cob, gumbo, hamburgers and ethnic specialties. All events for the price of a daily admission ticket, around $4. For specific dates, call the mayor's office, 744-5000.

# Cincinnati

Thanks to the Indian Mound Builders, who lived in this area centuries ago, Cincinnati, like Rome, is a city of seven hills.

It is also a city that remembers the past and continues to build on it. The land, which once sold for 66⅔ cents an acre at the spot where the Great Miami River enters the Ohio, is now weighed down by astronomically valuable, ever-changing and multiplying high-rise structures. This is a city that has overcome seven devastating epidemics of cholera, terrible floods, the lightning destruction of tornadoes, and has risen to better things.

For one reason or another, the city has always attracted people. In the era of Nicholas Longworth's vast vineyards, with the helping hands and minds of knowledgeable German immigrants, the city became the wine center of the country. After black rot wiped out the vineyards, an era of construction began, and with it came the Irish—good cooks, good builders and good minds. The wine center moved West, but German vigor, love of athletics and zest for good food and beer left a permanent stamp on the region.

The riverboat era and the opening of the Miami-Erie canal made Cincinnati a center of trade with the North, the East and the South. The city became the hog-butchering center of the country and was dubbed "Porkopolis." Spin-off industries flourished—soap and candles from the fat; shoes, harnesses and saddles from the hides. The city attracted immigrants from many parts of the world, all bringing part of their native culture to the Queen city, along with their tastes in food and drink.

Charles Dickens, Mrs. Frances Trollope of "bazaar" fame, Henry Clay and John Quincy Adams arrived by stagecoach. Here Stephen Foster wrote his "Oh! Susanna," and Harriet Beecher Stowe her nation-shaking *Uncle Tom's Cabin.*

As blacks came up from the South during the Civil War, Cincinnati learned and partook of soul food—of chitterlings and turnip greens.

Along with trade came cultural growth: churches, schools, universities, an opera house, a symphony orchestra, an art museum, botanical gardens and a zoo.

In 1850 the Burnet House was built, and *The Illustrated London News* described it as the "finest hotel in the world." Hebrew Union College was established in the city. Reform Judaism was born here, and kosher cooking had its place, too.

Cincinnati grew on the genius of its people—William Procter and James Gamble, founders of the Procter & Gamble Company; Anna and Andrew Jergens and their soap and lotion empire; the Fleischmanns of yeast fame; Salmon P. Chase, who helped found the Republican party here; Henry Huschard Mayer, a father of the meat-packing industry; Barney Kroger, who helped revolutionize the food merchandising business of the world; the Frank family and their spice company, and many others.

Restaurants in Cincinnati have always had an international flavor, from the time of the first German beer gardens. And so, today, among its more than a thousand restaurants, Cincinnatians can find dining to meet almost any taste—American, English, French, Chinese, Japanese, kosher, Lebanese, Greek, Italian and others.

During the past year, many new restaurants have opened in Cincinnati. Among these, two growing strongly in public favor, are House of Hunan (34 West 7th Street, second floor), with hot and hotter Chinese food, and Edwards (Fifth and Butler Streets, off Eggleston Avenue), with a menu featuring recipes of Southern France and Northern Italy.

The influences of the early days are still seen here, in the hush puppies and beaten biscuits of the South, Creole food from New Orleans, Sister Lizzie's sugar cream pie from the Shakers, German crispy pork schnitzels, hot potato salad and beer, Italian spaghetti and meatballs, fettuccine and lasagne, Greek baklava and Lebanese *kibbe* and stuffed grape leaves.

In the French restaurants of the city, a strict dress code is observed, with jackets and ties required. Elsewhere, the code is more—but never totally—relaxed. "Tier" tipping is not in general practice. One tip can say it all.

At Sixth and Vine streets, taxis are always lined up to carry passengers, at a reasonable fee, to any part of Greater Cincinnati. To get a cab there, go to the head of the line, at the southwest corner of the intersection.

# Restaurants and Food Sources
**(Area code: 513)**

# BIG DEAL

## WORTH IT

***The Maisonette,*** 114 East Sixth Street (721-2260). The restaurant makes dining an experience—quiet, relaxed, beautiful, unhurried. Continental style. At lunch, the *soufflé au fromage* ($6.25) may be the ambrosia of all soufflés. Crabmeat salad is highly popular, as is the *brochette de filet de boeuf, sauce bordelaise. Médaillons de veau sautés meunière* and tournedos Rossini are excellent dinner selections. The desserts are French works of art. An extensive wine list. Within walking distance of all major downtown hotels, the Cincinnati Convention Center and Riverfront Stadium, home of the Cincinnati Reds. Reservations necessary, also jacket and tie. Saturday, dinner only. Closed Sunday. Entrées from $5.75 (L), $10.50 (D). AE, DC, MC, V.

# INTERNATIONAL

## AMERICAN

***Chester's Road House,*** 9678 Montgomery Road (793-8700). An enterprise of the Comisars, proprietors of The Maisonette, this restaurant in an old home has genuine antique décor, a glass roof and lots of plants. A tree grows in the middle of the dining room. The rack of baby lamb is recommended, plus an excellent make-your-own-salad bar—all fresh ingredients. A blend of seven different liqueurs in their cappuccino makes this an after-dinner curiosity. Reservations recommended; none accepted Saturday. Dinner only. Open seven days a week. Entrées from $5.50. AE, MC, V.

# CHINESE

***Magic Wok,*** 8063 Montgomery Road (984-2222). A 10-minute drive from downtown Cincinnati: take I-71, get off at Exit 12 and turn right; about 300 yards on the left and you're there. Cantonese food expertly prepared by ten chefs draws politicians and sports figures to this large restaurant under the command of president Don Wong. They do a fine job with appetizers, especially a combination plate of delicate eggrolls, tempura shrimp, ribs and *Bali Maki* served in a flaming fire pot: for two, $3.25. For lunch the combination plate with shrimp chow mein is popular; at dinner it is *sub gum wonton* ($7.75). Before dinner try an Oriental Itch. Attire may be either casual or dressy. Reservations necessary on weekends. Open seven days a week. Entrées from $2.50 (L), $4.75 (D). AE, MC, V.

***Wah Mee,*** 515 Vine Street (579-0544). A center-city melting pot where shoppers and civic leaders enjoy the calm setting and soft Chinese music as they sample the varied Cantonese fare provided by chefs imported from San Francisco. Wah Mee steak is a specialty, as is stir-fried beef in oyster sauce. They serve Chinese whiskey—*um gai pei*—and Chinese wine, including *kao-liang-chiu,* which some find stronger than vodka. Watch out! It kicks hard. Reservations recommended. Open seven days a week. Entrées from $2.55 (L), $4.25 (D). AE, DC, MC, V.

***China Gourmet, Inc.,*** 3340 Erie Avenue, East Hyde Park Village Mall, about 10 minutes from downtown (871-6612). Devoted clientele claim this has the most refined Cantonese cooking in the area. Serves Szechuan, Mandarin and Hunan dishes as well. Shrimp Chinatown is extremely popular. Known for off-the-menu specialties, such as lobster Cantonese and yellow pike. Open seven days a week. Entrées from $2.50 (L), $4.25 (D). MC, V.

# ENGLISH

***The Sovereign,*** 810 Matson Place, Queen's Tower, in Price Hill area, 5 to 10 minutes by taxi from downtown (471-2250). High up, The Sovereign offers a beautiful view of the city. The décor is pub-type, Tudor-like with dark beams, and waitresses are dressed in Old English costumes. There are eighteen items to choose from at lunch, plus two specials and a businessman's lunch. Try crabmeat salad with avocado at lunch or individual beef Wellington at dinner. Unless you like Campari and grapefruit, avoid the "Sovereign," the house drink. The restaurant is known for large portions and the "biggest salad in town." Reservations suggested, but not required. Saturday and Sunday, dinner only. Closed Monday. Entrées from $3.50 (L), $7.25 (D). AE, DC, MC, V.

## FRENCH

***Pigall's,*** 127 West Fourth Street (721-1345). A consistent winner of major culinary awards, Pigall's is softly lighted with teardrop chandeliers. The background colors are deep rose and soft gray; choice linens and beautiful silver. Selections from a wide choice are expertly guided by waiters in black tie. Especially savory are *côte de veau sautée cardinale, filet de saumon cardinal* and *coquilles St.-Jacques à la crème.* For a twosome, roast rack of lamb *bouquetière* ($26.50) or *filet de boeuf Wellington, sauce périgueux* ($27.50). Reservations necessary, also coat and tie. Closed Sunday. Entrées from $6.75 (L), $11 (D). AE, DC, MC, V.

## GERMAN

***Lenhardt's,*** 151 West McMillan, near the University of Cincinnati (281-3600). Only minutes by taxi from downtown. Frequently seen here are Neil Armstrong, first man on the moon; Dr. Albert Sabin, discoverer of oral vaccine for poliomyelitis; opera stars appearing in Cincinnati; professors; lawyers; doctors; and on occasion, visiting members of European royal families. For lunch, try the sauerbraten with potato pancake; and for dinner, treat yourself to *Jaegerschnitzel* (veal with mushroom and parsley in sweet cream). Hungarian, German and Yugoslavian wines are featured. Homemade desserts here are outstanding, among them a superb Dobos torte—nine layers lined with chocolate butter cream. Weekend reservations suggested. Closed Monday. Entrées from $3.75 (L), $5.45 (D). No credit cards.

***Mecklenburg Gardens,*** 302 East University (281-5353). Only minutes from downtown. Close to the University of Cincinnati, this German restaurant has been a tradition in Cincinnati for one hundred years, although its offerings are becoming more international in character. From about May 1 into September or October, outdoor dining under a beautiful grape arbor is an added feature. Seafood omelet with seasonal vegetables is a popular luncheon selection. At dinner, try beef carbonade Flamande (beef braised in beer with pieces of bacon, onions and juniper berries). An effort is made here to use fresh foods, including fresh fish. Saturday, dinner only. Closed Monday. Entrées from $3 (L), $5 (D). AE, MC, V.

## ITALIAN

***Caruso's,*** 610 Main Street (421-1718). Italian food has been served here since 1886. Among the most popular dishes are veal *parmigiana, fettuccine romano* and fettuccine Alfredo with homemade noodles. The service is lively, yet the overall atmosphere is subdued and gracious. Extensive wine and cocktail lists. Reservations recommended. Saturday and Sunday, dinner only. Open seven days a week. Entrées from $2.95 (L), $7.50 (D). AE, MC, V.

***La Rosa's Italian Inn,*** 2409 Boudinot Avenue (451-1334). Fine Italian cooking in a Florentine setting. Music ranges from Mancini to Italian classics. Strolling violinists on occasion. Appetizers are excellent and veal dishes are a speciality. You can't go wrong with the *vitello Milanese* ($7.25). Party room available. Ten different sauces for pastas. Saturday and Sunday, dinner only. Open seven days a week. Entrées from $3.25 (L), $5.25 (D). AE, CB, DC, MC, V.

## JAPANESE

***Samurai Kabuki-Japanese Steak House,*** 126 East Sixth Street (421-1688). Delightful and exciting dining. Your own samurai chef works with a flying machete at the table in an elegant country-inn atmosphere. Try the *teppanyaki* sirloin strip steak with special mustard sauce for lunch. The samurai warrior dinner features an extra large cut of sirloin or filet plus a decanter of hot *sake,* grilled shrimp, soup, salad, vegetable, rice, tea and dessert. Plum wine is a nice added touch. Dress here is from dressy-casual to dressy. Reservations recommended. Saturday and Sunday, dinner only. Open seven days a week. Entrées from $3.65 (L), $8 (D). AE, DC, MC, V.

# SPECIALTY COOKING

## CHILI

***Skyline Chili, Inc.,*** 643 Vine Street (241-2020), and at 17 other locations. For the famous Cincinnati chili (not like Texas chili), try any one of the chili houses of Skyline Chili located throughout the city. Comes plain, in a bowl (95 cents) or two-way, three-way, four-way and five-way, the last of which is a slightly catsup-flavored spaghetti topped with large red beans, chili, chopped onion and a big and beautiful mound of shredded cheese. Get there on an off-hour—crowded at noon, but people stand and wait. Closed Sunday. Five-way chili, $1.60. No credit cards.

***Empress Chili,*** 30 West Fifth Street (421-1711), and at 10 other locations. This chili is similar to that of Skyline, but slightly spicier. Very popular, too; very Cincinnati. Open 8 A.M. to 11 P.M. Closed Sunday. No credit cards.

## CRÊPES

***The Saucy Crêpe,*** 3330 Erie Avenue (321-1961). Tasteful setting. Choice of six different crêpe dinners and six more traditional dinners, plus soups, salads and desserts. Filet of beef and chicken Florentine are excellent. Try the crêpe St.-Jacques—scallops, shrimp, mushrooms and béchamel sauce. Extensive wine and cocktail lists. Reservations for weekends only. Open seven days a week. Package dinner, with salads, rolls and butter $3.50 (L & D). AE, MC, V.

## DELI

***Temple Delicatessen, Inc.,*** 130 W. Seventh Street (621-6161). Specialities here are corned beef, pepper loaf, pastrami and tongue. Sandwich combinations include a great Reuben. Try the Temple Whopper—corned beef, tongue, salami and pastrami, double-decker on rye with Russian dressing ($2.75). The corned beef sandwich, for which the deli is famous, is $1.75. All meat, with the exception of ham, is kosher. Open 6 A.M. through late afternoon. Closed Sunday. Sandwiches from $1.15. No credit cards.

***La Rosa's Food and Wine Store,*** 2411 Boudinot Avenue (451-1520). Customers come from as far as 100 miles away to this deli in the western hills section that sells homemade bread, cookies, pastries, Italian hot and sweet sausage, cheeses, spices, 21 different antipasto salads, cooked pasta dishes and fresh pasta. More than 120 imported dried pastas, too. Buyers can consume their purchases next door in a La Rosa restaurant. Open seven days a week. AE, MC, V.

## HAMBURGER

***Incahoots,*** corner of Vine and Charlton, near the University of Cincinnati (861-2232). Top choices are burger with any kind of cheese, fresh mushrooms, avocado or the spicy ranchero burger. "The Potato" is a must here; it's cut across the width and home-fried. This ultramodern setting, with its platform areas and clever utilization of space, has won several awards. A nice place to sit, relax, talk and eat. Open seven days a week, until 1 A.M. Friday. The hamburgers are from $2.95 (L & D). MC, V.

## SEAFOOD

***Charley's Crab,*** 9769 Montgomery Road (891-7000). This is Nantucket Island in Ohio. Fresh fish brought in daily from the East Coast, the Gulf and the Great Lakes. Boston scrod, lemon sole, king salmon, striped bass, Lake Superior whitefish, lake trout and pickerel are among the choices. Brass oyster bar is exceptional. Casual dress, reservations recommended. Dinner only. Open seven days a week. Entrées from $8. One and a half Maine lobsters for $15.25. AE, CB, DC, MC, V.

## STEAK

***Thomas' F & N Steak House,*** Mary Inglis Highway (Ky. Route 8), eight miles from downtown Cincinnati and just east of Dayton, Ky. (261-6766). Beefeaters flock to this rustic roadside steakhouse with its six fireplaces, arriving by car or cruising up the Ohio to get here. Steaks are sold by weight, up to 32 ounces. All are aged and cut by F & N. Country-style vegetables are popular, too, especially the French-fried eggplant. Prime rib is roasted (10 roasts at a time) for 16 hours at 185 degrees. Results are terrific. Reservations recommended. Open seven days a week, until 1 A.M. Friday and Saturday. Try a 14-ounce T-bone at $6.95 or a prime rib ($5.95). Steak, with French-fried potatoes, salad and homemade buns, from $3.95 (L & D). AE, CB, DC, MC, V.

## VEGETARIAN

***New World Food Shop, Inc.,*** 347 Ludlow Avenue, Clifton area (861-1101). This small restaurant in the back of a health-food store can seat only sixteen, but it does a big carry-out business. A favorite is the Middle Eastern sandwich—*pita* bread with *homus* (chickpea spread) and *tabouli* (salad of cracked wheat, chopped greens and lemon). Fried rice is a specialty here; vegeburgers have wide popularity in the city. Homemade desserts include fruit pies, rice pudding, apple scrunch—all made without sugar. Spring water is used in all cooking. Complete line of natural foods in store in front of restaurant. Closes at 7:30 P.M. weekdays and all Saturday. Open 11 A.M. to 4 P.M. Sunday. Entrées from $2 (L & D). No credit cards.

***Spring Wheat,*** 22 Convention Way, on the Skywalk at Race Street (241-1600). Health-food shop and attractive, ample restaurant. While it serves some fish and dairy foods, there is much for the vegetarian to choose. Fruit and garden vegetable salads excellent. Calorie count provided with each item. Monday through Friday, lunch only. Saturday, juice bar only. Closed Sunday. Meatless Sloppy Joes $1.05, salads from $2.15. MC, V.

# FOR INDIVIDUAL NEEDS

## IF YOU HAVE TIME FOR ONLY ONE MEAL

***The Maisonette,*** 114 East Sixth Street (721-2260). (See description under BIG DEAL/WORTH IT.)

## BEST HOTEL MEAL

***Gourmet Restaurant,*** Terrace Hilton Hotel, 20th floor, Sixth and Vine streets (381-4000). Roast pheasant stuffed with forcemeat and truffles, and fresh lobster in champagne are specialties here. A dinner special—appetizer to dessert for $20—changes nightly. More than 150 different wines on the list. Dinner only. Closed Sunday. Entrées from $12. AE, CB, DC, MC, V.

## RESTAURANT NEAR AIRPORT

***Sky Chefs' River Queen Restaurant,*** at the Greater Cincinnati Airport, Covington, Ky. (1-606-283-3711). This large restaurant has the décor and design of an early riverboat. Turkey salad plate is a specialty at lunch, and a generous portion of roast beef is featured at dinner. Don't miss the black-bottom pie with its blend of vanilla ice cream and orange liqueur. Saturday, dinner only. Open seven days a week. Entrées from $2.50 (L), $5.45 (D). AE, DC, MC, V.

## BUSINESS BREAKFAST

***Palm Court,*** Netherland Hilton Hotel, Fifth and Race Streets (621-3800). Choose a Continental breakfast or a more leisurely one of pancakes and bananas. The setting is ornate, with wooden panels and murals. Coats and ties required for the most part. Open seven days a week. Continental breakfast $2.25. AE, CB, DC, MC, V.

## BUSINESS LUNCH

***Terrace Garden,*** Terrace Hilton Hotel, Sixth and Vine Streets (381-4000). Lovely, quiet setting, excellent service. Try the eggs Benedict or the broiled halibut. Their Netherland salad with special dressing is excellent—it has a slight touch of garlic. Excellent salad bar available with entrée. Reservations recommended. Open seven days a week. Entrées from $2.25. AE, CB, DC, MC, V.

## FAST, GOOD FOOD

***The Cricket,*** Sixth and Vine Streets (241-3949). An English pub setting with 400 seats and an excellent bar. The seafood bisque is excellent, as is poached salmon, but the menu is large. It fills quickly at noon, but the turnover is rapid. Sunday, dinner only. Open seven days a week. Entrées from $2.75 (L & D). AE, CB, MC, V.

## BEST WINE LIST

***Pigall's,*** 127 West Fourth Street (721-1345). (See description under FRENCH.)

## FOR DRINKS

***The Blind Lemon,*** 936 Hatch Street, in the Mt. Adams area (241-3885). A bistro atmosphere, but intimate. Live music at night. Popular with the younger set. Happy hour Monday through Friday from 4 P.M. to 7 P.M. Open seven days a week. No credit cards.

***Panorama Lounge,*** atop the Terrace Hilton, adjacent to The Gourmet Room, Sixth and Vine Streets (381-4000). Sedate, informal lounge. Old-fashioned arm chairs with satin covers. Racks of wine bottles. Browsing library of old books, chess tables and backgammon. Hors d'oeuvre served. George Corey, concert pianist. Open until midnight Monday through Friday, until 1 A.M. Saturday. Closed Sunday. AE, CB, DC, MC, V.

## RESTAURANT WITH MUSIC

***The Conservatory,*** 640 W. 3rd, next to the Holiday Inn, Covington, Ky. (491-6400). Dine here in casual elegance. Try the chicken Véronique or snapper amandine. After dining, there is a discotheque. Or stop in the enormous greenhouse, which contains a plant valued at $18,000. Jacket and tie preferred. Reservations recommended. Closed Sunday. Entrées from $3.25 (L), $5.95 (D). AE, MC, V.

## LATE-NIGHT SERVICE

***The Rib Pit,*** located in rear of 625 Walnut Street (721-9780). The barbecued baby ribs are exceptional, but steaks and seafood rate here, too. An Early American setting. Open seven days a week. Complete meals until 2 A.M. Entrées from $3.95, sandwich plate $2.25. AE, CB, DC, MC, V.

***L'Umbrella,*** off Skywalk (Stouffer's) or second floor, Stouffer's Hotel North Tower Lobby, 144 W. Sixth Street (352-2217). Open 24 hours a day. Breakfasts, sandwiches, light dinners and desserts available. Open seven days a week. Special late-night sandwich menu after 10 P.M. Sandwiches from $2.25. AE, CB, DC, MC, V.

## SUNDAY BRUNCH

***The Last National Bank Restaurant,*** 105 West Fourth Street (621-1811). Sunday brunch from 11 A.M. to 3 P.M. offers eggs Benedict, eggs Florentine, eggs Chateaubriand, steak and eggs, quiche, lox and bagels, and bankers' omelets. There is a minibreakfast for children. The restaurant setting is in an old bank. During the week there is dancing. Reservations recommended. Open seven days a week. Brunch includes blueberry muffins and coffee for $5.25. AE, CB, DC, MC, V.

***The Terrace Garden,*** 8th floor of Terrace Hilton Hotel, Sixth and Vine Streets (381-4000). Champagne brunch: beef Burgundy, chicken à la king or seafood Newburg, eggs Benedict or Florentine, scrambled eggs, sausage and ham, assorted cakes, rolls and fruit. Catawba wine served with brunch until 1 P.M.—champagne from 1 P.M. to 2 P.M. Brunch served from 9 A.M. to 2 P.M. Price $4.95, half price for children. AE, CB, DC, MC, V.

***The Celestial Restaurant,*** the Highland Towers, 1071 Celestial Street (241-4455). High up in the Mount Adams area with a view over the city, it's a site for relaxing, gracious dining. Arrive early for brunch if possible because empty trays may not be replenished in later hours. This is a good spot for a business luncheon, if you have time and transportation from the center city. Reservations recommended. Open seven days a week. Entrées from $3.50 (L), $8.75 (D). Brunch (11 A.M. to 3 P.M.) $6 for adults, $4 for children. AE, MC, V.

## SUNDAY-EVENING MEAL

***The Palm Court,*** Netherland Hilton Hotel, Fifth and Race Streets (621-3800). (See description under BUSINESS BREAKFAST.) Try rainbow trout, prime pepper steak or the house specialty, turkey Wellington. Reservations suggested. Open seven days a week until 10:30 P.M. Dinner entrées from $6.50. AE, CB, DC, MC, V.

## FOR FAMILIES WITH CHILDREN

***The Cricket,*** Sixth and Vine Streets (241-3949). (See description under FAST, GOOD FOOD.)

***Bob Evans Restaurant,*** 8057 Montgomery Road, exit 12 off I-71 going north (793-779); or 10 miles south of Cincinnati on Highway 42 in Florence, Ky. (606/283-2535). Beautiful red and white, down-on-the-farm-type structure. Family-style restaurant. Popular are the pioneer salad and the barbecued ribs, available weekdays after 4 P.M. and all day Sunday. Sugar-cured hams and salt-cured country hams featured. Homemade biscuits and honey. Closed Monday. Entrées from $2.25 (L & D). No credit cards.

## COUNTRY INN

***The Golden Lamb,*** 27 South Broadway, center of town on Route 48, Lebanon, Ohio (621-8373). Located about 30 miles north of Cincinnati, Ohio's oldest inn and restaurant shows strong Shaker influence in its menu. The roast duckling *à l'orange* is excellent and sugar-cream pie is much in demand. Homemade biscuits, apple butter. There is an extensive gift shop. You might have a 20-minute wait; reservations recommended. Open seven days a week. Entrées from $3.30 (L), $7.30 (D). AE, MC, V.

***The Heritage,*** 7664 Wooster Pike, eastern hills (561-9300). Historic homestead. Consistently excellent food. Try the beef tenderloin in Burgundy sauce or, from a new menu of *nouvelle cuisine,* the low-calorie chicken *au jus* or green pepper steak. Reservations recommended. Dress: jacket and tie. Saturday, dinner only. Closed Sunday. Entrées from $1.85 (L), $4.25 (D). AE, MC, V.

# MARKETS

***Findlay Market,*** Elder and Race Streets. Cincinnati's farmers market contains fourteen stores and hundreds of stalls passed on from generation to generation by farming families. Open 7 A.M. to

1:30 P.M., Wednesday and Friday; 7 A.M. to 6 P.M., Saturday. Closed all other days.

## GIFT FOODS/WINES

***Luxembourg House,*** 7789 Cooper Road (793-4133). More than fifty varieties of imported cheeses and wines from around the world. They will make up gift baskets. Closed Sunday. MC, V.

***Shillito's,*** Seventh and Race Streets (369-7000). One of the city's largest department stores contains a large wine shop and a gourmet shop on the first floor. Closed Sunday. No credit cards.

***H & S Pogue,*** Fourth and Race Streets (352-5589). Also a large department store with an epicure shop and Ohio's largest wine shop. Closed Sunday. No credit cards.

# SPECIAL EVENTS

***International Folk Festival,*** sponsored annually in early to mid-November by Cincinnati International Folk Festival, Inc. at the Cincinnati Convention Center. A three-day event in which 28 different ethnic groups in Greater Cincinnati participate. No set dates listed early. Call Convention Center (381-2210) for dates and time. Foreign foods, folk dancing, international disco featured. Nominal admission charge is for support of the festival.

***Sacred Heart Italian Church at Camp Washington,*** 2733 Massachusetts Avenue, early in April. Largest church dinner in United States. Italian cooks work day and night for four days preparing for the annual one-day event. For a recent dinner, volunteers cooked 460 pounds of spaghetti, 32,000 ravioli and 3,300 meatballs. Prices reasonable. Benefits church in poor area. Call 541-4654 for date and time.

# Cleveland

For its size, there is no other city in the U.S. with such complex and diversified ethnic communities as Cleveland. At last count 52 nationalities were represented here. Therefore it's not surprising that some of the best eating in the city is at neighborhood restaurants within these ethnic enclaves. The generation that initially operated many of them has begun to retire, and the shift of population to the suburbs has thinned the ranks, but restaurants such as the Hungarian **Balaton** continue to provide great quantities of fine food at astonishingly low prices.

Cleveland is made up of many smaller areas that have preserved their own identities; you will find a number of locales listed but all within a 45-minute drive from downtown.

Downtown itself, like other center-city areas across the nation, is trying to shed an image of decline and decay. Among the symbols of change a visitor will find the new Stouffer's Inn on the Square providing **The French Connection,** which is one of the finest restaurants in the city. The hotel lobby has a quiet bar and cozy seating areas where light luncheons are served. And, you can walk to nearby Higbee's to shop without going outdoors.

There is a sense of history, too. The nineteenth-century Herrman-McLean Feed Store, one of four stores on old Market Street, has become (along with the old-time bar next door) an exciting restaurant called **The Market Street Exchange.**

The Stouffer's chain began here and the popular place where Mother Stouffer first served her creations to the public is still in operation. Located at Shaker Square, the boundary separating Cleveland and Shaker Heights, it is sometimes wrongly demeaned as an "an old lady's luncheon room."

The area just east of Playhouse Square downtown contains several Oriental restaurants and food stores with their specialities.

Otto Mosher's, at E. 4th and Prospect, has been around for a century, and was one of the all-time great delis in the city. Truly extraordinary strudel can be purchased from three or four bakeries along Buckeye Road between E. 120th and 125th streets. The reason for such a wealth of Hungarian pastry is that, with the exception of Budapest, no other city in the world has a larger Hungarian population.

Just as the food-conscious visitor would be mistaken in thinking of Cleveland as only a Middle-American meat-and-potatoes town, he or she would be misinformed in thinking there is nothing distinctive here for the food shopper. After all, Cleveland is the home of the 3-foot salami. In addition to the Hungarian bakers, there are a number of superb Jewish bakers, whose handiwork may be found in the neighborhood of Taylor and Cedar roads. Lax and Mandel is probably the best known. For eat-in or carry-out delicatessen items, try **Corky and Lenny's** or **Bagel Nosh.**

Perhaps the prime target for a visiting shopper, however, should be the West Side Market at W. 25th Street and Lorain in "Ohio City." Old-fashioned, small-scale retailers survive, and one may browse among stands dedicated to fruits, vegetables, cheeses, sausages and cold cuts, plus many hard-to-find ethnic specialties.

Whatever Cleveland dining lacks in Continental sophistication is compensated for by its fascinating display of European simplicity and some straightforward American cooking. Cleveland's restaurants offer a cornucopia of flavors and nationalities, and dining out has become an important part of socializing. The restaurant population is growing in many neighborhoods. A section of Chagrin Boulevard has been dubbed "restaurant row" because so many restaurants of quality have sprung up there in the last few years.

# Restaurants and Food Sources

**(Area code: 216)**

## BIG DEAL

### WORTH IT

***The French Connection,*** Stouffer's Inn on the Square, 24 Public Square (696-5600). You might want to sink into one of the overstuffed chairs in the lobby for a cocktail before you dine; a harpist provides tranquil music. A gracious greeting and a comfortably elegant room with mirrors and watercolors. The food is fresh and attractively presented. Sauces are consistently good and vegetables are cooked only until crisp-tender. For appetizers, the game terrine is superb. Among the specialties are delicate quenelles topped with Nantua sauce, and duckling with green peppercorn sauce. The house dressing is a piquant, creamy vinaigrette. The dessert cart display includes crème caramel (topped with raspberry sauce) and a French fruit torte (it might be apple or apricot). Limited wine list, full bar. Chaîne des Rotisseurs. Reservations needed. Saturday, dinner only. Closed Sunday. Entrées from $5.75 (L), $9.75 (D). AE, MC, V.

### NOT WORTH IT

***Red Fox Inn Restaurant,*** Chagrin River Road, Gates Mills (423-4408). This was once considered one of the finest restaurants in northeast Ohio. The food was outstanding, the service and table appointments impeccable. It was the eating-meeting place for the horsey set and the well-heeled that live in the lovely area that surrounds the restaurant. For outsiders, the drive to Red Fox was almost as much pleasure as eating at the restaurant. But now the quality of the food is low, prices are high and the service is nothing like it was several years ago. Closed Sunday. Entrées from $4 (L), $6.50 (D). No credit cards.

# INTERNATIONAL

## CHINESE

***Pearl of the Orient,*** 21021 Van Aken Boulevard, Shaker Heights (751-8181). If you have time, order Peking duck (24 hours ahead), which is a house speciality and one of the best variations of this dish you'll ever taste ($21 for two or more). Szechuan cooking is the specialty here and it's very hot. Several meatless entrées are offered. Extensive take-out menu available. Wine list. Open seven days a week. Entrées from $4.75 (L & D). AE, MC, V.

***Pan Asia Restaurant and Lounge,*** 6080 Brecksville Road, Independence (524-6830). Extensive Oriental menu, very well prepared. Vegetarian, Szechuan and Hunan dishes. Full bar and wine list. Reservations recommended. Closed Monday. Entrées from $3.50 (L), $5.25 (D). AE, MC.

## CONTINENTAL

***Jim Swingos Keg and Quarter,*** 1800 Swingos Court (861-5501). Reservations are absolutely necessary if you are looking for dinner after a Browns game or following a show at the Hanna theater or the opera. At those times the lines waiting to get in are longer than those at the opening game of the World Series. Several of the entrées are prepared tableside, including the fettuccine, which is available in traditional preparation or with scallops, clams and shrimp. There is a fresh fish catch of the day. Veal Oskar is almost always reliable, as is the veal Milanese with lemon and wine. Excellent wine list, prices generally good. Sunday, dinner only. Open seven days a week, until 1 A.M. Friday and Saturday, until midnight the rest of the week. Entrées from $3.50 (L), $8.95 (D). AE, DC, MC, V.

## FRENCH

***Au Provence,*** 2195 Lee Road, Cleveland Heights (321-9511). One of only two places in town that serve authentic Creole cuisine. The restaurant is small (now seats 36) and reservations should be made well in advance, especially for Saturday evening when only two seatings (6:30 P.M. and 9:15 P.M.) are booked. It is a seven-course feast prepared by chef Richard Taylor, although only three entrées are offered. During the week the choice is broader. The owner, Dr. Thomas Wykoff, produces his own wine (Cedar Hill label). This wine is included on the wine list and you can also buy it next door at the Cedar Hill Wine Cellars (2197 Lee Road). Recommended: marinated shrimp au Provence—broiled shrimp served in the shell with some of the marinade for dipping—and the bread pudding with whiskey sauce. Dinner only. Closed Sunday. Entrées from $5.50; Saturday, fixed-price dinner $16.25. V.

***Au Père Jacques,*** 34105 Chagrin Boulevard, Chagrin Falls (831-8558). An outstanding wine list and a wine-gourmet store adjacent to the restaurant. Although the outside of the restaurant is sorely in need of a facelift, the menu inside is extensive and includes 34 variations of Dover sole. Everything is à la carte. Complete special house dinner with three wines on Saturday night, *Les Gourmets,* is $55. Late-supper special includes a large bowl of onion soup, Caesar salad, French bread and a carafe of Chablis for $5. Reservations necessary. Dinner only. Closed Sunday. Entrées from $5.85 weekdays, from $12.75 weekends. MC, V.

***Steffons Gourmet Wizardry,*** 29425 Chagrin Boulevard, Pepper Pike (464-2980). It's difficult to find the entrance to Steffons inside Executive Commons, but worth the search. The food is a combination of Northern Italian and country French and includes several selections of veal, with appropriate sauces, frogs' legs and veal sweetbreads. Vegetables are fresh and seasonal. Steak Diane is popular, as is the spinach salad for two. The Caesar salad tends to be overpowered by cheese. Numerous coffees from around the world at $2.95 each. Reservations suggested. Lunch in lounge only on Saturday. Dinner served until midnight. Closed Sunday. Entrées from $2.25 (L), $7.95 (D). AE, MC, V.

## HUNGARIAN

***Balaton Restaurant,*** 12521 Buckeye Road (921-9691). Menu changes daily but can include any of 20 to 25 house specialties. *Gulyas* (goulash) soup is made with tender chunks of beef and diced potato simmered in a rich paprikash broth. The house favorite is Wiener schnitzel served with applesauce and homemade dumplings. Don't overlook chicken paprikash or goulash (made with pork tips). The Hungarian platter is a combination of stuffed cabbage, chicken paprikash and goulash, plus dumplings, for $6.95. Homemade *Dobash* (*dobos*) torte is excellent. Strudels come from nearby

Lucy's Bakery and are outstanding. Closed Sunday and Monday. The kitchen closes at 8 P.M. Tuesday and Wednesday, and at 9 P.M. Thursday through Saturday. Entrées from $4 (L), $6.95 (D). No credit cards.

# ITALIAN

***Giovanni's,*** 25550 Chagrin Boulevard, Beachwood (831-8625). Call well in advance if you want to enjoy the fine Northern Italian food in this popular suburban restaurant. All the pasta is made on the premises and there are always house specials, depending upon what the chef and owner Luke Manfredi find desirable at the market that day. Escargots, *ostriche Fiorentina* (oysters with a delicious bacon-spinach topping), eight or more different veal dishes and nine pasta entrées. *Orata a cartoccio* is red snapper baked in parchment with shrimp and mushrooms. All entrées include Giovanni's house salad, fresh vegetable, potatoes of the day (which might be with hollandaise) and bread. The dessert cart is a knockout. It features homemade (and magnificent) cassata, a multilayered mousse cake and trifle. Ample wine list. Chaîne des Rotisseurs. Reservations necessary. Closed Sunday. Entrées from $2.50 (L), $6.50 (D). AE, DC, MC, V.

***Guarino's,*** 12309 Mayfield Road (231-9699 or 231-3100). Opened in 1918, Guarino's, in the heart of "Little Italy," is a traditional eating place for members of the Cleveland Orchestra and their fans. The outdoor garden is charming in the summer. Recommended: veal Marsala and veal Franchaise. Fettuccine Alfredo is the best in city; naturally the pasta is homemade. The house salad is simple—greens and red onion with olive oil, vinegar and oregano—but superb. (If Guarino's is filled, go across the street to the **Golden Bowl.** The outside garden is pleasing and there is a nice cocktail bar for drinks before dinner. Try the sausage with green peppers, onions and mushrooms. Good fettuccine, homemade pasta. Espresso prepared in one of those elegant machines.) Closed Sunday. Entrées from $6.25 (L & D). AE, CB, DC, MC, V.

# JAPANESE

***The Samurai Japanese Steak House,*** 23611 Chagrin Boulevard, Beachwood (464-7575). You'll be fascinated by the chef who skillfully prepares your entrée in front of you at the *teppanyaki* tables. Dinners include shrimp appetizer, soup, salad and dessert, along with one of seven entrées, which might be sesame chicken, shrimp flambé or one of three Kobe beef steaks. Japanese beer and sake available, plus a limited wine list and full bar. Great place for several couples. Open seven days a week. Entrées from $3.50 (L), $8 (D). AE, DC, MC, V.

## MIDDLE EASTERN

***The Middle East Restaurant,*** 1012 Prospect Avenue (771-2647). For 16 years Josephine Abrahams has turned out all the food for this restaurant in the downtown area. Like many of Cleveland's good ethnic restaurants, the emphasis is on the quality of food and not on atmosphere. An extensive menu includes Josephine's stuffed grape leaves, baked eggplant with pine nuts and meat, or stuffed zucchini with rice and lamb filling. The baklava is outstanding. Closed Sunday. Entrées from $2.95 (L), $4.95 (D). MC, V.

# SPECIALTY COOKING

## DELI

***Corky and Lenny's,*** 27091 Chagrin Boulevard, in Village Square, Woodmere (464-3838), 13837 Cedar Center, S. Euclid (321-3310). A superior selection of smoked fish, deli meats and salads. Chagrin Boulevard closed Monday; Cedar Center open seven days a week. Deluxe sandwiches from $2.50. No credit cards.

***Deli Nosh,*** 5110 Mayfield Road, Lyndhurst (461-2150). Terrific selection of sandwiches, all served on bagels or Kaiser rolls. (A sister restaurant, **Deli Nosh,** at 24127 Chagrin Boulevard, Beechwood (467-4177) is now open in Pavilion Mall.) Open seven days a week. Sandwiches from $2.25. No credit cards.

***Clifton Delicatessen and Epicure Shop,*** 11618 Clifton Boulevard (631-8899). Good assortment of deli foods and excellent sandwiches to carry out. Party trays, canapés. Excellent assortment of salads. Open seven days a week. Sandwiches from $1.90. V.

## HAMBURGER

***Hecks Café,*** 2927 Bridge Avenue (861-5464), 28699 Chagrin Boulevard, Woodmere (292-2545). Head to Hecks if everything else is closed late at night. The Bridge Avenue restaurant was the first place in the area to feature hamburgers with novel variations. A favorite is the El Ultimo (with Canadian bacon, mushrooms, *marchand de vin* sauce, lettuce, tomato and a "speck" of truffle on top). If you can't decide, there is a "U-Name-It-Burger." Piggy's

Delight, a selection from the soda fountain, contains five ice creams topped with hot fudge and six other sauces, plus whipped cream and Spanish peanuts. Daily specials are listed on blackboards. Fresh flowers on tables. Music from a 1940's jukebox. Try Julio's cheesecake, if available. Bring your own wine. Outstanding Sunday brunch. No reservations. Open seven days a week. Heck Jr. burger $1.70; entrées from $3.95 (L & D). AE, MC.

## SEAFOOD

***Pier W,*** 12700 Lake Avenue, Lakewood (228-2250). At least three fresh selections of fish and seafood each day, plus a fantastic view of Lake Erie and the city skyline. Some of the best service you'll find in town. In this nautical setting, the house specialty is bouillabaisse, which is served with hot French bread and salad. New England scrod—young cod—rolled lightly in fresh bread-crumbs and baked in drawn butter is delicate and flavorful. This is a Stouffer's restaurant, and, typically, portions are not too large but are satisfying. Warm gingerbread with lemon sauce is a refreshing and light ending to the meal. Car-parking service. Saturday, dinner only. Open seven days a week. Entrées from $2.95 (L), $4.95 (D). Outstanding Sunday brunch for $4.95. AE, CB, DC, MC, V.

***Charley's Crab,*** 25765 Chagrin Boulevard, Beachwood (831-8222). Fresh seafood daily with a raw oyster and clam bar, except on Sunday. The salad bar is well attended, reliably chilled and refilled as needed. In the evening there is soft piano music. Service is courteous and prompt. Reservations are a must. Open seven days a week. Entrées from $2.60 (L), $8 (D). AE, CB, DC, MC, V.

## VEGETARIAN

***Earth By April,*** 2151 Lee Road, Cleveland Heights (371-1438). The owners of this popular eatery are trying to get away from being known as just a vegetarian restaurant. They have introduced imaginative entrées with scallops, shrimp and sole. A salad bar and excellent dressings, including yogurt-cucumber. Fresh, warm bran muffins are the house bread. Vegetarian specialties include a delicious ratatouille served over brown rice with shredded cheese; vegetable tempura. Sunday brunch. Closed Monday. Entrées from $1.65 (L), $2.85 (D). AE, DC, MC, V.

# FOR INDIVIDUAL NEEDS

## IF YOU HAVE TIME FOR ONLY ONE MEAL

***Market Street Exchange,*** 2516 Market Street (579-0520). Located in "Ohio City" on the near west side. The restaurant is housed in two structures built in the 1830's. Inside, the rooms are decorated in turn-of-the-century antiques, including a magnificent solid mahogany backbar. This room is reputed to be the oldest continuously operated bar in Cleveland and, according to legend, was often frequented by Eliot Ness. The menu changes daily and features the imaginative concoctions of owner Jane Bowers. Vegetables are fresh, as is the fish; sauces are delicate. Try any of the iced soups, mushroom salad in mustard vinaigrette, crawfish, and bay scallops sautéed with bananas. The homemade ice cream is always a treat. By all means, wind up your meal with one of the flaming coffees. (A $5 dinner is served in the new Bistro bar—Wednesday through Saturday, 5 P.M. to midnight—Swiss raclette is featured.) Save enough time to visit the West Side Market at the end of the block. Reservations not always necessary, but suggested. Open seven days a week. Sunday brunch. Entrées from $2.95 (L), $7.95 (D). AE, MC, V.

## BEST HOTEL MEAL

***The French Connection,*** Stouffer's Inn on the Square, 24 Public Square (696-5600). (See description under BIG DEAL/WORTH IT.)

## RESTAURANT NEAR AIRPORT

***Brown Derby,*** 4998 Rocky River Drive (267-1744). (See description under FOR FAMILIES WITH CHILDREN.)

## BUSINESS BREAKFAST

***The Whole Grain,*** 55 Public Square in the Illuminating Building (861-0997). (See description under FAST, GOOD FOOD/BREAKFAST, LUNCH.)

## BUSINESS LUNCH

***The Theatrical Restaurant,*** 711 Vincent Avenue (241-6166). (See description under RESTAURANT WITH MUSIC.)

***Pat Joyce's Tavern,*** 602 St. Clair Street (771-6444), 1114 Chester Avenue (771-1010). Regulars call them "P.J.'s," and both these downtown Pat Joyce restaurants are crowded for lunch. A house specialty is Irish stew, and there are delicious hamburgers. P.J.'s is the most popular place in the city on St. Patrick's Day. Here, on most days, you'll find local TV and radio personalities and sports figures. Closed Sunday, except when there is a special event at the Convention Center across the street. Entrées from $1.75 (L), $3.95 (D). AE, DC, MC, V.

## FAST, GOOD FOOD/BREAKFAST, LUNCH

***The Whole Grain,*** 55 Public Square in the Illuminating Building (861-0997, or 861-0999 for take-out). Three hearty soups from a list of over 30 creations are offered each day to go along with either a salad or sandwich. Of the soups, which rotate regularly, the favorite is cheddar ale. Soup, salad and five-grain bread and butter, $2.95. Huge cookies and brownies for dessert, 40 cents each. Breakfast features assorted sweet rolls, cheese strata, English muffins, cereal and juice. Coffee is freshly ground. Breakfast from 7 A.M. to 9:45 A.M. Self-service lines move very quickly. Attractive butcher block, seed and pod décor. Courteous attendants. Open seven days a week. No credit cards.

## FAST, GOOD FOOD/DINNER

***Our Gang, Too,*** 20680 North Park Boulevard, University Heights (371-4700). This is the big brother of the original Our Gang (25100 Chagrin, 464-4848), which is housed in a former truck stop. Our Gang, Too is larger and is decorated with Art Deco and turn-of-the-century memorabilia. Within a block from John Carroll University. Good, fast service. A favorite hamburger is Dave's Burger, topped with Swiss cheese, sautéed onions, mushrooms and sour cream. Over a dozen other burgers are offered. Terrific appetizers, omelets, quiche and salads, plus great hot dogs. Frozen yogurt for dessert. Open seven days a week. Entrées from $2.25. MC, V.

## BEST WINE LIST

***Au Père Jacques,*** 34105 Chagrin Boulevard, Chagrin Falls (831-8558). (See description under FRENCH.)

## FOR DRINKS

***The Theatrical Restaurant,*** 711 Vincent Avenue (241-6166). (See description under RESTAURANT WITH MUSIC.)

## RESTAURANT WITH MUSIC

***The Theatrical Restaurant,*** 711 Vincent Avenue (241-6166). Along with superb food, touring jazz stars and good music make this restaurant desirable. You can always count on super steaks and outstanding lobster tails. The Theatrical is one of the best places to eat in downtown, although a bit noisy at times. A good meeting place for business lunch and dinner. Reservations suggested for lunch and dinner. Open until 2 A.M. Closed Sunday. Entrées from $2.95 (L), $7.50 (D). AE, DC, MC, V.

## ROMANTIC

***That Place on Bellflower,*** 11401 Bellflower Road (231-4469). One of the few quality restaurants near the culture-arts center of the city, the University Circle area. The restaurant is housed in an old coach house and has been very tastefully decorated by owner Isabelle Chesler with original contemporary artwork. In the summer, a patio garden area is open. The menu varies daily, with some unusual interpretations of classic dishes. Luncheon is well rounded with specialties such as lamb stew with puff-pastry topping and rare roast-beef sandwich with aioli sauce, hearty and robust with garlic. Full bar and good wine list. Chaîne des Rotisseurs. Reservations suggested. Closed Sunday. Entrées from $3.25 (L), $7.95 (D). AE, V.

## LATE-NIGHT SERVICE

***Hecks Café,*** 2927 Bridge Avenue (861-5464). (See description under HAMBURGER.)

## SUNDAY BRUNCH

***Port Brittany,*** Sheraton Hopkins Airport Hotel (267-1500). Choose the buffet if you are really hungry. Also, made-to-order omelets with choice of filling. Lovely pastry table with tempting éclairs and petits fours. Bottomless glass of champagne from 1 to 3 P.M. Complete brunch (11 A.M. to 3 P.M.) $6.95. AE, CB, DC.

***Market Street Exchange,*** 2516 Market Street (579-0520). (See description under IF YOU HAVE TIME FOR ONLY ONE MEAL.) Brunch is a New Orleans buffet including Creole gumbo, jambalaya, grits and Southern biscuits with Smithfield ham. Live Dixieland music adds to the fun. Brunch $6.95 adults, $3.95 children. AE, MC, V.

---

## SUNDAY-EVENING MEAL

***Brown Derby*** (See description and addresses under FOR FAMILIES WITH CHILDREN.)

---

## FOR FAMILIES WITH CHILDREN

***Brown Derby,*** Route 8 and Turnpike (656-3336), 2466 Fairmount (229-2477), 5142 Wilson Mills Road (442-8600), 5664 Brecksville Road (524-5300), Route 306 and I-90 (951-0574), 5445 Beavercrest Drive (835-2934), 4910 Northfield Road (475-1200), 19999 Center Ridge Road (333-4108), 4998 Rocky River Drive (267-1744), 29050 Lake Shore Boulevard (943-5686), plus more locations in Ohio, Pennsylvania, Michigan and Indiana. The first Brown Derby was opened in 1941 by Perris Girves in Akron across from the Goodyear Tire & Rubber Company. The restaurant chain has always specialized in steaks, but features some seafood now. USDA inspector at the commissary grades the prime or choice beef. No tenderizing here. There's a well-stocked salad bar. Special children's menu all day, every day, for $1.48. Strawberry-banana pie is made fresh at each location daily. Super-duper parfaits are 85 cents. Luv Pub or lounge cocktails (from 4:30 to 6:30 P.M.) are only 79 cents with free, hot popcorn. Good wine list at excellent prices. Open seven days a week. Entrées from $1.95 (L), $3.50 (D). AE, CB, DC, MC, V.

---

## WORTH THE TRIP

***Hunters Hollow Taverne,*** at Stepnorth, 100 N. Main Street, Chagrin Falls (247-5222). In a complex of appealing shops in a charming historical village about 45 minutes from downtown. There are more veal entrées on the menu than beef. The simplest is a lightly breaded cutlet, sautéed beautifully in butter and with no other detectable seasonings. Beef *funghetto* is popular and consists of sliced beef tenderloin in a fresh marinara sauce with mushrooms and wine. At noontime, crêpes are featured, along with eight sandwiches, salads and several entrées, including one for dieters. Good, if limited, wine list. Reservations necessary for dinner, suggested for lunch. Closed Sunday. Entrées from $2.45 (L), $8.75 (D). AE, MC, V.

## COUNTRY INN

***The Taverne of Richfield,*** Front Street, Rte. 176 at Rte. 303, Richfield (659-3155). The two-story building was erected in 1886. At one point, the Taverne was known as the most active social club of the region, offering grandiose supper feasts—lavish, gala affairs. The grand, barrel-vaulted ballroom is still used for social occasions. The historical Taverne is filled with antiques. Salad-and-sandwich-type menu for lunch with a few exceptions such as quiche and omelets. A bit more imagination at dinner. Entertainment. Sunday brunch. (In the basement is a Wine & Cheese cellar that is open until midnight Monday to Saturday. Raw-oyster bar and shrimp featured.) Entrées from $2.40 (L), $8.10 (D). AE, MC, V.

***The Inn at Fowler's Mill,*** 10700 Mayfield Road, Chardon (729-1313). The décor of this old tavern is typical of the 18th century. In the winter, a crackling fire warms the main dining room. And you may be able to watch skiers on the slopes at nearby Alpine Valley Ski Resort. The menu features daily specials, including fresh fish. House specialty is old-fashioned turtle soup with sherry. Omelets, when available, are light and nicely done. Lovely for luncheon in the fall or spring. Allow time to browse in the shops adjacent to the Inn. They are interesting and unusual. Wine list and full bar. Open seven days a week. Entrées from $2.95 (L), $8.95 (D). AE, MC, V.

# MARKETS

## GIFT FOODS

***Bavarian Pastry Shop,*** 17004 Madison Avenue, Lakewood (521-1344), 100 N. Main, Hudson (656-2696), and Stepnorth in Chagrin Falls (247-4086). Superior pastries of all kinds. Closed Sunday. No credit cards.

***Alesci's Imported Foods,*** 4333 Mayfield Road (382-5100), 6863 W. 130th Street (845-2700), 15800 Broadway (475-5252), 26367 Brookpark (734-7170), 29730 Lake Shore Boulevard (585-1112). Impressive selection of imported Italian foods, including cheese, olive oil, salami and hams. Imported cookware and stoneware serving pieces. Open seven days a week. MC, V.

## GIFT WINES

***Shaker Square Beverages,*** 13226 Shaker Square (561-5100). In business for more than 40 years and a favorite outlet for wines, particularly French and German. Good selection of kitchen equipment and gadgets, cookbooks. Closed Sunday. MC, V.

# Dallas

Until eight years ago the Dallas restaurant and entertainment industry was, like the rest of Texas, victimized by antiquated state liquor-control laws. According to these laws, a bar or restaurant could not serve a cocktail; they could serve only the setup and you had to bring your own booze. It was the age of the "brown bag."

Enlightenment, spurred by the need for convention trade in the state's major cities, came to the state legislature in 1971. The old liquor laws were abolished and in 1972 a new age began for the nightlife industry. However, the present law leaves a curious situation existing throughout Texas. The people of individual voting precincts are allowed self-determination by popular vote as to whether their district will be "wet" (commercial availability of wine and spirits) or "dry."

While Dallas has only one "wet" area, bounded roughly by the Trinity River on the south and west, Walnut Hill Lane on the north, and White Rock Creek on the east, within these boundaries lie some 95 percent of the city's major restaurants and entertainment spots. (The suburban town of Addison has also gone "wet" in recent years and represents a northern oasis of food and drink for the upper rim of the city.)

In restaurants in the outlying "dry" areas, patrons may drink only under the technicality of a private-club membership. Thus, these restaurants often offer a "temporary" club membership (usually for a fee of $5) that allows patrons to drink alcoholic beverages on the premises at least for that evening and often for a one-year period thereafter. Visitors will encounter this practice, for example, in the grouping of new hotels and restaurants centered on the north Dallas intersection of LBJ Freeway (Interstate 635) and Preston Road. In listings that follow, this procedure is indicated as "bar by membership." Even within the "wet" district, some restaurants are licensed to sell beer and wine only.

Mainly because of the years of liquor-law restraint, Dallas' restaurant heritage does not run deep. As recently as ten years ago, the scene was dominated by private country club activity and a few big names—the Town & Country, the Cipango Club, the Old Warsaw and others—most of which have since disappeared. But the new liquor laws and the population growth of Dallas and the surrounding region helped the restaurant business to explode. New restaurants are popping up almost daily. It is an entrepreneur's paradise—and a diner's jungle.

The bulk of the boom has been in two areas. The first and foremost is Greenville Avenue, an east Dallas north-south thoroughfare. From Ross Avenue at the south to Walnut Hill Lane at the north, the Greenville strip sports a continuum of restaurants and clubs ranging from seedy dives to chic pleasure palaces. The second major entertainment conglomeration is the Bachman Lake area in northwest Dallas. Its artery is W. Northwest Highway (Loop 12) between Marsh Lane and Denton Drive.

There are three smaller areas of activity, particularly in terms of good restaurants. Lovers Lane (near the Inwood Road intersection) is an older strip, featuring a few fine, older French standbys (Mr. Peppe, Marcel's and Ewald's) and other eating spots. A more recent area of growth in an older and more intriguing neighborhood is along McKinney Avenue from Maple Avenue north to Monticello Street, much of it the refurbishing of old houses and buildings. Perhaps Dallas' most diverse neighborhood is Oak Lawn, an area surrounding the intersections of Oak Lawn Avenue with Lemmon and Cedar Springs avenues. The nightlife is less ambitious, but more eclectic and, perhaps, eccentric.

Downtown Dallas, as any seasoned conventioneer can tell you, thrives by day, but dies by night. Concentrated efforts are under way to revitalize the city's core, but for now, options are limited mainly to hotel facilities and to several private professional clubs.

Dallas cuisine, if there is such a thing, represents an odd amalgam of cultures. It shows the influence of the Deep South—you'll find lots of fried chicken and often the breakfast option of grits and biscuits with cream gravy. It shows the influence of the "Chuck-wagon West"—there's barbecue galore—though it's not as easy to find a great steak as you might expect. Mexico is a strong influence. San Antonio is considered the home of "Tex-Mex," the now-standard Americanized version of Mexican cuisine, but Dallas may have more Mexican restaurants per capita than any city on earth—including Mexico City itself. For an ethnic treat (and there is precious little of the pure ethnic in this city), you might visit the predominantly Mexican-American neighborhood surrounding the intersection of Maple and Wycliffe avenues, and try one of the little Mexican cafés and their family-style home cooking (Herrera's, Escondido, Ojeda's are among them). And finally, the influx of people from the more cosmopolitan Northeast has spawned a rapidly expanding demand for fine European cuisine.

The two most satisfying French restaurants in the city, **Calluaud** and **Patry's,** are not luxury places. If you're looking for the trappings of elegance to accompany a French meal, you might consider the Old Warsaw or La Polonaise. Both are splendidly appointed with occasionally inspired cooking from the kitchen.

Dallas has a surprisingly large number of Chinese restaurants, though no concentrated Chinatown. It has a surprising dearth of good Greek or German food. Many ethnic cuisines (Lebanese, Japanese, Indian, Indonesian, Serbian) are barely represented, if at all. However, a new Japanese restaurant, Asuka (7236 Greenville Avenue, 363-3537), shows great promise and is undoubtedly the most attractive Oriental restaurant in town. And fine seafood is not common in landlocked Dallas, though a few places fly in fresh fish daily from the Gulf Coast. Anyone who cares asks about "fresh or frozen" before ordering seafood here.

If you choose to do your own food marketing, try the Farmer's Market in the southeast section of downtown (near Pearl and Cadiz streets), where fresh fruits and vegetables are trucked in daily from the surrounding countryside and sold in an open-air marketplace. **Kuby's,** in Snider Plaza off Hillcrest Road near Southern Methodist University, is a fine German-oriented delicatessen. Simon David (7117 Inwood Road) is an excellent specialty grocery. Antone's (4234 Harry Hines) and Al's (8209 Park Lane) offer a variety of imported goods. For cheese, visit the Cheese Shop in Preston Center, **Marty's** on Oak Lawn, or Neiman-Marcus in NorthPark. Marty's is also one of Dallas' better wine shops; the best volume wine dealers are Sigel's and Centennial, both chain operations with many locations.

# Restaurants and Food Sources

(Area code: 214)

## BIG DEAL

### WORTH IT

***Calluaud,*** 2619 McKinney (823-5380). The Calluauds, the young French couple who mastermind this fine restaurant, have had to move their establishment three times, always seeking a little more space to accommodate the crowds. This latest locale is certainly the most elegant; and fortunately, the kitchen is as excellent as ever—French specialties with a personalized touch. Favorite entrées include the quails in garlic and cognac, the veal Normande and the filet mignon *en croûte*. The red snapper pâté is a must, the omelets at lunch are the best in Dallas, and the little fruit tarts are a local legend. And what's best, the prices are reasonable—dollar for dollar, the best food in the city. Closed Sunday. Entrées from $3.50 (L), $7.50 (D). AE, CB, DC, MC, V.

### NOT WORTH IT

***Antares,*** Reunion Tower, Hyatt Regency Hotel (741-3663). This revolving restaurant atop Reunion Tower (inside the huge sphere that now dominates the city's skyline) has an almost irresistible attraction for visitors—and true, the trip up is fun and the view dramatic. But the food, an uninspired selection of American and Continental stand-bys, is average at best. And at prices that match the soaring locale. Much better to eat downstairs in the hotel at **Fausto**'s, which is quite good, and take an after-dinner ride to the **Top of the Dome** (the tower's bar) for drinks only. Entrées from $4.50 (L), $9 (D). AE, CB, DC, MC, V.

# INTERNATIONAL

## AMERICAN

***Arthur's,*** 1000 Campbell Centre (361-8833). From the sexy bar to the solid menu to the sophisticated service, this is a classy place. For starters, have the stuffed avocado or the elegant spinach salad. There are several splendid variations on mignons of beef, beautiful lamb chops and excellent calf's liver with bacon and chives. Many steak and seafood selections. A fascinating list of American wines only. Very masculine despite its elegance. The bar, with live entertainment, is warm and romantic. Sunday, dinner only. Entrées from $2.75 (L), $9.50 (D). AE, CB, DC, MC, V.

## CHINESE

***Hunan,*** 5214 Greenville Avenue (369-4578). The cuisine of Hunan province, laced with red peppers, will make your eyes water. Order it as hot as you like. The *pu-pu* tray of assorted appetizers is a good way to start. Choose at least part of the meal from the menu page marked "Chef's Specialties." Hunan lamb, abalone with chicken, and the spicy, crispy whole fish are particularly interesting. Small and comfortable, but with no real atmosphere. The Hunan has spawned several other restaurants (Chinese Pavilion, Central China and Szechuan) with similar menus and generally dependable performance. Open seven days a week. Entrées from $2.25 (L), $3.75 (D). AE, MC, V.

## FRENCH

***Patry's,*** 2504 McKinney Avenue (748-3754). A family operation from stove to table to cash register. Pride is evident, as is the expertise. The food, in provincial style, has a simple elegance. Hors d'oeuvre are exquisite: try stuffed leeks in cream sauce or rillettes of pork. Among the entrées, *escalope* of veal and the rich *coq au vin* are excellent. The place itself is quite small and displays a simple elegance; a loyal clientele returns again and again for the food and friendliness. Excellent wine selection. Dinner only. Closed Monday. Entrées from $7. AE, DC, MC, V.

# ITALIAN

***Il Sorrento,*** 8616 Turtle Creek Boulevard (352-8759). Some would argue this isn't the best Italian food in Dallas, but no one would deny this is the most fun place to eat it—a Disneyesque rendering of Venice, complete with strolling musicians and wandering bread vendors; tableside preparations, such as *tagliatelle,* are done with appropriate flair. A vast menu highlighted by the veal dishes (Marsala and piccata in particular) and the beef dishes (try the tournedos Rossini or the medallions of beef *frascati*). Always hopping. Even with reservations, you may have to wait. Dinner only. Open seven days a week. Entrées from $4. AE, CB, DC, MC, V.

***Lombardi's,*** 2815 McKinney Avenue (823-6040). Some would argue *this* isn't the best Italian food in Dallas, but no one would deny that it has never been served anywhere with more aplomb. The staff here has such style and grace, they could make a cold pizza seem like a royal banquet. In the warm confines of this refurbished old house, enjoy the *saltimbocca,* the unusual pork *parmigiana,* and the rich green noodle *fettuccine.* When they're available, don't pass up the mussels and langostinos or a delicious *zuppa de pesce.* Closed Sunday. Entrées from $4 (L), $5.50 (D). AE, DC, MC, V.

***Paisan's,*** 9405 Overlake (352-2765). The best, though not the most attractive Italian restaurant in Dallas. Set in an oddly remodeled Mexican restaurant, but who cares? Not with the *zuppa pavese,* the veal *Siciliano,* the beef rolls *alla Peppino,* spaghetti *alla Ciociara,* and sausage *alla Turiddu* to occupy your thoughts. For dessert, have the cheesecake with white raisins and pine nuts. Dinner only. Open seven days a week. Entrées from $4.95. AE, DC, MC, V.

# JAPANESE

***Fuji-Ya,*** 13050 Coit Road (690-8396). In the limited arena of Japanese food in Dallas, this is the best, though aficionados might be disappointed. There are some fine dishes—*sashimi, yakisoba,* and *tonkatsu* (a wonderful pork dish); for less adventurous tastes, the shrimp tempura and the *sukiyaki* are both excellent. Lunch is very limited, so visit at night. Unfortunately, an out-of-the-way location in far north Dallas. Closed Monday. Entrées from $1.95 (L), $2.95 (D). MC, V.

# MEXICAN

***Guadalajara,*** 3308 Ross Avenue (823-9340). If you like your Mexican food funky, this is the place. An old, high-ceilinged café complete with piñatas, Mexican comic books and impromptu singalongs. The clientele is mostly Mexican-American, including local cooks and chefs who stop in here after work, so you know you're eating the real thing. All the Tex-Mex standards plus some other goodies, such as *huevos con nopalitos* (eggs with cactus) and *carne asada* the way it's supposed to be. This isn't the nicest neighborhood in town, but it is perfectly safe. The place is open until 3:30 A.M.—and there are those who say if you've never experienced a Guadalajara *sopapilla* drenched in honey at 2 in the morning, you haven't lived. Closed Monday. Entrées from $1.95 (L & D). No credit cards.

***Chiquita,*** 3810 Congress (521-0721). If you like your Mexican food served with a touch of class, *this* is the place. A cheerful restaurant presided over by Mario, one of Dallas' venerable Mexican hosts. Old favorites: bean soup, tortilla soup, *chiles rellenos,* tacos *al carbon,* "Aztecs in a Blanket," and the *filete ala Chiquita.* Closed Sunday. Entrées from $2.35 (L), $3.65 (D). AE, MC, V.

***Javier's,*** 4912 Cole (521-4211). If you like Mexican food wrapped in elegance, *this* is the place. There's little in the way of Tex-Mex here; instead you'll find first-rate dishes such as red snapper Javier, shrimp broiled in garlic, fine chicken *mole*, and excellent Mexican beef dishes. Save room for the crêpes topped with *cajeta* (caramel) and flamed with Amaretto and brandy. Dinner only. Open seven days a week. Entrées from $4.95. AE, MC, V.

# SCANDINAVIAN

***Three Vikings,*** 2831 Greenville Avenue (827-6770). Run by a Swedish family, this charming little restaurant offers good Scandinavian cuisine. Top choices are two of the finest seafood dishes in town—the filet of sole with crab meat and the salmon steak in dill sauce, plus the house favorite, Swedish steak. Before you eat, enjoy a round of Aquavit (the traditional Scandinavian schnapps) and offer up a good "*Skoal.*" Dinner only. Closed Sunday. Entrées from $5.95. AE, MC, V.

# SPECIALTY COOKING

## BARBECUE

***Sonny Bryan's,*** 2202 Inwood Road (357-7120). To say one man's barbecue is better than another's is to ask for trouble (and there's good barbecue around every corner in Dallas). But Sonny puts out a big, fat, juicy sliced-beef sandwich that can't be beat. He's got ribs, ham, sausage and so much business he closes up when the stuff's all gone—usually about 7 P.M. A funky little smokehouse with no tables, just individual school-desk tops. Beer, but no hard liquor. Open seven days a week. Sandwiches from $1.25 (L & D). No credit cards.

## CHILI

***Frank X. Tolbert's Texas Chili Parlor,*** 802 Main Street (742-6336), 3802 Cedar Springs (522-4340). Frank Tolbert is the grand master of Texas chili, originator of the world-famous Terlingua Chili Cookoff. Chili-making is a mercurial art and the subject of interminable argument, but Frank's place puts out as consistently fine a blend as is to be had. And if you don't like chili, try Frank's Sonofabitch Stew. Tolbert has a second location (Cedar Springs), but the original is better. Chili from $2.25. Main Street: Lunch only. Closed Saturday and Sunday. No credit cards. Cedar Springs: Open seven days a week until 2 A.M. AE, CB, DC, MC, V.

## COUNTRY COOKING

***Gennie's Bishop Grille,*** 308 N. Bishop Avenue (946-1752). Deep in the heart of Oak Cliff, Gennie and her staff put out a Southern home-style spread that will warm your heart. Chicken-fried fried steak, chunky mashed potatoes, okra, zucchini, turnip greens, peanut-butter pie and banana pudding, just to name a few. The homemade rolls are out of this world. No bar. Lunch only. Closed weekends. Plate lunch from $1.95. No credit cards.

# CREOLE

***Broussard's,*** 707 N. Belt Line Road, 1 mile south of Route 183, Irving, (255-8024). Frenchy Broussard serves the best crawfish this side of Baton Rouge. Not to mention the wonderful sweet catfish, plump oysters (served raw or fried) and fantastic *piquante* and gumbo. The only treat that falls short is the jambalaya. A noisy, no-nonsense café. Bring your own liquor. Closed Sunday. Entrées from $3 (L & D). No credit cards.

# DELI

***Kuby's,*** 6001 Snider Plaza (363-2231). The accent is more German than kosher here. Order thick sandwiches (the pastrami is terrific) or the excellent homemade sausages (served with hot potato salad or sauerkraut—the choice is yours and it's difficult to make). Excellent pastries go fast, so come early. No bar. Lunch only. Closed Sunday. Sandwiches from $1.50. MC, V.

# HAMBURGER

***Stoneleigh P.,*** 2926 Maple (741-0824). You'll never get a consensus on the best hamburger in town, but try the provolone cheeseburger on pumpernickel bun here. A favorite Oak Lawn hangout, the Stoneleigh P. was originally a pharmacy and still has some pharmaceutical trimmings, plus a great jukebox selection and a magazine rack for browsing. Open seven days a week. Sandwiches from $1.75 (L & D). No credit cards.

# PIZZA

***Campisi's,*** 5620 E. Mockingbird (827-0355). Campisi's pizza (thin crust but with a flavor and style all its own) has fans lined up outside the door every night. Order a combination (the works) and dive in. It's a busy, noisy, steamy place with Italian family flair. Full Italian menu, too (try the crab claws), but the pizza is the prize. Open seven days a week. Entrées from $2.95. No credit cards.

## SEAFOOD

***S & D Oyster Company,*** 2701 McKinney Avenue (823-6350). A refurbished old brick warehouse (originally built as a livery stable), now handsomely appointed in New Orleans style. Oysters, as might be suspected, are the specialty—fresh, and delicious whether on the half shell or fried. Boiled and fried shrimp are also on the menu, along with a varying assortment of broiled fish depending on what is available fresh—usually it's flounder, snapper and trout. Or try the gumbo. Beer and wine only. Closed Sunday. Entrées from $3.65 (L & D). MC.

---

## STEAK

***Kirby's,*** 3715 Greenville Avenue (823-7296). One of the city's first true steakhouses and still the best. There's real nostalgia about the place, along with old-style country waitresses, sometimes gruff, sometimes motherly. Have the "extra cut" sirloin strip, baked potato with all the trimmings, and the creamy garlic salad dressing. Dinner only. Closed Monday. Entrées from $4. AE, CB, DC, MC, V.

---

# FOR INDIVIDUAL NEEDS

---

## IF YOU HAVE TIME FOR ONLY ONE MEAL

***Jean Claude,*** 2520 Cedar Springs (653-1823). Owner-chef Jean Claude Prevot prepares his splendid French cuisine in an open kitchen in the center of the small dining room, in an aura of polish and class. The menu changes daily, always featuring a choice of three hors d'oeuvre, three entrées, and three desserts. Whatever he happens to be cooking is marvelous, but a few standards of his repertoire are roast duck in ginger sauce, stuffed lamb, and pompano in a mousseline sauce. Price fixed at $20—and worth every penny. The one drawback is that the place is so small and in such demand, you may have to make reservations days in advance. Dinner only. Closed Sunday and Monday. AE, MC, V.

---

# BEST HOTEL MEAL

***The Pyramid Room,*** Fairmont Hotel, Ross & Akard (748-5454). The most sophisticated restaurant in Dallas, and the most complete dining experience the city has to offer. An aura of opulence and simple elegance pervades the dining room, an appropriate setting for a stunning meal. You really can't go wrong, but two dishes stand out: the *filet de sole en croûte* and the lamb loin baked in a pastry shell with tarragon sauce. For dessert, try the Grand Marnier soufflé. Impeccable service. Less glamorous, and less expensive, at lunch. Chaîne des Rotisseurs. Saturday and Sunday, dinner only. Open seven days a week. Entrées from $4.50 (L), $10 (D). AE, CB, DC, MC, V.

# BUSINESS BREAKFAST

***Brennan's,*** One Main Place (742-1911). This Brennan's is not a shining reflection of its illustrious namesake in New Orleans: lunch or dinner here is adequate at best. But the stylish dining room and a breakfast menu brimming with the famous Brennan's variations on poached eggs (Sardou is usually the best bet), turtle soup and several dessert flambés still make Brennan's the must for a morning downtown. Open from 9 A.M., seven days a week. Entrées from $3.25 (B). AE, CB, DC, MC, V.

# BUSINESS LUNCH

***Chateaubriand,*** 2515 McKinney (741-1223). A venerable Dallas institution, Chateaubriand doesn't always perform with the aplomb it once did. But at lunch it is still a very popular businessman's gathering spot. It offers a wide-ranging Continental selection, including several well-priced daily specials. Highly efficient service. Avoid the garish French provincial front dining room and dine in the more tasteful wood-paneled room behind. Closed Sunday. Entrées from $5.50 (L). AE, CB, DC, MC, V.

# FAST, GOOD FOOD/BREAKFAST

***Red Moon Café,*** 4537 Cole Avenue (526-5391). A charming little spot with a French-café feeling and a friendly staff. Omelets, eggs Benedict, grits, biscuits and fantastic chicory coffee. Open 7 A.M. Closed Sunday. Entrées from $1 (B & L), $1.75 (D). No credit cards.

## FAST, GOOD FOOD/LUNCH

***Highland Park Cafeteria,*** 4611 Cole Avenue (526-3801). A Dallas fixture, with some very exotic cafeteria food. A dazzling selection of salads at one end of the line and desserts at the other. In between are a host of vegetables (be sure to have the baked eggplant) and entrées, several prepared with a Southern touch (good chicken and dumplings). Usually a long line, but it moves fast. Closed Sunday. Entrées from $1.25 (L). No credit cards.

## FAST, GOOD FOOD/DINNER

***T.G.I. Friday's,*** Old Town, 5500 Greenville Avenue (363-5353). A lively spot with an equally lively menu—a little something for everybody, from soups to steaks, from *nachos* to rhubarb pie. Outstanding hamburgers and a huge chef's salad. Fairly priced and almost always well prepared. Open seven days a week. Hamburgers from $2.45. AE, MC, V.

## BEST WINE LIST

***La Cave,*** 2926 Henderson (826-2190). You don't just read the wine list here, you browse through the wine cellar itself. Choose from an excellent array of wines, and for a mere $1.50 corkage fee, sit down at your table and enjoy it. If you have any questions, François will be happy to guide you through the racks. An especially attractive selection of medium-priced wines ($5 to $10), but you also can purchase a 1934 LaTour, if you're so inclined. Light and stylish French foods and fine cheeses are served to accompany the wine. Wines may also be purchased retail. Closed Sunday. Entrées from $3. AE, MC, V.

## FOR DRINKS

***Andrew's,*** 3301 McKinney (526-9501). This warm and convivial bar rambles through a large old building that has been handsomely restored, predominately in bare, rough brick. A mixed and mixable clientele have made this place very popular, particularly during happy-hour. And if the weather's nice, Andrew's has a delightful outdoor courtyard for open-air sipping. They have an exotic group of strange specialty drinks in addition to the standards. Sandwiches, cheeses and snacks available. Open seven days a week, until 2 A.M. AE, MC, V.

***Arthur's,*** 1000 Campbell Centre (361-8833). (See description under AMERICAN.)

***Pyramid Lounge,*** Fairmont Hotel, Ross and Akard (748-5454). (See description under BEST HOTEL MEAL.) A dark and elegant piano bar adjacent to the Pyramid Room restaurant.

## RESTAURANT WITH MUSIC

***Strictly Ta-bu,*** 4111 Lomo Alto Drive (526-9325). A relic from the 1940's, still in its original pink-flamingo trappings, though a little worn on the edges. Good jazz every night beginning at 9 P.M., often talent from the renowned North Texas State music school. Nice homemade soups, great pizza, hamburgers, sandwiches, steaks. Open seven days a week. Sandwiches from $1.50. MC, V.

## ROMANTIC

***The Grape,*** 2808 Greenville Avenue (823-0133). A cozy and often crowded little spot tucked into a weathered and undistinguished old storefront building. Not glittery romantic, but intimate, dark and engaging. A vast selection of imported cheeses from which to create your own cheeseboard combinations. Also omelets, quiche and light entrées. The fresh-mushroom soup is a treat. Weekends, dinner only. Monday, lunch only. Open seven days a week. Entrées from $2.50 (L & D). No credit cards.

## LATE-NIGHT SERVICE

***Brasserie,*** Fairmont Hotel, Ross & Akard Streets (748-5454). A "coffee shop" extraordinaire, open 24 hours a day with a particularly impressive late-night (early-morning) menu. Lox and eggs and other hearty offerings, including eggs Benedict sprinkled with truffles. Nice pastries, but check to be sure they haven't been sitting out too long. Closed Sunday. Entrées from $2.25 (L & D). AE, MC, V.

***The Bronx,*** 3835 Cedar Springs (521-5821). A rustic-looking little bar that hides an unexpectedly good kitchen. Soups, salads, sandwiches. Order lox and bagels or an omelet with a side order of delicious Italian sausage. Beer (lots of imports) and wine only. Food is served until 12:30 A.M. on week nights, until 1:30 p.m. on weekends. Open seven days a week. Sandwiches from $2. MC.

## SUNDAY BRUNCH

***Bagatelle,*** One Energy Square, 4925 Greenville Avenue at University Drive (692-8224). The special Sunday attraction here is an omelet prepared to the diner's specification—choose whatever ingredients you like. Also crêpes, quiche, fruit salads. A very attractive and comfortable French restaurant. Sunday brunch 10:30 A.M. to 2 P.M. Brunch price $4.75. AE, MC, V.

## SUNDAY-EVENING MEAL

***Houlihan's,*** 4 NorthPark East, at Park Lane and Central Expressway (361-9426). The best thing about Houlihan's is that the menu offers a little bit of everything—and most of it is pretty good. You can eat light or heavy—from a cheese omelet to duck *à l'orange*—never extraordinary, but never disappointing either. No reservations, but a wait in the bar will provide you with excellent drinks. Open until 11 P.M. Sunday nights. Entrées from $2.50. AE, DC, MC, V.

## FOR FAMILIES WITH CHILDREN

***Celebration,*** 4503 W. Lovers Lane (351-5681). Not at all a "kiddies' " restaurant, but one that all can enjoy. They specialize in good ol' home cooking: pot roast, meat loaf, baked trout, chicken, spaghetti. All the trimmings are served family-style in big bowls, including three fresh vegetables, salad and biscuits. Plus pies and cobblers for dessert. All you can eat, so bring an appetite. Beer and wine only. No reservations. Dinner only. Open seven days a week. Entrées from $4.25, children from $1.75. MC, V.

## FORT WORTH

Fort Worth, Dallas' nearby neighbor to the west, is another culinary culture altogether. There is little need to venture to Fort Worth for food if what you're seeking is of the Continental or chic variety. But for a few traditional Texas treats, the 30-mile drive is worth making. Here are a few high spots.

***Angelo's,*** 2533 White Settlement Road (817/332-0357). Some say this is Texas' premier barbecue joint, a rambling, rickety building with sawdust on the floor and "cowboys" at the tables. Angelo's serves great spareribs, incredibly tender beef and huge glasses of cold beer. Closed Sunday. Entrées from $1.50 (L & D). No credit cards.

***Cattlemen's,*** 2458 N. Main (817/624-3945). The most famous name in Texas steakhouses, and this is the original, right in the heart of cowtown's legendary stockyards. Go with the ribeye or the Kansas City strip, and if you're adventuresome, try the calf fries, which are considered a frontier delicacy. Saturday, dinner only. Closed Sunday. Entrées from $2.50 (L), $3.50 (D). AE, CB, DC, MC, V.

***Kincaid's,*** 4901 Camp Bowie (817/732-2881). Kincaid's is a neighborhood grocery store, but it is also acclaimed as the home of Texas' greatest hamburger, served from behind the meat counter. Huge, fresh and mouthwatering, but be prepared to fight the crowds and eat standing up. Open from 10 A.M. to 6:15 P.M. Closed Sunday. Hamburgers $1.65. No credit cards.

***Massey's,*** 1805 Eighth Avenue (817/924-8242). If Texas had a state dish, it would surely be chicken-fried steak. Any of a hundred places claim to have the world's finest, and Massey's is a legitimate contender. Sample it in the folksy confines of a traditional Texas vinyl-boothed café. And don't forget to dip your biscuits in the cream gravy. Open seven days a week, from 6:30 A.M. Entrées from $1.75 (L & D). MC, V.

# MARKETS

## GIFT FOODS

***Goodies from Goodman,*** 12102 Inwood Road (major location) (387-4804); 8302 Preston Center E., at NW Highway (692-0773). Imported and gourmet foods and accompaniments. Cheeses, coffees, candies, etc. Closed Sunday. AE, MC, V.

***Epicure Shop,*** Neiman-Marcus, downtown (Main Street at Ervay Street) (741-6911); Neiman-Marcus, 400 NorthPark Center (N. Central Expressway at NW Highway) (363-8311). Imported and gourmet foods and accompaniments. Cheeses, coffees, candies, etc. Closed Sunday. No credit cards.

## GIFT WINES

***Marty's Wines & Liquors,*** 3316 Oak Lawn (526-7796). An excellent selection of wines, imported and domestic. Some cheeses, and gourmet "treats" also. Closed Sunday.

# Denver

Alferd Packer is Colorado's most famous diner. Packer and five companions set out on a Rocky Mountain gold-hunting expedition in the winter of 1874, the worst in the state's history, but only Alferd came back. Packer claimed luck had enabled him to survive two months in the deep snows and frigid weather without supplies. Others noted that his wallet and belly were fatter than they ought to have been after such an experience.

He was arrested and tried for murder and cannibalism. Before sentencing him to life imprisonment, the judge in Packer's trial is alleged to have scolded him: "They was siven Dimmycrats in Hinsdale County, but you, yah voracious man-eatin' son of a bitch, yah eat five of thim!"

It wasn't the worst anyone had eaten in the state.

The trip westward from Missouri and points east was far from easy. An early-day guide, Captain Randolph B. Marcy, advised: "It is a good rule to carry nothing more than is absolutely necessary for use. They should be used with economy, reserving a good portion for the Western half of the journey." Provisions for such a trip included a concoction known as pemmican, which consisted of buffalo meat cut into thin flakes and dried, then pounded between two stones to a powder. It was placed in a bag of animal hide (hair on the outside), melted grease was poured into it and the bag sewn up. Pemmican could be eaten raw, or mixed with flour and boiled. Marcy reported, "It is a very wholesome and exceedingly nutritious . . . and will keep fresh for a long time."

Other staples for the two-month trip across the prairie included bacon, pork, flour, butter, sugar, dried vegetables, wild onions, wild grapes and greens.

The settlers learned quickly from the inhabitants already living in the region. One-half bushel of a substance called Cold Flour was reputedly able to sustain a man thirty days. Cold Flour, used extensively by the area's Indians and Hispanos, was parched corn pounded to coarse meal. The addition of a little sugar and cinnamon made it "quite palatable."

When times got very tough, the prairie travelers resorted to eating the beasts of burden. ("We tried the meat of horse, colt and mules, all of which were in a starved condition, and of course not very tender, juicy or nutritious.") If there was no salt, the pioneers simply cooked the mule steaks and sprinkled the meat with gunpowder to produce a spicy taste.

Even after they arrived in Colorado, the earliest settlers continued to devour their means of transportation. A hardened prospector said, "The pioneer beefsteaks in Colorado were, in most cases, cut from bulls which had hauled the pioneers across from the plains. Firm in fibre as they were, they were generally made firmer still by being fried in lard. The meat was brought to the table in a dish covered with the drippings in which it had been hardened."

The prospector added, "Bad bread and bull beef did it. The powers of the human system were taxed to the uttermost to assimilate these articles. The assimilation of the raw material into bone, blood, nerve, muscles, sinew and brain were necessarily imperfect. Bad whiskey was then called upon for relief. This completed the ruin. Of course men would murder each other with such warring elements inside of them."

The populace of Denver didn't need much encouragement to put warring elements inside of them when "Uncle Dick" Wootten arrived in December of 1858 and set up a tent saloon from which he dispensed ten barrels of "Taos Lightning" he had brought up from New Mexico.

The early history of Denver dining is tied tightly to its saloons. Establishments like The Apollo, The Eldorado, The Mountain Boy's Saloon poured large amounts of whiskey. But none could touch the food at The Criterion, whose dining room was "supplied with all the delicacies of the country," including oysters, turkey, pineapple and champagne.

By the 1880's, approximately ten years after the railroad had linked Denver to the East, "variety saloons"—those lavish, gilded, red-carpeted palaces of music, food and drink popularized in novels and movies about the West—reached their height.

The Palace, Eugene Field's favorite hangout, boasted a bar with a sixty-foot mirror behind it and offered quail, roast turkey, breast of prairie chicken, venison, antelope cutlets and, of course, roast beef. Other notable establishments of the era were Tortoni's (spelled out in gold pieces on the floor), Gahan's, the Manhattan and the Navarre. When Colorado went "dry" in 1914, all of them died. Only a few reopened when Prohibition ended.

At the turn of the century, Denver had a reputation as a restaurant-oriented town. The Colorado Springs *Sun* reported, ". . . the great, big bustling part of Denver . . . rustles around when mealtime comes and goes to this place or that, wherever appetite and the condition of the pocketbook warrant. There is a collection of yawning mouths, if not stomachs, at every Denver restaurant three times a day, and sometimes all day."

Yet as late as the 1950's, a dining guide in the city was pressed to advise visitors to "dine in the Sky Chef Restaurant at the airport, where the fascination of the big aluminum birds . . . gives a twentieth-century seasoning to the meals." In 1952 there were only 1,400 restaurants licensed in Colorado. By 1976 the number had jumped to 5,000.

Thankfully, the city's restaurateurs seem to have outgrown the spasms of "theme" so popular in the 1960's, although restaurants like the 94th Aero Squadron (World War I France) and Casa Bonita (Sunny Mexico) still serve up visual diversions and food that is adequate. Others have died because an increasing number of restaurants present interesting meals, pleasantly served, and because customers have become more demanding.

There are three main groupings of restaurants in Denver. Larimer Square, a block-long area of restored Victorian-era buildings on Larimer Street between 14th and 15th Streets, houses a broad range of restaurants—from the Magic Pan (crêperie) at one end to **Laffite** (seafood) at the other. Between them are La Mancha (Mexican), Josephina's (Italian), **Café Promenade** (Continental), Basin Street (Creole) and the Bratskeller (German). Of these, only the Promenade presents a memorable eating experience; the specialties of the other places are done better elsewhere in the city. But an evening here would interest an out-of-town visitor because of the history of the streets and the small shops that line them.

About a fifteen-minute drive southeast of downtown is Cherry Creek, a pleasant neighborhood shopping area of exotic stores and some very good places to eat—**The Hatch Cover,** The Blue Bird Café and Bookstore, Stromberg's and The London House among them.

Another concentration is farther southeast, an area populated mainly by young singles. The Turn of the Century, Toby Jug, **Berel's,** Ichabod's and several others make up a wide choice for good but not exceptional dining. The nearby unincorporated city of Glendale is home for most of the city's discos and singles joints—The Dove, Bogart's, The Lift, **Bull and Bush** and Rosy Bottoms. All have frantic social scenes and most boast blaring disco-beat sound systems.

Reflecting Denver's casual frontier heritage—when the typical dining-out uniform consisted of a woolen shirt, rough pants, boots and a pair of six-shooters—relaxed atmosphere is the rule. **The Palace Arms** in the Brown Palace Hotel is probably the only place that still requires coat and tie. The city's top Continental restaurants (**Tante Louise, Normandy,** The Quorum, Le Profil) will accept diners in open-collar shirts. Even tipping is inconsistent, though 20 percent seems to be the coming thing. Outside the busiest eating times, reservations aren't required, except where recommended.

The region's Hispanic heritage produced myriad restaurants serving Mexican food, the most popular ethnic cuisine. Aficionados will defend unto their last enchilada their favorites: The Riviera, La Hacienda, The Satire Lounge, El Madero's, La Plaza and Monterrey House No. 2 are some of the most popular.

The visitor to Denver will have a bit of trouble trying to get to the city's better food stores. Wine is easy—the **Harry Hoffman** wine cellar is downtown, close to most hotels. The others will be harder to reach. The **Granada** market has no peer in dispensing fresh fish. Cheeses are available from **The Cheese People.** The best meats come from **Sid's** in South Denver or **Oliver's** near downtown.

# Restaurants and Food Sources

(Area code: 303)

## BIG DEAL

### WORTH IT

***Dudley's,*** 1120 E. 6th Avenue (744-8634). French with a strong leaning toward *nouvelle cuisine*—without pomp and nonsense. Informal setting (a converted neighborhood bar) with a wide-ranging menu that changes with the seasons and chef Orville Knight's inclination. Reservations a must because of small (48) seating capacity. Closed Sunday and Monday. Entrées from $3.75 (L), $7.50 (D). AE, CB, DC, MC, V.

### NOT WORTH IT

***Laffite,*** 14th and Larimer Streets (222-5811). A long-time Denver dining landmark, it appears to be suffering from rising prices and diminishing portions. A favorite hangout of Big Money from Texas. Features fish dishes, heavy on the Creole. Service is often perfunctory. Closed Sunday. Entrées from $4 (L), $7 (D). AE, CB, DC, MC, V.

## INTERNATIONAL

### AMERICAN

***Emerson Street East,*** 900 East Colfax Avenue (832-1349). Steak and prime ribs served amid a masculine setting of brick walls covered with photos of sports heroes from the past. Heavy drinks in the lounge, which draws post-swingles crowd and a smattering of local sports figures. Live music after 9 P.M. Tuesday to Saturday. Valet parking. Reservations requested for dinner. Sunday, dinner only. Entrées from $2.60 (L), $4.50 (D). AE, DC, MC, V.

## CHINESE

***Golden Dragon,*** 1467 Nelson Street (237-4144). Mandarin and Szechuan served in a casual helter-skelter atmosphere presided over by owner Jim Chang. Order the $7.50 family-style dinner (including appetizer, soup, and entrées such as *moo-shu* pork, sautéed shrimp, or hot shredded spice beef); assemble your own à la carte or "leave it up to your waiter." Scallion pancakes as an appetizer is a favorite. Closed Monday. Entrées from $3.25 (L), $4.35 (D). AE, CB, DC, MC, V.

## CONTINENTAL

***Café Promenade,*** 1430 Larimer Street (893-2692). Continental dishes, nicely served. An extensive wine list. Veal dishes are a specialty. Located in the reworked basement of an 1880's building in Larimer Square, a restored historic area. Tables outdoors for lunch (get there early) when the weather is right. Closed Sunday. Entrées from $4 (L), $6.75 (D). AE, CB, DC, MC, V.

## FRENCH

***Tante Louise,*** 4900 E. Colfax Avenue (355-4488). A small (it seats only 55) restaurant in a former private home, featuring provincial dishes including hare marinated in red wine. Fish dishes not up to the rest of the menu. Good selection of wines. Reservations recommended. Closed Sunday. Entrées from $3 (L), $6.50 (D). AE, CB, DC, MC, V.

***The Normandy,*** 1515 Madison Street (321-3311). Traditional French in a cozy setting. Speciality is *escalopes de veau* (veal scallops sautéed in butter, served in casserole with mushroom sauce, topped with cheese). Reservations recommended for dinner. Chaîne des Rotisseurs. Sunday, dinner only. Closed Monday. Entrées from $3.95 (L), $7.50 (D). AE, CB, DC, MC, V.

## GERMAN

***Bavarian Inn,*** 490 S. Colorado Boulevard (377-0208). Locals who know Germany swear this is "absolutely authentic." The menu offers seven appetizers, thirteen European entrées, eight specialties from the broiler and six desserts. Large portions of everything. Extensive list of German wines from the Rhine and Moselle valleys. Entrées from $2.50 (L), $4.95 (D). AE, DC, MC, V.

## GREEK

***The Athenian,*** 5501 E. Colfax Avenue (377-8478). A favorite meeting place of the city's Greek population, featuring lamb chops marinated in olive oil, moussaka. Without doubt one of the noisiest restaurants anywhere . . . . but fun. A belly dancer gets the crowd worked up. The usual drinks and wine, plus ouzo and retsina. Dynamite. Entertainment until 2 A.M. Dinner only. Closed Monday. Entrées from $6.50. AE, DC, MC, V.

## ITALIAN

***La Fontanella,*** 1700 E. Evans Avenue (778-8598). Northern Italian cookery a specialty, including *cannelloni fontanella* (spinach pasta filled with ground veal and beef and spinach, topped with two sauces), an excellent vegetable soup and a generous *antipasto misto,* at $4.95. Relaxed atmosphere with white stucco walls adorned with kitchen utensils and plants. Saturday and Sunday, dinner only. Open seven days a week. Entrées from $2.25 (L), $3.25 (D). MC, V.

***Berardi & Sons,*** 1525 Blake Street (623-7648). Son of the original Berardi & Sons in nearby Boulder, this place has fine veal dishes served in a cleverly remodeled meat-packing warehouse. A word of caution: Like the little girl with the curl, when Berardi's is good it is very, very good . . . Reservations a must on Friday and Saturday. Saturday and Sunday, dinner only. Open seven days a week. Entrées from $2.95 (L), $5.50 (D). AE, MC, V.

## JAPANESE

***The Kabuki House,*** 1561 Market Street (534-9194). Hard by Skid Row, this place was reclaimed from a dumpy bar and redecorated by two Japanese women. Throw yourself on the mercy of the chef and be surprised by dishes that include barbecued chicken, *sashimi* (raw tuna and octopus), soup, chicken. All cooked to order, so avoid it if you're in a hurry. Reservations requested. Saturday, dinner only. Closed Sunday. Entrées from $2.50 (L), $5.50 (D). AE, MC, V.

## MEXICAN

***Casa de Manuel,*** 2010 Larimer Street (629-6864). Like blazing Mexican food? Willing to venture to a less-than-fashionable address? Manuel (he's the one with the toothpick) serves a bean burrito covered with green chili unmatched in the Western Hemisphere. Also *barbacoa tacos:* soft-shelled corn tortillas, shredded beef and a separate pile of chopped onion, tomato and Chinese parsley. Both far outdistance the rest of the menu. Turquoise walls, fluorescent lighting and chrome chairs add to the atmosphere. Better for lunch than dinner. No liquor. Open until 11:30, Saturday. Closed Sunday and Monday. Entrées from $1.50 (L), $2.25 (D). No credit cards.

***Mama Elena's,*** 4575 E. Colfax Avenue (321-0146). Mexican in the Southern style: subtle sauces and hidden flavors. The enchiladas *verdes* and the combination dinners are tops. A wide range of Mexican and domestic beers and California wines. Tasteful, simple décor. Limited seating. Saturday and Sunday, dinner only. Open seven days a week. Entrées from $2.85 (L & D). MC, V.

## MOROCCAN

***Mataam Fez,*** 4609 E. Colfax Avenue (355-7037). No matter what your mother told you, you are expected to take your shoes off and eat with your fingers at the dinner table in this re-creation of a Moroccan home. Meals include soup, two kinds of salad, *pastella* (a mixture of eggs, chicken and nuts in a pastry), breads and mint tea. Reservations a must. Open seven days a week, from 6 P.M. to 9:30 P.M., Sunday through Thursday, and 6 P.M. to 10 P.M., Friday and Saturday. Twelve entrées, all $12, and a nightly special at $14. AE, MC.

# SPECIALTY COOKING

## BARBECUE

***Daddy Bruce's,*** 1629 E. 34th Avenue (623-9636). Official supplier of 'cue for the Denver Broncos, Bruce's is a Denver institution. Mostly take-out because the restaurant is quite small. Piquant sauce on big, meaty ribs. Open 11 A.M. to midnight. Closed Monday. Entrées from $3.15 (L & D). "No cards, no checks, just cash."

***Dewey's,*** 2216 Kearney Street (355-1438). A newcomer to challenge Daddy Bruce. Sauces hot and mild, though the meats are less generous. Slab of ribs is a money-saver at $10.50. Pork ribs $4.25, beef ribs $3.75. Open seven days a week. Closes at 6 P.M. on Sunday. No credit cards.

## DELI

***Bagel Nosh,*** 7777 E. Hampden Avenue (755-7550) and 1630 Welton Street (892-6881). Nearest thing to a New York deli in the metro area; the countermen are even surly. Welton Street: closed Saturday and Sunday. Hampden Avenue: open seven days a week. Entrées from $2.95 (L & D). No credit cards.

## HAMBURGER

***Berel's,*** 10005 E. Hampden Avenue (750-3500). Skip all the other offerings on the deli-oriented menu and head directly for "Sustainers," a variety of bountiful burgers. Also an extensive list of omelets. Open seven days a week. Entrées from $1.50 (L & D). AE, DC, MC, V.

## STEAK

***The Buckhorn Exchange,*** 1000 Osage Street (534-9505). The Buckhorn (founded in 1893 and holder of Colorado liquor license No. 1) is dispensing 24-ounce T-bone steaks in a cleaned-up but not cleaned-out atmosphere. The walls are lined with animal heads, souvenirs of the early owners' trophy hunts; and the place reeks with Colorado history. Order the T-bone pan-fried and they may mistake you for a habitué. Saturday and Sunday, brunch and dinner only. Closed Friday. Entrées from $1.30 (L), $8.95 (D). AE, MC, V.

## VEGETARIAN

***R. Valentino's,*** 1469 Pearl Street (722-1604), 1531 Glenarm Place (571-0823). Family-operated restaurants with an emphasis on Italian dishes, using tofu as a substitute for meat. Eggplant *parmigiana* and lasagne are two favorites. Also feature desserts made without sugar, using only honey. Pearl Street: dinner only. Closed Tuesday. Glenarm Place (mainly take-out): lunch only. Closed Saturday and Sunday. Both: entrées from $1.75 (L), $3 (D). No credit cards.

# FOR INDIVIDUAL NEEDS

## IF YOU HAVE TIME FOR ONLY ONE MEAL

***Café Promenade,*** 1430 Larimer Street (893-2692). (See description under CONTINENTAL.)

***Dudley's,*** 1120 E. 6th Avenue (744-8634). (See description under BIG DEAL/WORTH IT.)

## BEST HOTEL MEAL

***The Palace Arms,*** Brown Palace Hotel, 17th Street and Tremont Place (825-3111). Dining dignity remains alive at the city's only restaurant still requiring gentlemen to wear coat and tie at lunch and dinner. Beef dishes and Rocky Mountain trout are featured. Reservations almost a must. Open seven days a week. Entrées from $4.25 (L), $8.75 (D). AE, CB, DC, MC, V.

## RESTAURANT NEAR AIRPORT

***Open Season,*** 3333 Quebec Street (321-3500). Unusual "pioneer" favorites—wild pheasant, elk, buffalo steak, etc. Beef steaks and prime rib for the less adventurous. For the really adventurous there's rattlesnake (when available). Reservations suggested. Saturday and Sunday, dinner only. Open seven days a week. Entrées from $3.50 (L), $6.95 (D). AE, CB, DC, MC, V.

## BUSINESS BREAKFAST

***San Marco Room,*** Brown Palace Hotel, 17th Street and Tremont Place (825-3111). Much less formal than the hotel's Palace Arms, it nevertheless retains an elegant air of heavy silver utensils and extremely attentive service. Breakfasts range from simple pancakes (95 cents) to the city's best eggs Benedict ($5.25). Open seven days a week. AE, CB, DC, MC, V.

## BUSINESS LUNCH

***Downtown Broker,*** 17th and Champa Streets (893-5065). The site of a bank has been transformed into a plush below-street-level restaurant—a favorite of financial-district types, who flock here. Prime ribs are popular. Reservations advisable. Saturday, dinner only. Closed Sunday. Entrées from $3.20 (L), $9 (D). AE, MC, V.

## FAST, GOOD FOOD/BREAKFAST

***Cosmopolitan Hotel,*** Coffee Shop, 1780 Broadway (861-9000). Opens daily at 6:30 A.M. AE, MC, V.

## FAST, GOOD FOOD/LUNCH

***Temptry,*** 916 15th Street (893-5840), 1631 California Street (534-8734). A food-service experiment by Holiday Inns (independent of the hotels) that began in Denver, offers soup and sandwiches and a build-it-yourself salad bar. Quick, efficient and tasty. Open 7 A.M. to 3 P.M. Closed Saturday and Sunday. Sandwiches from 99 cents, soup 90 cents, salad bar $1.85. No credit cards.

## FAST, GOOD FOOD/DINNER

***Hatch Cover,*** 149 Steele Street (388-8181). Wend your way through the singles bar at the front of the place and go directly to the newly expanded dining room. Steaks a specialty. Swift service. No reservations. Open seven days a week. Entrées from $2.75 (L), $4.50 (D). AE, CB, DC, MC, V.

## BEST WINE LIST

***Café Promenade,*** 1430 Larimer Street (893-2692). (See description under CONTINENTAL.) A wide selection of European and California wines, vintage and *ordinaire,* goes well with the expansive menu.

## FOR DRINKS

***Bull and Bush,*** 4700 Cherry Creek South Drive (759-0333). Old-English motif and the center of Denver's dart-throwing activity. Lively singles atmosphere. Open seven days a week. AE, MC, V.

***Trader Vic's,*** Hilton Hotel, 1550 Court Place (893-6776). A large (100-seat) lounge in the traditional palm leaf and rattan setting. Open seven days a week, until 1:30 A.M. Monday through Saturday; until 11 P.M. Sunday. Also has a full lunch and dinner menu. AE, CB, DC, MC, V.

## ROMANTIC

***Downtown Broker,*** 17th and Champa Streets (893-5065). (See description under BUSINESS LUNCH.) Private booth tucked away in the restaurant's Vault Room. The house specialty, which is included with the dinner, is the large shrimp bowl.

## LATE-NIGHT SERVICE

***Royal Platte River Yacht Club,*** 1401 Larimer Street (893-1401). Located in a basement on Denver's historic Larimer Square. Favorite dishes include veal piccata with fettuccine, crab legs and steaks. Closed Sunday. Entrées from $2.25 (L), $6.50 (D). AE, MC, V.

## SUNDAY BRUNCH

***Fagan's,*** 1135 E. Evans Avenue (778-6426). Relaxed, rustic atmosphere. Eggs Benedict ($3.75) an overwhelming favorite, with good reason. Also omelets, cheese blintzes and quiches. No smoking in the dining area. Sundays only, beginning at 10:30 A.M. Entrées from $3.25. MC, V.

## SUNDAY-EVENING MEAL

***Berardi & Sons,*** 1525 Blake Street, Denver (623-7648) and 2631 Broadway, Boulder (449-9460). (See descriptions under ITALIAN and IN THE SUBURBS/BOULDER.)

## FOR FAMILIES WITH CHILDREN

***Hungry Farmer,*** 6925 W. Alameda Avenue (238-4321). Ample portions of soup, salad, chicken, etc., surrounded by children and grandmothers. Pleasant family atmosphere and a big favorite with kids. Very friendly service and reasonably priced. Dinner only. Open seven days a week. Entrées from $6.25. AE, DC, MC, V.

## COUNTRY INN

***Cottonwood Cottage,*** Niwot, Colo. (623-4713). Century-old farmhouse surrounded by cottonwoods. Basic menu, featuring fish, chicken and steaks. A 45-minute drive from downtown by taking the Boulder Turnpike to the Diagonal for Longmont. Closed Monday in winter. Entrées from $3.50 (L), $7.95 (D). MC, V.

# IN THE SUBURBS

## AURORA

***Sirloin House,*** 16000 Smith Road (366-6674). Also known as Emmerling's or Emil-lene's Steak House. Meat and potatoes in a 1950's roadhouse setting. Steaks, though expensive, are unbeatable; large cuts of aged beef. Closed Monday during football season. Entrées from $8.50. MC, V.

## BOULDER

***Berardi & Sons,*** 2631 Broadway (449-9460). Homemade Italian dishes, prepared fresh daily. Giant antipastos, rabbit and massive fettuccine Alfredo. Open seven days a week. Entrées from $2 (L), $4 (D). MC, V.

***Flagstaff House,*** Flagstaff Road (442-4640). Wide-ranging menu (*escargot* appetizers to crab Lausanne) and wine list. Reached via the Boulder Turnpike to Baseline Road, and west to Flagstaff Road. Dinner only. Open seven days a week. Entrées from $4.95. AE, CB, DC, MC, V.

***Red Lion Inn,*** Boulder Canyon Road (442-9368). Rustic, stone lodge setting. Menu ranges from elk steak to *coq au vin.* Boulder Canyon Road starts in downtown Boulder. Dinner only. Open seven days a week. Entrées from $6.50. AE, CB, DC, MC, V.

# MARKETS

## GIFT FOODS

***Sid's,*** 2700 S. Colorado Boulevard (757-7433). A bit out of the way in south Denver but worth the trip for superb meats and friendly service. Sid also carries a large line of fruits and vegetables and gourmet food items. Open seven days a week. AE, MC, V.

***Oliver's,*** 1312 E. 6th Avenue (733-4629). Operating since 1923, Oliver's is entering its fourth generation of family butchers. Friendly service still prevails and they happily butterfly roasts, bone breasts, etc. (Housed in the same building but not connected with Oliver's is **The Fruit Basket,** offering some of the freshest and most beautiful fruits and vegetables available in the city.) Closed Sunday. No credit cards.

***Granada,*** 1275 19th Street (534-5375). Top-quality fish, including most varieties fresh, in season, and clearly labeled as such. The shop's cleanliness is astounding. Closed Sunday. No credit cards.

***The Cheese People,*** 7400 E. Hampden Avenue (773-3477). Ninety kinds of cheese from all over the world. Also salami, bread, sweets, coffee beans and an eye-popping array of gourmet odds and ends. Open seven days a week. MC, V.

# GIFT WINES

***Harry Hoffman's,*** 511 18th Street (825-0111). Wide selection of imported and California wines. Premium California wines are cheaper in Colorado than on the Coast. They'll deliver free on orders over $30. No Sunday package sales in Colorado. No credit cards.

# Detroit

It all began in 1701 when Antoine de la Mothe Cadillac and his fellow French traders and trappers founded Ville d'étroit: City of the Strait. Then came the English, and as Detroit gradually became an industrial center, over sixty other ethnic groups made it their home. Today, the major groups include English, Canadians, Italians, Polish and Germans.

As Detroit became a trading and manufacturing center, inns, hotels and roadhouses sprang up along the routes to and from the city. They served hearty foods drawn from nearby forests and lakes—venison, quail, partridge, trout, perch and pickerel. Roadhouses, such as the famous Northwood, Eastwood and Westwood, were known for superb Michigan frogs' legs. Accompanied by huge relish trays, frogs' legs were served with chicken, with fish and with more frogs' legs. Unfortunately, this specialty is rarely found in local restaurants today.

In the late 1800's and early 1900's, Detroit's downtown hotels were praised for high-quality dining. Pioneers of the auto industry wined and dined in the fancy ones, such as the Russell House, which later was replaced by the even more elegant Hotel Pontchartrain. With Prohibition came a number of "blind pig" establishments (as speakeasies were called here) that earned a reputation for serving excellent steaks and chops. After Prohibition many became fine restaurants. The Commodore, Penobscot Inn, Gurney's and Pierre's were well known in the 1920's and '30s. About then, **Joe Muer** established his famous marble-topped oyster bar, which ran the length of his restaurant and which still stands (minus the marble) in its original location on Gratiot, now run by Joe's grandsons. Today's chop houses—**Carl's,** and the **London**—are all descendants of that era.

Above all, Detroit is known as a meat-and-potatoes town. The most popular restaurants are those serving steak and seafood, although some Continental-style restaurants are also doing well. Interesting food can also be found in many out-of-the-way, family-run restaurants that reflect the city's diverse population. Some are scattered around the city, others are found in the suburbs. Chinese restaurants are probably the most numerous, especially in the suburbs where they are thriving.

Growth is concentrated in Detroit's surrounding communities, although the downtown area has been infused with new vitality since the opening of the riverfront Renaissance Center, a complex of office buildings clustered around a 71-story skyscraper, the Detroit Plaza Hotel.

Eastern Market is the number-one spot for fresh produce—it's just a mile up Gratiot from the center of town. Recently spruced up with bright supergraphics (you can't miss the giant cow or the bright red-and-green watermelon), the market features open-air farmer stalls that do a bustling business every Saturday morning. It is surrounded by wholesale warehouses for produce, spices and nuts, cheese, meats, fish and poultry. A stroll over the walkway that crosses the freeway will bring you to Gratiot Market, with seafood, gourmet food, bakery and butcher shops all under one roof.

For imported cheese, try R. J. Hirt Co. in Eastern Market. Also in the market is the **Rocky Peanut Co.,** known for its selection of nuts, spices and dried fruits. For wine, continue up Gratiot to **Gibb's World Wide Wines.** It has the largest selection and most reasonable prices in Detroit. In the northern suburbs, Birmingham's Bottle and Basket has a good selection of wines.

For baked goods, Aliette's Bakery on Porter features excellent cream puffs, éclairs and French bread. **Aliette** also runs a small French restaurant with a limited menu.

The majority of Detroit restaurants require reservations for lunch and dinner. Prices are generally higher in the evening. Tips of 15 to 20 percent of the total meal cost are expected. Slacks for women are acceptable.

## GREEK

***New Hellas,*** 583 Monroe (961-5544). Just one of several good Greek cafés on an atmospheric block known as Greektown. Flaming cheese, Greek salad, moussaka, shish kebab and crusty light brown bread. If it's too crowded, neighbors Old Parthenon, Laikon and Grecian Gardens are just as good if less popular. Open seven days a week until wee hours of the morning. Entrées from $3.15 (L), $3.75 (D). DC, MC, V.

## HUNGARIAN

***Al's Lounge,*** West End at South (841-5677). Hidden away in Delray, the traditional Hungarian section of town, Al's features solid peasant cooking in a bar atmosphere. Chicken paprikash and stuffed cabbage, and a fish-fry every Friday. Hungarian wine by the glass. Open seven days a week. Entrées from $2.75 (L), $3.50 (D). No credit cards.

## INDIAN

***The Himalayas,*** 841 Ouellette, Windsor, Ontario, Canada (519/258-2804). It is just a short drive across the Detroit River to this old clapboard house converted into several funky dining rooms. The menu is an unusual combination of Indian with a smattering of French items. Try *samosas, tandoori* chicken and the vegetarian entrées. Top off the meal with a very untraditional but splendid baked Alaska. Service is slow. Dinner only. Open seven days a week. Dinners from $4. DC, MC.

## ITALIAN

***Aldo's,*** 19143 Kelly (839-2180). A warm, family-owned restaurant, specializing in veal and homemade pasta, cooked to order by Aldo himself. Excellent service and homey, white-linen-covered tables. The minestrone is recommended, along with antipasto, veal chops *alla Aldo* and subtle meat sauces for pasta. Popular with the Italian community. Dinner only. Closed Monday. Entrées from $9.75. No credit cards.

***Cardinali's,*** 3485 Mitchell, just off Gratiot (267-9622). Tiny and unimposing, but locally recognized for fine Northern Italian home cooking. Try the *lasagne verde,* fettuccine Alfredo and minestrone. A casual family spot. Closed Monday and Tuesday. Entrées from $4.75 (L & D). No credit cards.

## MEXICAN

***Mexican Village,*** 2600 Bagley (237-0333), located in Detroit's old Latin section not far from downtown. Nationalities mix here to eat excellent enchiladas, *chiles rellenos* (stuffed with cheese or meat), and the *botanas* (listed under appetizers but large enough for a meal for two). Good service. Open until 4 A.M., seven days a week. Entrées from $3.25 (L & D). AE, DC.

## POLISH

***Royal Eagle,*** 1415 Parker (331-8088). Costumed servers and a vintage setting of sparkling crystal and bright fresh flowers add ambiance to a fine menu of traditional dishes such as hunter's pancake, mushroom blintzes, roast duck and interesting soups including dill pickle and *czarnina* (duck's blood). Dinner only. Closed Monday and Tuesday. Entrées from $7.95. No credit cards.

# SPECIALTY COOKING

## DELI

***Stage Delicatessen,*** 13821 W. Nine Mile, Oak Park (548-1111). Just a mile north of Detroit, the Stage is a cheery restaurant noted for a range of sandwiches named after media personalities. Try the corned beef and the cheese cake. Usually jam-packed. Closed Monday. Entrées from $2.25 (L), $3.75 (D). No credit cards.

## HAMBURGER

***Diamond Jim Brady's,*** Seven Mile just east of Greenfield (272-2781). A tiny kitchen that has to share space with the bartender nonetheless turns out the Diamond Jim Special, renowned as one of the best hamburgers in a town that knows its chopped meat. The saloon setting harks back to the original Diamond Jim. Closed Saturday and Sunday. Entrées from $2.65 (L & D). AE.

## HOT DOG

***Lafayette Coney Island,*** 118 W. Lafayette (964-8198). Detroit's favorite dog. There is an *only* way to eat one while here. Take the regular dog and top it with a distinctive chili. Eat it with or without onions liberally sprinkled on top. Have it with beer at the counter or at a plastic-topped table. Dogs are $1. Open 24 hours a day, seven days a week. No credit cards.

## PIZZA

***Loui's,*** Dequindre just north of Nine Mile Road, Hazel Park (547-1711). A setting of friendly chaos, with tables set close together. Square pizza with chewy crust is the focus, along with big salads called antipasta. Small cheese, pepperoni and mushroom pizza is $3.75. Closed Monday and Tuesday. No credit cards.

## SEAFOOD

***Joe Muer's,*** 2000 Gratiot (962-1088). Fresh seafood from all coasts and a longstanding policy of no reservations. That may mean you'll stand in line a long time, but the food is worth it. The menu changes daily. Good service in handsome rooms with brick walls but no hokey trappings. Closed Sunday. Entrées from $5.25 (L), $8.50 (D). AE, MC, V.

## SOUL

***Mattie's Bar-B-Que,*** 11728 Dexter (869-6331). Old-fashioned recipes such as smothered steak, ribs, candied sweet potatoes and ham hocks offered at this straightforward family place. Check out the day's special. Open 24 hours a day, seven days a week. Entrées from $2.50 (L & D). No credit cards.

## STEAK

***Carl's Chop House,*** 3020 Grand River (833-0700). Beef is the name of the game in this barnlike room near Tiger Stadium. The steak is outstanding, but lots of businessmen and sports fans order the prime ribs. Reservations a must on game nights. Open seven days a week. Service is good. Entrées from $4.25 (L), $8.25 (D). AE, CB, DC, MC, V.

## VEGETARIAN

***Harvest Park,*** 15406 Mack, Grosse Pointe Park (343-0679). Just a dozen or so tables in a light, handsomely uncluttered room. Salads are as pretty as they are delicious. Vegetable soup is particularly good, as is the grilled vegie, a sandwich blending cheese and vegetables on whole-grain bread. Closed Monday. Entrées from $3.75 (L), $4.75 (D). MC, V.

# FOR INDIVIDUAL NEEDS

## IF YOU HAVE TIME FOR ONLY ONE MEAL

***Joe Muer's,*** 2000 Gratiot (962-1088). (See description under SEAFOOD.)

## BEST HOTEL MEAL

***La Rotisserie,*** Hyatt Regency, Fairlane Town Center, Dearborn (593-1234). An unusual Oriental and French menu served by teams of waiters in a contemporary setting with glass ovens, through which you can watch the ducks searing. Dinner only; Sunday, brunch only. Entrées from $4.95 (L), $11.75 (D). AE, CB, DC, MC, V.

## BUSINESS BREAKFAST

***Dearborn Inn,*** 20301 Oakwood Boulevard, Dearborn (271-2700). (See description under COUNTRY INN.)

## BUSINESS LUNCH

***Caucus Club,*** 150 W. Congress (965-4970). Under the same management as the London Chop House and right across the street, the club draws many bankers and lawyers to its comfortable leather chairs. Hearty sandwiches and corned-beef hash are the most popular items. Sunday and Monday, lunch only. Entrées from $5.50 (L), $6.75 (D). AE, CB, DC, MC, V.

## FAST, GOOD FOOD

***Ham Heaven,*** 70 Cadillac Square at Bates (961-8818). Just about any dish, as long as it includes ham in some form, is served from a bleary-eyed 6:30 A.M. until 5 P.M., Monday through Friday, at this cheery downtown spot that offers real value. Bean soup is consumed at the rate of 250 bowls a day. Entrées from $1.50 (B, L & D). No credit cards.

## BEST WINE LIST

***The London Chop House,*** 155 W. Congress (962-0277). (See description under BIG DEAL/WORTH IT.)

## FOR DRINKS

***Traffic Jam,*** Second at Canfield (831-9470). Decorated with urban artifacts plucked from the teeth of bulldozers when old turn-of-the-century Detroit buildings were coming down, this Wayne State University hangout is popular with faculty and students. An adjoining bakery in a renovated Victorian house provides bread *du jour.* The menu is varied with lots of vegetarian choices. No sign outside. Closed Saturday and Sunday. Entrées $2.50 (L & D). MC, V.

***Lindell AC,*** 1310 Cass Avenue (964-1122). Must be the second home for Detroit jocks and jock-followers, including members of the press. Sports memorabilia and photos hang everywhere, but it's usually so crowded they're hardly noticed. Great place for people-watching and a hamburger with fries for $1.85. Open seven days a week until 2 A.M. No credit cards.

## RESTAURANT WITH MUSIC

***The Money Tree,*** 333 W. Fort Street (961-2445). (See description under CONTINENTAL.) Classical guitar and flute duo every evening.

## ROMANTIC

***Pontchartrain Wine Cellars,*** 234 W. Larned (963-1785). Not really a cellar, but dark and cozy bistro atmosphere with excellent Continental and French food and good wine list. This is where Cold Duck originated. Rack of lamb, *ratatouille* and seafood are top choices. Saturday, dinner only. Closed Sunday and holidays. Entrées from $3.60 (L), $7.95 (D). AE, DC, MC, V.

## LATE-NIGHT SERVICE

***New Hellas,*** 583 Monroe (961-5544). (See description under GREEK.)

***Mattie's Bar-B-Que,*** 11738 Dexter (869-6331). (See description under SOUL.)

## SUNDAY BRUNCH

***La Rotisserie,*** Hyatt Regency Hotel, Fairlane Town Center, Dearborn (593-1234). A lavish array of dishes ranging from eggs Benedict and crêpes to fresh fruit and cheese, plus a dessert table. Buffet-style service from 10:30 A.M. to 2:30 P.M., Sunday only. Brunch is $7.50; for those under 12 years, $4.95. AE, CB, DC, MC, V.

## SUNDAY-EVENING MEAL

***Mario's,*** 4222 Second (833-9425). All the classic Italian dishes plus some French, great mixed-at-each-table salads. The staff is friendly, informal but professional. Sunday dinner from 2 P.M. to midnight. Entrées from $4 (L), $6.50 (D). AE, CB, DC, MC, V.

## FOR FAMILIES WITH CHILDREN

***Pacifico's Pasta Village,*** Maple Road just west of Livernois, Troy (362-1907). Lots of Italian village atmosphere, including a gondola in which families may dine under a mural of Venice. Pasta dishes of all sorts, with a pasta-maker working in view of the customers. Entrées from $3.75 (L & D). AE, CB, DC, MC, V.

## COUNTRY INN

***Dearborn Inn,*** 20301 Oakwood Boulevard, Dearborn (271-2700). Authentic Early American inn near historical Greenfield Village. Only 15 minutes from downtown. Buffets at lunch feature seafood and prime rib. New England clambake, planked Lake Superior trout are good dinner choices. You may wish to stay the night in the inn or in historic cottages behind the inn. The inn also serves an excellent Sunday brunch. Open seven days a week. Entrées from $3.90 (L), $10.25 (D).AE, DC, MC, V.

# IN THE SUBURBS

## BIRMINGHAM

***Tweeny's,*** 280 N. Woodward (644-0050). In an airy, yet elegant, courtyard setting, chef Yvonne Gill Davis serves luncheon and dinner using only the freshest of ingredients and her own flair for European cooking. The menu changes every day. The complete Boulevard Supper served from 5:30 P.M. to 7 P.M. is a bargain at $12.50. Closed Sunday and Monday. Entrées from $4.50 (L), $12.50 (D). MC, V.

## LIVONIA

***Moy's Japanese Steak House,*** 16825 Middlebelt just south of Six Mile (427-3170). Bump elbows with strangers around a table that encloses a huge *teppan* grill on three sides. The chef cooks the meal in front of you—steak, chicken or shrimp and vegetables. Lots of showmanship. Another dining room offers Cantonese specialties. No reservations—be prepared to wait on weekends. Closed Monday. Steakhouse entrées from $6 (L), $9.50 (D); Chinese food $3.50 (L & D). AE, DC, MC, V.

---

## MADISON HEIGHTS

***Mandarin Dining,*** 31742 John R. (585-6071). Ignore familiar Cantonese selections and choose from the Mandarin menu. Try the spicy ginger beef, smooth and subtle garlic chicken, fried dumplings, or Three Delicacies Soup to feed four, or call ahead to order whole steamed fish in brown sauce. Typical Chinese décor, and good service. Open seven days a week. Entrées from $1.85 (L), $4.50 (D). No credit cards.

---

## NOVI

***Ah Wok,*** 41563 W. 10-Mile (349-9260). Cantonese, Mandarin and Szechuan food. Ask the chef to prepare something of his choice, or order Peking duck ahead for four or more. Also try the hot-and-sour soup, meats over crackling rice and beef with broccoli. Tucked into an out-of-the-way shopping center, nothing special about the décor. The food makes the drive worth it, though. Closed Monday. Entrées from $2.75 (L), $3.75 (D). AE, DC, V.

---

## SOUTHFIELD

***Golden Mushroom,*** 18100 W. 10-Mile (559-4230). The fine European chef is more classically inclined than the informal setting would lead one to believe. He has a way with veal Oscar and rack of lamb as well as seafood. Closed Sunday. Entrées from $4.25 (L), $7.50 (D). AE, DC, MC, V.

---

## WINDSOR, ONTARIO, CANADA

Only a 75-cent bridge or tunnel toll away from downtown Detroit.

***Ye Olde Steak House,*** 46 Chatham Street West (519/256-0222). A most popular steakhouse for Canadians and Americans alike, this provincial-looking spot serves both U.S. and Canadian beef accompanied by French onion soup, dill pickle, salad and French-fried onion rings at reasonable prices. Friendly service. Closed Sunday. Entrées from $3.50 (L), $5.25 (D). AE, DC, MC, V.

***Cheshire Cat,*** 131 Riverside Drive West (519/256-4621). Not as tiny as it once was, and now serving beer and wine as well as many varieties of tea, it is still charming in its cellar quarters at Place Riviere, a mini shopping spot carved out of two restored brick buildings. Homemade soups and sandwiches. Closed Sunday. Snacks from 95 cents. No credit cards.

# MARKETS

## CARE PACKAGE

***Rocky Peanut Co.,*** 2453 Russell (962-5925). In the Eastern Market complex. Stock up with over two dozen kinds of nuts, large dried fruits, spices, extracts, seeds and old-fashioned hard candies. No credit cards.

## GIFT FOODS

***J. L. Hudson's Pantry Shop,*** 1206 Woodward (223-5100). Detroit's largest department store offers a wide selection of imported foods, exotic coffees, wine, baked goods, cheese and sausages. Within walking distance of downtown hotels. No credit cards.

## GIFT WINES

***Gibb's World Wide Wines,*** 9999 Gratiot (921-6581). Largest selection of imported and domestic wines in the city, often at bargain prices. Closed Sunday and Monday. No credit cards.

# Florida's West Coast

The megalopolis that makes up the Suncoast on the west coast of Florida and the Tampa Bay area—St. Petersburg, Tampa, Gulf beaches, Sarasota and Clearwater—offers the diner a huge variety of restaurants. Because the area is so large, discerning diners may drive distances of up to 45 miles to reach their chosen restaurant. However, there are several factors that hold true throughout the area.

The early settlers on the west coast found they could use the bountiful seafood from the Gulf of Mexico to sustain their families. Even the Crackers (named for the huge bullwhips they cracked over oxen hitched to their wagons) brought their families to the Gulf beaches from central Florida during the summer months. Here they caught mullet, oysters, clams and other varieties of seafood to be preserved for the winter months ahead. Smoked mullet and mackerel are still popular with Suncoast residents and can be found in specialty restaurants.

Population growth has pushed the citrus groves further and further from the beach areas and since frozen concentrate came along, there is little fresh-squeezed juice served in restaurants. But you can still find some roadside stands where fresh juices are served.

Seafood is one of the first things a visitor looks for when he eats out on the Suncoast. Like the juice, much of it is frozen, but there are restaurants that make a fetish of fresh fish—sometimes even buying it right off the boats. More than 500 varieties of fish and shellfish swim in the Gulf of Mexico and its inlets. Blue crab and stone crab are favorite shellfish, along with shrimp and oysters.

In the settlement of Tarpon Springs, a Greek influence can be found in the language, on the sponge docks and in food. Tampa's Ybor City still has many Cuban and Spanish residents, and the restaurants feature famous dishes of these countries. But most of them, including the well-known Columbia, aren't what they once were. These ethnic cuisines have now spread to other parts of the Suncoast, and Greek and Spanish food can be found in many locations.

Through all of this run threads of Southern and Northern American cooking, since this part of Florida has many modern-day settlers from northern as well as southern states.

# Restaurants and Food Sources
**(Area code: 813)**

## BIG DEAL

### WORTH IT

***Bill Nagy's,*** 10400 Gandy Boulevard, St. Petersburg (577-1565). Near Derby Lane dog track. In a remodeled steakhouse. Nagy's Czechoslovakian touches are marvelous (Spaetzle, hearty borscht with meat, paprika schnitzel). Also recommended: poached chicken with vegetables, sautéed scallops, puff pastry, appetizers, Russian eggs and a wide range of steaks. Mystère Belle Hélène contains chocolate sauce and meringue. Black Forest cake is popular as are the dessert coffees. Candlelight, nice paintings, graceful plantings and mounted birds and animals make for an extra helping of ambience. Reservations necessary. Open seven days a week. Saturday and Sunday, dinner only. Entrées from $2.95 (L), $5.95 (D). AE, MC, V.

***Bern's Steak House,*** 1208 South Howard Avenue, Tampa (251-2421). Bern Laxer has created a memorable restaurant that features fine steaks (aged and fresh). Order them by weight and cut. The wine list—contained in a 4½-pound book—may be the most extensive in the world. Organically grown fresh vegetables arrive daily from Laxer's own farm. Teas are blended on the premises. Glorious desserts include Blue Bern (with two liqueurs), banana, chocolate or lemon cheese pies. Rococo décor and furnishings in the bar and various dining rooms in which smoking is prohibited. Reservations necessary. Dinner only. Open seven days a week. Entrées from $6.71. AE, DC, V.

***Café L'Europe,*** 431 Harding Circle (St. Armand's Circle), Sarasota (388-4415). Beautiful appointments plus fresh flowers and green plants. This little jewel of a restaurant features Continental service, veal specialties, duckling, sweetbreads, crêpes, a good house dressing for crisp, attractive salads, homemade pastries. At Easter time, view 2,000 imported Dutch tulips. Reservations a must. Open seven days a week. Entrées from $3.75 (L), $7.95 (D). AE, DC, MC, V.

***The Wine Cellar,*** 17307 Gulf Boulevard, North Redington Beach (393-3491). Ted and Liesel Sonnenschein's international restaurant includes numerous dining rooms, each with the décor of a different country. An "alley" with food displays leads to the large bar-lounge. Appetizers include clams oregano and casino, escargots and mushroom caps stuffed with veal ragoût. Beef Wellington is popular as is the Chef's Surprise. Schnitzel à la Holstein and rack of lamb are good choices. For dessert try Baked Alaska made at tableside or chocolate mousse. Reservations suggested. Dinner only. Closed Monday. Entrées from $4.95 (early dinners) to $12.50. AE, DC, MC, V.

***Baumgardner's,*** 924 McMullen-Booth Road (North Haines Road), Clearwater (726-3312). Part of the Kapok Tree Inn complex. Beautiful, with Old World elegance. Skylights give a view of the old oak trees that tower above the building, drinks arrive in stemmed goblets. Dignified waiters and waitresses bring appetizers of crêpes, vichyssoise, fruit in orgeat syrup before your order of *steak au poivre* or boned chicken breasts with grapes and white wine sauce. Reservations suggested. Dinner only. Closed Monday. Entrées from $6.75. AE, CB, DC, MC, V.

## NOT WORTH IT

***The Kapok Tree Inn,*** 923 North Haines Road, Clearwater (726-4734). A popular place for visitors, but the food is paid for at the entrance, giving an assembly-line feeling. There is scenery (a huge kapok tree is spectacular when in bloom the last part of February and into March), and a gift shop for souvenirs. The various dining rooms usually are crowded, service is too fast, and one visit will last you for years. Entrées (chosen at the door) include shrimp, chicken, steak. Corn fritters a specialty. Open seven days a week. Dinner only. Entrées from $4.95. AE, MC, V.

# INTERNATIONAL

## AMERICAN

***Siple's Garden Seat,*** 1234 Druid Road, Clearwater (442-9681). For 50 years the Siple family has served good prime ribs, seafood, steaks and ham dinners as well as special pies for dessert—macadamia nut is the customer's favorite. Reservations suggested. Open seven days a week. Entrées from $2.65 (L), $3.95 (D). AE, MC, V.

## CONTINENTAL

***Peter's Place,*** 208 Beach Drive Northeast, St. Petersburg (822-8436). Intimate and elegant. The menu at this small restaurant changes daily with entrées of seafood, beef, chicken, capon and crab in crêpes, with rice (in ramekins), most sauced. Reservations necessary. Monday through Wednesday, lunch only. Closed Sunday. Complete lunch from $6, fixed-price dinner $15.50. AE, CB, DC, MC, V.

***Bon Appetit,*** 148 Marina Plaza, Dunedin (733-2151). Looks out over the Intracoastal Waterway to the Gulf of Mexico. An appetizer cart features house pâté. Other offerings vary daily. Veal Oskar and Zingara (wine, shallots, ham and paprika) are specialties. Dessert cart offers pecan pie, mousse, strudel. Reservations suggested. Open seven days a week. Dinner only. Entrées from $6.95. MC, V.

## FRENCH

***Rollande et Pierre,*** 2221 Fourth Street North, St. Petersburg (822-4602). This cozy place offers French provincial décor, several dining rooms, steaks (a wise choice is *au poivre*), red snapper, pompano, scallops, chicken Elizabeth (with cheese or with green grapes). Cherries Jubilee and crêpes Suzette are flamed tableside. Dinner only. Closed Sunday. Entrées from $6.95. AE, CB, DC, MC, V.

***Le Pompano,*** 19325 Gulf Boulevard, Indian Shores (596-0333). A new and handsome wooden structure looks out over the Intracoastal Waterway and features, of course, pompano. Other fish and seafood (with sauces or broiled) are featured on the entrée list. Michel

Denis is the owner and chef. Dinner only. Closed Sunday. Entrées from $5.75. AE, CB, DC, MC, V.

***L'Auberge du Bon Vivant,*** 7003 Gulf of Mexico Drive, Long Boat Key, Sarasota (383-2481). Customers come in droves to this enticing little spot near the Gulf of Mexico. Uncluttered inside with nice lamps and dark timbers on the walls. A brace of husbands cook while their wives work as hostesses. Vegetable side dishes such as sliced potatoes, onion and green beans; green salad with a lovely lemon dressing and carefully sliced tomatoes and cucumbers show the chefs' broad tastes. Vichyssoise, veal scaloppini, *coquilles St.-Jacques,* and a trifle with grapes and almonds are popular choices. Reservations a must. Dinner only. Closed Sunday. Entrées from $6.75. AE, MC, V.

## GREEK

***Louis Pappas,*** 10 West Dodecanese Boulevard, Tarpon Springs (937-5101). There are other Greek restaurants in Tarpon Springs, but begin with this one. It's the largest, and the newest, and dominates the scene. Pappas Greek salad (which includes shrimp and potato salad) was originated with the first Pappas restaurant years ago, and is now a specialty of the whole Sun Coast area. Order it for any number. Steaks, moussaka, pastichio and honey-sweet baklava are popular. Open seven days a week. Entrées from $3.25 (L), $4.25 (D). AE, DC, MC, V.

## ITALIAN

***Campanella's,*** 6665 Park Boulevard, Pinellas Park (546-3101). Ralph and Rita Campanella make all the pasta, soups, bread: "Everything is homemade," they say. While the small dining room may be crowded, it is a cozy and happy place. You get a lot of food for your money. Try tortellini *in brodo, fettuccine alla Campanella* and one of the crêpes with cheese and tomato sauce. Veal is a specialty, too. The dessert list features Italian rum cake. Pizzas are superior. Closed Monday. Entrées from $2.95 (L), $3.60 (D). MC, V.

## SPANISH

***Café Pepe,*** 2006 West Kennedy Boulevard, Tampa (253-6501). Black beans and rice, a big paella, shrimp in a special batter, flan, sangría. White-washed walls, crowded and noisy. House specials are shrimp à la Pepe, rich with lobster stuffing, and shrimp Suprema, wrapped with bacon. Flan, coconut ice cream and cheesecake. Closed Sunday. Entrées from $2.70 (L), $5.40 (D), paella $19.95 for two. AE, DC, MC, V.

***Pepin's,*** 4125 Fourth Street North, St. Petersburg (821-3773). Popular for both lunch and dinner. Salad Sevillana is a luncheon favorite. Shrimp Almendrina (with almonds) and shrimp Suprema (with bacon) are specialties of the house. Good sangría. Don't fail to order black beans and rice, or chicken with yellow rice. No reservations. Closed Monday. Entrées from $1.50 (L), $3.95 (D), paella $19.75 for two. AE, MC, V.

***Tio Pepe,*** 2930 Gulf-To-Bay, Clearwater (725-3082). Remodeled house with Spanish décor, and a bake oven beside the door for homemade breads. Owner José Rodriqez, a brother of Pepin (above), has a similar menu. The dark bread is a house specialty along with shrimp Suprema and fish dishes such as trout à la Rusa, topped with breadcrumbs. No reservations. Closed Monday. Entrées from $2.95 (L), $6.65 (D), paella $19.95 for two. MC, V.

# SPECIALTY COOKING

## SEAFOOD

***Fisherman's Inn,*** 9595 Fourth Street North, St. Petersburg (576-4252). Near the turn-off for Gandy Bridge-Causeway and Derby Lane dog track. Several dining rooms with beautiful wood and stained glass. The large bar-lounge is now a discotheque; a room next to it has a popcorn machine, huge TV screen, aquarium. Seafood specialties include fried mullet, scamp, catfish, grouper, lobster, several kinds of crab, shrimp. Sunday, dinner only. Open seven days a week. Entrées from $2.25 (L), $2.95 (D). MC, V.

***Heilman's Beachcomber,*** 447 Mandalay Avenue, Clearwater Beach (442-4144). A dependable, large restaurant. Stone crab claws (in season), frogs' legs, shrimp Rockefeller, grouper, red snapper. Maine lobster and Alaska King crab for bored natives. Dessert treats include Alaska meringue pie and an ice-cream-filled pastry shell topped with chocolate sauce. Reservations suggested. Open seven days a week. Entrées from $3 (L), $6 (D). AE, DC, MC, V.

***Marina Jack,*** Marina Plaza, downtown Sarasota (365-4232). A modernistic building with several levels and a beautiful view of water and skyline. Large menu carries 40 items with seafoods featured (red snapper, grouper, and some good *au gratins*). Homemade desserts include Black-Bottom and Derby pies, plus a great, authentic Key lime pie. Reservations necessary. Open seven days a week. Entrées from $3 (L), $5.25 (D). No credit cards.

***Gene's Lobster House,*** 565 150th Avenue, Madeira Beach (391-0238). Recently remodeled, the dining rooms have a California-Danish look and offer views of the Intracoastal Waterway. Escargots are served on mushrooms. Fish specials change daily. Steaks are charbroiled as are grouper filets and swordfish. Crab Imperial and shrimp Madeira are justly popular. Desserts are made on the premises and include Key lime pie and orange-chocolate mousse. Reservations suggested, especially during the winter visitor season. Open seven days a week. Entrées from $1.80 (L), $4.95 (D). AE, MC, V.

***Crawdaddy's,*** 2500 Rocky Point Road, Tampa (885-7407). On the east side of Courtney Campbell Parkway. Dinner in an old fish house on the bayou? Not really, but it's fun. This new building looks ancient with an old bus and chickens in the yard, and a creaky front porch. Inside, memorabilia hangs, peers, drapes, lies and folds around corners, walls, shelves, pipes and railings on seven dining levels. You may have a "show" out the window—crab fishermen wading in Tampa Bay or a thundershower across the way. Crawdaddy pie with seafood and potatoes, crunchy bass, lobster Whiskey, shrimp Newburg and steaks are featured. Reservations for seven or more only. Open seven days a week. Entrées from $2.95 (L), $6.95 (D). AE, MC, V.

***Sea Wolf,*** 4115 East Busch Boulevard, Tampa (985-3112). Here's a dining adventure coupled with some good food. The mammoth parking area is usually filled and so are the waiting rooms, but there are aquariums and plenty to look at: a stuffed Kodiak bear, a mountain goat, a lion and moose heads decorate the Teddy Roosevelt lounge where you wait and watch a screen for your number to be called. A salad bar in each dining room precedes a platter of beautiful rock lobster tail, shrimp in ramekin, scallops in butter, stuffed mushrooms and corn fritters. Steaks, chicken and ham are also featured. Open seven days a week. Entrées from $2.15 (L), $3.89 (D). AE, CB, DC, MC, V.

## SMOKED FISH

***Ted Peters,*** 1350 Pasadena Avenue South, South Pasadena (381-7931). This small restaurant features an outdoor dining area, a smokehouse and a ranch-style indoor dining room. Smoked fish is a popular Gulf Coast specialty. Here the choices are mullet and mackerel. Eat the fish with German potato salad and order enough to take home. Smoked fish freezes nicely. Informal attire and pleasant aroma of smoking fish. Closed Tuesday. Entrées from $2.95 (L), $3.95 (D). No credit cards.

# FOR INDIVIDUAL NEEDS

## IF YOU HAVE TIME FOR ONLY ONE MEAL

***Bill Nagy's,*** 10400 Gandy Boulevard, St. Petersburg (577-1565). (See description under BIG DEAL/WORTH IT.)

***Bern's Steak House,*** 1208 South Howard Avenue, Tampa (251-2421). (See description under BIG DEAL/WORTH IT.)

***The Wine Cellar,*** 17307 Gulf Boulevard, North Redington Beach (393-3491). (See description under BIG DEAL/WORTH IT.)

***Café L'Europe,*** 431 Harding Circle (St. Armand's Circle), Sarasota (388-4415). (See description under BIG DEAL/WORTH IT.)

## BEST HOTEL MEAL

***Don CeSar Beach Resort Hotel,*** 3400 Gulf Boulevard, St. Petersburg Beach (360-1881). The "Pink Palace," as it is called, is an historical landmark worth visiting. Food quality varies, but chicken Florentine (with ham and almond sauce) is a favorite. Veal Oscar, prime ribs. Fifth-floor restaurant: dinner only. Open seven days a week. Entrées from $8.50. Bistro: Open seven days a week. Entrées from $2.95 (L), $4.25 (D). AE, CB, DC, MC, V.

***The Peppercorn Restaurant,*** Hyatt House, 1000 Boulevard of the Arts, Watergate Center, Sarasota (366-9000). Duckling a specialty—Madagascar, l'Orange, Scandinavian (with lingonberries) or roasted with honey and almonds. Open seven days a week. Entrées from $3.25 (L), $9.95 (D). AE, CB, DC, MC, V.

## BUSINESS BREAKFAST

***Owl Restaurant,*** 241 Fourth Street North, St. Petersburg (822-3542). Thirty-one years in same location, near downtown. The homemade donuts are famous. Numerous shelves are populated by all manner of owls. Open all night, but checks are paid before food is brought to the table. Open seven days a week. Breakfasts from $1.25 (one egg, strip bacon, grits, toast, coffee refilled) to $4.80 (steak, eggs). No credit cards.

***Ponce de Leon Hotel Corner Café,*** 95 Central Avenue, St. Petersburg (822-4139). Newly redecorated coffee shop with cheerful palm-tree wallpaper, plants. Rolled blueberry pancakes a feature. Convenient for sportsfishermen and sailing crews from city marina nearby. Open seven days a week during winter visitor season. Breakfast from $1. MC, V.

***The Loading Dock,*** 100 Madison East, Tampa (223-9540). Small, modern restaurant in renovated brick building, nice wood, plants. Danish pastry, ham, egg-and-cheese breakfast sandwich. Closed Saturday and Sunday. Breakfasts from $1.25. No credit cards.

***Robby's,*** 10925 Gulf Boulevard, Treasure Island (360-4253). Waffles, English muffins and pancakes, including chocolate, blueberry, banana, strawberry and others. Open seven days a week. Breakfasts from $1.30. No credit cards.

***Palmer House,*** 1 North Trail, Junction Highway 41 and Gulfstream (955-6384). Motel coffee shop with steak and eggs, pancakes, omelets. Open seven days a week. Breakfast from $1.49. MC, V.

## BUSINESS LUNCH

***Ten Beach Drive,*** 10 Beach Drive Northeast, St. Petersburg (894-6398). Downstairs in Ponce de Leon Hotel. Early-American décor. Small bar, cheerful management. Large sandwiches, excellent potato salad, daily specials. Closed Sunday. Entrées from $1.75 (L), $4.95 (D). MC, V.

***Peter's Place,*** 208 Beach Drive Northeast, St. Petersburg (822-8436). (See description under CONTINENTAL.)

***Tower Eight,*** First Financial Tower Building, 8th floor, Tampa (223-5451). Reasonably priced cafeteria, favorite of office workers from nearby. Antipasto, beef stew, country steak, homemade pies, cobblers, puddings. Menu changes daily. Lunch only. Closed Saturday and Sunday. Entrées from $1.35. No credit cards.

***Gene's Lobster House,*** 565 150th Avenue, Madeira Beach (391-0283). (See description under SEAFOOD.)

***Colombia,*** Harding Circle (St. Armand's Circle), Sarasota (388-3987). Spanish food draws shoppers. Black bean soup, Spanish bean soup, Cuban sandwiches, chicken and yellow rice. Open seven days a week. Entrées from $3.95 (L), $6.50 (D). AE, CB, DC, MC, V.

# FOR DRINKS

***CK's,*** atop the Host International Hotel, Tampa Airport (879-5151). Striking, modern décor in a revolving dining room with airport view. Open seven days a week. AE, CB, DC, MC, V.

***Rollande et Pierre,*** 2221 Fourth Street North, St. Petersburg (822-4602). (See description under FRENCH.) A popular postwork watering hole for local businessmen.

***Don CeSar Beach Resort Hotel,*** 3400 Gulf Boulevard, St. Petersburg Beach (360-1881). (See description under BEST HOTEL MEAL.) A comfortable fifth-floor bar in a refurbished '20's boom-time hotel. A combo plays for dancing during the season.

# SUNDAY-EVENING MEAL

***Bill Nagy's,*** 10400 Gandy Boulevard, St. Petersburg (577-1565). (See description under BIG DEAL/WORTH IT.)

***Bern's Steak House,*** 1208 South Howard Avenue, Tampa (251-2421). (See description under BIG DEAL/WORTH IT.)

# FOR FAMILIES WITH CHILDREN

***Old Swiss House,*** Busch Gardens (988-9161). A colorful glassed-in room overlooking the veldt with all the animals at Busch Gardens. Sauerbraten and steak Diane a dinner specialty. Reservation not necessary. Open seven days a week. Entrées from $3.50 (L), $7.50 (D). AE, CB, DC, MC, V.

# LATE-NIGHT SERVICE

***Ten Beach Drive,*** 10 Beach Drive Northeast, St. Petersburg (894-6398). (See description under BUSINESS LUNCH.) At night, tableside cooking, with steak Diane, *au poivre,* veal. Dinners until midnight, seven days a week. Entrées from $4.95. MC, V.

***Malio's Steak House,*** 301 South Dale Mabry Highway, Tampa (879-3233). Part of the building is now a private club, but anyone can eat in the large bar-lounge. Steaks, ribs, veal, chicken Florentine. Closed Sunday. Full meals until 11 P.M. Entrées from $3.25 (L), $6.50 (D). AE, CB, DC, MC, V.

***The Buccaneer,*** 595 Dream Island Road, Long Boat Key, Sarasota (383-1101). Resort-marina motel has large dining room. Lobster, steaks, chops, prime ribs. Full service until 11 P.M. Late supper menu with sandwiches; try a Pirate Beef sandwich on French bread.

Open seven days a week. Entrées from $4.50 (L), $7 (D); supper entrées from $5.95. AE, CB, DC, MC, V.

***Lenny Dee's King's Inn,*** 10551 Gulf Boulevard, Treasure Island (360-3660). Lenny Dee entertains at the console organ. Steaks, chops. Dancing. Full service until midnight. Dinner only. Closed Sunday and Monday. Entrées from $5.95. AE, MC, V.

# MARKETS

***Fonte's Finer Foods,*** 4910 Central Avenue, St. Petersburg (345-1756). This family store offers ethnic foods from around the world. Closed Sunday. No credit cards.

***Whaley's Produce Market,*** 533 South Howard Avenue, Tampa (257-5171), 4205 North Florida Avenue, Tampa (239-9914). Pick out citrus here to carry home. Special bags provided. Closed Sunday. No credit cards.

## GIFT FOODS/WINES

***Imperial Chateau,*** 2600 Fourth Street North, St. Petersburg (822-9520). Wines from around the world and wine-oriented accessories. Closed Sunday. MC, V.

***Swiss Colony,*** 130 Clearwater Mall, Clearwater (726-4026). Cheese and assorted sausages boxed for mailing. Candy and petit fours. Open seven days a week. MC, V.

***Gourmet Wine and Cheese Shop, Inc.,*** 301 Westshore Boulevard, Tampa (879-4696). Gift baskets from $20, with cheese, wines, gourmet canned foods and mustards. Open seven days a week. MC, V.

# Honolulu

Although it has often been said, and with good reason, that one can't eat the ambience, the two often are inseparable in Hawaii's best restaurants. Most travelers, including business visitors, tend to select establishments that combine good cuisine with a sense of place—a dream of Hawaii, if you will. In a few publicized restaurants the dream is considerably more substantial than the victuals, but in others the merger succeeds.

The fact that hotel restaurants tend to dominate the culinary scene sets Honolulu apart from most mainland cities. There is good reason for this. Prior to the great tourist influx in the years since World War II, restaurant fare in Hawaii ranged from bad to a good deal worse. Only the pre-Sheraton Royal Hawaiian, then the Queen of Waikiki Beach, set a respectable table, save for **Wo Fat** and one or two other Cantonese establishments. It is significant that the few survivors of a 1932 dinner served to 100 people by dredging tycoon Walter Dillingham remember the tablecloth—a two-inch-thick blanket of pressed orchids—but not what was on it.

The Royal has long since been eclipsed, but hotels—or restaurants located in hotels—still set the gastronomical pace. From 1964 until the early '70's, the Kahala Hilton was the acknowledged leader, and its **Maile Room** and **Hala Terrace** are still in the top bracket; but they are no longer unchallenged. The oddly named **Bagwell's 2424** at the Hyatt Regency (with Honolulu's best wine list) and **The Third Floor** at the Hawaiian Regent rate with the Kahala rooms as the *luxe* Continental restaurants in Honolulu. (Given Hawaii's complex racial mix—a plurality of minorities—it is hard to designate *any* restaurant as "American," whereas "Continental," a grab-bag term on the mainland, has a more precise meaning in the Islands: a mixture of the cuisine of two continents, the American and European.)

The postwar years have also brought a great expansion of ethnic restaurants, led by the Chinese and the ascendant Japanese. The **Mandarin Palace,** with its Hong Kong distillation of many regional cuisines, has moved to the front in a mere three years; but **King Tsin** and **Winter Garden** provide excellent Northern and Western cuisine. The Mandarin and Maple Garden are equally esteemed by many. Most Japanese restaurants attempt to combine menus that are rigorously separated in Japan itself, with **Kyo-ya** (Classic), **Mon Cher Ton Ton** (modern), and **Ideta** (a little of both) exemplifying this trend. Osaka Yakiniku and **Furusato Sushi** are still dedicated to specialty cooking. Thus far only two good Filipino restaurants have surfaced—**Barrio Fiesta** in Waikiki and Mabuhay downtown in Mamie Stover country. The Portuguese, who in 1979 celebrated their centennial in Hawaii, have yet to open a good restaurant (several Portuguese favorites, notably bean soup, sausage and tripe, have been co-opted by other ethnic groups). And although there are many Puerto Ricans in the Islands, there is no Caribbean *restorán.*

During the '50's and early '60's there were two exceptions to hotel dominance: the authentically French restaurants of Michel Martin, whose **Chez Michel** remains at the top of an expanding category (a tiny bistro, **Le Café de Paris,** is rising fast), and Canlis, a steakhouse now in decline, though it serves some fine pan-fried seafood. **Matteo's** has forced both Trattoria and Rudy's to raise their Italian sights, but not high enough. In an ocean full of fish, **Nick's Fishmarket** is the only world-class fish house.

Two "hot food" restaurants, the Korean **Ji Young** and the Thai **Mekong,** are both hotter and better than most of the many Mexican cantinas, though **Popo's** offers good if relatively mild Guadalajara dishes. Pubs abound, but only **Dickens** is really serious about food. Beware fake ethnics—the ubiquitous "Smorgies" are second-rate cafeterias masquerading as *smörrebrod.* There are a number of other "pseudos," the best-attended (and worst) begin the hotel *luaus* (feasts) where catered—and emasculated—Hawaiian food is served. If you want to try the native dishes, go to **Helena's** or **The Willows.**

Some Hawaiian words may confound the first-time visitor, especially the universally applied synonym for hors d'oeuvre—*pu-pu's.* So may the *pu-pu* bar, a Hawaiian version of Ginza (and mainland) strip-tease-cum-B-girl establishments. There are hundreds, providing "free" *pu-pu's* with overpriced drinks. Many legitimate bars offer excellent (and really free) *pu-pu's* at Happy Hour, when bar drinks are doubled in size.

Food shoppers will find the **Ala Moana Farmers' Market** rewarding, and **Tamashiro's** fish market an astonishing visual experience. There are no gift wine shops worth the shipping costs, and no wide-spectrum gourmet-food gift establishments (Maui's celebrated potato chips are obtainable only on Maui).

Honolulu is an early town (business hours often run from 7:30 A.M. to 3:30 P.M.), and restaurant hours reflect that fact. The few restaurants that do not serve liquor permit you to bring your own and will supply glasses. In Waikiki, tips of at least 20 percent are expected; in downtown restaurants and smaller, ethnic establishments 15 percent will do (there is no formal captain-waiter split in Hawaii).

# Restaurants and Food Sources

**(Area code: 808)**

## BIG DEAL

### WORTH IT

***The Hala Terrace,*** Kahala Hilton Hotel, 5000 Kahala Avenue (734-2211). The seaside terrace at the Kahala is a big deal gastronomically all day long, but the finest hour for Executive Chef Martin Wiss comes just after sunset. At 7 P.M., the Hala is transformed into a dinner showcase for entertainer Danny Kaleikini, and at about the same time Wiss begins serving an elaborate (and much admired) repast in the nearby Maile Room (see description under CONTINENTAL). His menu for the terrace is limited, but it offers some 36 choices—Westphalian ham with asparagus, filet of *mahi mahi* (the best in the Islands) and rum-flavored macadamia-nut soufflé. The Kaleikini show, with three talented (and sexy) hula dancers, a fire dancer and the ingratiating Kaleikini singing and playing the Hawaiian nose flute, is the most stylish in Hawaii. Cover charge, $6. Make reservations at least one day ahead. Chaîne des Rotisseurs. Closed Sunday. Entrées from $4 (L), $14.75 (D). AE, CB, DC, MC, V.

***Nick's Fishmarket,*** Waikiki Gateway Hotel, 2070 Kalakaua (955-6333). (Valet parking on Kuhio Avenue.) An extraordinary restaurant, which already has branched out to Beverly Hills and Chicago. Scampi, *sashimi,* fresh Blue Points, recognizable oysters Rockefeller, and many fish from Hawaiian waters—*ulua* (jack), *ono* (wahoo), *opakapaka* (snapper), *mahi mahi* (dolphin), swordfish, Maui catfish, prepared in a variety of ways. Softshell crabs and turtle steaks are flown in from the East Coast and Grand Cayman, as well as lobsters from Maine ($22.50) and Louisiana prawns, frogs' legs and oysters. Steaks for non-fish eaters; Greek-accented salads. The wine list is particularly strong in whites, ranging from La Blanc de Blanc, Wente Brothers ($9) to Batard Montrachet, Joseph Drouhin ($50). The best-drilled waiters in Hawaii are omnipresent but unintrusive. Dinner only. Open seven days a week. Table d'hôte from $17.75, entrées from $11.50. AE, DC, MC, V.

# BIG DEAL

## NOT WORTH IT

***Michel's at the Colony Surf,*** 2895 Kalakaua Avenue (923-6552). If ambience were the only measure, this elegantly appointed, crystal-chandeliered seaside room—billed as "Hawaii's very French restaurant"—would win going away. By day Michel's provides an intimate view of the golden crescent of Waikiki; by night the lights dance before your eyes (but so do the dinner prices, many of them sky-high for food that can be excellent but often is mediocre). But Michel's main flaw, pretensions aside, is its unimaginative, uninformative and often misspelled wine list. Stick to California wines. Michel's is better in daylight (see descriptions under BUSINESS BREAKFAST and SUNDAY BRUNCH). Jackets required at dinner. Saturday, dinner only. Open seven days a week. Entrées from $5 (L), $12 (D). AE, CB, DC, MC, V.

***All commercial luaus*** (hotel or other).

# INTERNATIONAL

## BRITISH

***Dickens British Pub,*** 1221 Kapiolani Boulevard (531-2727). An oasis for Britishers homesick for fog (in short supply here), Dickens is a pub in name only, though it does have a fine selection of English and Irish beers and ales. An extensive menu lists 18 identifiably British dishes, including cock-a-leekie soup, beefsteak-and-kidney pie, angels on horseback, Toad-in-the-Hole. The Colonies Beef Burger has enough chopped choice for five Big Macs. Ten varieties of after dinner coffee. Open seven days a week, late supper until 1 A.M. (see description under LATE-NIGHT SERVICE). Entrées from $3.95 (L & D). AE, CB, DC, MC, V.

# CONTINENTAL

***Bagwell's 2424,*** Hyatt Regency, 2424 Kalakaua Avenue (922-9292). Bagwell's is beautifully appointed, decorated with tiny, twinkling lights and luxurious lounge-chair seating; but the real beauty is in the food—Hawaiian *sashimi* (raw fish), *opihi* (limpet), octopus and seaweed salad, country pâté and a "gazpacho cocktail" that evoked a whole column by James Beard. Among entrées: roasted quails basted with muscat, sweetbreads sautéed *beurre noir* and a three-pepper steak. The wine list is unequaled in Hawaii (for details see BEST WINE LIST). Jackets suggested, reservations required. Chaîne des Rotisseurs. Dinner only. Open seven days a week. Entrées from $13. AE, CB, DC, MC, V.

***The Third Floor,*** Hawaiian Regent Hotel, 2552 Kalakaua Avenue (922-6611). This spectacular room, with its three-story-high beamed ceiling and a horn-of-plenty entrance display of fresh fruit, seafood, breads and fresh-cut flowers, promises a bit more than it delivers. Its relish tray and *naan* bread—with a delicate, spreadable pâté—are a delight, but entrées can be inconsistent and service slow. Usually reliable: rack of lamb Provençale (ask for caper sauce), and medallions of venison forestière, in a cream sauce with chanterelles. Desserts are upstaged by ice-cream bonbons, floating on a tray of smoking dry ice. Jackets recommended. Chaîne des Rotisseurs. Dinner only. Open seven days a week. Entrées from $15.75. AE, CB, DC, MC, V.

***Maile Room,*** Kahala Hilton, 5000 Kahala Avenue (734-2211). Dinner at the Maile is prix-fixe at $24.50, reasonable enough given the *nouvelle cuisine* artistry of Chef Martin Wiss. Gleaming crystal, crisp napery and an atmosphere of understated, unhurried elegance provide an appropriate setting for such Wiss creations as oysters Florentine on Pernod-flavored spinach, and *opakapaka* Kahala (medaillons of fresh Island pink snapper in a creamed white-wine sauce). Jackets recommended. Reservations required. Dinner only. Open seven days a week. AE, CB, DC, MC, V.

# CHINESE

***Mandarin Palace,*** Miramar Hotel, 2345 Kuhio Avenue (922-1666). If the Palace did nothing else, its instant (and perfect) Peking duck would make it the best Chinese restaurant in Hawaii. The duck ($22, serves six) is not really "instant," but it is offered on a half-hour's notice. The cuisine is a fusion of Mandarin, Hunan, Szechwan, Shanghai and Cantonese styles. Bean curd stuffed with shrimp, minced squab, sizzling beef in satay sauce. Braised imperial shark's fin soup for four ($39.80), vagabond's chicken for six ($25). Bilingual, Shanghai-born Nancy Chu presides over the Mandarin's handsome dining room. Chaîne des Rotisseurs. Open seven days a week. Buffet lunch, $4.75; entrées from $4.75 (D). AE, DC, MC, V.

***King Tsin,*** 1486 South King Street (946-3273). The only elegance in this small storefront restaurant is in the menu, dedicated to Northern, Hunan and Szechwan food of unimpeachable quality. Szechwan steamed five-spice duck, Hunan ham with leeks, a deluxe cold combination plate (drunken chicken, smoked fish, five-spice beef, Hunan preserved hog, jellyfish and abalone). Chef's deluxe 12-course dinner for 10, $150. Reservations required. Open seven days a week. Entrées from $2.95 (L & D), with more than 100 choices. AE, DC, MC, V.

***Winter Garden,*** Kahala Mall (Waialae at Kilauea), (732-5505). Under the redoubtable Nancy Chu, now at the Mandarin Palace, the Winter Garden was Honolulu's temple of Northern and Western cuisine. It sagged with her departure, but is now recovering. Spring rolls, shredded beef with chilis, Chinaman's Hat (named for a local island—shredded pork and vegetables in a light, rolled crêpe), bean curd and minced meat with noodles. (Chili dishes are softened for Western palates unless you specify "hot hot.") Sunday, dinner only. Open seven days a week. Entrées from $3.50 (L & D). AE, DC, MC, V.

***Wo Fat,*** 115 North Hotel Street (533-6393). Honolulu's oldest Chinese restaurant (since 1882), a garish, pagoda-roofed shrine to undiluted Cantonese cuisine. At the epicenter of the one-time red-light district, now devoted to watching (porn movies) and walking (street). Wo Fat has an enormous menu, but to enjoy Cantonese *haute cuisine* go with a friend who speaks the dialect. Tourists served with considerable surliness. Open seven days a week. Entrées from $2.60 (all day). Nine-course dinners (for 10) from $85 to $300. AE, CB, DC, MC, V.

***Asian Garden,*** 1110 McCully (955-6674). Basically Cantonese but with many Northern dishes. The best meal-in-itself Chinese dish in Honolulu is *wor gau gee* (specify no noodles). A full 32 ounces of savory fish broth, stocked with *gau gee* packets (translucent steamed dough wrappers around minced pork), *char siu* (sweet pork), *bok choy,* water chestnuts, bamboo shoots, twice-cooked pork, sliced carrots, mushrooms, and shrimp. It costs $2.50. *Jook*—a rice soup that supposedly enhances virility—is available from 8 P.M. on. Open seven days a week, until midnight Sunday through Thursday, until 1 A.M. Friday and Saturday. Entrées from $2.75 (L & D); seven-course dinner (for 10) $105. MC, V.

***Yong Sing,*** 1055 Alakea Street (531-1336). (See description under DIM SUM.)

## FILIPINO

***Barrio Fiesta,*** 1887-A Kalakaua Avenue (941-9794). The first Filipino restaurant to make the quantum jump from the downtown Tenderloin to Waikiki, the Fiesta offers reassurance for the timid visitor and a challenge to the daring. *Kare-kare* (oxtails, tripe and crisp green beans in a mild, peanutty gravy) and *bangos sinigang* (imported milk-fish steaks in a zesty peppery fish broth) should frighten no one. Neither would *di-nugu-an,* if the diner would just eat and not ask what the menu notation "Filipino Chocolate Meat" really means (pig intestines in a rich, dark sauce somewhere between *en su tinta* and *mole*). For dessert don't miss *halo-halo,* a lovely mess of fresh fruit, imported Magnolia (brand) ice cream, and shaved ice. No liquor. Open seven days a week. Entrées from $3.50 (L & D). No credit cards.

## FRENCH

***Chez Michel,*** 2126-B Kalakaua Avenue (923-0626). Michel Martin, the volatile Niçois who presides over this tiny *boîte* (which shares a Waikiki *cul de sac* with the Parisian Body Rub Parlor), operates on the better mousetrap principle. He introduced French cuisine to Hawaii in 1946 at remote Wahiawa, near Schofield Barracks, spent a few spotlighted years endowing Michel's at The Colony Surf with his name and the reputation it still enjoys, and then tried to hide again here. No mice have come, but prides of lions (social and culinary) have entered Chez Michel's tender trap to feast on fresh mountain trout, real scampi (*langoustine*), home-style vichyssoise, and an endive-mushroom salad bathed in Michel's marvelously herbed vinaigrette dressing. An extensive wine list for a small restaurant, all good and some great. Closed Sunday. Entrées from $5.25 (L), $8.50 (D). AE, CB, DC, MC, V.

***Le Café de Paris,*** 1778 Ala Moana Boulevard at Discovery Bay (947-6467). During the seven years he served as sommelier at the

Kahala Hilton's Maile room, Belgian Claude Leruitte dreamed of marrying Yoshiko, a beautiful Kyoto-born Japanese waitress, and starting his own restaurant. Now he has achieved both, and the couple's tiny Café de Paris, a self-proclaimed bistro, is serving dishes (and sauces) never before seen in Honolulu: a superb *confit de canard,* red snapper in a variation on sauce poulette, and *coquilles St. Jacques* in a light, delicate cream of curry. Chef Girard Reversade, who was brought from Biarritz two years ago as chef *saucier* for an ambitious venture that failed, has had much to do with the bistro's success. Reservations only until 7:30 P.M. Dinner only; late supper till 1:30 A.M., Friday and Saturday. Closed Sunday. Entrées from $10. AE, MC, V.

***Le Bistro,*** 1647 Kapiolani Boulevard (955-3331). (See description under LATE-NIGHT SERVICE.)

## HAWAIIAN

***Helena's Hawaiian Foods,*** 1364 N. King Street (845-8044). Helena Chock, a Chinese, has operated Honolulu's most authentic Hawaiian restaurant in ramshackle Kalihi for 33 years. Such aboriginal dishes as *laulau* (pork and taro leaves wrapped in ti leaves and steamed for hours), *opihi* (limpet) and *poi* (which should be considered an accompaniment, like potatoes in Western cuisine) are served in an almost bare room. *Pipikaula,* a moist Hawaiian version of beef jerky, is barbecued to make a delicious *pu-pu* (hors d'oeuvre). *Haupia,* the native coconut pudding, is the best in town. Helena's serves no drinks. Closed Sunday through Tuesday. Entrées from 85 cents (L & D). No credit cards. A comparable menu at somewhat higher prices (from $1.75) with liquor and wine is available at **Hanks,** 1137 Eleventh Avenue (735-1755). Or, if you just want to dip one toe in the Hawaiian culinary pool, you can do so at the **Poi Bowl** (from $1.50), a tiny but good fast-food outlet in the vast Ala Moana Center (no phone, no liquor, no reservations).

***The Willows,*** 901 Hausten Street (946-4808). If Helena's offers infinite culinary riches in an austere atmosphere, the Willows reverses the process. Most of the time it serves mediocre Caucasian food in an ambience of great beauty, but it is partially redeemed on Friday and Saturday by a $9 "Hawaiian dinner" (both days) and a "Hawaiian lunch" (Saturday only). *Laulau,* sweet potato, lomi salmon, *pipikaula,* chicken luau (cooked with taro leaves), poi and *haupia* (coconut pudding), all done reasonably well. Closed Sunday. Entrées from $3.50 (L), $7 (D). AE, CB, DC, MC, V.

## ITALIAN

***Matteo's,*** Marine Surf Hotel, 364 Seaside Avenue (922-5551). (Valet parking at Kuhio Avenue entrance.) Matteo's is likely to appease, if not entirely satisfy, visitors who are nostalgic for New York, San Francisco or Los Angeles. It offers a mixture of Neapolitan and Northern Italian cookery, none of it original but all of it sound. *Saltimbocca* and other scaloppine dishes are deservedly popular. The wine list is short. (Matteo's has a downtown branch at 2 Merchant Street, 524-4870, which serves lunch. It is closed Saturday and Sunday.) Dinner only. Open seven days a week, until 12:30 A.M. Entrées from $5.75. AE, CB, DC, MC, V.

## JAPANESE

***Kyo-ya,*** 2057 Kalakaua Avenue (947-3911). This pagoda-roofed restaurant, authentic both in cuisine and in its spare, *shoji*-screened décor, has the look of Old Japan. It combines most of Japan's specialities in one menu. *Tonkatsu* (fried pork cutlets, currently a rage in Tokyo), butterfish *misoyaki* (in miso sauce), tempura, *shabu-shabu* and *unagi* (broiled eel). Kyo-ya also has wells for stiff Caucasian legs under some of its teahouse tables. Closed Sunday. Entrées from $3.75 (L), $7.50 (D). AE, DC, MC, V.

***Mon Cher Ton Ton,*** Ala Moana Americana Hotel, 410 Atkinson Drive (955-4811). Several Waikiki hotels have Japanese restaurants, but none quite compare with this serene, high-ceilinged and sparely-but-authentically decorated room, either in quiet ambience or diversity of cuisine. A popular half-way house between Waikiki and downtown Honolulu for business people, Mon Cher Ton Ton offers tempura, *shabu-shabu, yakitori, kushiyaki, teppanyaki* and the look of New Japan. Chaîne des Rotisseurs. Saturday, dinner only. Closed Sunday. Entrées from $4.75 (L), $8.75 (D). AE, CB, DC, MC, V.

***Irifune,*** 563 Kapahulu Avenue (737-1141). This badly decorated little box (it seats only 24) is in a storefront a half-mile from Waikiki, but it has one of the most varied of Japanese menus. Chef Hitoshi Ishizawa prepares tempura, *tonkatsu, yosenabe, kushiyaki, donburi, teriyaki,* curry, *yakitori*—available individually or in plate combinations from $2.50 (L & D). No liquor. Sunday, dinner only. Closed Tuesday. No credit cards.

***Miyako,*** Kaimana Beach Hotel, 2863 Kalakaua (923-4739). One of the first Honolulu restaurants to serve *shabu-shabu,* now featured in many restaurants. *Takara nabe,* another self-cooked meal (on a gas wok), confronts the diner with raw chicken, squid, octopus, king crab, shrimp, long rice, scallops, fish cake, cabbage, watercress, mushrooms and tofu. Tempura (first rate), *sashimi* and other delicacies à la carte. Sake and beer, along with full bar. No wine list. Dinner only. Open seven days a week. Entrées from $8.50. AE, CB, DC, MC, V.

***Furusato Sushi,*** Hyatt Regency, 2424 Kalakaua Avenue (922-4991—ask for the *sushi* bar). First Japan-quality *sushi* bar in Waikiki. *Sushi* is butterflied, mostly raw seafood impacted in cold vinegared rice, secured with *nori* (seaweed). Color photographs of available ingredients (order à la carte by pointing—Chef "Goro" Uyehara has flying fingers but speaks little English). Beer and sake only. *Sushi* selections from 90 cents (L & D). AE, CB, DC, MC, V.

## KOREAN

***Ji Young,*** 1677 Kapiolani Boulevard (946-7868). An uncompromising, utterly Korean restaurant that does not temper its basically flame-hot cuisine, though there are some mild dishes. Try fish in hot seasoned soup (listed under "stew"), barbecued short ribs, and steamed cold pork with a fiery dipping sauce. All meals accompanied by *namul* (spicy), *kim chee* (hot) and other definite vegetables. Wine by the glass, sake. Closed Sunday. Open until midnight Monday through Thursday, until 5 A.M. Friday and Saturday. Entrées from $2.50 (L & D). V.

## MEXICAN

***Popo's,*** 2112 Kalakaua Avenue (923-7355). A chef from Guadalajara provides credentials that make this airy, small but decorative room the best of many. Medium-hot food. *Nachos, burrito de cerdo* and *chalupa* are wise choices. Mexican beer, sangría, full bar. Sunday, dinner only. Open seven days a week. Entrées from $2.50 (L), $4.50 (D). AE, DC, MC, V.

## MOROCCAN

***Marrakech,*** 1855 Kalakaua Avenue (955-5566). The skillful belly dancer is the least novel part of this gaudy nightclub restaurant, its décor a well-cushioned mating of Louis XIV and Moorish harem. Marrakech not only prints its menu both in English and Arabic but compels you to eat with your fingers. Try Royal *b'stilla* (*pastilla* on the menu), chicken with figs and almonds, lamb with eggplant M'Derbel. Two shows: 7:30 and 9:30 Monday through Friday, 7 and 9 Saturday and Sunday. Reservations necessary. Dinner only. Open seven days a week. Table d'hôte from $15.50. AE, DC, MC, V.

---

## PAKISTANI

***Shalimar,*** 450 Lewers Street (923-2693). This superb restaurant, like the Indian subcontinent, is a bit schizophrenic—most of the time it labels itself "Pakistani," but it also proclaims "the authentic cuisine of India and Pakistan." *Naan, chapati* and *poori* breads, tandoori *murgh* (yogurt-marinated spiced chicken baked in the clay oven), *sag gosht* (tender chunks of lightly curried lamb buried in a creamed spinach). An unlisted (and unsurpassed) ice cream called *kulfi* that is heavier and richer than the American confection. Multilingual staff (one waiter speaks ten languages). Reservations recommended Saturday and Sunday, dinner only. Open seven days a week. Entrées from $3.25 (L), $4.50 (D). AE, CB, DC, MC, V.

---

## THAI

***Mekong,*** 1295 S. Beretanie Street (521-2025). About 45 diners can be accommodated in this recently expanded, gaily decorated duplex. The diner is invited to specify mild, medium or hot (a thoughtful precaution for tender palates). Risk the fire—especially with Evil Jungle Prince sliced meat (beef, pork or chicken) in hot spices with hot or sweet basil, or *Chieng Mai* meat salad set aflame by "a special Thai ingredient." A pleasant counterpoise: Thai garlic beef, pork or chicken, fragrant and relatively mild. Some 58 dishes, plus a special vegetarian menu. No liquor (but bring cold beer from the supermarket across the street; you'll need it). Saturday and Sunday, dinner only. Open seven days a week. Entrées from $2.50 (L & D). AE, MC, V.

# SPECIALTY COOKING

## DELI

***New York Deli,*** 1778 Ala Moana Boulevard (949-6661). Not quite Lindy's, but Manhattan street and subway signs, bagels, lox and cream cheese galore, stuffed cabbage, chopped liver, gefilte fish, kosher-style meat sandwiches, and chicken in the pot with matzoh ball. Large take-out and delicatessen counter. Full bar. Open seven days a week, 18 hours a day. Hot entrées from $4.95 (L & D). MC, V.

***Middle East Delicatessen & Bakery,*** 747 Queen Street (524-6823). Delicious *pita*-pocket sandwiches with *hommus, baba ghunoug, falafel, kibbee bi sa, neeye* and other exotics. Delicatessen includes Armenian string cheese, a dozen varieties of Greek and Middle Eastern olives and all of the sandwich ingredients. *Pita,* baklava and *maumoul* cookies baked on premises. Open 8 A.M. to 6 P.M. Closed Sunday. Entrées from $1.80. AE, CB, DC, MC, V.

## DIM SUM

***Yong Sing,*** 1055 Alakea Street (531-1366). Yong Sing is a full-service restaurant, but its specialty is *dim sum*—and you can order one or 30 of the little steamed or fried dumplings, each with a different filling. Open seven days a week, from 7:30 A.M. to 9:30 P.M. *Dim sum* from 30 cents to $1.40 per item. MC, V.

## SAIMIN

***Tanoue's in Kaimuki,*** 3538 Waialae Avenue (737-3939). A local corruption of "ramen" (the delicate, thin Japanese noodle), *saimin* (sye-min) is to Hawaii what the hot dog is to mainland America. Sold everywhere—at baseball and football games, hundreds of coffee counters and small stands. At worst it tastes like noodles warmed in dishwater. At best, which is to say Tanoue's, it is offered in five versions, all begun with a delicate fish broth and firm noodles. Toppings may include baby shrimp, shredded egg, the traditional *char siu* pork, green onions, seaweed and many others. No liquor. Sunday and Tuesday, breakfast and lunch only. Open seven days a week. Saimin from $1.75 (B, L & D). No credit cards.

## SANDWICH

***Heidi's,*** Ala Moana Building, 1441 Kapiolani Boulevard (949-2768). Begun a few years ago as a European bakery, Heidi's has grown to five locations, partly on the strength of its French, German and sourdough breads, and partly because it offers any of these oven delights wrapped around the best delicatessen meats available in Hawaii. Party platters catered. Open from 7:30 A.M. to 5 P.M. Closed Sunday. Sandwiches from $1.85. No credit cards.

## SEAFOOD

***Nick's Fishmarket,*** Waikiki Gateway Hotel, 2070 Kalakaua (955-6333). (See description under BIG DEAL/WORTH IT.)

***Ray's Seafood Restaurant,*** Waikiki Shopping Plaza, 2250 Kalakaua Avenue (923-5717). A serious—but still distant—challenge to Nick's Fishmarket, Ray's features a delectable, light, slightly lemony seafood soup, fresh Island fish, notably broiled *kahala* (amberjack), and Sam's special, which combines shrimp, zucchini and mushrooms. It's baked in a ceramic boat and topped with parmesan cheese and an excellent hollandaise. Huge oval bar with two "happy hours" (4 to 6 P.M., 10 P.M. to 1 A.M.). Saturday and Sunday, dinner only. Late supper served until 1 A.M. Open seven days a week. Entrées from $2.95 (L), $9 (D). AE, MC, V.

## STEAK/AMERICAN

***Bobby McGee's Conglomeration,*** 2885 Kalakaua Avenue (922-1282). One would hardly expect gourmet food at this island offshoot of a Western disco chain, but some of the dining rooms not only are almost out of earshot of the disco but all are out of sight for steaks—flavorful filet, tender sirloin. Deep-fried zucchini, a salad bar with fresh spinach and mushrooms, and hot apple pie in a honey-rum sauce. Wine list limited. Dinner only. Open seven days a week. Entrées from $7.95. AE, DC, MC, V.

## STEAK/JAPANESE

***Kobe Japanese Steak House,*** 1841 Ala Moana Boulevard (941-4444). The rage continues for *teppanyaki* (shrimp and steaks cut into bite-sized pieces by acrobatic chefs and grilled at special hot-slab tables, and usually served with bean sprouts and sliced onions, mushrooms and green peppers). The Kobe has no Kobe beef (rare even in Tokyo), but it has lobster and its table-chefs are skillful and relatively restrained. Reservations required. Dinner only. Open seven days a week. Entrées from $7.90. AE, CB, DC, MC, V.

***Tokyo Joe's,*** 1909 Ala Wai Boulevard (947-2848). Has equally good food but also features real gymnastics. Chefs juggle spatulas, play bongo solos on the hot slab while salting and peppering your beef, and occasionally flip a shrimp into a shirt or hip pocket. Dinner only. Open seven days a week. Entrées from $7.95. AE, DC, MC, V.

## VEGETARIAN

***Laulima,*** 1824 S. Beretania Street (947-3844). A skillful chef demonstrates some epicurean dimensions of vegetarian cookery. Avocados are employed in salads, sandwiches and, of course, guacamole; a papaya half is filled with fruits and topped with yogurt, nuts and honey; a "tasty *tostado*" brings a corn tortilla with refried beans, cheese, guacamole, tomato, sprouts and Laulima's own hot sauce. Closed Monday. No meat, no smoking, no reservations, no credit cards and no liquor. Entrées from $2.75 (L); special 6 P.M. dinner, $6.50.

# FOR INDIVIDUAL NEEDS

## IF YOU HAVE TIME FOR ONLY ONE MEAL

***The Hala Terrace,*** Kahala Hilton, 5000 Kahala Avenue (734-2211). (See description under BIG DEAL/WORTH IT.)

## BEST HOTEL MEAL

***Bagwell's 2424,*** Hyatt Regency Hotel, 2424 Kalakaua Avenue (922-9292). (See description under CONTINENTAL.)

## RESTAURANT NEAR AIRPORT

***Ideta,*** 620 Kohou Street (847-4844). A culinary pearl in the muddy sea of Kapalama. Great *sushi* bar, superb tempura (seven kinds), and a fantastic seafood stew, *chiri naba,* cooked for two on a table burner. Monday, lunch only. Sunday, dinner only. Open seven days a week. Entrées from $3.75 (L), $5.75 (D). AE, DC, MC, V.

## BUSINESS BREAKFAST

***Michel's at the Colony Surf,*** 2895 Kalakaua Avenue (923-6552). (See description under SUNDAY BRUNCH.) Quiet and pleasant setting, exceptional eggs Florentine, *opakapaka*, fresh strawberries, and, of course, fresh Island fruit.

## BUSINESS LUNCH

***Merchant Square Seafood Restaurant and Oyster Bar,*** 923 Nuuana Street (523-7906). Located in a historic downtown Honolulu area now being restored and revitalized, the Merchant Square Oyster Bar (most people drop the rest of the name) serves both lunch and dinner from the same pleasantly varied menu. It includes Island oysters, clams casino (unminced, uncrumbed, with a tiny curl of bacon), scallops *au gratin* with a touch of curry, and the fresh fish of the day. Large, well-lighted but patterned with a maze of booths that provides considerable privacy. Saturday and Sunday, lunch only. Entrées from $4.50 (L), $6.50 (D). DC, MC, V.

***Mon Cher Ton Ton,*** Ala Moana Americana Hotel, 410 Atkinson Drive (955-4811). (See description under JAPANESE.)

## LEISURE BREAKFAST/LUNCH

***The Hala Terrace,*** Kahala Hilton, 5000 Kalaha Avenue (734-2211). By day a breezy, canvas-roofed seaside lanai enriched by sparkling surf, lush plantings, startling bikinis and fine food and drink. Breakfast: fresh tropical fruits, pancakes with coconut syrup, sautéed *mahi mahi,* Portuguese sausage, eggs Benedict. Lunch: seafood salad, matchless filet of *mahi mahi,* cold prime rib, a galaxy of superior sandwiches and daily specials—*osso buco,* veal kidneys and more mid-ocean rarities. Satiated (or, sometimes, saturated) patrons are encouraged to stroll past the Kahala's penguins and tortoises to view—but not join—the bottlenose dolphins frolicking in the world's only hotel porpoise pool. Open seven days a week. Complete breakfasts from $4.75. Lunch entrées from $3.50; sandwiches (after 2:45 P.M.) from $3.50. AE, CB, DC, MC, V.

## FAST, GOOD FOOD/BREAKFAST

***Canterbury Coffee House and Tavern,*** 1910 Ala Moana Boulevard (941-5277). (See description under LATE-NIGHT SERVICE.)

## FAST, GOOD FOOD/LUNCH

***Canoe House Buffet,*** Ilikai Hotel, 1777 Ala Moana Boulevard (949-3811). An opportunity to sample many ethnic cuisines—Japanese, Chinese, Hawaiian, Italian, American—at one's own pace. Standouts: sausage salad, *namasu* (pickled cucumbers and seaweed), *sushi, sashimi,* Chinese red duck, sweet/sour *mahi mahi,* curry (bland). Best desserts: plain cream puffs, napoleons, apple or chocolate layer cake. Full bar. Reservations recommended. Chaîne des Rotisseurs. Lunch only. Open seven days a week. Fixed-price lunch $6.95. AE, CB, DC, MC, V.

## FAST, GOOD FOOD/DINNER

***South Seas Village,*** 2112 Kalakaua Avenue (923-8484). This flagrantly misnamed restaurant is housed in a replica of a Japanese country inn, and offers a helter-skelter menu that should be awful. It isn't. Its Japanese *shabu-shabu* is the equal of any and is offered in single servings at a handsome oval counter that seats 24, each seat with an individual copper broth pot. Superlative dipping sauce. Best bet: Queen (all-beef) *shabu-shabu.* Tell the waiter to hold the incongruous Western salad—there are quite enough vegetables (bok choy, mushrooms, watercress, tofu) on the platter. Japanese beer or sake, full bar. Sunday, dinner only. Open seven days a week. Entrées from $3.75 (L), $4.95 (D); *shabu-shabu* $5.95 (L), $8.95 (D). AE, CB, DC, MC, V.

## BEST WINE LIST

***Bagwell's 2424,*** Hyatt Regency, 2424 Kalakaua Avenue (922-9292). A superior selection of quality wines, divided into two lists, the first offered to all diners, the second—the Sommelier's Selection—only on request. By itself, the standard collection would justify Bagwell's rating, with fine reds ranging from a 1967 Château La Mission-Haut-Brion at $50 to a 1974 Freemark Abbey Cabernet Bosche at $19. The "private stock" second list carries the unusual caution that all of its wines are considered purchased when opened—surely justified for the 1870 Lafite-Rothschild, at $1,700, or the 1949 Château Latour at $610, but a bit presumptuous for the excellent California wines that conclude the list. (For details on menu offerings, see description under CONTINENTAL.) Dinner only. Open seven days a week. Entrées from $13. AE, CB, DC, MC, V.

---

# FOR DRINKS

***Jameson's Irish Coffee House,*** 16 Merchant Street (538-7630). The downtown gathering place for upward-achieving young career people and for singles—although this is not a singles bar in the pejorative sense. Jameson's pioneered the local rescue of Irish coffee from aerosol foam whip. Closed Saturday. Lunch from $3.95; dinner (corned beef and cabbage, mulligan stew) $4.95. AE, CB, DC, MC, V.

***Trappers,*** Hyatt Regency, 2424 Kalakaua Avenue (922-9292). This Art Deco gin mill attracts people of all ages to listen to Hawaiian guitars or New Orleans jazz during Happy Hour (4:30–9:30 P.M.). At 10 o'clock Jimmy Borges, Hawaii's leading vocalist, takes the stage, and the drinking, listening and dancing (no disco) goes on until 4 A.M. New York, Las Vegas and Hollywood stars, in Honolulu for concert shows or vacations, usually show up late to jam with Jimmy. Closed Sunday. Bar drinks $2.75. AE, CB, DC, MC, V.

***Bagwell's 2424,*** Hyatt Regency, 2424 Kalakaua Avenue (922-9292). (See description under CONTINENTAL and BEST WINE LIST.) The cocktail lounge that adjoins the restaurant is an oasis of quiet, luxurious charm and comfort, with a soft guitar the only distraction. A refuge for the mature, a rendezvous for young lovers. Well-stocked bar, open until midnight, sometimes later, seven days a week. AE, CB, DC, MC, V.

***Beach Bar,*** Moana Hotel, 2365 Kalakaua Avenue (922-3111). Five generations of residents and visitors have drunk their "sundowners" under the giant banyan in the tacky courtyard of Waikiki's oldest hotel (1896). Almost at the water's edge, the bar erodes in early evening when a Hawaiian show occupies the interior court. But few World War II veterans will want to miss one nostalgic sunset drink here. Open seven days a week. AE, CB, DC, MC, V.

## ROMANTIC

***Rex's Ristorante,*** 2310 Kuhio Avenue (923-7618). If there is such a thing as a hideaway in bustling Waikiki, this is it. Small, intimate, with a remarkable menu and a modest but respectable wine list. An admirable rack of lamb, cooked precisely to order, abundant but subtle caper sauce on request. Unbeatable (even in Paris or New York) crêpes suzette. Reservations necessary. Saturday and Sunday, dinner only. Open seven days a week, until 1 A.M.. Entrées from $5.50 (L), $9.50 (D). AE, DC, MC, V.

## LATE-NIGHT SERVICE

***The Bistro,*** 1647 Kapiolani Boulevard (955-3331) (Valet parking on Kona Street.) Modestly billed as "mostly French," this cushioned little cocoon's major reputation rests on its supper menu (11 P.M. to 1:30 A.M.) with French onion soup reminiscent of Les Halles, snails Bourguignonne, and a filet steak sandwich béarnaise. Wine list inconsistent, few vintage designations, but reasonable. Sunday, dinner only. Open seven days a week. Entrées from $4.95 (L), $7.95 (D), $2.50 (S). AE, CB, DC, MC, V.

***Dickens British Pub,*** 1221 Kapiolani Boulevard (531-2727). (See description under BRITISH.) Dickens not only serves lunch and dinner but also offers a late supper (10 P.M. to 1 A.M.)—a collection of cheeses, omelets, sandwiches, soups and savories, mostly variations on its lunch and dinner offerings, but with some additions, notably Cornish pasty and Scotch eggs. Open seven days a week. Supper entrées from $1.50. AE, CB, DC, MC, V.

***Canterbury Coffee House and Tavern,*** 1910 Ala Moana Boulevard (941-5277). This 24-hour restaurant serves breakfast, lunch, dinner and snacks and breakfast dishes all night. Mexican *nachos,* sliced beef with fresh vegetables (chopped steak Hawaiian), Scottish bangers, smoked pork chops, Texas-style French toast, and hamburgers with cheese, chili, avocado, and teriyaki sauce. Full bar in Tavern. Open seven days a week. From 80 cents for soup (cup) to $7.75 (New York steak). AE, CB, DC, MC, V.

## SUNDAY BRUNCH

***Michel's at the Colony Surf,*** 2895 Kalakaua Avenue (923-6552). On the seventh day Michel's virtually escapes its dubious dinner distinctions and presents a superb brunch. The presentation is equal to the restaurant's splendid vista of surf, sea and sand, and is marred only by its "champagne brunch" cocktail. Broiled grapefruit with sherry, faultless eggs Benedict and spring lamb chops (three) cooked with care and served with a crumbled mint leaf sauce. Opt for a *mai tai* or New Orleans fizz. Chaîne des Rotisseurs. Entrées $6.50. AE, CB, DC, MC, V.

***Quinton's,*** Ward Warehouse Shopping Center, Ward at Ala Moana Boulevard (536-3656). (See description under FOR FAMILIES WITH CHILDREN.)

## SUNDAY-EVENING MEAL

***Rex's Ristorante,*** 2310 Kuhio Avenue (923-7618). (See description under ROMANTIC.) Rex's serves full dinners until 1 A.M.

## FOR FAMILIES WITH CHILDREN

***Quinton's,*** Ward Warehouse Shopping Center, 1050 Ala Moana Boulevard (536-3656). This cheerful, relatively inexpensive restaurant defines itself as "a taste of America." That apparently means English-style beef, Maine lobster, Italian fettuccine, Australian steak 'n' eggs, Russian crêpes à la Kiev and marvelous, featherlight Mexican *quesadillas.* On Sunday, from 7 A.M. to 3 P.M., Quinton's offers a "Brunch 'n' Lunch" at considerably lower prices than Michel's—of some interest if you're feeding more than one. All of the cuisines are creditably represented, both at lunch and dinner. Open seven days a week, from 6:30 A.M. to 1 A.M. Entrées from $1.50 (B), $2.50 (L), $5.75 (D). AE, CB, DC, MC, V.

# IN THE SUBURBS

## HAWAII

***Garden Pavilion,*** Mauna Kea Beach Hotel, Kawaihae, Hawaii (882-7222). This remote destination resort, originally a Rockefeller enterprise, was sold recently to Western International hotels, with no discernible effect on its elaborate cuisine—always slightly overrated. Even so, the Mauna Kea is the only game in town on the Big Island, and its dinners—changing each night to emphasize French, Swiss, Tahitian, Italian and German specialties—boast some unusual dishes, among them pheasant pâté, Tahitian fish and almond soup, stuffed palmetto squab, baked papaya and *mahi mahi en coulibiac.* The wine list, however, is shocking—dozens of wines are identified only as "vintage" (no dates), the list is carelessly organized, and there are surprising inaccuracies. Chaîne des Rotisseurs. (The buffet lunch is second only to Honolulu's Ilikai Canoe House in variety and quality.) Open seven days a week. Fixed-price meals $11.50 (L), $19.50 (D). No credit cards.

## MAUI

***Chez Paul,*** Olowalu (661-3843). This tiny café, tucked into a weathered row of attached buildings that look like a set for *The Petrified Forest,* is six minutes and 6,000 miles from Lahaina's tourist restaurants. Authentic French cuisine by Mme. Paul Kirk, wife of a dour Scot who loves good wine and keeps most of it at home. *Anguille fumé* (smoked eel), *cuisse de grenouille* (frogs' legs), *roulade de jambon à la Flamande* (Belgian endive rolled in ham), and fresh Maui catfish *sauté meunière.* Reservations essential. Dinner only. Closed Sunday and Monday. Entrées from $10.25. AE, MC, V.

## OAHU

***L'Auberge,*** 117 Hekili Street, Kailua (262-4835). A mom 'n' pop restaurant with a difference—mom and pop being Elvie and Marcel Balzar, both of whom trained in Europe (Marcel was once a captain at Maxim's). Fillings for their many crêpes include coq au vin, *poulet à l'estragon* and *coquilles St. Jacques.* Dessert crêpes. Modest wine list. Reservations required (allow a half hour for the drive over the Pali to Windward Oahu). Dinner only. Closed Monday and Tuesday. Entrées from $6. MC, V.

# MARKETS

***Ala Moana Farmer's Market,*** 1020 Auahi Street. A colorful bilingual version of the old Chinatown market in downtown Honolulu, and a fine source for cooks frustrated by "Chinatown only" recipe ingredients: star anise, lily flowers, red dates, five-spice powder, etc. You can nibble *sushi, shoyu* chicken, *mahi mahi,* long rice, raw squid, king clam *poki* or octopus *poki* (raw with soy and seaweed), lomi salmon and Hawaiian *laulau.* None over $1.85.

Open seven days a week, from 6:30 A.M. to 6 P.M. (1 P.M. on Sunday).

***Tamashiro Market,*** 802 North King (841-8047). Hawaii's most resplendent and abundant fish market—almost every edible reef and open-sea fish or mollusk on sale and display. A huge sign provides translations of Hawaiian fish names—a handy identification tool for snorkelers. Also, live Dungeness crabs, Maine lobsters, Oregon king clams and fresh Alaska salmon. Open seven days a week.

***Cindy's Lei Shoppe,*** 1034 Maunakea Street (536-6538). Time was when Kalakaua Avenue abounded in lei stands, and visitors and residents alike wore plumeria, ginger, pikake and other Island flowers (at about $1 per lei). The Waikiki stands are mostly long gone, but Cindy's and several other shops flourish on Maunakea Street in downtown Honolulu. Only carnation leis know no season and hence provide a good standard of price measurement: Cindy and friendly rivals, $4; the official airport stand, just short of the terminal, $6; Greeters of Hawaii, the terminal monopolist, $10. Shop early (leis will keep for hours in plastic bags). Cindy's open seven days a week, 6:30 A.M. to 9 P.M.

## GIFT FOODS

***Macadamia Nut Factory,*** 2430 Kalakaua Avenue (922-5306) and 2200 Kalakaua (923-9811). Nearly 300 gift products, created by the Hawaiian Holiday Macadamia Nut Co. of Honokaa, Hawaii, most of them variations on "the perfect nut," as Luther Burbank christened the Australian seed that is now a virtual Hawaii monopoly. Priced from $1.95 (4-oz. bar) to $495 (60-pound chocolate-macadamia bar). World-wide mail-order service. Open seven days a week, from 8 A.M. to midnight. AE, DC, MC, V.

# Houston

Gulf Coast Texans have been known as meat-eaters since the seventeenth century when the Karankawa Indians were supplementing their diet of alligator, oyster and locust with rack of enemy. Two centuries later, Houstonians still hanker for good red meat, but also take a liking to caviar (at $215 for a 14-oz. jar at **Jim Jamail and Sons Food Market**), milk-fed veal, soufflés, blinis, quiches and *zabaglione.*

The Houston restaurant business was born in pioneer boardinghouses. From 1837 to 1839, when it became the capital of the Republic of Texas, Houston was nothing more than a village of mud, tents (the largest one, the Round Tent, was a saloon), log government offices, mosquitoes, water moccasins and udder-deep mud. At the beginning of 1837 the population was 500; by the end of the year the government moved in and the town grew to 1,500. Food was scarce as hen's teeth in the boom town. Chickens went for $1 each, eggs were $1 a dozen, and butter was 75 cents a pound. The one bargain was range beef at 2 cents to 4 cents a pound. Table board at Mann's or Canfield's boardinghouses ran $2 a day.

In the 1840's, while New Englanders were dining on roast duck and freshly pressed apple cider at the Wayside Inn in Massachusetts, and while the American Philosophical Society was savoring oyster croquettes and imported wine in Philadelphia, Houstonians were scrambling after bear meat, venison, wild turkey, armadillo and even mustang. Visitors could get room and board at the Mansion House, which was owned by Mrs. Pamelia Mann, who could drive oxen, wield a derringer and bowie knife, and "fork a broncho"; at the City Hotel, where fourteen men could sleep side by side in attic accommodations; and at the Houston House, which was locally famous for pork "dodgers," chicken "fixins" and corn bread.

By the turn of the century, although many of Houston's rough edges had worn down, unpaved streets still compelled dandies to wear boots instead of fashionable black patent shoes, and ladies had to be hauled to dances in ox carts, since trotting horses with carriages floundered in the mud. However, mansions flourished on Quality Hill, ice tinkled in julep glasses, and black "mammies" presided over huge kitchens where wild game was still a staple. Food and wine service became more refined.

Bars stayed open all night and specialty restaurants proliferated. For a taste of the exotic, diners went to Okasaki Tom Brown's Japanese Restaurant. The Turf Exchange, offering "direct wires to all race tracks throughout the country," employed a bookie and a cook. Fifty-cent dinners at the Grand Central included suckling pig, larded quail, green goose with calf's-foot jelly, English plum pudding and fresh strawberries. Colby's café, famous for wild-game dinners, displayed partridges, snipes, turtles, venison, ducks and geese outside and had a large tank of bullfrogs inside from which customers could choose their victims personally. During watermelon season, waiters at Colby's skated from table to table on melon juice.

Houston and its restaurant population grew slowly for the next fifty years. After wild game petered out, steak and fried chicken became the mainstays. Anything approaching *haute cuisine* was confined to private homes and clubs. It wasn't until the 1950's, when **Maxim's** opened, that Houston's public restaurant image began to change. Maxim's owner, Camille Bermann, a transplanted Parisian, began to serve *escargots, poulet aux herbes* and *coupe de marrons.* He eventually added steaks, but he had singlehandedly changed the taste of Houston's dining public.

In 1972, liquor-by-the-drink became legal in Texas for the first time since before Prohibition, and cocktails could be served outside of private homes and clubs. This, together with the city's phenomenal growth, resulted in a rapid proliferation of restaurants. There are now in excess of 3,800 eating establishments. You can order beluga caviar, crawfish *étouffée,* 1,000-year-old egg with jellyfish, turtle steak, *cabrito, raita, tiropitakia,* tempura, knockwurst and fondue. You can dine in a train, a mine, a stable, a chalet, an English manor, a hacienda, or a hobbit hole.

Among the cuisines that appear to have blossomed here of late are Indian, and Northern and Szechuan Chinese. Substantial Indian and Chinese populations no doubt account for part of the interest, but the willingness of the Texas palate to embrace chiles in almost any form has helped.

Except for the Alley Theater, Jones Hall, and Maxim's, downtown Houston virtually closes down at night. Most of the city's fancy restaurants are located to the west and south of town, with more and more opening farther and farther to the west as the city sprawls toward San Antonio. Currently, Houston restaurants are spread out over more than sixty miles from east to west, with the greatest single concentration in the Galleria area. Be sure to ascertain the location of a restaurant before you start out. You could go home to Cincinnati for lunch for the price of cab fare from the Hyatt Regency to **Foulard's.**

People tend to dress for dinner here. Leisure suits are on the wane and restaurants like **Brennan's** request that men wear coats and ties. Ladies should bring along sweaters or stoles because air conditioners run almost year round.

# Restaurants and Food Sources
(Area code: 713)

## BIG DEAL

### WORTH IT

***Tony's,*** 1801 S. Post Oak (622-6778). Tony's is fresh flowers, vintage claret walls, seasoned waiters, lighting that enables you to see and be seen, and a full house on Wednesday at 10 P.M. The clientele includes jet setters, ranchers from the Valley (Rio Grande), men from the fields (oil), the chic of Araby and anyone else who seeks the best in *haute cuisine,* service and surroundings—and is willing to pay for it. The à la carte Continental menu includes lobster bisque, tomatoes *émincés* (sliced tomatoes, minced green onion, heart of palm, crab meat and a vinaigrette), red snapper *noisette* (with seasoned lump crab meat), capon with black cherries, veal Oskar (with brown sauce and lobster) and Grand Marnier soufflé. The wine cellar has one of the finest stocks in the city and serves as a private dining room for parties of 14 or more. The house wine is consistently the best in town. Reservations advised. Chaîne des Rotisseurs. Saturday, dinner only. Closed Sunday. Entrées from $5.95 (L), $10 (D). AE, MC, V.

***Ché,*** Plaza Hotel, 5020 Montrose (524-9071). Muted gray walls and upholstery provide the perfect foil for the vaulted, ornate ceiling of this small, elegant restaurant nestled on the second floor of the Plaza Hotel. The menu changes seasonally, offering perhaps pear and apple soup in the spring or a hearty *l'ouille* (barley and mushroom soup) in the fall. Preparation of standard items also varies so that rack of lamb might be graced with herbs one season and with green peppercorn sauce the next. Frozen Amaretto soufflé and New England maple mousse should be tried if they are available. Service is excellent. Reservations advised. Dinner only. Closed Sunday. Entrées from $13. AE, MC, V.

## NOT WORTH IT

***La Hacienda de los Moralos,*** 10440 Deerwood (780-0933). Luxuriating on a multimillion-dollar 10-acre site along Buffalo Bayou, La Hacienda de los Moralos is a heroic re-creation of Mexico City's sixteenth-century plantation-turned-restaurant of the same name. Although the food (Continental with a few Mexican dishes) falls short of the magnificent surroundings, the *ambiente* itself is stunning. If you're invited, go for a margarita (avoid the frozen ones) or for the noon buffet ($6.75) or the Sunday brunch buffet ($7.25) so that you can pick and choose. Saturday, dinner only. Closed Monday. Entrées from $1.75 (L), $8.25 (D). AE, CB, DC, MC, V.

# INTERNATIONAL

## CHINESE

***Shanghai East,*** Third Level, Galleria, 5015 Westheimer (627-3682). This Northern Chinese restaurant, relocated in the Galleria after many years in New York, captivates taste buds with *liang mien* (cold noodles served with bean sprouts, shredded chicken and ham and hot sauce), eggplant Szechuan with pork, Mongolian hot pot and twice-cooked chicken or pork with pine nuts. Cantonese fare is not the forte here. Closed Sunday. Entrées from $3 (L), $4.50 (D). AE, DC, MC, V.

***Hunan Restaurant,*** 1713 S. Post Oak (965-0808). Explore the elegant cuisine of Hunan Province at this attractive, competent restaurant with dishes like Empress Tsu'shi's shrimp (with ham, bamboo shoots, and puffs of egg white); spicy Hunan beef with fresh Chinese cabbage or watercress (avoid the small dark peppers if your fire insurance isn't paid up); and marinated duck (rosy slices of duck served cold in an assertive five-spice sauce). Open seven days a week. Entrées from $2.70 (L), $5 (D). AE, DC, MC, V.

***Hunan East,*** 10001 Westheimer (789-6424). Hunan East occupies a cavernous space in Carrillion West shopping center on the far Westheimer frontier. Ambience is negligible in spite of a lava-rock fountain and lanterns, but the lengthy menu sparkles with seldom encountered gems—squid, tripe, kidneys—as well as with delicious versions of smoked tea duck, country-style bean curd, Hunan lamb, won ton soup and *gan shao* fish. Open seven days a week. Entrées from $3 (L & D). AE, DC, MC, V.

## FRANCO-TEXAN

***Maxim's,*** 802 Lamar (658-9595). Don't let Maxim's nouveau bordello décor put you off. The kitchen, although not infallible, treats Gulf Coast bounty in a French manner with delicious results such as shrimp rémoulade, red snapper excelsior (with Gulf crab meat and artichoke hearts) and oysters Bourguignonne. Vegetables are religiously overcooked. Reservations advised. Closed Sunday. Entrées from $6.25 (L), $9.75 (D). AE, CB, DC, MC, V.

## FRENCH

***Foulard's,*** 10001 Westheimer (789-1661). Chef Foulard was performing for Houstonians before the Galleria was even a gleam in Gerald Hines's eye. In his current spacious establishment, Foulard features his renditions of escargots Bourguignonne, oysters Foulard, duck Normande (with apples and brandy) and cheesecake laced with orange liqueur. Beef Wellington and lamb persille require two days notice and a fat bankroll. Reservations advised. Chaîne des Rotisseurs. Open seven days a week. Entrées from $3.75 (L), $9 (D). AE, CB, DC, MC, V.

## GREEK

***Zorba the Greek's Café,*** 202 Tuam (528-1382). There is nothing about Zorba's weathered-wood, contemporary outside that prepares you for Zorba's inside. Menu offers melt-in-your-mouth *tiropitakia* (cheese puffs), roast lamb, and the city's best fried shrimp and scallops. At noon opt for fresh Gulf fish if it is available. Prices will please your Spartan budget. Closed Sunday and Monday. Entrées from $3.95 (L & D). No credit cards.

## INDIAN

***The Tandoor,*** 3901 Westheimer (960-8472). Houston's only Indian restaurant is a notable one, featuring such marvels as *alu chaat* (chunks of boiled potato in a highy seasoned sauce spiked with cilantro), chicken *sagwala* (chicken cooked in spinach with spices) and *boti kebab* (cubed leg of lamb roasted on a skewer), *dal maharani* (don't let the fact that this translates as creamed lentils deter you), six kinds of bread, and *raita* (yogurt with tomatoes, potatoes, cucumbers and mint). Meats cooked in the *tandoor* (Indian oven) have an intriguing flavor and color (red), but tend to be dry. Saturday, dinner only. Open seven days a week. Entrées from $2.95 (L), $4.95 (D). AE, DC, MC, V.

## ITALIAN

***Arno's,*** 5213 Cedar (668-4299). In pleasant, unpretentious surroundings, Arno's Northern Italian menu changes daily according to what seafoods, fruits and vegetables are available and what herbs are coming up in the garden. Always offered are spinach gnocchi, marinated mushrooms and homemade *fettuccine al pesto;* and often available are calf's liver with sage, veal kidneys marsala and *zuppa di cozzi* (a tomato-based broth bristling with fresh New England mussels). Saturday, lunch only. Closed Sunday and Monday. Entrées from $3.25 (L), $5.95 (D). MC, V.

## JAPANESE

***Tokyo Garden,*** 4701 Westheimer (622-7886). East meets West in this spacious, pleasantly metamorphosed steel building in which tatami seating wraps around a large carp pond. The *sushi, sashimi* and *shabu-shabu* are excellent, as is the tempura. Apparently convinced that Texans want quantity, portions are enormous and chicken *teriyaki* comes with almost every entrée. If you have arthritis or poor circulation, ask for American-style seating. Saturday and Sunday, dinner only. Open seven days a week. Entrées from $1.75 (L), $5.75 (D). AE, CB, DC, MC, V.

## MEXICAN

***Ninfa's,*** 2704 Navigation (228-1175), 6154 Westheimer (781-2740), 9333 Katy Freeway (932-8760), 8507 Gulf Freeway (943-3183). Ninfa's has revolutionized Tex-Mex food in Houston by proving that orange grease is not an essential ingredient. In spite of a host of imitators, Ninfa's is still *numero uno* when it comes to *tacos al carbon* (barbecued beef or pork wrapped in a tortilla), *queso a la parilla* (melted white cheese to be eaten with tortillas), chicken *chalupas* and *empanadas* filled with bananas, raisins and pecans, and dusted with powdered sugar and cinnamon. At the Navigation location (the original), fat *gatos* and big *quesos* eat elbow to elbow with little *pescados*. The branches have more homogeneous clienteles and are heavier on décor. Open seven days a week. Entrées from $2.75 (L & D). AE, CB, DC, MC, V.

***Las Casuelas,*** 2221 Fulton (223-0095). When you're feeling the need for a guacamole fix, drop into this 24-hour *taqueria* in the heart of the Mexican-American community. Make your way past the glass-walled kitchen, through the Spanish magazines, records and tapes, and around the rack of *guayaberas* to the large, bright dining room to feast on tortas, *burritos,* enchiladas, *chiles rellenos, caldo de res* and *cabrito.* Wash it all down with margaritas, cerveza Mexicana, or tamarind juice. Open seven days a week. Entrées from $1.50 (L & D). MC, V.

***Primo's Mexican Restaurant & Outdoor Cantina,*** 519 Rosalie (528-9158). Small and informal, this pleasant, 12-table establishment is a favorite with Tex-Mex fans for fresh, tasty fare. Try the *fajitas,* a skirt steak grilled to perfection to be cut up, swaddled in a tortilla with a dab of guacamole, and relished. Doctor your Tecaté beer with a dash of salt and a squeeze of lime—a poor man's margarita. Closed Sunday. Entrées from $2.95 (L & D). MC, V.

# SPECIALTY COOKING

## BARBECUE.

***Otto's,*** 5502 Memorial (864-2573). A prime contender for the city's best barbecue title, Otto's piles 1,400 pounds of beef on the fire daily and serves it counter-style. The sauce is on the sweet side, as is most all of the sauce in town, a sure sign that Houston is in East Texas (sauces start getting tart just west of here). Hamburgers are served separately (up front) but are equally fine specimens of their genre. Eat in or take out to nearby Memorial Park. Closed Sunday. Barbecue from $1.45. No credit cards.

## CRAWFISH

***Ray Hay's Cajun Po-Boys,*** 4302 Richmond (623-6321), 6718 Hillcroft (772-2441), 22215 Katy Freeway (392-0452). Houston rides the western edge of bayou country, so make a point of visiting this Cajun-style roadhouse for a long-neck beer and a bucket of boiled, peel-'em-yourself crawfish (December through early June). If you are still hungry, fill up on boudin, red beans and rice, and oyster po' boys. Fast, cafeteria-style service. Closed Sunday. Crawfish from $2.75 (1½ pounds). No credit cards.

***Don's,*** 3009 S. Post Oak Lane (629-5380). (See description under CREOLE.)

# CREOLE

***Brennan's,*** 3300 Smith (522-9711). Like its New Orleans counterpart, Brennan's is known for Creole dishes and Southern charm. Sip a Sazarac on the patio before moving inside the New Orleans-style building, which originally housed the Houston Junior League. Dinner favorites include turtle soup, oysters Bienville, trout with pecans, and bread pudding. For an especially civilized weekend brunch, start with oyster soup, proceed to eggs Nouvelle Orléans (with Gulf crab meat and brandy), and finish yourself off with crêpes Fitzgerald (strawberries and sour cream). A jazz group sparks Saturday's brunch. Reservations advised. Open seven days a week. Entrées from $3.95 (L), $9 (D). AE, CB, DC, MC, V.

***Don's Seafood Restaurant & Steakhouse,*** 307 North Belt East (931-7654). Jambalaya, crawfish pie, and filet gumbo constitute staples at this branch of the Landry brothers' famous Lafayette restaurant. Dive into oysters on the half shell or a bowl of oyster and shrimp gumbo. In crawfish season (December through early June, depending on the weather) move on to étouffée or a combination plate with samples of all of Don's crawfish specialties. Off season (or if you don't relish crawfish), try the broiled flounder or the fried shrimp. Open seven days a week. Entrées from $5.25 (L & D). AE, MC, V. There is a second Don's, 3009 S. Post Oak (629-5380), owned by a Landry nephew. Overall it falls short of the first but in crawfish season is worth a visit, and the lump crab-meat salad is excellent. Open seven days a week. Entrées from $7.50 (L & D). AE, DC, MC, V.

# DELI

***New York Deli,*** 5016 Westheimer (622-5760). Complete with caricatures and noise, this haven for displaced New Yorkers packs 'em in for potato pancakes, fine smoked-fish platters, first-rate pastrami sandwiches, the city's best dill pickles and tomatoes, chocolate creams and devastatingly delicious chocolate cheese cake. The kitchen has no talent for soups and hot dishes, however. Open seven days a week. Entrées from $1.95 (L & D). AE, CB, DC, MC, V.

# HAMBURGER/PLAIN

***Otto's,*** 5502 Memorial (864-2573). (See description under BARBECUE.)

## HAMBURGER/FANCY

***Mason Jar,*** 9005 Katy Freeway (461-9005). You'll flip your lid over the open-face mushroomburger on an English muffin at this New York East Side-style establishment. The day's clam chowder supply is depleted by 2 P.M., so aim for an early lunch. The reasonably priced steaks merit your attention. Open seven days a week. Entrées from $2.65 (L), $5.29 (D). AE, MC, V.

## HOME-STYLE

***Nanny's,*** 4729 Calhoun (741-7085). Near town (off I 45 S) and just across from the University of Houston, Nanny's dishes up the kind of food you hope you'll get every time you are suckered in by a "home cooking" sign. At Nanny's there isn't a puddle of floury gravy, a scoop of instant potatoes, or a canned vegetable in sight. Instead, you'll find plate-engulfing, fork-tender chicken-fried steaks and Texas-sized servings of tender, well-trimmed liver cooked to order and heaped with sautéed onions, along with deli-style sandwiches, steaks and salads. Closed Sunday. Entrées from $2.35 (L & D). AE, CB, DC, MC, V.

## OYSTERS

***Captain Benny's Half Shell,*** 7409 S. Main (795-9051). Drop anchor alongside this shrimper moored on Main Street and fill your hold with the city's best oysters on the half shell (from Matagorda Bay), fried oysters, gumbo, and cold boiled shrimp. With only seven stools, it's usually SRO on this ship of foods, but no one seems to mind. Fast service. Closed Sunday. Oysters on half shell from $2.25 (½ doz). No credit cards.

## SEAFOOD

***San Jacinto Inn,*** San Jacinto Battleground, off Hwy. 225 (479-2828). A vast, turn-of-the-century raised wooden structure, the San Jacinto Inn is an all-you-can-eatery featuring Gulf seafood. Roll up your sleeves and ride wave after wave of oysters on the half shell (September to April), cold boiled crab (summer), cold boiled shrimp, fried redfish, chicken, and potatoes; biscuits and strawberry jam; and sherbet. The trip from town includes a swing through the sprawling refinery area (a fairyland of lights at night), an optional tour of the battleship *Texas,* and a jaunt through the San Jacinto Battleground where Texans routed Santa Anna. Dinner only. Closed Monday. Fixed price: adults $12.50, children (2–11) $4. AE, CB, DC, MC, V.

# SOUTHERN

***Confederate House,*** 4007 Westheimer (622-1936). Summertime (all eleven months of it), and the livin' is easy with Old South service, crystal chandeliers, and a portrait of the President (Davis). Native Houstonians have been eating here on the maid's night out for two generations, thanks to straightforward quality fare with scarcely an artery-clogging sauce in sight; hickory-smoked shrimp, Confederate-trim steak, fried shrimp, broiled Gulf fish, broiled lamb chops, prime rib. A first-class fresh fruit salad with poppy-seed dressing is available only at lunch. Saturday and Sunday dinner only. Open seven days a week. Entrées from $3.50 (L), $6.75 (D). AE, DC, MC, V.

---

# STEAK

***Brenner's,*** 10911 Katy Freeway, I-10 W (465-2901). Brenner's has been catering to West-siders since 1937 when a meal ran 37 cents. The current menu, recited by nurse-efficient waitresses, includes four cuts of steak which come with German fries and salad (go with the Roquefort dressing). Save room for the luscious apple strudel and ice cream. Garden vista by Black Forest elves. By reservation only. Saturday, dinner only. Closed Monday. Steaks $13 & $14 (L & D). AE, DC, MC, V.

***Ruth's Chris Steak House,*** 6213 Richmond (782-2453). Like its progenitor in New Orleans, Ruth's deals in huge, butter-bathed steaks. High prime-rib eyes, sirloin strips, and filets go for $13 each but can be shared at noon for an ample lunch à deux; and there are also Porterhouse steaks for two ($26), three ($39) or four ($52). Outside, Ruth's is office-building contemporary. Inside, oil company logos pass for décor and the waitresses are down-home friendly. Side dishes leave a lot to be desired although the salad is one of the few bowls of iceberg around with any character, and the pecan pie is worth the calories. Saturday and Sunday, dinner only. Open seven days a week. Steaks from $13 (L & D). AE, CB, DC, MC, V.

---

## STEAK/TEXAS STYLE

***The Hofbrau,*** 1803 Shepherd (869-7074). Platter-sized steaks cut from young local-feedlot beef are a ubiquitous feature of roadhouses all over Texas. The genre reaches its zenith at the Hofbrau in Austin as well as at this authorized copy founded by a couple of enthusiastic University of Texas Ex's. The 17-ounce T-bone ($5.95) is the best pick—flavorful and on the tender side. Other cuts taste good but can be chewy. An iceberg and green-olive salad and home fries come with the entrées. The décor is basic roadhouse, the service is friendly, the beer is cold, and the music is C&W. Closed Sunday. Entrées from $2.95. AE, MC, V.

## VEGETARIAN

***Hobbit Hole,*** 1715 S. Shepherd (528-3418). Well-dressed matrons and jeans-clad students alike hole up here for mouth-expanding sandwiches constructed with bean sprouts, cheese, mushrooms, tomatoes, avocado, and tabouli on slabs of homemade bread. Fresh fruit smoothies, especially (in summer) peach, would make even Smaug purr. Closed Monday. Entrées from $1.30. No credit cards.

# FOR INDIVIDUAL NEEDS

## IF YOU HAVE TIME FOR ONLY ONE MEAL

***Tony's,*** 1801 S. Post Oak (622-6778). (See description under BIG DEAL/WORTH IT.)

## BEST HOTEL MEAL

***Trader Vic's,*** Shamrock Hilton, 6900 S. Main (668-9211). In spite of its touristy connotations and Polynesian polyglot décor (right down to the tiki salt shakers), Trader Vic's offers a softly lit, comfortable milieu in which to explore the delights of Indonesian, Continental and Chinese cuisines. Even local folks stop in regularly for the Indonesian dry-roasted lamb or pork, the green pepper steak, sea scallops in white wine, the limestone lettuce salad with bay shrimp, and the unusual vegetable selections—snow peas with water chestnuts, glazed artichoke bottoms with creamed spinach, sautéed bananas. Saturday and Sunday, dinner only. Open seven days a week. Entrées from $4.95 (L), $6.50 (D). AE, CB, DC, MC, V.

## RESTAURANT NEAR AIRPORT

***Don's Seafood Restaurant & Steakhouse,*** 307 North Belt East (931-7654). (See description under CREOLE.)

## BUSINESS BREAKFAST

***Hunt Room,*** Warwick Hotel, 5701 S. Main (526-1991). Ease yourself into the day and a business discussion in handsome, clublike surroundings with fresh orange juice, melon and berries in season, and a pecan waffle or Spanish omelet. Excellent service. Open seven days a week. Entrées from $3.35. AE, CB, DC, MC, V.

## BUSINESS LUNCH

***Brennan's,*** 3300 Smith (522-9711). (See description under CREOLE.)

***Confederate House,*** 4007 Westheimer (622-1936). (See description under SOUTHERN.)

## FAST, GOOD FOOD

***Andre's Swiss Candies and Pastry Shop,*** 2515 River Oaks Blvd. (524-3863). Luncheon in this Swiss-efficient bakery-cum-tearoom means a choice of entrées—perhaps sausage with noodles; quiche; *croque monsieur;* or a ham, cheese, and mushroom omelet. Salad, a beverage and a selection from a pastry tray laden with Linzer torte, napoleon, mocha tart, rum balls and such. Lunch only. Closed Sunday and Monday. Fixed price: $3.60. No credit cards.

***Captain Benny's Half Shell,*** 7409 S. Main (795-9051). (See description under OYSTERS.)

***Luther's,*** 3100 Fountain View (789-0360), 9797 Westheimer (780-0081), 8560 Gulf Fwy. I-45 S (947-2783), 51 Woodlake Square (789-1820). Comfortably understated frontier-town style, with wood walls and floors and counter service, makes Luther's ideal for an uncomplicated meal. The barbecue is lean and tender, generously portioned, and comes by the sandwich or the platter. If your sidekick or the kids have an aversion to barbecue, they can line up at the hamburger counter across the room. Open seven days a week. Barbecue from $1.10. No credit cards.

## BEST WINE LIST

***Tony's,*** 1801 S. Post Oak (622-6778). (See description under BIG DEAL/WORTH IT.)

## FOR DRINKS

***Cody's,*** 3400 Montrose (522-9747). A downbeat crowd flocks to this treetop spot for topnotch jazz, dancing and the view. Dress ranges from Calvin Klein jeans to black tie. Steaks and seafood served. Closed Sunday. Entrées from $7.95. AE, DC, MC, V.

***Ché,*** Plaza Hotel, 5020 Montrose (524-9071). (See description under BIG DEAL/WORTH IT.) Comfortable sofas, elegant appointments, well-modulated lights and piano music add up to an intimate spot for cocktails or an after-dinner brandy. The concomitant restaurant is excellent. Closed Sunday. AE, MC, V.

## ROMANTIC

***The Rainbow Lodge,*** 1 Birdsall (861-9407). (See description under WITH A VIEW.)

## LATE-NIGHT SERVICE

***Ruggles,*** 903 Westheimer (524-3839), 6540 San Felipe (977-4949). Relaxed surroundings, attentive service and consistency have netted Ruggles a large and devoted following. Dishes such as trout *meunière, poulet au poivre* and *côte de porc Zingara* save the famished before or after the theater, while eggs Sardou, a sirloin steak sandwich or an order of beignets suits the smaller appetite. "Mud" pie hits the spot anytime. Saturday, dinner only. Open seven days a week, Sunday through Thursday until 1 A.M.; Friday and Saturday until 3 A.M. Entrées from $3 (L), $6.50 (D). AE, CB, DC, MC, V.

***Harlow's Third Avenue Delicatessen,*** 3100 Hillcroft (780-9500). 1930's movie memorabilia set the scene for deli sandwiches, three-egg omelets and a fine Greek farmer's salad. Breakfast served anytime. Open seven days a week, from 11 A.M. to 5 A.M. Entrées from $2.95 (L & D). AE, CB, DC, MC, V.

## SUNDAY BRUNCH

***Brennan's,*** 3300 Smith (522-9711). (See description under CREOLE.)

## SUNDAY-EVENING MEAL

***Ruggles,*** 903 Westheimer (524-3839), 6540 San Felipe (977-4949). (See description under LATE-NIGHT SERVICE.)

## FOR FAMILIES WITH CHILDREN

***Don's,*** 307 North Belt East (931-7654), 3009 S. Post Oak (629-5380). (See description under CREOLE.) Both locations have special children's menus for coloring while waiting.

***San Jacinto Inn,*** San Jacinto Battleground, off Hwy. 225 (479-2828). (See description under SEAFOOD.)

## WITH A VIEW

***The Rainbow Lodge,*** 1 Birdsall (861-9407). A renovated, old two-story manse that overlooks rolling lawns, azaleas, woods and Buffalo Bayou, as do many of the city's finest estates just upstream. The menu avoids the usual culinary clichés and delights tastebuds with marinated vegetables, a fragrant mushroom soup, carefully cooked fish and superb calf's liver in a rich brown sauce (ask for it to be cooked rare unless you want it really well done). Vegetables are a forte here, as is the whole-wheat-crusted apple pie. Reservations advised. Saturday, dinner only. Closed Monday. Entrées from $4.75 (L), $7.50 (D). AE, MC, V.

# IN THE SUBURBS

## CLEAR LAKE/NASA

***Gabriel's,*** 810 Nasa Road One (488-7722). Gabriel DiCesare's apprenticeship as general manager of Tony's is evident in this smoothly run establishment. The Continental menu owes much to Tony's, although the prices are lower and vegetables and salad come with each entrée. Seafood is impeccably fresh and you shouldn't miss the crab meat crêpe, the flounder *noisette* with lump Gulf crab meat, or the red snapper Pontchartrain. Also good is the veal *piccata Ramsnitzel* with mushrooms. The Swiss chocolate mousse is world class. Saturday, dinner only. Closed Sunday. Entrées from $4.50 (L), $8.50 (D). AE, MC, V.

# MARKETS

## GIFT FOODS

***Jamail's,*** 3114 Kirby (523-5535). Houston's mecca for cheese, fresh produce, meat and imported items, Jamail's also has an in-house chef who prepares take-out food ready-to-eat (from canapés to beef Wellington) and frozen (sauces, soups, entrées, desserts). Arcane items are usually cheaper and fresher here than elsewhere in town due to rapid turnover. Jamail's will prepare and deliver gift baskets and will ship anywhere. Closed Sunday.

***Fiesta Mart,*** 3140 Fulton (224-1535). Stock up here on *chilis, tomatillos, jicamas, achiote,* plantains, mangos, papayas, tamarind, *nopales, epazote* and all of those other exotic ingredients Diana Kennedy specifies. Open seven days a week.

***Ed's Farmer Market,*** 1800 Westheimer (528-6444). Texas produce including Ruby Red or Star Red grapefruit ($2.25 to $3.19 per 18-lb. bag). Closed Sunday.

***Glatzmaier's,*** 809 Congress (223-3331). Have your briefcase fitted with a pound of crab meat or of red snapper at this downtown market. Closed Sunday.

***Fishery,*** 9521-A Westheimer (781-1931). A comprehensive West-side seafood market. Closed Sunday. MC, V.

## GIFT WINES

***Spec's,*** 2410 Smith (526-8787), and 19 other locations. Warehouses full of wine, whiskey and beer. Best prices in town. Closed Sunday.

***Richard's Liquors and Fine Wines,*** 5630 Richmond (783-3344), and three other locations. Distinctive selection, knowledgeable help. Closed Sunday.

# Indianapolis

Indianapolis' first restaurant of any pretension was established by Mr. John Crowder in 1838. In 1840 an Englishman, John Hodgkins, bought the restaurant, added a confectionary, and created the city's first ice-cream garden, where couples could stroll along graveled paths that wound among the arbors and flower gardens, and sample the new frozen delicacy in the garden's gazebos.

After completion of the railroad to Indianapolis in 1847, the restaurant and hotel business really began to grow. In 1851 the German Turngemeinde club was founded by the growing number of German immigrants. They served German foods and "an effort was also made to accustom the German stomach to American beer through frequent practice." The Athenaeum Turners, a club still in existence downtown, traces its history back to these early settlers. The membership is trying to revive the German menu and *Gemütlichkeit* and willingly opens the doors of the club to visitors.

Oysters were brought to Indianapolis in the mid-1880's by James Blake—described in historical references as a town gallant. Settlers sneered at the Eastern delicacy, but by the time the railroads could successfully transport seafood, oysters had replaced pheasant as the choice of the city's connoisseurs. Imported lobsters, salt-water seafood and lake fish continued to be popular through the Gay Nineties.

When the first pork house was built in the center of town, it signaled the end of fishing in downtown White River. Pollution from the slaughterhouses and manufacturing drove the bass and redeye upstream.

In the 1880's, beer gardens flourished. According to a 1924 newspaper recollection of the era, the beer garden was "an enclosed space set with trees, where of summer evenings patrons could sit about in neighborly groups at little tables sipping their mugs of beer, enjoying each other and whatever entertaining was offered . . . usually vaudeville." Dramatic performances were often given in German.

For the non-imbibing, the Woman's Christian Temperance Union ran a dining hall that in 1884 was considered one of the best in the city.

The Grand Hotel, which had been the celebrity hostelry since 1873, opened a café in 1896. Owner H. J. Hyde raised all the fruits and vegetables for his restaurant. The location of the restaurant was South Illinois (near what is now Union Station), which was hotel and restaurant row during the nineties. **St. Elmo Steak House** survives on this street in an 1872 edifice.

World War I brought inflation to Indianapolis. Mrs. Schlegel, who ran a restaurant at **City Market,** raised her lunch from 15 to 25 cents. The meal consisted of roast beef, roast pork or veal loaf; green beans or butter beans; mashed potatoes; and homemade pie. Restaurants such as the now-departed Canary Cottage and Fendrick's faced a crisis in 1945, when shortages and OPA restrictions left 85 percent of the restaurants without beef. Downtown hotels such as the razed Lincoln and Claypool as well as the fashionable Marott fed only registered guests during the shortage years of the 1940's.

In the mid-1950's, Continental cuisine was introduce to the Marott Hotel's Driftwood Room, and the Seville's owner, M. J. Comisar, adopted a Continental menu and renamed his redecorated restaurant the **King Cole.** The King Cole survives, but the Driftwood Room, the Graylyn Hotel's Blue Room, La Rue's Supper Club and the Keys, all popular dining spots of this era, are gone.

The 1960's brought concept or theme restaurants to town. Today you can dine in a railway car, a cave, a stable or several seafaring spots. The menus are the same—steak, seafood and salad bar—and the food all tastes similar.

A rash of new restaurants has spotted the suburban scene in Indianapolis during the past few years. Some are sisters of successes in other Midwestern cities. Others are classier cousins of casual local eateries.

Devotees of family-style fare remain loyal to Hollyhock Hill and the Iron Skillet, home-style restaurants that began in the 1950's, whose menus of Hoosier fried chicken, mashed potatoes, green beans and corn never change.

Men dress in suits and ties at the better restaurants, and women are dressing up more in dresses instead of pants. Dress is casual in the neighborhood niches.

Expense-account Continental restaurants want dinner reservations every evening, and you'll need weekend reservations at all of the popular restaurants. One tip for drinks and dinner will suffice, and the going rate is 15 percent, with 20 percent favored at the higher-priced Continentals.

Take time to shop at City Market—an 1867 building that's been renovated and that offers produce, meat, poultry and seafood stands; ethnic groceries and snackeries; specialty shops, and stand-up eateries. Tony's pizza at the Grand Prix Pizza stand is some of the best in town.

# Restaurants and Food Sources
**(Area code: 317)**

# BIG DEAL

## WORTH IT

***Glass Chimney,*** 1037 W. Main Street, Carmel (844-0921). Chef-owner Dieter Puska produces the best and most consistent Continental fare in town. The décor of the dining rooms remains dismal, but the extensive menu and creditable wine list compensate. The chef's seasonings and sauces have character and balance. Start with a house pâté, *coquille St.-Jacques* or lobster bisque. Recommended entrées include *mahi-mahi* sautéed with banana, *Fasan auf Jägermeister Art,* lamb chops *à la boulangère* and *rognons de veau sauce moutarde.* The French and Austrian veal dishes are popular. Entrées include an excellent green salad maison, potato or rice, vegetable and croissant or German rye rolls. Reservations a must on weekends. Dinner only. Closed Sunday. Entrées from $8.50. AE, MC, V.

## NOT WORTH IT

***La Tour,*** Indiana National Bank Tower, One Indiana Square (635-3535). Panoramic views from the 35th floor, excellent French menu and wine list, and an ambience of refined elegance. Personalized matches, fresh flowers for the ladies and impeccable appointments are solicitous touches that promise perfection, but, unfortunately, meals are not always well-prepared. Dishes may be over- or undercooked, for instance. The $10.95 four-course twilight dinner, served from 6 to 7 P.M. with limited choices, is the best buy.

Reservations recommended. Saturday, dinner only. Closed Sunday. Entrées from $3.85 (L), $8.50 (D). AE, CB, DC, MC, V.

# INTERNATIONAL

## AMERICAN

***Dodd's Towne House,*** 5694 N. Meridian Street (255-0872). An enduring eatery favored for steaks and Hoosier home-style cooking. Betty and Jim Dodd, who founded the country predecessor of the Towne House in 1948, still run the restaurant and bake the outstanding pies. Faded and modest décor in an unpretentious frame home on a fashionable suburban street. No liquor. Dinner only. Closed Monday. Complete dinner from $4.50. MC.

## FRENCH

***Chanteclair sur le Toit,*** Holiday Inn Airport, 2501 S. High School Road (244-7378). Impressive menu in a sophisticated dining room. Distinctive offerings include *viande de grison hors d'oeuvre,* shark-fin soup, *mignonettes de chevreuil* and *ris de veau Madère.* The *escalope de veau* Parisienne and *entrecôte farcie* are specialties of the Swiss chef. Some of the best prepared and presented choices are the entrées for two, which include loin of veal, rack of lamb, pheasant and venison. The clientele is largely on expense accounts, but service is polite and hospitable. Reservations a must. Dinner only. Closed Sunday. Entrées from $9. AE, DC, MC, V.

***Chez Jean Restaurant Français,*** Indiana 67 in Camby, north of Mooresville (831-0870). Convenient from airport. The quaint French-provincial dining rooms are rendered in plastic, but the cuisine prepared by the owner-chef remains consistent and popular. The sweet *canard à l'orange* is the house specialty, but the lemon-touched *moules marinière, tournedo sauté chasseur, steak au poivre vert* and *médaillons de veau aux chanterelles* are popular choices, too. Reservations required. Dinner only. Closed Sunday and Monday. Dinners from $10.95 include soup, salad, puff potatoes, vegetables and coffee. AE, DC, MC, V.

## MEXICAN

***Chi-Chi's Restaurante,*** 6110 E. 82nd Street, Castleton (842-4597). The most attractive and popular of the many local Mexican spots. There's good taste in the décor as well as on the tables. Tex-Mex and Southern California tortilla-type fare. Try the *quesadilla, chim-*

*ichanga,* super *burro,* chicken *flauta* and fried ice cream but skip the *chile relleno.* Open seven days a week. Large, individual servings from $1.35, combination plates, $2.40 (L & D). AE, DC, MC, V.

# SPECIALTY COOKING

## CRÊPES

***Magic Pan Crêperie,*** 6101 N. Keystone in Glendale Shopping Center (259-4335). Cheery country-French dining rooms and consistent crêpe dishes that draw diners for lunch, dinner, after-theater desserts and Sunday brunch. More than 20 crêpe choices including some almost irresistible desserts. Good soups and salads, too. Open seven days a week. Crêpes from $2.75 (L & D). AE, DC, MC, V.

## DELI

***Shapiro's,*** 808 S. Meridian Street (631-4041). The spiffy new façade disguises this deli's 1905 origins. The quality of the carry-out and cafeteria modified kosher cooking and sandwiches remains unchanged. The clientele is broad, ranging from the elderly to harried executives. Expect a line at lunchtime. Open seven days a week, from 7 A.M. until 7:45 P.M. Entrées from $1.95, plate lunches from $2.65 (L & D). No credit cards.

## HAMBURGER

***T.G.I. Friday's,*** Bazaar in Keystone at the Crossing, Keystone and 86th Street (844-3355). Consistently popular mingling place for young adults. Antique, New York-style stand-up bar. Thick burgers served on English muffin or sesame bun. Choice of 19 different toppings, including a make-your-own-burger choice. Menu includes steaks, shrimp, sandwiches, salads, soup, omelets and Tex-Mex specialties. Over 21 only. Open seven days a week, until 2 A.M. Monday through Saturday with food service until 1 A.M.; bar open until midnight Sunday, food service until 11 P.M. Hamburgers from $3.25 (L & D). AE, MC, V.

## SEAFOOD

***New Orleans House,*** 8845 Township Line Road (298-9670). A sumptuous seafood smorgasbord that features an entrée choice of fresh Maine lobster or a filet mignon and dozens of seafood samplings from the buffet extravaganza. Count on five trips to the buffet tables and three hours to try all the treats. Reservations required. Dinner only. Closed Sunday and Monday. One price for all, $17.95. AE, MC, V.

## STEAK

***St. Elmo Steak House,*** 127 S. Illinois Street (637-1811). This New York Gay Nineties steakhouse and bar, its décor somewhat faded these days, has been popular since 1902. Select an aged New York strip, filet mignon or porterhouse, and watch the cook broil it. Pork chops, lobster tail, Florida red snapper, French fried shrimp and fried chicken also on the menu. Be wary of the fresh horseradish seafood sauce—it's powerful. Dinner only. Closed Sunday. Steaks from $9 to $17. AE, DC, MC, V.

# FOR INDIVIDUAL NEEDS

## IF YOU HAVE TIME FOR ONLY ONE MEAL

***Glass Chimney,*** 1037 W. Main Street, Carmel (844-0921). (See description under BIG DEAL/WORTH IT.)

## BEST HOTEL MEAL

***Harrison's,*** Hyatt Regency Indianapolis in Merchants Plaza, 155 W. Washington Street (632-1234). This is not the usual epicurean eatery. It's an eclectic entity that dares to dish up 19th-century American décor seasoned with Scandinavian. The appetizer *kold bordt* is outstanding. The limited menu features four different ducklings, rack of lamb, lobster thermidor, Chateaubriand, steaks, seafood and veal. Adequate wine list. Open seven days a week. Saturday and Sunday, dinner only. Entrées from $4.95 (L), $8.50 (D). AE, CB, DC, MC, V.

## BUSINESS BREAKFAST

***Marten House,*** 1801 W. 86th Street (259-4111). Fast and efficient service in recently redecorated Sir John Sexton dining room and attractive new Art Deco coffee shop. Comfortable and commodious seating. Seven complete breakfast combinations plus customary à la carte selections, including popular homemade German kuchen. Adequate if not excellent food. Extensive Sunday brunch. Open seven days a week, from 6:30 A.M. Monday through Saturday; from 7 A.M., Sunday. Breakfasts from $1.55. AE, MC, V.

## BUSINESS LUNCH

***King Cole,*** 7 N. Meridian Street (638-5588). A perennial award-winner that remains a favorite for business lunches. English library atmosphere in a subterranean setting. Luncheon specials change daily. A wise choice is the fresh fish. Good wine list. French and American offerings on evening menu. Reservations recommended. Closed Sunday. Entrées, with salad and vegetable, from $4.50 (L), $9.45 (D). AE, CB, DC, MC, V.

## LATE-NIGHT SERVICE

***T.G.I. Friday's,*** Bazaar in Keystone at the Crossing, Keystone and 86th Street (844-3355). (See description under HAMBURGER.) Food service until 1 A.M. Monday through Saturday, until 11 P.M., Sunday. Large menu with reasonably priced, consistent food. Entrées from $1.95. AE, MC, V.

# MARKETS

***City Market,*** 222 E. Market Street (633-3209). More than 60 individually owned and operated stands for meats, poultry, fish, eggs, cheeses, produce, ethnic groceries, baked goods, fast and ethnic foods and boutique items. The Grand Prix Pizza serves superb pizza. Open 6 A.M. until 6 P.M. Monday through Saturday, though most fresh-food stands only operate Tuesday, Thursday, Friday and Saturday. Closed Sunday. No credit cards.

## GIFT FOODS

***Around the World Food Shop,*** 1760 E. 116th Street in Carmel (846-4208). Wines, cheeses, homemade breads, shellfish, live lobsters, sausages, coffee, epicurean foods. Party platters and catering. Open seven days a week. No credit cards.

***Whistle Stop,*** 901 E. 64th in Broad Ripple Village (251-1932). Sausages, cheeses, a few frozen entrées, deli salads and meats, few epicurean foods, coffee and wines. Party trays and catering. Closed Sunday. MC, V.

***Parthenon Grocery,*** 3805 Central Avenue (283-3010). Greek and Middle Eastern foods. Greek and Turkish coffees; Spanish, Greek and Italian olive oils; homemade Syrian and Greek breads; *filo* and *katafi;* Greek, Syrian, Armenian cheeses; bulk spices and grains. Open seven days a week. No credit cards.

***Heidelberg Café and Bakery,*** 7625 Pendleton Pike (547-1230). Authentic French and Austrian pastries and tortes. German gift shop, imported epicurean foods, a few European-style breads. Browse the bakery museum and sample the sweets, or snack on German lunches in the café. Open seven days a week. No credit cards.

***Holland American Pastry Shop,*** 6315 Guilford Avenue in Broad Ripple Village (251-4913). Neat blue-and-white shop with authentic Dutch pastries and cookies. A few imported Dutch foods. Closed Sunday. No credit cards.

***Klemm's Sausage and Meat Market,*** 315 E. South Street (632-1963). Thirty types of excellent homemade German sausage. Family owned and operated, in the old-world tradition. Closed Sunday and Monday. No credit cards.

# Kansas City

1776 was the coming of age for America. 1976, the year in which Kansas City welcomed the Republican Convention, was the coming of age for Kansas City. Kansas Citians, always a mite touchy about their national image as hicks, Indians and desperados, launched a campaign for the convention to astonish both patronizing Easterners and trendy Westerners. The local enthusiasm transcended party lines and political ties. Volunteers planned spectacular entertainments for the visiting press and dignitaries. The goal was not only to demonstrate that Kansas City was sophisticated and swinging, cultural and chic, but also to answer the nagging question, "Is everything up-to-date in Kansas City?" Yes.

The present city got its start as Westport Landing, a Missouri River port developed to import supplies to ship down the Santa Fe Trail. Westport was also the last shopping opportunity for the westward-bound prairie schooners. Thus the city has always faced southwest, and its finest eating traditions have been beef, barbecue and Mexican food.

In 1839, when the town fathers decided to rename the area, there was a groundswell movement to christen it Possum Trot, which happily failed. But illogically they chose "The City of Kansas," which ever afterwards has caused confusion and needed explanation, since Kansas City is in the state of Missouri.

As a central depot for trade, agricultural products and livestock, Kansas City quickly established sophisticated eating habits. Oysters and fresh seafood were shipped in from New Orleans. The City Market, still in existence and a colorful Saturday-morning adventure, provided fresh vegetables, poultry and fruit. As a national center for livestock butchering, the city had an abundance of pork and beef.

Kansas City has long enjoyed fine eating, but because entertaining was primarily done in private homes and clubs, visitors have been forced to rely on a few restaurants. Nevertheless, there were excellent restaurants. Fred Harvey's had its origins in Kansas City and flourished here until the 1950's. In 1903, **The Savoy,** a restaurant still popular, was opened. Its terrazzo floors, frontier murals and Tiffany glass provide a charming nostalgia that enhances its admirable steaks and seafood.

Then the Muehlbach Hotel opened. Every President since Teddy Roosevelt has been a guest at the Muehlbach, although it was particularly identified with Harry Truman. It, too, offered elegant dining, a cabaret and orchestra. Recently remodeled as the Radisson Muehlbach, it has **Le Carrousel,** which offers Continental dining with live music and an extremely popular Sunday brunch.

In the 1930's, Kansas City was the home of some of the best jazz in the country. Count Basie, Charlie "Bird" Parker and Louis Armstrong are strongly identified with the city's jazz history. Older residents fondly recall the Chesterfield Club, where waitresses wore nothing but shoes. Few patrons ever mentioned the food.

In September 1977, Kansas City was the victim of a devastating flood. Happily, restoration was so speedy that now only bronze plaques in some restaurants show the water marks, and a visitor is once again able to choose from a broad range of cuisines and dining experiences over a large area of the city. Overall, most restaurants, many of them family oriented, emphasize décor and solid food. Steaks, chicken, Mexican and Italian dishes are the most popular. The atmosphere is easygoing and friendly. Prices, by East or West Coast standards, are moderate.

The Plaza, the nation's first suburban shopping center, has more than a score of restaurants. Spanish architecture and fountains contribute to an elegant atmosphere. On Thanksgiving Evening, 152,000 Christmas lights are switched on, outlining the Plaza's buildings. In the summer, one can people-watch and dine from open-air patios, at **Fred P. Ott's,** the German Butcher's or **Putsch's Coffee House.** Japanese, French, Italian and Continental restaurants are to be found here in addition to steak and salad places. On Saturday afternoons, live music invigorates the Seville Square. Here, too, is **Biba's, Dirty Sally's** and **Houlihan's.** Near the Plaza is Tiffany's Attic, a dinner theater, which serves good food.

Crown Center, developed by the Hall family of Hallmark Cards, boasts the city's most elegant restaurant, **The American;** along with a **Trader Vic's, The Signboard Bar,** featuring live music, and the International Café, which offers eight different ethnic styles clustered around a central core of butcher-block tables. Every weekend during the summer, Crown Center presents a festival, often featuring ethnic food fairs.

Westport, a historic landmark area, is enjoying a renaissance. Gaslights and mellow brick enhance its shops, galleries and restaurants. Kelly's, primarily a bar that also serves sandwiches, is housed in the oldest building in Kansas City. Young singles will find an active nightlife in the New Stanley, Stanford and Sons, and **The Prospect,** an exquisitely designed restaurant, which opens its patio in the summer for romantic dining under the stars. Two new restaurants that show promise of becoming popular favorites are Papillon and Raisin Rack.

One of the best-kept secrets in town is lunch at the William Rockhill Nelson Gallery. Modestly priced, simple and hearty fare offers a chance to eat without having to leave the Gallery.

Family restaurants are found throughout the greater metropolitan area. **Mrs. Peters'** in Kansas City, Kansas, **Stephenson's** near Independence, and Leona Yarborough's in Fairway are just three of the many choices.

Downtown has several fine restaurants. The premier dining experience is at **La Bonne Auberge.** The **Italian Gardens,** family owned and operated, offers good food and fast service. Here, too, are **The Savoy** and **Le Carrousel.**

Farther south, in Waldo, are the city's best Chinese restaurant, the **Princess Gardens,** and **Jasper's,** an expensive, very good Italian restaurant. For those (with cars) who want fine American cooking in a totally relaxed roadhouse setting, there is **Jess and Jim's** for steaks and **R.C.'s** for fried chicken.

Kansas City has some exciting markets for those who wish to take food home. At **Fritz's,** the smoked hams, turkeys and sausages are superlative. Call the **Williams Meat Company** for outstanding beef, packed to order for shipping or carrying home. **Crown Center Marketplace** carries a multitude of imported luxury foodstuffs as well as an excellent variety of cheeses and sausages. Chinatown offers the exotic from China, India and Vietnam. **The Classic Cup** grinds fresh blends of coffee to order. Candy lovers should drop into Halls and personally select a pound or two of chocolates, or some Bogdon's Sticks—an inexpensive gift for anyone with a sweet tooth. And at any grocery store in the city one can purchase Wolferman's English Muffins, which are superior to any in the country.

Berbiglia and Happy Hollow cater to wine fanciers.

Dining in Kansas City is relaxed and fairly informal. However, all of the better restaurants and discos have strict, enforced dress codes. Coats and ties—no jeans, cords or halter tops—and an appropriate dress or pants suit are in order. Tipping is generally 15 percent of the bill.

# Restaurants and Food Sources
(Area code: 816)

# BIG DEAL

## WORTH IT

***The American,*** 2450 Grand Avenue (471-8050). Exquisite wooden fan-vaulting, glass walls overlooking Crown Center Square, formal service and beautiful appointments enhance elegant dining. People dress up here; men are required to wear coat and tie. Specialties are unusual delicacies such as Montana elk with lingonberries, New Orleans Carpetbagger steak, roast rack of lamb, as well as steaks and chops. Chocolate Velvet is a marvelous choice for dessert. There is a private dining room; arrangements must be made in advance. For private parties, request *torta primavera*—it is gorgeous and good. Buffets are managed in European and lavish style. Reservations a must. Closed Sunday. Entrées from $2.95 (L), $9.50 (D), fixed-price lunch $4.95. AE, CB, DC, MC, V.

## NOT WORTH IT

***Le Jardin,*** 9200 Metcalf, Overland Park, Ks. (649-7000). Pretty surroundings, but pretentious. The food is fair, service indifferent at best, prices very high. Saturday, dinner only. Closed Sunday. Entrées from $2.65 (L), $6.95 (D). AE, DC, MC, V.

# INTERNATIONAL

## AMERICAN

***Plaza III,*** 4749 Pennsylvania (753-0000). On September 12, 1977, Plaza III was hit full force by the flood. It was closed for months but is reopened now and provides one of the city's nicest evenings. Live music is featured every night but Sunday. The bar is ample and active. Dark wood, bricks, brass and hanging lamps give a warm and inviting air. For lunch, one cannot do better than the steak soup and Plaza III garden salad. The seafood crêpe is also tasty. Fresh fish is featured in the evening, as is chicken breast Eugenie and prime rib. After dinner, slip downstairs to Biba's, Kansas City's "in" disco. Reservations recommended. Sunday, dinner only. Open seven days a week. Entrées from $3.50 (L), $8.95 (D). AE, DC, MC, V.

***Houlihan's Old Place,*** 4743 Pennsylvania (561-3141). Favored by those who enjoy loud music, lively socializing and good food. Graffiti and wooden sculpture are mainstays of the funky décor. A sign tells how many days to St. Patrick's Day, the major celebration of the year at this watering hole. The food is savory, abundant and served piping hot. Especially recommended are the spinach salad, quiches, the Nickelodeon and French onion soup. The omelets are light and tasty. Houlihan's also offers a delicious Sunday brunch featuring such hearty fare as the Bourbon Street Breakfast and eggs Houlihan. Reservations a must. Open seven days a week. Entrées from $3.50 (L & D). AE, CB, DC, MC, V.

***The Prospect,*** 4109 Pennsylvania (753-2277). Housed in one of the city's older buildings in historic Westport, this delightful, spacious restaurant is a tribute to historic preservation. Plants, flowers, natural wood and a well-planned use of space add to the charm. In the summer you can sit under the stars in the courtyard. The salads are particularly refreshing and the quiches very good. Portions are huge and the desserts are sinfully fattening—especially mocha Suisse. Wine list outstanding. Reservations recommended. Open seven days a week. Entrées from $2.75 (L), $5 (D). AE, MC, V.

## ARGENTINIAN

***Los Gauchos,*** 128 West 63rd Street (361-6525). Recently opened, this family-owned restaurant serves one of the most delicious meals in the city. Terrazzo floors, arched glass walls with wrought-iron detailing, Latin American music and flowers on the table combine to provide a pleasant backdrop for the excellent dishes. There are offerings from Spain, Brazil and Uruguay. Particularly satisfying are the *pollo con arroz al azafrar* (lemon chicken with saffron rice and shrimp) and *costilla de cordento al chimichurri* (rack of lamb). The entrées come planked with the day's vegetables, and the presentation is elegant. Since each order is cooked individually, service is leisurely; plan to spend some time here. Closed Sunday. Entrées from $1.95 (L), $7.15 (D). MC, V.

## CHINESE

***Princess Gardens,*** 7351 Wornall Road (444-3709). There are not many outstanding Northern Chinese restaurants in the Midwest, but this is one of them. Located in a shopping center, it has stereotype Chinese restaurant décor. Almost everything on the extensive menu wins praise; but if you wish, call Robert and order any of the following ahead: lobster with wine-and-garlic sauce, pork with melon, spicy shrimp with eggplant, *chiao-tzu,* shrimp Peking, lake-style fish. Casual dress is acceptable. No reservations. Sunday, dinner only. Open seven days a week. Entrées from $3.65. AE, MC, V.

## CONTINENTAL

***Nabil's,*** 4735 Wyanotte (931-7959). Brick floors, brightly colored cloths, hanging plants and "medieval" frescos. Mediterranean, French and Spanish dishes dominate the menu. A good choice is leg of lamb Greek style. Others are shrimp à la Gello, trout stuffed with crab meat or Spanish paella. The house salad is colorful, crisp and tangy. Classical-guitar music. No reservations. Sunday, dinner only. Open seven days a week. Entrées from $2.95 (L), $7.95 (D). MC, V.

## FRENCH

***Le Méditerranée,*** 4742 Pennsylvania (561-3016). Country-French furnishings and rich cooking with an emphasis on sauces make for a pleasant meal. Recommended are *salade canaille, médaillons de veau* Oscar, Dover sole *belle meunière au citron.* Lunch service is quick and good. Reservations recommended. Chaîne des Rotisseurs. Saturday, dinner only. Closed Sunday. Entrées from $3.25 (L), $8.25 (D). AE, MC, V.

# ITALIAN

***Jasper's,*** 405 West 75th Street (363-3033). Italian restaurants abound in Kansas City, but this one offers exceptional food combined with opulence. Red is the predominant color and fresh flowers are on every table. Especially recommended is the pasta, particularly the *cannelloni al Romano,* fettuccine Pope John XXIII and the *paglia e fieno.* The veal dishes are also very good. Desserts are flamboyant and delicious. Closed Sunday. Entrées from $3.95 (L), $9.50 (D). AE, DC, MC, V.

# JAPANESE

***Gojo's,*** 4193 Broadway (561-2501). In the heart of Westport, in a converted Oriental rug emporium. Don't be put off by the hideous green exterior. This is a restaurant especially delightful for children who will adore the waterfall, complete with Japanese *koi*—colorful and friendly fish. Be sure to mention if you are celebrating a birthday; the waiters put on a parade complete with "Happy Birthday" in Japanese. One is seated in large, open wooden booths at tables for eight, with the *teppan* grill in the center of the table. The service is particularly friendly, and the chef puts on a show. There is a children's portion (chicken or minute steak), which includes soup, salad, ice cream, rice and tea for $4.50. Saturday, dinner only. Closed Sunday. Entrées from $3.50 (L); complete dinner—with soup, salad, shrimp, entrée, ice cream and tea—$7. AE, CB, MC, V.

# LEBANESE

***Nabil's,*** 3605 Broadway (531-0700). This branch of Nabil's is for those who enjoy Middle-Eastern and Mediterranean cooking. Many locals prefer this small, cozy restaurant to the larger, more Continental Nabil's at 4735 Wyandotte. The shish kebab is excellent, as is the lamb. Saturday, dinner only. Closed Sunday and Monday. Entrées from $3 (L), $7 (D). No credit cards.

# MEXICAN

***Patricio's,*** 9849 Holmes (942-4443). If you want a casual meal serving spicy Mexican food, Patricio's is your best bet. The décor is indifferent, but the food is fine. Try the *tostadas, burritos, chalupas* or taco salad. American foods are also available. No reservations. Open seven days a week. Entrées from $2.65 (L), $4.50 (D). MC, V.

## MOROCCAN/MEDITERRANEAN

***The Olive Tree,*** 4916 Main (753-1332). Moorish décor, hanging copper pans, stained glass, Mediterranean plants and an excellent belly dancer Wednesday through Saturday give a flavor of Morocco. Foods choices vary from Moroccan to Greek, French and Spanish. Dolmas, *couscous* and *felafel* are good choices. So are the lamb kebab, rack of lamb and sole Louise. Dinners include salad and vegetables. The desserts are luxurious. Reservations a must. Saturday, dinner only. Closed Sunday. Entrées from $2.95 (L), $5.25 (D). MC, V.

## POLYNESIAN

***Trader Vic's,*** Crown Center Hotel (474-4894). The usual Polynesian South Seas décor, but the service is well managed, efficient and friendly, and the food and drinks are fine. Open seven days a week. Entrées from $3.75 (L), $6 (D). AE, CB, DC, V.

## SWISS

***André's,*** 5018 Main Street (561-3440). A replica of a Swiss chalet, with tiled floors, hanging Swiss flags, wooden chairs and tables. The food here is excellent: the quiches (four choices every day) are light and satisfying. Good salads, too. Freshly made pastries and candies are sold to take home, as are European chocolates and other luxury foodstuffs. Pastry and coffee served before and after lunch. Lunch Monday through Saturday. Dinner, Friday only (6 to 8 P.M. October to May). Closed Monday during summer and Sundays. Entrées from $3.50 (L), $6.50 (D). No credit cards.

# SPECIALTY COOKING

## BARBECUE

***Arthur Bryant's Barbecue,*** 1727 Brooklyn (231-1123). Purists will admit to no other barbecue than the legendary Bryant's. Calvin

Trillin is such a devotee that for the publishing party of his book *American Fried,* 95 pounds of ribs and beef were flown to New York. The décor is so nonexistent that it's camp. Everyone waits in line; no celebrity treatment. Everything is recommended, especially the free "brownies," which are the crisp ends of the brisket. Gigantic sandwiches, abundant ribs, terrific smoked ham, French fries and iced beer. The sauce is rich, thick and hot, and available to take home. Casual dress prevails. No reservations. Closed Sunday and during January, when Bryant goes on vacation. Prices start around $2 (L & D). No credit cards.

## CHICKEN

***R.C.'s,*** 411 East 135th Street (942-4999). Take a ride out in the country and fill up on real country crispy-fried chicken, crackling potatoes and the house salad. Beef is available. The surroundings are country casual, the music is bluegrass. A fine family outing. Reservations necessary. Open seven days a week. Entrées from $2.50 (L), $3.25 (D). No credit cards.

## DELI

***Fiddler on the Square,*** 500 Nichols Road, Seville Square. This deli is good by Midwestern standards. Buffet line with hot dogs, cheeses, sausages, deli sandwiches on your choice of onion roll, bagel, rye or pumpernickel. There is a blintz platter, noodle pudding and good potato salad. Dr. Brown's Creme Soda and Cel-ray Tonic and beer. Carry out. Open seven days a week. Entrées from $1.69 (L & D). No credit cards.

## HAMBURGER

***Fred P. Ott's,*** 4770 J. C. Nichols Parkway (753-2878). Marilyn Monroe photographs, cheesecake posters, campy old signs, electric TV games, pinball and baseball machines give an eclectic charm to Fred P. Ott's. Add to that enormous juicy hamburgers, huge smoked hot dogs and crunchy French fries and onion rings, all at inexpensive prices. Tables are scarce, be prepared to share. A young crowd; loud music vibrates. Self-service and a computer bar system. Dress is casual. No reservations. Closed Sunday. Beer is 59 cents; mixed drinks, 89 cents. Entrées from $1.50 (L & D). No credit cards.

## PIZZA

***Minsky's,*** 5105 Main (561-5100), and 10630 Metcalf (341-9292). Minsky's serves no ordinary pizza. The crust is thick, the topping is savory and the ingredients, such as cheese and sausage, are unusually good. Two hungry people will be satisfied with even a small pizza. There are also salads and sandwiches. Beer and soft drinks only. Jeans or chinos are the rule here. No reservations. Open seven days a week. Entrées from $2.50 (L & D). No credit cards.

## SEAFOOD

***The Savoy,*** 9th and Central (842-3890). Tiffany glass, terrazzo floors, dark wood and frontier murals provide a nostalgic charm in this restaurant opened in 1903. Lobster is flown in daily and the seafood gumbo is thick and tangy. Beef here is top quality. The service is courtly and can be efficient. There are several rooms, including a small private dining room and a large one for parties. Reservations recommended. Closed Sunday. Entrées from $2.60 (L), $5.25 (D). AE, CB, DC, MC, V.

***Tony's,*** (a/k/a Antoine's on the Boulevard), 423 Southwest Boulevard (471-9833). Tony's started as a neighborhood saloon. Now it serves three meals a day and features all the shrimp you can eat for $8. Other excellent choices include veal Parmesan and the broiled sirloin steak. Dinner comes with a dip, salad, vegetables, bread and half a watermelon filled with fruit and liqueurs. The décor includes an enormous jar for tips ("For Antoine's Great Bartenders"). Tony himself comes over to see how things are progressing. He wears a hat because he is the chef, but his is an old golf hat. Casual fun with good food as a plus. Reservations recommended. Closed Sunday. Entrées from 90 cents (L), $4 (D). No credit cards.

## STEAK

***Golden Ox,*** 1600 Genessee (842-2866). This venerable steakhouse, located in the heart of the old stockyards, has long been famous for its quality beef. It is a short walk from the Kemper Arena. Décor is determinedly Western, and in addition to beef, seafood and chicken are on the menu. Friendly service and an informal air make it a comfortable family place. Reservations necessary. Open seven days a week. Entrées from $1.45 (L), $4 (D). AE, DC, MC.

***Hereford House,*** 2 E. 20th Street (842-1080). Many people believe this is the best beef in the Kansas City area. Western style is also evident here. Excellent and quick service make it feasible to eat quickly. Chicken and lobster are also favorites. Dinner includes salad, potatoes and fresh-baked bread. The menu is in the shape of a cow. Reservations recommended. Closed Sunday. Entrées from $1.95 (L), $5.95 (D). AE, CB, DC, MC, V.

***Jess and Jim's,*** 135th and Locust (942-9909). Maybe the best steak anywhere, mouth-watering cottage fries (ask for them extra-crisp), pickled beets and terrific cole slaw. The chicken is good and seafood is available. Sample steaks are on display. It's a 45-minute drive from downtown, so the patrons represent a cross-section of city and country. A train may rumble by, it's next to the tracks. Everybody is friendly and welcoming. Service is quick and well managed. They take no reservations, but the wait is worth it. No desserts. Closed Sunday. Entrées range from $3 for chicken to $5.75 for a steak. No credit cards.

## VEGETARIAN

***Golden Temple of Conscious Cookery,*** 4059 Broadway (561-6440). The members of the 3HO (Healthy, Happy, Holy Organization) prepare and serve all the food in this vegetarian restaurant. *Tostada* Ram Das, a dish made of tortillas, refried beans, cheese, salad, tomatoes, scallions and sour cream, is a specialty. Service is adequate, but dishes are prepared to order so it can be slow. There is a health-food store on the premises with a variety of organic foods for sale. Reservations accepted for more than twenty people. Closed Sunday. Entrées from $1.95 (L & D). No credit cards.

# FOR INDIVIDUAL NEEDS

## IF YOU HAVE TIME FOR ONLY ONE MEAL

***La Bonne Auberge,*** Ramada Inn, 6th and Washington (474-7025). Owner-chef Augustin Riedi has a gift for presenting fine French cookery with fresh ingredients. The location is strange and one has to parade through a dingy lobby, bar and coffee shop. But it is worth the dispiriting journey. Veal Maurice is a prime favorite, but one has to ask for it. Other choices include the *caneton* Bonne Auberge, and fish dishes. The pièce de résistance is the chocolate soufflé, which you should order when reserving a table. Reservations necessary. Dinner only. Closed Sunday and Monday. Entrées from $10.75. AE, MC, V.

## BEST HOTEL MEAL

***Alameda Roof,*** Alameda Hotel, Wornall Road at Ward Parkway (756-1500). Spanish tiles, lavish use of cinnamon coloring, ornate chandeliers, heavy molding and large chairs provide the Spanish influence in this rooftop restaurant with its unparalleled view of the Plaza. Service is competent, the food is beautifully served. A special luncheon salad is the South Pacific; the Fiesta Mexicana is also a good choice. A dinner selection might be scampi à la St. Valery or *beurre d'escargot.* There are three beautiful private dining rooms, and the hotel does an exceptional job with private parties. Live music and dancing in the bar. Reservations recommended. Open seven days a week. Entrées from $2.75 (L), $7.95 (D). AE, DC, MC, V.

## RESTAURANT NEAR AIRPORT

***Cascone's,*** 3733 Oak Trafficway (454-7977). Fifteen minutes from KCI, this restaurant has live music in a traditional country-Italian setting. Baked cannelloni and veal Leonora Limonada are excellent. For a special treat, call at least 24 hours in advance and order the special seafood platter. It includes antipasto, Italian salad, scampi, stuffed crab, deviled crab, stuffed clams, frogs' legs, Alaskan King crab claws and legs, shrimps and lobster tails. With dessert and coffee it costs $19.95 per person. Open seven days a week, September through May; closed Sunday in summer. No reservations. Banquet facilities. Entrées from $1.95 (L), $3.95 (D). AE, CB, DC, MC, V.

***Frolics Restaurant and Bar,*** 7007 N.W. Barry Road at I-29 (587-0808). A ten-minute drive from KCI, Frolics' specialties range from steak fingers to Pompous Pineapple. The Frolics' omelet or Pablo Diablo are other good choices. Be sure to leave room for Platte County Pie—a confection of pecans, chocolate chips and butter—and *do* ask for the recipe. Reservations accepted. Open seven days a week, with Sunday brunch. Entrées from $2.95 (L & D). AE, MC, V.

## BUSINESS BREAKFAST

***Alameda Coffee Shop,*** Alameda Hotel, Wornell Road at Ward Parkway (756-1500). Spacious, light, with a view of the Plaza. Specialties include Chilachiles omelet and eggs Benedict, although any omelet can be prepared. French toast, pancakes and hot and cold cereals add to the variety. Casual, no reservations. Open seven days a week, at 6 A.M. Entrées from $2.95. AE, DC, MC, V.

## BUSINESS LUNCH

***Italian Gardens,*** 1110 Baltimore (221-9311). Family owned and operated, this Italian restaurant is located in the heart of downtown. Unpretentious décor but fast, competent service, and consistent food. There are both Italian and American dishes on the menu. The Italian steak, spaghetti and Italian sausage are all fine choices. The bread is delicious. Reservations accepted for large groups only. Closed Sunday and holidays. Entrées from $2.25 (L), $3.75 (D). MC, V.

***Mario's,*** 4747 Wyandotte (931-4500). Mario's on the Plaza offers fast, efficient service and excellent food. Salads are good, the sandwiches innovative—especially the sausage grinder. The pasta is delicious, particularly manicotti and *fettuccine al Mario.* Also, lobster Diavolo or the filet of sole *della Nonna Scaglia.* Plants, trees and Italian flags mixed with rich colors provide a cheerful décor. Reservations recommended. Closed Sunday. Entrées from $2.85 (L), $5.50 (D). AE, MC, V.

## FAST, GOOD FOOD

***Putsch's Coffee House,*** 333 W. 47th Street (753-3345). The food is always simple, but good. Open from 6 A.M. to 2 A.M., seven days a week. Dinners from $2.50. MC, V.

## BEST WINE LIST

***Alameda Roof,*** Wornall Road at Ward Parkway (756-1500). (See description under BEST HOTEL MEAL.)

## FOR DRINKS

***Alameda Roof,*** Wornall Road at Ward Parkway (756-1500). Here is an oasis for a leisurely drink combined with mellow music, sometimes jazz, sometimes more of the pop variety. Dancing. It all takes place with a spectacular view of the Plaza and is a pleasant way to end any evening. Open seven days a week. AE, DC, MC, V.

***Biba's,*** 4749 Pennsylvania (753-0000). Located in the Plaza III, this disco is decorated in sophisticated style: mirrors, burgundy and silver, fountains and sliding doors. A private club, it is open to the public only on Monday, Tuesday and Thursday. Dress code is strictly enforced: suits and ties are required, suitable attire for women. No reservations. Closed Sunday. AE, DC, MC, V.

***Dirty Sally's,*** 614 W. 48th Street (753-2402). A disco mostly for singles who like backgammon mixed with loud music. Open until 1:30 A.M. Closed Sunday. No credit cards.

***The Signboard Bar,*** 1 Pershing Road (474-4400). Located in Crown Center, this bar is for those who enjoy live music presented in a variety of styles. There is a buffet lunch at $4.25, which includes roast beef, chicken, ham, salads and desserts. The music runs from 4:30 to 7:30 P.M. and 9 P.M. to 1 A.M. The stage is in the round, so all tables have a good view. No reservations. Closed Sunday. AE, CB, DC, MC, V.

## LATE-NIGHT SERVICE

***Granfalloon,*** 611 W. 48th (756-7850). Terrific place for after a show or movie, casual but classy décor. Good bar, loud music and limited menu that includes a Reuben burger and spinach salad, chili and frankfurters. Dress casual. No reservations. Open seven days a week. Entrées from $2.95 (L & D). AE, MC, V.

***Nichols Lunch,*** S.W. Trafficway and 39th (561-8871). Open 24 hours a day, Nichols offers a good, simple meal any time. In business 56 years, it draws a crowd of aficionados. Breakfast dishes are especially good; there is a daily special luncheon and deli sandwiches. Casual in the extreme. No reservations. Entrées from $1 (B), $1.30 (L & D). No credit cards.

## CONTINENTAL BREAKFAST

***La Bonne Bouchée,*** 618 Ward Parkway (931-5230). A true French *boulangerie,* it boasts two French bakers who arrive at midnight to prepare pastries and breads for the morning's delectation. Croissants melt in the mouth, brioches beg to be eaten, the tarts are flaky and mouth-watering. Long loaves of wheat-stalk bread. Coffee and tea are featured. The take-home section is perfect for the traveler who wants something in the room for a Continental breakfast. Clean, airy and light, it provides a charming break for shoppers at the Plaza. Closed Monday. No credit cards.

## SUNDAY BRUNCH

***Le Carrousel,*** Radisson Muehlbach Hotel, 12th and Baltimore (471-1400). The fixed-price ($4.95) brunch is served from 10:30 A.M. to 2:30 P.M. It also serves a lunch and dinner with live music during the week. Reservations a must. Closed Monday. AE, CB, DC, MC, V.

## SUNDAY-EVENING MEAL

***Mrs. Peters' Chicken Place,*** 4960 State Avenue, Kansas City, Ks. (827-7711). If you're crazy about down-home American cooking mixed with American Gothic décor, served family style, Mrs. Peters' is for you—and the family. Gingham tablecloths, gingerbread moldings, cheerful and clean surroundings set the mood for good eating. Everything is fresh and homecooked. There are only three choices: Southern-style fried chicken, pork chops and chicken-fried steak. Homemade beaten biscuits, coleslaw, mashed potatoes and corn are side dishes. The ice cream is homemade, the Dutch apple pie and peach cobbler are fine. Lunch offers soups, salads, sandwiches and desserts. Children welcome, a child's portion, including lemonade, is ample and costs only $2.50. There is a gift shop. Reservations a must. No liquor. Open seven days a week. Entrées from $2.50 (L), $6 (D). MC, V.

***Golden Ox,*** 1600 Genessee (842-2866). (See description under STEAK.)

## FOR FAMILIES WITH CHILDREN

***Stephenson's,*** 40 Highway & Lee's Summit Road (373-5400). Convenient to the Truman Library and Fort Osage. The atmosphere is old-fashioned country inn. There are a myriad rooms. Crowded seating but rapid—sometimes too rapid—service. The chicken and apple dishes are famous. The owners have their own orchards, and apple butter and apple jellies are for sale. All foods are homemade; they hickory smoke many of the meats. So popular that reservations are necessary. Open seven days a week. Entrées from $2.95 (L), $5.25 (D). AE, CB, DC, MC, V.

***Mrs. Peters' Chicken Place,*** 4960 State Avenue, Kansas City, Ks. (827-7711). (See description under SUNDAY-EVENING MEAL.)

# MARKETS

***Crown Center Marketplace,*** 2450 Grand (471-1783). One can purchase anything from soup to nuts. Fresh flowers, fresh fish and imported luxury items are all available. For cheese and sausages, see George Detsios. He stocks a bewildering variety. At the pastry shop, chocolate Swiss tortes, petits fours and cookies compete for attention. Wine and spirits shops as well.

## GIFT FOODS

***The Classic Cup,*** 5 Westport Square (913/561-7478). Features imported coffees, ground to order. No credit cards.

***Williams Meat Company,*** 1101 South 5th Street (913/371-8255). Williams packs and ships the beef that made Kansas City famous. Some of the choices are beef tenderloin, Kansas City sirloin strips and porterhouse. If you plan to travel home with the beef, call the day before and it will be packed and ready for you. Closed Saturday and Sunday. No credit cards.

***Fritz's,*** 10326 State Line (913/381-4618). Worth a special trip. The sausage, hot dogs, knockwurst are all worthy of mention; the smoked meats are mouth-watering; the cold cuts are excellent. Everything is cooked in the shop, which is scrupulously clean. Call Elmer if you want it packed for travel or shipping, it will save time. Try to avoid Saturday mornings, it's jammed. Closed Sunday and Monday. No credit cards.

# Las Vegas

Las Vegas, the largest city in Nevada, has evolved from the railroad town it was at the turn of the century, into one of the world's most glamorous tourist attractions, known for superstars, neon lights and football-length casinos.

This transformation brought with it a move away from a small-town diet to cuisines catering to international high rollers, business executives and wide-eyed conventioneers. But the "Strip" has not erased the past totally. Locals, all too familiar with the clang of slot machines and the rattle of dice, seek less flamboyant, out-of-the-way dining.

Tourist areas of Las Vegas are generally divided into two locations—the "Strip" and "Glitter Gulch." The Strip refers to a line of hotels along Las Vegas Boulevard South beginning with the Sahara Hotel at Sahara Avenue and stretching south to the Hacienda Hotel some seven miles away. Glitter Gulch is in downtown Las Vegas. Drive or ride north on Las Vegas Boulevard to Fremont Street and look left (or west) and there it is. Undoubtedly the largest concentration of neon lights in the world, Glitter Gulch is a blazing area of wall-to-wall casinos complete with restaurants, coffee shops and a few hidden delights for the palate such as **Cosmo's,** an Italian restaurant located beneath the street level and featuring "Mama's" cooking.

A third area is beginning to develop along the Boulder Highway (U.S. 95-93) leading from Las Vegas to Henderson and Boulder City. At the intersection of Fremont Street and Charleston Boulevard, where U.S. 95-93 begins, you will find The Green Shack. Casual, unaffected, a favorite of many "old-timers" and one of southern Nevada's oldest restaurants, The Green Shack looks exactly like its name and has good chicken.

The Showboat Hotel, known among locals for its nearly 24-hour buffet, is the largest hotel-casino on the Boulder Highway, and farther out is Sam's Town, a hotel-casino recently opened by long-time gaming figure Sam Boyd. The menu, which features Western cooking, is still unproven.

Hungry travelers will never starve in this city of no clocks. Hotel room service and coffee shops in major resorts all operate 24 hours a day. So do many outlying restaurants, such as Port Tack, Starboard Tack, El Jardins, The Flame and Good Time Charlie's (closed only from 10 P.M. Sunday to 6:30 A.M. Monday). The food at these places, though not exciting, is acceptable, the lights are dim, the cocktails plentiful and the service friendly.

Those losing at the gambling tables should tuck a buck away for a cheapie pre-dawn breakfast, which ranges in price from 49 cents at the Bingo Palace (3 to 6 A.M.) to slightly less than $1 for eggs and bacon or sausage at Circus Circus, Flamingo Hilton, Fremont Hotel, Hacienda Hotel, Holiday Casino (24 hours), Jolley Trolley, Royal Inn, Silver City (24 hours), Silver Nugget or the downtown Union Plaza, which serves steaks, eggs, juice and coffee for 96 cents (4 to 10 A.M.).

Public transportation in Las Vegas is difficult and inadequate except for bus service from the Strip to downtown. Taxicabs are expensive. Surprisingly, 61 percent of the city's 10 million annual tourists arrive here by car. The layout of the city is easy to follow with a good street map.

The "come as you are" motto of a few years ago is no longer quite as appropriate as it once was, but is still acceptable. In Strip hotel gourmet rooms, a suit and tie are more common than a sports jacket. Seldom, however, is anyone turned away for lack of a tie—and never if the hungry customer is known to the hotel management as a high roller with a fat wallet. In the casinos, women wear anything from floor-length evening dresses or pants suits to disco tights.

Most of the food consumed in southern Nevada is imported from nearby agricultural states, and fresh fish more than likely is "fresh frozen." Dinner served in hotel showrooms is, to some extent, prepared in advance in order to serve as many as 1,000 people in the 60 to 90 minutes before curtain time. Showroom service lacks class and is sometimes irritating, but the customer—for $20 to $30 a person, plus tips and beverages—goes away with a full stomach and the memory of watching one of the world's best-known stage names. Showroom wines, however, are overpriced and selections are limited. Top line wines from nearby California usually are the best bet.

# Restaurants and Food Sources
**(Area code: 702)**

## BIG DEAL

### WORTH IT

***Palace Court,*** Caesars Palace Hotel, 3570 Las Vegas Boulevard South (731-7110). A red-carpeted winding staircase with marble banisters leads to this second-floor room, frequented by high rollers and superstars. The vermeil flatware, hand-blown crystal and white-glove service lend an elegance that is rare if not unique in these parts. Highlights of the extensive menu: Maine lobster *au gratin* or flambéed in Cognac, steak Diane, steak tartare, twin tournedos with foie gras, veal kidney in mustard sauce, rack of baby lamb. Sommeliers pour your choice from a list of 100 different wines, some priced at $100 or more. Dessert soufflés, fruit and cheese or flaming coffee are alternative ways to complete one of the most expensive yet "worth the money" treats in Las Vegas. No fixed-price meals. The menu is à la carte. Chaîne des Rotisseurs. Monday and Tuesday, dinner only. Open seven days a week. Entrées from $8 (L), $16 (D). AE, CB, DC, MC, V.

## INTERNATIONAL

### AMERICAN

***Golden Steer,*** 308 West Sahara Avenue (384-4470). Excellent New York steaks and seafood served in a casual atmosphere just off the Strip. Italian entrées also on the menu include clam linguine and various pastas. Featured is the giant pound-and-a-half prime rib served with baked potato (which weighs about a pound). The restaurant has been in operation since the early 1960's, the "boom" days of the Strip. The cocktail lounge was recently expanded to accommodate the waiting dinner crowd. Reservations necessary. Dinner only. Open seven days a week, until midnight. Entrées from $6.95. AE, DC, MC, V.

***Phillips Supperhouse,*** 4545 West Sahara Avenue (873-5222). A Victorian San Francisco-style house with turn-of-the-century décor. The atmosphere is right for a romantic evening or a private, uninterrupted business meeting. Some booths literally take on the character of a small, individual dining room. New England shore dinner is a specialty, along with steaks, baked Maine lobster and tournedos of beef (served with a special sauce that takes three separate steps and two days to prepare). Reservations suggested. Dinner only. Open seven days a week, until midnight. Entrées from $9.95. AE, MC, V.

## GERMAN

***Alpine Village Inn,*** 3003 Paradise Road, across the street from the Las Vegas Hilton (734-6888). This family-run Swiss-German restaurant started small but because of its popularity has expanded into a near-Strip restaurant. Waiters and waitresses are dressed in Alpine attire, and the décor in the entrance-level dining room has a German flavor. Try chicken supreme soup and smoked pork chops. Service is polite, friendly and efficient. Downstairs in the Rathskeller, a room with red-checkered tablecloths, a piano goes nightly for a singalong crowd. There is also a separate cocktail lounge with Alpine backdrop. Weekend reservations suggested. Dinner only. Open seven days a week, until midnight. Entrées from $2.25 in the Rathskeller and from $5.50 in the main dining room. AE, CB, DC, MC, V.

## ITALIAN

***Battista's Hole in the Wall,*** 4041 Audrie, across from the M-G-M Grand Hotel (732-1424). The family-operated restaurant is comfortable, friendly and tastefully decorated. The dull exterior opens into several rooms suggesting old Italy. The homemade fresh pastas became so popular as appetizers that some now are listed as entrées. Waiters and waitresses in native dress invite tables of four to share the entrées—cheese-filled crêpes, seafood combinations, veal, scampi or eggplant dishes—family style. Fresh bread, soup, salad, complimentary house wines and *cappuccino* accompany every meal. Reservations suggested. Dinner only. Open seven days a week. Entrées from $8. AE, DC, MC, V.

***Cosmo's Underground Ristorante & Lounge,*** 32 East Fremont, under the Sundance Casino (382-0330). This relatively new restaurant in the heart of Glitter Gulch is operated by seven members of the Ruffino family. A few steps below street level, it is literally underground and one must look closely to find the Cosmo's sign. Attractive patio décor. The Italian food is prepared by "Mama." Her chicken Angelo is recommended but don't hesitate to try any of the veal dishes. Dinner only. Open seven days a week, until midnight. Pasta entrées from $3.50. MC, V.

# SPECIALTY COOKING

## DELI

***Max C's Corned Beef Junction,*** 221 Bridger Street (386-0224). This deli is located in the shadow of the downtown Clark County Courthouse and specializes in giant sandwiches named after local characters and celebrities. Max's lively patter keeps customers entertained as they wait for him to slice corned beef, turkey, tongue and all kinds of cheeses for his jawbreaker-sized sandwiches. They come with a kosher pickle and potato salad. Call ahead to avoid a wait. Closed Saturday and Sunday. Entrées from $1.75 (L & D). No credit cards.

## OMELET

***Alias Smith & Jones,*** 541 E. Twain Avenue (732-7401). Come here for the "MMM Omelet"—named for the sounds of satisfaction that it will evince. The ingredients include an unknown number of eggs, mushrooms, three cheeses, avocado, tomato, bacon and olive. Other menu choices include ribs and a vegetarian sandwich. Located in a small shopping center. Open seven days a week, until 6 A.M. Cocktail lounge open 24 hours a day. "MMM Omelet" is $4.95. MC, V.

## ROAST BEEF

***Coachman's Inn,*** 3240 Eastern Avenue (734-9767). This off-Strip restaurant has Christmas every day, with a lighted tree and fireplace. It offers steaks, seafood and prime rib. The queen-sized prime rib ($9.95) and the king-sized rib ($12.95) shouldn't be attempted unless you have a hearty appetite; each weighs over two pounds and comes with baked potato, soup, salad and dessert. At lunch try the cold roast beef sandwich. Sunday, dinner only. Open seven days a week. Cocktail lounge open until 2 A.M. Entrées from $2.95 (L), $7.95 (D). MC, V.

***Golden Steer,*** 308 West Sahara Avenue (384-4470). (See description under AMERICAN.)

## SEAFOOD

***Dome of the Sea,*** Dunes Hotel, 3650 Las Vegas Boulevard South (737-4110). This dome-shaped restaurant features broiled Maine lobster for $25, but it also serves an acceptable bouillabaisse. The menu is primarily à la carte, but dinner includes potato and vegetable. Dinner is served in the midst of an undersea kingdom with a mermaid harpist floating in a small central pool and flying fish projected on the walls about you. Dinner only. Closed Tuesday. Entrées from $13.50. AE, CB, DC, MC, V.

## STEAK

***Spanish Steps,*** Caesars Palace Hotel, 3750 Las Vegas Boulevard South (731-7110). Named for the Spanish Steps in Rome, this new Strip restaurant shines with $650,000 worth of copper décor. Primarily a steakhouse, with prime cuts, although a wide variety of fish and fowl are offered as well. Plan on ceviche or shrimp with wine sauce and garlic for starters. Dinner only. Open seven days a week. Entrées from $7.50. AE, CB, DC, MC, V.

# FOR INDIVIDUAL NEEDS

## IF YOU HAVE TIME FOR ONLY ONE MEAL

***Palace Court,*** Caesars Palace Hotel, 3570 Las Vegas Boulevard South (731-7110). (See description under BIG DEAL/WORTH IT.)

# BEST HOTEL MEAL

***Sabre Room and Middle East Room,*** in the Aladdin Hotel, 3667 Las Vegas Boulevard South (736-0111). Below-casino-level dining here is an escape from the shouts of the winners and groans of the losers. The softly lit dining area is divided into two sections—the Sabre Room with Continental food, and the more intimate Middle East Room with its Lebanese and French flavor. Devour shish kebab or stuffed grape leaves under the Middle East Room's Arabian Nights canopies. Overstuffed booths, subtle lighting and attentive waiters in the Sabre Room. Steak Diane flambé and veal Oskar are favorites on the à la carte menu. Reservations necessary. Dinner only. Open seven days a week. Entrées from $12.95. AE, CB, DC, MC, V.

***Regency Room,*** Sands Hotel, 3355 Las Vegas Boulevard South (733-5000). Virtually every major Strip hotel and downtown hotel-casino has more than one dining room—some as many as seven or eight. Rating them would require a lifetime of eating; among them, however, the Regency Room stands out as one of the best. Its ambitious menu features French and a few American dishes—tournedos Rossini, *escalopes de veau* epicurean, Chateaubriand *bouquetière,* chicken Kiev, scampi Provençale, stone crab with mustard sauce and butter sauce, steak *au poivre,* beef Wellington. Reservations suggested. Dinner only. Open seven days a week. Entrées from $15. AE, CB, DC, MC, V.

# RESTAURANT NEAR AIRPORT

***Jubilation Restaurant,*** 75 East Harmon Avenue (733-8822). (See description under LATE-NIGHT SERVICE.) The restaurant is about three miles from McCarran International Airport and would be a highlight of a stopover in the nation's gambling capital. Go here for dinner after satisfying your gambling hunger at the airport slot machines.

# BUSINESS BREAKFAST

***Garden Room,*** Sands Hotel, 3355 Las Vegas Boulevard South (733-5000). The indoor-outdoor atmosphere of this bright room is highlighted by fresh flowers and well-appointed tables. Manny Armijo has commanded the room for 16 years with tender, loving care and has maintained its quality through several hotel ownerships. Telephone outlets are convenient for those conducting

observe the activity from a gallery lined with food stands offering everything from *carnitas*-filled soft tacos to headily flavored bowls of fish stew and exotic fresh fruit drinks.

While a large segment of the population consumes junk food with a vengeance, another sizable segment is equally into health food. This is Tinsel Town, after all, and the pressure to be beautifully fit is enormous. At Ruffage, in Beverly Hills, a former fatty, pleased with his new self, is now running a serious exercise class and an elegant, high-quality salad bar. At The Thinnery, ingeniously tasty, low-calorie specialties are served. At The Source, overindulged locals seek to restore themselves over toasted cheese and alfalfa sprouts on whole-grain bread, in the questionably healthy outdoors of the Sunset Strip. And, although Los Angeles is a melting pot of foreigners, you can count on your fingers the fine Italian restaurants. The gifts of the Orient are endless, however. The array of Japanese, Korean, Vietnamese and Thai food, as well as Chinese, is practically limitless. The best Japanese restaurants are found in a large "little Tokyo" area. The best Chinese restaurants, however, are *not* found in the city's sizable Chinatown. Conveniently, the Thais have settled everywhere, so that Angelenos from El Monte to the San Fernando Valley can include good, inexpensive Thai meals in their ethnic dining.

One thing Los Angeles is short on is tradition. It is true that forty years ago Alex Perino opened a dignified Continental restaurant next to his Hancock Park neighbors; it is still one of the best in town. Downtown, **Original Pantry** has been open continuously for fifty years. And **Musso and Frank's Grill,** the place that gave Hollywood its own version of the Algonquin's Round Table, is a Hollywood Boulevard landmark. But outside of these and a handful of others, most of Los Angeles is born yesterday. Perhaps the city's greatest contribution to dining has been the creation of the single-entrée restaurant (a dubious achievement). Living testimony to this contribution is the original Lawry's Prime Rib, founded in 1958, which is still one of the most popular places in town. The "secret" of its success is that a great many people prefer to know exactly what they're getting into when they go out to eat. And there are no surprises on Lawry's straightforward menu. But then, if it's salad, prime rib, potato and vegetable that you're after, there is probably no reason to go elsewhere.

In short, Los Angeles is not much different from anyplace else in America, only larger. Meanwhile, travel, plus the rage (and social pressure) to cook well at home, are creating a generation of more aware diners.

Enforced dress codes are rare in Los Angeles, but people seem to be dressing up more, at least for the finer restaurants. Some places, **Scandia** for instance, insist that gentlemen wear jackets, and shirts buttoned up to the chin. At other places—The Tower, L'Orangerie, L'Ermitage—it simply would be tasteless to dress *very* casually. Reservations are almost always necessary, and all but a few places try to honor them. Tipping is about the same as it is in New York or other large cities. Fifteen percent, to be divided between waiter and captain, is expected for good service. Some restaurants provide checks with separate lines for different tips, but if not, the tips may properly be combined. Maître d's and sommeliers may be given a cash tip, if it is deserved; sommeliers are routinely given one or two dollars for each bottle opened.

# Restaurants and Food Sources
(Area code: 213)

## BIG DEAL

### WORTH IT

***Perino's,*** 4101 Wilshire Boulevard (383-1221). Perino's graceful oval dining room is from a more civilized age. The service is formal but not intimidating. The need to request anything is rare. And the à la carte Continental menu reflects a classical cuisine that was stylish when the restaurant opened forty years ago. The food can be exquisite: still-cool ocean-fish oysters under a silken sauce Mornay, *consommé bellevue,* a cream-of-pea soup that may be the best you've tasted. Favored entrées include saddle of baby lamb carved into long, even slices, squab grilled with bacon, and veal Cordon Bleu, a dish that usually is mundane elsewhere. The menu is enormous: fifteen fresh vegetables are listed, sixteen salads. There are nine preparations of potatoes, but not to order the faultless *pommes soufflées* is to make a big mistake. Perino's dessert chef is a master soufflé maker. Perino's is very expensive, with dinner entrées ranging from $8 (for pasta) to a rather startling $26 (veal *noisette*). Saturday, dinner only. Closed Sunday. Lunch entrées from $5. AE, CB, DC, MC, V.

### NOT WORTH IT

***Chasen's,*** 9039 Beverly Boulevard (271-2168). The famous chili parlor has assumed pretensions of cuisine as well as grandeur so severe that the dish that made Chasen's reputation appears on the after-10 P.M. supper menu only. Someone, it seems, has decreed chili an inelegant dinner dish; however, it will be served (somewhat grumpily) earlier on request. Go if you insist on seeing the famous feeding, but avoid any Continental folderol in favor of simple American food, such as the founder's hobo steak or the excellent chicken potpie. Banana shortcake, a fresh but unsophisticated concoction, is the favored dessert. Rudeness on the part of Chasen's help should not be taken personally; celebrity treatment is reserved for celebrities. Dinner only. Closed Monday. Entrées from $9. No credit cards.

# INTERNATIONAL

## AMERICAN

***Musso and Frank's Grill,*** 6667 Hollywood Boulevard, Hollywood (467-7788, 467-5123). A genuine Hollywood landmark since 1919, Musso's has a large menu with the kinds of dishes your mother made—if she was a good American cook—and the kind of faded comfort that would make even your old Auntie from Biloxi feel at home. Daily specials include a thick-crusted and generously filled chicken potpie and corned beef and cabbage. Mainstays are excellent calf's or steer's liver, thick-cut loin lamb chops, fried smelts, or sautéed sand crabs. No meal is complete without Musso's incomparable nutmeg-edged creamed spinach. Some of the waiters may be grumpy, but few of them will mix up your orders. Closed Sunday. Entrées from $3 (L), $5 (D). AE, CB, DC, MC, V.

## CHINESE

***Chung King,*** 11538 Pico Boulevard, West L.A. (477-4917). Chung King was serving uncompromising Szechuan food long before it was much of a fashion in Los Angeles. This restaurant separates the sissies from the serious. Classic dishes such as chicken with tangerine flavor and steamed fish in a dark, oil-rich sauce are complicated, reflecting the cuisine's reliance on contrasts of taste and texture. Green bean-thread noodles, a specialty that must be ordered in advance, is extraordinary, but so searingly hot that it should be eaten as a final, separate course. Saturday and Sunday, dinner only. Open seven days a week. Entrées from $3 (L & D). No credit cards.

***Mandarin,*** 430 North Camden Drive, Beverly Hills (272-0267). This is uptown Chinese, with a menu that will appeal to broader tastes. The Mandarin is elegant, with peach-colored linens, tile floors and considerate service. If you have time to order in advance, the

Peking duck here is exquisite both to taste and look at. Minced squab is combined with rich spices and rolled in fresh Boston lettuce leaves. A favorite lunch is the Mandarin's mustard-spiked chicken salad with crisp noodles, and spinach with garlic and cellophane noodles; or, when it is in season, crisp, cold asparagus. Sunday, dinner only. Open seven days a week. Entrées from $4.25 (L), $4.75 (D). AE, CB, DC, MC, V.

***Gung Hay,*** 14800 Crenshaw Boulevard (770-3777). The regular menu at this suburban Los Angeles restaurant is an enormous, sophisticated and handily executed introduction to authentic Cantonese food. Beyond that, the restaurant's nine chefs (all trained by a master from Hong Kong) will, on 48 hours' notice, turn out far more esoteric dishes, such as taro root "bowls" filled with abalone in a delicate oyster sauce; stuffed, crisp-fried squabs; or boned duck filled with Chinese ham, barley, lotus seeds, mushrooms and exotic spices. Open seven days a week. Entrées from under $3 (regular menu), special dishes from $15 (for six or more). AE, DC, MC, V.

## FRENCH

***L'Ermitage,*** 730 N. La Cienega Boulevard (652-5840). A serenely beautiful decorator's dream of an elegant French country house. There are fresh flowers everywhere, and painted ones on the service plates; the windows are curtained in sheer, shirred cotton. The signature dishes here include the aquavit- and dill-cured *gravlax,* the delicate puff-pastry layers sandwiching asparagus, or silky, barely cooked scallops and braised spinach, and the rare duck breast in Médoc. But owner-chef Jean Bertranou has exhaustive energy for tracking down ingredients and creating new dishes, and the menu changes to include such items as fresh-killed California squabs roasted with garlic, wild hare from Scotland, or goose from Wisconsin; fresh shrimp, scallops and fish of all kinds are flown in from the East Coast and France. Bertranou started his career as a pastry chef and now trains and employs two or three at a time; they make everything from the slivers of tomato quiche or other amusements that are passed with apéritifs in the little waiting bar, to the staggering daily display of desserts and the elegant cookies that arrive with the homemade fruit sherbets—five or six flavors, including fresh cassis, are routinely included. Dinner only. Closed Sunday. Entrées from $12. AE, MC, V.

***Ma Maison,*** 8368 Melrose Avenue (655-1991). Famous for years as a favorite Hollywood hangout, this funky little bungalow with its plastic-encased front garden (which functions as the main room of the restaurant) also has recently emerged as a terrific place to eat. Fish dishes—from simply poached scallops with vegetables or fresh sting ray sauced with butter and vinegar to the elaborate specialty, whole fish *en croûte* stuffed with *mousseline*—are among the best. A two-stage duck entrée (the rare breast in a simple, Armagnac-laced sauce, followed by the grilled leg and a salad of chicory garnished with bits of fried duck skin) is excellent. Favored desserts include fruit tarts, a sinful marjolaine and little puff-pastry containers filled with fruit and light pastry cream. Closed Sunday. Entrées from $7 (L), $12 (D). AE, CB, MC, V.

## ITALIAN

***Peppone,*** 11628 Barrington Court, Brentwood (476-7379). The creation of a young Venetian, this also ranks as one of Los Angeles' best fish restaurants. Cioppino with halibut, clams and shrimp in a rich tomato sauce, octopus stewed in a richly herbed broth, and broiled shark are routinely available. For meat-eaters there are chicken and specially made sausages or tender tripe cooked in a light, peppery tomato sauce. Pasta is prepared with tuna from Genoa, imported *porcini* mushrooms or, more simply, with peas and cheese. Be sure to consult with the captain before you order at Peppone; the menu is often no more than a starting point for what's available. The wine list includes the best of California, and a good variety of Italian. Saturday and Sunday, dinner only. Closed Monday. Entrées from $6 (L), $8 (D). AE, DC, MC, V.

***La Famiglia,*** 453 N. Canon Drive, Beverly Hills (276-6208). Wonderful pasta, if you remind them that you want it cooked *al dente:* fresh, firm *tagliarini* with sweet butter and chives; tender *tortellini,* which can be ordered plain, or with sauce *all' arabiata,* a spicy hot tomato sauce which is sometimes served with the additions of tuna or *calamari.* In season, *linguine al pesto* is a treat. La Famiglia specializes in a simple but sophisticated style of Italian home cooking. Grilled chicken with garlic and herbs, a carefully prepared New York steak with gently sautéed green peppers, zucchini *fritto* and fresh spinach sautéed with olive oil and plenty of garlic. La Famiglia is Beverly Hills casual, with gingham tablecloths, fresh flowers and friendly, competent waiters. Saturday, dinner only.

Closed Sunday. Entrées from $5.95 (L), $7.95 (D). AE, CB, DC, MC, V.

# JAPANESE

If you are anywhere in Los Angeles, you are in the neighborhood of a very good *sushi* bar.

***Hamayoshi,*** 3350 West 1st Street (384-2914), and the nearby **Shibucho,** 3114 West Beverly Boulevard (387-8498), both attract a large Japanese clientele and routinely offer a large assortment of fish—the mild-flavored tuna called *maguro* as well as the fattier and stronger tasting *toro;* sea bass, mackerel, halibut and so on—as well as more esoteric items such as cockles, octopus, giant Japanese clams, fresh abalone, and the roe of salmon, crabs or herring. The *sushi* bar at the **Inagiku** restaurant in the Bonaventure Hotel, 5th and Flower streets (624-1000) is equally well-stocked, and, when they have the time, some of the chefs can be very creative. There are also some rare ingredients, like salt-cured salmon, which is combined with a thin slice of onion and a strip of *nori,* and smoked Japanese scallops. The refreshing *sunomono*—cold dishes of seafood and cucumbers dressed with rice vinegar—are elegantly arranged; *sashimi* and *chirashi* (a *sushi*-style dish in which the ingredients are presented over the rice) are excellent. **Tokyo,** 9561 Wilshire Boulevard, Beverly Hills (274-7568) or 621 South Olive (687-9606), offers a wide and classy assortment of *sushi* ingredients; the sea urchin, the salmon roe (top either with a raw quail's egg yolk) and the cooked eel, *anago,* to be warmed and bound to its rice with a strip of *nori* and topped off with sweet soy sauce are particularly fine. *Sushi* prices start at around 75 cents per piece, though many restaurants traditionally regard one order as consisting of two pieces.

***A Thousand Cranes,*** New Otani Hotel, 120 South Los Angeles Street (629-1200). For full-course Japanese dinners. The menu here is large and exotic, and the pretty, contemporary dining room faces a roof-top garden complete with waterfall (there are also traditional, private *tatami* rooms). Appetizers include at least half a dozen different *sunomono,* briny fresh seaweed and excellent green tea noodles. The *shabu-shabu* and the *yosenabe,* an elaborate fish and shellfish stew, are among the best entrées; both include a staggering selection of vegetables as well as tofu, ginkgo nuts and cellophane noodles. Open seven days a week. Complete meals from $4.50 (L), $7.50 (D). AE, CB, DC, MC, V.

## MOROCCAN

***Dar Maghreb,*** 7651 Sunset Boulevard (876-7651). The owner of San Francisco's famous Marakesch has moved his act down to Los Angeles, and outstripped anything he did before. At Dar Maghreb, ambience is as important as food. The rooms are lavishly decorated with imported tiles, and the diners sit on low banquettes or floor cushions and eat a communal meal with flatbread or fingers. The multicourse dinner is fixed: cold vegetables, *b'stilla* (a delicious flaky pastry enveloping shredded chicken) and *couscous.* Only the main course—chicken, squab, rabbit or lamb—is chosen by the party, and everyone must decide to have the same thing. Dinner only. Open seven days a week. Complete dinners from $12.50. MC, V.

## RUSSIAN

***Kavkaz,*** 8795 Sunset Boulevard, West Hollywood (652-6582). The best Russian restaurant in town also commands a beautiful city view from just above the Sunset Strip. Lamb marinated in pomegranate juice is a constant winner; so is the chicken Kiev, and the borscht, a thick blending of cabbage and grated beets in a rich stock. Order baklava for dessert. Dinner only. Closed Monday. Complete dinners from $6. AE, CB, DC, MC, V.

## THAI

***Tepparod,*** 4649 Melbourne Avenue (666-9919), 147 S. Fairfax Avenue (932-9552), and 5151 Hollywood Boulevard (660-9800). There are so many really splendid Thai restaurants in Los Angeles that it is difficult to single out one; but the Tepparod on Melbourne was one of the first to open and has grown to a mini-chain of three. The latest, on Fairfax Avenue, is across the street from the Farmer's Market. The Tepparods are carefully designed (the Hollywood Boulevard location is the least attractive) and the service, often by beautiful young women, is refined. The hot-and-sour shrimp is classic, a sophisticated balance of tastes punctuated by lemon grass and dried lime leaves and a bit of cilantro. Other favorites are chicken with mint, and *phat thai,* a noodle dish made with bean sprouts and a spicy peanut sauce. The Melbourne Avenue branch is closed Monday; the Fairfax Avenue branch is closed Tuesday; and the Hollywood Boulevard branch is open seven days a week. Entrées from $3 (L & D). V.

## VIETNAMESE

***Saigon Flavor,*** 1044 South Fairfax (935-1564). A very fine, family-run restaurant. Best dishes are seafood: the roast crab with butter, spices and garlic; the shrimp wrapped around crab claws, then deep-fried; and the shrimp, charcoal-broiled with fresh sugar cane and served in rice paper with cucumbers, mint and green apple slices are extraordinary. Modest surroundings but lovely service. Closed Tuesday. Entrées from $4 (L & D). AE, MC, V.

# SPECIALTY COOKING

## DELI

***Nate 'n Al,*** 414 N. Beverly Drive, Beverly Hills (274-0101). This is supposed to be the New Yorker's home away from home, but by New York standards it is an average deli. However, some dishes are quite good. Quality is high, sandwiches are enormous, and eggs, lox and onions can be admirable. The place is often mobbed, and on Sunday morning the inevitable 30- to 45-minute wait for a table becomes an opportunity to observe Beverly Hillers in action. It's not your usual deli crowd. Open seven days a week. Dishes from $2.50 (L & D). DC.

## HAMBURGER

***Cassell's Patio Hamburgers,*** 3300 W. 6th Street (480-8668). Cassell's has been declared the best hamburger place in Los Angeles—and possibly the world—so many times that writing about it seems redundant. But it is indeed the best in L.A. The prime beef is trimmed of all fat and ground on the premises daily. If there is one criticism of Cassell's, it is that the meat is possibly *too* lean. But the rare burgers are juicy, and the thin, 10-ounce patties are also good raw. There are also gigantic baked-ham sandwiches on egg bread. And there is homemade lemonade, as well as homemade potato salad with homemade mayonnaise, tomatoes, onions, etc., on the help-yourself buffet. Lunch only. Closed Sunday. Burgers from $2.05. No credit cards.

## HOT DOG

***Pink's Famous Chili Dogs,*** 711 North La Brea (931-4223). In Los Angeles, the hot dog is more a matter of art than substance; what you put on is more important than the dog itself. Pink's specializes in a spicy chili topping, which is definitely not made for children. Pink's serves hamburgers as well as hot dogs, but you'll seldom see anyone eat one. One suspects that the help, who are less than polite to begin with, could turn real nasty with anyone who ordered one. Open seven days a week, until 3 A.M. Chili dog, 90 cents. No credit cards.

---

## SEAFOOD

***Gladstone's 4 Fish,*** 146 Entrada Drive, Santa Monica (454-3474—GL 4-FISH). Gladstone's does serious daily negotiating to have the largest possible variety of fresh fish and seafood. But the abilities of the kitchen are limited, so demands upon it should be kept to a minimum. Best bets are shark or sea bass from the mesquite charcoal broiler, or simple fries. Special efforts should be made to avoid the chowder. Dinner only. Open seven days a week. Entrées from $3.95. MC, V.

---

## SOUL

***South Town,*** 1515 N. Wilcox Avenue, Hollywood (461-3245). When fresh catfish are in town, they show up at South Town, where they are delicious fried and served in small, medium and large sizes, priced accordingly. The pan-fried pork chops are also great, and, on Friday, aficionados check in for the filé gumbo. Dinners are served with two vegetables—collard greens and red beans or black-eyed peas are best, unless you have meat loaf, in which case mashed potatoes and gravy are essential. South Town is open 24 hours a day and serves breakfast anytime. Two eggs, grits and corn muffins or homemade biscuits can be had for about a dollar. For a little more, you can add the eye-opening spicy Louisiana hot links. Open seven days a week. Entrées from $2 (B, L & D). AE, CB, DC, MC, V.

---

## STEAK

***Palm,*** 9001 Santa Monica Boulevard, West Hollywood (550-8811). Why should Los Angeles be different? This Palm is as good as any other city's, and therefore, the best steak in town. The nostalgia here is spanking new, with a decided Hollywood cast, but the noise level is equal to New York's. Even more important than steak is access to fresh Maine lobster, carefully prepared. They are gigantic (four pounds for about $25 and up). Steaks are priced from $12. Cottage fries and crisp onion rings are fine side dishes. Open seven days a week. Entrées from $4.50 (L), $7 (D). AE, CB, DC, MC, V.

## VEGETARIAN

***Two Worlds,*** 8022 W. 3rd Street (653-4212). Also strictly kosher, with a large menu featuring meatless enchiladas, lasagne, moussaka, as well as omelets, salads, soy meat sandwiches. Friday, lunch only; Saturday, dinner only. Full meals from $4, snacks from $1.50, sandwiches from $2.25 (L & D). No credit cards.

# FOR INDIVIDUAL NEEDS

## IF YOU HAVE TIME FOR ONLY ONE MEAL

***Scandia,*** 9040 Sunset Boulevard, West Los Angeles (272-9521, 278-3555). Scandia is a revelation for anyone whose association with Scandinavian cuisine has been confined to the pickled herrings on the smorgasbord. Ken Hansen, one of this country's premier restaurateurs, opened Scandia more than 40 years ago and only recently sold it; but he still oversees the restaurant's daily operation. At times, it seems the fine edge of precision is off the service, but mainstays from the menu—the poached turbot with the impeccable hollandaise; the silky *gravlax* served with a boiled potato, a bit of fried salmon skin and mustard-dill sauce; the Danish apple cake—are as good as ever. Beyond old Scandinavian favorites, however, Scandia is truly Continental, and the menu continues to change daily, mostly to reflect fluctuations in the fresh-fish market. The wine inventory is enormous, and the prices on the list often reflect a less inflationary buying time. Scandia's after-10 P.M. supper menu offers forty open-faced sandwiches, and a startling but successful plate of spicy chili and homemade veal sausages. Reservations are imperative; if you plan to be in town for only a few days, call before you get to Los Angeles. For quality, Scandia is probably the best buy in town, with full dinners averaging $15 to $18. Open until 2 A.M. Closed Monday. Entrées from $4 (L & D). AE, CB, DC, MC, V.

## BEST HOTEL MEAL

***Bernard's,*** The Biltmore, 515 South Olive, downtown (624-0183). The classy old Biltmore has undergone a thorough renovation, and Bernard's is the stunning signature of the project. Its contemporary chic décor includes Mies van der Rohe chairs, rust linens and live trees; the menu is largely influenced by *nouvelle cuisine.* Of the fish dishes, which far outnumber the meat, a trio of slices from tiny fish terrines, saffron-scented scallops atop puréed endive, and poached salmon with kiwi are among the best. A smooth kiwi sherbet is served between courses in the antique silver-plated sherbet cups from the Biltmore's halcyon days. Bernard's is frequently booked a week in advance, so make reservations as soon as possible. Closed Sunday. Entrées from $8 (L), $11 (D). AE, CB, DC, MC, V.

## RESTAURANT NEAR AIRPORT

***Tracton's,*** 3560 South La Cienega Boulevard (931-1581). The standard serving of prime rib here weighs in at two pounds; with it, you get an overgrown baked potato and an overwhelming salad, with what is said to be the authentic formula for Green Goddess dressing. For a $3 service charge, you can share the whole thing with a friend, even a very hungry friend. For seafood lovers, there are enormous Australian lobster tails (frozen), or the better choice (and one that made Tracton's famous), fresh stone crabs, flown in from Florida. Save room for the Florida Key lime pie. Open seven days a week. Entrées from $5 (L), $11 (D). AE, CB, DC, MC, V.

## BUSINESS BREAKFAST

***Don Hernando's,*** Beverly Wilshire Hotel, 9500 Wilshire Boulevard (275-4282). There's no problem deciding what to order. Don Hernando's serves some of the world's greatest corned beef hash. Open from 7 A.M. Closed Sunday. Complete breakfast from $5. AE, CB, DC, MC, V.

***The Polo Lounge,*** Beverly Hills Hotel, 9641 Sunset Boulevard (276-2251). The food is incidental but adequate. The scene is pure Hollywood. Earth-shaking deals are struck over breakfast at the

Polo Lounge. Have you ever wondered where all those "calls to the Coast" go? Most of them go to the private phones in the Polo Lounge. Open seven days a week, from 7 A.M. Complete breakfast from $5 to $10. AE, CB, DC, MC, V.

## BUSINESS LUNCH

***The Bistro Garden,*** 176 North Canon Drive, Beverly Hills (550-3900). For a business lunch, or a shopper's lunch, or any other kind of lunch, try this offshoot of the famous Bistro restaurant up the street. This is undoubtedly the prettiest garden café in the city, and the interior a pared-down but no less charming version of the Bistro's Grand Vefour glamour. Fresh fish, the famed Bistro chickenburger, cold roast chicken, a cold plate of grilled bratwurst, cheese and salad, even a yummy *tostado* are listed on the eclectic menu. The same individual deep chocolate soufflés that became synonymous with "The Bistro" are served here. Closed Sunday. Entrées from $6.50 (L), $10 (D). AE, CB, DC, MC, V.

## FAST, GOOD FOOD

***Michel Richard,*** 310 S. Robertson Boulevard (275-5707). An authentic French *pâtisserie-charcuterie* with various quiches (spinach with hard-boiled eggs is superb), a torte Milanese (*pizza rustica*), crêpes, pâtés, omelets, and what is certainly among the best pastry available, anywhere. For breakfast, the fresh-from-the-oven croissants and espresso are perfect. Richard has been a chef at Le Nôtre, the famous Paris caterer; the quality here is tops. Carryout available. Closed Sunday. Entrées from $4, croissants 55 cents. MC, V.

***Me & Me,*** 465 North Fairfax (655-4748), 6687 Hollywood Boulevard (464-8448), 10975 Weyburn Ave., Westwood Village (478-6616). One of those little local enterprises that grew into a local mini-chain, Me & Me offers a viable alternative to junk food. The greaseless fried *felafel,* the searingly hot Turkish salad (tomatoes, scallions, chilis), the chopped eggplant salad, the *tahini,* to combine and eat from a plate or stuff into *pita* bread all are excellent, and the quality of the ingredients is consistent at all outlets. Open seven days a week, from 11 A.M. to 12 midnight, Hollywood Boulevard until 1 A.M. *Pita* sandwiches from around $2. No credit cards.

***Clifton's Cafeteria,*** 648 S. Broadway (627-1673); Century City Shopping Plaza (879-9966); 515 W. 7th Street (485-1726). Homemade bread and soups, fresh fish and vegetables, and sandwiches. Basic, hearty, home-style cooking. Days and hours differ. Entrées from under $3. No credit cards.

## BEST WINE LIST

***Pacific Dining Car,*** 1310 W. 6th Street (483-6000). A wide selection of the best California labels, as well as an extraordinary range of French whites, champagnes, and—most important—big reds to go with the Dining Car's prime, aged-on-the-premises lamb and beef. Some of the wines are rare. Prices consequently are high but fair, all things considered. Be emphatic about how you want your meat cooked, and do try the creamed spinach, the cottage-fried potatoes or French-fried onion rings. Sunday, dinner only. Open seven days a week. Entrées from $4 (L), $7.50 (D). MC, V.

## FOR DRINKS

***The Saloon,*** 9390 Santa Monica Boulevard, Beverly Hills (273-7155). The great round mahogany bar is a popular meeting place for celebrities, people-watchers and singles. The simpler dishes, such as the very good hamburgers, raw clams and oysters on the half shell, are most successful. Supper until 11:30 P.M., drinks until 2 A.M. Sunday, dinner only. Entrées from $4 (L), $7.50 (D). AE, CB, DC, MC, V.

***Yamashiro,*** 1999 North Sycamore Avenue (off Franklin), Hollywood (466-5125). An authentic Japanese mansion originally built as a private home. Situated in acres of gardens, Yamashiro offers—especially on smogless evenings—a breathtaking view of Los Angeles. There is a heated terrace. Staying for dinner is *not* recommended. MC, V.

***The El Padrino Room,*** Beverly Wilshire Hotel, 9500 Wilshire Boulevard (275-4282), the **Polo Lounge** (of course) and **Perino's** cocktail lounge (which has homemade potato chips and a piano player on weekends) are also great for drinks. For a good, rollicking—and loud—saloon, try the transplanted (from New York) **Ginger Man,** 369 North Bedford Drive, Beverly Hills (273-7585). The Ginger Man offers a stage-set 3rd-Avenue ambience, good drinks, a large assortment of domestic and imported beers, and the strong possibility of seeing co-owner-actors Carroll O'Connor or Patrick O'Neal behind the bar.

## ROMANTIC

***Albion's,*** 13422 Ventura Boulevard, Sherman Oaks (981-6650). Interior architecture combining late Victorian and Art Nouveau styles is the backdrop for plush cameo-back chairs, soft lighting, potted plants, and exquisite table appointments. The emphatically romantic mood is underscored by gentle music, fine service and luxurious French food. Desserts are especially seductive. As for wine, this is a room for champagne. Dinner only. Closed Monday. Entrées from $9.75. AE, CB, DC, MC, V.

## LATE-NIGHT SERVICE

***Le Dome,*** 8720 Sunset Boulevard (659-6919). Le Dome, one of the stars of the 1978 season, which gave L.A. a handful of dazzling new restaurants, combines chic décor, a smart, young clientele, correct but friendly service and a very good kitchen in an old bank building. Best choices for late suppers: grilled blood sausages served with sautéed apples and mashed potatoes, grilled fresh tuna fish, chicken roasted with mustard. Some of the hors d'oeuvre and salads are substantial enough for a light meal; best of the homemade daily desserts are the excellent fruit tarts. Food is served continuously from 11:45 A.M. until 1 A.M. (bar service till 2) and the prices are reasonable, considering the quality and style of the place. Closed Sunday. Entrées from $5 (L), $8 (D). AE, MC, V.

***Café Moustache,*** 8155 Melrose Avenue (651-2111). A friendly café atmosphere, with a heated front garden, and a stylish young crowd, the Moustache serves continuously, from the same menu from 11:30 A.M. until 1 A.M. There is a wide assortment of egg dishes, salads, crêpes and sandwiches, as well as more substantial entrées. Best bets: spinach salad, *moules marinière,* chopped steak Provençal with *pommes frites,* charcoal-grilled sea bass, and *coq au vin.* Stay away from anything pretentious. Open seven days a week. Prices are reasonable, from around $4 for entrées, all day. MC, V.

***Original Pantry,*** 877 S. Figueroa Street, downtown (972-9279). The Pantry is a plain, middle-class grill that has been open continuously for over fifty years. Meals begin with big baskets of fresh sourdough bread and bowls of iced carrots, celery and radishes. The no-nonsense menu concentrates on pan-broiled steaks and chops of good quality, simple stews and fabulous hash-browned potatoes.

The T-bone is the best steak. Breakfast is excellent, with ham the star attraction. There's no liquor, but the Pantry's iced tea is fine, and the coffee supply endless. No reservations. Open 24 hours a day, seven days a week. Breakfast from 95 cents. Entrées from $3 (L & D). No credit cards.

## SUNDAY BRUNCH

***Hotel Bel-Air,*** 701 Stone Canyon Road, L.A. (472-1211). The Bel-Air is isolated, elegant and a bit expensive, but the fresh fish, a decent wine list and the view of the resident swans make it worthwhile. Don't bother with dinner here; it's too unpredictable. Reservations recommended. Open seven days a week from 11 A.M. to 11 P.M. Brunch from $6.50. AE, CB, DC.

## SUNDAY-EVENING MEAL

***Scandia,*** 9040 Sunset Boulevard, West Los Angeles (272-9521, 278-3555). (See description under IF YOU HAVE TIME FOR ONLY ONE MEAL.) Best buy on quality food, but reservations are necessary unless you go quite late. Supper menu starts at 10 P.M. and is available until 1 A.M. CB, MC, V.

## FOR FAMILIES WITH CHILDREN

***Victoria Station,*** 3850 Lankershim Boulevard, Universal City (760-0714). This is the flagship of the chain; and it is convenient for anyone taking the Universal Studios Tour or attending a concert at the Universal Amphitheater. The familiar prime-rib and salad-bar menu is mounted on an extravagantly well-done railroad theme—all the artifacts are authentic British Railway fixtures, and the clock and the indicator board that dominate the bar area once hung in the real Victoria Station. You can even dine in real cars from the famous "Flying Scotsman." The baby rack of lamb, broiled to order with a gentle Dijon mustard and breadcrumb crust, is excellent. Some reasonably priced California wines, too. Children's menu. Open seven days a week. Entrées from $4 (L), $8 (D). AE, MC, V.

# MARKETS

***Farmer's Market,*** 3rd and Fairfax (933-9211). You'll find retail merchants in the stalls, not farmers. The prices are well above average (the Market is not competitive), but the fresh produce is the best since the Garden of Eden. Many of the stalls make up gift packages and will mail them long distances. Dozens of spots for inexpensive snacks, lunches. Closed Sunday.

## GIFT FOODS

***Tudor House,*** 312 Wilshire Boulevard (451-4107). A great selection of British tinned foods and other specialties: biscuits, crackers, teas, jams, beers and ales. Cakes and meat pies are made on the premises. Open seven days a week. Tearoom closed Monday. MC, V.

***Beverly Hills Cheese Shop,*** 419 N. Beverly Drive (278-2855). Hundreds of varieties. Knowledgeable and friendly salespeople. Imported New York cheesecake. Closed Sunday. MC, V.

***Bagatelle,*** 8690 Wilshire Boulevard, Beverly Hills (659-0782). French deli. Pâtés, prepared salads, catering. Closed Sunday. MC, V.

***Le Grand Buffet,*** 9527 Santa Monica Boulevard, Beverly Hills (278-4674). French pâtés, cold dishes, excellent chicken salad with white raisins. Closed Sunday. MC, V.

***Krön,*** 9529 Santa Monica Boulevard, Beverly Hills (278-4061). The famous *chocolatier* prepares fresh-dipped strawberries or oranges and will write your message on a slab of chocolate and mail it off in a special little wooden crate. Closed Sunday. MC, V.

***Monaco Grocery,*** 8513 Santa Monica Boulevard (654-7414). French and Italian canned goods, Niçoise olives, olive oils, imported sardines, etc. Good sandwiches, and a few select cheeses. Closed Sunday. No credit cards.

## GIFT WINES

***Wine Merchant,*** 9701 Santa Monica Boulevard, Beverly Hills (278-7322). Excellent selection of California and imported wines; high class but competitively priced. Also pâté, fresh beluga caviar and a few cheeses. Closed Sunday. AE, MC, V.

***Greenblatt's,*** 8001 Sunset Boulevard (656-0606). Excellent wine and liquor, large selection of champagne on ice, along with a good deli that stocks fresh caviar (sometimes it's on sale). Open seven days a week. MC, V (with $5 minimum purchase).

***Wally's West,*** 10811 West Pico Boulevard, West Los Angeles (475-0606). Steve Wallace is just wild about California wines. A fine palate, and continual research and tasting make it possible for him to shepherd you through a staggering inventory. Open seven days a week. MC, V.

# Louisville

After a long spell of favorite old restaurants going out of business fast, Louisville is witnessing a boom in quality dining places. Granted, some places emphasize the décor over the food and certain entrepreneurs think the freezer and microwave oven are better than a chef in the kitchen. But that is just as true elsewhere.

The proliferation of restaurants hasn't brought about an equivalent variety, however. Middle Eastern, Vietnamese, Japanese or Spanish cuisine is nonexistent here. Even good Southern and soul cooking is hard to find outside of a private home.

Old-timers claim it wasn't always so, and they sigh for the long-vanished Restaurant Vatel, a French establishment; the Seelbach Hotel dining room, a bastion of Southern and seafood dishes; the Old Vienna restaurant; and the English Grille of the Brown Hotel.

If the world thinks of Kentucky at all in terms of food (tobacco, bourbon whisky, and the Kentucky Derby are more likely to come to mind), it is probably the picture of the Colonel with the white goatee and the finger-lickin'-good fried chicken.

Louisville *does* have some claims to regional culinary fame. The Hot Brown sandwich, born at the Brown Hotel (a favorite of the Bluegrass horsey set), is chicken breast and bacon swathed in a mornay sauce, served brown and bubbling on toast. Louisville is also the home of Modjeskas, caramel-coated marshmallow candies named for the Polish actress Helena Modjeska. And cheeseburger fanciers may be interested to know that a Louisville restaurant called Kaelin's claims to have invented the cheeseburger.

For a city that is approximately one-third Catholic, Louisville is singularly poor in restaurants featuring fish and seafood. The best of them is an invitation to gluttony—all you can eat for $17.95.

A boomlet in Chinese restaurants has brought with it some timid experimenting with Szechuan and Hunan dishes, but Cantonese cuisine still prevails.

Dress codes are generally lenient; some places are so relaxed they only ask you not to show up barefooted or in tanktops. Many places encourage you to linger after dinner to hear soft rock, pop or jazz. You can drink until 2 A.M. (or 4 A.M. if the bar has a special, costlier, license), but no drinks are served on Sunday. Tipping follows a rule practiced generally: one tip for the whole meal, with 15 percent the bottom line. Luncheon prices are modest; dinner prices soar.

Shoppers in quest of specialty foods, wines, cheeses, and fancy kitchenwares will find the purveyors have scattered into suburbia. There is a remnant of a downtown farmers' market called the Haymarket, and a trip there can be interesting.

# Restaurants and Food Sources
(Area code: 502)

## BIG DEAL

### WORTH IT

***Casa Grisanti,*** 1000 E. Liberty (584-4377). Years ago this was a family-run factory where ornamental plaster moldings were created. It has become one of the city's best restaurants—and one of its most expensive. The Grisanti family is still in charge. There is one room in glossy Art Deco style and another with dark wood and black vinyl. Tableside service is exemplary. The dinner-jacketed waiters are efficient and courteous but unobtrusive. Chaîne des Rotisseurs. Bar and wine list. Reservations are a must. Dinner only. Closed Sunday. Rack of lamb for two is $25; tournedos da Vinci $10.25. Entrées from $6.25 (pasta). AE, CB, DC, MC, V.

### NOT WORTH IT

***The Chapel Restaurant,*** at The Cloister, 800 E. Chestnut (584-7488). A declining neighborhood and a declining enrollment forced a Roman Catholic girls' school to shut down. The chapel that once served school and convent is now a restaurant. Mixed drinks and wine are served. The stained-glass windows remain and would divulge the room's past even if an historical note in the menu did not. The expansive menu aims high but the delivery stops considerably short of acceptable, especially considering the prices. The waiters wear monkish garb, but those wide sleeves are hard to manage when serving food. The room is noisy. Closed Sunday. Dinner entrées from $7.75. AE, MC, V.

# INTERNATIONAL

## CHINESE

***The Jade Palace,*** 9713 Taylorsville Road (267-9778). Although individual dishes vary, the overall standard here is quite high, higher than the unprepossessing surroundings would indicate. Seafood and vegetables (*Chow Sam Seen*) are carefully and quickly cooked. Four Seasons is a combination of beef tenderloin, chicken, shrimp, pork and Chinese vegetables. At $6.15 it is a bargain. Also recommended are shrimp Royal Cashew and the spicy hot-and-sour soup. Servings are very generous. Beer is the only alcoholic beverage available, and it goes well with the food. Sunday, dinner only (noon to 10 P.M.). Open seven days a week. Entrées from $1.60 (L), $3.15 (D). No credit cards.

## FRENCH

***La Cuisinière,*** 1285 Bardstown Road (456-6815). French cuisine prepared by a highly qualified chef. His kitchen offers seafood, chicken, veal and beef dishes prepared in ways worthy of the prices—not cheap—that are charged. The sauces are exemplary. Salads are beautiful to look at and tasty. Beer and wine are available. Dinner only, except brunch on Saturday and Sunday. Closed Monday. Entrées from $4.95 (brunch), $6.50 (D). AE, DC, MC, V.

## GERMAN

***Kienle's German Delicatessen & Restaurant,*** Shelbyville Road Plaza (897-3920). Delicious German food—sauerbraten, beef rouladen, Wiener schnitzel, stuffed veal—and not a bit heavy. Dinners include soup, salad, two vegetables and German breads. The Mozart torte and Black Forest cake (at $1.50) are desserts to dream about. There are fresh flowers and the table appointments are handsome. Mrs. Kienle is strict about dress: jacket and tie required;

no jeans need apply. No alcoholic beverages except German beer. Dinner only. Closed Sunday and Monday. Entrées from $9.95. No credit cards.

## HUNGARIAN

***Soos' Inn,*** 617 Jefferson Street, LaGrange, Ky. (222-1568). Only the adventurous, or those of Hungarian background, are likely to search out Stefan Soos' modest mecca of sour cream and cabbage cookery. The cooking is very good. By all means have Soos' goulash soup, which is lighter by American standards than the great Hungarian stew of the same name. Eschew the Americanisms on the menu and stick with the native cuisine. Save room for the desserts; you will be glad you did. No alcoholic beverages served. The Wedding Feast for two is $18. Closed Monday. Complete lunch from $3.30, entrées from $1.45 (L), $2.50 (D). MC. V.

## INDIAN

***The Curry House,*** 3044 Huntsinger Lane (454-0291). If you are not knowledgeable about curried food, ask the waiter. Shrimp, beef and chicken dishes are available, prepared in various ways. There are authentic Indian vegetarian dishes as well. A hotter sauce is available for those who prefer very spicy curries. Dinner only. Closed Monday. Entrées from $3.95. No credit cards.

## MEXICAN

***Tumbleweed Mexican-American Restaurant,*** 1900 Mellwood Avenue (896-9143). A taste for jalapeño peppers, tacos, *burritos* and the rest cuts across class lines at this hacienda, set between a packing house and a TV station. You will see teased hairdos as well as the fashionably streaked locks of suburbia, the gent in penny loafers as well as the dude in boots. There's a jukebox but there's also as good an array of Mexican food as you will find in town. You won't pay more than $3.50 for any Mexican dinner. Service is variable. Bar service and beer. Closed Sunday. No credit cards.

# SPECIALTY COOKING

## HAMBURGER

***Bennigan's Tavern,*** 4000 Dutchmans Lane (893-0333). If you tell somebody you ate here they'll ask, "What kind of banana dessert did you order?" You can eat Mexican (sort of) here with an array of tortillas, beef, refried beans, cheese, and guacamole, but why not go for the specialty, the Super Chopper? It is an astonishing hamburger creation that will fill you up or bowl you over. And do order a banana dessert. Open seven days a week. Super Chopper, $4.95. AE, CB, DC, MC, V.

## QUICHE AND CRÊPES

***Jocelyn's,*** 9944 Linn Station Road, Plainview Village Center (425-7101). The name belongs to Mrs. Jocelyn Levitt, whose pastry is renowned, even among restaurants. In this establishment she has turned her talents to making a variety of quiches and crêpes, with both delicate and robust fillings. Finish your meal with one of Mrs. Levitt's confections. Closed Sunday. Friday and Saturday, open until 1 A.M. Entrées from $2.50 (L & D). AE, MC, V.

## SEAFOOD

***New Orleans House East,*** 9424 Shelbyville Road (426-1577) and ***New Orleans House Downtown,*** 412 W. Chestnut (583-7231). A gourmand's dream. The self-service buffet serves cold shrimp, oysters on the half shell, herring, scallops, crab, salads, cheeses, barbecued ribs, deviled eggs . . . and on and on. Then comes a choice of lobster or steak, if you can face it. Dessert is pineapple and strawberries. The total tab is $17.95, a bargain if you have an expandable belt. The décor is forgettable and in the rush of things it may get a little messy. Bar and wine list. Reservations are a must. Dinner only. Closed Sunday. AE, MC, V.

## STEAK

***Kunz's The Dutchman,*** 526 River City Mall (584-1158). A Louisville institution that doesn't try to be more than it is, a steakhouse of modest pretentions. The 16-ounce T-bone is $10.25 and the Chateaubriand for two is $22.50. There are plenty of in-between steak sizes, too. Chaînes des Rotisseurs. Bar service. Closed Sunday. AE, DC, MC, V.

# FOR INDIVIDUAL NEEDS

## IF YOU HAVE TIME FOR ONLY ONE MEAL

***The Fig Tree,*** 234 W. Broadway (583-1522). In its brief four-year reign as the most imaginative dining room in Louisville, this sophisticated eating place has become a landmark. From soup to dessert, Fig Tree dinners are planned as ensembles. The management sometimes goes overboard on innovation, but the success level is high. And there is variety. The menu changes nightly. A new jazz club on the premises is open seven days a week, with music, drinks, light food; beer only on Sunday. Saturday, open for dinner only. Closed Sunday. Fixed-price dinner $13.75, lunch entrées from $3.75. AE, CB, MC, V.

## BEST HOTEL MEAL

***Lambs,*** Hyatt-Regency Hotel, Fourth and Liberty (587-3434). Expensive. Dinner and drinks for two can easily come to $60. The array of entrées is limited for so flossy a setting: roast duckling, rack of lamb, veal Oskar, quail, pompano *en papillote* among them. With the entrées, the customer has access to a handsomely stocked salad bar (little shrimp, herring, bacon are among offerings), vegetables with the main course, and a scoop of sherbet to cleanse the palate before dessert. Saturday, dinner only. Closed Sunday. Entrées from $3.95 (L), $12.50 (D). AE, CB, DC, MC, V.

## BUSINESS BREAKFAST

***Turner House,*** 970 S. Third (583-8015). Virtually all of the big motels downtown and at the edge of the city serve standard American breakfasts, but if you are of a mind to have a "down home" breakfast, try this tiny spot. The sign out front promises "The best breakfast in Kentucky," especially if you love hash-browned potatoes. Opens at 6 A.M. Closed Sunday. Breakfast entrées from 65 cents. No credit cards.

## BUSINESS LUNCH

***The Savoy,*** 727 West Main Street (583-3341). There's a shabby burlesque house with the same name operating a few blocks east, but this stunningly decorated new place knows few rivals, even on revitalized Main Street. Housed in fashionable Main Street's old buildings (whose cast-iron façades are much admired by architectural historians) are a number of bars and restaurants popular with executives from downtown business firms. The Savoy is one of the best, and it takes more pains with food than most others. The salads are excellent, the vegetables are served crisp. Steak tartare is on the menu; so are duck, sole, soft-shell crab, steaks and lamb chops. Saturday, dinner only. Closed Sunday. Entrées from $3.25 (L), $8.25 (D). AE, MC, V.

## LATE-NIGHT SERVICE

***Charley's,*** 530 West Main Street (585-5300). The management thoughtfully keeps Charley's bar open until early morning and the chef usually stays on until midnight to turn out the menu's appetizing crêpe dishes. Another Main Street transformation, this is a warehouse that was turned into a restaurant. The menu plays up the local history, and the décor includes the massive bar than once graced the English Grille in the Brown Hotel. Closed Sunday. Entrées from $2.25 (L), $5.50 (D). AE, DC, MC, V.

## COUNTRY INN

***Old Stone Inn,*** Simpsonville, via U.S. 60 or I-64 (722-8882). About 25 miles east of Louisville and a restaurant for 58 years, the Old Stone Inn is housed in a pioneer-days building that is a national landmark. Fried chicken, country ham and sirloin strip compete for your palate with deep-fried shrimp and sautéed chicken livers. The corn pudding or eggplant casserole, homemade rolls and berry cobblers are legendary. Reservations needed on weekends. Open for dinner only, from late March to the end of November; closed Monday and Tuesday. Entrées from $8. AE, DC, MC, V.

# MARKETS

## GIFT FOODS/WINES

***The Delikatessen,*** 2222 Dundee Road (452-1707). Coffee roasts of international variety; sausages and country ham, cheeses, gift items. Closed Sunday. MC.

***The Cheddar Box,*** 3907 Chenoweth Square (893-2324). Imported cheese, fresh French bread, sausages, dried fruits. Closed Sunday. MC.

***Stewart's,*** 501 River City Mall (584-3261). Imported cheese, bakery goods, gift food items. Closed Sunday. No credit cards.

***J.B.'s Larder,*** 4160 Shelbyville Road (895-5481). Well-stocked wine and liquor shelves; 160 varieties of cheese; international variety of roasted coffee; prosciutto, Westphalian ham; fresh French bread. Closed Sunday. AE, MC, V.

***Beam Liquor, Inc.,*** 3634 Brownsboro Road (896-6309). Tries to keep as wide a selection of California and imported wine as any in the city. Closed Sunday. No credit cards.

# Miami

For a city its size (just over one million in Dade County alone), Miami has more than its fair share of good places to eat. The trouble is, they're not located in any kind of central "restaurant row," but scattered in little pockets of gastronomic interest all over the place. If you do not have the use of a car, be prepared for a healthy cab fare to most places.

One section of town blessed with a surfeit of good food, however, is Coral Gables. Within a square-mile area are ten excellent restaurants, among them three French (**Le Festival,** Vinton's and Le Petit Bistro), two Greek (Zorba's and Sparta), and one each among Continental (**Whiffenpoof**), Indian (**House of India**), Mexican (Mexico Lindo), Spanish (**Madrid**), vegetarian (**Spiral**) and one of the few surviving old-fashioned coffee shops serving real food (Tiger's), not to mention the best pastry shop in town (Andalusia Bakery).

But such an area is the exception. There is no Chinatown to act as a focus for Cantonese and Mandarin food, so the best restaurants are miles apart. The Italian community, loosely centered in the north end of the county, is still too spread out for there to be a discernable rationale for the location of good restaurants.

The stars of the local dining scene are the Latin places, primarily Cuban. Almost a third of Miami's population is Latin, and a stroll down Little Havana's main thoroughfare, Southwest Eighth Street, becomes heady with the aromas of roasting pork and fresh coffee.

Miami's Latins tend to dine late, virtually leaving the restaurants to the Anglos before 9 P.M. Take advantage of this to try black- or white-bean soup, garlic soup, roast pork, *palomilla* steak (a thin cut with onion, parsley and lime juice), fried red snapper, spicy roast chicken with saffron-tinted rice, flan and, of course, tiny demitasses of thick Cuban coffee.

Cubans argue about the best of their restaurants, but the names that most often come up are La Tasca on Flagler Street; **Centro Vasco,** Lila's and the **Malaga** on SW Eighth Street, El Cortijo on Coral Way, **Madrid** on Douglas Road and **El Segundo Viajante** in Hialeah.

South Florida boasts several excellent French restaurants. In addition to the long-established Cordon Bleu in Dania (Broward County) and Le Parisien in Miami Beach, there's the **Café Chauveron** (transplanted in 1972 on Bay Harbor Isle from its original home in Manhattan) and **Les Trois Mousquetaires** in Fort Lauderdale. Less formal and more inventive are **La Bohème** on Biscayne Boulevard and **Le Festival** in Coral Gables.

Miami's unrivaled stunt pilot of creative cuisine is **Raimondo.** The restaurant that bears his name is a remarkable Northern Italian enclave that has become a local gastronomic mecca. Other Italian restaurants are not as exciting, but one of the more reliable is Gatti's. The rambling old house on a Miami Beach side street is one of the town's worst-kept secrets. Others are Tullio and Andrée's, a Franco-Italian hybrid in an unreconstructed downtown speakeasy that dates back to Prohibition days.

At the southern tip of Miami Beach is **Joe's Stone Crab.** As an index of its landmark status, the place has been specially exempted from the redevelopment plans that have been set for the tawdry neighborhood that surrounds it. The Florida stone crab is king here, but Joe's also turns out other good, simple fresh seafood specialties. A word of warning, though: get to Joe's before 7 P.M., if you can. Any later and the wait can be lengthy.

Another Miami Beach landmark is The Embers, which has built up a devoted clientele that keeps coming back for steak and ribs. Newer, but as impressive, is **The Forge,** a showplace of Victorian opulence and fine American food. It also prides itself on its 1,000-entry wine list, which can be as daunting in its prices as in its breadth.

Chinese food is still a good gastronomic value in Miami at the handful of first-rate restaurants in town—**Wong's** and **Tiger Tiger Teahouse** for the eclectic hodge-podge of dishes that goes by the name of "Mandarin" cuisine and the **Kowloon** for *dim sum* tea brunch. Christine Lee's reputation for traditional Cantonese specialties is far exceeded by the prices. In Fort Lauderdale, The Forbidden City turns out a long menu of quite presentable dishes.

Dining habits in South Florida tend more toward nighttime meals. This is not an elaborate lunch town, except in the downtown area. Most of the best dinner restaurants are not even open for lunch, and those that are tend to offer pared-down and relatively unexciting menus.

Mode of dress in Miami's subtropical climate is casual. Not even the most elaborate restaurant will require a tie, although fancier places might insist upon a jacket. Women have been wearing pants suits to better restaurants here for years. Many restaurants do not take reservations for lunch, but dinner reservations are advisable almost anywhere they are accepted.

# Restaurants and Food Sources

(Area code: 305)

## BIG DEAL

### WORTH IT

***Raimondo,*** 201 N.W. 79th Street (757-9403, 759-9071), Brooklyn-born Northern Italian chef Raimondo is the most imaginative around. He's in a rotten neighborhood, but don't let that deter you. His blackboard specials are often the best, but such menu fare as fettuccine Organic John, *zuppa di pesce,* veal chops with *cèpes* and morels, pompano *en papillote* are exceptional. For dessert, his meringue with grated chocolate is sinful, or try anything with *zabaglione.* Reservations required. Chaîne des Rotisseurs. Dinner only. Open seven days a week. Entrées from $5.50 (for pasta). No credit cards.

### NOT WORTH IT

***Chez Vendôme,*** David William Hotel, 700 Biltmore Way, Coral Gables (443-4646). One of the pioneers in *haute cuisine* in Miami. Unfortunately the kitchen now takes too many shortcuts and the service is overly obsequious, but the prices remain stiff. Sunday, dinner only. Open seven days a week. Entrées from $3 (L), $8 (D). AE, CB, DC, MC, V.

## INTERNATIONAL

### AMERICAN

***The Forge,*** 432 Arthur Godfrey Road, Miami Beach (538-8533). Decorated in San Francisco Victorian excess, this is still a comfortable if potentially noisy Miami Beach restaurant serving first-class steaks, a few imaginative dishes (including chicken with macadamia nuts) and a dessert orgy that includes chocolate crêpes and the world's best black-bottom pie. Wine list is staggering in size, as are some prices. Chaîne des Rotisseurs. Dinner only. Kitchen closes at 2 A.M. Open until 5 A.M., seven days a week. Entrées from $8.95. AE, CB, DC, MC, V.

## CHINESE

***Tiger Tiger Teahouse,*** 2235 Biscayne Boulevard (573-2689) and 14059 Kendall Drive (274-4585). There are a few pitfalls on this menu—notably overstarched soups and heavy-handed deep-fried dishes—but some choices at this family restaurant are first-rate. If you can plan ahead, order a Peking duck or Peking hot pot a day in advance. Otherwise, try cashew chicken or twice-cooked pork from the à la carte menu. Lo mein is a good bet for lunch. Biscayne: Saturday and Sunday, dinner only. Closed Monday. Kendall: Sunday, dinner only. Closed Monday. Entrées from $1.95 (L & D). AE.

***Wong's,*** 12420 Biscayne Boulevard (891-4313). Crowds back up into the parking lot outside waiting for tables in this cramped little shopping-center storefront. Be prepared to wait at dinnertime. Pass up the combination dinners in favor of such à la carte specialties as hot and sour soup, General Cheng's chicken, bean curd with black mushrooms and bamboo shoots, and shrimp with black beans. Reservations are accepted for tables of six or more. Open seven days a week. Entrées from $4 (L & D). No credit cards.

## FRENCH

***Café Chauveron,*** 9561 E. Bay Harbor Drive (866-8779). Classic dishes prepared by the book and served impeccably. Craig Claiborne called it "an oasis in a gastronomic desert," a fascinating bit of hyperbole. Try the *soupe de poisson,* and its grand cousin, bouillabaisse; *quenelles Nantua;* roast lamb and sometimes venison. The dessert soufflés are outstanding. The wine cellar is far-ranging and somewhat overpriced. Dinner only. Open seven days a week. Closed June 1 to October 15. Entrées from $9.50. AE, CB, DC, MC, V.

***Le Festival,*** 2120 Salzedo Street, Coral Gables (442-8545). Immensely popular little place, only opened in late 1975, on a quiet side street. Small and comfortable, and even the cheapest entrée, *poulet Normande,* is delicious. Try *escargots* in a puff pastry, snapper in champagne sauce, steak with green peppercorns, super napoleons for dessert, good *tarte Tatin.* Saturday, dinner only. Closed Sunday. Entrées from $2.50 (L), $6.50 (D). AE, MC, V.

## INDIAN

***House of India,*** 22 Merrick Way, Coral Gables (444-2348). Behind a storefront, this tiny restaurant on a Miracle Mile side street serves up a wonderfully hot, fragrant chicken vindaloo. It will send tears of joy (perhaps pain) rolling down your cheeks, to be remedied by dollops of cool yogurt. Lamb curry, *samosas,* mulligatawny soup, three kinds of Indian bread, and a yogurt drink called *lhassi* that is soothing to a parched palate. Sunday, dinner only. Open seven days a week. Entrées from $1.75 (L), $5 (D). CB, DC, MC, V.

## SCANDINAVIAN

***Prince Hamlet,*** 8301 Biscayne Boulevard (754-4400). Usually crowded and noisy, but a spectacular *koldtbord* offers unlimited black and red caviar; smoked and poached salmon; sturgeon and whitefish; innumerable kinds of herring; salads; and on Mondays, Tuesdays and Wednesdays, there's a chef opening fresh oysters. It's all included with the price of entrées, which include duck Danoise, excellent veal Oskar, good beef dishes. Have an akvavit and a Carlsberg. The bar is superior. Chaîne des Rotisseurs. Dinner only. Open seven days a week. Entrées from $9.50. AE.

# LATIN RESTAURANTS

## BEST FOOD

***El Segundo Viajante,*** 2846 Palm Avenue, Hialeah (888-5465). Bright, garish, superbly efficient and incredibly cheap. Try *sopa de fabado,* oxtails, fried whole snapper, roast pork or shrimp in garlic sauce. Have beer, not wine, and for dessert *pudin diplomatico* and Cuban coffee (a must). Service is extraordinarily competent. Open seven days a week for lunch and dinner. Entrées from $2.95. AE, CB, DC, MC, V.

***Malaga Restaurant,*** 740 SW Eighth Street (858-4224 or 854-9101). The kitchen is bigger than the dining area in this tiny family-run transplant from Old Havana. Small wonder, considering the caliber and variety of dishes that are turned out there. You can't go wrong ordering the special of the day. Otherwise try the rice with squid in its own ink; the boiled smoked ham hocks; or the beef kidneys in wine sauce. There is a superb chicken casserole with yellow rice, but give the restaurant a half day's notice or more when you order it, and bring along at least three sturdy trencherpersons to help you put it away. For dessert, try the rice pudding. Open seven days a week. Entrées from $2.45 (L), $3.95 (D). AE, CB, DC, MC, V.

### VARIETY

***Madrid,*** 2475 Douglas Road (446-2250). Once upon a time, this place was behind a tiny storefront on SW Eighth Street, even before the Cuban migration. Though it's now moved to larger quarters, it still has the distinction of being Miami's first Spanish restaurant, and still one of the very best. The menu lists some Mexican dishes (*taquitos* with *mole* sauce recommended), but the stars are Spanish specialties such as shrimps enchiladas, octopus *marinara,* fried garlic pork chunks. Closed Sunday. Entrées from $1.75 (L), $3.25 (D). AE, DC, MC, V.

### BASQUE

***Centro Vasco,*** 2235 SW Eighth Street (643-9606, 642-2672). Specialty is sangría made fresh at your table in this old, rather rambling restaurant that seems to be transplanted from old Havana (where a small Basque community thrives). Snapper in green sauce, fried snapper chunks, chicken *basquaise.* Open seven days a week. Entrées from $2.50 (L), $4.50 (D). AE, CB, DC, MC, V.

## SPECIALTY COOKING

### BARBECUE

***Hitching Post,*** 445 E. Okeechobee Road (887-6012). Just north of the airport, this is your stereotype BBQ joint—cowboy murals on the walls, wooden picnic tables, the works. But the spareribs are the best in town, and the barbecued pork sandwich is piled a mile high. French fries are good, but the onion rings tend to be greasy, although they are homemade. Key lime pie is first-rate. Closed Monday. Entrées from $1.79, sandwiches; and $4.39, ribs (L & D). No credit cards.

# DELI

***Rascal House,*** 17190 Collins Avenue, Miami Beach (947-4581). Perched way up in the northern marches of Miami Beach, this first-rate deli is a mecca, day and night. Be prepared for a wait. It's worth it: the sandwiches are deep-pile, the pot roast and matzoh-ball soup are home-style and the desserts are knockouts. Open seven days a week. Sandwiches from $1.95, entrées from $3.95 (L & D). No credit cards.

# HAMBURGER

***Gibby's,*** 901 5th Street, Miami Beach (673-2351). The house special is topped with fried onions and green peppers on a kaiser roll, and it's the best burger in town. The place is clean and has an old-fashioned charm. You'll love the onion rings. Order beer with your burger. Closed Saturday and Sunday. Hamburgers from $2.35. No credit cards.

# SEAFOOD

***Joe's Stone Crab,*** 227 Biscayne Street, Miami Beach (673-0365). The quintessential old South Florida restaurant (it's been there since you had to take a boat to get to Miami Beach), high-ceilinged and somewhat noisy, it has a personality of its own, and tuxedoed waiters, yet. The stone crabs are unbeatable, but expensive. Florida fish, such as red snapper, yellowtail, pompano, even mackerel, are fresh-fresh. Try the cottage-fried sweet potatoes for an interesting treat. A specialty is hash-brown potatoes. Key lime pie is a must. Dinner only. Open seven days a week. Closed May 15 to October 15, approximately. Entrées from $3.50 (for fried oysters). AE, DC, MC, V.

# STEAK

***The Depot,*** 5830 S. Dixie Highway (665-6261). The gimmick here is a railroad theme, but not a lineup of boxcars. It's a room with tables that are actually glass-topped model-train layouts. The second room is a converted old-style dining car. Steak and sautéed crab meat is a special treat, and the seafood is generally well prepared. Dinner only. Closed Monday. Dinners from $14.95. AE, CB, DC, MC, V.

# VEGETARIAN

***Spiral,*** 1630 Ponce de Leon Avenue (446-1591). This small Coral Gables storefront presents Miami's first and still best meatless menu. Tempura is a specialty. There's an appealing house salad, and the daily soups and specials are always first-rate. Sunday, dinner only. Open seven days a week. Entrées from $2.95 (L & D). No credit cards.

# FOR INDIVIDUAL NEEDS

## IF YOU HAVE TIME FOR ONLY ONE MEAL

***Whiffenpoof,*** 2728–32 Ponce de Leon Boulevard, Coral Gables (445-6603). A German chef and a British maître d' make for a winning combination. This reliable, always crowded but not terribly noisy place in a quiet part of Coral Gables (only 10 minutes from the airport) shows more than a little imagination in such dishes as red snapper caprice (filet of fresh local snapper draped with thin banana slices and broiled), more than passable sauerbraten, steak *au poivre,* onion soup, chocolate mousse. Closed Monday and from July 1 to October 1, approximately. Entrées from $3.25 (L), $7.95 (D). AE, DC, MC, V.

## BEST HOTEL MEAL

***Horatio's,*** 2649 S. Bayshore Drive (858-2500). This rooftop restaurant, perched atop the Coconut Grove Hotel, has finally had to forego its weekly changing fixed menu, but the à la carte offerings are almost as attractive. Try the lobster tarragon or, if you're prepared to go halves with your dining partner, the saddle of lamb. Dinner only. Closed Sunday. Entrées from $8.95. AE, CB, DC, MC, V.

## RESTAURANT NEAR AIRPORT

***Chalet Gourmet,*** 1470 NW LeJeune Road (871-4944). A refreshing oasis in one of the city's grimmest gastronomic deserts, where the rent-a-car lots back up against the runways. Luncheon menu is long on salads, seafoods, egg dishes (try the spinach omelet). Dinner features steaks and lobsters, attractively sauced. Saturday, brunch and dinner only. Closed Sunday. Entrées from $3 (L), $15 (D), $5.95 brunch. AE, CB, DC, MC, V.

## BUSINESS BREAKFAST

***Café Brasserie,*** Coconut Grove Hotel, 2649 S. Bayshore Drive (858-2500). Open seven days a week. Breakfast from $1.75. AE, CB, DC, MC, V.

# BUSINESS LUNCH

***Café 18,*** 1 SE Third Avenue (577-6613). Unbeknownst to most passersby 18 stories below, this cut-above-average cafeteria hides out high up in the First Federal Savings Building, which passes for a skyscraper in Miami's somewhat stunted downtown. The windows command a 270-degree view (with a little craning) from Biscayne Bay to the fringe of the Everglades. Food is simple, fresh and very reasonably priced. Trays are brought from the end of the cafeteria line to your table by liveried waiters (who expect tips). Breakfast and lunch only. Closed Saturday and Sunday. Daily special complete meals at about $2.75 (L). No credit cards.

# FAST, GOOD FOOD/BREAKFAST

***Sam and Carl's Delicatessen,*** 6751 SW 57 Avenue (665-1631 or 667-9578). Either go with the $1.89 breakfast special, which includes toast, potatoes, eggs and coffee, or order from the extensive à la carte breakfast menu. Everything from lox and eggs to smoked kippers is offered at fairly reasonable prices. Closed Monday. MC, V.

# FAST, GOOD FOOD/LUNCH

***Pete Sauer's Sandwich Shop,*** 3806 NE 1st Avenue (576-6565). Small but beautifully designed shop in Decorator's Row makes eye-popping sandwiches, salads, especially chopped liver, roast beef, pastrami, lobster salad. Closed weekends. Sandwiches from $1.65. No credit cards.

# FAST, GOOD FOOD/DINNER

***La Crêpe,*** Dadeland Shopping Mall, N. Kendall Drive at Palmetto Expressway (661-6051). Crêpes, soups, bread and desserts are reliable, tasty. Open seven days a week. Entrées from $2.70. AE, DC, MC, V.

# BEST WINE LIST

***Bodega,*** 9801 S. Dixie Highway (667-2574) and 5911 NW 36th Street (871-2764). Other branches in Broward County and Orlando. The wine list at these chain steakhouses is not the most elaborate in town, but it is a model of selection and fair pricing. A frequent rendezvous for the local chapter of Les Amis du Vin. Steaks and prime ribs are fair enough. Dinner only. Open seven days a week. Entrées from $4.95. AE, MC, V.

## FOR DRINKS

***Cye's Rivergate,*** 444 Brickell Avenue (358-9100). A stained-glass ceiling dominates a huge bar. Lots of young singles, and hot hors d'oeuvre around 5 P.M. to 7 P.M. Modern restaurant is reliable, too. Closed Sunday. AE, DC, MC, V.

## RESTAURANT WITH MUSIC

***Les Jardins,*** 1546 NW LeJeune Road (871-3430). The best of the local jazz and disco groups play this place regularly, clashing somewhat with a décor that's billed as "French country inn." The cuisine, too, falls a little short of what you'd expect at a Gallic auberge, but some dishes are good bargains. Saturday and Sunday, dinner only. Open seven days a week. Entrées from $2.95 (L), $7.95 (D). AE, CB, DC, MC, V.

## ROMANTIC

***La Bohème,*** 2937 Biscayne Boulevard (573-3864). Cozy little place with a fireplace, high-backed booths, efficient service and a spectacular French menu that's a bit on the expensive side. Steak with green peppercorns, snapper *en croûte, truite au bleu,* curried scampi. Closed Sunday. Entrées from $5.95 (L), $12.95 (D). AE, MC, V.

## LATE-NIGHT SERVICE

***The Forge,*** 432 Arthur Godfrey Road, Miami Beach (538-8533). (See description under AMERICAN.)

***Ham And Eggery,*** 530 NE 167 Street (947-1430). "Welcome to Cholesterol Heaven" reads the hand-painted sign emblazoned over the doorway of this 24-hour dive. That and the name of the place should tip off the menu: long on breakfast foods with a slightly Southern accent. Two-fisted coffee cups big as beer steins, quickly replenished. Eclectic wee-hours clientele ranges from prom dates to pimps, motorcyclers to cops. Open seven days a week. Entrées from $1.65. No credit cards.

## SUNDAY BRUNCH

***Courtyard Inn,*** 2451 Brickell Avenue (858-5770). Great display of shrimp, salads, sausage, etc., to go with your scrambled eggs. Beautiful San Francisco-type setting with stained glass and lots of unfinished wood. Complete brunch from $5.95. AE, CB, DC, MC, V.

***Kowloon,*** 930 East Ninth Street, Hialeah (885-6376). Buried in the industrial heart of Spanish-speaking Hialeah, this converted Frosty Kone parlor has become a meeting place for South Florida's widely scattered Chinese community every Saturday and Sunday morning. That's when they break out the special menu for *dim sum,* the little platters of assorted dainties that Cantonese love to wash down with tea in a long, leisurely brunch ritual. The menu loses a lot in the English translation, but at 80 cents to $1 per platter, you can afford to order blindly just to experiment. Try the fried taro, the duck feet, the "chicken bundle" and the steamed shrimp roll, for starters. The untranslated ball-point scrawlings on the front of the menu are names of various kinds of noodles and rice porridge for those who need more substantial fare than hors d'oeuvre. These, too, are delicious. No credit cards.

# IN THE SUBURBS

## BROWARD COUNTY-CENTRAL

***New River Storehouse,*** Marina Bay Club, State Road 84 (behind Holiday Inn) at I-95 (791-7600). Restaurant is open to the public at dinner, but only members can make reservations, so go early, unless you know a member. American food with lovely South Florida touches, excellent bar. Open seven days a week. Entrées from $6.95. AE, DC, MC, V.

## FORT LAUDERDALE

***Les Trois Mousquetaires,*** 2447 E. Sunrise Boulevard (564-7513). Superb French food in a bistro atmosphere, absolutely first-rate in every way. Veal with *chanterelles,* lobster thermidor made from scratch, roast chicken, cake-type chocolate mousse. Chaîne des Rotisseurs. Saturday, dinner only. Closed Sunday. Entrées from $3.50 (L), $6.50 (D). AE, DC, MC, V.

# MARKETS

## GIFT FOODS

***The Cheesery,*** Jordan Marsh Omni, 1501 Biscayne Boulevard (377-1911). Fourth-floor shop-within-a-store has bulging cases full of well-cared-for cheese, best selection in town. Also imported crackers, freshly baked bread, etc. Open seven days a week. AE, DC.

***Epicure Market,*** 1656 Alton Road, Miami Beach (672-1861). The number-one market for people who care about quality at a price. Lots of homemade food in the Hostess Pantry ready to heat up, good cakes and other desserts; the whole place has a faintly homey, Jewish feeling. Closed Sunday. MC, V.

***Coffee, Etc.,*** Dadeland Shopping Mall (665-7779). Reliable supply of best-known varieties of beans, some unusual ones, too. Owner is a blending wizard. Also paraphernalia for enjoying tea, coffee, etc. Open seven days a week. MC, V. .

## GIFT WINES

***Foremost Sunset Corners,*** 8701 Sunset Drive (271-8492). Best selection in town of French, German, California wines, including a number of exclusives. Sales help knows whereof it speaks, and the German selection is astounding. Closed Sunday. No credit cards.

# Milwaukee

To a large extent, the food and special dishes typical of Milwaukee restaurants today reflect the multinational character of the city's population. Three major groups—the Germans, Poles and Italians—settled in Milwaukee in the mid-1800's. From 1844 to 1878, German immigration to Milwaukee outnumbered that of all other nationalities; and by 1870, Milwaukee had the largest German settlement in the United States. Polish immigration to Milwaukee began in 1848, and between 1870 and 1880, they came in numbers that made them second only to the Germans. Heavy Italian immigration—mostly fishermen, sailors and farmers—took place from 1900 to 1910.

Through the years many other nationalities have contributed their traditions to the city and have kept them alive in restaurants. Among them are Norwegians, Scots, Welsh, Russians, Finns, Serbs, Croats, Czechs, Swiss, Mexicans, Greeks, Chinese, Turks, Syrians and Armenians. The German influence continues to predominate, however. Nearly every menu has a few German specialties—sauerbraten or Wiener schnitzel, Milwaukee rye bread, tortes and cheesecakes—even if the restaurant isn't devoted to German cooking. Italian food is also found everywhere in Milwaukee, with many restaurants making their own pastas.

In addition to the influence of strong ethnic backgrounds, Milwaukeean attitudes toward food have been shaped by and deeply rooted in the productivity of its rich farmlands. The state's dairy industry provides an abundance of distinctive regional cheeses; Milwaukee's three breweries, Schlitz, Pabst and Miller, sustain an interest in fine food as well as beer; and meat packers, who have been active here since 1844, produce excellent meat, especially pork, and an uncommon variety of sausages and smoked meats. The city also reaps benefits from the waters of Lake Michigan. Fishing, once a larger industry than it is today, provides lakefish—trout, salmon, whitefish—all favorite menu offerings. (Friday fish fries abound throughout the city). Wild game, as in the city's early years, is still essential to many ethnic dishes. Venison, goose, duck and pheasant are commonly found on menus.

Milwaukee's finest restaurants are spread throughout the city—in specific ethnic areas, or in the North Shore suburbs, or west, to Oconomowoc. However, the East Side (east of the Milwaukee River) has restaurants well worth a visit—**Karl Ratzsch's, Jean-Paul Restaurant Français, Grenadier's, Nicolo, Pandl's** in Whitefish Bay and **Boder's on the River** in Mequon. On the near South side is **Old Town Serbian Gourmet House.**

Restaurant growth in Milwaukee has steadied in the last five to ten years. There is an upsurge in fast-food restaurants, but they don't seem to be a threat to Milwaukee's older, family-owned, ethnic restaurants.

Weekend reservations are essential at the more popular downtown restaurants and at certain times during the week. Tipping is in the 15 percent range for dinner; somewhat less for lunch. Most restaurants are in the same price range, usually averaging around $9 for an entrée (with soup, salad and beverage). Ethnic entrées and specialties are frequently economically priced.

Dress is casual. Jackets with ties or turtlenecks are worn by men in downtown restaurants; pants suits on women are acceptable, although they are not seen as often as they were in past years. Some restaurants outside the downtown area are even more relaxed.

Many of the best produce, meat and cheese markets are located in Milwaukee's downtown and East Side areas—Sendik's (produce), The Coffee Trader and Wisconsin Cheese Mart (cheeses), and Blair's (meats)—although there are many family-owned and -run food specialty shops throughout the city.

Pay a special visit to Milwaukee's downtown Third Street—the 1000 block to be specific. There you will find **Usinger's Fine Sausage** shop, a family-owned business that makes what Milwaukeeans and others consider to be some of the finest sausage in the country. A visit to the store will take the tourist back in time to an Old World sausage shop.

Across the street is Mader's German restaurant, styled in the Bavarian fashion. Like many of Milwaukee's other distinctive restaurants, food shops and specialty stores, Mader's has developed an extensive gift shop featuring German wares.

In the 1100 block of Third Street, across from each other are the Asian Mart and Hong Fat Co.—both excellent shops for Oriental food and wares.

# Restaurants and Food Sources

**(Area code: 414)**

## BIG DEAL

### WORTH IT

***Karl Ratzsch's Restaurant,*** 320 E. Mason (276-2720). A restaurant that should not be missed. Ratzsch's superb German cuisine is served in an authentic German atmosphere, complete with a string trio playing nightly and on Sunday afternoons. Dirndl-skirted waitresses provide quite good service. One of Milwaukee's family-owned restaurants, Ratzsch's is known for its roast goose, sauerbraten, liver-dumpling soup and hot-bacon salad dressing. Reservations are essential. Chaîne des Rôtisseurs. Open seven days a week, until midnight. Entrées from $2.50 (L), $7.75 (D). AE, DC, MC, V.

## INTERNATIONAL

### AMERICAN

***Jack Pandl's Original Whitefish Bay Inn,*** 1319 E. Henry Clay (964-3800). Exceptionally fine home cooking in a comfortable, cozy atmosphere. Just off Lake Michigan, the restaurant is tastefully decorated. Big windows line the dining room, making it possible to appreciate the flowers that abound on the premises, in season. Take the Lake Drive route from downtown Milwaukee to look at some of the old mansions that line the street. Pandl's is known for its whitefish. Another specialty is a German pancake large enough to cover the plate; desserts are homemade. Late Fridays and Saturdays it is also possible to order sandwiches, and they are good. Service is friendly. Reservations are recommended. Closed Sunday. Entrées from $3.95 (L), $6.95 (D). AE, DC, MC, V.

## CHINESE

***China Palace Restaurant,*** 4511 N. Oakland Avenue (332-2024). A blend of Cantonese, Szechuan, Hunan and Mandarin cuisines at this comfortable and clean Chinese restaurant. Also an American menu, but the emphasis is on Chinese food. Carry-out or eat there. Dinner only. Open seven days a week. Entrées from $2.25 (L), $3.25 (D). MC, V.

## FRENCH

***Jean-Paul Restaurant Français,*** 811 E. Wisconsin Avenue (271-5400). Milwaukee's only real French restaurant. Chef-owner Jean-Paul Weber, formerly a captain at Maxim's in Paris, features French cuisine with many personally created specialties. The décor is elegant. The canopied bar is a good place to relax before lunch and dinner, and a piano bar provides tasteful music nightly. Servers are informed and friendly. The menu has been recently revised and is now 40 percent *nouvelle cuisine.* In addition, there is *le grand diner,* a nine-course meal with carefully limited quantities in each course. The French onion soup is superb and the house dressing, a creamy tarragon blend, is delightful. A good wine list is available, too. Reservations are recommended. Chaîne des Rotisseurs. Saturday, dinner only. Closed Sunday. Entrées from $4.25 (L), $8.85 (D). AE, MC.

## GREEK

***Kosta's White Manor Inn East,*** 1234 E. Juneau Avenue (272-4029). Small and intimate, located off Lake Michigan, the emphasis here is on Greek food. Try Greek salad, lamb shanks with artichoke hearts, lamb *exohiko, soutsoukakia* (spiced lamb meatballs in tomato sauce), fish kebab of red snapper, mushrooms, peppers and tomatoes; and *dolmades* (beef-stuffed grape leaves). Reservations are recommended. Sunday, dinner only. Open seven days a week. Entrées from $2.50 (L), $6.50 (D). MC, V.

## ITALIAN

***Nicolo Ristorante Internazionale,*** 1332 E. Brady (276-7477). A remodeled, spacious, comfortable restaurant. The bar is a great place to relax. Waitresses can steer the diner to the best the kitchen has to offer. A variety of pasta is available along with lasagne and manicotti. Veal entrées are superb. For an appetizer, try French-fried eggplant or mozzarella marinara. Clams and squid are prepared in imaginative ways. Sandwiches, too. Reservations recommended, especially on weekends. Dinner only. Closed Sunday. Entrées from $3.95 (L), $6.25 (D), AE, MC, V.

## SERBIAN

***Old Town Serbian Gourmet House,*** 522 W. Lincoln Avenue (672-0206). On Milwaukee's near South Side. Stucco walls are lined with art. Specialties are lamb *moussaka;* beef, cheese or spinach *boerek;* chicken paprika; veal cutlets and duck. Homemade strudels and tortes shouldn't be missed. A strolling trio plays Friday, Saturday and Sunday evenings. Service is good and can be fast. Chaîne des Rotisseurs. Saturday and Sunday, dinner only. Closed Monday. Entrées from $3 (L), $5 (D). AE, MC, V.

# SPECIALTY COOKING

## CHILI

***Real Chili Restaurant,*** 1625 W. Wells Street (342-6955), and 419 E. Wells Street (271-4042). Small, brightly lit, clean and friendly places with good service. Chili is the only business here and it's made to suit many tastes. Mild to medium is $1.25, hot is $1.77 and all-meat sauce is $2.50. (L & D). Chili dogs and burgers also available. Open until 2 A.M. Closed Sunday. No credit cards.

## DELI

***Jake's Delicatessen,*** 1634 W. North Avenue (562-1272). Seats about 55 at tables, booths and a lunch counter. Lunch is the main meal of the day. Be sure to have Jake's corned beef—it's cooked on the premises and sliced in front of the diner. Baked short ribs are good, as are homemade soups, the contents of which vary from day to day. Carry-out service. Closed Sunday. Entrées from $2.25. No credit cards.

## HAMBURGER

***Major Goolsby's, Inc.,*** 340 W. Kilbourn Avenue (271-3414), and ***Someplace Else, Inc.,*** 634 N. Water Street (273-6473). Both are clean, pleasant bars with tables and booths. Major Goolsby's has a garden room. A limited menu of sandwiches, hamburgers and chili is served. Salads are served at lunch on weekdays; ice-cream drinks for $1 on Wednesdays. Hamburgers ($1.50) and cheeseburgers ($1.70) are made of ⅓-pound pure ground beef and are outstanding. Both restaurants closed Sunday, but open until 2 A.M. the rest of the week at Someplace Else, and until 3:30 A.M. at The Major. Food always available. The Major: AE, DC, MC, V. Someplace Else: AE, CB, MC, V.

## KOSHER

***Jewish Community Center Kosher Restaurant,*** 1400 N. Prospect Avenue (276-0716). Milwaukee's only kosher restaurant. Popular items are whitefish, brisket and chicken. The dining room, pleasant and clean, overlooks Lake Michigan. Lunch only. Closed weekends and all Jewish holidays. Entrées from $2.75. MC, V.

## PIZZA

***Allegretti Pizzaria,*** 8030 N. 76th Street (354-4940). Allegretti's specializes in thick-crust, deep-dish pizza, served in hefty portions. The restaurant is small and reservations are not accepted, so don't be surprised if you have a short wait. Pizzas start at $4 and range to $7.50. Carry-out available. Closed Monday. Entrées from $2.25 (L), $3.50 (D). No credit cards.

## SEAFOOD

***Anchorage Restaurant,*** 4700 N. Port Washington Road (962-4710). Overlooking the Milwaukee River and owned by the adjacent Hilton Hotel, this is a pleasant seafood house that's comfortable and tastefully decorated along nautical lines. Steaks, veal and duck are available, but seafood is the forte here. Try cioppino, any of the clam entrées or scrod à la Oskar. The Anchorage prepares crab, lobster, scallops, shrimp and clams in entrées ranging from *au gratin* to Creole. Homemade desserts include cheesecake, strawberry *Schaumtorte,* Bavarian tortes and Brandy Alexander pie. Breakfast, 6:30 A.M. to 11 A.M., features omelets. Reservations recommended for lunch and dinner on weekends. Open seven days a week. Entrées from $3.95 (L), $7.95 (D). AE, CB, DC, MC, V.

## SOUL

***Toran's Tropical Hut,*** 2901 N. 5th Street (264-6590). Looks like a frame house from the road, but it has a front bar, a back dining room and patio dining in the summer. Basically a neighborhood tavern with excellent soul food, Toran's is clean and comfortable. There are no waitresses or waiters; customers place orders in the kitchen and select table service and condiments in the dining room. Lunches are more elaborate than dinners. Dinner entrées are mostly short-order, including fish, chicken, pork chops and shrimp. Specialties include catfish and buffalo fish, huge fried shrimp, a variety of greens, corn bread and black-eyed peas. Homemade desserts include peach cobbler, deep-dish apple pie and sweet-potato pie. Saturday and Sunday, dinner only. Open seven days a week: until 2 A.M. Sunday to Friday; until 3:30 A.M. Saturday. Entrées from $3.25 (L), $3 (D). No credit cards.

## STEAK

***Friendly Inn Supper Club,*** 4034 W. Good Hope Road (352-2535). Comfortable, pleasantly decorated and has good service. Call for reservations, especially on weekends. Steaks and beef are prime and usually cooked perfectly. Dessert tortes and pies are homemade and delicious. Saturday and Sunday, dinner only. Closed Monday. Entrées from $2.90 (L), $6.25 (D). MC, V.

***Jake's,*** 6030 W. North Avenue (771-0550) and 21445 Capitol Drive (781-7995). Same menu at both and each has a good wine list. Jake's is famous for its tenderloin steak that comes with a mountain of thin, crisply fried onion rings. Both restaurants open seven days a week. Entrées from $3.50 (L), $4.95 (D). AE, MC, V.

## SUBMARINES

***Cousins Submarine Sandwiches,*** 1634 W. Wisconsin Avenue (933-0480); 5121 W. Howard Avenue (321-4650); 1673 N. Farwell Avenue (272-7220); 5560 N. 60th Street (464-3110); 4134 W. Villard Avenue (527-1501); 2867 S. Kinnickinnic Avenue (747-0800); 5158 S. 108th Street (425-3140); and 3074 E. Layton Avenue (481-8700). Nothing fancy as far as décor, but they make the best Eastern-style submarine sandwiches in Milwaukee. The basic sub is $1.25 (half), $2.50 (whole). Carry-out or eat there. You can also buy a 4-foot or 6-foot sandwich—ideal for a large group—but give them a day's notice. Italian salamis as well as cheese, turkey, ham, etc. Call individual branches for hours. No credit cards.

# FOR INDIVIDUAL NEEDS

## IF YOU HAVE TIME FOR ONLY ONE MEAL

***Karl Ratzsch's Restaurant,*** 320 E. Mason (276-2720). (See description under BIG DEAL/WORTH IT.)

## BEST HOTEL MEAL

***Anchorage Restaurant,*** 4700 N. Port Washington Road (962-4710). (See description under SEAFOOD.)

## RESTAURANT NEAR AIRPORT

***Selens House of Prime Ribs,*** 3107 E. Layton Avenue (744-7890). A clean, comfortable restaurant. Service can be speedy if you let them know you're in a hurry. Prime rib is the best. Reservations recommended. Saturday and Sunday, dinner only. Closed Monday. Entrées from $2.95 (L), $5.25 (D). AE, CB, DC, MC, V.

## BUSINESS BREAKFAST

***Seven Eighty North,*** 780 N. Water, in Marshall & Isley Bank (276-8384). Privacy and good food are the keynotes. One can select a continental breakfast, or omelets, quiche Lorraine, eggs Benedict. Average omelet is $2. Available for private parties in the evening. Breakfast, 7:30 A.M. to 10 A.M., Monday through Friday. AE, MC, V.

## BUSINESS LUNCH

***Grenadier's,*** 747 N. Broadway (276-0747). Beautifully decorated with nice bar for relaxing. There are six specialties of the day in addition to Caesar Salad with Crab Meat. Specialties are $4.95. Lots of fresh fish, too. Reservations are recommended for lunch and dinner. Chaîne des Rotisseurs. Saturday, dinner only. Closed Sunday. Entrées from $3.95 (L), $9.95 (D). AE, MC, V.

## FAST, GOOD FOOD/BREAKFAST

***JoJos Restaurants,*** 5470 N. Port Washington Road (332-4030), 15280 Blue Mound Road (786-0475), 9075 N. 76th Street (354-1328), 5300 S. 76th Street (421-7530), and 230 W. Layton Avenue (483-7008). Breakfast is served 24 hours a day. Luncheon and dinner menus available, too. Breakfast begins at $1.75. Open seven days a week, 24 hours a day. Entrées from $3.45 (L), $3.75 (D). MC, V.

## FAST, GOOD FOOD/DINNER

***Towne Room East,*** Milwaukee Inn, 916 E. State Street (276-3345). Good Italian food and a variety of steaks well prepared in a minimum of time. Open seven days a week. Entrées from $2.95 (L), $4.95 (D). AE, MC.

## BEST WINE LIST

***Karl Ratzsch's Restaurant,*** 320 E. Mason (276-2720). (See description under BIG DEAL/WORTH IT.) Ratzsch's has by far the most extensive wine list, offering both good vintages and good values.

## FOR DRINKS

***Safe House,*** 779 N. Front Street (271-2007). Styled after a speakeasy with emphasis on gangland mobsters. Entrance is through what looks like an office in which a false bookcase opens to the bar and restaurant. Food is secondary to drinks. Monday, lunch only. Bar open from 11:30 A.M. to 2 A.M., Monday through Friday; Saturday from 5 P.M. to 3:30 A.M.; Sunday from 5 P.M. to 1:30 A.M. AE, MC, V.

***Bryant's Cocktail Lounge, Inc.,*** 1579 S. 9th Street (383-2620). Known for 350 or more drinks, many creations of the bartenders. Pleasant, comfortable surroundings. Open until 2 A.M., Monday through Friday; until 3:30 A.M., Saturday; until 2 A.M., Sunday. Most mixed drinks begin at $1.50. Elaborate, mostly tropical drinks range from $1.50 to $3.50. MC, V.

## RESTAURANT WITH MUSIC

***Karl Ratzsch's Restaurant,*** 320 E. Mason Street (276-2720). (See description under BIG DEAL/WORTH IT.)

***Old Town Serbian Gourmet House,*** 522 W. Lincoln Avenue (672-0206). (See description under SERBIAN.)

## ROMANTIC

***Alpine Retreat,*** 1380 Friess Lake Road, Hubertus (628-1909). A cozy, small, log-cabin restaurant (about a 45-minute drive from downtown Milwaukee) that has a limited menu, but all items are done very well. Most popular are tenderloin filet ($7.75), and the Surf and Turf ($10.95). Dinner only. Closed Monday. AE, MC.

## LATE-NIGHT SERVICE

***Karl Ratzsch's Restaurant,*** 320 E. Mason (276-2720). (See description under BIG DEAL/WORTH IT.)

***Nicolo Ristorante Internazionale,*** 1332 E. Brady (276-7477). (See description under ITALIAN.)

***Major Goolsby's,*** 340 W. Kilbourn Avenue (271-3414). (See description under HAMBURGER.) Hamburgers available until closing.

***Someplace Else,*** 634 N. Water (273-6473). (See description under HAMBURGER.) Hamburgers available until closing.

## SUNDAY BRUNCH

***Eggcetera,*** 424 E. Wisconsin Avenue (273-8222). In the Café Rouge of the Pfister Hotel. About 67 different items are offered, including omelets, sausages, bacon, ham and chicken, hash browns, a variety of cold salads, lox spread and bagels, smoked fish and a variety of desserts. Elegant surroundings. Reservations are recommended for a large party. Adults, $6.95; children under 12, $4. AE, CB, DC, MC, V.

## SUNDAY-EVENING MEAL

***Old Town Serbian Gourmet House,*** 522 W. Lincoln Avenue (672-0206). (See description under SERBIAN.)

***Anchorage Restaurant,*** 4700 N. Port Washington Road (962-4710). (See description under SEAFOOD.)

## FOR FAMILIES WITH CHILDREN

***JoJos Restaurants,*** five locations in Milwaukee. (See description under FAST, GOOD FOOD/BREAKFAST.) During bar hours, parents can have a drink with their meal as the kids eat.

## COUNTRY INN

***Fox & Hounds Restaurant,*** 1298 Friess Lake Road, Hubertus (251-4100). In the beautiful Holy Hill area of suburban Milwaukee—a 45-minute to 1-hour drive from downtown. Comfortable, spacious, tastefully decorated and the service is prompt. Try duck or stuffed pork chops. Desserts, as well as soups, are homemade and delicious. Reservations essential on Saturday; recommended otherwise. Dinner only. Open seven days a week. Complete dinner from $8. AE, DC, MC, V.

# IN THE SUBURBS

## BAYSIDE

***George Pandl's in Bayside,*** 8825 N. Lake Drive (352-1430). A large, attractively decorated restaurant about 20 minutes from downtown Milwaukee. Wednesday night (5 P.M. to 9 P.M.) there is a very good buffet with fresh shrimp, crab, smoked trout or salmon in addition to expertly prepared entrées. Service is good. Try whitefish, the specialty. Reservations recommended. Sunday brunch. Closed Monday. Entrées from $5 (L), $7.25 (D). AE, MC, V.

## BROOKFIELD

***The Proud Popover,*** 17700 Capitol Drive, Brookfield (781-1776). The Colonial décor is appropriate to the house specialty—giant, delicious popovers. Good main dish choices include quiches, prime rib and leg of lamb. Sunday brunch (not buffet style). Dinner reservations recommended. Open seven days a week. Entrées from $3.50 (L), $6.25 (D). AE, DC, MC, V.

## MEQUON-THIENSVILLE

***Boder's on the River, Inc.,*** 11919 N. River Road, 43W (242-0335). About 30 minutes from downtown Milwaukee, located in a rambling farmhouse on the Milwaukee River. Old-fashioned elegance and leisurely dining are the hallmarks in rooms paneled with dark wood. Very generous dinners are served, so bring your appetite along. Boder's is famous for whitefish, corn fritters, a house salad of fresh fruit, and hot, freshly baked blueberry and black-cherry muffins that come with every dinner. Homemade desserts. Reservations recommended. Closed Monday. Entrées from $7.50 (L), $8.95 (D). "Luncheonette" (smaller portions) at $5.50. No credit cards.

## WAUKESHA

***The Depot Restaurant,*** 319 Williams (547-1722). A restaurant built in old railroad cars, about a 20-minute drive from downtown Milwaukee. Favorites here include barbecued ribs and baked duck. Saturday, dinner only. Sunday, brunch only. Monday, lunch only. Open seven days a week. Entrées from $3.25 (L), $5.95 (D). MC, V.

# MARKETS

## GIFT FOODS

***Usinger's Fine Sausage,*** 1030 N. 3rd Street (276-9100). Superb homemade sausages—about 80 different kinds. Usinger's sends gift assortments all over the country and delivers in the Milwaukee area. Orders can be placed by phone if time is at a premium; however, try to visit this Old World sausage company if possible. Gift assortments range from $7.50 to $22.50. Closed Sunday. No credit cards.

***Larry's Brown Deer Market,*** 8737 N. Deerwood Drive (355-9650). A small, extremely friendly country grocery with shelf after shelf of food specialties. An extensive line of cheeses from around the world, wines, fresh fruit and fresh imported French pâtés are available. Prices begin at about $15 for these individual gifts. Closed Sunday. No credit cards.

## GIFT WINES

***Mason Street Liquors,*** 226 E. Mason (272-1900). Will make up gift wine selections from their extensive stock. Closed Sunday. MC.

# SPECIAL EVENTS

***Holiday Folk Fair.*** Each year, the International Institute and the Joseph Schlitz Co. co-sponsor the Holiday Folk Fair in which more than 45 ethnic groups provide a food-and-ethnic craft booth at the fair. It's not to be missed for those interested in good ethnic food. Always Friday, Saturday and Sunday before Thanksgiving at MECCA (Milwaukee Exposition & Convention Center & Arena).

# Minneapolis/St. Paul

"Say, where does one get a good Scandinavian meal in the Twin Cities?" Don't ask.

Many visitors consider Minnesota the land of Swedes and Norskis, but not when it comes to restaurants. When a restaurant named The Stockholm serves Chinese food, it's a clue that the tourist's best hope for a Scandinavian meal is to be invited home to dinner by someone of Swedish or Norwegian descent. As far as restaurants go, it's a Swedish meatball here, a bit of *lefse* there and that's about it.

For good reason. The Twin Cities are a cosmopolitan area with a varied ethnic heritage. Restaurants follow suit: they range from Afghani fare to Vietnamese meals, with Indian, Mexican, Italian, Irish and German in between.

Minneapolis and St. Paul have gained a glamour image. If one can ignore the miseries of winter, the area oozes quality of life. Economy and industry are strong, government is progressive, the arts are vibrant. Local residents are willing to spend for a good meal; though by New York standards, prices are quite reasonable.

Even in frontier Minnesota a "steak and potatoes" reputation was not the local culinary curse. Riverboats and wagons brought barrels of oysters and a tremendous variety of exotic foods to augment what the fields and rivers could supply. Then came railroads, which brought more provisions and a standard of dining-car excellence that still is mourned by those who remember its heyday.

Hotels such as the Ryan, the Park Place, the Windsor in St. Paul, the Nicollet House in Minneapolis, offered caviar, quail, buffalo tongue and saddle of antelope with French peas. People ate well to compensate for the cold winters. Subconsciously, perhaps, Twin Citians still do. Any visitor should try local specialties such as walleye pike (the state's official fish) or wild rice.

The metropolitan area stretches forty miles, with three main commercial areas: the downtowns of St. Paul and Minneapolis, and The Strip, which skirts Interstate 494 from the airport for about eight miles due west.

Most of the restaurants suggested are found in the downtown areas for the convenience of carless travelers. The two mentioned for families with children are farther afield, assuming a traveling tribe will have their own transportation.

However, anyone with a liberal expense account can wine and dine endlessly along The Strip. Eddie Websters, Steak and Ale, **Camelot, L'hotel de France,** Howard Wong's, **Lincoln Del** and motel fare keep the traveler well sustained.

There is a wealth of imaginative, youth-oriented theme restaurants offering filling, fresh food. **Sgt. Preston's of the North, Rudolph's,** W.A. Frost and Garuda are worth seeking out.

The center for trendy dining in Minneapolis has become St. Anthony on Main, a restored mattress factory now well padded with shops and restaurants such as **Taiga, Anthony's Wharf,** GuadalaHarry's, and nearby **Pracna on Main.**

The Twin Cities also has two underground restaurants. In St. Paul, Castle Royal is a revival of a Prohibition era dine-and-dance spot built into former mushroom caves fronting the Mississippi. It's the coolest place in town in hot July. On the western reaches of Minneapolis is Amalgamated, built to look like an underground iron mine of the early days of Minnesota's mining industry.

Amalgamated is one of the Restaurants No Limit group of innovative eateries including Pracna on Main, **Forepaugh's,** Lord Fletcher's (on Lake Minnetonka—great spot during the boating season), and D. B. Searle's in St. Cloud, 60 miles northwest. The only other organization that feeds as many people (excluding burger chains) is the Radisson Corp., which owns the Twin Cities' major hotels and eating magnets such as **The Flame Room,** the **Haberdasheries,** the Shipside seafood restaurant, **Le Carrousel** and many more.

Nicollet Mall, which wends through downtown Minneapolis, is a prime shopping area. Wander through the Crystal Court at the IDS Tower—everyone else does—or stop for a drink and snack at the Crossroads Bar overlooking the enclosed city square. A fifty-story elevator ride will give a panoramic view of the area—on a clear day Stillwater, 20-plus miles away, is visible.

Shoppers who enjoy boutiques in neighborhood settings should head for Grand Avenue near Lexington Avenue in St. Paul, or 50th and France in Edina. Both cities have renovated warehouses full of shops and eateries. In St. Paul there's Park Square Court; in Minneapolis, Butler Square where one must try D. B. Kaplan's or Caffé di Nichelini.

The serious diner will find a tie appropriate in the more formal spots at dinner, although it's rarely essential. One tip, after dinner, is the custom.

# Restaurants and Food Sources

**(Area code: 612)**

## BIG DEAL

### WORTH IT/MINNEAPOLIS

***New French Café,*** 128 N. Fourth Street, Minneapolis (338-3790). Never mind the warehouse district location (6 blocks from midtown) or the dreary hallway you must traverse. Once inside, the restaurant is sparkling white. The superb food is prepared in an open kitchen by the two women owners. Their loving and imaginative approach makes this the "in" place to dine among younger Twin Citians. Selections change regularly and there's a fixed-price dinner each evening; everything else is à la carte. Homemade French bread, *escargot en casserole,* salmon mousse, excellent soups, *nouvelle cuisine* approach to entrées, exciting vegetables, brilliant desserts. Dinner with wine and tip will average about $20 per person. Lunch with changing daily selections is unpretentious, reasonable, from $5. Homemade croissants served only at daily Continental breakfast from 8 A.M. Sunday brunch menu offers omelets, *gravlax,* oyster stew, from $5. Reservations recommended. Closed Monday. AE.

***510 Haute Cuisine,*** in lobby of apartment building at 510 Groveland Avenue, Minneapolis (874-6440). Genteel, chandeliered dining room and a top-notch chef in the kitchen. Dinner is fixed-price ($17.50 for four courses excluding dessert), with selections changing daily. Fanciful dessert tortes are irresistible. Wide selections of wines at agreeable prices. Lunch menus include daily specialities such as cassoulet, goulash, navarin of lamb (in $5 to $6 range) along with regular crêpes, quiches, soups, and baked hot sandwiches. Caters to after-Orchestra Hall and Guthrie Theater clientele with late light-meal service. Reservations suggested. Saturday, dinner only. Closed Sunday. AE, DC, MC, V.

## WORTH IT/ST. PAUL

***The Blue Horse,*** 1355 University Avenue, St. Paul (645-8101). Outstanding food and tableside service in subtle yet plush setting. Consistent award winner for such offerings as West Coast seafood, roast duck, fettuccine, Chateaubriand. Crab Louis and walleye pike popular with lunch crowd. Superb Caesar salad served with entrées. Ask waiter for house specialties not listed on menu if you hunger for something elaborate. Reservations essential. Closed Sunday. Entrées from $3.95 (L), $7.50 (D). AE, CB, DC, MC, V.

# INTERNATIONAL

## AFGHANI

***Caravan Serai,*** 2046 Pinehurst Avenue, St. Paul (698-9941). *Morgh kebab* (breast of childen marinated, then broiled) plus lamb specialties are enjoyed by the nimble who recline and dine on floor pillows (tables and chairs available, too). Homemade baklava. Afghani Feast available with 24 hours' notice. Wine served. Saturday, dinner only. Closed Monday. Entrées from $1.85 (L), $5.95 (D). AE, CB, MC, V.

## AMERICAN

***Charlie's Café Exceptionale,*** 701 Fourth Avenue S., Minneapolis (335-8851). Patriarch of Twin Cities fine dining for four decades. Always good, always crowded despite its size. Huge kitchen, their own bake and butcher shops. There is an immense menu of steaks, seafoods and specialties such as roast peppered ribeye, Dover sole, walleye pike, steak Diane. Everyone loves Charlie's potato salad. Start with the posh appetizer tray. Late-evening snack, dessert and coffee menus, too. Saturday, dinner only. Closed Sunday. Entrées from $4.75 (L), $8.25 (D). AE, CB, DC, MC, V.

***Forepaugh's,*** 276 S. Exchange Street, St. Paul (224-5606). Fans of Victoriana, lace curtains and antiques will be delighted with this century-old mansion. Cozy dining areas on three floors plus a trio of cocktail settings on first level. Food has been upgraded in elegance with tableside service at dinner. Sitdown Sunday brunch averages $4.95 for adults, $3.25 children. Reservations suggested. Open seven days a week. Entrées from $2.95 (L), $8.95 (D). AE, DC, MC, V.

## CHINESE

***Taiga,*** 201 S.E. Main Street, Minneapolis (331-1138). An across-the-river Oriental twin to Fuji-Ya (see JAPANESE). Built in the dungeons of the former mattress factory that is now trendy St. Anthony on Main, Taiga has stone walls balanced with warm décor. *Kung Pao* chicken a favorite on menu that features Cantonese, Mandarin and Szechuan items. *Dim sum* served during brunch hours. Entertainment nightly. Open seven days a week. Entrées from $3.95 (L), $4.50 (D). AE.

## FRENCH

***L'hotel de France,*** 5601 W. 78th Street, Bloomington (835-1900). The complete French dining experience, no matter the hour or finances. Formerly known as L'hotel Sofitel, this first French hotel to be built in the U.S. offers three enticements. **Le Café** is a glittering, mirrored setting. An elaborate, expensive *haute cuisine* menu is augmented by weekly specialties, often based on French regional fare. Impressive cellar of French wines. Closed Sunday. Entrées from $3.95 (L), $11.25 (D). **Chez Colette** exudes the essences of a bistro, including the aroma of onion soup dripping with cheese; French specialties vary daily. Entrées from $2.25 (B), $2.95 (L), $7.25 (D). The place to be seen late hours is **La Terrasse,** an enclosed version of a sidewalk café. Open seven days a week, from 11 A.M. through the night to 6:30 A.M., with a special, elegant late-hours snack menu. Regular menu entrées from $3.10 (L & D); Sunday brunch is $4.50; snacks from $1.50. L'hotel also has take-out service for French specialties and their crusty baguettes. Chaînes des Rotisseurs. AE, CB, DC, MC, V.

## GERMAN

***Black Forest Inn,*** 1 E. 26th Street, Minneapolis (823-2747). Colorful crowd gathers daily for sauerbraten with red cabbage, bratwurst, strudel and tap brews. Good wine list; liquor, too. Mad King Ludwig's castle mural decorates exterior; outdoor beer garden for summer sipping and dining. Sensational onion rings available after 9 P.M. Open seven days a week, except on major holidays. Prices are moderate, $3.40 for a plate special (L) to an average of $6 (D). AE, CB, DC, MC, V.

## GREEK

***Acropol Inn,*** 748 Grand Avenue, St. Paul (225-1989). Modest setting for Greek goodies such as *moussaka, souvlaki,* baklava and gyros. Excellent Greek salad. American choices, too. Closed Sunday. Entrées from $2.35 (L), $3.50 (D). No credit cards.

## IRISH

***MacCafferty's,*** 788 Grand Avenue, St. Paul (227-7328). Favorite hangout for citizens of St. Paul, which proves its ethnic bias annually with a large and rowdy St. Patrick's Day parade. Lively, foot-stomping Irish music nightly (Tuesday through Saturday) woos the drinking crowd. Dine on Scotch eggs, mixed grill, steak and mushroom pie, and soda bread. Open seven days a week. Kitchen closes at 8 P.M. Sunday brunch ($4.75) from 11 A.M. to 2 P.M., then "pub grub" from 2 to 8 P.M. Entrées from $2 (L), $3.95 (D). MC, V.

## ITALIAN

***Sammy D's,*** 1301 Fourth Street S.E., Minneapolis (331-5290). Located in the heart of University of Minnesota's Dinkytown shopping area, attractions are not only a full menu of Italian dishes (including an outstanding antipasto salad) but also charming, outspoken matriarch Mama D, cookbook author and TV talk-show personality. Ask for something special and she might go into the kitchen to cook it herself. Upstairs is Bootleg Sam's for wet goods. Open seven days a week. Entrées from $3 (L & D). No credit cards.

## JAPANESE

***Fuji-Ya,*** 420 First Street S., Minneapolis (339-2226). This is the dining house that Japanese war-bride Reiko Weston built. Sukiyaki and tempura are favorites in sit-on-the-floor *O-Zashiki* room upstairs. Downstairs, amid old mill foundations with a view of St. Anthony Falls, steak and shrimp are served *teppanyaki* style. Closed Sunday. Entrées from $2.95 (L), $7.50 (D). AE.

## MEXICAN

***Esteban's,*** 901 Marquette Avenue, Minneapolis (338-3383), 100 E. Main Street, Anoka (427-1970), 6042 Nicollet Avenue S., Richfield (866-3622). Serene stucco and greenery setting, exciting Phoenix-style fare. You could take a bath in their 27-ounce margarita. Use it to quench the fire from the tangy dip served with hot tortilla chips. Best bets on the menu are the *flauta* and *chimichanga,* but combination plates sell well, too. Sunday, dinner only. Open seven days a week. Entrées from $1.95 (L & D). AE, MC, V.

***Boca Chica,*** 11 Concord Street, St. Paul (222-9696). Run by the second generation of the Coronados, first family of Twin Cities' Mexican food. Simpie country-Mexican restaurant. Sunday breakfast is a favorite of the large St. Paul Mexican community. Liquor. Open seven days a week, until after midnight Friday and Saturday. Complete meals from $2.50 (L), $3.50 (D). No credit cards.

# SPECIALTY COOKING

## DELI

***Lincoln Del,*** original at 4100 W. Lake Street, St. Louis Park, just across Minneapolis line (927-9738) with newer locations at 5201 Wayzata Boulevard, Golden Valley (544-3616), and 4401 W. 80th Street, Bloomington (831-0780), that both serve liquor. The absolute temple of Reubens and blintzes in the Twin Cities. Soups are excellent, bakery items and desserts are wonderfully rich. Diet afterwards. Prices, commensurate with superb quality, start at $2.25 (L), and $4.95 for a complete dinner. Open seven days a week. No credit cards.

***Cecil's Back Room,*** 651 S. Cleveland Avenue, St. Paul (698-9792). Good Jewish food prepared the old-fashioned way. Chopped liver, cabbage borscht, potato latkes, blintzes, omelets, salads, homemade soups, handmade desserts (that don't spare the whipped cream). Be prepared to wait in line at lunchtime. Full take-out deli up front. Open seven days a week. Sandwiches from $1.25 (L & D). No credit cards.

## HAMBURGER

***Annie's Parlor,*** 406 Cedar Avenue, Minneapolis (339-6207). A modest ice-cream parlor that draws crowds from the University of Minnesota. Surroundings are casually decrepit but hamburgers compensate. Massive malts, home-cut, skin-on French fries and honest burgers cause nostalgia for those who remember the pre-Golden Arches era. Open seven days a week, until midnight. Sandwiches from $1.25. No credit cards.

***Mayor T. R. Potts,*** 193 S. Robert Street, St. Paul (226-8804). Just across the river from downtown St. Paul and named for the city's first mayor, the eatery looks like an old-fashioned firehall on the exterior and is pleasantly arrayed inside, with vintage wallpapers and stained glass. Well-stacked hamburger best sellers include the Crazy Harold and Sirloin Royal. Good salad bar and full dinner menu, too. Open seven days a week, 24 hours a day. Bar open 10:30 A.M. to 1 A.M. Entrées from $1.65 (L), $3.80 (D). AE, MC, V.

## PIZZA

***Green Mill,*** 57 S. Hamline Avenue, St. Paul, half a block from Grand Avenue (698-0353), 26th and Hennepin Avenue, Minneapolis (374-2131). Supreme deep-dish Chicago-style pizza in the Twin Cities and no slouch on flat pizzas, either. Full menu of salads, pot pies, well-garnished hamburgers at budget prices. Seafood bar in Minneapolis. Noisy, young crowd, always a wait for a table evenings, but you can order your pizza on arrival and sip beer or wine until there is a free table. Open seven days a week. Pizza take-out orders taken at 690-0539 until midnight; pick-up location at Hamline Avenue. Hamburgers from $2.30. AE, MC, V.

## SEAFOOD

***Anthony's Wharf,*** 201 S.E. Main Street, Minneapolis (378-7058). Draws diners into the St. Anthony on Main whirl. If possible, get a booth where built-in aquarium provides ever-swimming décor. Seafood is as fresh as possible 1,500 miles from any ocean; daily specials are based on what's available. At dinner, steamed lobster and grilled swordfish are favorites. In the summer, dine on a terrace overlooking the Mississippi. No reservations for dinner, so expect to wait. They do take lunch reservations. Open seven days a week. Entrées from $2.95 (L), $5.95 (D). AE, MC, V.

***Horatio Hornblower's,*** 345 Wabasha Street, St. Paul (227-8781). A favorite lunch spot downtown, and mecca for those who like seafood and sassy dancing music in the evening. Excellent salads at lunch; pan-fried scallops are delightful, too. Fish and beef entrées at night. Diners are seated in paneled, comfortable areas, including an intimate library that might have been in the Captain's own mansion. Reservations essential. Closed Sunday. Entrées from $2.95 (L), $7.95 (D). AE, DC, MC, V.

## STEAK

***Murray's,*** 26 S. Sixth Street, Minneapolis (339-0909). Famous for their Silver Butter-Knife Steak for two, so tender you can cut it with a you-know-what. Quality salads, great garlic toast, kitchen-made onion rings. Draws women for its afternoon cocktail lunch and early hours Queen's dinner. Music in dining room and bar. Kitchen open until midnight. Closed Sunday. Entrées from $2.95 (L), $6.95 (D). AE, CB, DC, MC, V.

***Lindey's Prime Steak House,*** 3610 N. Snelling Avenue, Arden Hills (633-9813). Only three items are on the menu: prime chopped sirloin, prime sirloin, Lindey's special sirloin. Your choice comes sizzling, with garlic toast and salad. Dinner only. Closed Sunday. Entrées from $8.65. No credit cards.

## VEGETARIAN

***Prashad Kitchen,*** 3415 W. 44th Street, Minneapolis (926-7890). No matter the ethnic origin—Mexican, Middle Eastern, Chinese, European—the food is always good, filling, inexpensive and dedicatedly meatless. Open seven days a week. Entrées from $2. No credit cards.

# FOR INDIVIDUAL NEEDS

## IF YOU HAVE TIME FOR ONLY ONE MEAL

***International Rosewood Room,*** Northstar Inn, 618 Second Avenue S., Minneapolis (338-2288). Plan on leisurely dining in this elegant, award-winning seventh-floor mecca for local gourmets. Just reading the extensive menu will take you through the first cocktail. It offers pages of European and American specialties, with emphasis on French. Food is almost always superb. Northstar salad is a must-order. They bake their own French bread and pastries. Chaîne des Rotisseurs. Reservations essential. No Saturday lunch during summer. Open seven days a week. Entrées from $4.75 (L), $9.75 (D). AE, DC, MC, V.

***The Lexington,*** 1096 Grand Avenue, St. Paul (222-5878). Long the favorite restaurant for residents of St. Paul's Historic Hill district, this genteel establishment with its handsome paneled bar has a wide menu selection. Favorites include eggs Benedict at lunch, Columbia River salmon, steaks and seafood for dinner. At the center of an area popular for boutique shopping. Reservations suggested. Closed Sunday. Entrées from $2.50 (L), $5.75 (D). No credit cards.

## BEST HOTEL MEAL

***International Rosewood Room,*** Northstar Inn, 618 Second Avenue S., Minneapolis (338-2288). (See description under IF YOU HAVE TIME FOR ONLY ONE MEAL.)

## RESTAURANT NEAR AIRPORT

***Gannon's,*** 2728 W. Seventh Boulevard, St. Paul (699-2420). A great haven for anyone who loves a thick liver steak, smothered in onions, one of the house specialties. About 2 miles from the airport. Closed Sunday. Bar opens at 8 A.M. Entrées from $2.60 (L), $6.25 (D). No credit cards.

## BUSINESS LUNCH

***Gallivan's,*** 354 Wabasha Street, St. Paul (227-6688). Boisterous watering spot for local City Hall and journalist types. Fried shrimp, omelets, walleye pike are noon favorites; prime rib is the dinner specialty, also torsk and ribs. Closed Sunday. Entrées from $2.55 (L), $5.95 (D). AE, DC, MC, V.

***Jax Café,*** 1928 University Avenue N.E., Minneapolis (789-7297). In "nordeast" section, "where everything swings," yet an easy cab ride from downtown, Jax food has been drawing crowds for more than three decades. Rainbow trout taken fresh from their own pool are available (when the pool isn't frozen over). The "lunch in a kettle," offering chicken and dumplings, stew, tenderloin tips, is a favorite of businessmen. They have Weight-Watchers selections for dieters. Closed Sunday. Entrées from $3.25 (L), $5 (D). AE, CB, DC, MC, V.

## FAST, GOOD FOOD/LUNCH

***The Four Inns,*** 220 American National Bank Skyway North, downtown St. Paul (225-9453). Always a line at lunch but service is amazingly fast, food is exceptionally good and inexpensive. Daily soup specials, fish sandwich on Friday. Closed weekends and two weeks in July. Open from 7 A.M. to 4 P.M. Entrées in $2 range. No credit cards.

***Sgt. Preston's of the North,*** 221 Cedar Avenue, Minneapolis (338-6146). Canadians would feel at home surrounded by décor that features Mounties memorabilia. One portion of the colorful bar is devoted to sandwiches and soups that are generous and satisfying. French-Canadian onion soup is super. Soup (whole or half bowls) and sandwiches can be ordered in endless combinations of healthy ingredients. Cafeteria service. Open seven days a week. Entrées from $2.30 (L & D). AE, CB, DC, MC, V.

## FAST, GOOD FOOD/DINNER

***Becky's Cafeteria,*** 1934 Hennepin Avenue, Minneapolis (871-

8500). Tasty, substantial cafeteria food but the dining room itself is the real attraction: antiques, chandeliers, artwork, cabinets full of curios. Open seven days a week. Entrées from $3. No credit cards.

## BEST WINE LIST

***The Wine Cellar,*** Northstar Inn, 618 Second Avenue S., Minneapolis (338-9351). Let maître d' Marcel help you choose from an extensive wine list, and from the nightly list of five entrées (emphasizing *nouvelle cuisine*) that star in five-course dinners. Full price (excluding wine) is $19 to $24. Reservations a must for this intimate, elegant spot. Dinner only. Closed Sunday. AE, DC, MC, V.

## FOR DRINKS

***Haberdashery,*** Radisson Hotel, 45 S. Seventh Street, Minneapolis (333-2181), 1501 Washington Avenue S., Minneapolis (333-6303), 395 Wabasha, downtown St. Paul (222-7855). Decorated as an old-time clothing store, the Habs draw a young crowd of lunch and after-work drinkers. Good hamburgers and light meals, too. Open seven days a week from 11:30 A.M. to 1 A.M.; but St. Paul location closed Sunday. Food from $2.35. AE.

***The Little Prince,*** 1403 Harmon Place, Minneapolis (338-0900). Opulent stone mansion on fringe of downtown, dripping with impressive architectural amenities, including a dark-paneled library-bar that's a sophisticated setting for older adults longing for a quiet and elegant drinking spa. Expensive meals are also featured in the privacy of former bedrooms turned dining areas. Décor is inspired, food sometimes not. Frequented by expense-account crowd. Open seven days a week. Entrées from $1.95 (L), $7.95 (D). AE, CB, DC, MC, V.

## RESTAURANT WITH MUSIC

***Flame Room,*** Radisson Hotel, 45 S. Seventh Street, Minneapolis (333-2181). More than two million patrons have heard the eight violins, two pianos and bass collectively known as the Golden Strings. Devoted crowds, especially birthday and anniversary celebrants, come to revel in the music, red-velvet décor and opulent food. Veal Oskar is popular. No music at lunch. Golden Strings play two shows Friday and Saturday at dinner, cover charge. Chaîne des Rotisseurs. Reservations essential. Saturday, dinner only. Closed Sunday. Entrées from $3.35 (L), $9.50 (D). AE, CB, DC, MC, V.

## RESTAURANT WITH A VIEW

***Orion Room,*** 50th Floor, IDS Tower, downtown Minneapolis (372-3772). Wild-rice soup, pheasant in puff paste and flaming desserts draw attention away from the "see forever" view atop the Twin Cities' loftiest building. Dining areas are tiered to emphasize the feeling of height. If not hungry, enjoy the view from the adjacent Orion Penthouse Lounge. Reservations suggested. Saturday, dinner only. Closed Sunday. Entrées from $3 (L), $9.50 (D). AE, DC, MC, V.

***Le Carrousel,*** Radisson Hotel, Wabasha at Kellogg Boulevard, St. Paul (222-7711). Beautiful view of the Mississippi from the 22nd floor. The room, elegantly adorned in refined brass-wood-greenery style, has a revolving center section for changing city and river panoramas. At dinner, steak Diane, poulet Oskar, batter-fried walleye pike and duckling *à la bigarade* are notable. At lunch there is a buffet, design-your-own omelets and appealing sandwiches. Sunday brunch. Dancing music for dinner. Saturday, dinner only. Open seven days a week. Entrées from $3.50 (L), $9.50 (D). AE, CB, DC, MC, V.

## ROMANTIC

***Pracna on Main,*** 117 S.E. Main Street, Minneapolis (379-3200). A saloon in the 1890's, then a warehouse, now a comfortable, busy restaurant bursting with plants and memorabilia. In the basement, booths have closeable curtains for privacy. Simple but excellent sandwiches, soups, and light meals, from $2.50. Third floor has steak and seafood menu, starting at $6.95. Open seven days a week. AE, DC, MC, V.

## LATE-NIGHT SERVICE

***Rudolph's Barbecue,*** 1933 Lyndale Avenue S., Minneapolis (871-8969), 475 Fairview Avenue, St. Paul (698-5503), 815 E. Hennepin Avenue, Minneapolis (379-4900). Barbecued ribs are the specialty although there's a full menu and mighty ice-cream desserts. Posters of namesake Rudolph Valentino and Hollywood stars of his era. Minneapolis locations are open until 3 A.M. Monday through Saturday, until 2 A.M. Sunday. St. Paul location open from 4 P.M.

until midnight, seven days a week. Entrées from $2.50, with daily specials for $1.95. No credit cards.

***Mayor T. R. Potts,*** 193 S. Robert Street, St. Paul (226-8804). (See description under HAMBURGER.)

## SUNDAY BRUNCH

***The Curtis Hotel,*** Tenth Street and Third Avenue S., Minneapolis (340-5300). Extensive choices offered in the hotel's Cardinal room. Hot dishes, meat items, eggs, breads, fruits, dessert crêpes. Served buffet-style for $5.50 adults, $3.75 kiddies, from 11 A.M. to 2 P.M. AE, MC, V.

***The Restoration,*** 653 Grand Avenue, St. Paul (225-5441). Charming, small restaurant in an old house offers imaginative egg dishes, casseroles, crêpes and such delights as apple-cheese pancake. Breakfast breads and sweets, too. Also highly recommended for daily lunch and dinner when beef Wellington is a specialty. (Downstairs is **Just Desserts,** featuring sublime tortes.) Reservations advised. Brunch prices from $2.95. AE, V.

## SUNDAY-EVENING MEAL

***Forepaugh's,*** 276 S. Exchange Street, St. Paul (224-5606). (See description under AMERICAN.)

***Becky's Cafeteria,*** 1934 Hennepin Avenue, Minneapolis (871-8500). (See description under FAST, GOOD FOOD/DINNER.)

## FOR FAMILIES WITH CHILDREN

***Aquila,*** 1330 Highway 96, 2 blocks east of I-35E, White Bear Lake (429-5564). Futuristic geodesic dome, talking robot maître d', and a children's hostess dressed as an apple or carrot, delight kids. Parents are attracted by very reasonable prices and by healthful emphasis on four food groups. Menu items carry symbols so it's easy to select a balanced meal. Crêpes, salads, entrées and sandwiches have outerspace names. Yummy fountain creations. Open seven days a week. Breakfast served all day. Breakfast special 99 cents, sandwiches $1.60 (L), entrées $3.95 (D). No credit cards.

***Arboretum Tea Room,*** near Chaska and Chanhassen, west of Minneapolis on Highway 5, west of Highway 41 (443-2460). Entrance fee to University of Minnesota Landscape Arboretum (open year round) is $2 per car; lovely grounds to explore. When everyone's hungry, homemade breads, soups, entrées (which change daily) and exceptional desserts are served à la carte and buffet-style in the main building. Light breakfast and lunch only. Closed Monday. Entrées from $2.25. No credit cards.

## COUNTRY INN

***The Lowell Inn,*** 102 N. Second Street, Stillwater, about 20 miles east of downtown St. Paul (439-1100). Called the "Mount Vernon of the Midwest," a series of gracious dining rooms rich with silver and china collections are the setting for refined food. The Garden Room has an indoor trout pool. Matterhorn Room serves multicourse beef fondue dinner with appropriate wines for $22.50 per person. Hot rolls, tasty relishes and irresistible desserts. Outstanding wine selection. Open seven days a week. Chaîne des Rotisseurs. Entrées from $6 (L), $7.50 (D). AE, MC, V.

***The Anderson House,*** Wabasha, about 80 miles south of St. Paul, on the Mississippi River (612/565-4524). Lovely drive along Highway 61, especially in autumn. Oldest continually operating hotel in Minnesota, now designated National Historic Landmark. Rooms are full of antiques and quilts; dining room bulges with good, hearty food, homemade breads and desserts that deny calories exist. Breakfast rolls are immense. Crowded Sunday but worth the wait. Entrées from $4.95 (D). Rooms start at $12. MC, V.

# IN THE SUBURBS

## BLOOMINGTON

***Camelot,*** 5300 W. 78th Street (835-2455). Dine at a round table in a castle decorated with suits of armor and numerous awards for excellence. Cuisine includes crab meat imperial and rack of lamb. Entertainment and meals in cabaret, too. Chaîne des Rotisseurs. Closed Sunday. Entrées from $3.45 (L), $6.95 (D). AE, CB, DC, MC, V.

## LITTLE CANADA

***Venetian Inn,*** 2814 Rice Street (north of St. Paul) (484-7215). Really hungry? Try the seven-course dinner *alla Siciliana.* Otherwise, there's a huge menu of Italian, American and seafood items offered by the Vitale family, who have been in business for a half century. Closed Sunday. Entrées from $3.25 (L), $4.50 (D). AE, CB, DC, MC, V.

## MAPLEWOOD

***Bali Hai,*** 2305 White Bear Avenue (777-5500). Polynesian food of quality and even greater quantity. The Pu-Pu Platter of snacks is enough for a meal. House special and flaming ambrosia are entrées not to be missed. Open seven days a week. Entrées from $2.25 (L), $5.25 (D). AE, V.

## WAYZATA

***Chouette,*** 739 E. Lake Street (473-4611). Chouette may offer the most attractive setting for dining in the area; elegant and expensive. Cocktails are served in the courtyard in summer. Menu changes daily, but favorites are Long Island duckling and veal Florentine, saddle of lamb béarnaise. Dinner is à la carte. Wine list is a fine one. Chaîne des Rotisseurs. Reservations recommended. Closed Sunday. Entrées from $4 (L), $12 (D). AE, MC, V.

# MARKETS

## GIFT FOODS

***Hello Minnesota,*** Butler Square, 100 N. Sixth Street, Minneapolis (332-1755). Everything sold here is made in or is about Minnesota. Open seven days a week. AE, MC, V.

***Wood's Chocolate Shop,*** St. Paul locations at 4 W. Fifth Street (222-7679) and in Park Square Court, 225 E. 6th Street (224-2216), where you can watch candy being made. Also in Edina, at the Galleria shopping center (925-3325). Everything made with pure butter and whipping cream. Victoria Brittle is their finest achievement. MC, V.

## GIFT WINES

***Haskell's,*** 23 S. Seventh Street, Minneaplis (333-2434), 12900 Wayzata Boulevard, Minnetonka (544-4456), 2151 Ford Parkway, St. Paul (698-8844). Excellent selection of domestic and imported wines, including some new Minnesota vintages. Closed Sunday. MC, V, with $10 purchase minimum.

# Monterey/Carmel

John Steinbeck set three novels and numerous short stories here, and Robinson Jeffers' poetry is full of passionate reference to this coastline. Robert Louis Stevenson and Jack London, both enamored of the geography, hung around the area for lengthy periods. Furthermore, 11 million annual tourists can't all be wrong. The Monterey Bay and coastline is one of the most beautiful landscapes in the world—with some of the best restaurants in the West.

On the southern curve of Monterey Bay lie the cities of Monterey and Pacific Grove, curious neighbors of early California adobe and manicured Victorian homes set high above the sidewalks. On the bay in Monterey is Fisherman's Wharf, the dictate of the local cuisine. It is an active fishing center with an abundance of excellent seafood restaurants, many of which have been around for decades, like **Mike's.** The wharf is rustic and informal, popular with local people for family dining. Here, from October to April, the fish markets sell the gigantic bay prawns with roe. They are delicious sautéed in olive oil and seasoned with coarse salt. Nothing can compare with them outside of Spain or Portugal.

Close to Pacific Grove and also on the water is Cannery Row. Massive wooden buildings that once contained flourishing fish canneries now house some of the most elegant and large dinner restaurants on the peninsula. Many have been there for a long time, but there is always room for another, or for a refurbishing like the recent extension of the popular **Whaling Station Inn.** A tourist promenade during the day, Cannery Row satisfies more formal tastes in the evening, catering to the international palate, too, with Asian, Polynesian, French and Italian menus.

Over the hill and through the forest of Pebble Beach is Carmel-by-the-Sea, located on a small bay of white sand and green water. It was settled first by Franciscan Fathers, although the Spanish influence is seen more in Monterey, which was the area's port and the first capital of California. Carmel's shaded terrain is covered with small but elegant homes and charming cottage-type motels for honeymooners. It is like a European village; almost all the restaurants are styled like cafés, bistros, or French or Italian country inns. Even the newer, popular additions like **Casanova** affect an atmosphere of intimacy and antiquity. The locals laugh that there are more restaurants than permanent residents in Carmel, but you rarely see an empty house. The major shopping/dining area extends only a few blocks, and the menus are posted outside of the restaurants. One popular, old-time stop is the **Mediterranean Market** on Ocean and Mission. Here you can get sandwich or picnic fixings and any wine or gourmet-food item you desire.

Cross the coast highway and drive into Carmel Valley, and you will find more restaurants, from country cooking to *haute cuisine.* Or drive down to Big Sur to the spectacular vistas from **Nepenthe** or the **Ventana Inn.** If San Francisco is your destination, take Highway 1 north through Castroville, the "Artichoke Capital of the World," where it is possible to buy bargain bags of fresh artichokes and French-fried artichoke hearts from stands on the highways. Have dinner in Santa Cruz on the north side of Monterey Bay at the popular **Shadowbrook** or **Crow's Nest** restaurants. No one need leave the north coast with a hunger pang.

# Restaurants and Food Sources

(Area code: 408)

## BIG DEAL

### WORTH IT

***Whaling Station Inn,*** 763 Wave Street, one block above Cannery Row, Monterey (373-3779). In an area where dining establishments are a big deal both in price and size, here is a really well-run restaurant that lives up to its PR. The décor is of a whaling station at the end of the 19th century. Features steaks and fish broiled on a grill over oak wood and grape cuttings. The result is magnificent. Try salmon if it is in season. Reservations suggested. Open seven days a week. Entrées from $3.75 (L); complete dinners from $9.95. AE, DC, MC, V.

### NOT WORTH IT

***Sardine Factory,*** 701 Wave Street, Monterey (373-3775). Once, but not now, this was one of the best Continental restaurants around. The menu is hearty (fish and shellfish, beef and veal) as are the prices, but the preparation is poor and the service inconsistent. If you must look in, try the sardine sandwich, it's the only deal left. Open seven days a week. Entrées from $3.50 (L); complete dinners from $8.50. AE, DC, MC, V.

## INTERNATIONAL

### AMERICAN

***General Store,*** 5th and Junipero, Carmel (624-2233). The new, old look for informal dining. This friendly and well-run restaurant is one of the newer, more popular hangouts in the area. The menu is imaginative and extensive, and they are known for their spinach salad and fish entrées. Open seven days a week. Sunday brunch. Entrées from $2.25 (L), $6.95 (D). MC, V.

## FRENCH

***Patisserie Boissière,*** Mission between Ocean and 7th, Carmel (624-5008). A highly successful French pastry shop expanded into a lunch and dinner restaurant in Louis XIV décor. There are elegant hors d'oeuvre, soups, a salad and a selection of eight entrées. The sweetbreads are popular. Apéritifs, an adequate wine list and wine by the glass. A small, very reasonable and well-maintained establishment. Closed Wednesday. Entrées from $3.25 (L & D). No credit cards.

## ITALIAN

***Bertolucci's,*** 208 Forest Avenue, Pacific Grove (373-8116). An uptown Italian restaurant known for its seven choices of veal and excellent pasta. The attention is good, though the hours are short—5:30 P.M. to 9 P.M., with reservations very much suggested. Dinner only. Closed Sunday and Monday. Complete meals from $6.25. No credit cards.

## JAPANESE

***Shabu-Shabu,*** Carmel Plaza, Mission between Ocean and 7th, Carmel (625-2828). This is a tasteful, traditional Japanese country restaurant with three selections cooked at your table. *Shabu-shabu* is the specialty (steak, tofu and vegetables). Dinner only. Closed Tuesday. Complete meals from $7.75. MC, V.

## MEXICAN

***El Topo,*** San Carlos between 5th and 6th, Carmel (624-7388). It is odd that with such a Spanish heritage here, there are so few Mexican restaurants. El Topo has an extensive menu with standard items like enchiladas, tacos, tostadas, and many specialties. The chili *verde* is good and not too hot for the novice. Open seven days a week. Entrées from $4.25, complete meals from $5.65, children's plate $2.50 (L & D). MC, V.

# SPECIALTY COOKING

## DELI

***Mediterranean Market,*** Ocean at Mission, Carmel (624-2022). A long-popular stop for tourists to stock up on imported meats, cheeses, wines, and coffees. This is a perfect place to buy ingredients for sandwiches for a picnic on the Carmel Beach. A good selection of fresh breads, cold beverages (including small bottles of wine for just such an occasion). The atmosphere is friendly, they encourage browsing and don't mind small orders. Open seven days a week. No credit cards.

***Mediterranean Market,*** Del Monte Center, Monterey (373-0555). Owned by the brother of the Carmel operation. Located in a shopping mall near freeway and hotels. Here, too, they have a full supply of imported cheeses, meats, wines, coffees and condiments, and specialize in sandwiches served there and box lunches made to order. They also make up small buffets and cocktail trays for parties and business gatherings in hotels. Open seven days a week. MC, V.

## SEAFOOD

***Mike's Seafood,*** on Fisherman's Wharf, Monterey (372-6153). Since 1929 this restaurant has been satisfying tourists and locals with simple, but deliciously prepared, fish and shellfish. Try the squid dishes. Open seven days a week. Entrées from $4.25 (L & D). AE, MC, V.

***The Rogue,*** on Wharf #2, Monterey (372-4585). Overlooks the yacht harbor and serves all manner of seafood with an excellent lobster Thermidor. Appetizers include Calamari Puffs. Reservations suggested. Open seven days a week. Entrées from $2.75 (L), $6.95 (D). AE, DC, MC, V.

## VEGETARIAN

***Cornucopia,*** in the Barnyard Shopping Center, Rio Road and Highway 1, Carmel (625-1454). An extensive vegetarian menu in pleasant surroundings. The food is well prepared and served. The lunch-special sandwiches are creative and ample, dinner entrées are well seasoned. Also special Mexican plates. Open seven days a week. Entrées from $2.50 (L), $4.50 (D). MC, V.

# FOR INDIVIDUAL NEEDS

## IF YOU HAVE TIME FOR ONLY ONE MEAL

***Casanova,*** Fifth between San Carlos and Mission, Carmel (625-0501). A relatively new restaurant, though the chef-owner has been in the area for several years. Specializing in Italian and French cuisine, Casanova is a satisfying experience in food, service and atmosphere. Suggestions for lunch are the calamari or the chicken in pastry. For dinner the veal and lamb are both excellent. No reservations. Open seven days a week. Brunch on Sunday and afternoon tea every day (3 to 4 P.M.). Entrées from $2.50 (L), $7.75 (D). MC, V.

## BEST HOTEL MEAL

***The Pirates Cove,*** Del Monte Hyatt, One Old Golf Course Road, Monterey (372-7171). One of the more elegant dining rooms in the area. The Pirates Cove has an excellent menu, basically Continental. The roast duckling and sweetbreads are hard to choose between. A relaxing view of the golf course included. Reservations suggested. Open seven days a week. Entrées from $3.75 (L), complete dinners from $8.95. AE, CB, DC, MC, V.

## BUSINESS BREAKFAST

***Pine Inn,*** on Ocean Street between Lincoln and Monte Verde, Carmel (624-3851). A charming old Victorian inn and a local landmark, the regulars still rate the dining room as the best breakfast around. The menu is simple to elegant with shirred eggs and eggs Benedict and a couple of steak and egg specialties. The service and setting is dignified and toast is always warm. A serene atmosphere for conversation. Open seven days a week. Special brunch on Sunday starts at 11:30. From $2.10 for the Continental breakfast. AE, MC, V.

## BUSINESS LUNCH

***Hog's Breath Inn,*** San Carlos Street between 5th and 6th, Carmel (625-1044). One of the business partners is Clint Eastwood and that attracts a crowd, but it's a good lunch spot by any name. Specializing in sandwiches and salads, they also have a green-chili and sour-cream omelet and fish entrée. Dining is both indoor and out on the shaded patio where seating is on several levels. The bar has its own little building. Service is good and there is no attempt to push you on. Many locals hang out all afternoon and drink wine. Open seven days a week. Entrées from $1.95 (L), $6.75 (D). AE, MC, V.

## LATE-NIGHT SERVICE

***Jack London,*** San Carlos Street between 5th and 6th, Carmel (624-2336). Tucked back in one of the many little-shop malls is a rare night-owl spot in the area. It's comfortable, too. Pizza, hamburgers, steak sandwiches are most popular. Open seven days a week until 1 A.M. Entrées from $2.75 (L & D). MC, V.

# ALONG THE HIGHWAY

## SOUTH TO BIG SUR

***Ventana Inn,*** Highway 1, 3 miles south of Big Sur (667-2332). This is a hotel with a restaurant that has a panoramic view of the Pacific. (*Ventana* means "window" in Spanish.) An interior of cedar and warm colors. Brunch, lunch and dinner served to the motoring public. A spacious deck accommodates more in the good weather. There is live entertainment at both lunch and dinner. Enchiladas, quiche, sandwiches, steaks, chops, chicken—all entrées are ample and well prepared. One feature is fresh trout from nearby Garrapata Creek. Drinks are expensive—but that may be a safety valve, considering the winding road to and from. Weekend dinner reservations. Open seven days a week. Entrées from $4.50 (L), $8.50 (D). AE, CB, DC, MC, V.

***Nepenthe,*** Highway 1, Big Sur, just ¼ mile beyond the Ventana Inn (667-2345). A heavy-timbered rustic building perched on the ocean side of the Coast Range, the Nepenthe is a favorite spot for diners and drinkers who wish to gaze at the spectacular coastline south. A slim but adequate menu of beef, chicken and fish, informally served. Nice gift shop on the premises. Open seven days a week. Entrées from $3.50 (L), $4.50 (D). AE, MC, V.

## NORTH TOWARD SAN FRANCISCO

***Shadowbrook,*** 1750 Wharf Road, Capitola-by-the-Sea (475-1511). This is an old favorite with locals as well as summer tourists, and famous for its lush, hanging begonias and cable-car descent from the parking area. (There are steps for the hardy or timid.) Primarily fish and meat; features tender abalone, steaks and generous prime rib. Reservations recommended. Dinner only. Open seven days a week. Entrées from $6.95. AE, MC, V.

***Crow's Nest,*** 2218 East Cliff Drive, Santa Cruz (476-4560). A consistently good lunch and dinner spot on the jetty at the Yacht Harbor. It is possible to eat outside year-round (except when it rains) under the overhead heaters. A first with a salad bar in the area, the Crow's Nest stays reasonable in price. Salmon is a favorite when available, and the Catch of the Day (usually cod) is always well prepared. No reservations. Open seven days a week. Entrées from $2.60 (L), $3.95 (D). AE, MC, V.

***Cedar Street Restaurant*** (and Gallery), 411 Cedar Street, downtown, off the Mall, Santa Cruz (423-2087). A tasty, tasteful restaurant tucked in two rooms of a graceful Victorian home that has been converted to an art gallery. The dining area extends to a shaded brick patio in the summer. Menu is simple, one or two specials of the day, one or two soups, and a large lunch salad. Food is consistently well prepared and nicely served on stoneware made by the gallery owners. Good house wine. Lunch only. Open seven days a week. Entrées from $3.95. Fixed-price Sunday brunch, $4.95. No credit cards.

Two *gemütlich* stops heading north to San Francisco from Santa Cruz are located in the Linda Vista Shopping Center, just where Mission Street (the Highway 1 artery through town) turns into Highway 1 proper:

***Hugo's Armenian Restaurant*** (423-5536) serves authentic Armenian dishes. You can load up or eat lightly on *kufta, dolmas, plaki* and the like. Entertainment. Dinner only. Open seven days a week. Entrées from $3. MC, V.

***El Azteca*** (423-2515) is a popular and busy Mexican restaurant (a couple of doors down from Hugo's) with efficient service and not-overly *picante* standard dishes—tacos, tamales, enchiladas, and a Friday-night special of red snapper. Open seven days a week. Entrées from $1.20, combination plates from $3.50 (L & D). No credit cards.

# MARKETS

## GIFT FOODS

***Mediterranean Markets,*** Carmel and Monterey. (See description under DELI.) Wide selection of gourmet gift foods and wines. The prices are as good as you will find in discount stores. Both stores are a pleasure to visit.

***The Cheese Shop,*** Carmel Plaza in Carmel, opposite the center fountain (625-2272). This is an extensive cheese store. They say they have over 300 varieties from all over the world. Biscuits, crackers, caviar, bread and wine. Stop in and sample the cheese. Open seven days a week. AE, MC, V.

# Montreal

Montreal's Gallic mystique is such that back in 1972 a delegation of gourmets with ponderous titles crossed the Atlantic for one of those solemn no-flowers-on-the-table-please assemblies. After the salad, the mineral water and all went round, they proclaimed "la Métropole," as Montreal is called, "la première ville gastronomique d'Amérique du Nord."

A prime case of Gallic hyperbole? Very likely. The city is coming along, however.

If certain chefs are serving the ubiquitous frozen sole amandine and the ersatz escargot, others are plotting small culinary insurrections that merit looking into. The French have always been partial to a revolution—particularly in the kitchen—and Montreal is the second largest French-speaking city in the world.

The congenital obsession traces back to 1606 when Samuel de Champlain, bored to distraction in the wilderness, founded L'Ordre du bon temps. Literally: the Order of the Good Time. Fifteen colonists and an Indian chief convened regularly over beaver, wild goose, sturgeon and whatever firewater was going.

In 1759, the Battle of Quebec altered the course of things. General James Wolfe defeated le général Louis-Joseph de Montcalm and gastronomy went Anglo for a time. A certain Beaver Club came into existence that specialized in uproarious annual dinners of beaver tail, buffalo and the like. At the 1808 dinner at the Montreal Hotel, "the meal for 32 included 29 bottles of Madeira, 19 bottles of port, 14 bottles of porter, 12 quarts of ale, and unspecified quantities of brandy, gin, and something called negus."

The diet of the average settler, however, was sober fare—the fruits of a now-you-see-it growing season and long winters. A kind of survival cuisine was developed with a character all its own. Traces of this traditional cuisine can still be found on country tables and in the rare Montreal restaurant.

Gradually, English and French elements settled into their own peculiar dining habits. The English acquired their Drury's, and their Mother Martin's for a decent mutton chop and a respectable joint of beef. Mother Martin's, having crossed the street, is still a matriarch of sorts today—a number of chairs carry plaques church-pew fashion inscribed with the names of the faithful. Mr. James Keep has been sitting in his for 50 years.

The English also had a grande old dame, the Windsor Hotel. It's on the shabby genteel side these days. However, Fred Mercier, who serves lunch weekdays at the Lantern Bar, could tell you a thing or two about the good years. Fred is 86 as this edition goes to print.

The French, by far the majority in the province, rallied at Chez Pauzé for the freshest in seafood (still around but no fireworks). And, as of 1866, at a certain Maison Dorée, a restaurant of *"haute gastronomie."*

The best meals of all, however, were meals on wheels—the famous dining car of the Canadian National Railroad on trips to Quebec and back.

As far as the city today is concerned, there are facts that it helps to know: 1. At press time, the Canadian dollar was down in the cellar. Where U.S. visitors are concerned, the entire city is on sale, 15 percent off on everything. 2. All names and titles are in the process of going *français* in a slightly frenetic, province-wide, save-the-language campaign. Time-honored traditions such as Ben's Delicatessen are undergoing transformations despite themselves. Le Delicatessen de Ben?

There have been other changes . . . the legendary André Bardet of **Chez Bardet,** the controversial *numéro un* in the city, has just sold out to Daniel Dunas and has retired to his native Touraine. Dunas, once chef at Blenheim Palace and at the Connaught Hotel, was snatched by the Tavern on the Green for a hundred thousand per annum, dropped it like the proverbial hot potato and purchased Chez Bardet. The man has hardly begun, but the prognosis is promising.

The tour of the city . . .

There are three rooftop restaurants with the usual mezzo-mezzo cuisine à go go. Good for getting bearings but don't count on the sauces.

The old city, southward, skirting the river, merits at least one visit. Sidewalk cafés, none of them serious, the rising star of **Le Fadeau** restaurant, the classic St-Amable sitting on its laurels and always, always packed.

The Chinese *quartier* is a short step northward from Old Montreal at Clarke and Lagauchetière. Purists can't agree on any single ne-plus-ultra house. Pot luck is the order of the day.

For a sampling of the city's own French flavor at its piquant best, move eastward to St. Denis Street just south of de Maisonneuve. Left-bank cafés, original little restaurants, going bourgeois but not there yet.

For a counterculture Québécois diversion, on the other hand, travel a mile north of center to Prince Arthur Street. The artisans in the kitchen and the fauna in hats are worth the trip.

Downtown. You have your Crescent Street night life with its Corvette Set out pub crawling—**Les Halles** (reserve), **Les Beaux Jeudis** (you *can't* reserve), the reliable, never-changing Chez la Mere Michèle further west and the up-again-down-again Tiffany's. And uptown, the Italian quarter—ten minutes north of downtown at St. Lawrence Boulevard and Jean Talon; simpatico, with plenty of homemade pasta and interesting market finds.

On restaurant evenings, wear a jacket to be on the safe side and plan on a 15 percent tip.

For delicacies to take home—**Chocolat Andrée** (chic), **Stilwell's Home Made Candy** (inverted chic) and a government monopoly polished up for visitors, **La Maison des vins.** With your 15 percent built-in discount, you may forage out a deal or two here.

# Restaurants and Food Sources

**(Area code: 514)**

**Note:** Prices given are in Canadian dollars

## BIG DEAL

### WORTH IT

***The Beaver Club,*** Hotel Queen Elizabeth, 900 Dorchester Boulevard West (861-3511). The Beaver Club is size extra large, and in a hotel. It seats 240, a far cry from the 60 to 80 limit of French, three-star-caliber houses. It's a good thing that chef Albert Schnell has never let these facts interrupt him. One of the city's handful of purists, he has turned the system upside down and is now allowed to run his prestige restaurant his own way. Fresh sole and true bouillabaisse fish are flown in, season permitting; market seafood and seasonal finds are trucked in daily; fresh herbs flourish year round in the kitchen; sauces are finished to order. The *cervelas* of *fruits de mer* is to be tried, as are the house sherbets—pear, mango, etc. Décor is hotel executive clubbish; service is geared to the mogul who feels reassured when his name is repeated each time a dish comes around. Slightly unwieldy (there are occasional slips between cup and lip), but undisputed as one of the city's top choices. Saturday, dinner only. Open seven days a week. Business lunch from $11.50, entrées from $12.50 (L & D). AE, CB, DC, MC, V.

### NOT WORTH IT

***Le Tour de Ville,*** Hotel Régence Hyatt, 777 University (879-1370). This rotating restaurant has what it takes to divert the bus tours—turning tables thirty stories up, a glass-walled elevator cum space capsule to fire you up there. The rub: dishes are cooked well in advance in the ground-floor central kitchen and carted up to be reheated. If, however, Aunt Hattie is counting on her "tour of the city" and insists on going, stick to the steaks—a safe bet grilled to order on the spot—the reliable cold fare, and the locally celebrated chocolate cheesecake. Saturday, dinner only. Open seven days a week. Fixed-price lunch buffet, weekdays $7.50. Dinner entrées from $8.75. AE, CB.

# INTERNATIONAL

## FRENCH

***Les Halles,*** 1450 Crescent Street (844-2328). The place for restaurant theatrics. It has sparkle; it has éclat; it has waiters in long aprons with faces by Toulouse-Lautrec rattling off house specialties without their prices. Imagination runneth over, sometimes to the point of overkill. Escargots with three sauces; a tournedos with four. The owners find rare seasonal produce with dexterous sleight of hand and stand on their heads (all but literally) to please. An attractive duck steak with mangoes and leeks for example, and quality pastry. Topflight for original productions. Second string for purists. Kitchen-to-dining-area size ratio is such that no chef could prepare everything to order. Saturday, dinner only. Closed Sunday. Business lunch from $6.50, entrées from $7.75 (D). AE, DC, MC, V.

## JAPANESE

***The Katsura,*** 2170 Mountain Street (849-1172). The best of the genre at the moment. Part of the Prince Hotel chain, but there's no evidence of cloning chain tendencies in the cuisine. Excellent, varied *sashimi* carved in full view; conservative, Tokyo-style *sushi,* tempura at its delicate best (by Montreal standards) and traditional *sukiyaki* and *shabu-shabu* prepared more or less classically at the table in a subdued Japanese-Modern ambience. Remind the waitress to add the meat in stages; there's a tendency to throw it all in to save time. Service can be brusque. Saturday and Sunday, dinner only. Open seven days a week. Business lunch from $3.95, entrées from $7 (D). AE, CB, DC, MC, V.

## LEBANESE

***Mont Liban,*** 7495 St. Denis Street (273-3381). Small-time pool-hall dimensions and elemental bric-à-brac of ethnic restaurants before they go bourgeois. Mama Atmé is in the kitchen. The trick is to accost the solid lady over the stove with Arabic translator: "Mama, make me a whatsit the way I like it." She can be persuaded occasionally to bake *markouk* bread on a wooden plaque over an open fire (in the kitchen) the way mountain people do it. She works only with *samne hamawie,* butter clarified with cracked wheat. The delicate crust of her *fatayer,* a spinach and meat pie, is unique. Moreover, she is in the process of inventing a *nouvelle cuisine libanaise* straight off the top of her head. Service depends on which of her nine children you happen to draw. Open seven days a week. Business lunch from $3.50, entrées from $3.10 (L & D). AE, CB, DC, MC, V.

## SWISS

***William Tell,*** 2055 Stanley Street (288-0139). You'll find the cowbells and the air-dried beef, and the convincing Swiss travel brochure trappings here, *but . . .* owner-chef Peter Muller, a far cry from a conservative Swiss in the kitchen, has a disconcerting Archimedean side. He has contrived a filet of pork variation arranged on apple-stuffed crêpes and garnished with grapes steeped in wine; and a chicken breast on a corn-meal crêpe with oranges and Triple Sec. Only the beginning. And they work. Sauces are on the rich side by modern standards, all prepared to order with prime ingredients. Matterhorn classics are here as well, and a roster of tortes kill you kindly. Saturday, dinner only. Closed Sunday. Business lunch from $4.75, entrées from $7.25 (D), AE, CB, DC, MC, V.

# SPECIALTY COOKING

## PASTRY

***La Patisserie Belge,*** 3487 Park Avenue (845-1245). The Patisserie Belge is a high-gloss dieters' Waterloo. Pass beyond the pastry section into a lovely glassed-in restaurant area, Chez Gautier. The pastries are close to the best in town. The Patisserie creates its own attractive fish terrines that are sauced lightly in *beurre blanc,* also *charcuteries,* fresh asparagus in season, light quiches and the like. On the way out, shelves of attractive gourmet imports for your suitcase corners. Closed Saturday for dinner and Sunday. Entrées from $3.50 (L & D). MC, V.

## QUÉBÉCOIS

***Au Quinquet,*** 354 St. Joseph Boulevard West (272-4211). The place to discover the elusive flavors of rural Québec cooked more or less the way grand'mère used to. No subtle gourmet fare here. Sample Québec's traditional holiday tourtières (meat pies), *la cipaille* (thin layers of game under a golden crust in a terra-cotta crock), solid Québec-style farm cake under an eiderdown of warm white fudge, or cod tongues—if you have the gumption. Service more amateur than professional. Saturday, dinner only. Closed Sunday. Business lunch from $4.50, entrées from $5.95 (D). AE, DC, MC, V.

***Le Jardin St-Denis,*** 1615 St. Denis Street (288-2023). The antithesis of Au Quinquet. An amusing example of what original Québécois cuisine can be today—open ended, with creative soufflé starters: apples and herbs, smoked salmon and sour cream. Light-handed entrées sauced while you wait; vegetables seared in a smoking skillet for 60 seconds flat. *Cuisine minceur* experiments and born-in-Montreal conceptions. A designer's eye look and a clientele to match. Dinner only. Closed Sunday. Closed Monday during summer. Entrées from $7.75. AE, MC, V.

## SEAFOOD

***Chez Delmo,*** 211-215 Notre Dame Street West (849-4061). Half of Montreal can't go to Delmo's any more: the owner has the proverbial short fuse. The other half, and those who go crawling back, persist because this is one seafood house in the city where quality isn't iffy. Aficionados follow the seasons with consuming interest—the oyster months, the arrival of the Pacific salmon in March, the Atlantic salmon in May. The vintage oyster-bar entrance is something of a period piece with its mahogany, mirrors and tile-work, plus tycoons from surrounding power palaces queueing up for a turn. Better to avoid the saucy choices and to savor Delmo's quality *au naturel*—grilled, poached, or meunière. Saturday, dinner only. Monday, lunch only. Closed Sunday. Entrées from $4.75 (L), $8.25 (D). AE, CB, DC, MC, V.

## SMOKED MEATS

***The Montreal Hebrew Delicatessen (Schwartz's),*** 3895 St. Lawrence Boulevard (842-4813). (See description under LATE-NIGHT SERVICE.)

## STEAKS

***Moishe's,*** 3961 St. Lawrence Boulevard (845-1696). Moishe and his family have been rugged do-it-yourselfers since 1938. They choose and hang their own beef, pickle their own herring, make their own coleslaw, applesauce and schmaltz salmon (salty as the dickens). They also bake their own rolls and pastry, but don't cross town for the latter. Moishe's is upstairs in a decidedly colorful market neighborhood. The big, elbow-to-elbow dining room began with a very central wood stove and now has face-lifts as regularly as an aging movie queen. Color it copper, cranberry and taupe at the moment, slightly brassy. Steaks are A-1 and the *kanatzlech* could be the best in town. As for ambience, it's a psychiatrist's delight. Nobody is repressed at Moishe's. Open seven days a week. Entrées from $9 (L & D). AE, CB, DC, MC, V.

***Gibby's,*** 298 Place d'Youville (282-1837). The foil for Moishe's, this is the city's steakhouse showplace. It's in a historical monument-caliber fieldstone house in the old *quartier.* The business is operated on oiled rubber wheels with big-business efficiency and a menu designed for hungry North America along bigger-is-better lines. Salads are mostly iceberg, the pastries in cinemascope are better off left in the kitchen, but the steaks are big, impeccable and served with all the calorie-rampant trimmings you can manage. Open seven days a week. Complete lunch from $4.95, entrées from $8.95 (D). AE, CB, DC, MC, V.

## VEGETARIAN

***Vent d'Est,*** 964 Rachel Street East (524-2100). Vent d'Est has its own inscrutable *philosophie de la cuisine.* East meets West with Japanese macrobiotic overtones. Controversial spin-offs on the menu include a meatless *québécois pot-au-feu,* a New Brunswick algae salad under Japanese plum vinaigrette, natural apple "Jell-o" sweetened with local maple syrup and set with agar-agar. Bizarre-bizarre—but creative. If reactions are mixed re the cooking, the look of the place seldom fails to delight. Homey with an artist's touch and a clientele that goes beyond the strict vegetarian set. Saturday, dinner only. Closed Monday. Entrées from $1.50 (L & D). No credit cards.

# FOR INDIVIDUAL NEEDS

## IF YOU HAVE TIME FOR ONLY ONE MEAL

***Le Fadeau,*** 423 St. Claude Street (878-3959). Le Fadeau's star is on the rise at the moment. The dinner to try for is Henri Woczik's *menu de dégustation* (taster's menu). All house originals. (Better if you are three people or more.) He caught diners' attention with a butterless béarnaise mounted with vegetable purée, and an array of savory, cloudlight flans—chicken liver with morels, salmon with dill. He recently perfected a lightly sautéed scallop and rolled Chinese mustard-green arrangement that is a rare treat. You may not cotton to everything—the deboned chicken leg stuffed with a mousse of scampi for example—but certain variations are sure to delight. For example, his quatuor of lamb filets enveloped in mousse of lamb, rolled in marinated vine leaves and baked to a tender rose in a pastry case. The restaurant, a historic stone house in Old Montreal, seats 50. The wine list is récherché. Now for the buts: service needs working on; it tends to flag toward the end. And the fireworks don't always unfurl as planned. Saturday and Sunday, dinner only. Open seven days a week. Business lunch from $5, entrées from $10 (D). AE, CB, DC, MC, V.

## BEST HOTEL MEAL

***The Beaver Club,*** Hotel Queen Elizabeth, 900 Dorchester Boulevard West (861-3511). (See description under BIG DEAL/WORTH IT.)

## RESTAURANT NEAR AIRPORT

***Au Coin du Feu,*** Hilton International Dorval, 12505 Cote de Liesse (631-2411). Hilton again. But probably your best bet. Said to be the first restaurant in North America to grow fresh herbs via hydroponics in the kitchen. Market fish daily (try the seafood pot-au-feu, cooked lightly), a terrine of not particularly wild boar, lovely house sherbets, quality pastry. Dorval lacks the luster and the light-fingered artistry of the Beaver Club downtown, but sound, basic principles are applied at both. An unloveable 1950's-modern look clings relentlessly to the place despite concerted efforts of hotel makeup artists. Saturday, dinner only. Open seven days a week. Business lunch from $8.50, complete dinner from $12.25, entrées from $9.65 (D). AE, CB, DC, MC, V.

## BUSINESS BREAKFAST

***The English Room,*** Ritz-Carlton Hotel, 1228 Sherbrooke Street West (842-4212). Not what it was in the old Ritz Café days, with loose sugar and imported Dundee marmalade in pots, but the best breakfast of the genre anyway, in a hunting scene ambience. Whether or not you'd consider ordering any of them, proper cocoa, earnest kippers, finnan haddie, breakfast steak and kidneys and bacon stare up reassuringly from the menu. Naturally, the eggs-and-croissant route is available too. Open seven days a week, from 6:30 A.M. to 10:30 P.M. Complete breakfast from $4.75. AE, DC, MC, V.

## BUSINESS LUNCH

***The Beaver Club,*** Hotel Queen Elizabeth, 900 Dorchester Boulevard West (861-3511). (See description under BIG DEAL/WORTH IT.) For business people sensitive to pecking orders, here are the territorial imperatives. The left wing area is inner corporate circle. As one member of the cognoscenti puts it, "anything to the left of the buffalo head is Camelot." If Camelot is booked solid, repair to the Ritz' Maritime Bar. It has just been refurbished. The sole variations are reliable, and powers that be are sitting almost anywhere at the moment.

## FAST, GOOD FOOD/BREAKFAST

***Beauty's,*** 93 Mount Royal Avenue West (849-8883). Beauty's is a socio-cultural phenomenon of sorts. The sandwich counter was opened 35 years ago by Beauty himself in a neighborhood where anybody who was anybody had a nickname. Today, sports people make detours to down gallons of Beauty's pulpy fresh orange juice. Rag-trade moguls cross town to the old neighborhood to savor Beauty's famous mishmash, an omelet with chutzpah, and its old ninety-fiver, cream cheese, lox, tomato and onion on a toasted bagel, which is a two-twenty-fiver these days. Counter, stools, booths, the pop-culture works, and a line out the door most Sundays. Open seven days a week. Sandwiches from $2. No credit cards.

## FAST, GOOD FOOD/LUNCH

***Chez Delmo,*** 211-215 Notre Dame Street West (849-4061). (See description under SEAFOOD.) Delmo's has a great oyster bar; its popularity is such that you *have* to eat fast.

## FAST, GOOD FOOD/LUNCH, DINNER

***The Coffee Mill Espresso,*** 2046 Mountain Street (288-3546). Hungarian bistro with a décor of hat-shaped tortes and colorful clients. You'll find neon, counter, stools, and *ludlab*—a rummy, cherry-poked chocolate confection that now has its own underground cult in the city. The menu commits the gourmet faux pas of listing 50 choices with a Hungarian accent, but more or less carries them off with quantities of fresh mushrooms and 35 percent cream. Fast service, great European-style cheesecake, and incidentally, also a nice quick breakfast bet with its bakery in the back. Closed Sunday. Entrées from $2.95 (L & D). No credit cards.

## BEST WINE LIST

***Chez Bardet,*** 591 Henri Bourassa Boulevard East (381-1777). Daniel Dunas, who has just taken over the legendary André Bardet's kitchen, found 15,000 bottles in the cellar (it was a celebrated cellar) and ordered 20,000 more. And not just at random. The prestige Bourgogne bottlers are represented—Domaine de la Romanée-Conti, Marquis de la Guiche, Hospices de Beaune; the decent years. Nothing is a steal, but the selection is more than respectable, and prices, if you consider your exchange, are competitive in many cases. Saturday, dinner only. Closed Sunday. Business lunch from $8.50, entrées from $12 (D). AE, DC, MC, V.

## FOR DRINKS

***Friday's,*** 636 Cathcart Street (866-4979). Solid with high-gloss, low-gloss and matte-finish Montrealers making it. An interesting place to look into for the twenties-thirties crowd—if you can stand that old beer-5¢ painted-mirror routine and matching nostalgia one more time. The volume of music and voice-over exchanges gives pub crawlers with lip-reading experience a distinct advantage. The food has a certain pizazz. There's an hors d'oeuvre of snails in a hat-shaped *feuilleté* that can hold its head up. The *steak-frites* are Paris bistro quality—except that they're tender—and the crab pancake would rate a safe pass almost anywhere. Closed Sunday. Business lunch from $4.50, entrées from $3.25 (L & D). AE, DC, MC, V.

***Café de Paris,*** Ritz-Carlton Hotel, 1228 Sherbrooke Street West (842-4212). Shhh. Subdued. Velour divans, appropriate canapés (pâté, smoked salmon, occasionally caviar) and at the piano, a light-fingered South American named Jorge Garcia, whose claim to fame is that once he played for Callas on Onassis's yacht. Open seven days a week. AE, DC, MC, V.

## RESTAURANT WITH MUSIC

***The Troika,*** 2175 Crescent Street (849-9333). The duo at the Troika used to be a trio years ago until the celebrated defection: the violinist went over to the Montreal Symphony Orchestra and is there still. Meanwhile, Sacha and Vladislav, in peasant blouses with guitar and accordion, have established a running love-hate relationship with management, defecting periodically, and then repenting. The ambience in the restaurant is thick as the borscht with shoulder clod in it. Pre-revolution, pleasantly decadent, with touches of Old World crimson and tapestry chairs. A proper chicken Kiev splashes butter when all goes well, blinis and blintzes are savory, and exclusive house vodkas could bowl over a Volga boatman—112-proof Krepkaya, Polish bison vodka (complete with herb in the bottle) and pepper vodka, appropriately red. Saturday and Sunday, dinner only. Complete lunch from $4.95, entrées from $10.95 (D). AE, DC, MC, V.

***Pierre de Coubertin,*** Hotel Le Quatre Saisons, 1050 Sherbrooke Street West (284-1110). A touch of class. Potted palms and dinner dancing to a discreet society band in black tie plus chanteuse. Generous-plus armchairs, sky-high ceilings and plate glass, and tables islands apart. Moreover, the cuisine has just slipped into the No. 2 hotel place (after the Beaver) in the city, with herbs sprouting year round in the kitchen and possibilities such as fresh sole with chives, a house *terrine* of lobster and gemlike vegetables, and grapefruit rolled with almonds. Alongside these *nouvelle cuisine* variations you'll find a small roster of quinquagenarian classics, courtesy of Maxim's. Billy Bi soup for example, and sole Albert, named after history's most tyrannical maître d'hotel. Saturday, dinner only. Closed Sunday. Business lunch from $6.50, complete dinner from $15.50, entrées from $7.50 (L & D). AE, CB, DC, MC, V.

## LATE-NIGHT SERVICE

***Les Beaux Jeudis,*** 1449 Crescent Street (849-5635). *Très in. Pas de réservations.* The youthful Who's Who stands and waits, and although its pricey nostalgia and architectural antique décor now border on the kitsch, the faithful remain undiscouraged. The cuisine is fairly imaginative and turned out with a certain flair, circus conditions taken into account. The bad signs: asparagus and artichoke hearts on the standing menu. You know where those come from. Good signs: smoked trout with horseradish, and lobster, either in brioche or *au vin fou* (crazy with wine). Attempts at conversation without ear trumpet and megaphone will fail. Sunday, dinner only. Open seven days a week, until 1 A.M. Entrées from $3.75 (L & D). AE, CB, DC, MC, V.

***The Montreal Hebrew Delicatessen (Schwartz's),*** 3895 St. Lawrence Boulevard (842-4813). Purveyors par excellence of Montreal's own deli spoiler, the smoked-meat sandwich. Smoked meat isn't pastrami; it isn't corned beef. It's a savory relation—quality brisket smoked on the premises and marinated for two weeks in an Old Country spice formula, kept under wraps. The décor here is so neon rudimentary it's almost a bad dream, but dinner jackets with wives in 14-carat heels cue up into the small hours anyway, sometimes out the door. The meat has been slivered by hand with the same precision knifework, tucked between seedless rye slices and squirted with screaming yellow mustard, for the last 40 years. Steaks, the alternative, are fine too if you can face the complement of coleslaw and 7-Up. Open seven days a week: until 12:45 A.M. Sunday through Thursday, until 2:45 A.M. Saturday. Smoked-meat sandwiches from $1.80. No credit cards.

## SUNDAY BRUNCH

***The Beaver Club,*** Hotel Queen Elizabeth, 900 Dorchester Boulevard West (861-3511). (See description under BIG DEAL/WORTH IT.)

## SUNDAY-EVENING MEAL

***The Beaver Club,*** Hotel Queen Elizabeth, 900 Dorchester Boulevard West (861-3511). (See description under BIG DEAL/WORTH IT.)

## FOR FAMILIES WITH CHILDREN

***La Petite Halle,*** 1425 Bishop (849-1294). La Petite Halle was designed, the owners claim wryly, to whet the appetites of the next generation of Les Halles diners (see description under FRENCH). The menu presents a choice of light, bright things: fresh fruit juices frothed to decorator colors, milk shake combinations the likes of which no drugstore ever saw. Raclettes, baguette sandwiches, crêpes bretonnes, and more than respectable house pastries. In short, this and that, nicely done in a pearl of an old graystone on a block to match. Closed Monday. Entrées from $1.75 (L & D). AE, DC, MC, V.

## AL FRESCO

***The Ritz Garden/Le Jardin du Ritz,*** Ritz-Carlton Hotel, 1228 Sherbrooke Street West (842-4212). The Ritz Garden has been called an à la carte mirage. The set is belle époque Cesar Ritz, with rock garden, waiters in livery, gold and white awnings and a duck pond (inhabited). Service is hit or miss. They round waiters up when the weather permits. For seating there is an obscure but unbending pecking order. Geneviève Bujold et al. are ringside near birds; visiting firemen are seated off in Siberia. Cuisine is elemental Ritz à gogo—chef's salad (fresh crudités and canned asparagus), salmon mayonnaise, etc. The flora has charm; the fauna, chic. You get what you pay for—and that isn't your cold salmon mayonnaise. Open seven days a week during summer months. Entrées from $6.75 (L), $10.50 (D). AE, DC, MC, V.

## COUNTRY HOTEL

***La Sapinière Hotel,*** Val David (866-8262, direct line). One of the province's serious houses with a longstanding reputation, although competition is stiffer these days. Canadian Culinary Olympic team captain Marcel Kretz, in the kitchen here for nearly 20 years, is your perennial anxious man. He refuses to coast: grows his own herbs (summer), runs an open-minded kitchen and discovers seasonal produce. The menu changes completely from day to day, geared to what's fresh, but you'll find Jell-O on it, and chocolate sundaes (for the locked-in conventioneers who eat here lunch and dinner, lunch and dinner). The hotel is tucked away in the Laurentian Mountains an hour from town. Manicured, with stables, pool, the works, and dining room with view of lake. You can generally count on gourmet finds and Kretz originals (veal with leek, an experimental seafood *terrine*). Open seven days a week. Complete lunch $9.80, $15.80 on Sunday; complete dinner $18.80. AE, MC, V.

# IN THE SUBURBS

## HUDSON

***Maison Bradley,*** 64 Selkirk Street, Hudson (458-7727). Hidden away in the proverbial white storybook village half an hour from the city, Maison Bradley is worth the junket. It offers a limited menu with original touches and changing seasonal produce, cooked to order, down to the last green bean. Waits between courses are such that it helps to be in love. The pheasant pâté is something of a coup—in a decorated crust bejeweled with pistachios and a rosy *pâté de foie* centerpiece. The house sole (in parchment *papillote* on fresh spinach with mounted butter) may not be inventive, but it's consistently delightful. A Delft-blue ambience with crackling fire, and Gallic moustaches at your beck and call. Dinner only. Closed Monday. Entrées from $9.50. AE, MC, V.

# MARKETS

## GIFT FOODS

***La Patisserie française au duc de Lorraine,*** 5002 Cote des Neiges Road (731-4128). The duc himself, Jean Adam, has just sold his famous pastry shop. However, the patisserie continues to go through 750 pounds of Grade A butter a week and limits its clientele to individuals. Hotels and restaurants? No and no. The patisserie would grow too big. Quality would suffer. You may find more brilliant work in other cities, but this is one of the last honest houses. True liqueurs and no cut corners. Closed Sunday and Monday, and from June 23 to July 23. No credit cards.

***Stilwell's Home Made Candy,*** 5123 Wellington Street, Verdun (766-4481). Twenty minutes from town. Back in 1933, Richard Thomas Stilwell, a violinist by profession, began selling fudge on a bicycle. (The Depression hit Montreal rather hard.) Gladys Adelaide, his daughter, took over the copper pots in the Stilwell kitchen and wrote her short stories on weekends. Gladys' sister, Kathleen, is still at it, working on an antique coke-burning candy stove turning out fudge, the Queen Ann bars, etc. Nothing chichi. English-style Candy People's candy. Stilwell humbugs are famous in both senses of the word. Closed Sunday and Monday, and July and August. Opens "at tennish." No credit cards.

***Café Toman,*** 1421 Mackay Street (844-1605). To the regret of local art lovers, the Picasso of Pastry, Miroslav Toman has retired (for years he rose at 4 A.M.), but the irresistible little Czech pastries he made famous are still confected in the old, expensive way. "Little baskets" (shortcrusts filled with almond paste spiked with Slivovitz), *vanilkove rohlicky* (classic crescent cookies). Chilled cucumber soup in the summertime and a handful of tables and chairs. Closed Sunday and Monday. No credit cards.

***Chocolat Andrée,*** 5328 Park Avenue (279-5923). Andrée Farand and her sister Juliette have been fashioning delightful chocolate miniatures in this thumbsized store for nearly 40 years, working over the same Neanderthal stove, using the same prehistoric mixer. Chocolates are hand-confected without preservatives—true maple syrup, coffee milled in the house. Gift packages have a jewel-box look, studded as you choose with truffles, pralines, miniature marzipan fruits, etc. Closed Sunday, and Monday during the summer. No credit cards.

## GIFT WINES

***La Maison des vins,*** 600 President Kennedy Avenue (873-2274). Countless *grands vins* growing old gracefully in temperature- and humidity-controlled comfort. Something of a showplace what with the plate glass and the wall-to-wall, but the facts are these: liquor is strictly a government monopoly in Canada, and prices tend to be significantly higher than they are for the careful buyer in the U.S. There are deals to be found, however, if you're conversant with your vintages and know your Burgundy bottlers. Check out the Musigny Blanc, rare now in the U.S., the Cognac selection and the Champagnes. Closed Sunday and Monday. No credit cards.

# New Orleans

New Orleans has more good restaurants per capita than any other city in America—products of a deeply ingrained tradition of eating that is two centuries old. They spring—like the city itself—from an entirely separate set of roots than those that fostered the rest of the country. The same culture that produced jazz also gave birth to Creole cuisine.

That word "Creole" means something only outside New Orleans. In the city itself, trying to define "Creole" is like trying to describe air. About all you can say is that it's everywhere. French and Spanish colonizers planted culinary seeds to be cultivated by blacks from both Africa and places like Haiti (the only other place in the world with terrific red beans and rice). To this day the practitioners of Creole cuisine—the guys in the kitchen—are almost all black. And it's the rule rather than the exception that even in such diverse kitchens as Chinese and Italian, the cooks are black. New Orleans food is black food.

The cuisine draws its raw materials from two sources. The first is the incredibly bountiful supply of fresh seafood all year round from Lake Pontchartrain, the bayous and the Gulf of Mexico. Trout, red snapper ("redfish"), flounder and pompano are always on hand. Crabs—hard and soft—are plentiful and cheap. Shrimp and crawfish are caught by the millions in season. And oysters are taken in such numbers that downing several dozen as a snack is not a luxury but the norm. The second rich supply of foodstuffs is from the great commerce, particularly in vegetables, that passes through the port.

The first entrepreneurial codifier of Creole cooking was Antoine

Alciatoire, an aggressive, talented French-Italian who had a piece or all of the action in several restaurants around town in the early 1800's. His magnum opus quickly became and still is the quintessential New Orleans restaurant. **Antoine's** opened in 1840, when the very concept of restaurant dining was decidedly avant-garde. Antoine adapted French cuisine to local conditions—in searching for a snail substitute he invented oysters Rockefeller. Under his son Jules, Restaurant Antoine entered the 1900's as the prime inspiration for the restaurant business here, and its influence is still in evidence.

There was new blood in the twentieth century. **Galatoire's** in the first decade, **Arnaud's** in the twenties and **Brennan's** in the forties were noteworthy innovators who added branches to the tree. The current trendsetter is Warren Le Ruth, chef-proprietor of **Le Ruth's** on the West Bank; it is generally agreed that his ten-year-old restaurant serves the best food in New Orleans.

The New Orleans palate, always discriminating, has in the past few years become multifarious. Ethnic cuisines in their relatively pure forms, previously eclipsed by Creole cooking, have appeared and been well received. And for the first time the seeming taboos against elaborate surroundings and service in New Orleans restaurants are being challenged beyond mere pretension. Ten years ago you couldn't find a captain in any restaurant here; now, full French service can be had at a number of restaurants. And it's catching on.

The pantheon of great New Orleans dishes is huge, but few local specialties are skillfully executed across the board. For example, trout amandine—a sautéed filet with lemon butter and toasted almonds—is on virtually every Creole menu in town, but in most places it's merely a demand item. For trout amandine, go to Galatoire's, where it's a real specialty. In most cases (with Antoine's a notable exception), it's relatively easy to tell from the menu what the kitchen cares most about; but some notable dishes are mentioned in the restaurant list that follows.

The best guideline to remember is that Creole food is simple food, and beware of the grandiose. Pompano *en papillote* gets high praise from waiters, and makes a great show at the table as the parchment bag the fish was cooked in is opened steaming. However, in all but one small, out-of-the-way Gretna place (Berdou's), it tastes terrible. Also beware of shrimp Creole, which nobody makes well. And if a restaurant advertises Cajun food, realize that it is only a watered-down version of the real thing, which is only available in the Cajun country, which begins at its closest 40 miles outside the city limits.

The heart of New Orleans, both physically and psychically, is the Vieux Carré, the French Quarter. Far from a mere tourist attraction, it is the densest residential section of town, with people on the streets around the clock. Walking about, therefore, is safer than it looks under the dim old lights. The architecture is principally early-nineteenth-century Spanish with some eighteenth-century French; some blocks of Royal Street are a veritable jungle of beautiful iron grillwork.

Most of the older restaurants and nightspots are in the French Quarter. A disarming array of both is on or just off Bourbon Street between Canal and St. Peter—six blocks with a high sleaze quotient but with pockets of pure joy. The older jazz spots—Maison Bourbon, Crazy Shirley's, The Famous Door, The Paddock and The Blue Angel—offer strictly authentic Dixieland jazz played by the same old guys who've been honking for decades; the drink prices are high but worth it. The strip places are all right for satisfying a moment's curiosity, but you're almost sure to be disappointed. Several of the restaurants we list are here on Bourbon.

Where the Vieux Carré meets the Mississippi is the French Market. The circa-1824 structures were recently extensively refurbished and are very pleasant, with gift shops and several good restaurants, not to mention the all-night coffee-and-doughnut place, Café Du Monde. Across the street is a variety of little shops, restaurants and groceries; don't miss walking through the **Central Grocery,** home of the muffuletta sandwich. On the Canal Street end of the Market there is the Moon Walk, an enjoyable place to stroll along the river and see the ships in port. The Walk crosses the flood wall and actually goes down into the swirling, muddy waters of the river, where some people like to wade.

If you're looking to buy foodstuffs at retail, you will find good merchants. The best grocery is Langenstein's on Arabella Street uptown; it specializes in fancy meats of all varieties. Fresh vegetables can be bought around the clock from the stalls in the French Market. The **Central** and Progess groceries across Decatur Street from the Market are jammed with spices, imported (especially from Italy) meats and cheeses, pasta, coffee and fancy vegetables. For fresh seafood, visit the many markets in Bucktown near West End.

The dominant wine store in selection and price is **Martin Wine Cellar** on Baronne uptown; it also has the best cheeses. A smaller but interesting store for French and German bottles is the Wine and Cheese Co., also uptown, on Magazine Street. In Metairie is a new, small, but excellent store called The Vintner.

You are as likely to run into one of the best restaurants in the suburbs (Metairie, Algiers and Gretna, especially) as in the center of town. Heavy concentrations of restaurants, particularly if they are similar, are to be avoided (*e.g.*, West End, where eight of the ten seafood houses overlooking Lake Pontchartrain serve mediocre seafood).

Unlike other cities, New Orleans does a bigger restaurant volume at dinner (reservations essential) than at lunch (reservations unnecessary). There is an advantage in this to the visitor; in many of the better places the food and prices are the same at lunch as at dinner, with a less frenetic pace and more casual dress. For dinner, men should wear a jacket and, in some places, a tie.

Traditionally, the restaurants here are rather matter-of-fact about ambience and service. Appreciating the stark, eccentric décor at Galatoire's is an acquired taste, and when the waiter at Antoine's leans with both hands on your table as he listens to (but does not write down) your order, accept it not as carelessness but as the New Orleans way of doing things.

# Restaurants and Food Sources

**(Area code: 504)**

## BIG DEAL

### WORTH IT

***Antoine's,*** 713 St. Louis (581-4422). Plenty of tourists but an equally large crowd of Orleanians fill the huge restaurant with, respectively, puzzlement over the all-French menu and speculation about the future of the place under the management of young, fifth-generation proprietor Roy Guste. The system whereby one's personal waiter sneaks one past the line outside through the back door is not essential; go at lunch, when the menu and prices are the same but the food is better and the atmosphere less frenetic. The waiter will strike you as almost rude in his casualness, but put up with it. He will also recommend a seafood entrée, but restrict your fish eating to the superb appetizers (oysters Rockefeller, oysters Foch, crawfish *cardinale,* and a highly unusual escargots bordelaise). The best main dishes are meats and fowls: tournedos *marchand de vin,* chicken Rochambeau, lamb *noisettes Maison d'Or.* On the side, have an order of the soufflée potatoes. For dessert, order a Baked Alaska in advance. A huge and growing wine cellar is good both to select from and look at; the rest of your tour should include the surfeit of Mardi Gras paraphernalia about. No reservations. Closed Sunday. Entrées from $8.00 (L & D). AE.

### NOT WORTH IT

***The Court of Two Sisters,*** 613 Royal (522-7261). A beautiful restaurant with a model New Orleans courtyard and a reputation for good food everywhere but in New Orleans. The best thing that can be said is that the place is inconsistent; the likelihood of getting a fully excellent meal for two is remote. The Court seems to be content with its busloads of tourists, most of whom have no great Creole food to compare this with. The service is clattering and clumsy. Open seven days a week. Entrées from $4.25 (B & L), $7.75 (D). AE, CB, DC, MC, V.

# INTERNATIONAL

## CHINESE

***Dragon's Garden,*** 3100 17th, Metairie (834-9065). Highly imaginative and deft handling of Mandarin and Szechuan dishes in a small, casual dining room. Peking duck (order a day in advance), *moo shu* pork, shrimp with sizzling rice, fried pork string, Szechuan beef are best choices from a large menu of fine food. Closed two or three months in summer for the chef's annual visit to Taiwan. Saturday, dinner only. Closed Sunday and Monday. Entrées from $4.75. No credit cards.

## CONTINENTAL

***Jonathan,*** 714 N. Rampart (586-1930). A thoroughly innovative restaurant from the ground up. Easily the architectural gem among New Orleans restaurants, Jonathan's Art Deco theme makes the place a time machine. The kitchen, however, is unfettered and the chef's imagination is brilliant. A good portion of the menu consists of items seldom if ever heard of before in these parts: lamb curry, ceviche, filet with cold béarnaise, and the best liver dish in town, sautéed liver *à l'orange.* Freshly baked bread, excellent and unusual desserts, and a great wine list round out an exciting restaurant, located across the street from the Theatre for the Performing Arts. Saturday and Sunday, dinner only. Open seven days a week. Entrées from $4 (L), $9 (D). AE, CB, DC, MC, V.

## FRENCH

***Crozier's Restaurant Français,*** 9301 Lake Forest Boulevard (241-8220). A tiny room in a strip shopping center camouflages one of the two or three best kitchens in town. Chef Gerard Crozier purveys the only pure provincial-French food in the city. Begin with the pâté maison, the soup du jour, and the great romaine salad. Among the dozen or so entrées, the best are tournedos Gerard, *entrecôte au poivre, escalopes de veau,* the trout with fennel and a definitive *coq qu vin.* The modest surroundings are made immensely pleasant by the chef's wife, a friendly woman with a great sense of elegance. Dinner only. Closed Sunday and Monday. Entrées from $8. MC, V.

***Louis XVI,*** 829 Toulouse Street (581-7000). The most expensive place in town, attached to a small hotel. A scrupulous maître d' and the best French chef in town create full French service in comfortable but not terribly elaborate, small dining rooms. Wonderful *terrine,* fresh vegetable cream soups, watercress-and-mushroom salad. Two delicious racks of lamb: the one *en croûte* is the best lamb dish in town. Live Maine lobster Américaine for seafood eaters. Excellent dessert crêpes, complimentary Goldwasser *digestif.* Chaîne des Rotisseurs. Saturday and Sunday, dinner only. Open seven days a week. Entrées from $5 (L), $9.50 (D). AE, CB, DC, MC, V.

## FRENCH/CREOLE

***Brennan's,*** 417 Royal (525-9711). One of the most profitable and busy restaurants in the world, this big and beautiful place serves all three meals, but the one to come for is the justifiably legendary breakfast. This is really an all-morning meal, the highlight of which is rare feats performed with eggs. Eggs Hussarde and eggs Sardou are rich items, terrific with hot loaves of French bread and cup after cup of the strong addictive coffee. Dessert with breakfast may sound odd, but you'll be glad you ordered bananas Foster. Problems: some inconsistency in the food (so much so at lunch and dinner as to make those meals here chancy) and long waits for tables even when you have a reservation. Excellent wine list. Chaîne des Rotisseurs. Open seven days a week. Complete meals from $11.75 (B, L & D), à la carte entrées from $7.95 (L & D). AE, MC, V.

***Commander's Palace,*** 1403 Washington Avenue (899-8221). A beautiful Garden District landmark is the flagship for the elder branch of the Brennan family. What the Brennan's on Royal Street lacks at lunch and dinner, Commander's makes up for. Especially at lunch, when the garden aspects of the place are a suitable setting for the long-lunching habits of the uptown Orleanian. Try oysters 2-2-2, crab meat and corn chowder, tournedos Stanley, filet mignon with "debris," trout with pecans and veal Kottwitz. Try not to fill yourself up on the slices of great garlic bread and eggplant sticks served with cocktails. A shade inconsistent, but an immensely pleasing restaurant. The jazz brunch on Sunday mornings features the Brennan breakfast dishes along with two fine, Dixieland trios. Reservations essential. Open seven days a week. Sunday brunch. Entrées from $4 (L), $7.50 (D). AE, CB, DC, MC, V.

***Galatoire's,*** 209 Bourbon (525-2021). The thing to eat is fish: outstanding shrimp *rémoulade,* gumbo, bouillabaisse; the definitive trout *meunière,* amandine and Marguery. Even a plain broiled pompano is great here. Strange desserts: crêpes maison, princess cup. Thick, good coffee. The very plain mirrored dining room, brightly lit, is as far from private as it could be. Convivial, bustling; a long line outside. Come at an off-hour to avoid a wait—they serve all afternoon. No reservations. Closed Monday. Entrées from $5 (L & D). No credit cards.

## GERMAN

***Willy Coln's Restaurant,*** 2505 Whitney Avenue, Gretna (361-3860). Sauerkraut, beef stroganoff, beef roulades and other German dishes nobody ever made well before in New Orleans. A fabulous soup: Bahamian seafood chowder. A wonderful cold first course: Mexican ceviche. Good steak *au poivre* made with Louisiana hot peppers, and jaeger schnitzel made with five kinds of mushrooms. Good pastries. Dinner only. Closed Monday. Entrées from $7.75. MC, V.

## GREEK

***Royal Oak,*** Oakwood Shopping Center, Gretna (362-4592). Looks like a suburban theme restaurant, but has authentic Greek cuisine. *Taramasalata,* spinach pie, stuffed grape leaves with *avgolemono,* and a superb Greek salad highlight a fine selection of first courses. The roast rack of marinated lamb is the best in town. Other entrées include strikingly successful Creole specialties such as barbecued shrimp and trout amandine. For dessert: *galaktoboureko,* a flaky custard pie. Closed Sunday. Entrées from $3 (L), $5.50 (D). AE, CB, DC, MC, V.

## ITALIAN

***Pascal's Manale,*** 1838 Napoleon Avenue (895-4877). An established uptown meeting place, with most of the meeting occurring during an inevitable one- to two-hour wait for dinner seating in a well-worn bar with good oysters and a cocktail-party ambience. Worth the wait for barbecue shrimp. They are buttery and peppery, peeled and eaten with fingers and by half the diners here. (Count the bibs.) Also good red-sauce dishes such as stuffed tufoli and brisket marinara; good veal. Fresh marinated salads. Closed Sunday. Entrées from $3.50 (L), $8 (D). AE, MC, V.

## MEXICAN

***Castillo's,*** 620 Conti (581-9602). Far beyond enchiladas, although they are really terrific. *Mole poblano* (chicken with chocolate sauce), *chilmole de puerco* (pork with burned peppers), and a spicy, cool *guacamole* are excellent as well. A popular, casual French Quarter lunch and late-dinner spot. Open seven days a week. Entrées from $3 (L & D). AE, CB, MC, V.

## SPANISH

***España,*** 2705 Jefferson Highway, Jefferson (835-1502). A recently spruced-up restaurant, previously quite seedy, that serves delicious *arroz con calamares, arroz con pollo, carne asada* and a handful of other authentic dishes. From time to time there's live flamenco center stage. Dinner only. Open seven days a week. Entrées from $3.50. V.

## YUGOSLAVIAN

***Drago's Lakeside Seafood Restaurant,*** 3232 N. Arnoult, Metairie (887-9611). The Yugoslavians are the fishermen of Southeast Louisiana, hence the original theme of this large family place. Recent emphasis on Yugoslavian specialties has brought to surface some good food; you can sample a lot of it—beef, lamb and pork—in a single platter, or go for individual items such as *musaka,* cabbage rolls, or any of several preparations of squid. Excellent Creole seafood dishes, too. Closed Sunday. Entrées from $3.25 (L), $4.25 (D). AE, CB, DC, MC, V.

# SPECIALTY COOKING

## CRAWFISH

***Bon Ton Café,*** 401 Magazine (524-3386). The place bills itself as a Cajun restaurant, but, while good, it's nothing like the Cajun food you'll find in Acadiana. However, the crawfish platter in season is a delight, with six different preparations. Shrimp *étouffée* and redfish Bon-Ton are also good, and the highly alcoholic bread pudding is excellent. Very crowded at all hours. Closed Saturday and Sunday. Complete dinners from $7.25 (L & D). AE, V.

## HAMBURGER

***Port of Call,*** 838 Esplanade Avenue (523-0120). A bar with a steakhouse in the back. From the charcoal grill come hamburgers ground on the premises and cooked thick to order, served with a baked potato. No dressings needed on this sandwich. Open seven days a week, until around 2 A.M. Entrées from $3 (L & D). AE, MC, V.

## ICE CREAM

***Angelo Brocato,*** 617 Ursulines (524-2731). Authentic Italian *gelati,* with freshly made impeccable *spumone, cassata, terrancino, bisquit tortoni* and *cannoli.* Fresh-fruit ices: they go so fast that half the time the place is out. The unshaven guy in the T-shirt is the second-generation owner; his antique parlor is a gem. Open seven days a week. From 45 cents. No credit cards.

## OYSTERS

***Casamento's,*** 4330 Magazine (895-9761). A peculiar-looking tiled restaurant. While waiting in the first room for a table in the second, have a few (dozen) raw oysters on the half shell, opened before your eyes, with a sauce (mix it yourself) of lemon, horseradish, Tabasco and catsup. Inside Room Two get a fried oyster loaf for two, and beer. Closed Monday; also closed all summer. Entrées from $3.75 (L & D). No credit cards.

***Acme Oyster House,*** 724 Iberville, in the French Quarter (523-8928). Have exceptionally good, salty and well-shucked oysters while standing up at the bar. Poor-boy sandwiches are served too, but they're of no great note. Closed Sunday, and by 8:30 P.M. other days. A dozen raw oysters sell for about $3.50; $2 a half dozen, fried. No credit cards.

***Felix's,*** 739 Iberville, in the French Quarter (522-4440). Offers a stand-up bar with excellent oysters. Also, a full seafood menu with good oysters Rockefeller, but the place is so busy that the wait in line is not worth the whole meal. You can get oysters on the half shell very quickly and be gone. Open late. Closed Sunday. A dozen oysters go for about $2.50. AE, V.

## PASTRY

***La Marquise,*** 625 Chartres (524-0420). A tiny, crowded area of small tables before a glass case filled with excellent croissants, brioches, tarts, Napoleons and other sweet pastries of remarkable description and taste. Quarterites sit for hours discussing calligraphy and working crosswords. Bohemian. Closed Wednesday. Pastries from 30 cents. No credit cards.

## SANDWICHES

***Central Grocery,*** 923 Decatur (523-1620). (See description under GIFT FOODS.)

***Mother's,*** 401 Poydras (523-9656). The line at lunch is long, but it only takes at most twenty minutes to get through it—local businessmen usually get a beer before queuing up. Almost too-large sandwiches of freshly carved roast beef and baked ham on excellent French bread. Ask for gravy and "debris," the stewed, tasty leftovers of yesterday's roast. Also good plate lunches, red beans on Tuesday. Breakfast and lunch only. Closed Sunday and Monday. Entrées from $1.65 (B & L). No credit cards.

***Parasol's,*** 2533 Constance (899-2054). The classic roast beef poor boy is sold here under the classic poor-boy circumstances: those of a neighborhood bar. You must wait about 30 minutes for serving, but the neighborhood is the colorful Irish Channel and there are lots of characters to watch. Closed Sunday and Tuesday. Entrées from $2 (L & D). No credit cards.

## SEAFOOD

***Lakeview Seafood Restaurant,*** 7400 Hayne Boulevard (242-2819). A white shack, sometimes with a small line outside, with distinctive New Orleans proletariat interior décor. What most eat here is a fried seafood "boat"—a hollowed-out, unsliced white-bread loaf filled with shellfish (oysters, shrimp or both), beautifully fried and seasoned. Closed Sunday. Entrées from $3 (L & D). No credit cards.

***Swanson's,*** 540 West Roadway, West End Park (288-4411). Not much on looks or view of the lake, but the fried seafood is excellent and the boiled seafood is served hot, cooked to order and well seasoned. The waitress will show you how to crack a crab's shell, and you'll be glad you learned. Avoid anything fancy. Dinner only. Closed Monday and Tuesday. Entrées from $5.25. AE, MC, V.

## SOUL

***Chez Hélène,*** 1540 N. Robertson (947-9155). The name is no affectation; many Creole blacks in New Orleans speak French.

Race does not bear on the service you receive here: it's always rather slow. The menu is a startling amalgam of cuisine you might find in the best restaurants with dishes you'd read on a corner joint's blackboard. Start with oysters Rockefeller, then get fried or boiled chicken with a stuffed pepper, and bread pudding for dessert. Delicious food. Open late Tuesday through Sunday, Monday till 6 P.M. Entrées from $2.50 (L & D). No credit cards.

***Eddie's Restaurant and Bar,*** 2119 Law (945-2119). A wonderful kitchen is hidden on a hard-to-get-to side street inside a building with no sign outside—nor, for that matter, any indication that the place isn't deserted. Inside, however, is a nice dining room where you can have textbook examples of red beans and rice, gumbo and fried seafood, all thoroughly New Orleans in style. Open seven days a week. Entrées from $1.50 (L & D). No credit cards.

## STEAK

***Ruth's Steak and Lobster House,*** 1100 N. Broad (822-9750). Small, somewhat the worse for wear, with private curtained booths along one wall. Large U.S. prime steaks, served sizzling in butter and parsley. Fresh lobster, also sizzling and buttery. Closed Monday. Entrées from $11 (L & D). AE, CB, DC, MC, V.

## VEGETARIAN

***Schan's Natural Foods,*** 1414 Veterans Boulevard, Metairie (837-8444). Small dining room attached to a large health-food store; all ages and descriptions of diners. Good vegetable casseroles, quiche, artichoke spaghetti with meatless meatballs, mock veal, terrific blintzes on Sunday, and fresh-fruit drinks and smoothies. Some fish is served. Lunch only. There is a Thursday night dinner–buffet for $5.50. Closed Saturday. Entrées from $3. MC, V.

# FOR INDIVIDUAL NEEDS

## IF YOU HAVE TIME FOR ONLY ONE MEAL

***Le Ruth's,*** 636 Franklin, Gretna (362-4914). A singularly modest house in a nondescript neighborhood has what is generally agreed to be perhaps the best food in town. Reservations, if made several days in advance for one of the two nightly seatings, will gain you a table a little too close to the next one, a view of an original Picasso and a table d'hôte dinner of great size and merit. First course: crab meat St. Francis or hearts of artichoke. Move on to *potage* Le Ruth, an oyster-artichoke broth, then the green salad with avocado dressing. Favorite entrée choices are sautéed soft-shelled crab with crab meat meunière, trout Oliva, or tournedos béarnaise. Mandarin ice and great coffee. The best wine attic (no cellars in New Orleans) in town. Closed Sunday and Monday. Dinner only, from $13.95. MC. V.

## BEST HOTEL MEAL

***Caribbean Room,*** Pontchartrain Hotel, 2031 St. Charles Avenue (524-0581). Very uptown establishment clientele, very original and good food. Recommended starters are shrimp Saki (hot) or crab meat Biarritz (cold); good entrées are trout Véronique or trout Eugène. Try Mile High Ice Cream Pie for dessert. Sunday, there's a lavish buffet with some excellent dishes and several that are not-so-excellent. Some new waiters are slipshod, but the non-food aspect is generally good. Open seven days a week. Entreés from $4.50 (L), $7.50 (D). AE, CB, DC, MC, V.

## RESTAURANT NEAR AIRPORT

***John Charles,*** 2300 Airline Highway, Kenner (721-9524). Good fried seafood. Open seven days a week. Entrées from $2.50 (L), $3.25 (D). AE, CB, DC, MC, V.

***Andy Messina's,*** 2717 Williams Boulevard, near the north entrance of the International Airport near I-10 (729-7373). Basically Italian in thrust, this place also does well with seafood and makes great poor-boy sandwiches. Spaghetti, lasagne, stuffed artichokes and veal dishes are all excellent. Open seven days a week. Entrées from $2.25 (L), $3.50 (D). AE, CB, DC, MC, V.

## BUSINESS BREAKFAST

***Bailey's,*** Fairmont Hotel, 123 Baronne (529-7111). Tables well separated, ambience cheerful, food passable to very good. Open 24 hours a day, seven days a week. Entrées from $2. AE, DC, MC, V.

## BUSINESS LUNCH

***Tommye's Ridgelake Restaurant,*** 1917 Ridgelake (831-7700). Quite possibly the best food in New Orleans' large Metairie suburb, but only open for lunch. Breathtaking Creole cooking served in large portions promptly and with minimal fuss. Menu consists of daily specials, seafood and poor-boy sandwiches. Lunch only.

Closed Saturday and Sunday. Entrées (including soup) from $3. AE, CB, DC, MC, V.

## FAST, GOOD FOOD/BREAKFAST

***Toney's Spaghetti House,*** 212 Bourbon (561-9253). The best biscuits in the city, big platters of sausage and ham at dirt-cheap prices but, strangely, no eggs. (Also good for lunch or supper, with excellent pizza after 5 P.M.) Closed Sunday. Open at 7 A.M. From 30 cents. No credit cards.

## FAST, GOOD FOOD/LUNCH

***Wise Cafeteria,*** 909 S. Jefferson Davis Parkway (488-7811). From the unlikely cafeteria format come really fine Creole items: boiled beef, trout, red beans, soups, fresh vegetables, great bread pudding. Many septuagenarians eat well here. Closed Saturday. Entrées from $1.85 (L & D). No credit cards.

## FAST, GOOD FOOD/DINNER

***Camellia Grill,*** 626 S. Carrollton (866-9573). Strong contender for best hamburger—hand-formed, good meat. Also good is the cannibal special, a steak tartare sandwich. Soufflé-like omelets, plate specials and deli sandwiches are served you at a counter after you are seated by a maître d'. Linen napkins. Very popular. Open seven days a week, until 2 A.M. Entrées from $1.50 (B, L & D). No credit cards.

## BEST WINE LIST

***Le Ruth's,*** 636 Franklin, Gretna (362-4914). (See description under IF YOU HAVE TIME FOR ONLY ONE MEAL.) About 25,000 bottles, representing the great vintages of the great châteaux, well priced.

## FOR DRINKS

***Napoleon House,*** 500 Chartres (523-0371). A crumbling, non/air/conditioned, open-door, eighteenth-century relic popular with two disparate crowds: the 25-to-35 and the over-60. Classical music. Muffuletta sandwich—three Italian meats and two cheeses on a huge round loaf with olive salad—feeds two. Open seven days a week. Sandwiches from $1.25. No credit cards.

***Que Sera,*** 3636 St. Charles Avenue (897-2598). A very casual lounge spilling out onto the sidewalks of St. Charles Avenue, where the streetcar ridership can watch you down good drinks and good light food from a small menu with particularly good salads. The population is half under 30 and half from the staffs of the large hospitals nearby. Open seven days a week. Entrées from $3 (L & D). AE, MC, V.

***Forty-One Forty-One,*** 4141 St. Charles Avenue (891-9873). Classy uptown lounge with a disco. Areas available for talking without having to scream over the music. Good drinks at dear prices. (Stephen and Martin's restaurant adjacent. See description under LATE-NIGHT SERVICE.) Open seven days a week. AE, CB, DC, MC, V.

## ROMANTIC

***Bistro Steak Room,*** 1098 Fourth Street, Westwego (347-3117). The epitome of the underground restaurant: you walk through a truck stop called the Riviera through a neon-marked door, and find a French-Moroccan restaurant, very quiet, low-key, and exciting. Start with a French-fried parsley basket, kosher eggs Benedict (with smoked salmon) and oysters Riviera. Steaks are excellent, as are the double lamb chops. Good seafood and a remarkable veal Normande. Closed Sunday. Entrées from $3.50 (L), $7 (D). MC, V.

## LATE-NIGHT SERVICE

***Stephen and Martin*** 1613 Milan (897-0781). Good earthy New Orleans dishes such as barbecued shrimp, fried-seafood platters, steak *au poivre* with lemon, and oysters on the half shell. The dining room is a vaguely Art Deco indoor garden. Open Monday through Wednesday until 2 A.M., Thursday through Saturday until 4 A.M., and until 11 P.M. on Sunday. Entrées from $4.50 (L & D). AE, CB, DC, MC, V.

***Bailey's,*** Fairmont Hotel, 127 Baronne (529-7111). (See description under BUSINESS BREAKFAST.) Fried seafood, red beans and rice, poor boys, good desserts in sparkling surroundings.

***Camellia Grill,*** 626 S. Carrollton Avenue (866-9573). (See description under FAST, GOOD FOOD/DINNER.)

## SUNDAY BRUNCH

***Brennan's,*** 417 Royal (525-9711). (See description under FRENCH/CREOLE.)

***Commander's Palace,*** 1403 Washington Avenue (899-8221). (See description under FRENCH/CREOLE.)

## SUNDAY-EVENING MEAL

***Galatoire's,*** 209 Bourbon (525-2021). (See description under FRENCH/CREOLE.)

***Jonathan,*** 714 N. Rampart (586-1930). (See description under CONTINENTAL.)

***Caribbean Room,*** Pontchartrain Hotel, 2031 St. Charles Avenue (524-0581). (See description under BEST HOTEL MEAL.)

## FOR FAMILIES WITH CHILDREN

***Delmonico,*** 1300 St. Charles Avenue (525-4937). An old-fashioned Creole restaurant with consistent, excellent food at very low prices. Table d'hôte service includes shrimp rémoulade, excellent Creole soups, a good fresh vegetable salad, and a variety of seafood, chicken and meat dishes. Duck with fruit, catfish meunière, veal Cordon Bleu are particularly good. Busy with uptown families who have been coming for years. Very comfortable and distinctly New Orleans surroundings. Open seven days a week. Entrées from $3 (L), $4.50 (D). AE, V.

***Maylie's,*** 1009 Poydras (525-9547). Even more old-fashioned, this 100-year-old restaurant is an incredible antique. Best bet is the boiled beef dinner, encompassing eight small courses of good Creole food. Also good are the fried seafood, oysters on the half shell, and poor-boy sandwiches. Closed Saturday and Sunday. Table d'hôte lunches from $3, dinners from $6. AE, CB, DC, MC, V.

## COUNTRY INN

***La Provence,*** U.S. 190, Lacombe, across the lake (1-626-7662). Get there via the 24-mile Lake Pontchartrain Causeway. Here's another very impressive kitchen, turning out magnificent French food with the very slightest touch of Greek influence. Outstanding duck, veal and lamb; superb wine list. A cozy little cabin in the woods, popular among pilgriming cognoscenti. Dinner only. Closed Monday and Tuesday. Entrées from $6.95. V.

# IN THE SUBURBS

## LAPLACE

***Roussel's,*** U.S. 61, 30 minutes from downtown (1-652-9910). Looks like a truck stop. The nearest real Cajun food; exemplary crawfish *étouffée* and *andouille* gumbo. Open seven days a week. Entrées from $2.50 (L), $5.95 (D). AE, CB, V.

## MANCHAC

***Middendorf's,*** U.S. 51 and Interstate 55, 45 minutes from downtown (1-386-6666). Catfish. Get a large order, fried, thick; precede it with a beer and a dozen raw oysters. Very large but still busy—sometimes the restaurant's patrons exceed the population of the town. Open seven days a week. Entrées from $3 (L & D). MC, V.

## MARRERO

***The Lido,*** 1019 Avenue C, 20 minutes from downtown (347-8203). Italian cuisine with good tomato sauces. Best lasagne and manicotti in the area, some unusual veal dishes. Saturday, dinner only. Closed Sunday. Entrées from $2 (L), $4.50 (D). No credit cards.

## PORT SULPHUR

***Sig's,*** La. 23, 40 minutes from downtown (1-564-3181). They manufacture an orange wine here that compares favorably with imported Tokay. Prime steaks, which rival the best in town, and seafood. Closed Monday. Entrées from $9 (L & D). AE, CB, DC, MC, V.

## WAGGAMAN

***Mosca's,*** U.S. 90 West, 30 minutes from downtown (436-8942). Far and away the most original and best Italian restaurant in the vicinity, but the environment may put you off. It's miles into the swamp to an old, beat-up white house that's very hard to find, with a stark, noisy interior. Emphasis is on seafood, with marinated crab claws and Italian oyster or shrimp pan roasts topping the bill. Huge servings. Don't miss spaghetti bordelaise—homemade pasta with an ideal garlic-and-oil component. Dinner only. Closed Sunday and Monday. Entrées from $8. No credit cards.

# MARKETS

## GIFT FOODS

***Central Grocery,*** 923 Decatur (523-1620). The most important item here is the muffuletta sandwich, the original, filling, delicious one with freshly carved meats. Besides that, there are imported meats and cheese in bulk, pasta, spices dispersed from jars, coffees of all types, fancy vegetables, pâté, just about any foodstuff from Italy, and much from all over the rest of the world. Closed Sunday. No credit cards.

## GIFT WINES

***Martin Wine Cellar,*** 3827 Baronne (899-7411). Huge selection, well priced; incredible specials and finds. Also very good cheese and gourmet groceries. Open 7 days a week, Sunday 10 A.M. to 2 P.M. AE, CB, DC, MC, V.

# SPECIAL EVENTS

***New Orleans Food Festival.*** Held in July in the Rivergate convention facility, this consists of some hundred booths dispensing small portions of Creole and not-so-Creole specialties to a throng jam-packed into a large and messy hall. Sounds like a culinary adventure, but it's really more successful as a profit-maker for the participants.

***France-Louisiana Festival.*** Held in May or June in the Rivergate convention facility. A handful of French restaurants serves samples of excellent dishes to a restrained crowd. There are also cooking demonstrations, cookbooks, and tallow-and-ice sculptures.

# New York

A list of New York restaurants reads like an atlas. The ingredients that have been accumulating in the pot over the years never managed to melt; even today they retain their individual and often fiercely ethnic identities. The result is an international banquet unmatched by any other city in the world.

Earlier eras boasted taverns (dispensing man-sized portions, buffet-style, to an all-male clientele) and hotels (serving on the "American plan"). Along Canal Street there were oyster houses galore, the fast-food joints of their day. The brothers Delmonico are credited with being the first to offer well-prepared meals to the public in gracious surroundings. That was in 1831. There were eleven subsequent editions of Delmonico's from William Street to 44th Street. A vague echo still inhabits the corner of Beaver and William. Look but don't taste. The Delmonicos maintained their monopoly on fine food for several decades but gradually the competition gathered steam.

By the 1880's ostrich-plumed operagoers and top-hatted tycoons supped on Continental spectaculars at Louis Sherry while Lüchow's established a beachhead for German dining. Across the East River in the city of Brooklyn, **Gage & Tollner** and **Peter Luger** opened their doors with less fanfare. They have survived for nearly a century with both cuisine and credibility intact. While some contend that one need never leave Manhattan and its marvelous array of restaurants, these two are worth the trip.

In time, New York society danced and drove its way uptown. Wall Street was once a wall—the city limits. Then 14th Street, Madison Square (at 23rd Street), 34th Street, 42nd Street and 59th

Street took their turns as hubs of fashionable activity. Today the Metropolitan Opera, once the geographic bellwether, is located at West 63rd Street, while expensive French restaurants dot the East Sixties, Seventies and Eighties. Recently, however, eyes have turned far downtown once again toward **Windows on the World.** This magnificent restaurant complex on the top (107th floor) of the World Trade Center has become a symbol of the vitality of both New York City and the food service industry, and is an attraction to New Yorkers as well as out-of-towners. Even the main concourse of the Trade Center draws crowds to a medley of food establishments that include **The Market Dining Rooms and Bar,** Nature's Pantry, The Deli, Ice Cream Parlor, Seafood Bar and Coffee Exchange. Another new complex of restaurants and food shops is in the striking Citicorp Center (Lexington Avenue and 53rd Street).

In a city of so many moods and with so many choices available, it is not surprising that restaurantgoers are fickle. Restaurants where people go to see or be seen change often. Reservations that were precious a year ago may be old hat today. Critics argue in print about the merit of this place and that. The instability of local Italian kitchens only fans the flames of controversy, as does the lack of a superb seafood restaurant.

The loss of Le Pavillon, Café Chauveron and even Reubens has thinned the ranks of dining meccas; but discriminating palates still rely on **Lutèce, The Coach House** and **Christ Cella.** To offset memories of past glory, we can point with pride to the revitalization of the Grand Central **Oyster Bar** and **The Four Seasons** as well as the stubborn determination of **P. J. Clarke's** to survive.

No longer is it absolutely necessary to be inconvenienced by a trip to Chinatown or Little Italy for good Chinese or Italian food, although a well-chosen restaurant will certainly be cheaper and possibly more interesting within the boundaries of those neighborhoods. Among them, Chinatown still reigns supreme. Once occupying six or eight cluttered blocks bordered by Canal Street on the north and the Bowery on the east, it has now spilled beyond those limits. The choice of cuisines is like the map of China itself and includes Cantonese, Shanghai, Peking (Mandarin), Hunan, Szechuan, Fukien, Taiwanese, Mongolian; the choice of meals ranges from a bowl of noodles or a dumpling lunch to a ten-course banquet. Nearby, Little Italy still provides hearty Neapolitan meals or snacks of pastry and inky coffee. The press periodically identifies this or that restaurant as a Mafia hangout, which only appears to make it more romantic to the public.

While the Yorkville area (the far east Seventies and Eighties) has lost much of its ethnic identity, hearty Slavic and German dishes are still available, served to the strumming of a zither or the rhythm of an oom-pah-pah band. There are other pockets of international kitchens: Greek and Thai restaurants share 8th Avenue above 42nd Street with the skin-flick houses. West 46th Street has become little Brazil. And the entire midtown area seems to have been taken over by a *sushi* storm—nearly every block boasts a restaurant catering to the New Yorker and the native Japanese alike. Atlantic Avenue, Brooklyn, is a Levantine oasis; and in Astoria, Queens, one dines to the beat of Greek bouzoukis. A few places, such as Rao's (a tiny Italian restaurant on East 114th Street), are excellent, but so small and so out-of-the-way that they are best approached in the company of a native guide.

It is not only the ethnic meal that captures the imagination and tempts the palate in New York. Cachet is quickly bestowed on cleverly successful restorations, groovy little bistros or the gleaming butcher-block-and-tile places offering innovative menus that may draw on many different cuisines.

Only the theater district remains largely beyond the pale for serious diners, but an occasional bright spot illuminates the area.

While a well-endowed pocketbook or expense account and a polyphagic palate are helpful when dining in New York, they are not *de rigueur.* Just as important is enough willpower to avoid highly touted tourist traps (Mamma Leone's is the quintessential example), the confidence to breach some frighteningly exalted enclaves (Lutèce or The Four Seasons, for example) and enough sense of adventure to head off into the wilds (SoHo, for instance, boasts some highly individualistic and good food; and the grimy streets are safe). You can also improve your lot by ignoring reviews pasted to the windows of restaurants. Almost inevitably they are weatherworn and outdated.

Make reservations whenever possible for both lunch and dinner and expect to wait for a table at places that do not accept them. Except for theatergoers bolting a meal before curtain time, the customary dinner hour is 7 P.M. at the earliest. Ask the restaurant about dress codes when you reserve. Although the tie-and-jacket or skirt dictum of another era has been relaxed, you will find some midtown restaurants fairly dressy. In most other parts of the city, with the exception of some French restaurants, you would not feel out of place in your most casual duds.

Once at table, inquire as to specials of the day and request explanations of any unfamiliar dishes on the menu. Except for clam chowder with tomatoes, New York does not boast a local specialty. (The "New York cut" steak is a boneless sirloin usually known elsewhere as the Kansas City strip.) Out-of-towners are impressed by New York's "delis" and by the availability and quality of smoked salmon and hot pastrami. As the funnel through which most of the imported food for the Northeast is poured, there is a staggering variety constantly on hand. Shops in almost every block and street vendors testify to just how strongly New York loves food and eating.

This selection of New York's distinctive restaurants represents approximately .4 percent of the 25,000 possible bites of the Big Apple.

# Restaurants and Food Sources
(Area code: 212)

## BIG DEAL

### WORTH IT

***The Four Seasons,*** 99 E. 52nd Street (754-9494). The stunning, high-ceilinged dining room in the Seagram Building, with a pool as a centerpiece, has regained all of its former splendor under the guidance of Tom Margittai and Paul Kovi. If its traditions of cuisine and service are largely European, its architecture (by Philip Johnson), vitality and occasional unrealized pretensions are all American. It's a restaurant that could exist only in New York and therefore a very New York restaurant. The menu is highlighted by imaginative seasonal variations—it changes four times a year—and co-owner Kovi's wide expertise is well reflected on the wine list. *Charcuterie* (*terrines,* sausages), seafood (scallops and snapper) and duck are prepared with great skill. Lunch is agreeable, but evening somehow dresses up the restaurant. Chaîne des Rotisseurs. One way to experience The Four Seasons without placing undo strain on the pocketbook is to reserve for the before- (5 P.M. to 6:30 P.M.) or after- (10 P.M. to 11 P.M.) theater supper. The fixed price for pre- and after-theater supper, with several alternative choices, is $19. Closed Sunday. Everything is à la carte. $6.95 (L), $8.75 (D). For the Grill Room see BUSINESS LUNCH. AE, CB, DC, MC, V.

***Windows on the World,*** 1 World Trade Center (938-1111). Whisk up 107 floors to this extraterrestrial aerie and you are no longer a mere mortal. You are seated in a beautiful, terraced spaceship with a uniformed crew tending to your needs. The breath-taking view offers compensation when the cooking is less than fit for the gods, though food quality is high and the menu admirably free of clichés. Broiled meats and poached fish are the most popular entrées. The dessert display competes with the view and contains some jewels. Everyone is a tourist. Chaîne des Rotisseurs. Dinner on Saturday takes advance planning—one to two weeks to realize your reservation. Entrées from $5.95 (L), $8.95 (D). Also lunch buffet $10.95, complete dinner $19.50. Club members only at certain hours. There is a $7.50 surcharge per person for nonmembers at lunch—they may be admitted at any time, but a reservation is mandatory. Dinner seating every half hour from 5 P.M. to 6:30 P.M. and from 8:30 P.M. to 10 P.M. Open seven days a week. For The Hors d'Oeuverie, see FOR DRINKS. AE, CB, DC, MC, V.

## NOT WORTH IT

***"21,"*** 21 W. 52nd Street (582-7200). Famous since Prohibition days, it still functions as a club of sorts. Insiders feel welcome, but others might be advised not to waste their time because the ambitious food has little to recommend it. Open until 12 P.M. Closed Sunday, and Saturday and Sunday during the summer. Entrées from $9 (L), $10.75 (D). AE, CB, DC, MC, V.

***Tavern on the Green,*** Central Park West at 67th Street (873-3200). Someday this dream may come true. The utterly glorious and extravagant decorations—greenery, crystal, statuary—make this a spectacular setting. The kitchen still has not gotten its act together, and with the enormous volume of business, it will be difficult. Worth seeing. Go for cocktails. Open seven days a week. Brunch on Saturday and Sunday. Entrées from $5 (L), $7 (D). AE, CB, DC, MC, V.

# INTERNATIONAL

## AMERICAN

***Market Dining Rooms and Bar,*** 1 World Trade Center, Main Concourse (938-1155). Bustling and informal. Designed as a tribute to market restaurants of a bygone era, though simple simplicity has become elegant simplicity. Broiled meats and fish are featured on a menu that contains an imaginative array of appetizers. Top-quality ingredients. The house drink is an outsized bourbon sour. Closed Sunday. Entrées from $4.95 (L), $5.95 (D). AE, CB, DC, MC, V.

***The Coach House,*** 110 Waverly Place (777-0303). This is the New Yorker's automatic response to a request for "American" food; but more accurately it is a French-Continental melting pot, despite black-bean soup, crabs, superb grilled lamb and pecan pie. If a choice has to be made, hazelnut meringue *dacquoise* is probably the best dessert. A good selection of American wines is available. Sedately conservative, pleasant dining in "the Village." Closed Monday. Dinner only. Entrées from $8.50. Complete 3-course dinner from $20.50. AE, DC, MC.

***Gage & Tollner,*** 374 Fulton Street, Brooklyn (875-5181). A gaslit survivor of the 1880's with décor intact and the best traditional American food in all the five boroughs. A good excuse to cross the bridge; handy to the Brooklyn Academy of Music's gorgeous theater. Fish and seafood are the specialties in more styles than you thought possible, steaks and chicken also recommended. Saturday and Sunday, dinner only. Closed Sunday during July and August. Entrées from $6.50 (L & D). AE, DC, MC, V.

***Restaurant Leslie,*** 18 Cornelia Street (675-1255). Created by Leslie Revsin, the first women chef at the Waldorf, and a band of dedicated friends, this small (30 seats), understated and cozy Greenwich Village storefront is a rendezvous for those who admire culinary craftsmanship and innovations. Chef Revsin prepares some intricate personal creations—quenelles of scallops, Roquefort beignets, quail with port and cranberry, lemon-rum torte among them. While she has been inspired by the *nouvelle cuisine* chefs, her cooking and her restaurant are both Europe-tinged American-contemporary, not traditional. The prices scarcely reflect the effort she expends. Reservations recommended. Dinner only. Closed Sunday. Entrées from $6. AE, MC, V.

## ARMENIAN

***Dardanelles,*** 86 University Place (242-8990). Dependable and delightful Near Eastern oasis. White tablecloths, good service. Assorted appetizers—especially the flaky, warm *boerek,* the *kofte* and the *kebabs. Ekmek kedaif* with *kaymak* is a dessert not to be missed. Sunday, dinner only. Open seven days a week. Closed Sunday in July and August. Entrées from $3.95 (L), $4.95 (D). AE, CB, DC, MC.

## BRAZILIAN

***Brazilian Pavilion,*** 141 E. 52nd Street (758-8129). There is more to South America; but in these northern latitudes, Brazilian is best. Hearty helpings of rich meats and inky black beans, seasoned with fire and spice. Chicken bossanova, *churrasco* steak, shrimp Baina served in a pleasantly tropical room. Closed Sunday. Entrées from $4 (L), $6 (D). MC, V.

## CHINESE

***David K's,*** 1115 Third Avenue, at 65th (371-9090). There are a dozen or so Chinese restaurants in America that have discarded the clichés of decoration along with menu clichés and have become stratospheric temples of *haute cuisine.* David K's is among them; some think it is first among them. The waiters and the well-spaced tables are dressed to suit an occasion. There is Western piano music in the bar Wednesday through Saturday and wine on many tables. Luxury, at luxurious prices, though the bite is less at lunchtime. What to order? Dumplings (in one of three styles), hot-and-sour fish soup, shellfish, squab, orange beef and any vegetable dish. Reservations suggested for dinner. Open seven days a week. Entrées from $9 (L & D). AE.

***Shun Lee Palace,*** 155 E. 55th Street (371-8844). Shiny and shimmery, the Palace is midtown elegant, but doesn't try to hide its roots. Skip the combination plates however, and take aim at Chef Wong's specialties, or those from Hunan. Slippery chicken, heavenly fish filets and even *moo-shu* pork are outstanding, as are the chef's frogs' legs, the pearl ball appetizers and the three-delicacy cold platter. If you have resisted liver or veal in Chinese restaurants, try them here. There are layers of service. Go in a group for larger tables and a wider range of dishes. Reservations suggested. Open seven days a week. Entrées from $3.50 (L), $6.50 (D). AE, CB, DC.

***Say Eng Look,*** 1 E. Broadway (732-0796). It's right out of central casting: one room, simple, stark and uncompromising. The waiters are indifferent to the niceties of pleasing tourists—a distinct minority of the clientele here. But a bit of courage and the willingness to ask for advice will take you a long way in this fine, Shanghai-oriented Chinatown landmark. The specials are special, especially fish pieces deep-fried in a skin of bean curd, bean curd "puff" (with a sauce containing chopped pork), Shanghai-style spareribs, Chinese string beans and broccoli or giant casserole (subgum or fish head). Portions are large. The restaurant often is crowded to overflowing. Beer and soft drinks served. No wine or liquor. Open seven days a week. Entrées from $2.25 (L & D). MC.

***Szechuan Cuisine,*** 30 E. Broadway (966-2326). Restaurants claiming to re-create the food of China's spiciest province are scattered like peppercorns throughout Manhattan. This unimposing Chinatown spot may be the best of them all. The fish—from shrimps to carp—is exceptional here, as are appetizer dumplings and steamed buns. Also, don't pass by the eggplant and bean curd. Bring your own wine or beer. Closed Thursday. Entrées from $2.95 (L), $3.75 (D). No credit cards.

***Hee Seung Fung,*** 46 Bowery (374-1319) and ***H.S.F.,*** 578 Second Avenue, at 32nd (689-6969). The owners use only initials in their midtown location, but at either, the Cantonese *dim sum* are outstanding. In Chinatown there are two dining rooms on either side of an arcade, and crowds of people. Unless you arrive with a crowd of your own, expect to share one of the large round tables with strangers. Uptown, it's more stylish and some very Chinese dishes, such as ducks' feet and pigs' ears, are missing among the 65 they offer downtown. You may choose egg rolls, spring rolls, vegetable rolls, baby shrimp rolls, Phoenix rolls and more and more. Shellfish, spareribs and noodle dishes are worthwhile, too. *Dim sum* from 50 cents. Bowery open seven days a week. No credit cards. Second Avenue open seven days a week. AE, DC, MC, V.

***Yun Luck Rice Shoppe,*** 17 Doyers Street (571-1375). A small, crowded Cantonese restaurant tucked into a side street in Chinatown. Luncheonette décor. Avoid the Occidental menu and order from the Chinese listing, which boasts authentic dishes such as spareribs with black-bean sauce; and pepper shrimp, snails, steamed flounder with scallions, ginger and soy sauce. Also specify that you want everything Chinese-style (unaltered for Western tastes). No desserts or alcoholic beverages are served, but you may bring beer or wine. Open seven days a week; Saturday, until 1 A.M. Entrées from $2.25 (L & D). No credit cards.

## FRENCH

***Lutèce,*** 249 E. 50th Street (752-2225). Utterly, Frenchly charming. Dine in a greenhouse garden or in one of two formal upstairs rooms in what once was an East Side town house. Owner/chef André Soltner is highly regarded by his peers here and in France. His menu isn't vast, but it is always supplemented by daily specials and contains surprising delights, the most famous being an appetizer mousse of pike and salmon. Soltner has a way with vegetables and takes great pride in his desserts. Memorable dining usually worth the considerable expense. Closed Sunday, and Saturday and Sunday in June and July. Fixed-price lunch, $16.75; dinner (à la carte only) entrées $16–$17. AE.

***La Caravelle,*** 33 W. 55th Street (586-4252). Probably the most traditional and possibly the most consistent French restaurant in New York. Food service, table appointments and atmosphere are all in classic good taste. Specialties change every day, but *mousse de brochet,* tournedos, duckling and fish are fixtures. The cooking is skillful, though less inspired than in years gone by. Excellent but expensive wine list. Closed Sunday all year; Saturday, too, in summer; and all major holidays. Dinner only. À la carte entrées from $18.50. No credit cards.

***Raoul's,*** 180 Prince Street (966-3518). Not only is this the odds-on choice for best bistro in SoHo, it is the best restaurant in the area. Very French despite the Ballantine Beer neon signs in the window, Raoul's has the warm feeling of a place that's worn but cared for. Eat steak and *pommes frites* at the bar or excellent duck or fish dishes at a table. The menu changes daily; the crowd is often the same—a good sign. Reservations necessary. Dinner only. Open seven days a week. Entrées from $8.50. AE.

***Le Lavandou,*** 134 E. 61st Street (838-7987). If *The New Yorker* magazine were to do a cartoon of the archetypical New York French restaurant, it would probably resemble this small, streamlined room. Red banquettes line the walls; there is a small bar in a corner near the entrance and fresh flowers everywhere. Chef Jean-Jacques Rachou is an artist whose presentations are carefully arranged and unfailingly attractive. His food is classic in inspiration rather than regional, with poached fish (hot or cold), puréed vegetables and chicken in pastry showing his talents to good advantage. The restaurant attracts a cross-section of customers, perhaps preserving the serving personnel from snobbism, a disease all too common in restaurants of this caliber. With the fixed-price luncheon at $12.50, and dinner at $23, Le Lavandou represents relative value for money. Closed Sunday. AE.

***Le Cirque,*** 58 E. 65th Street (794-9292). The clientele is very well-heeled and it shows—the mink coats crowd almost atop one another in this pretty but noisy dining room. Prices are a step or two below Le Cirque's competitors for the carriage trade however, and some of the specialties—including pasta primavera, lamb, and dessert soufflés—are among the best in town. Reservations necessary. Closed Sunday. Fixed-price lunch $12.75. Entrées from $6.75 (L), $9.75 (D). AE, DC.

***Café des Artistes,*** 1 W. 67th Street (877-3500). Restaurant entrepreneur George Lang gave this West Side landmark a massage and a face-lift not too long ago, and New Yorkers have flocked in to admire his handiwork ever since. (Murals by Howard Chandler Christy and mirrors are the chief decorative features.) The restaurant is convenient to Lincoln Center, though most diners choose to stay put for a relaxed meal that is more in keeping with the tempo of the service. The ambience is that of a French café, but the menu is determinedly international, with specials changing daily. *Pâtés* and sausages, *gravlax,* sometimes sturgeon, and duck and beef are featured. Wine specials are on display in wicker baskets. However, the food is not as consistently pleasing as the setting. Saturday, dinner only. Brunch served Saturday and Sunday. Open seven days a week. Entrées from $5.50 (L), $9.50 (D). Fixed-price complete meal, $9.25 (L), $12.75 (D). AE, DC, MC, V.

***Café des Sports,*** 329 W. 51st Street (581-1283). Don't expect the elegant France of Cardin and Bocuse. The Café is on the edge of the theater district, just beyond two other French restaurants that are less homespun and more expensive. There is a collection of sports trophies here and enough genuine French people smoking Gauloise cigarettes to make the place smell authentic. The food is unspectacular but honest, to excavate a phrase from another era. Try the soups and pâtés, homemade sausage, steak and fried potatoes. It's open late so you can squeeze in after the final curtain. Reserve for dinner. Saturday and Sunday, dinner only. Open seven days a week. Entrées from $4 (L), $4.75 (D). AE.

***The Palace,*** 420 E. 59th Street (355-5152). If money is no object, here is where to buy an evening of total culinary theater, though for some it is musical comedy instead of the Comédie Française. Splendid food is magnificently presented and served by clusters of gracious attendants. Seven courses of luxury with manageable quantities bestowed in measured rhythm. The full dinner (without wine) is priced at $90 per person, but there are no supplementary charges, even for the excellent caviar. Here money does buy respect. If you plan forty-eight hours in advance for this special occasion, you can order "*sur commande,*" a list that greatly expands the main-course choices. Wines are outrageously expensive. The Palace truly is unique. It should be shared with someone whose company you enjoy and who doesn't object to excess.

Chaîne des Rotisseurs. Dinner only. Closed Sunday. $90 per person, without liquor, plus a 23 percent "suggested" service charge. AE, CB, DC, MC, V.

# GREEK

***Pantheon,*** 689 Eighth Avenue, between 43rd and 44th (840-9391). Immaculate, unpretentious, pleasant, convenient to Broadway theaters and a favorite of the Greek community. *Avgolemono, moussaka, taramasalata, dolmadakia, spanatakopita,* all full of flavor. No reservations. Open seven days a week. Entrées from $4.75 (L & D). AE, MC, V.

# HUNGARIAN

***Csarda,*** 1477 Second Avenue, at 77th (472-2892). The setting is bright and clean and uncluttered. The food is Hungarian tavern-style—filling, fun and not overly ambitious. Roast stuffed chicken is marvelous here, as is the veal shank and the onion rings. A dish called *lecsos kabbasz* features sausage; liver is a good choice among the paprikash dishes; and the stuffed cabbage is so ample it's best to have an appetizer portion. Begin with brains and eggs, or any of the soups. Have cheese strudel or chocolate cake for dessert and waddle away humming. Dinner only, Monday through Friday. Dinner served from noon on Saturday and Sunday. Entrées from $5.95. AE.

# INDIAN

***Gaylord,*** 50 E. 58th Street (759-1710). Warm, comfortable and somewhat exotic without becoming bizarre. This London import was the first to install the clay *tandoor* oven. Watching the chefs impale chickens on long wooden skewers or fashion the *tandoori* bread, *naan,* on the palms of their hands is a delightful diversion—not that the delicious, well-prepared food can't stand on its own. Saturday, dinner only. Sunday, brunch and dinner. Open seven days a week. Entrées from $3.95 (L), $4.75 (D). Brunch, $4.95. AE, CB, DC, MC, V.

***Raga,*** 57 W. 48th Street (757-3450). This is a spacious, subdued and graciously elegant setting for the complex and spicy cuisine of India. The *tandoori* (clay-oven) cooking of the North, seafood specialties of Goa, and both mild or volcanic dishes from other regions are excellently prepared, garnished and served. Follow the waiter's suggestions in coordinating the meal. The more people in your party, the more interesting it will be, since the dishes can be shared. Crabs Goa, a hot appetizer; *murg tikki makhani,* a specially sauced *tandoori* chicken; *barra kebab, tandoori* lamb; peppers stuffed with spices and potatoes; interesting breads, condiments and desserts. Saturday and Sunday, dinner only. Open seven days a week. Complete business lunch, weekdays, $8.50. Entrées from $6.50 (L & D). AE, CB, DC, V.

***Madras Woodlands,*** 310 East 44th Street (986-0620). (See description under VEGETARIAN.)

# ITALIAN

***Salta in Bocca,*** 179 Madison Avenue, between 33rd and 34th. (684-1757). A very busy place at luncheon, this comfortable, well-run restaurant relaxes somewhat week nights and is an ideal site for a leisurely dinner with a Northern Italian accent. Among pastas, don't overlook the tortellini. Fish (striped bass Livornese in a spritely, caper-flavored sauce), veal or superbly sautéed chunks of liver are recommended entrées. As should be the case in a fine Italian restaurant, fresh vegetables are excellent. The wine list is strong in reds, with several older vintages of Barolo and Spanna represented. Reservations are recommended. Closed Sunday. Entrées from $7.50 (L & D). AE, DC, MC, V.

***Parioli Romanissimo,*** 1466 First Avenue, between 76th and 77th (288-2391). With almost a surfeit of imagination, Mr. Rossi has created and maintained a softly lit, romantic restaurant in miniature where the service and food are consistently excellent. Veal *scaloppine capriccio, cannelloni,* exquisite pastas superbly sauced. A favorite of the socially prominent, tables may be hard to come by. Dinner only. Closed Sunday and Monday. Entrées from $9.50. AE, CB, DC.

***Trattoria da Alfredo,*** 90 Bank Street, corner of Hudson Street (929-4400). Some of the most original Italian food in New York is served in this tiny, triangular corner restaurant. The surroundings are simple—uncarpeted stone floor, hanging plants. The food is lovingly described at tableside by the waiter or, often, by owner Alfredo Viazzi. *Carpaccio* (thin, pounded, uncooked sirloin), a medley of fresh vegetables, pasta of whatever style with whatever sauce of the day and veal Milanese are special here; desserts are to be resisted only at the risk of a broken heart. Moderate prices, no liquor or wine (there is a shop next door). Reservations necessary for dinner, advisable for lunch. Closed Tuesday. Entrées from $4

(L & D); minimum charge per person $5 (L), $9 (D). No credit cards.

***Forlini's,*** 93 Baxter Street (349-6779). Typical of the heavy, hearty red-sauce cooking that goes on in Little Italy, the kitchen at Forlini's has more finesse than most others. Through almost continual expansion and face-lifting, the place has emerged attractive. Try pasta with seafood, *saltimbocca* or *lasagne.* Although closer to Chinatown than Little Italy (it is south of Canal Street), you can always stroll across the border to Café Roma or Ferrari's afterwards for a cup of espresso. Open seven days a week. Closed first two weeks in August. Entrées from $4.25 (L), $4.50 (D). AE, CB, DC, MC, V.

***Patrissy's,*** 98 Kenmare Street, near Mulberry (226-8509). One of Little Italy's institutions, Patrissy's is proud of its "45-foot full bar," separate from the restaurant. In the latter, you might select roast peppers and anchovies, *frito misto* of vegetables, chicken cacciatore or a specialty such as linguine or steak Patrissy. Cheesecake is a sure winner for dessert. No reservations accepted Saturday. Open seven days a week. Closed last week in July and first week in August. Entrées from $5 (L), $5.50 (D). AE, CB, DC, MC, V.

***Gino's,*** 780 Lexington Avenue, between 60th and 61st (223-9658). Italian restaurants are divided into reds and whites. This is red, robust and vigorous. Popular, but the noise can be a drawback. To perform another act of division, a meal here is more like eating than dining, but the food is good. *Paillard* of beef as well as veal. No reservations. Open seven days a week. Entrées from $7 (L & D). No credit cards.

## JAPANESE

***Kitcho,*** 22 W. 46th Street (575-8880). Frequented primarily by Japanese—an auspicious sign. Three floors comprise a modern ground-floor dining area and two stories decorated in the traditional manner where guests remove their shoes and sit on *tatamis.* Any dish in this handsome restaurant can be ordered with confidence, and they are exquisitely presented. Exceptional appetizers include *yaki-hama* (broiled clams with lemon, served with a spicy sauce) and *shitashi* (braised spinach). The *teriyakis,* tempura and *sushi* are all above average. Desserts include unusual ice creams. Reservations a must. Sunday, dinner only. Closed Saturday. Complete meals from $7.50 (L), $10 (D).. Entrées from $3.50 (L & D).

Special "chef's choice" dinners, ranging in price from $20 to $50 per person, may also be ordered. AE, DC.

***Nippon,*** 145 E. 52nd Street (758-0226). Restful, gracious surroundings where the food, like art, is expensive and beautiful. Superb *sushi, sunomono, shabu-shabu.* Saturday, dinner only. Closed Sunday. Complete lunch from $7.50, dinner from $10. A la carte dinner from $7. AE, CB, DC, MC, V.

***Hatsuhana,*** 17 E. 48th Street (355-3345). An excellent choice for *sushi* or tempura. Service at either table or a bar, where you can watch the *sushi* being sliced and shaped in highly artistic fashion. They prepare delicious broiled seafood as well, but humdrum sukiyaki. It's usually crowded and can be noisy. No reservations. Saturday, dinner only. Closed Sunday. Fixed-price meals $5 (L), $7 (D). Entrées from $4 (L), $6 (D). AE, CB, DC, MC, V.

## JEWISH

***Sammy's Restaurant,*** 157 Chrystie Street (673-0330). Hearty East European/Jewish dining on Manhattan's Lower East Side. *Mushk* steak, Rumanian tenderloin, chicken livers, garlic-flavored sausage, boiled beef and potato pancakes are among the specialties. Real seltzer water, and liquid chicken fat in syrup dispensers (for the potatoes, of course). Music from an electric piano Wednesday through Sunday. Take a cab to and from the restaurant. Dinner only, from 4 P.M. to midnight. Open seven days a week. Entrées from $6.95. No credit cards.

## MEXICAN

***El Parador Café,*** 325 E. 34th Street (679-6812). Mexican food all dressed up in a three-piece suit. It's dark here, but stylishly so. It's not dingy. There is a ritual wait at the bar among convivial company—about two drinks long—before you are seated. But the drinks are good and the food that follows, particularly anything involving guacamole, is more than passable. (New York is no distant province of Mexico, nor Texas, for that matter). The *nachos royale* is a form of Mexican pizza. Fried chicken is quite tasty. No reservations. Dinner only. Closed Sunday. Entrées from $6. No credit cards.

***Zapata's,*** 330 E. 53rd Street (223-9408). Narrow, dim, almost cellar-like, this is not sunny Mexico but an intensely brooding place dominated by a stern portrait of the mustachioed revolutionary. A good setting for a conspiracy. The lunch menu is a taco-enchilada combination-plate affair, but horizons expand at dinner, with *moles* and *cabrito* (baby goat), the rich chunks of meat stewed to a deep mahogany and served with delicate flour tortillas. The enchilada department produces as creditable results as you might expect this far north of the border. Be assured of copious quantities of reasonably well seasoned food. Start with a plate of excellent *nachos*—tortilla chips heavy with black beans, melted cheese and pepper. Open seven days a week. Entrées from $3.75 (L), $5.50 (D). AE, DC, MC.

***El Tenampa,*** 304 W. 46th Street (586-8039). The restaurant is small and unpretentious, but it has attracted a faithful following for consistently well-prepared and well-spiced *mole verde, chiles en nogada,* enchiladas, and so forth. Convenient to theaters. Closed Sunday. Entrées from $3.50 (L), $3.75 (D). DC.

## RUSSIAN

***Russian Tea Room,*** 150 W. 57th Street (265-0947). Famous and festive, crowded with somebodies and nobodies supping on *blini, pierogi,* borscht and *shaslik* before, instead of and after the theater. Caviar and vodka? Why not? They never take down the Christmas decorations, so every day is a party. Late supper, 9:30 P.M. to 12:30 P.M.; 1:30 A.M., Saturdays. Open seven days a week. Entrées from $5.75 (L), $8.75 (D). AE, CB, DC, MC, V.

## SPANISH

***Rincón de España,*** 226 Thompson Street (475-9891, 260-4950) and 82 Beaver Street (344-5228). There's a constant turnover of tables, with those waiting crowded in the doorway or at a small but comfortable bar along with carry-out customers. The waiters, who do their jobs very well, are in uniform. There the elegance ends; dress is as informal as the food. The chef's strong suit is seafood, particularly mussels and shrimps in sauces he has created. (The mussels à la Carlos are particularly good.) Among the meat entrées, veal with Spanish sausage and barbecued pork with almond sauce stand out. While the various paella dishes don't set new culinary standards, they are made to order and ample. In fact, portions here are generous enough to share. Don't stint to save room for desserts. They are not special. Beaver Street: Closed Saturday and Sunday. Thompson Street: Dinner only; open seven days a week. Entrées from $5.50 (L & D). AE, CB, DC, MC, V.

***Tres Carabelas Restaurante,*** in Casa de España, 314 E. 39th Street (689-6388). Pretend you are on one of Columbus' Three Ships when you try to find this restaurant. It's hidden in the heart of the Spanish Cultural Center without a sign on the street to guide you. Once inside however, with a pitcher of sangría near at hand, you are on a relatively inexpensive visit to Spain. The wine list has good selections priced from $6.50 to $7.50. Most appetizers and the ritual salad are dull but several of the main courses are so good and served in such ample portions you can forgive—or skip—the banal beginning. Order *zarzuela* (fish and clams with rice), paella, baby lamb chops or beef on the bone, sliced tableside. For dessert try the superior bread pudding or flan. Lunch is less ambitious and less expensive than dinner (which is a bargain). Closed Monday. Entrées from $6 (L), $12 (D). AE.

## SWISS

***Chalet Suisse,*** 6 E. 48th Street (355-0855). With the Tyrolean kitsch kept to a pleasant minimum, the stuccoed and beamed chalet emphasizes carefully prepared, meticulously served food. In the Swiss tradition, the dollar does not go very far. Cheese-and-onion pie, veal *à la suisse,* bratwurst, fondue, ice cream with Swiss chocolate. Chaîne des Rotisseurs. Closed Saturday and Sunday. Fixed-price dinner $16.50. Entrées from $7 (L), $7.50 (D). AE, CB, DC, MC.

## THAI

***Bangkok Cuisine,*** 885 Eighth Avenue, between 52nd and 53rd (581-6370 or 840-8777). Thai food represents the city's most recent Oriental fad. This is as good a place as any to sample dishes that can be dominated by fiery peppers or are spicy and fragrant with rare aromatics such as lemon grass. Worth enjoying in these pleasant, dim surroundings are lemon-steamed fish, Thai curries, dumplings, meat patties. Closed Sunday. Entrées from $3.45 (L & D). AE, DC, MC, V.

# SPECIALTY COOKING

## DELI

***Second Avenue Kosher Delicatessen and Restaurant,*** 156 Second Avenue, at 10th (677-0606). Corned beef, pastrami, brisket, salami, pickles, sauerkraut. The cooking is lighter than is normal with Jewish cuisine, and there's a wonderfully improbable explanation: the chef is Chinese. Sandwiches on rye with Dr. Brown's Cel-Ray are still one of the best ways to dine in New York. Open seven days a week. Entrées from $5.50. No credit cards.

***Carnegie Delicatessen,*** 854 Seventh Avenue, at 55th (757-2245). A real boon for concert-goers or those who wander north of the theater district in search of deli food. They prepare decent soup and salads, but you should go directly to the pastrami or corned beef on rye, wash it down with beer or a Cel-Ray tonic and have a piece of cheesecake. Open seven days a week, 6:30 A.M. to 4 A.M. Sandwiches from $2.95. No credit cards.

***Madison Avenue Delicatessen,*** 1175 Madison Avenue, at 86th (369-6670). If hunger strikes while touring the Metropolitan or Guggenheim museums, relief is not far away. This large deli has a take-out counter and table service is prompt. The soups, pickled herring, chicken giblets—yes, chicken giblets—and blintzes are fine, as are the large sandwiches. Here as elsewhere, smoked fish is very expensive. Unlike most other delis, the rye bread is sliced thin and meats are cut the way you ask for them. Open seven days a week. Sandwiches from $2.50. No credit cards.

## HAMBURGER

***Friday's,*** 1152 First Avenue, at 63rd (832-8512). The singles' scene along First Avenue in the '70's is now part of New York folklore. Somehow, amidst all the diversions, Friday's offers a very good hamburger for $2.75, and they'll serve it your way—with chili, onions, bacon or whatever, without jacking up the price. Chicken wings should please those not of the beef persuasion. Calm at lunch. Noisy at night. Open seven days a week, until 3 A.M. AE, CB, DC, MC, V.

***Barrymore's,*** 267 W. 45th Street (541-4500). Theatrical it should be and theatrical it is. In the John Barrymore tradition, the management sends apples to the casts of Broadway shows on opening nights. They give patrons a fine hamburger, hash of the day and other type-cast entrées at a fair price. You'll find a comfortable bar, memorabilia on the walls and lower prices than at several better-known theater watering holes nearby. Reserve before and after theater. Open seven days a week. Closes at 8 P.M. Sunday. Entrées from $4 (L & D). AE, DC, V.

***Maxwell's Plum,*** 1181 First Avenue, at 64th (628-2100). (See description under LATE-NIGHT SERVICE.)

# HOT DOG

***Nathan's Famous,*** Surf and Stillwell, Brooklyn (266-3161); Broadway and 43rd Street at Times Square (594-7455); 6 East 58th Street (751-9060); 881 Third Avenue at 53rd Street (752-6881). Once a pilgrimage to Coney Island was necessary to get a Nathan's hot dog, now Nathan's has come to Manhattan and Queens. Still the best hot dog in the world—also, great fries, good pastrami, edible corn and tasteless hamburgers. Brooklyn: 8 A.M.–2 A.M.; Friday and Saturday till 5 A.M. Times Square: 8 A.M.–2 A.M. 58th Street: 8 A.M.–2 A.M. 53rd Street: 7 A.M.–2 A.M. A hot dog costs 75 cents. No credit cards.

# KOSHER

***Lou Siegel,*** 209 W. 38th Street (947-1262). Not *glatt,* but strictly kosher. Food is competently prepared, especially the simple, serve-from-the-pot dishes: brisket, chicken, meatballs. Closed Saturday. Entrées from $4.75 (L), $10.50 (D). AE, DC, MC.

# OMELET

***Madame Romaine de Lyon,*** 32 E. 61st Street (758-2422). Impossible to recommend which of the nearly 600 omelet possibilities to order. You're on your own, but you should plan on ordering one—it's all Madame serves as an entrée. There are salads, croissants, wines and desserts. No reservations for parties of less than four. Lunch only. Open seven days a week. Omelets from $3.25. No credit cards.

# PIZZA

***Fiorello,*** 1900 Broadway, between 63rd and 64th (595-5330). When they sing arias in this "Roman Café" across from Lincoln Center, it's only for the pizza. But the pizza is a surprise, an enlightening change from the Naples-style pizza sold throughout Manhattan Island. The base is thin and more like pie crust than bread dough. Toppings are made up of first-class ingredients. They aren't as big as most pizzas, but they are better. Open seven days a week. Pizzas $6.95 and $8.95. AE, MC, V.

# SEAFOOD

***Oyster Bar & Restaurant,*** at Grand Central Station, lower level, 42nd Street and Lexington Avenue (532-3888). This revitalized dining landmark within the famous train station is bright, busy and was never better. Plates of assorted oysters, she-crab soup, sturgeon, shad in season are among the prodigious variety on the daily changing menu. American wines featured on a fine list. Go early—lunch is crowded (and noisy), dinner is served only until 9:30 P.M. Closed Saturday and Sunday. Entrées from $5.75 (L & D). AE, CB, DC, MC, V.

***King Crab,*** 871 Eighth Avenue, at 52nd (765-4393). Crab, and its subjects in the realm of seafood, are all treated royally here. They're fresh-cooked with a minimum of fuss and served up in an eclectic dining room with real gas lamps and track lighting, young plants, a variety of old furniture. There are only five listings under lunch, but "fish of the day" may be as many as ten different species and the "seafood combination" is really a large delicious broth and fish mixture. In fact, large portions seem to be a custom here. Mussels are a good appetizer choice. Bluefish is outstanding. Potato or saffron rice and a vegetable are served with lunch; you get a salad and vegetable with dinner. Shell steak is the only non-fish entrée. Prices are very reasonable. Saturday and Sunday, dinner only. Open seven days a week. Entrées from $3.35 (L), $4.95 (D). AE, CB, DC.

***Hisae's Place,*** 35 Cooper Square (228-6886), ***Hisae's Lobster House,*** 13 E. 37th Street (889-9862). East meets West in the kitchen of these cleverly conceived restaurants which manage to give equal status to fish and vegetables. Some preparations are Oriental in inspiration, others are European or mid-ocean. You will probably have to wait, even with reservations, both before and after being seated. The décor is a mish-mash, but the cooking is fine—with occasional lapses. Portions are large, so split orders of scungilli, broccoli in garlic oil, large salads, mussels or mixed vegetables. Share only a few spoonfuls of the scallop chowder at the Lobster House. Keep the rest for yourself. The fish is fresh and well prepared, although lobsters may be overcooked (something hard to overlook even at a bargain price). Desserts are homemade. Hisae's restaurants have opened, closed or changed location with some frequency. The menu concept and standards of quality remain consistent, however. Hisae's Place: dinner only. Open seven days a week. Entrées from $4.95. No credit cards. Hisae's Lobster House: Sunday, dinner only. Open seven days a week. Entrées from $4.50 (L & D). AE, MC, V. Hisae's Restaurant: Saturday and Sunday, dinner only. Open seven days a week. Entrées from $4.95 (L), $6.95 (D). AE, CB, DC, MC, V. All: reservations necessary.

***The Captain's Table,*** 410 Sixth Avenue, between 8th and 9th (473-0670), and 860 Second Avenue, at 46th (697-9538). There are nice touches in the décor at these two attractive restaurants. The selection is broad and the simple preparations show off the fresh fish best. Some are for two or four persons. There are flaws, however, and the non-fish side dishes and desserts often look better than they taste. Sixth Avenue: closed Monday. Entrées from $6.75 (L & D). Second Avenue: closed Sunday. Entrées from $7.95 (L & D). Reservations recommended at both. AE, DC, MC, V.

## SOUL

***West Boondock Lounge,*** 114 10th Avenue, at 17th (929-9645). Located among packing houses and trucking depots, about as far west as one can get in Manhattan. Ample portions of fried chicken, barbecued ribs, ham hocks or chitterlings as well as steak, other meats and fried fish. All entrées are accompanied by corn bread and a choice of two vegetables from among collard greens, yams with apples, black-eyed peas and potato salad. Sandwich platters also on the menu. This hospitable restaurant provides good solid food at a reasonable price, along with modern jazz in the form of a piano and bass from 8:30 P.M. until 2 A.M. Sawdust on the floor, black-painted walls, red tablecloths and candlelight set the mood. Saturday and Sunday, dinner only. Entrées from $2.95 (L), $4.95 (D). AE, CB, DC, MC.

## STEAK

***Christ Cella's,*** 160 E. 46th Street (697-2479). The argument will never cease, but many connoisseurs call this the ultimate. Steaks are flawless and so is nearly everything else: lobsters, chicken, fish, vegetables and salads. There's no menu and there is reason to be fearful of the prices. The choices are suggested and served by utterly professional waiters in subdued dining rooms. Jacket and tie required. Saturday, dinner only. Closed Sunday. Entrées from $11 (L), $12.50 (D). AE, CB, DC, MC, V.

***Palm,*** 837 Second Avenue, between 44th and 45th (687-2953). The sawdust-strewn floor and cartoon-scribbled walls have uncompromising style matched by titanic lobsters (four-and-one-half pounds, about $30 at this writing) and highly praised steaks. Sharing is permitted, which is logical, since the portions are massive. Determined diners will suffer the wait for tables (no reservations for dinner, although reservations are accepted for lunch), and have to pry details of the lengthy unwritten menu from taciturn waiters—if they can hear over the din. Lamb chops and some Italian dishes are seldom ordered but worthy. **Palm Too,** 840 Second Avenue, between 44th and 45th (697-5198), is the spinoff across the street from the Palm. Saturday, dinner only. Closed Sunday. Closed Saturday and Sunday during the summer. Entrées from $6.50 (L), $8.50 (D). AE, CB, DC, MC, V.

***Peter Luger,*** 178 Broadway, Brooklyn (387-7400). One of Brooklyn's oldies but goodies with mainly turn-of-the-century dark woodwork. Steaks, the bigger the better to share, are sliced up by stern, unsmiling waiters. Also roast beef and a salad of equal-sized tomato and onion slices. Skip dessert. Open seven days a week. Entrées from $3.50 (L), $9.50 (D). No credit cards.

## VEGETARIAN

***Madras Woodlands,*** 310 E. 44th Street (986-0620). There's no meat served here, but you won't miss it. The cuisine's inspiration is Southern India. There are a variety of breads, several filled crêpes and lovely fried vegetable appetizers. The curries are spiced to match your internal thermometer. It's not a fancy place, nor is it expensive, so allow the amicable staff to guide you. Liquor is served. Be sure to try Indian beer. Open seven days a week. Entrées from $2.25 (L & D); complete meals from $3.35 (L), $4.95 (D). AE, CB, DC, MC, V.

***Hisae's Place,*** 35 Cooper Square (228-6886), ***Hisae's Lobster House,*** 13th E. 37th Street (889-9862), ***Hisae's Restaurant,*** 45 E. 58th Street (753-6555). (See description under SEAFOOD.)

# FOR INDIVIDUAL NEEDS

## IF YOU HAVE TIME FOR ONLY ONE MEAL

***Windows on the World,*** 1 World Trade Center (938-1111). (See description under BIG DEAL/WORTH IT.)

***The Four Seasons,*** 99 E. 52nd Street (754-9494). (See description under BIG DEAL/WORTH IT.)

## BEST HOTEL MEAL

***The Restaurant,*** Hotel Carlyle, 35 E. 76th Street (744-1600). Elegance and breeding, in chocolate-brown suede surroundings. The setting for tastefully conceived, beautifully presented lunches and dinner. The Oak Room at the Plaza may be more handsome, but you cannot eat the ambience. The food at the Carlyle is better. Rack of lamb, succulent and perfectly pink tournedos, fresh asparagus (in season), cold poached salmon. Entrées from $5 (L), $8 (D). AE, CB, DC, V.

## BUSINESS BREAKFAST

***Hotel Regency,*** 540 Park Avenue and 61st Street (759-4100). This is a good place to start the day with a sense of well-being. There's a lot of elegance in the air and you pay for it. Good food, too, great coffee, flawless service in a gracious setting. Open from 7 A.M., seven days a week. Entrées from $2.25 (B), $6.50 (L), $8.50 (D). AE, DC, MC, V.

***Edwardian Room,*** Plaza Hotel, Fifth Avenue, at 59th (759-3000). Elegant and predictably costly, considering the view into Central Park. (Ask for a window table when reserving.) The service, ample space between tables and fresh orange juice all are from another era. The menu caters fairly well to the full range of appetites. Open seven days a week, with brunch on Sunday. Complete breakfast $4.95. Entrées from $6.75 (L), $10.75 (D). Sunday brunch entrées from $6.75. AE, CB, DC, MC, V.

## BUSINESS LUNCH

***The Grill Room at The Four Seasons,*** 99 E. 52nd Street (754-9494). You might deduce what deals are being made by whom you see, not by what you hear. There's nothing garish and tables are well-spaced. Luxuriously simple food (*paillard* of veal, grilled fish, *gravlax* with mustard sauce). Excellent desserts and wine list. Closed Sunday. Entrées from $6.75. AE, CB, DC, MC, V.

***Market Dining Rooms and Bar,*** 1 World Trade Center, Main Concourse (938-1155). (See description under AMERICAN.)

## FAST, GOOD FOOD/BREAKFAST

***Brasserie,*** 100 E. 53rd Street (751-4840). The classiest fast breakfast in town is "The Continental" at the counter of this indefatigable establishment. Fresh orange juice, croissant or brioche, sweet butter and jam, coffee and a linen napkin. To start the day off really right, order the cappuccino instead of the regular coffee; and, if you need it, you can request a shot of vodka in your O.J. Toast (French and otherwise) is made with French bread. There are various egg preparations, sandwiches and pastries as well. Breakfast served until 11 A.M. Open 24 hours a day, seven days a week. Breakfast items from $1.25. AE, CB, DC, MC, V.

## FAST, GOOD FOOD/LUNCH, DINNER

***Pot au Feu,*** 123 W. 49th Street (765-4840). The "soup for lunch" formula here is expanded to include stews. Located within a couple of blocks of the theater district, this is a good place for enough sustenance to last several acts. Cafeteria-style (the sometimes long lines move rapidly). Complete meal with soup, including bread, salad, dessert and beverage, $3.95 (L), $4.02 (D); with stew, $4.39 (L), $4.95 (D). Open until 9 P.M. Closed Sunday. No credit cards.

***Oyster Bar & Restaurant*** at Grand Central Station, 42nd Street and Lexington Avenue (532-3888). (See description under SEAFOOD.) Stand up for window service or sit at stretches of counter for shellfish freshly opened or pan-roasted before your eyes. Oyster stew and poached or broiled Atlantic seafood treated with proper respect in spite of the rush. There is usually a wait at lunchtime, but efficiency reigns once you are seated.

***Dosanko Larmen,*** 423 Madison Avenue, between 48th and 49th (688-8575), 341 Lexington Avenue, between 39th and 40th (683-4740), 135 E. 45th Street (697-2967), and 19 Murray Street (964-9696). We gave the Japanese McDonald's, they gave us Larmen, transplanted from a Tokyo-based chain. Deep bowls of noodles in rich, spicy broth with various toppings; dumplings; stir-fried noodles. Open for lunch and dinner with counter and table service. Closed Sunday. Entrées from $2.25. No credit cards.

***SoHo Charcuterie,*** Ann Taylor, 3rd level, 3 E. 57th Street (832-1246). A pricey restaurant on a pricey street, but shoppers who can afford the neighborhood will find signs of quality in the physical aspects of the tiny restaurant and in the food. Salads, sandwich meats (the hero sandwich is for real); a vegetarian hero. Other options: tarragon chicken in brioche or a sampler platter of pâtés. Reservations necessary, though there is a fast service window for carry-out. Lunch only. Closed Sunday. Entrées from $4.50. AE, MC, V.

## BEST WINE LIST

***Windows on the World,*** 1 World Trade Center (938-1111). (See description under BIG DEAL/WORTH IT.) As a symbol of America on the shores nearest to Europe, Windows on the World has carefully balanced its French, German and Italian selections with a comprehensive presentation of quality American wines. The extremely fair prices are intended to encourage the consumption of wine, which they do. A special multicourse dinner built around wine is served in the glass-enclosed "Cellar in the Sky" for a fixed price of $50. AE, CB, DC, MC, V.

***The Four Seasons,*** 99 E. 52nd Street (754-9494). (See description under BIG DEAL/WORTH IT.) A mix of rare and expensive vintages and representative European and Californian wines. A well-thought-out list. In general, prices are not excessive. AE, CB, DC, MC, V.

***One/Fifth,*** 1 Fifth Avenue, at 8th (260-3434). Over one hundred wines, including many handsome American, at moderate but not bargain prices to accompany everything from full-course dinners to snacks. Decent food. The décor is vintage H.M.S. *Caronia*. Open seven days a week. Entrées from $3.50 (L), $8.95 (D). AE, CB, DC, MC, V.

***Oyster Bar & Restaurant,*** at Grand Central Station, 42nd Street and Lexington Avenue (532-3888). (See description under SEAFOOD.) Others have discovered America by now, but the Oyster Bar was one of the first here to offer a comprehensive list of quality California wines. The list still is among the best and prices are very fair. AE, CB, DC, MC, V.

# FOR DRINKS

***P. J. Clarke's,*** 915 Third Avenue, at 55th (759-1650). This quintessential Third Avenue bar is such an institution that a skyscraper was built around it, and an exact replica installed in Macy's new food cellar. Locals stay loyal long after they become account executives. Fight your way through the front-room crowd for table service in the white-tiled middle room (preferred) or the dim, checker-tableclothed back room. Open until 4 A.M., seven days a week. Entrées from $3.20 (L), $4.40 (D). No credit cards.

***Lion's Head, Ltd.,*** 59 Christopher Street (929-0670). You step down into the properly unimposing world of Greenwich Village writers, their neighbors and friends. Dust jackets from patrons' books are on a wall facing the bar. Beer and conversation are the staples here, though if you prowl awhile, you'll find some tables and a waitress ready to bring *escargots* or, more appropriately, a hamburger. Weekdays, dinner only; brunch and dinner weekends. Open seven days a week until 3 A.M. for food, 4 A.M. for drinks. Hamburgers for $2.25. AE, DC, V.

***Windows on the World (The Hors d'Oeuverie),*** 1 World Trade Center (938-1111). Lacking a dinner reservation, head for this smaller perch on the 107th floor. Cocktail hour verges on mealtime. There is a changing selection of international tidbits—of varying quality and fairly steep prices—to nibble on with drinks while enjoying the view. The sunsets are memorable. Music begins around 7:30 P.M. and continues until 1 A.M.; a small dance floor encourages full appreciation of the beat. Tea-dancing on Sundays from 4 to 6 P.M.

***Hotel Algonquin,*** 59 W. 44th Street (840-6800). The small Blue Bar is off to one side and the dining rooms are on the other, but the hub of activity is a lobby as comfortable and well-worn as tweeds. Once associated with the literary famous, it remains a good place for cocktails on the edge of the theater district. Late in the evening, it becomes a setting for informal buffet supper. Open until 3 A.M.; breakfast, 7:30 A.M. to 11:30 A.M. Sunday, no dinner. AE, CB, DC, MC, V.

***Bemelmans' Bar,*** Carlyle Hotel, Madison Avenue, at 76th Street, (744-1600). The walls are covered with magnificent murals by Ludwig Bemelmans, which makes this bar a work of art in itself, as well as the perfect place to celebrate a purchase from an East Side art gallery or from Parke-Bernet across the street. It's very classy and very quiet. If you linger until 9:30 or so, the live music begins. No food served. Open seven days a week. AE, CB, DC, MC, V.

## RESTAURANT WITH MUSIC

***Monsignore II,*** 61 E. 55th Street (355-2070). A swath of soft apricot velvet spiked with silver and blue is the scheme of things. Enlivened by a guitarist threading his way between tables, who will strum and sing your requests in Italian, English, French. The food is less international, more exclusively Italian and excellent. Carefully made, complex sauces on pasta—*penne all'arrabbiata* (a highly spiced tomato sauce) for example. Striped bass Livornese, *scaloppine de maiale pizzaiola,* mussels, impeccable vegetables, superb pastries. Saturday, dinner only. Closed Sunday. Complete lunch from $10.25. Dinner entrées from $10.75. AE, CB, DC, MC, V.

***West Boondock Lounge,*** 114 10th Avenue, at 17th (929-9645). (See description under SOUL.)

***Bradley's,*** 70 University Place (228-6440). The jazz sounds continue from 9:30 P.M. till 2:30 A.M., and fill the front bar (dark wood with a full-length mirror behind) and a back room. The music is invariably good and the customers present a scene in themselves. Beef, in either steak form or as hamburger, is the featured food attraction. Saturday and Sunday, dinner only. Open seven days a week. Hamburgers from $2.75 (L), $3.75 (D). AE.

## ROMANTIC

***Orsini's,*** 41 W. 56th Street (757-1698). You'll find red-velvet-covered walls and cozy loveseats in the dim recesses of the ground-floor dining room. (Upstairs all is golden and brightly tiled.) Now that the movable chic have found new kitchens to feed from, you are more likely to have your pick of alcove and table. The competently prepared food is gracefully delivered by proper professionals. *Spiedini, mozzarella in carrozza, crostini*—varieties of cheese melting over toast—are suitable first courses. *Fettuccine,* veal scaloppine, steak, fish. Dinner until 1 A.M. Closed Sunday. Complete lunch from $10.25; dinner entrées from $10.75. AE, CB, DC, MC, V.

## LATE-NIGHT SERVICE

***Russian Tea Room,*** 150 W. 57th Street (265-0947). (See description under RUSSIAN.)

***Maxwell's Plum,*** 1181 First Avenue, at 64th (628-2100). The quintessential Upper East Side singles party, created by showman Warner LeRoy. If you have a reservation or patience, there is something for everyone, including eminently decent dinners in the dining room, informal café food and a stand-up crush at the bar, although *New York Magazine* has reported an absence of liquor in tested Bloody Marys and fruit drinks. Sometimes the pace is too brisk and kitchen performance wavers. Meals are served until midnight, lighter fare in the Café until 1:30 A.M. Open seven days a week. Entrées start at $5.85, but run as high as $29.50 (L & D). AE, CB, DC, MC, V.

***Hotel Algonquin,*** 59 W. 44th Street (840-6800). (See description under FOR DRINKS.) After-theater buffet Monday through Saturday evenings, 9:30 P.M. to 12:30 A.M. Reservations necessary. Entrées from $6.75. AE, CB, DC, MC, V.

***Serendipity III,*** 225 East 60th Street (838-3531). After almost two decades, Serendipity (once the newest, most with-it boutique-cum-restaurant) is still with-it and with us. Imaginative omelets, sandwiches and desserts highlight the complex menu; items in the latter category (pecan pie, chocolate cake) are smothered with real whipped cream. Ice cream and coffee fantasies, assorted teas, indulgence for adults, treats for kids. Open until midnight, Sunday through Thursday; until 1 A.M., Friday; until 2 A.M., Saturday. Dessert items from $2. DC, MC, V.

***Ruskay's,*** 323 Columbus Avenue, between 75th and 76th (874-8391). The main idea is "less is more," and it works. Open 5 P.M. to 5 A.M. Monday through Friday and 24 hours on weekends, with a limited menu in a dim, narrow, Art Deco storefront complete with pressed-tin ceiling. Dinner is an $11, five-course affair, appetizer through dessert ($12 for steak, always available) and done with imagination, but it's not always successful. Morning, afternoon and late choices run to excellent omelets, salads, desserts. Breakfast (Continental or full-course) from 1 A.M. Music on the balcony from 7 P.M. to 11 P.M. Monday through Wednesday, 7 P.M. to 3 A.M. Thursday through Saturday, at brunch on Saturday and Sunday. Convenient before or after performances at Lincoln Center. Entrées from $4.50. No credit cards.

## SUNDAY BRUNCH

***Village Green,*** 531 Hudson Street (255-1650). This enchanting brick-walled place adorned with pewter, brass and greenery sustains the pretty-restaurant trend that rolled east from California. The restaurant also maintains a commendable kitchen. Dinner may falter, but brunch is a delight. Quiches, crêpes and egg dishes—Benedict, Sardou, *hussarde* and Chenier—are good Sunday starters in a part of town where the shops are open for browsing afterwards. Sunday brunch, noon to 3:30 P.M. Entrées from $6.50 (L), $9 (D). AE, MC, V.

***Market Dining Rooms and Bar,*** 1 World Trade Center, Main Concourse (938-1155). (See description under AMERICAN.) Whether you are a tourist planning to see the sights of lower Manhattan or a native New Yorker who has never seen fruit and produce selling at 1884 prices, the World Trade Center is a good choice on Sunday. In addition to the food stalls, the Sunday visitor is likely to find a jazz band and old-time games. Have brunch in the Market Dining Rooms (from noon to 4 P.M.), or lighter fare in the Bar Room or one of the specialty food stands in the Big Kitchen. Reservations necessary for the Market Dining Rooms. Entrées from $7 (L), $8 (D). Fixed-price brunch $11.75. AE, CB, DC, MC, V.

## SUNDAY-EVENING MEAL

***David K's,*** 1115 Third Avenue, at 65th (371-9090). (See description under CHINESE.)

***Market Dining Rooms and Bar,*** 1 World Trade Center, Main Concourse (938-1155). (See description under AMERICAN.)

***Coach House,*** 110 Waverly Place (777-0303). (See description under AMERICAN.)

## FOR FAMILIES WITH CHILDREN

***Metropolitan Museum of Art,*** Fifth Avenue, at 82nd (879-5500). The fountain restaurant is pleasant enough for lunch but one of the best buys for dinner (Tuesday evenings only). Good roast beef and other entrées served cafeteria-style and consumed at white-draped poolside tables. Full bar. Closed Monday. Entrées from $3.50 (L & D). No credit cards.

***Maxwell's Plum,*** 1181 First Avenue, at 64th (628-2100). (See description under LATE-NIGHT SERVICE.) Maxwell's stays open late, but it also opens early and the broad menu allows a family with financial resources to suit their individual tastes. For the kids, there are large, very good hamburgers, along with first-rate French fries and onion rings.

# MARKETS

## GIFT FOODS

***Les Trois Petits Cochons,*** 17 E. 13th Street (255-3844). A serious *charcuterie* with pâtés, *terrines,* sausages for princely *pique-niques.* Expensive but worth it. Closed Sunday. No credit cards.

***Murray's Sturgeon Shop,*** 2429 Broadway, between 89th and 90th (724-2650). Sublime sturgeon and smoked salmon, enbageled or not, can become midflight manna when stowed in the carry-on luggage. Murray's does it all the time for fussy travelers. Closed Monday. No credit cards.

***Dean & DeLuca,*** 121 Prince Street (254-7774). A winning combination of food shop and equipment store in deepest SoHo, it is every bit as interesting as the nearby art galleries. The cheese display and specially made pastries are marvelous, but there is lots more—fresh, canned, wrapped and unwrapped. The staff is pleasant, so is the place. Open seven days a week. No credit cards.

***Bloomingdale's,*** 59th Street and Lexington Avenue (223-7111, main number). Even Elizabeth II knew enough to head for "Bloomie's." "Delicacies" is the name of the basement market. Concentrate on breads, imported delicacies, chocolates, candies and clever packages. Open Monday and Thursday until 9 P.M. Closed Sunday. No credit cards.

***The Cellar,*** in Macy's, 34th Street and Broadway (971-6000). A full range of gourmet goodies in Macy's basement, along with a replica of P. J. Clarke's (see description under FOR DRINKS). AE.

***Zabar's,*** 2245 Broadway, between 80th and 81st (787-2000). The "nosher's" dream, an indoor bazaar hung with salamis and culinary gadgets, stacked with breads and cheeses, lined with barrels of coffee and sides of salmon, all in astonishing array. For serious shopping, avoid the weekends, when celebrities vie with the sturgeon for attention. Quality is invariably good, prices both reasonable and high. Open Friday until 10 P.M. and Saturday until midnight; until 7:30 P.M. Sunday through Thursday. AE, DC, MC, V.

## GIFT WINES

***Sherry-Lehmann, Inc.,*** 679 Madison Avenue between 61st and 62nd (838-7500). Esteemed, classy, interesting shop. There are some good bargains, but don't be surprised to discover you can pay for the name. Closed Sunday. No credit cards.

***Park Avenue Liquor Shop,*** 292 Madison Avenue, between 40th and 41st (685-2442). A good spot for old Sauternes, vintage Port and classic wines (some of them in outsized bottles). Closed Sunday. No credit cards.

***Morrell & Co.,*** 307 E. 53rd Street (688-9370). Specializes in rare and exclusive wines. Reliable. Closed Sunday. No credit cards.

***Astor Wines & Spirits,*** 12 Astor Place (674-7500). By far the cheapest prices in Manhattan. Good selection. Closed Sunday. No credit cards.

***Sixty-Seven Wine and Liquor Shop,*** 179 Columbus Avenue, at 68th (724-6767). An excellent wine shop with an emphasis on American, German and Bordeaux wines; they stock many hard-to-find American vineyards. Closed Sunday. No credit cards.

# SPECIAL EVENTS

***Ninth Avenue International Food Festival,*** Ninth Avenue from 37th to 57th streets. For dates and further information, call 581-7029. This enormous food fair, begun in 1974, is now attended by 25,000 people annually. Cars are banned on the one-mile expanse of Ninth Avenue from 11 A.M. to 7 P.M. one weekend each May. The 40 restaurants and 250 stores within this 20-block stretch offer some of the best ethnic food and produce in town. In addition, scores of outdoor stands offer tastes of many cuisines including Italian, Greek, Turkish, Caribbean, Korean, Filipino and Irish.

***Feast of San Gennaro,*** on Mulberry Street from Park Street to East Houston Street. For dates and further information, call 698-2064. The city's oldest and most popular festival is an 11-day eating bonanza in New York's Little Italy. The more-than-50-year-old festival starts sometime between September 13 and 23 (be sure to check the dates) and attracts an annual crowd of four million. Strings of lights illuminate the 200 food stands that line Mulberry Street, and the area's restaurants usually feature a special festival menu. You'll get mostly Mom's Italian home cooking—which will surpass your wildest (and most fattening) dreams—but a number of other ethnic cuisines are offered as well. Food vendors donate money to the Church of the Most Precious Blood, so this is a charitable, not commercial, venture. Fun begins at 9 A.M. daily and goes until midnight on weekdays, until 2 A.M. weekends.

# Philadelphia

In the past decade Philadelphia has changed from a culinary caterpillar into a butterfly. The old town that used to lead the nation as a butt of bad jokes has emerged from its cocoon, and today may be the most interesting, as well as one of the best, of our restaurant cities.

A spectacular example of how the city has changed was the first Philadelphia Restaurant Festival, held on a Sunday afternoon in October 1978. Despite unseasonably chilly weather, some 500,000 hungry citizens flooded the broad, befountained Benjamin Franklin Parkway to sample the wares of more than 50 restaurants, served at booths and impromptu sidewalk bistros.

More than 300 new restaurants have opened in downtown Philadelphia since 1970. All but perhaps two dozen are still in operation. This would be an amazing success rate even without a shortage of first-class hotel rooms that is only now being alleviated with the opening of the swank Fairmont on Broad Street and the construction of two other luxury hotels, the Rittenhouse and Franklin Plaza, elsewhere in the central business district.

The menus range from Alsatian and Basque to Burmese, in addition to the more familiar classic French, Chinese and Italian. But much of Philadelphia's restaurant vitality lies in the dozens of small, storefront restaurants (several of them without liquor licenses) operated by young, imaginative people who have created "Philadelphia cuisine," a homogeneity of French, Middle Eastern and Oriental styles and dishes.

All this is part of a general awakening of the nation's first capital. Twenty years of massive, ongoing redevelopment has turned a dowdy, dusty city into a lively and dramatic mixture of old and new.

Regal office and apartment towers have risen above sidewalks that bustle in a fashion unknown in this city since Prohibition. In the Olde City, quaint cobbled streets ramble through refurbished Colonial-era neighborhoods and past historic shrines (Independence Hall, the Betsy Ross House, etc.). New Market, a glass palace of restaurants and shops overlooking the Delaware River, and **The Gallery,** which features about 20 different ethnic fast-food outlets in a dramatic setting, have brought fun and commerce to areas that used to be little more than slums.

It is by no means a city without blight. Urban decay grips vast sections of north and west Philadelphia. But the process has been reversed in many areas, and the midcity streets may be the safest of any metropolis in the land.

If Philadelphia's "Restaurant Renaissance" had an instigator, it was Peter von Starck. In the late 1960's, when most Philadelphians who had the money to dine elegantly did so in private clubs or at home where they had domestic cooks, von Starck opened a restaurant the likes of which had never been seen in the city: an elegant, highly expensive, classic French dining room called **La Panetière.** It was an almost instant success and can be credited with providing the inspiration for the following waves of quality-oriented restaurateurs.

Much of the credit was due to chef Georges Perrier. When La Panetière moved to larger and even more elite quarters, Perrier kept the old location and renamed it **Le Bec-Fin.** For the past several years Le Bec-Fin has been acclaimed as the best restaurant in Philadelphia and one of the best in North America. Over the years von Starck and Perrier have imported and "graduated" European-trained chefs and dining-room professionals who today own or operate the majority of the city's other good French restaurants.

For generations the visitor's choice of what and where to eat was almost no choice at all: the two landmark seafood houses, **Bookbinder's Seafood House** and Old Original Bookbinder's, a few steak and oyster places, and the hotel dining room. Today the choice can be bewildering. The French and "Philly" restaurants have been augmented by a blossoming crop of fine Italian dining rooms and a veritable United Nations of authentic ethnic places.

There is one lingering problem. While the "blue laws" that once banned everything from drinking to night baseball are long gone,

Philadelphia remains in the grip of the Pennsylvania state-store liquor distribution system, the biggest, most bureaucratic and probably most slothful operation of its kind in the free world. Building a good wine cellar costs time, paperwork and patience, as well as money, and while the best places have made these investments, the average wine list is comparatively short and basic. There are no good liquor stores.

Gourmet food shops, however, abound in the downtown area. There is also the **Italian Market** on S. 9th Street, two solid blocks of open-air produce stands and specialty shops for cheeses, meats and fish. This is an authentic re-creation of a Neapolitan shopping area and is as entertaining a place to shop as you are likely to find.

The Italian Market is also home of the cheese-steak sandwich—chipped beef, molten cheese and a variety of pepper, onion and sauce toppings served on a long Italian roll—which is regarded by the natives as the *pièce de résistance* of street foods. Other sidewalk specialties are water ices made of shaved ice and fruit syrups, and the soft pretzel (try one with mustard). In warm weather these delicacies are flogged by vendors all over the city.

Tipping and dress policies are the same as in New York, Washington and other Middle Atlantic cities. Women can be comfortable in slacks or dresses at most places, and while few places demand it, a coat and tie is the norm. One 15 percent tip is sufficient for all services.

Prices are as varied as the restaurants. Dinner at one of the top French restaurants can cost $50 or more per person. At the same time, a light meal can be had in handsome surroundings at **Barry's** disco-restaurant for less than $4. Par for a middle-range restaurant is $9 to $14 for dinner, sans drinks or tip.

# Restaurants and Food Sources

(Area code: 215)

## BIG DEAL

### WORTH IT

***Le Bec-Fin,*** 1312 Spruce Street (732-3000). Tiny and almost precious in décor with its rose-ivory color scheme and abundant flora, it has earned and retains its reputation as a truly great restaurant. The service is silky, the classic French cuisine as good as is to be found in this country. The clientele is urbane, serious about food and necessarily well-heeled. The price of a six-course dinner is $44 at this writing, and does not include service or wine. Unless the chef has other suggestions, try the *quenelles de brochet* as an early course. Among the entrées, *canard* is a specialty and is served in various ways—all glorious—on various nights. If there is a weakness here it is in the desserts, but you can count on the Grand Marnier soufflé. Reservations are a must and should be made at least a week in advance, especially for a Friday or Saturday. Dinner only. There are two seatings, at 6:30 and 9 P.M. Closed Sunday. Takes lots of money; credit cards are not accepted.

***Déjà-Vu,*** 1609 Pine Street (546-1190). It is small, French and nationally acclaimed, but there the similarity to Le Bec-Fin ends. The décor is baroque Russo-Franco, with heavy silk drapes, a hand-painted picture ceiling, Oriental carpets and old, gilt-framed oils on the dark-paneled and brickwork walls. It is almost too exquisite. The food is *cuisine Montez,* sometimes Asian-influenced variations on the French culinary theme devised by the inventive owner-chef Sal Montezinos. Purified water and organic produce are used in all cooking. Game is often featured and Indonesian-style sweet curries are unabashedly added to veal, chicken and beef dishes. At last report the fixed price for dinner was $30, not counting the temptations of the city's most extraordinary, most expensive wine cellar. *Le délice de foie d'oie* is a recommended appetizer and *les noisettes de chevreuil* with lingonberries is one of the favored main courses. Advance reservations are advised. Dinner only. Seating 6 to 9:30 P.M. Closed Sunday and Monday. AE, CB, DC, MC, V.

## NOT WORTH IT

***Elan,*** the Warwick Hotel, 17th and Locust Streets (546-8800). Poses as a club and charges nonmembers $10 admission to a very sleek, pretentious restaurant-lounge-disco complex. The food is good but expensive ($15 to $22 per person), and the drinks are mostly in the $3 range. The general effect is that of a gourmet singles bar. Hotel guests do not pay the entry fee. Open seven days a week. AE, MC, V.

# INTERNATIONAL

## AMERICAN

***Riverfront Restaurant,*** Delaware Avenue at Poplar Street (925-7000). Elsewhere in this sprawling building one finds a dinner theater and dance bar, but despite such frivolity, the Main Deck dining room is a serious effort at quality food and service. The riverside wall is mostly glass, looking out on a summertime promenade patio and the Delaware itself, where ships great and small drift past in a steady, if sporadic procession to remind you that Philadelphia is, after all, the world's largest inland port. Aside from excellent American and Continental menus, there is a daily luncheon buffet and nightly specials that have included amazingly good green turtle steak and other expertly prepared exotica. Good bar. Fairly good wine list. Lots of free parking, but taxi service can be slow. Chaîne des Rotisseurs. Sunday, dinner only. Closed Monday. Entrées from $3.50 (L), $6.50 (D). Complete "early gourmet" dinner $9.95 (5:45 to 6:30 P.M. Tuesday through Saturday). AE, DC, MC, V.

***Mitchell's,*** 207 S. Juniper Street (735-1299). Reliable quality in steaks, chops, lobster and other familiars in a cathedral-ceilinged, somewhat chapel-like dining room. Excellent liver and onions. Mitchell's has a reputation for never doing anything badly, the result of its conservative menu and long experience. Good after-theater place. Closed Sunday. Entrées from $3.50 (L), $6.50 (D). AE, CB, DC, MC, V.

## AUSTRIAN

***Ripplemyer's Café Vienna,*** 1300 Pine Street (546-0777). A lot less formal than most Viennese dining rooms, this cozy little café is no café at all in as much as it has no liquor license. It does, however, have the city's best schnitzels as well as several Greek specialties. Try the curried chicken salad among the appetizers or the *rahmschnitzel* among the main courses. Closed Monday. Entrées from $3 (L), $4.50 (D). No credit cards.

## CHINESE

***The Mandalay Inn,*** 214 N. 10th Street (627-3834). In the heart of Chinatown, this little restaurant offers Burmese as well as Cantonese and Mandarin cooking. Some of the Burmese dishes, notably the house soup, are quite hot and the food is generally spicier than other Cantonese-style places, No liquor. Open seven days a week. Entrées from $3.50 (L), $4 (D). No credit cards.

***Imperial Inn,*** 941 Race Street (925-2485). Is a fair-sized, handsomely done restaurant with a lengthy menu of Szechuan, Cantonese and Mandarin dishes. Shrimp in all forms is recommended. One of the few Chinatown restaurants with a liquor license. Open seven days a week. Entrées from $3.50 (L), $4.50 (D). AE.

***Mayflower Restaurant,*** 1010 Cherry Street (923-4202). Big, ornate and one of the best Cantonese kitchens in town. The Imperial Chinese banquet is a specialty, but is served only to groups of four or more with at least 24 hours' notice. Also has a bar. Saturday and Sunday, dinner only. Open seven days a week. Entrées from $3.25 (L), $4 (D). AE, DC, V.

## CONTINENTAL

***Charles',*** 1523 Walnut Street (567-5484). Redecoration has lightened the almost museumlike atmosphere that detracted from this solid, consistent downtown restaurant. Specialties such as Lobster Jamaican and lamb in mustard sauce are available at affordable prices (entrées from about $7). The carrot blinis are a favorite fixture for lunch or as dinner appetizers. Saturday, dinner only. Closed Sunday. Entrées from $4 (L), $7 (D).

***Parson's Table,*** 26 Front Street (925-4447). One of Society Hill's first good restaurants, it is still among the best. The menu ranges from Spanish paella and San Franciscan cioppino to a very good rack of lamb. Good bar. Saturday, dinner only. Sunday, brunch only. Closed Monday. Entrées from $3.75 (L), $7 (D). Sunday brunch prices from $4.50. AE, DC, V.

# FRENCH

***Maureen,*** 11 S. 21st Street (567-9895). The chef, Steve Horn, is American, and so is his wife Maureen, who is the manager. The food is definitely French, though, and even if success has bred somewhat higher prices, it is one of the most delicious values in town. Puff pastry is an art form here, and some of the stuffed fish dishes served in this flaky crust are real ambrosia. Or try the veal Maureen, or the duck with fresh strawberries. Dinner only. Closed Sunday and Monday. Entrées from $9. AE, MC, V.

***La Truffe,*** 10 S. Front Street (627-8630). Charming, handsomely appointed surroundings, good service and rather straightforward French cuisine. Specialties include *homard thermidore, canard au poivre vert* and lamb. Fairly expensive. Saturday, dinner only. Closed Sunday and Monday. Entrées from $5 (L), $10 (D). AE, DC, MC, V.

***La Panetière,*** 1602 Locust Street (546-5452). The Maxim's of Philadelphia. Very elegant, very social and very expensive. The most opulent luncheon place in the city, and the ritziest bar. This was the birthplace of *haute cuisine* here, and if it has been outstripped by some of its progeny, it is still a restaurant to be reckoned with. The old town house has been done up in regal, impeccable taste. Lamb, lobster and pheasant are prevalent. Good wine list. Saturday, dinner only. Closed Sunday. Entrées from $7 (L), $12 (D). AE, DC.

# GREEK/LEBANESE

***The Middle East,*** 126 Chestnut Street (922-1003). Full of politicians, tourists, Oriental artifacts and belly dancers. A good place to get into the Zorba spirit. Better-than-average Lebanese food, *kibbe, hummus,* and shish kebab. Fair wine list and bar. Sunday, dinner only. Open seven days a week into the wee hours. Entrées from $3 (L), $6 (D). AE, CB, DC, MC, V.

***Onassis,*** 1735 Sansom Street (568-6960). This plaster grotto full of the young, the hungry and fun-loving was once the cheapest restaurant in town. You can still eat here for less than $3, but most prices are in the $4.50 to $7 range. The *psaristo ladoharto* and the *taramasalata* are specialties. Sunday, dinner only. Open seven days a week, until 2 A.M. AE, CB, DC, MC, V.

## INDIAN

***Siva's,*** 34 S. Front Street (925-2700). Behind a beaten brass door lies one of the finest classic Indian restaurants this side of New Delhi, which is where the chefs come from. None of those rough Southern Indian curries here. The *tandoori* oven produces delicious chicken, lamb and even beef dishes, along with the traditional plain and filled breads—*naan, poori* and *paratha.* Decent bar. Sunday, dinner only. Closed Monday. Entrées from $4 (L), $7.50 (D). AE, CB, DC, MC, V.

## IRISH

***Downey's,*** 526 S. Front Street (629-0526). The bar used to be the counter of a Dublin bank, and it's almost always crowded. Good steaks, chops, stews, corned beef and cabbage. Open seven days a week. Sunday brunch. Entrées from $4 (L), $6.50 (D), Sunday brunch from $4. AE, CB, DC, MC, V.

## ITALIAN

***Cous' Little Italy,*** 901 S. 11th Street (627-9753). Cous (a/k/a Vince Pilla) is the Caesar of Italian cooking in Philadelphia, and this large, white, archwayed restaurant is a fitting setting for him. He names his culinary creations after favorite little girls, politicians and racketeers, and everything from the antipasti to the ziti asparagus is worth a taste. Wonderful shrimp dishes, first-class veal (try the veal *bella buco*). Dinner only. Open seven days a week. Entrées from $5. No credit cards.

***Il Gallo Nero,*** 254 S. 15th Street (546-8065). Excellent, plentiful Northern Italian cuisine in a bright, attractive setting. The best Italian wine list in town. The *osso buco* is wonderful. So is the *cannelloni.* Fine desserts. Closed Sunday. Entrées from $3 (L), $6 (D). AE, DC, MC, V.

## JAPANESE

***Kanpai,*** in New Market mall, off Head House Square (925-1532). One of those *teppanyaki* where the chef does knife tricks at the table and doles out steak, shrimp and chicken like a Vegas croupier. This one is in an all-glass shopping and restaurant complex that overlooks the Delaware River. Good bar. Saturday and Sunday, dinner only. Open seven days a week. Entrées from $3.50 (L), $7 (D). AE, DC, MC, V.

***Chiyo,*** 8136 Germantown Avenue, Chestnut Hill (247-8188). A delicate blossom of a restaurant in one of Philadelphia's most interesting old shopping areas. Classic tempura and *teriyaki* dishes. No liquor license, but they will warm your sake or chill your wine, if you bring it. Dinner only. Closed Monday and Tuesday. Entrées from $6. No credit cards.

## MEXICAN

***Los Amigos,*** 50 S. 2nd Street (922-7061). The only Mexican restaurant in town, and not a bad representative. Authentic, if basic, Mexican cooking, good margaritas and Mexican music on weekends. Closed Sunday. Entrées from $4.50 (L & D). AE, CB, DC, MC, V.

## SPANISH

***Mesón Don Quijote,*** 110 Chestnut Street (925-1889). A nicely turned out Castillian bistro that offers a pretty fair *zarzuella de mariscos* and a not-so-authentic paella. There is flamenco music and dancing. Good wine list. Dinner only. Closed Monday. Entrées from $7.50. AE, CB, DC, MC, V.

***Pyrenees,*** 627 S. 2nd Street (925-9117). This interesting place has a dramatic staircase that leads into a two-level cellar and requires a bit of mountaineering to negotiate. The paella is good, and so are many of the other Basque and coastal Spanish dishes. Nifty little bar. Dinner only. Closed Monday. Entrées from $7. No credit cards.

## THAI

***The Thai Restaurant,*** 23rd and Sansom Street (567-2542). Offers deep-fried pompano in a wickedly hot sauce, soft-shell crabs and lots of the spices of Southeast Asia. Not for everyone, but quite interesting. No liquor, but you can take your own. The recommended beverage is beer. Saturday and Sunday, dinner only. Open seven days a week. Entrées from $2 (L), $5 (D). AE, DC, MC, V.

# SPECIALTY COOKING

## DELI

***Famous Delicatessen,*** 700 S. 4th Street (922-3274). Great Jewish soul food. Roast beef, corned beef, knishes, *et al.* Open 7 A.M. to

6 P.M., Monday through Saturday; 7 A.M. to 3 P.M. Sunday. Sandwiches from $1.75. No credit cards.

## HAMBURGER

***H. A. Winston's,*** Front and Chestnut streets (928-0660), and 1500 Locust Street (546-7232). Offers more than a dozen varieties of freshly-ground gourmet burgers (with caviar and sour cream, for instance) in various sizes. Both places have bars. Open seven days a week. Burgers from $2.50 (L & D). AE, DC, MC, V.

## HOT DOG

***Levis,*** 507 South 6th Street (627-2354). A Philadelphia tradition. Sandwiches are pretty good, too. Open seven days a week. Hot dogs still 60 cents at last report. No credit cards.

## PHILADELPHIA COOKING

***Frog,*** 264 S. 16th Street (735-8882). This is the most popular, and one of the best of the "New Philadelphia" restaurants. The cuisine is basically French with Middle- and Far-Eastern accents. Excellent wine list. Veal and poultry dishes abound, as do fruit soups and exotic salads. The décor is lush with greenery. Crowded. Reservations usually required. Saturday, dinner only. Closed Sunday. Entrées from $5 (L), $8 (D). AE, DC, MC, V.

***Black Banana,*** 201 S. 3rd Street (925-4433). Off the beaten path, but worth the excursion if you like beautifully prepared, exotic food cooked with a French flair. The décor is Art Deco, and there is a disco upstairs. Prompt radio taxi service is promised. Sweetbreads in port sauce is one of the best first courses to be found in the city. Dinner only. Open seven days a week, until 2 A.M. for late supper Monday through Saturday. Entrées from $8.50. AE, DC, MC, V.

## SALAD BAR

***Wildflowers,*** 514 S. 5th Street (923-6708). The salad bar is only one of the attractions of this large and lovely "new wave" restaurant, but it is a main one. For $2.45 with dinner or $5.95 without other order, you get your fill of sundry cheeses, beans, greens, anchovies, pimientos, tomatoes and other fresh makin's. The rest of the fare here is described as "country French," but the spices and cooking styles of several other lands, especially Asian, have been included. Very good bar. Good wine list. Chaîne des Rotisseurs. Dinner only. Sunday, brunch only. Open seven days a week. Entrées from $6.50, fixed-price brunch $8.50. AE, MC, V.

## SEAFOOD

***Bookbinder's Seafood House,*** 215 S. 15th Street (545-1137). A big, rambling landmark that serves top-quality oysters, clams, lobster and other fruits of the sea. Fine steaks, too. Preferred over Old Original Bookbinder's, 2nd and Walnut streets (925-7027) because of its less touristy, friendlier atmosphere and service. Sunday, dinner only. Open seven days a week. Entrées from $4 (L), $7.50 (D), but most meals cost considerably more. AE, CB, DC, MC, V.

## STEAK

***Maxwell's Prime,*** 623 South Street (923-6363). One of the few places anywhere that still serve a full 16-ounce New York cut of properly aged, well-trimmed prime beef cooked the way you want it. The rest of the meal is good too. But it's expensive. Most cuts are about $16. Good bar and adequate wine list. Also features a few lamb and seafood selections. Dinner only. Open seven days a week. AE, DC, MC, V.

# FOR INDIVIDUAL NEEDS

## IF YOU HAVE TIME FOR ONLY ONE MEAL

***The Garden,*** 1617 Spruce Street (546-4455). This lovely restaurant could also be listed in the Big Deal, French or Philadelphia Cooking categories, since it offers some of the best of each. Housed in a fine old brownstone that used to be the Philadelphia Musical Academy, it offers formality in the main dining room, a cozy club atmosphere in the front oyster bar, and in warm weather, the delights of dining in the backyard garden. The cooking is mostly French, but there are some "Philly" innovations. Try one of the unusual and everchanging soups, oysters (raw or delicately cooked in several ways), poached sea bass or one of the classic lamb or beef dishes. The menu changes frequently. Closed Sunday. Late after-theater supper Saturday. Entrées from $4.50 (L), $7 (D). AE, MC, V.

## BEST HOTEL MEAL

***Versailles,*** in the Fairmont, Broad and Walnut Streets (893-1776). Recently open. Millions of dollars have been spent in completely renovating this grand old hotel. It seems safe to say that this French-style "gourmet room" will offer the best hotel food and service in town. Dinner only. Open seven days a week. Entrées from $7.50. AE, CB, DC, MC, V.

***The Barclay,*** 18th Street on Rittenhouse Square (545-0300). The main dining room of this medium-sized, decorous and extremely elegant hotel is the epitome of "Olde Philadelphia" dining. The menu is Continental, the service generally good. The food is ample and well prepared, if not always exciting. Open seven days a week. Entrées from $4 (L), $7 (D). AE, CB, DC, MC, V.

## RESTAURANT NEAR AIRPORT

***The New Leaf,*** in the Sheraton Airport Hotel across from the International Air Terminal (365-4150). Offers truly first-class service and fare. The menu is French-Continental, the décor clubby and the service designed to massage the ego. There is a free panatella for him, a rose for her, and personalized matchbooks for those who make reservations a day ahead. Dinner only. Closed Sunday. Entrées from $8. AE, CB, DC, MC, V.

## BUSINESS LUNCH

***The Garden,*** 1617 Spruce Street (546-4455). (See description under IF YOU HAVE TIME FOR ONLY ONE MEAL.)

## FAST, GOOD FOOD/LUNCH, DINNER

***Barry's,*** 1918 Chestnut Street (561-3636). Sleek, two-story drinking, dining and late-hour dancing establishment. There is comparative quiet—along with plump chicken breasts beneath various "gourmet" toppings (mushroom, onion, Madeira wine sauce) and probably the best spareribs in the city. Also omelets and burgers. Open until 2 A.M. Closed Sunday. Entrées from $3.25 (L & D). AE, DC, MC, V.

## BEST WINE LIST

***Déjà-Vu,*** 1609 Pine Street (546-1190). (See description under BIG DEAL/WORTH IT.)

***Frog,*** 264 S. 16th Street (735-8882). (See description under PHILADELPHIA COOKING.)

## FOR DRINKS

***Happy Rooster,*** 118 S. 16th Street (563-1481). Listed here because it is too tiny (maybe 24 seats) and too popular as a restaurant to stand much additional food trade. Much of the crowding is because wine racks have encroached from behind the bar all over the little room (the list is exceptional). It is easily the best-stocked bar in the city. The bar Scotch is single malt (one of nearly 40 brands carried). There are all sorts of imported vodkas, and a veritable museum of old cognacs and Armagnacs, some selling for $15 and more per generous snort. The food is Hungarian-Continental and fairly expensive. The bar, booths and fittings are solid rosewood, brass and wrought iron. Closed Sunday. Sandwiches from $3, dinner entrées from $6. AE, DC, V.

## RESTAURANT WITH MUSIC

***Le Bistro,*** 757 S. Front Street (389-3855). A cute, cozy restaurant has added a large annex that is more like a greenhouse overlooking the Delaware River. The food is "Philly-French" and very good. The music is big-league jazz and contemporary. Large, good bar. Dinner only. Late supper until 1 A.M. Tuesday through Saturday. Sunday brunch. Closed Monday. Entrées from $7, Sunday brunch from $4.25, late supper from $3.50. AE, MC, V.

## ROMANTIC

***Morgan's,*** 135 S. 24th Street (567-6066). Down by the Schuykill (skoo-kill) riverside, almost lost among warehouses and other grim buildings, this cozy spot looks like an English pub, but is really *nouvelle* French. The menu is exotic, freewheeling and changes every six weeks. High-backed booths add to the privacy. If you don't want to be found, they'll need bloodhounds to track you here. And it's really good. Saturday, dinner only. Late supper 10:30 P.M. to 1 A.M. Tuesday through Friday. Closed Sunday. Entrées from $4 (L), $7.50 (D). AE, DC, MC, V.

## LATE-NIGHT SERVICE

***Frankie Bradley's,*** 1320 Chancellor Street (545-4350). Favorite after-theater restaurant for performers as well as show patrons. Good steak and lobsters featured in a long and varied menu. Fair wine list and busy, attractive bar. Open seven days a week, 11:30 A.M. to 2 A.M. Entrées from $3.75 (L), $6.50 (D). AE, CB, DC, MC, V.

***Barry's,*** 1918 Chestnut Street (561-3636). (See description under FAST, GOOD FOOD/LUNCH, DINNER.)

## SUNDAY BRUNCH

***Le Bistro,*** 757 S. Front Street (389-3855). (See description under RESTAURANT WITH MUSIC.) Brunch with music, too.

***Top of Centre Square,*** 41st floor, First Pennsylvania Tower, 15th and Market Streets (569-9494). Provides an unmatched view of William Penn, standing atop City Hall, and the north and western city vistas. Big, quite handsome and comfortable. The food is conventional, but wholesome and generally good. Good bar, which opens at 1 P.M. Sunday. Sunday, brunch and dinner only. Open seven days a week. Entrées from $3.50 (L), $6 (D), Sunday brunch from $2.50. AE, DC, MC, V.

## SUNDAY-EVENING MEAL

***Frankie Bradley's,*** 1320 Chancellor Street (545-4350). (See description under LATE-NIGHT SERVICE.)

## FOR FAMILIES WITH CHILDREN

***The Gallery,*** in Market Street East, 9th and Market Streets. This is a subterranean United Nations of fast-food and sit-down restaurants. There are a score of stands that specialize in foods from Japanese chicken *yakitori* to French crêpes and Mexican tortillas, along with a good oyster and seafood bar and The Newsstand, a restaurant-bar with good sandwiches and light dishes. Surrounding all this is the dramatic architecture of a huge urban shopping mall. All restaurants are open seven days a week.

## HIGH TEA

***The Crystal Room,*** 9th floor at John Wanamaker's, 13th and Market Streets (422-2813). The closest thing this city has to the lobby of the Peninsula Hotel in Hong Kong or the Kranzler in Berlin. Monster, sparkling chandeliers, prim waitresses, matrons with furs and crocodile handbags, sandwiches and all sorts of mega-calorie desserts *mit schlag* and apéritifs. Closed Sunday. Lunch (11 A.M. to 2:30 P.M.) and tea (2:30 to 3:30 P.M.) served Monday through Saturday. Dinner (4:30 to 7:30 P.M.) served on Wednesday only. Entrées from $2.50 (L). AE, MC, V.

## COUNTRY INN

***Coventry Forge Inn,*** Coventryville, 15 miles west of Valley Forge Park on Route 23 (1-469-6222). Run by a family named Callahan—so naturally it's Provincial French. The *truite au bleu,* steak *au* *poivre* and various game dishes, plus a fine wine cellar make it worth the hour's drive from downtown. Lovely rolling countryside and fine service add to the pleasure. Overnight accommodations. Reservations a must. Dinner only. Closed Sunday, May through October; closed Monday and Sunday the rest of the year. Entrées from $8.50, weekdays; Saturday fixed-price dinner $21. No credit cards.

***The Inn at Philips Mill,*** N. River Road, New Hope (1-862-9919). Actually a rebuilt stone barn, vintage 1750 or thereabouts. The food is French and good. There is a big working fireplace and summer dining on the terrace. This is one of the best spots in a very rustic, arty area. No liquor license, but you can take your own, and set-ups, chilling, etc. will be taken care of. Five guest rooms and continental breakfast is served to overnight guests. Dinner only. Closed Tuesday. No credit cards.

***Joe's,*** 7th and Laurel Streets, Reading (1-373-6794). The real reason to buy the Reading Railroad in a Monopoly game is to have a free pass to visit Joe's. The town has seen better days, but Joe's is alive and charming. Jack Czarnecki has taken over from his father, Joe (in the kitchen); and his wife, Heidi, runs the dining room and makes the pastries. This is a restaurant with a most unusual theme—mushrooms. Joe Czarnecki began collecting them in nearby fields and forests years ago and the hunt continues. They turn up on the menu inside appetizer pastries, pickled in salad, in a wonderful wild-mushroom soup and as garniture or stuffing for fowl, meat or game. Tables are well spaced, service from carts is by amiable waitresses. Reservations suggested. Dinner only (until 9 P.M.). Closed Sunday and Monday. Entrées from $11.50. AE, DC, MC, V.

# IN THE SUBURBS

## DOYLESTOWN

***Conti's Cross Keys Inn,*** Routes 611 and 313 (1-348-3539). A Bucks County landmark, this big, handsome restaurant offers a Continental menu that touches all bases from Italian to Parisian. The quality and service are amazingly good for a place of this size. Good wines, bar drinks. Chaîne des Rotisseurs. Saturday, dinner only. Closed Sunday. Entrées from $3.50 (L), $7 (D). AE, DC, MC, V.

## GLENSIDE

***La Petite Ferme,*** 245 S. Easton Road (576-5117). Small and cozy, with a fireplace room and a French-Continental menu that features topnotch lamb and duck, plus seafood and veal, pork and beef. No liquor, but set-ups and service are provided. Saturday, dinner only. Closed Sunday. Dinner seatings at 6 P.M. and 8:30 P.M. Friday and Saturday. Entrées from $3.50 (L), $7.50 (D). No credit cards.

## MAIN LINE

***Helen Sigel Wilson's l'Auberge,*** Spread Eagle Village, Strafford (687-2840). A modern rendition of a French country inn. The décor is charming, the food strongest on quiches, soufflés and mousses. Good wine list and bar. Closed Sunday and Monday. Entrées from $3.50 (L), $7.75 (D). AE, DC.

## NORRISTOWN AREA

***Blue Bell Inn,*** Skippack and Penlyn Pikes, Blue Bell (646-2010). There are plenty of historic inns in suburban Philadelphia. The Blue Bell (built in 1743) is one of the oldest and best. Excellent steaks, seafood and Continental-American dishes. Good bar, wine list. Big and comfortable. Closed Sunday and Monday. Entrées from $3.50 (L), $7 (D). AE.

***Jefferson House,*** 2519 DeKalb Pike (Route 202), Norristown (275-3407). This is a large old mansion, elegantly furnished and smoothly run. The menu is Continental-Italian, offering all sorts of well-prepared, well-presented beef, veal, seafood and pastas. Fine bar. Saturday and Sunday, dinner only. Open seven days a week. Entrées from $3.50 (L), $6 (D). AE, DC, MC, V.

## VALLEY FORGE

***The Sting,*** Route 363, King of Prussia (265-2550). Excellent steaks and a singing dining-room staff. Lively bar. Saturday, dinner only. Closed Sunday. Entrées from $3 (L), $7.50 (D). No credit cards.

# MARKETS

***The Italian Market*** district, in the area surrounding 9th and Katherine. (See INTRODUCTION.)

# Phoenix

The hungry gourmet will find slim pickin's in Phoenix. But the hungry traveler—along with newcomers, tourists and retirees—will find many eating treats. Within the last five years, restaurants have sprung up everywhere, and dining out has become a kind of sport in Phoenix. The style is usually very casual and the emphasis is on Mexican and Western foods.

A first-time visitor should not pass up a chance to taste "Mexican" food. Phoenicians use the word loosely and usually mean Arizona-Mexican food. The most popular Arizona invention is a chimichanga (pronounced chee-mee-CHAHNG-ah). It is a flour tortilla filled with a meat or bean mixture and deep-fried. A chimichanga is usually served on a bed of shredded lettuce and topped with sour cream or guacamole. Some restaurants serve chimichangas with a whipped cream cheese mixture and others serve them with a red chile sauce.

A favorite appetizer is a "Mexican Pizza," called a cheese crisp. This is a large flour tortilla covered with cheese, usually Cheddar or Monterey Jack, and broiled until the cheese is melted. Additional toppings include chopped green onion, diced tomatoes, strips of red and green chiles or chorizo sausage. The fare at most Mexican restaurants is bountiful and even with current inflation, $6 will cover an appetizer, main course and perhaps a margarita.

Visitors who want a great Mexican meal should try **Garcia's.** There is usually a waiting line at both the Scottsdale and Phoenix locations and no reservations are accepted. Garcia's is known for its margaritas. Drinking one is a good idea while you wait to be seated; two undoubtedly will affect your appetite.

Phoenicians who are real Mexican-food buffs prefer places such as Rosita's or The Matador. Atmosphere is lacking, an ability to speak Spanish is helpful, and the food is very typical of the Sonora region of Mexico.

Downtown Phoenix is undergoing a revitalization program. The Civic Plaza, Symphony Hall and two new hotels—the Hyatt Regency and the Adams—make up the core of the area. There are few shops, and tourists are advised not to venture on foot beyond the confines of the immediate hotel area at night. The **Compass** at the Hyatt (Arizona's only revolving restaurant) and the Golden Eagle in the Valley National Bank Building provide interesting views of the city. On a clear day, of which there are many, visibility is often sixty to seventy miles. The food at both places is good, but rather expensive by Phoenix standards. The Compass is a nice choice for a nightcap. The Sandpainter in the Adams has Continental cuisine of consistently high quality.

A Phoenix institution is **Monti's La Casa Vieja.** Built in 1871, it was originally the southern station for Hayden's Ferry across the Salt River. The river only rarely sees water these days, but the restaurant is a mecca for history buffs.

The Arizona Biltmore has a reputation for fine chefs and excellent Continental cuisine as well as being an outstanding luxury resort. Its up and coming competition is the Registry Resort in Scottsdale, where the **La Champagne** restaurant has drawn rave reviews. Not worth it however is the Registry's Phoenician Room. It draws name entertainment, but the cover charge is between $10 to $15, depending on the performer, plus a very expensive and not terribly good dinner menu. Seating is very crowded and the service lacks the flair and elegance of La Champagne.

Excellent fish or seafood restaurants have been practically nonexistent, but a new place, the Hungry Tiger, at the Lakes in Tempe, has been offering a good selection of fresh fish and seafood flown in from the West Coast. The restaurant is part of a California chain by the same name. The setting at the Lakes is charming and romantic.

The best Cantonese food is found at the **China Doll;** for Mandarin specialties, try the Golden Phoenix. Despite its outstanding food, most Phoenicians would not recommend Riazzi's for Italian food because it is a hole-in-the-wall place that natives think only *they* can appreciate. **Avanti** is more elegant, and more expensive.

Dining customs are more informal in Phoenix than in other cities. Restaurants requiring sports jackets are few. Leisure suits and sports shirts without ties are normal attire for men. Pants suits or casual dresses are appropriate at most places for women, although there is a trend to dress-up at some places, especially at those with adjoining disco dance floors.

While the climate may seem extremely warm, restaurants are often cold. Take a sweater or light wrap for protection against excessive air conditioning.

A 15-percent gratuity is standard, and there is a 5-percent tax on restaurant meals. Popular restaurants are particularly crowded during the height of the tourist season—January to March. Dining after midnight is limited to coffee shops and a few after-hours taverns.

Phoenix has no farmers' market area, but a good selection of wines, cheese and other foods is available at the **Duck and Decanter** on Camelback Road. Niccoli's Italian Grocery, the Oriental Food Center and Nakatsu Farms provide some interesting ethnic shopping. Arizona-grown citrus is available at numerous roadside markets, especially along Baseline Road from December to April. Eastern visitors will find Phoenix supermarkets larger and newer than those at home. They often contain separate deli and bakery sections, making them good places to pick up competitively priced items for snacks and picnics.

When natives talk about Phoenix they are usually referring not only to the town itself but also to a larger area often called the Valley of the Sun. Included in the Valley are Tempe, Mesa, Scottsdale and Glendale. More outlying areas include Sun City, Litchfield Park, Carefree and Apache Junction.

For restaurant-hopping—or any kind of touring of the city—an automobile is essential. Many restaurants are clustered in Scottsdale, about 10 miles from downtown Phoenix, but few are close together there or even near boutiques or shops of interest.

Good restaurants in the outlying areas are few and generally not worth the trip for a visitor on a limited time schedule.

# Restaurants and Food Sources

(Area code: 602)

## BIG DEAL

### WORTH IT

***La Champagne,*** Registry Resort, 7171 N. Scottsdale Road, Scottsdale (991-3800). Handsome atmosphere with Thai silk wall fabrics, crystal chandeliers and a tempting *haute cuisine* menu. The restaurant serves no more than its capacity (150) in an evening. Specialties include *médaillons de veau marchand de vin,* abalone Nantua with lobster mousse and roast sirloin with sauce bordelaise. Dinner only. Closed Monday during the summer. Entrées from $11. AE, CB, DC, MC, V.

### NOT WORTH IT

***Hugo's,*** Hyatt Regency, 2nd Street and Adams (257-1110). Somehow this restaurant has not attained the excellence of Hugo's in other Hyatts around the country. The service is very personal, but the food lacks luster. Dinner only. Closed Sunday. Entrées from $8.75. AE, CB, DC, MC, V.

## INTERNATIONAL

### AMERICAN

***Gregory's Penthouse,*** 2333 E. Thomas Road (956-8740). A popular gathering place for business people, particularly those who are traveling on the road. The specialty is prime rib. Open seven days a week. Entrées from $2.95 (L), $5.95 (D). AE, CB, DC, MC, V.

## CHINESE

***China Doll,*** 3336 N. 7th Avenue (264-0538). A favorite for lovers of Cantonese cuisine with specialties ranging from lobster Cantonese style to beef with oyster sauce, sweet and sour pork, and almond duck. Spacious dining rooms, excellent service. Open seven days a week. Entrées from $2.85 (L), $5.50 (D). AE, CB, DC, MC, V.

## FRENCH

***La Chaumière,*** 6910 Main Street, Scottsdale (946-5115). Outstanding food in a French cottage nestled among a grove of orange trees. Outdoor dining or indoor country-French elegance. The rack of lamb for two ($23.50) is a treat. For dessert try the calorie-rich *mousse au chocolat.* Dinner only. Open seven days a week. Entrées from $7.25. MC, V.

## GERMAN

***Felsen Haus,*** 1008 E. Camelback Road (277-1119). The most authentic German food in Phoenix. Wiener schnitzel, sauerbraten and rouladen are specialties. Chaîne des Rotisseurs. Open seven days a week. Entrées from $1.75 (L), $2.95 (D). MC, V.

## ITALIAN

***Avanti,*** 2728 E. Thomas Road (956-0900). Green plants set against a black and white motif. Many veal specialties including *osso buco.* Saturday and Sunday, dinner only. Open seven days a week. Entrées from $3.25 (L), $7.50 (D). AE, CB, DC, MC, V.

## JAPANESE

***Asia House,*** 2310 E. McDowell (267-7461). A real experience in dining; excellent service. *Sukiyaki* is the Japanese specialty, served in traditional style at low tables. Also special rooms for Cantonese food and a Mongolian barbecue. Dinner only. Closed Monday. Fixed-price dinner $8.25. AE, CB, DC, MC, V.

## MEXICAN

***Garcia's Del Este Restaurant,*** 7633 E. Indian School Road, Scottsdale (945-1647). A taste of Arizona-Mexican food in a nice setting, a treat for visitors. Albondigas soup, *quesadillas* and chimichangas would be ideal for first-timers. Very crowded, no reservations. Open seven days a week. Entrées from $.60, complete meals from $3 (L & D). AE, CB, DC, MC, V.

***George's Ole,*** 7330 N. Dreamy Draw Drive (997-5776). This is a good place to try a chimichanga. Fast service, large portions. Also American food. Open seven days a week. Entrées from $2 (L & D). AE, MC, V.

***Conquistador,*** 605 E. Missouri (277-7471). Their *carne asada* is very good; have a cheese crisp as an appetizer. Saturday and Sunday, dinner only. Entrées from $2.50 (L), $3.50 (D). AE, MC, V.

# SPECIALTY COOKING

## BAGELS

***Jumbo Bagel Deli,*** 1352 E. Apache, Tempe (966-8482). Eight different kinds of bagels including pumpernickel, raisin and onion. Bagels baked fresh every 20 minutes. Sandwiches on bagels available. Open seven days a week, from 7 A.M. Jumbo bagels are $1.80. No credit cards.

## DELI

***Duck and Decanter,*** 1651 E. Camelback Road (274-5429). Billed as the "Complete Gourmet," this place offers fine sliced meats and cheeses as well as a large selection of wine and beer. Open seven days a week. Sandwiches from $2. MC, V.

## HAMBURGER

***Lunt Avenue Marble Club,*** 1212 E. Apache, Tempe (967-9192), and 2 E. Camelback Road, Phoenix (265-8997). The burgers extraordinaire are outstanding. Try "The Awful Burger" for a real surprise. Menu includes crêpes, omelets, quiche and pizza in a pan. Unusual atmosphere, reasonable prices, friendly service. Open seven days a week. Hamburgers from $2.35. MC, V.

## HOT DOG

***Fire House,*** 1639 E. Apache, Tempe (966-4531). This used to be a fire station, but has been converted into a cozy restaurant. Good, fast service. Open seven days a week. Firedog including salad and chili is $2.50. Also a good selection of steaks from $3.95. No credit cards.

## NATURAL FOODS

***Earthen Joy,*** 36 E. Fifth Street, Tempe (968-4710). Close to Arizona State University. The soups are delicious and filling; unusual teas. Serves both vegetarian and meat dishes. Closed Sunday. Soup and sandwich about $3. No credit cards.

## STEAK

***Monti's La Casa Vieja,*** 3 W. First Street, Tempe (967-7594). A rare combination: Good steaks and low prices, plus a special dining room for nonsmoking patrons. Open seven days a week. Steaks start at $3.65 including salad and baked potato. Entrées from $1 (L), $2.75 (D). AE, CB, DC, MC, V.

# FOR INDIVIDUAL NEEDS

## IF YOU HAVE TIME FOR ONLY ONE MEAL

***GuadalaHarry's,*** 4949 E. Lincoln Drive, Scottsdale (959-4650). Beamed ceilings, lots of plants and a number of small, intimate rooms make this restaurant an excellent choice for a taste of Arizona-Mexican cuisine. The service is very prompt, the quality of the food is consistently good. This is where visitors must try chimichangas, an Arizona specialty. Their margaritas are also very good. Open seven days a week. Entrées from $2.50 (L), $3.25 (D). AE, MC, V.

## BEST HOTEL MEAL

***Orangerie,*** Arizona Biltmore, 24th Street and Missouri (955-6600). Excellent food; salmon Wellington is outstanding. Pastries made daily at the hotel. Excellent bar, too. The setting is a stunningly beautiful example of the Frank Lloyd Wright school of architecture. Piano music until 10 P.M. nightly. Jacket required for dinner. Chaîne des Rotisseurs. Open seven days a week. Entrées from $5 (L), $15 (D). AE, MC, V.

## RESTAURANT NEAR AIRPORT

***Newton's Prime Rib,*** 915 E. Van Buren (254-7268). About 3 miles from airport. Excellent prime rib; black-bottom rum pie is delicious. Chaîne des Rotisseurs. Open seven days a week, from 6 A.M. Entrées from $1.50 (B), $2.95 (L), $4.95 (D). AE, MC, V.

## BUSINESS BREAKFAST

***Boojum Tree,*** Doubletree Inn, 2nd Avenue and Osborne Road (248-0222). Cozy, sunny atmosphere makes this a pleasant place to discuss business. Open seven days a week, from 6 A.M. on weekdays, 7 A.M. weekends. Entrées from $1.55 (B). AE, CB, DC, MC, V.

## BUSINESS LUNCH

***Navarre's,*** 52 E. Camelback Road (264-5355). Consistently good food with Continental overtones. Chicken Kiev, sweetbreads, good salad specialties with outstanding house dressing. Sunday, dinner only. Open seven days a week. Entrées from $2.50 (L). AE, CB, DC, MC, V.

## FAST, GOOD FOOD/BREAKFAST

***The Citrus Grove,*** Adams Hotel, Central and Adams (257-1525). Open seven days a week, from 6:30 A.M. AE, CB, DC, MC, V.

## FAST, GOOD FOOD/LUNCH

***Green House Restaurant,*** 139 E. Adams (252-2742). Bountiful salads, sandwiches in *pita* bread from $1.75. Closed Saturday and Sunday. No credit cards.

## FAST, GOOD FOOD/DINNER

***Caf' Casino,*** 1312 N. Scottsdale Road, Scottsdale (947-4100), 4824 N. 24th Street, Phoenix (955-3430), 10030 Metro Parkway East (997-2544). Authentic French food in a cafeteria setting. Open seven days a week. Dinners with wine for under $5. No credit cards.

## FOR DRINKS

***Bogarts,*** 4821 N. 20th Street, in the Town and Country Shopping Center (957-1684). Popular gathering place for the young business disco crowd. Backgammon tables are an added attraction. No jeans; most of the crowd is rather dressed up. Open seven days a week. AE, MC, V.

***Compass,*** Hyatt Regency, 122 N. Second Street (257-1110). Phoenix's only revolving restaurant. A great view of the city—the city lights at night are romantic. Lunch and dinner are served, but they are willing to serve cocktails only. Open seven days a week. AE, CB, DC, MC, V.

## RESTAURANT WITH MUSIC

***Pointe of View,*** 7277 N. 16th Street (997-5859). Jazz quintet on Sunday and Monday from 9 P.M. to 1 A.M., disco music the rest of the week. Nice view of the city. Saturday and Sunday, dinner only. Open seven days a week. Entrées from $2.50 (L), $6.25 (D). AE, DC, MC, V.

## ROMANTIC

***Figg Tree,*** 4110 N. 49th Street (959-9140). Hidden among the trees, this restaurant has a living-room lounge, outdoor patio with live entertainment. Small dining rooms, excellent service. Dinner only. Open seven days a week. Entrées from $5.95. AE, MC, V.

## LATE-NIGHT SERVICE

***BB Singer's Pub and Restaurant,*** 7071 3rd Avenue, Scottsdale (947-2405), 4321 North Central, Phoenix (279-9567). Dining for every taste, from an elaborate meal to a light snack. Relaxing atmosphere. The crêpes are delicious. Open seven days a week, until 2 A.M. Sunday through Thursday, until 3 A.M. Friday and Saturday. Entrées from $2.95 (L & D). AE, MC, V.

## SUNDAY BRUNCH

***The Other Place,*** Fiesta Inn, 2100 S. Priest, Tempe (967-8721). Good food in a festive setting. Also a fine choice for a business lunch. Sunday brunch from 10 A.M. to 3 P.M. for $5.25. AE, MC, V.

## SUNDAY-EVENING MEAL

***John's Green Gables,*** 2345 E. Thomas Road (956-5581). Quiet, not too crowded, consistently good food. Prime rib is a specialty; complimentary dessert bar guaranteed to stretch your waistline. Saturday and Sunday, dinner only. Open seven days a week. Entrées from $3.50 (L), $5.95 (D). AE, CB, DC, MC, V.

## FOR FAMILIES WITH CHILDREN

***Spaghetti Company,*** 1418 N. Central Avenue, Phoenix (966-3848). Naturally spaghetti, with a variety of sauces, is the main feature. Sunday, dinner only. Open seven days a week. Entrées from $1.80 (L), $1.95 (D). MC, V.

# IN THE SUBURBS

## APACHE JUNCTION

***Mining Camp Restaurant,*** four miles north of Apache Junction on the Apache Trail (982-3181). Western fare: Barbecued ribs, chicken and dressing, roast beef. Baked ham served on Sunday. Also steaks and prime rib. A convenient stop on the way back from Canyon or Apache Lakes. Food is served family-style. Dinner only. Closed Monday. Entrées from $5.50. Children under 2 free, children 10 and under $2.50. No credit cards.

## CAREFREE

***Elbow Bend,*** 7210 E. Elbow Bend Road, Carefree (488-9495). Relaxing outdoor patio for brunch; lively entertainment inside on Friday and Saturday night. Steak Diane prepared at the table; daily house specials. Friday fish fry ($4.50). Open seven days a week except in summer, when closed Monday. Entrées from $2 (L), $5.50 (D). AE, DC, MC, V.

## SUN CITY

***King's Inn,*** 10660 Grand Avenue (977-7261). Usually crowded with visitors as well as residents of this retirement community. Wide variety of entrées including steak, chicken and seafood. Open seven days a week. Entrées from $2 (L), $4.75 (D). AE, CB, DC, MC, V.

# MARKETS

## GIFT FOODS

***Sunny Hills Farm,*** 3224 E. Baseline Road (276-9558). Organically grown citrus, dates, nuts and honey. Closed end of May to beginning of November. No credit cards.

## GIFT WINES

***Brookside Winery,*** 10240 N. 27th Avenue in Metrocenter (943-0972), 1131 West Broadway Road, Tempe (967-9836). Tasting rooms with over 100 varieties. Part of a California chain. Open seven days a week. No credit cards.

# Pittsburgh

When George Washington stood on top of what is now called Mt. Washington and gazed down on the confluence of three great rivers, he could scarcely have envisioned the row of restaurants that would grow up in that very spot. But Pittsburghers are proud of their view, equating it with that of San Francisco; and visiting guests are generally treated to a ride up the mountainside on the incline to enjoy a drink and dinner overlooking the city and rivers below.

The Monongahela and the Allegheny meet precisely in the middle of Pittsburgh's downtown area to form the Ohio River. The resulting point is the site of the Golden Triangle, built after World War II when the unlikely coalition of big business and a Democratic Administration decided to clean up the smog and dirt. The Pittsburgh renaissance has served as a model to other cities, despite the lingering image of the area as choked with smoke and grit, and visitors are surprised at the beauty of this important industrial city.

Pittsburgh is a city of neighborhoods, pockets of homes and small businesses tucked away in the valleys and atop the hills. The boundaries are sometimes ethnic, sometimes geographic, and the most interesting restaurants reflect this pattern. The downtown area has few good restaurants, so the best food requires a little travel. The Oakland and Shadyside areas, east of downtown, the North Side and the South Side, are all rewarding to the diner willing to ride for fifteen minutes or so.

In a city that prides itself on its ethnicity, most people expect to find charming Czech, Polish or Hungarian restaurants dotted around town. But except for **Sarah's,** a Balkan-style restaurant specializing in the food of Yugoslavia, they do not exist. Sarah Evosovich devotes most of her time to catering, but her attractive South Side restaurant serves dinner and lunch by reservation only.

What the town lacks in this department, however, is more than made up in Italian restaurants. **Tambellini's** on Wood Street is close to major hotels and theaters and provides excellent seafood as well as Italian dishes. A short cab ride from downtown Pittsburgh is the east end's New Meadow Grill, with excellent food but totally lacking in atmosphere and with eccentric service; and the Tivoli, which serves a fine Southern-style fish soup and pasta with *pesto* sauce. Somewhat farther out, La Cresta and **Flavio's** offer excellent Northern Italian cooking. Il Geranio, an attractive new restaurant at river's edge in Sharpsburg, shows great promise, with a variety of veal dishes along with some French specialties. The diner must be wary, however, as Pittsburgh's Italian restaurants tend to be heavy-handed with thick tomato sauce and a firm commitment to a philosophy of "more is better." A simple request for butter or oil and cheese on one's side dish of pasta is usually received pleasantly.

The most unusual group of ethnic restaurants is Middle Eastern. In Oakland alone, ten minutes from downtown, there are eight thriving Syrian and/or Armenian-style restaurants, with at least five others in various parts of the city. The menus are similar, with the differences shown by the size and thickness of *pita* bread, the succulence of the lamb or beef shish kebabs, and the décor, or lack of it. Middle Eastern food in Pittsburgh is undoubtedly the best buy in terms of quantity as well as quality.

Until recently, the city lacked a good French restaurant. Now **La Normande** has filled that important gap, providing a constantly changing menu of seafood, duck, beef, lamb and veal specialties, with outstanding hors d'oeuvre and desserts. A few good restaurants such as **De Foro's, The Common Plea** and the **Park Schenley** specialize in "Continental" food, a combination of French- and Italian-style cooking, with an emphasis on the latter.

Pittsburgh's reputation as a "shot-and-a-beer" town persists. There are neighborhood bars around the steel mills where workers still drop in for that Pittsburgh specialty called a boilermaker everywhere else. There is an excellent local beer named, appropriately, Iron City.

Market Square, downtown, is an attractive cobble-stoned area abounding in modest nightclubs, jazz spots and a few restaurants. One of Pittsburgh's landmarks there is the Oyster Bar, a crowded and noisy drop-in tavern with a fifty-foot bar and a reputation for serving the best fish sandwich in town. Chesapeake Bay oysters, clam rolls and first-rate French fries can be washed down with a beer or—of all things—cold buttermilk. It's a meeting place for the famous and the infamous, and a good spot to think about what Pittsburgh might have been like in the 1870's when the Oyster opened its doors.

Meanwhile, back on Mt. Washington, the diner can select from among the overpriced, glass-walled Le Mont's, **Christopher's,** The Tin Angel and the Celestial. Or, at more modest prices, Cliff Side and Georgetowne Inn. The view is the same. Tucked behind the hill without a view are several good restaurants, the most outstanding being another **Tambellini's,** where the Italian specialties vie with fine seafood for popularity.

Despite the presence of wealthy families such as the Mellons, the Carnegies, the Fricks and the Scaifes, Pittsburgh is essentially a simple town, gastronomically speaking. It isn't difficult to find a good steak or roast beef, and oddly enough in this inland city, excellent fish. Dress codes are relaxed. Only in the most expensive restaurants are jackets required. Turtlenecks for men are generally accepted in lieu of ties. Women can go anywhere in pants suits.

Tipping customs are standard—a single tip of 15 percent. The gratuity is rarely added to the bill automatically. Many Pittsburgh restaurants do not accept reservations, a source of some dismay when the diner in a hurry is confronted with a long line in popular places such as the Seventh Street Restaurant, **The Common Plea** and **Tambellini's.**

Farmers' markets are popular shopping spots for Pittsburghers; and the open-air Common Market on the North side, a five-minute ride or fifteen-minute walk across the Allegheny from downtown, is a pleasant place to spend an hour or so on Saturdays or in the early evening. In addition to fresh produce, homemade sausages, cold meats and cheeses, homemade bread, cookies and pastries are also sold. **The Strip District,** a short walk to the east from downtown, is a fascinating series of wholesale and retail markets specializing in fresh produce, fine fresh fish as well as walk-away fish sandwiches and crab cakes, cheeses, and Greek and Italian groceries.

Gourmet food shops tend to be located in the suburbs, but the hungry hotel-dweller need not starve. The Bank, a downtown shopping complex, has a small but good cheese-and-sausage shop, while all of the department stores have substantial food departments.

Wine and liquor in Pennsylvania must be purchased through state stores, not known for their wide selections. Beer in less than case lots may be purchased in any bar for take-out purposes, but beer by the case must be bought from beer distributors.

There is a small but steady growth of restaurants in Pittsburgh including an interesting trend toward reconstructions and recyclings similar to San Francisco's Ghirardelli Square. In the downtown area, the Bank complex is in a turn-of-the-century bank building. The fine marble columns and stained-glass skylights remain, while multilevel shops and eating places offer the shopper or browser hours of pleasure. In Shadyside's Walnut Street area, where boutiques and other fine shops abound, a former theater has been renovated to provide three levels of shopping plus a crêpe restaurant, and one of the city's better food shops, Mr. Pumpernick. It sells a vast array of sausages, cheeses, salads and other delicatessen goodies, including a soup of the day.

The most ambitious of these reconstructions is Station Square, the elegant Edwardian Pennsylvania, Lackawanna and Erie Railroad Station just across the Monongahela River from downtown Pittsburgh. Now housing the **Grand Concourse Restaurant** and the **Gandy Dancer Saloon,** Station Square will eventually contain more than one hundred shops and restaurants.

# Restaurants and Food Sources
(Area code: 412)

## BIG DEAL

### WORTH IT

***De Foro's,*** Lawyers Building, Forbes Avenue, downtown (391-8873). The menu is just a starting point for an excellent blend of Italian and French cooking with a dash of Swiss for good measure. Along with always-available entrées of veal Cordon Bleu, tournedos Rossini and rack of lamb for two, the chef presents daily seasonal specialties such as a whole sea bass, freshly poached salmon, crisp fresh vegetables. Try the seafood crêpes as an appetizer, or the homemade vichyssoise. Lunch features a selection of omelets, pasta and salads. Excellent European-style service. Closed Sunday. Entrées from $3 (L), $7.50 (D). AE, MC, V.

### NOT WORTH IT

***Christopher's,*** 1411 Grandview Avenue, Mt. Washington (381-4500). A penthouse restaurant at the top of Mt. Washington, overpriced and pretentious with only slightly better-than-average food. Sweetbreads with pilaf and mushrooms, and the fresh spinach salad with hot herb dressing are stand-outs; but the menu promises far more than it delivers. The view of the city is superb, but you can have the same thing for less money elsewhere. Take the glass elevator up to the bar for a drink. Closed Sunday. Entrées from $3.75 (L), $8.95 (D). AE, CB, DC, MC, V.

## INTERNATIONAL

### AMERICAN

***The Colony,*** Greentree and Cochran Roads, Scott Township (561-2060). About a 15-minute cab ride from downtown, the Colony features an open-hearth grill and a specialized menu of steaks, liver and fish, all cooked with care. A miniature salad bar is brought to each table. Desserts arrive in the form of large trays of French pastry and fresh fruits. Décor is modern and comfortable, the service smooth and effortless. The maître d' is nice to strangers. Reservations required; difficult on Saturdays. Dinner only. Closed Sunday. Complete dinners from $11.75. AE, CB, DC, MC, V.

## BALKAN

***Sarah's Ethnic Restaurant,*** 52 S. Tenth Street (431-9307). Primarily Yugoslavian, Sarah's food reflects the diversity of cultural influences within the country, with Greek, Turkish and Slavic accents. Specialties include *sarma* (cabbage leaves stuffed with rice and pork); *trke podvarku* (turkey stuffed with sauerkraut—far better than it reads); moussaka, apple strudel and feather-light *palacsintas* (a form of crêpe with sweet fillings). Hungarian and Greek wines only, somewhat overpriced. Friendly atmosphere, with Sarah usually there to greet you and explain the dishes. Coat and tie required. Lunch and dinner by reservation only. Closed Monday. Complete meals from $5 (L), $12 (D). No credit cards.

## CHINESE

***Anna Kao's,*** 1034 Freeport Road, O'Hara Township (782-3010). You have to travel if you want good Chinese food in Pittsburgh, but this place is usually worth the 30-minute drive from downtown. Unusual dishes from many regions of China including lemon chicken, hot ginger shrimp puffs, firecracker fish Szechuan style, a fried combination of flounder, shrimp and meat called Treasure Fish, Mandarin beef and a smashing bamboo-stick soup. Décor is standard Chinese-American. Anna Kao will help you select your dinner. Reservations recommended. Dinner only. Closed Monday. Entrées from $6.95; complete dinners from $10.50. No credit cards.

## FRENCH

***La Normande,*** 5030 Centre Avenue (621-0744). A 15-minute cab ride from downtown brings you to such French specialties as galantine of chicken with pistachios, poached trout in aspic and a Normandy pâté for starters; boeuf Bourguignonne, poached mussels in cream, roast duck with green peppercorn sauce, rack of veal with Dijon mustard and calvados, *cassoulet,* sautéed kidneys, braised sweetbreads or calves liver for entrées; and a fine Grand Marnier soufflé for dessert. Menu changes daily. Excellent wine list. Good service. 15 percent gratuity added. Reservations suggested. Dinner only. Closed Monday. Entrées from $8.75. AE, MC, V.

## GERMAN

***Max's Allegheny Tavern,*** Middle and Suismon Streets, North Side (231-1899). Tiffany lamp shades, a huge mahogany bar, tiled floors and four-bladed ceiling fans combine to re-create a turn-of-the-century feeling in this old hotel tavern. Enjoy weisswurst, knockwurst, sauerbraten, red cabbage, homemade applesauce and a variety of other German dishes, plus draft beer in frosty mugs. The price is right. No reservations. Closed Sunday. Entrées from $1.75 (L), $3 (D). No credit cards.

## ITALIAN

***Alex Tambellini's Wood St.,*** 213 Wood Street, downtown (281-9956). (See description under SEAFOOD.)

## MIDDLE EASTERN

***Samreny's,*** 4808 Baum Boulevard, Oakland (682-1212). The granddaddy of Pittsburgh's Middle Eastern spots and many say the best. If you can handle the chrome-and-vinyl drugstore décor, you'll find classic renditions of *kibbe,* shish kebab, Syrian salad, *nis-oo-nis* and baklava. Waitresses are cheerful and very helpful to first-timers. Very informal. Closed Monday. Complete meal from $6 (L & D). No credit cards.

***Palmyra,*** 370 Atwood Street, Oakland (621-6400). (See description under FOR FAMILIES WITH CHILDREN.)

# SPECIALTY COOKING

## DELI

***Richest's Downtown Restaurant,*** 140 Sixth Street (471-7799). Not fancy, but plenty of corned beef and other kosher standbys; bagels and rye bread, cole slaw and the like. Sit-down service, with bar, or take-out service. Open until 12:30 A.M. Closed Sunday. No credit cards.

***Aunt Fanny's Nosheria,*** Baum Boulevard and Roup Street, Shadyside (687-5600). Bagels, lox, knockwurst, salads, sandwiches, daily special hot plates and larger-than-life chocolate-chip cookies.

All this and draft beer, too, with plenty of antiques to stare at as you munch. Parking. Open seven days a week. No credit cards.

## HAMBURGER

***C. J. Barney's Wooden Keg,*** 3905 Forbes Avenue, Oakland (621-2149). Limited but good menu of mostly hamburgers with special toppings such as chili, cheese, bacon or ham. The same toppings are available for omelets. Attractive Victorian décor; friendly service; crowded. No reservations. Open seven days a week. Entrées from $2.25 (L & D). No credit cards.

## SEAFOOD

***Alex Tambellini's Wood St.,*** 213 Wood Street, downtown (281-9956). Even though first-timers might be drawn to the fine Italian specialties, best bets are the seafood dishes: poached salmon with hollandaise, oysters Bienville with crab and shrimp stuffings, *langostina alla Fiorentino,* Spanish scampi, Boston scrod, and on and on. Good house wine; very large portions of everything. Small dining room with cozy feeling, filled with serious eaters. Friendly and efficient service. No reservations. Closed Sunday. Entrées from $3.75 (L), $7.25 (D). No credit cards.

## SOUL

***Southern Platter Restaurant,*** 625 N. Homewood Avenue, Homewood (241-2505). Grits, ribs, crackling bread, Hopping John, greens and sweet-potato pie. It's all good. Open seven days a week. Entrées from $2.25 (L), $3.50 (D). CB, DC, MC.

## STEAK

***The Colony,*** Greentree and Cochran Roads, Scott Township (561-2060). (See description under AMERICAN.)

## VEGETARIAN

***Cornucopia,*** 328 Atwood Street, Oakland (682-7953). The only vegetarian restaurant in town, but good nonetheless. It's pleasant in the bright and airy dining room; relax and enjoy an exotic tea or coffee. Food includes homemade pasta with spicy vegetable sauces, Brazilian black beans and rice, cheese enchiladas and wholewheat tortillas, a variety of vegetable and fruit juices, homemade ice cream, cakes, and whole-wheat bread with a superb texture. Fresh baked pastries for late breakfast. Service by students is cheery and helpful. No liquor, but diners may bring wine. No smoking. Closed Monday. Entrées from $2.75, sandwiches and salad from $1.10 (L & D). No credit cards.

# FOR INDIVIDUAL NEEDS

## IF YOU HAVE TIME FOR ONLY ONE MEAL

***The Common Plea,*** 308 Ross Street, downtown (281-5140). Patronized by politicians and lawyers, this small, pleasant restaurant presents three appetizers before the entrée (which might be bouillabaisse, scallops and shrimp Norfolk, veal roulades stuffed with crab, or a fine broiled seafood platter). Desserts are tempting: huge goblets of fresh strawberries doused in white wine, parfaits and cheesecake. Good service from attentive waitresses. The no-reservation policy means a wait at the bar, especially at lunch and weekends. Closed Sunday. Entrées from $2.75 (L), $6.95 (D). No credit cards.

***Louis Tambellini's,*** 160 Southern Avenue, Mt. Washington (481-1118). No view but excellent seafood and Italian specialties such as baked baby *langostino* and salmon poached with vegetables and herbs. Sole is sautéed whole in oil, garlic and herbs. Plenty of other fish, much of it with shrimp and crab meat placed under, over or in between a variety of sauces. Extra touches include crisp spinach salad, homemade *gnocchi* and a large pot of espresso coffee. Informal friendly service and clientele. No reservations, so a long wait at the bar is almost inevitable. Saturday, dinner only. Closed Sunday. Entrées from $3.75 (L), $6.75 (D). No credit cards.

## BEST HOTEL MEAL

***Hugo's Rotisserie,*** Pittsburgh Hyatt House, Chatham Center, downtown (391-5000). Duck, beef and other meats roast on spits before your very eyes, served with a variety of sauces. Unusual salad and hors d'oeuvre bar includes shrimp, avocado, cheese and a wide selection of greens and other vegetables. Do-it-yourself desserts, with soft ice cream and yogurt plus sauces. Open seven days a week. Entrées from $3.75 (L), $9.50 (D). AE, DC, MC, V.

## RESTAURANT NEAR AIRPORT

***Myron's,*** Airport Ramada Inn, Beers School Road, Coraopolis (264-8950). Pleasant, subdued décor with good selection of standards (pastas, steaks, seafood) plus specialties (tournedos in two sauces, veal Veronique, lamb *noisettes*). Good wine list, domestic and foreign, at reasonable prices. Open seven days a week. Entrées from $3.25 (L), $6.75 (D). AE, DC, MC, V.

***Hyeholde,*** 190 Hyeholde Drive, Coraopolis (264-3116). (See description under COUNTRY INN.)

## BUSINESS LUNCH

***Park Schenley,*** 3955 Bigelow Boulevard, Oakland (681-0800). A big menu featuring French and Italian dishes, generally well prepared, including sole Véronique, thick slices of calves' liver and onions, chicken in white wine and vegetables, veal Oskar, *grillades* of steak, lamb and lobster, and a good mixed grill. Rich desserts, good wine list. Efficient, unhurried service, with tables far enough apart for conversation. Chaîne des Rotisseurs. Closed Monday. Entrées from $3.35 (L), $7.75 (D). AE, CB, DC, MC, V.

## FAST, GOOD FOOD/BREAKFAST

***Ritter's Diner,*** 5221 Baum Boulevard Oakland (682-4852). A Pittsburgh institution, with the best breakfast in town—be it eggs, and home fries, pancakes or whatever—available at any hour, along with hamburgers and other usual diner items. Open seven days a week, 24 hours a day. Complete breakfast from $1.75. No credit cards.

## FAST, GOOD FOOD/LUNCH, DINNER

***Café Cappuccino,*** The Bank, 414 Wood Street, downtown (261-1008). A pleasant "sidewalk café" inside the restored Bank shopping complex, serving interesting and well-prepared crêpes, including a superb *ratatouille.* Long list of exotic coffees, substantial salads, cheese boards and fondues. Tables are tiny, waiters friendly, service prompt. Sometimes there's music. Closed Sunday. Entrées from $2.65 (L & D). AE, MC, V.

## BEST WINE LIST

***Ben Gross,*** Route 30, Irwin (271-6696). Some distance from downtown Pittsburgh. Wide selection of French and German wines plus the best of California makes it worthwhile. Big menu, big portions of specialties such as soft-shell crabs, roast duckling in elderberry-ginger sauce, sherried oysters with mushrooms and cheese, sliced tenderloin with wild rice. Unusually good steaks and prime ribs. Desserts are apt to be flamed. Entrées from $1.95 (L), $6.50 (D). AE, DC, MC, V.

***Wooden Angel,*** West Bridgewater Street, Beaver (774-7880). (See description under IN THE SUBURBS/BEAVER.) An unusually large selection of American-only wines.

## FOR DRINKS

***The Rusty Scupper,*** The Bank, 311 Fourth Avenue, downtown (765-2590). Where the swingers like to meet in a nautical setting that also includes food, mostly steak and seafood. No reservations, always crowded. Open seven days a week. AE, MC, V.

***The Gandy Dancer Saloon and Oyster Bar,*** One Station Square, P & LE Station (261-1717). An elegant Edwardian bar with shining brass and frosted glass, once the baggage room of the old railroad station. Generous drinks, draft beer, fine fresh oysters, shrimp, clams, mussels and crab, plus sandwiches. Cocktail hour piano. No reservations. Open seven days a week. Adjoins the ***Grand Concourse Restaurant,*** specializing in seafood, including lobster, a hearty seafood chowder, finnan haddie, bluefish, scrod and smelts, among others. Reservations advised. Open seven days a week. Entrées from $3.95 (L), $7.25 (D). AE, DC, MC, V.

## RESTAURANT WITH MUSIC

***Encore I,*** 5505 Walnut Street, Shadyside (683-5656). Light-jazz quartet with occasional big names. Sandwiches, steaks, shrimp and other steakhouse fare. Open seven days a week. Entrées from $2.50 (L), $3.95 (D). AE, CB, MC, V.

***Encore II,*** 629 Liberty Avenue, downtown (471-1225). Dixieland, country-and-western and light jazz with a different group weekly. Closed Sunday. Same menu as Encore I. AE, CB, MC, V.

## LATE-NIGHT SERVICE

***The Top Shelf,*** 606 Liberty Avenue, downtown (566-2900). A profusion of cheese boards, fish boards, hot appetizers, fondues and crêpes are served. Service is barely adequate in this starkly modern black-and-silver dining room. Steaks featured for lunch and dinner. Snacks later. Weekend entertainment, mostly jazz. Closed Sunday. Entrées from $2.75 (L), $6.75 (D). AE, CB, DC, MC, V.

## SUNDAY BRUNCH

***Café Stephen B's,*** 5847 Ellsworth Avenue, Shadyside (361-0188). A bright, modern restaurant transformed from an old warehouse, with a pleasing mixture of textures and colors. Chowders, salads, sandwiches and unusual entrées for daily lunch and dinner, but Sunday brunches feature three-egg omelets with fillings ranging from sausage and apples, to white asparagus to Canadian bacon and strawberries. Or try eggs Benedict or quiche. Open seven days a week, Sunday brunch from 11 A.M. Brunch entrées from $2.75. AE, MC, V.

## SUNDAY-EVENING MEAL

***Hugo's Rotisserie,*** Pittsburgh Hyatt House, Chatham Center, downtown (391-5000). (See description under BEST HOTEL MEAL.)

***Park Schenley,*** 3955 Bigelow Boulevard, Oakland (681-0800). (See description under BUSINESS LUNCH.)

## FOR FAMILIES WITH CHILDREN

***Palmyra,*** 370 Atwood Street, Oakland (621-6400). For a change from the fast-food route, take the kids to an informal Middle Eastern restaurant where they can have plain shish kebab and superior French fries, with gooey desserts such as baklava or honey cookies. More adventurous adults will go for tabouleh, fresh kale, artichoke salad with tahini. No liquor, but diners often bring their own beer and wine. Open seven days a week. Mid-Eastern buffet on Sunday. Complete meals from $4.95 (L), $5.50 (D). AE, MC.

## COUNTRY INN

***Hyeholde,*** 190 Hyeholde Drive, Coraopolis (264-3116). Very near the airport. Set in spacious grounds, this gracious home offers excellent food in a relaxed atmosphere of candlelight and classical music. Steak, lobster, squabs in Champagne sauce, duck and rack of lamb are the mainstays, but seasonal specialties and the chef's "feast" change often. Meal prices include a good sherry bisque, an assortment of well-cooked vegetables, and rich desserts such as *zuppa inglese* and trifle. Reservations only. Closed Sunday. Complete meals from $3.95 (L), $12.50 (D). MC, V.

# IN THE SUBURBS

## APOLLO

***Flavio's,*** 212 N. Warren Avenue (478-2961). Mostly Northern Italian and French cooking, with *baccala* and *polenta; lasagne Abruzzese* with three kinds of cheese and miniature meatballs; homemade pasta and rich desserts. Dinner only. Closed Monday. Entrées from $6.25. AE, CB, DC, MC, V.

## BEAVER

***Wooden Angel,*** West Bridgewater Street (774-7880). Wooden beams, low lights, plenty of open space and good food combine to make this one of the area's best restaurants. Hot appetizers with crabs and clams, homemade chicken pâté, variety of steaks and chicken plus cheesecake are all outstanding. A big draw is the unusual American wine cellar, with reasonable prices. Dinner only. Closed Sunday and Monday. Entrées from $6.85. AE, MC, V.

## IRWIN/GREENSBURG

***Ben Gross,*** Route 30, Irwin (271-6696). (See description under BEST WINE LIST.)

# MARKETS

***The Strip District,*** beginning around 17th Street on Penn Avenue near downtown. Pittsburgh's wholesale produce markets generally welcome retail shoppers as well. Within a four-block area you can buy fish sandwiches and crab cakes at **Robert Wholey and Company** fish market; bag and weigh your own fresh fruit and vegetables at **Keystone Produce;** trade jokes with the friendly folk at **Allesandro Sausage Company** while picking out your cheeses and coffee; or buy three kinds of Greek olives, sesame oil and sesame *pita* at **Stamoolis Brothers** grocery.

## GIFT FOODS

***À La Carte,*** The Bank, 414 Wood Street, downtown (261-1262). Good cheese, sausages and breads in bewildering variety. Closed Sunday. No credit cards.

# SPECIAL EVENTS

***Pittsburgh Folk Festival,*** held annually in late May for three days, features food specialties from more than twenty different countries, including Croatian and Hungarian pastries, Irish scones, Indian curries, Latvian ham baked in rye dough, Philippine chicken adobo, Polish stuffed cabbage, Serbian pancakes, Ukrainian honey cake. Each booth has a dozen or more specialties and the event works like a gigantic smorgasbord as you pick up your goodies, buy a draft beer and sit at a picnic table, listening to strolling musicians. There's folk dancing, too, every evening of the Festival. Admission charge. Civic Arena, downtown.

# Portland, Oregon

Dining out in Portland has improved immeasurably in the past twenty years. Not long ago, members of even the most chauvinistic old families complained that one had to go to San Francisco for a truly enjoyable and varied restaurant experience. Now the choice of fine eating places is limited only by considerations of time and pocketbooks—or expense accounts.

Nature has blessed Oregon with an abundance of ingredients for good eating. Mention the Columbia River and most people will think of the huge fish that astounded Lewis and Clark. Salmon still come to spawn, although in greatly reduced numbers; in season, there's nothing better than a dinner of grilled or poached fresh Columbia River salmon.

Pioneers who followed the Oregon Trail found sturgeon in the Columbia in addition to salmon, and trout and crayfish in the lesser streams. (In September, chefs come from all over the United States to compete in the Crayfish Olympics at Sun River, a resort town in central Oregon's high country.)

When those early settlers reached the Oregon coast, they found a wealth of seafood: clams, tiny North Pacific shrimp, oysters and, best of all, the sweet Dungeness crab. Oregonians who have developed a taste for the succulence of the crab native to their shores are hard put to accept substitutes elsewhere. Offshore, Oregon's trawlers bring in catches of a wide variety of ocean fish.

The Oregon cuisine, if it can be called that, began when 19th-century pioneers adapted their traditional dishes to native foods. Since many of the settlers came from the New England States, Oregon cooking has been characterized—by its detractors, at least—as an illegitimate child of Northeastern forebears.

This oversimplification neglects many other ethnic influences, including the native Indians, whose salmon "bakes" over fires of seasoned alderwood are legendary.

Like most major West Coast cities, Portland has always had a fair-sized Oriental population. As late as the 1940's, a "Chinatown" existed near the Willamette River waterfront in a now-restored downtown area known today as "Old Town," which still contains a core of Chinese restaurants.

After World War II, interned Japanese-Americans returned to the truck gardens and berry fields of the Columbia flatlands, rejoining the sons and daughters of other early settlers who had found the area suited to vast fruit and nut orchards. By this time, too, the cattle and wheat industries had been well established by homesteaders in the eastern part of the state, rounding out the sources of home-grown foods for Oregon's tables. Scandinavian fishermen on the Columbia and along the coast added their touches to the regional cuisine.

Southern "soul" food came to Portland when workers for the wartime shipbuilding industry were recruited from the South during World War II.

Probably the earliest fine dining establishment remembered by present residents of the city was the Portland Hotel, where generations of citizens were introduced to what passed for *haute cuisine.* The elegant dining room was full of tables dressed in snowy linens and had windows that looked out on a garden in the center of the city's growing business district. Around the turn of the century, the Portland's chef was Anton Slavich. His grandsons, Tony and Jerry, still follow the family cooking tradition.

The old hotel has now been replaced by a parking lot. Its place in dining history was filled by the Benson Hotel when owner Chester Benson persuaded a French-trained Swiss chef named Henry Thiele to leave the Fairmont in San Francisco and take over the newer hotel's kitchen.

"A great, creative chef," Portland native James Beard called him, praising Thiele's way with salmon and his Princess Charlotte pudding, a dessert Beard says he has tried to duplicate without success. The creamy bavaroise with fruit sauce, incidentally, is still being made by the chef's widow at **Henry Thiele's,** which she has operated since his death over a quarter century ago.

The Benson Hotel is still a Portland landmark, and the **London Grill,** its principal dining room, remains a popular gathering place for business breakfasts and lunches as well as for dinner. Its special Thanksgiving and Christmas feasts are reserved for weeks in advance.

In Portland today there are numerous good restaurants in the downtown area as well as in suburban neighborhoods. The trends recently have been to large establishments, heavy with atmosphere (some with disco lounges), or to small, ethnic, open-on-a-shoestring restaurants. Among the latter, loyal followings have been won by the Korea House (2534 S.E. Belmont Street), Thanh Truc, a Vietnamese restaurant (1227 S.E. Powell Boulevard) and the K-Y restaurant (322 N.W. Broadway). The owner-chef of the K-Y is Jeri Sipe, a Taiwanese woman noted by Craig Claiborne as one of the best Chinese cooks west of the Mississippi. She is seeking larger quarters, so the address may change.

For weekend diners, reservations are essential at most popular eating houses; during the week, same-day reservations usually are obtainable, particularly for early dinner.

The last remnants of the old Portland market are located downtown, on Yamhill Street between 4th and 5th avenues. Unfortunately, urban renewal has shrunk its size, but you can browse among open-front shops that sell fresh produce, meats, fish and flowers. Nearby are several delicatessens selling Italian, Greek, Middle-Eastern and some kosher-style foods. Like ethnic restaurants, small delicatessens have sprung up throughout the city.

# Restaurants and Food Sources

(Area code: 503)

## BIG DEAL

### WORTH IT

***Pettygrove House,*** 2287 N.W. Pettygrove Street (223-6025). In a residential neighborhood, with no sign outside, this 19th-century mansion is the corner house next to 23rd Avenue. Menu changes according to the season, but the food—a choice of four entrées—is pure satisfaction: fresh ingredients, nicely garnished and skillfully served. Reservations recommended. Dinner only. Closed Sunday through Tuesday. Complete dinner (including appetizer, first course, soup, salad, entrée, good bread and beverage) $16–$19. MC, V.

### NOT WORTH IT

***Couch Street Fish House,*** 105 N.W. 3rd Avenue (223-6173). Before this eating house opened in an elegantly refurbished building in "Old Town," it was touted as the most pretentious, highest-priced restaurant in Portland, and that's what it is. Fish and seafood entrées are generally of good quality, however. Service sometimes is overbearing. Dinner only. Open seven days a week. Entrées from $9.95. AE, MC, V.

## INTERNATIONAL

### AMERICAN

***John's Meat Market,*** 115 N.W. 22nd Avenue (223-2119). Good, solid food, served against a background of polished wood décor. Steaks and beef ribs are served by waiters in black butcher aprons. Broiled salmon in season and assorted skillet dishes are good, too. A plateful of sautéed-to-order mushrooms, ordered à la carte, almost can be a meal in itself. Open seven days a week. Entrées from $3.45 (L), $7.95 (D). AE, DC, MC, V.

***The Woodstove,*** 2601 N.W. Vaughn Street (227-6956). Cozy atmosphere with a subtle smell of woodsmoke from the huge fireplace where meats are actually roasted on a hand-wound, counterbalanced spit, or grilled over the coals. Fresh foods on a seasonal menu that changes often. The owner calls it *nouvelle cuisine* with Northwest foods, but the emphasis is not particularly French. Dinner only. Closed Sunday. Dinners from $8.95. AE, MC, V.

## CHINESE

***Pot Sticker and Sizzling Rice,*** 228 N.W. Davis Street (248-9231). Northern Chinese cuisine in a restored building in Portland's "Old Town," once the center of the local Chinese community. The menu is extensive, including, of course, pot-stickers (meat and vegetables wrapped in wonton skins, steamed and sautéed) and sizzling rice. Mongolian and Szechuan beef, *moo shu* pork, braised sea cucumber, Peking duck (must be ordered in advance). Closed Sunday. Entrées from $2.25 (L), $4.25 (D). No credit cards.

## CONTINENTAL

***L'Omelette,*** 815 S.W. Alder Street (248-9661). "New cooking" is what L'Omelette calls its adaptations of French *nouvelle cuisine:* tarragon chicken, scallops *minceur,* veal scaloppine with artichoke hearts. Classic European dishes fill other parts of the menu. There is a good wine list, with a well-informed wine steward. Closed Sunday. Omelets from $3.50, entrées from $4.25 (L), $5.25 (D). AE, MC, V.

## FRENCH

***L'Auberge,*** 2180 W. Burnside Street (223-3302). Discouraging décor, but time, effort and money not spent on the setting have been spent on high-quality food and a good menu. The chef offers a set menu, with a choice of several entrées that change weekly: mushroom-stuffed trout in season, duck with orange sauce, Dungeness crab could be part of the six-course dinner. Dinner only. Sunday, brunch only, 10:30 A.M. to 2 P.M. Closed Monday. Brunch varies from $4 to $6. Dinners from $14. MC, V.

***L'Escargot,*** 1987 N.W. Kearney Street (223-6964). Classical French food in a simple country atmosphere. The dinner menu, though it changes seasonally, always includes a rack of lamb, which is unequaled in Portland. Dessert profiteroles bring raves. Soups and salads for lunch, with a daily special. Saturday, dinner only. Closed Sunday and Monday. Entrées from $4.50 (L), $9 (D). V.

## GERMAN

***The Rheinlander,*** 5035 N.E. Sandy Boulevard (288-5503). Hearty food such as sauerbraten, rouladen and Wiener schnitzel served with potato pancakes, noodles and red cabbage. Price of entrées includes cheese fondue, a bowl of lentil soup, salad, a sweet bread and dessert. A roving accordionist and a dining room staff that bursts into song at the slightest provocation make it a favorite spot for families. It's not a place for quiet conversation, however. Dinner only. Open seven days a week. Entrées from $5.95. AE, MC, V.

## ITALIAN

***Genoa,*** 2832 S.E. Belmont Street (238-1464). A seven-course set menu that changes often, it's a Northern Italian feast: fresh vegetables with *bagna cauda,* soup, pasta, fish, entrée, dessert and fruit in season. To find out what's being served on a given night, ask when you call for reservations (essential). Genoa is open Monday for "international night" with a menu that changes monthly. Dinner only. Closed Sunday. Monday entrées from $12; Tuesday through Saturday, fixed-price dinners $17. AE, MC, V.

## JAPANESE

***Bush Garden,*** 900 S.W. Morrison Street (226-7181). Walk through a miniature Japanese garden, enter a dining cubicle (after first removing your shoes), sit on cushions at low tables (the floor is recessed for seating comfort). A kimono-clad waitress serves course after course, cooking some at the table, after discreetly closing the screens. Tempura, *teriyaki, sashimi* are excellent. Portland's oldest authentic Japanese restaurant, destroyed by fire in 1976, has a beautiful new location, complete with *sushi* bar. Open seven days a week. Entrées from $3.75 (L), $8 (D). MC, V.

## MEXICAN

***Mexico City Dinner House,*** 5145 S.E. McLoughlin Boulevard (238-0859). For Mexican-food lovers: tacos and *chiles rellenos, gallina en mole* and *camarones rancheros.* The unprepossessing building looks like an old-time roadhouse; inside, the décor is south-of-the-border red and black. Dinner only. Closed Monday and Tuesday. Entrées from $5.50. MC, V.

## NORWEGIAN

***A Bit of Norway,*** 5440 S.E. 82nd Avenue (771-3124). Set back from the road on this city-long street of used-car lots and flashing neon, this is one of the few restaurants in America that serves *lutefiske* regularly. A diner finds trolls and Viking ships and authentic Norwegian foods such as *farr i kaal* (braised lamb and cabbage), Bergen *kjottballer* (meatballs) and *fruktsoppe* (fruit soup). Homemade breads, including *lefse,* and pastries. Open at 7 A.M. for breakfast. Closed Sunday. Entrées from $2.75 (L), $5 (D). MC, V.

# SPECIALTY COOKING

## HAMBURGER

***Stanich Ten Till One Tavern,*** 4915 N.E. Fremont Street (281-2322). Beer and wine help wash down this burger, modestly called "the world's greatest." It contains bacon, cheese, ham, onion, pickle, fried egg, tomato, lettuce and—oh, yes—hamburger, too. It's indecent and hard to eat. There are less gigantic burgers and other sandwiches for the faint-hearted. Closed Sunday. The big one costs $2.30 on premises, $2.40 to go. No credit cards.

***Yaw's Top Notch,*** 2001 N.E. 40th Avenue (281-1233). Generations of Portlanders have grown up on Yaw's hamburger WGOO ("We grind our own") and accept no substitutes. There's a sauce that will run down to your elbows if you're not careful and it costs $1.95. Open seven days a week. AE, MC, V.

## RIBS

***Geneva's Food and Drinks,*** 4228 N. Williams Avenue (282-6363). Hot and spicy barbecued ribs are the specialty here. Jazz sessions Sundays at 7 P.M. (Disco dancing other nights.) Wide-screen TV for sports events. When Portland's NBA Trail Blazers are playing at home, a free "soul train" (a decorated bus) carries fans from Geneva's to the Memorial Coliseum and back. Open seven days a week. Entrées from $2 (L), $3.75 (D). AE, MC, V.

## SEAFOOD

***Dan and Louis Oyster Bar,*** 208 S.W. Ankeny Street (227-5906). Four generations of the Wachsmuth family have been in the oyster business. They operate their own oyster "farm" in Yaquina Bay on the Oregon coast. Their oyster stew ($1.70, or $2.70 with a double dose of oysters) is a Portland tradition. Diners share long tables to savor the stew as well as clam chowder and other seafoods served as the weather and good fishing permit. Walls are nearly covered with Wachsmuth family memorabilia dating back to 1865 when great-grandfather Meinert, a sailing man, was shipwrecked in Yaquina Bay. Open seven days a week. Entrées from $3.75 (L & D). AE, MC, V.

***Jake's Famous Crawfish,*** 401 S.W. 12th Avenue (226-1419). Dates back to the 1890's and to old-timers who wore bibs to eat their barbecued crab and succulent crawfish. The latter are still served in season, early summer to early fall. Salmon is baked, poached or broiled—this, too, in season. Bouillabaisse and sourdough bread are excellent. Good wines, with a separate list of Oregon wines. There are steaks for unyielding meat-lovers. Impeccable service. Open seven days a week. Entrées from $3.75 (L), $6.95 (D). AE, MC, V.

## STEAK

***The Ringside,*** 2165 W. Burnside Street (223-1513), ***Ringside East,*** 14021 N.E. Glisan Street (255-0750). Recent redecoration mellowed the atmosphere but didn't change the excellent quality of the beef. New York-cut is a favorite. Superb onion rings are another specialty. Burnside Street: dinner only. Glisan Street: lunch and dinner. Both: open seven days a week. Hamburgers $2.50 (L), steaks from $7.95 (D). AE, MC, V.

## TACOS

***Heavy Number Taco Company,*** 2088 N.W. Lovejoy Street (222-2913). A variety of tacos, including vegetarian, to take out or eat on the premises (take them out). The premises are a remodeled service station that looks like a remodeled service station. Order Heavy No. 2, lots of beef, refried beans, lettuce, tomato and onion with sour-cream sauce in a soft, flour tortilla. Open seven days a week. Tacos from 40 cents; Heavy No. 2 $1.25 (L & D). No credit cards.

# FOR INDIVIDUAL NEEDS

## IF YOU HAVE TIME FOR ONLY ONE MEAL

***L'Escargot,*** 1987 N.W. Kearney Street (223-6964). (See description under FRENCH.) Write or call ahead for Friday- and Saturday-night reservations; Tuesday through Thursday, reservations are usually available one day ahead. Dinner only.

## BEST HOTEL MEAL

***London Grill,*** The Benson Hotel, 309 S.W. Broadway (228-9611). Portlanders who've been faithful to the Grill for decades agree it is better than it has been for a while. Service is casual and friendly at breakfast and lunch; more formal, still friendly, at dinner. A new dinner menu features lighter entrées, more seafoods. Poached or baked salmon is a standby, as are steaks, but there is also sautéed chicken with tarragon, fillet of red snapper with ginger, pan-fried veal dishes and lobster flown in from Maine. Entrées from $2.95 (B), $3.80 (L), $8.50 (D). AE, CB, DC, MC, V.

## RESTAURANT NEAR AIRPORT

***Telstar Room,*** Airtel, 6221 N.E. 82nd Avenue (255-6511). A phone in the terminal baggage pickup area will summon a van for transportation to this restaurant-hotel that features steaks, prime rib and seafoods in relaxed surroundings. There is an assortment of flaming fruit desserts. Sunday and Friday buffets. Open seven days a week. Entrées from $2.75 (B), $3.85 (L), $6.95 (D). AE, CB, DC, MC, V.

## BUSINESS BREAKFAST

***The Original Pancake House,*** 8600 S.W. Barbur Boulevard (246-9007). "Original" in this case means not-part-of-a-chain, fresh and delicious. On a weekend or holiday, the wait will be a long one; Portlanders flock there. But Wednesday through Friday it's less crowded, and it's a haven for those who love fresh fruits and juices and unbelievable pancakes. The omelets are creditable, but out-classed. Closed Monday and Tuesday. Pancakes from $1.65. No credit cards.

## BUSINESS LUNCH

***Rian's Eating Establishment,*** 515 S.W. Broadway at Morgan's

Alley (222-9996). Downtown and convenient, Rian's is frequented at lunch by well-dressed business and professional types. Specialties are tasty sandwich offerings, quiches, chicken and crab Kiev (you're in Oregon, remember?) and low-calorie lunches for "thin-thinkers." At dinner, half-portions of entrées may be ordered at reduced cost. Closed Sunday. Entrées from $3.50 (L), $7 (D). MC, V.

## FAST, GOOD FOOD

***Henry Thiele's,*** 2305 W. Burnside Street (223-2060). An old Portland standby with one of the most extensive menus in town. It's still run by the widow of its founder, one of the city's early chefs of note. Interspersed with its original *frikadeller,* sauerbraten and Wiener schnitzel are entrées such as sautéed crab legs, veal scaloppini, Chinese skillet steak and hamburger Louisiana, along with the house specialty—an immense, baked German pancake. Open seven days a week. Entrées from $1.65 (B), $2.75 (L), $2.95 (D). AE, CB, DC, V.

## BEST WINE LIST

***London Grill,*** The Benson Hotel, 309 S.W. Broadway (228-9611). (See description under BEST HOTEL MEAL.) Considered by many to be the best in the Northwest, the wine list offers a fine selection of more than 150 Burgundies and Bordeaux with an outstanding assortment of German, California, Oregon and Washington wines. The knowledgeable sommelier will describe others that are in the cellar but not on the list. Open seven days a week.

## FOR DRINKS

***Jake's Famous Crawfish,*** 401 S.W. 12th Avenue (226-1419). (See description under SEAFOOD.) Since the main lounge is always crowded—standing room only at the long 1890's bar—Jake's has a second area, the 1220 Room, open after 6 P.M. for cocktails and snacks, too.

***The Princess,*** 1 S.W. Columbia Street (222-1881). Comfortable seating with a stunning view of Willamette River bridges and city lights; drinks are also served on an outside terrace in the summer. Hot and cold appetizers may be ordered in the bar. The restaurant offers a Continental menu. Saturday, dinner only. Sunday, brunch and dinner. Open seven days a week. Entrées from $3 (L), $8.95 (D). AE, MC, V.

## ROMANTIC

***Captain's Corner,*** 1201 S.W. 12th Avenue (224-9877). You may not be recognized in these dark-red booths that are dimly candlelit—for intimacy, one assumes, since the food is high quality and could bear examination under brighter light. Steaks are best here; skewered scallops and sautéed mushrooms are good bets, too. Closed Sunday. Entrées from $2.95 (L), $5.75 (D). AE, DC, MC, V.

## LATE-NIGHT SERVICE

***Valentino's,*** 555 S.W. Oak Street (226-3312). In the downtown business district, Valentino's serves omelets, lunch, snacks or dinner from 11 A.M. to 1 A.M.. Disco lounge. Saturday, dinner only. Sunday buffet brunch. Open seven days a week. Entrées from $2.95 (L), $6.50 (D). AE, CB, DC, MC, V.

## SUNDAY BRUNCH

***Nendel's Inn,*** 9900 S.W. Canyon Road (297-2551). A groaning table that supports brunch fare from hominy, ham and eggs to fresh salmon. Cold fresh fruit and excellent pastries. Open seven days a week. Fixed price $5.75 (adults), $4 (children under 8). AE, CB, DC, MC, V.

## SUNDAY-EVENING MEAL

***Valentino's,*** 555 S.W. Oak Street (226-3312). (See description under LATE-NIGHT SERVICE.)

## FOR FAMILIES WITH CHILDREN

***River Queen,*** 1300 N.W. Front Avenue (228-8633). An elegant retired ferryboat that plied the waters of San Francisco Bay and Puget Sound, the River Queen is moored in the Willamette River and retains its nautical gear and ornate décor, complete with gangplank entrance. Window seats offer a water-level view of boat traffic (Portland is a Pacific Ocean port). Children's menu (for subteens) at dinner only; entrées from $3.50. There are hamburgers, too. Adult dinners feature steaks and seafood; try the crab-stuffed baked trout. Open seven days a week. Adult entrées from $3.85 (L), $5.85 (D). AE, DC, MC, V.

## COUNTRY INN

***Aurora Colony Inn,*** 108 Main Street, Aurora (678-1300). This antique-filled old house retains some of the flavor of the German Mennonite communal society that flourished here in the 19th century. The society's Ox Barn Museum complex and antique shops are nearby. Hearty food, well-prepared. Homemade breads and pastries. Closed Monday though Wednesday. Dinner served until 6 P.M. Sunday; until 9 P.M. Thursday through Saturday. Entrées from $3.75 (L), $7 (D). MC, V.

***Forest Inn,*** Highway 26, east of Portland, at Alder Creek (668-6079). Nearby Mount Hood is a logical target for a drive outside Portland, and this scenic inn makes a good stopping place on the return trip. The country atmosphere has a Continental flavor; seafood encased in pastry and tournedos Rossini are worthwhile. The cooking is fine, and there are wood-paneled walls and a big stone fireplace. Dinner only. Open seven days a week. Entrées from $7.90. MC, V.

# IN THE SUBURBS

## BEAVERTON

***Rian's Fish and Ale House,*** 6620 S.W. Beaverton-Hillsdale Highway (292-0191). Pub-style atmosphere with Oregon-timber-country wood décor. Freshwater fish and seafood, from fish and chips to broiled scallops and the area's best cioppino. For non-fish-lovers, a Rian's hamburger is worth the trip. Open seven days a week. Entrées from $3 (L & D). MC, V.

## LAKE OSWEGO

***B. Street Bistro,*** 148 S.W. B Street (636-7500). More than its name implies, offering full-course dinners in a pleasant, semi-formal, country-French atmosphere. The menu leans toward the French, too, ranging from broiled veal or lamb shank to roast duckling (escargots Bourguignonne are offered as an entrée). Dinner only. Closed Sunday and Monday. Entrées from $7.95. MC, V.

## TIGARD

***Tebo's,*** 15900 S.W. 116th Avenue (620-0225). This is a suburban haven for hamburger lovers, most of whom save room for delicious fresh-fruit pies. Cafeteria-line service. Steaks, Reubens, hot dogs and home-crafted French fries. Open seven days a week. Hamburgers from $1.55 (L & D). MC, V.

## WEMME

***Chalet Swiss,*** Welches Road off Highway 26, east of Portland (622-3600). Mostly Continental food served in a chalet setting. Try the veal scallops with fresh mushrooms (*Zürcher Geschnitzeltes*). Dinner only. Closed Monday and Tuesday. Entrées from $5.50 (D). MC, V.

# MARKETS

## GIFT FOODS/WINES

***4th & Salmon Deli and Wine Cellar,*** 922 S.W. 4th Avenue (227-3189). Box lunches, gift baskets, buffet trays, imported foods. Wines and imported beers. Closed Sunday. MC, V.

***Meier & Frank,*** 621 S.W. 5th Avenue (227-4411). Good selection of packaged Oregon fruits and other specialties, and imported products. They do an extensive mail-order business. Cheeses, wines and delicatessen foods. Closed Sunday. No credit cards.

***Portland Fish Company,*** 301 S.W. 3rd Avenue (224-1611). Will ship gift packages of fish and seafoods anywhere in the U.S. Prepare whole salmon for shipping yourself or carrying home on the plane. Closed Saturday and Sunday. No credit cards.

***Harris Wine Cellars,*** 2300 N.W. Thurman Street (223-2222). Full selection of more than 375 wines, imported and domestic, also coffees, teas, cheeses. Soups, sandwiches, quiches served on premises for lunch or early supper. Closed Sunday. MC, V.

# St. Louis

People who have spent little or no time in St. Louis usually think of it as a German city. Indeed, it still has its fine old German neighborhoods full of sturdy stone and brick houses, it still boasts the largest brewery in the country, and German names help fill the phonebook.

But, gastronomically, St. Louis is an Italian city. There are bad Italian restaurants in St. Louis, but not many. And there are dozens and dozens of fine ones, not just on "the Hill," the hub of the Italian community, but in the suburbs and downtown. Even the better "Continental" menus in town have an Italian accent.

Italians came to St. Louis rather late in its history, however. Fur traders from New Orleans founded the city in 1764, and a succession of Spanish viceroys governed it until 1804. Westward expansion gave St. Louis the name "Gateway to the West"; and the Mississippi River, running along its eastern boundary, made it a major trading center.

Local larders of that riverside crossroads never suffered a lack of ingredients. Indians and settlers alike brought fish, wild game and produce to St. Louis to barter for the coffee, sugar and flour that were carried upriver by the Mississippi steamboats.

River life at this level was luxurious, and riverboat meals were extravagant. Tables were beautifully set, and bars were stocked with the finest wines and liquors. Boat captains vied for fine chefs, and local aristocrats did their best to emulate the style of the river. They entertained with a touch of Southern grace and charm—which still exists in St. Louis today.

Because of its position as a thriving port, St. Louis's industries expanded rapidly, attracting a large immigrant population. By 1860, St. Louis had more foreign-born residents than any other city, just over half of whom were German or Italian. With those immigrants came not only a solid Democratic conservatism but great bakers and candymakers and plenty of family-owned restaurants.

Family life in St. Louis has always centered around the kitchen table (large clans still gather for homemade Sunday dinner); and many South St. Louis restaurants are simply extensions of that tradition.

There are many "neighborhoods" in St. Louis, but the best known, most easily identifiable one is the Italian "Hill," roughly bordered by Kingshighway and Interstate 44 and Hampton Avenue. Its streets are lined with neat workmen's bungalows that surround an old spaghetti factory. While tourists may come here to view Joe Garagiola's and Yogi Berra's childhood homes, St. Louisans come to the Hill to eat. It seems every other storefront is either a restaurant, bakery, sausage shop or caterer.

"Toasted ravioli" (actually deep-fried) is a purely local concoction, a hybrid of Italian and American tastes. Other culinary contributions made by St. Louisans include angel-food cake, peanut butter (designed by a sympathetic dentist concerned about the nutrition of his toothless patients), Planter's punch and iced tea. An enterprising sausage peddler, Antoine Feuchtwanger, is credited by some with the invention of the hot dog at the St. Louis World's Fair in 1904. He was giving customers white gloves to protect their fingers when they picked up his sizzling sausages. When the gloves became a major expense, he talked his wife into making long buns to hold the meat.

The ice-cream cone also made its debut at the Fair where, according to one report, a waffle concession was located next to an ice-cream vendor. When some unknown genius purchased a penny waffle, rolled it into a cone and filled it with ice cream, both vendors noticed and quickly joined forces.

In spite of a population shift to suburbs after World War II, famous old watering spots in St. Louis's downtown continued to prosper. Gaslight Square was a nationally prominent entertainment center into the late '60's, when urban blight finally eroded the surrounding neighborhood. A few years ago, the last restaurant on Gaslight Square, **O'Connell's Pub,** turned out its lights and relocated in midtown.

Not far away, however, in the city's West End, a variety of small restaurants and pubs prosper today. Running along Euclid, several blocks on either side of Lindell Boulevard, sit such restaurants as Balaban's, **Duff's,** El Maya and **Sunshine Inn,** and pubs such as Llewelyn's Welsh Pub, Culpepper's and Tom's Bar & Grill.

Downtown, just across Washington Avenue from the city's gleaming Arch, another restaurant and entertainment center is coming to life. Called Laclede's Landing, this redevelopment area is a combination of businesses, antique shops, restaurants and bars, all housed in restored warehouses lining cobblestone streets. At the foot of the Landing, an authentic riverboat offers theater melodrama, while several handsome replicas offer lunch and dinner.

And, as business and residential development has continued to move west, restaurants and night spots have sprung up, too—in Westport Plaza and along Olive Street Road.

Nonetheless, some of the best food in the city is still to be found in private clubs—the Stadium Club, St. Louis Club and Missouri Athletic Club, among others.

Many worthwhile St. Louis restaurants continue the irritating practice of not taking reservations. On weekends, and sometimes even on week nights, the only way to avoid a frustrating wait in the bar is to arrive early—before 7 P.M. Tipping practices are standard, dress codes are nil with only the most formal spots requiring jackets or ties.

In the days before air conditioning, torrid heat from June to September made it too hot to cook indoors. Today the aroma of piquant barbecued pork wafts gently over every neighborhood throughout the summer. The enterprising visitor can share the fun by attending one of the street festivals held in one neighborhood or another almost every weekend of the summer. Sponsored by churches, community organizations and foreign-language clubs, they are reminders of the city's heritage.

For the shopper, excellent produce is available at Soulard Market (7th Street and Lafayette, downtown) open Friday evening and Saturday. The spice shop there is recommended. On the Hill, inexpensive Italian groceries are found at Viviano's (5147 Shaw Avenue); Italian sausage and prosciutto at John Volpi (5258 Daggett Street); and pastries or bread at the Missouri Baking Co. (2027 Edwards Avenue). Lindy's Meat and Sausage Market (3401 Winnebago Avenue, and Louisiana Avenue, on the south side) has been in business since 1904, and makes fine German sausages. **Randy's Cheese Shop** in Union Market (Delmar and Sixth Street) is a good place to find cheese. **The Epicure Ltd.** (9807 Clayton Road, mid-county) also offers a wide variety of cheese, coffees and homemade sorbets.

# Restaurants and Food Sources

(Area code: 314)

## BIG DEAL

### WORTH IT

***Tony's,*** 826 N. Broadway, downtown (231-7007). Diners are treated as pampered guests at this restored French row house near the riverfront. Dimly lit Italian Renaissance setting, impeccable, ostentatious service and an imaginative menu create a romantic ambience. The veal dishes, *tagliatelle* with marinara sauce, *cavatelli* with broccoli, salads and *zabaglione* are especially good. Many items prepared at tableside, often under the supervision of owner Vincent Bommarito. Reservations are not accepted, so unless you want to jeopardize a potentially good dinner with too many cocktails, arrive around 5 P.M. It will be very crowded by 6:30 P.M., especially on weekends. Chaîne des Rotisseurs. Dinner only. Closed Sunday and Monday. Pasta from $9; entrées, with vegetable, from $11; everything à la carte. AE, MC, V.

### NOT WORTH IT

***Stouffer's Top of the Riverfront,*** 200 S. 4th Street, downtown (241-3191). If only the food matched the view in this rooftop revolving restaurant near the Arch and the Mississippi. The specialty on the Continental menu is an artichoke and crab-meat combination, but the food seems to have a sameness true of many hotel dining rooms. Open seven days a week. Entrées, with salad, from $8.25 (L & D). AE, DC, MC, V.

# INTERNATIONAL

## AMERICAN

***Jefferson Avenue Boarding House,*** 3265 S. Jefferson Avenue, south city (771-4100). A restored, turn-of-the-century storefront. Menu changes daily, with at least three offerings each day. Typical entrées might be Chicken Tony Faust (chicken breast wrapped in ham in orange sauce) and baked pike meunière. Dinners include vegetables and salad. Appetizers and dessert extra. Reservations suggested, especially on weekends. Tuesday through Saturday, dinner only. Sunday, brunch and dinner. Closed Monday. Dinner entrées from $7.50, brunch entrées from $6.50. MC, V.

## CHINESE

***Yen Ching,*** 1012 S. Brentwood Boulevard, Richmond Heights, mid-county (721-7507). Simple Oriental décor. The Peking and Szechuan-style dishes are authentic, beautifully turned out, graciously served and delicious. Sweet-and-sour fish, served whole, is a ritual, and very good. Recommended also are Mongolian beef and sizzling-rice soup. Closed Monday. Entrées from $2.15 (L), $4.55 (D). MC.

***China Garden,*** 8600 Delmar Boulevard, University City, Mo., west county (997-0906). On the ground floor of the Montmartre Apartments, this Northern Chinese restaurant is simple and quiet. Pot stickers (crescent-shaped pastries filled with ground meat) and the Chinese dumplings are magnificent. The aromatic garlic chicken is also very good. Saturday and Sunday, dinner only. Closed Monday. Entrées from $2.75 (L), $4.55 (D). AE, DC, MC, V.

## FRENCH

***L'Auberge Bretonne,*** 13419 Chesterfield Shopping Plaza, Olive Street Road at Woods Mill, Chesterfield, west county (878-7706). A quietly elegant dining room in a sterile suburban plaza. The food is excellent, with friendly service. Despite the name, the menu is not regional but classic. There are salmon *quenelles,* oysters marinated in red wine, lobster bisque, red snapper in lobster sauce, roast duck and a different pastry daily. Reservations suggested. Dinner only. Closed Sunday. Entrées, with salad, from $9.35. AE, DC, MC, V.

# GERMAN

***Eberhard's,*** 117 N. Main Street, Columbia, Ill., a 20-minute drive from downtown (618/281-5400). Despite the owner's penchant for Bavarian memorabilia, the décor does not distract one from the food. The accompaniments, including potato or bread dumplings, chunky homemade applesauce or *Spaetzle* (tiny homemade dumplings), are a meal in themselves. Of the entrées, *Hasenpfeffer* is particularly good. Sauerbraten every night. Save room for dessert. At least 15 German beers and many German and French wines available. Reservations suggested on weekends. Dinner only. Sunday dinner begins at 11:30 A.M. Open seven days a week. Entrées, including side dishes, from $4.75. AE, CB, MC, V.

# ITALIAN

***Cunetto House of Pasta,*** 5453 Magnolia Avenue, on the Hill (781-1135). *Linguini sotto mare* (pasta with seafood sauce) is the house specialty. Also recommended are the pastas with vegetable sauces such as cauliflower, fresh asparagus, fresh tomato or pea. Reservations not accepted and you can expect a wait. Parking is also a problem on the narrow streets of this ethnic neighborhood, especially near such a popular restaurant. Closed Sunday. Sandwiches from $1.75 (L), pasta from $3 (D). AE, DC, MC, V.

***Kemoll's,*** 4201 N. Grand Boulevard, midtown-north (534-2705). Large, well-established, family-run restaurant with an extensive menu representing many regions of Italy. The homemade green fettuccine, served with a variety of sauces, is a real treat. Monthly "gourmet nights" feature six to ten courses and a different cuisine, not always regional Italian ($13.75). Reservations suggested. Closed Sunday. Entrées from $3.10 (L), pasta from $6 (D). AE, DC, MC, V.

***Dominic's,*** 5101 Wilson Avenue, on the Hill (771-1632). Expensive, elegant restaurant featuring excellent veal dishes, homemade pastas. Reservations accepted except Saturday. Dinner only. Closed Sunday and Monday. Entrées from $10.50, pasta from $8.50. AE, MC, V.

# JAPANESE

***The Mikado,*** 18 S. Kingshighway, midtown (367-1266). Diners may choose between a traditional *tatami* room, requiring the removal of one's shoes, or a conventional table. Bamboo screens separate the tables into intimate alcoves. The fried dishes are excellent, but it is a shame not to try the more unusual offerings such as *sashimi* or chicken and red snapper poached with vegetables. Dinner only. Closed Monday. Entrées with soup, salad and rice, from $6.75. AE, MC, V.

## LEBANESE

***St. Raymond's Maronite Church,*** 1020 S. 10th Street, downtown, across from Checkerboard Square, Ralston Purina's headquarters (621-0056). The women of the church shape the traditional *pita* bread by tossing it in the air, then rolling it on their arms. *Kibbe*—raw or baked—cabbage rolls, pilaf, spinach or meat pies are always featured along with other specialties. Wednesday and Friday, lunch only. All day on the last Sunday of each month, dinner only, 11 A.M. to 7 P.M. Entrées from $1.25. No credit cards.

## MEXICAN

***Hacienda,*** 2435 Woodson Road, Overland, northwest county (426-4569). A large cheerful restaurant that features a dinner plate with choice of three items. Diners are given the choice of domestic or Mexican cheeses. A tortilla factory next door is open to the public Monday through Friday. There is a sister restaurant at 9748 Manchester Road, west county (962-7100). Both restaurants: Open seven days a week. Dinner plate $3 (L & D). AE, MC, V.

## POLISH

***Little Poland,*** 3557 Delor Street, south city (353-9584). A simple neighborhood tavern that has good sauerkraut, soup and dumplings. Also a Warsaw Special that features Polish specialties, including pirogis. Polka music Friday and Saturday. Closed Sunday. Sandwiches from $1 (L), entrées from $1.90 (D). No credit cards.

# SPECIALTY COOKING

## BARBECUE

***Mo Jo's Barbecue,*** 3417 Lindell Boulevard, midtown (371-9249). A carry-out place, painted bright orange but otherwise not too cheerful. The ribs are wonderful, however. Closed Sunday. Open until 2 A.M. Thursday through Saturday. Entrées, with cole slaw, from $2.75. No credit cards.

# DELI

***Posh Nosh,*** 8115 Maryland Avenue, Clayton, mid-county (862-1890). Cheerful neighborhood gathering spot with a few extra tables for dining outside during summer months. Good hot dogs, thick pastrami sandwiches. Pickles and sauerkraut with all orders. Open seven days a week. Sandwiches from $1.10. No credit cards.

***Dunie's,*** 1215 Delmar Boulevard, downtown (231-8294). Look for a small beige building with auto graphics on one wall, standing alone in the middle of a parking lot. The location, across the street from the town's two major newspapers, makes it a favorite of local journalists. Try the chicken-noodle soup, one of the thick sandwiches or the marvelous cheese cake. Lunch only. Closed Saturday and Sunday. Sandwiches from $1.25. MC.

# HAMBURGER

***O'Connell's Pub,*** 4652 Shaw Avenue, midtown (773-6600). The last to leave Gaslight Square, this tavern reopened immediately just a block off "the Hill." The jazz-era furniture is still around; nostalgia is for real. A limited menu, but everything is good, especially the drinks. Hamburgers made from fresh, coarsely ground meat. Very thick, rare roast beef sandwiches. Outstanding French fries, fried mushrooms and onion rings. Closed Sunday. Sandwiches from $1.50 to $3. No credit cards.

# HOT DOG

***Kelly's Korner,*** 723 Market Street, downtown (421-9707). A dingy bar filled with pictures of local sports figures. Its location, a block from Busch Memorial Stadium, makes it a favorite of fans, sportswriters, and even coaches. Hot dogs—substantial, all-beef ones—are the only food served. 75 cents and served on a napkin. No credit cards.

# SEAFOOD

***Port St. Louis,*** 15 N. Central, Clayton, mid-county (727-1142). Some people say this elegant, expensive restaurant, filled with antiques, is the best place to eat in town. Service is impeccable, the wine list large. Stuffed Shrimp Antoine is a favorite. Dinner only. Open seven days a week. Entrées, with salad and vegetables, from $8.95. AE, CB, DC, MC, V.

## SOUL

***Crown's Cafeteria,*** Jefferson Avenue at Martin Luther King Drive, midtown (535-0590). Great corn bread as well as ham hocks, greens, biscuits, cobbler and pecan pie. Fish on Fridays, fried chicken every day, barbecue in the summer. Open 6 A.M. to 11 P.M., seven days a week. A complete meal costs about $3.50. No credit cards.

## STEAK

***Tenderloin Room,*** Chase-Park Plaza Hotel, 212 N. Kingshighway, midtown (361-2500). The dark mahogany bar, red velvet and chandeliers create a formal setting appropriate to this old hotel; and this dining room is by far the best of several in the house. Hack, the maître d', knows "everybody in town," so they say. Entertainers and politicians are seen at the best tables. The pepper steak is a favorite, but save room; the dessert cart is irresistible. Steak from $3.75 (L), $6.25 (D). AE, CB, DC, MC, V.

## VEGETARIAN

***Sunshine Inn,*** 8½ S. Euclid Avenue, midtown (367-1413). Once strictly vegetarian, this friendly, "earthy" restaurant now has some meat dishes as well. Hearty soups, fresh, hot whole-wheat breads. Sunday, dinner only. Closed Monday. Entrées from $2.75 (L & D). No credit cards.

# FOR INDIVIDUAL NEEDS

## IF YOU HAVE TIME FOR ONLY ONE MEAL

***Anthony's,*** Equitable Building, 10 S. Broadway, downtown (231-2434). Although it's in the heart of the downtown business district, Anthony's is still an elegant, sophisticated hideaway. The smoked glass and steel décor, illuminated by tiny lights, makes it seem as though every table were floating in space. Waiters drift in and out of view; service is impeccable. Owned and operated by Vincent and Anthony Bommarito, who also own Tony's. The menu is Continental. Wonderful soups and salads, scallops poached in white wine, scampi in mustard sauce. Reservations suggested. Saturday, dinner only. Closed Sunday. Entrées, with vegetables, from $8 (L), $10 (D). AE, MC, V.

## BEST HOTEL MEAL

***Tenderloin Room,*** Chase-Park Plaza Hotel, 212 N. Kingshighway, midtown (361-2500). (See description under STEAK.)

## RESTAURANT NEAR AIRPORT

***The Hangar,*** Marriott Hotel, Interstate 70 at Lambert-St. Louis International Airport (423-9700). Decorated with old airplane memorabilia. Saturday, dinner only. Brunch on Sunday. Open seven days a week. Soup and salad bar $3.75 (L), brunch from $6.25, entrées from $7.25 (D). AE, CB, DC, MC, V.

## BUSINESS BREAKFAST

***Cheshire Inn,*** 6306 Clayton Road, mid-county (647-7300). At the edge of Forest Park and decorated in Old English style with many fine antiques, this is a "Miss Hulling's" restaurant, part of a local chain known for its superb baked goods. There is a bakery outlet next door. Chaîne des Rotisseurs. Open from 7 A.M. weekdays; 7:30 A.M. Saturday, 8:30 A.M. Sunday. Buffet brunch, $3.90 Monday through Saturday; $5.80 on Sunday. AE, DC, MC, V.

## BUSINESS LUNCH

***Stan Musial & Biggies,*** 5130 Oakland, midtown (652-2626). Popular with businessmen and clubs, partly because of generous portions, partly because of central location. Sandwiches, omelets, chops, steaks (the specialty), and a daily special. Reservations suggested. Sunday, dinner only. Open seven days a week. Sandwiches from $1.95, pasta from $5.25, steaks from $9.25. AE, CB, DC, MC, V.

## FAST, GOOD FOOD/BREAKFAST

***Miss Hulling's Cafeteria,*** 1105 Locust Street, downtown (436-0840). Spotlessly clean, with fresh flowers on the tables. Wonderful baked goods, also available for carry-out from the bakery outlet next door. Portions not large, but food is always good. Open at 6:30 A.M. Closed most Sundays. Entrées from $1.75 (L & D). AE, DC, MC, V.

## FAST, GOOD FOOD/LUNCH

***Famous Barr.*** A local department-store chain with branches throughout the metropolitan area. Most have dining rooms open in the evenings. Rich, filling French onion soup, crusty French bread, good omelets, their own ice cream, acceptable salads. Meals are often accompanied by wonderful blueberry muffins. Closed Sunday. French onion soup, $1.50. Entrées from $2.45 (L), $3.75 (D). No credit cards.

## FAST, GOOD FOOD/DINNER

***Rich and Charlie's Pasta House,*** 8213 Delmar Boulevard, University City, mid-county (991-2022). One of a local chain of 10 pasta restaurants (some are called the Pasta House Co.), this casual restaurant offers some of the best food in town for the price. Portions are gigantic. Customers bring their own wine or beer here, but others in the chain serve liquor. Dinner only, here; lunch at others in chain. Open seven days a week. Pasta from $3.25; half orders available for some dishes. MC, V.

***Duff's,*** 392 N. Euclid, midtown (361-0522). Casual restaurant where either blue jeans or business suits are at home. Wonderful homemade soups and salads, well-cooked fresh vegetables. Entrées change bi-monthly. Reservations suggested. Closed Monday. Entrées, from $1.95 (L), $4.95 (D). MC, V.

## BEST WINE LIST

***Al Baker's,*** 8101 Clayton Road, Clayton, mid-county (863-8878). Fussy, memorabilia-laden setting inside a plain building. An Italian menu with a few Continental touches. Expensive. A wide selection of European labels. Reservations recommended. Dinner only. Closed Sunday. Pasta from $6.95, entrées from $8.95. AE, DC, MC, V.

## FOR DRINKS

***Fox and Hounds,*** Chesire Inn, 6306 Clayton Road, mid-county (647-7300). Part of an Old English-style hotel and restaurant complex, this bar is warm, cozy and full of antiques. Bill Benson, who sings and plays the piano, is a local institution. Full lunch, but in the evening, limited snacks only. Open from 11:30 A.M., Monday through Saturday. Closed Sunday. AE, DC, MC, V.

***Burnham's St. Louis Opera House,*** 314 Westport Plaza, west county (434-9040). The country-rock music is live Tuesday through Saturday and the foot-stomping, hand-clapping crowd is packed in shoulder-to-shoulder. Blue jeans are in order. So is singing along. No cover. No credit cards.

***TGI Friday's,*** 12398 Olive Street Road, west county (878-2220).

This modern, plant-filled bar usually has a line of young people waiting to get in. Voices tend to drown out the stereo music. Lunch and dinner are served but are not the main attraction. Open from 11:30 A.M., seven days a week. AE, MC, V.

## ROMANTIC

***Busch's Grove,*** 9160 Clayton Road, Ladue, west county (993-0011). This white frame restaurant has been around for more than 85 years and is a landmark. Although the food is short of terrific, regular patrons are very loyal. From early May to late September, ask for seating in one of the screened-in private dining rooms out back. Some are small enough for parties of two. Reservations essential. Closed Sunday and Monday. Entrées from $2.50 (L), $6 (D). No credit cards.

## LATE-NIGHT SERVICE

***Caleco's Restaurant and Saloon,*** 3818 Laclede Avenue, midtown (534-7878). Best pizza in town; choose either deep-dish or thin crust. Ample salads, fried mushrooms, toasted ravioli and other pasta. Dining rooms separate from attractive bar that has live music Tuesday through Sunday. Dinner until 1:30 A.M. Open seven days a week. Entrées from $2.95, pizza from $3.85 (L & D). MC, V.

## SUNDAY BRUNCH

***Houlihan's Old Place,*** 104 West County Center, west county (821-0900). Casual, funky, crowded restaurant filled with Art Deco posters and hanging plants. Plan on arriving right at 10 A.M. for the buffet because crowds are enormous. Reservations not accepted. $4.95 for adults, $2.95 for children. Also open for lunch and dinner, Monday through Saturday. AE, DC, MC, V.

## SUNDAY-EVENING MEAL

***Lt. Robert E. Lee,*** foot of Wharf Street on the riverfront, downtown (241-1282). Replica of an old sternwheeler riverboat, containing a seafood restaurant, a steak restaurant and a bar. Restaurant is always crowded, but if weather allows, you can walk along the levee while you wait. Reservations on a limited basis. Open seven days a week. Sunday dinner begins at noon. Entrées from $3.25 (L), $6.95 (D). MC, V.

# FOR FAMILIES WITH CHILDREN

***Belle Angeline,*** 800 N. Wharf Street, downtown ( handsome replica of the riverboats that once plied th this restaurant has several dining rooms. Families Eads Bridge Room most; it is warm, casual and has a An oyster bar with banjo and piano music is open months, when the riverfront restaurants get very cro vations not accepted on Saturday. In warm weather days a week. During winter months, closed Sunday. $3.95 (L), $7.50, with salad and vegetable (D). AE, [

***The Carriage House of the Chatillon-DeMenil M*** DeMenil Place, south city (771-5829). Only a few mir Busch brewery on Broadway, this restored mansion a would appeal more to families with older children. Bu and five hot entrées. During warm weather, diners ca or outside on a covered terrace. Reservations sugg only, but plans call for dinner one night weekly. T information. Closed Sunday and Monday. Sandwiche MC, V.

# COUNTRY INN

***Elsah Landing,*** 18 LaSalle Street, Elsah, Illinois, 18 Alton, Illinois, about 45 to 60 minutes from downto (618/374-1607). Franco-American and Gothic Revival are represented among the homes in this small ninete village, the site of Principia College. The Landing is a rustic lunch counter in an 1894 storefront. Run b women, the fare includes several varieties of hot, fres breads; outstanding soups including cream of lettuce with bacon; and dessert. In the fall, the road to El Highway 100 is ideal for viewing the colorful folia Mississippi's bluffs. Usually crowded for lunch. Ope to 8 P.M. Closed Monday. Bread and soup prices fro credit cards.

# TEAROOM

***André's Swiss Candies and Pastry,*** 7721 Clayton Rc mid-county (727-9928). Entrées vary, but often include or omelets. Choose from a pastry tray for dessert. A adjoins the lunchroom. Monday through Saturday, Closed Sunday. Entrée, salad, vegetable, beverage a $3.65. MC.

# N THE SUBURBS

## T. CHARLES

**e Mother-In-Law House,** 500 S. Main Street (724-9279). One of veral restored houses in St. Charles's commercial district. The nu includes beef, seafood and poultry. Reservations suggested. turday, dinner only. Closed Sunday. The luncheon buffet is 95; dinner entrées, with a salad bar, from $5.50. DC.

# MARKETS

## IFT FOODS

**rl Bissinger's,** 4742 McPherson Avenue, midtown (361-0647). so in Plaza Frontenac, mid-county (361-0647). Beautiful French nfections; chocolate-covered molasses lollipops. Closed Sun-y. MC, V.

**icure Ltd.,** 9807 Clayton Road, Ladue, mid-county (997-6668). de selection of cheeses, coffees, as well as homemade sorbets, tés, salads to take out. Will mail almost anywhere. Open seven ys a week. MC.

**rb's Candies,** 4000 S. Grand Boulevard, south city (832-7117). so shops at 103 Concord Plaza, south county (842-4644), 590 rissant Meadows Shopping Center (837-2324) and 12710 Olive eet Road (434-2213). Novelty chocolate molds a specialty. Open ven days a week. MC, V.

**ndy's Cheese Shop,** Union Market, 6th Street and Martin Luther ng Drive, downtown (621-7024). Many imported and domestic eeses are available. Closed Sunday. No credit cards.

## IFT WINES

**ople's 905, Le Château,** 10405 Clayton Road, west county (993-55). Large selection of wines and cheeses. One of many 905 res in area, this shop is located in a small shopping mall that o contains **Boucair's,** a French restaurant and sidewalk café. osed Sunday. MC, V.

# Salt Lake City

Salt Lake City has grown up. It is a far cry from what it was in 1847 when Brigham Young and the band of Mormon followers came upon the valley.

It has an extraordinary past and an unusual present. Salt Lake City was settled by orderly and industrious members of the Church of Jesus Christ of Latter-day Saints whose influence is still strongly felt. Today there are a vast number of nonmembers living in the city, but most things that happen in the state are affected in some way by the rules and customs of the Mormon church.

The food is no exception. There was a day when strangers spending a few days in the obviously prosperous city were surprised at so few good restaurants. Family-oriented Mormons had been taught to eat at home. And although they ate extremely well, what they consumed was also related to their religion.

The state of Utah is dry. Liquor by the drink is prohibited, although most restaurants now have liquor stores on the premises where minibottles and wine may be purchased.

Downtown Salt Lake City is now dotted with large new buildings, housing numerous regional and national headquarters offices. There are fine new stores, whole blocks of new and rebuilt shops and a new downtown mall. Main Street has undergone simultaneous modification and beautification. Hundreds of parking spaces have been added. High-rise hotels have been built and the expansion in motels and restaurants cannot seem to keep pace with the demand. There has been a steady expansion of restaurant, private club and entertainment facilities.

The suburbs also bring eating pleasures. There are delightful restaurants in the ski areas, which offer not only fine food but fantastic scenery. Visitors should try to visit one of these close-to-town ski resorts.

Steak-and-potato restaurants and family-type eating establishments are plentiful. Most hotel restaurants have ordinary food—nothing to rave about, but acceptable and moderately priced.

Tables in the most popular restaurants in Salt Lake City are more available for dinner than lunch, generally speaking. Reservations are recommended for either meal. One tip for the meal is acceptable. Pants suits are in order for women, and jackets with ties, or turtlenecks, for men.

# Restaurants and Food Sources
**(Area code: 801)**

# BIG DEAL

## WORTH IT

***La Caille at Quail Run,*** 9565 S. Wasatch Boulevard (942-1751). Housed in a replica of an eighteenth-century French château, La Caille features fine country dining. Formal gardens. Dinner specialties include veal Marsala, duck *à l'orange,* rack of lamb. Liquor store with minibottles, wine. Dinner only, except brunch on Sunday. Open seven days a week. Basque dinners (including special breads) available on Sunday, from 6 P.M. to 9 P.M. Regular dinners from $13.75, Basque dinner $11. Sunday brunch (featuring crêpes *crustaces*), $8.50. MC, V.

## NOT WORTH IT

***Royal Palace,*** 249 South 4th East (359-5000). Unusual restaurant located in what once was a Jewish synagogue. Owner-chef is a Persian with multinational point of view and menu—which is a bit too diversified and expensive. Valet parking. Entrées from $8.95. AE, MC, V.

# INTERNATIONAL

## AMERICAN

***Balsam Embers,*** 2350 Foothill Drive (466-4496). The captivating décor is Victorian and comfortable. Special rooms for private parties and meetings. Specialties include prime rib, *médaillons de veau* Oskar, scallops. Liquor store on premises. Dinner only. Closed Sunday. Complete meals from $8. AE, MC, V.

## FRENCH

***Le Fleur de Lys,*** 338 South State (359-5753). *Haute cuisine* in the heart of the city. Menu offers pheasant, beef Wellington, roast duckling, veal Viennoise. Top-quality wines, liqueurs. Fine linen, silver service, crystal glassware. Harp music nightly. Valet parking. Dinner only. Closed Sunday. Entrées from $8. AE, DC, MC, V.

***Rustler's Lodge,*** Alta Resort, Little Cottonwood Canyon (532-4061). Rustic décor in a beautiful mountain setting. The cooking is French. Excellent service. Minibottle service. Summer, dinner only. Open seven days a week. Entrées from $3 (L), fixed-price entrées $11 (D). MC.

## ITALIAN

***Ristorante Della Fontana,*** 336 South 400 East (328-4243). Seasoning and recipes from the Mediterranean: minestrone and antipasto are among the best house specials. Also consider stuffed breast of chicken, lasagne, halibut. Seven-course dinners with a lot of food. Wine available. Closed Sunday. Complete dinner from $4.60. AE, V.

## JAPANESE

***Mikado,*** 67 West First South (328-0929). Private Japanese *zashiki* rooms or private booths. Kimono-clad hostesses. Eat at the grill table or in traditional, shoes-off fashion at a low table. Steak *teriyaki,* sukiyaki or *shabu-shabu* (vegetables and meat cooked in broth at the table) are recommended. Dinner only. Closed Sunday. Entrées from $7.25. AE, DC, MC.

## MEXICAN

***Sophie Garcia's Mexican Restaurant,*** 150 West 600 South (521-2145). South-of-the-Border décor complements excellent Mexican food served. Live music. Open seven days a week. Complete meals from $3.50 (L & D). AE, MC, V.

# SPECIALTY COOKING

## DELI

***Marianne's Delicatessen,*** 149 West 2nd South (364-0513). Delightful deli specialties. German-type foods are featured, but most other styles of delicatessen are available as well. Closed Sunday and Monday. No credit cards.

***Luxury Dornbush Delicatessen and Foods,*** 163 E. 3rd South (363-8261). Jewish specialties featured—bagels, sandwiches garnished "as you like it." Closed Sunday. MC.

## HAMBURGER

***Cotton Bottom Inn,*** 2820 E. 6200 South (277-0017). Beautiful canyon setting. Excellent hamburger, cheeseburger, hot dogs—with variations to all. Beer served. Open seven days a week until 1 A.M. Hamburgers from $1.25. No credit cards.

## SEAFOOD

***The Towne Hall,*** Salt Lake Hilton, 151 West 5th South (532-3344). Cape Cod cuisine. Fresh fish, including lobster, flown in daily from the East Coast. Oyster stew a specialty. Also prime rib and other beef entrées. A Sunday brunch is dedicated to seafood: halibut casserole, creamed lobster. Liquor store on premises. Open seven days a week. Wednesday evening buffet. Continental breakfast, Monday through Saturday. Entrées from $3 (L), $8.50 (D). AE, CB, DC, MC, V.

## STEAK

***Steak Pit,*** Snowbird Resort, Little Cottonwood Canyon, east of the city (521-6150). Informal, comfortable, appropriate décor. Beautiful setting. Excellent steaks, steak-and-Alaskan-crab combination, and *teriyaki* chicken. Steaming hot artichokes and sautéed mushrooms are specialties. Mingle with skiers in season, but popular all year. Dinner only. Open seven days a week. Entrées from $7.50 (D). AE, MC, V.

## VEGETARIAN

***Morning Star Natural Foods Restaurant,*** 154 East 2nd South (532-9118). This place is modern—elegantly plain, white and clean, and it caters to the recent vogue for organic foods. Try *falafel* served in *pita* bread. Closed Sunday. Entrées from $3.50 (L & D). No credit cards.

# FOR INDIVIDUAL NEEDS

## IF YOU HAVE TIME FOR ONLY ONE MEAL

***The Roof Restaurant,*** Hotel Utah, Main Street and South Temple (531-1000). Panoramic view of Temple Square, the city skyline and western mountains. Superb food, excellent service, beautiful view. Specialties, rack of lamb, roast duckling, baked halibut. Dinner only. Open seven days a week. Complete meals from $7.95. AE, CB, MC, V.

## BEST HOTEL MEAL

***Little America Restaurant,*** 500 South Main (322-1941). Elegant, traditional décor. Excellent food and service. Specialties include salmon, prime rib, New York sirloin steak, pepper steak, abalone. Open seven days a week. Entrées from $4.95 (L), $9.95 (D). AE, CB, DC, MC, V.

## BUSINESS BREAKFAST

***Lamb's Grill,*** 169 South Main (364-7166). Fine linens and china; quiet and secluded. Excellent service. Close to in-town hotels and motels. Open from 7 A.M. to 9 P.M. Closed Sunday. Breakfast from $2.35. AE, MC, V.

## BUSINESS LUNCH

***Hilton Hotel,*** 150 West 5th South (532-3344). Typical coffee-shop fare is served at the **Cream and Sugar,** but it's good. Business types also enjoy the **Room at the Top** because it's quiet. Relatively light lunch offerings such as fried oysters, clams or scallops are available at the **Oyster Bar** in the restaurant. Shish kebab is popular, too. Liquor store on premises. Open seven days a week. Entrées from $2.95 (L). AE, CB, DC, MC, V.

## LATE-NIGHT SERVICE

***Bill and Nadas,*** 479 South 6th East (359-6984). Specialties: Two and Two (pancakes and eggs), ham and eggs. Coffee is the best in town. Breakfast anytime. Open 24 hours a day, seven days a week. No credit cards.

## SUNDAY-EVENING MEAL

***La Caille at Quail Run,*** 9565 S. Wasatch Boulevard (942-1751). (See description under BIG DEAL/WORTH IT.)

# MARKETS

***Trolley Square,*** 602 East 500 South (521-9877). Close to the heart of the city. Features meats, cheese, fish, produce, deli and general commodities. Gift packages. Open seven days a week. AE, CB, DC, MC, V.

# San Antonio

Just a little more than a decade ago, the number of quality restaurants in San Antonio could almost be counted on one hand.

The HemisFair in 1968 put San Antonio on the map. That event, plus the renovation of La Villita (San Antonio's Old Town) and the creation of the downtown River Walk, had a major influence on the city's restaurant business. But it was not until the liquor-by-the-drink laws came into effect in 1972 that things really began to change: the restaurant business all over the state was rejuvenated.

Up until then, San Antonio's major restaurants included La Louisiane (a French restaurant opened in 1937 that has received national recognition for its cuisine), **Naples** Italian restaurant, Barn Door Steakhouse, **Old San Francisco Steak House,** Casey's John Charles (which has one of the most extensive wine collections in South Texas this side of Houston), the Grey Moss Inn (which began as a stagecoach stop) as well as Casa Rio, La Fonda, Karam's, **Mi Tierra,** Mario's and the Pan American—all large Mexican restaurants popular with tourists. Except for these restaurants and numerous coffeeshops, almost every other dining option was a tiny Mexican café. There are still literally hundreds of small Mexican-American cafés on the south and west sides of the city.

However, with the new liquor laws came a population explosion of restaurants and clubs along North Loop 410, and today that several-miles-long strip of expressway is known as Restaurant (or Nightclub) Row.

Starting a restaurant is, of course, only part of the story. Survival is the rest of it, the key to which not many have found. For every new major restaurant that has succeeded in the past 10 years, probably five—at least—have died. An amazingly large number never see that first birthday. Many, many more never see the second. Those that see the third usually continue to see more.

For this reason, choosing a list of "Best Restaurants" in San Antonio is difficult. One of the best restaurants the city has ever had, Mel's (which specialized in Continental cuisine) didn't even last a year. It went out of business early in 1979. Half a dozen of what would have been the top restaurants in the city just a year and a half ago are no longer in business.

In spite of the restaurant growth in San Antonio, the city's Mexican heritage is still a major influence. More than 50 percent of the population of the 10th largest city in the nation is Mexican-American. The Mexican food served in San Antonio is known as Tex-Mex. A few places offer dishes from northern Mexico, but even these are so influenced by local taste that much of the authenticity is lost. For real Mexican food, go to central Mexico. For Texas-style Mexican food at its best, head for San Antone! And before leaving San Antonio, be sure to try *menudo*—a treat that tastes much better than it sounds. Cow belly (tripe) is cut into small pieces and simmered for several hours until tender, then seasoned with chili pods, paprika, oregano, garlic, other spices and white hominy

San Antonio also has a strong German heritage, but the best German restaurants are found in the smaller communities grouped around San Antonio. Somehow enchiladas and *menudo* haven't made way for German cuisine in the city itself.

# Restaurants and Food Sources
(Area code: 512)

## BIG DEAL

### WORTH IT

***Little Rhein Steak House,*** La Villita, 231 S. Alamo, two blocks south of the Alamo (225-2111 or 225-1212). Located on land that belonged to the first mayor of the Alamo, the building that houses this superb restaurant was built in 1847, or thereabouts, and was probably the first two-story structure in San Antonio. Dine on the River Walk almost year round, or indoors when the weather is less pleasant. Steaks, chicken, pork and lamb chops, shrimp and lobster are the main menu items. High prices for San Antonio, but moderate for a major American city. A combination of good food, good service and unique atmosphere. Beer, wine list, full bar. Reservations recommended. Dinner only. Open seven days a week. Entrées from $7.45. AE, CB, DC, MC, V.

### NOT WORTH IT

***Tower of the Americas Restaurant,*** HemisFair Plaza (223-3101). Built for the 1968 world's fair, the tower has become a San Antonio landmark. Ride up the elevator to the top and view the city from the observation deck. Have a drink and dance in the discotheque located on the floor above the restaurant, but dine elsewhere. (Elevator ride to restaurant and discotheque, 50 cents; to observation deck, $1.) Full bar. Open seven days a week. Entrées from $2.75 (L), $6.25 (D). AE, CB, DC, MC, V.

# INTERNATIONAL

## CHINESE

***Hung Fong Chinese and American Restaurant,*** 3624 Broadway (822-9211). In operation since 1942, this is the oldest Chinese restaurant in San Antonio and it is practically an institution among the city's restaurants. Other Chinese restaurants have sprung up around the city in the last few years, and even months, but none has maintained the consistent quality of this restaurant. Expect a crowd at any hour. There will be a wait for a table during peak hours and often even late at night. The servings are generous—two light eaters will be able to share one entrée. Beer, wine. Open seven days a week, until 1 A.M. Saturday, and until midnight the rest of the week. Entrées from $2.15 (L & D). No credit cards.

## FRENCH

***Chez Ardid,*** 7701 Broadway (824-6567). The best French restaurant in the city. Good service, good food and an intimate atmosphere. Most popular items are the filet of red snapper and the *escalope de veau* in cream or Marsala sauce. Wine list. Reservations recommended. Closed Sunday and Monday. Entrées from $4.50 (L), $8 (D). MC, V.

## ITALIAN

***Paesano's,*** 1715 McCullough (226-9541). The shrimp Paesano cannot be matched. Other favorites are filet of red snapper, plain or with mushroom sauce, beef steak pizzaiola, beef steak Italiana, veal scaloppini (Marsala, Francesca or Cristina). Try to avoid dining at peak hours or you will have to wait for a table in this small, intimate restaurant. Informal. Beer and wine. Reservations recommended. Saturday and Sunday, dinner only. Closed Monday. Entrées from $2.50 (L & D). MC, V.

***Naples,*** 3210 Broadway (826-9554). The 30-year-old Naples is large and decorated with an incredible collection of antiques that belong to the owner. Naples draws crowds but is so big it handles them well. The *conchiglia* of shrimp Naples, an appetizer, is one of the best dishes, and oysters oreganato are a specialty. Vegetable dishes, omelets, seafood, steaks, veal, pizza and traditional Italian pastas. Superb desserts. Reservations recommended. Dinner only. Closed Monday. Entrées from $1.10. AE, MC, V.

## MEXICAN

***El Bosque Mexican Restaurant and Patio,*** 12656 West Avenue (494-2577). This small restaurant, located in a beautiful forested area on the north side of town, is considered by many local Mexican food buffs to have the best enchiladas in the city. And everything served is made from scratch in this family-owned and -operated restaurant. One may dine indoors or on the huge patio under the giant trees, weather permitting. Try the *carne guisada* (a Mexican beef stew), made with beautifully trimmed round steak. About a quarter pound of meat is served in each *carne guisada* taco, for only 80 cents. American hamburgers, cheeseburgers and steak are also popular items. Closed Monday and Tuesday. Entrées from $2.10 (L & D). CB, DC, MC, V.

# SPECIALTY COOKING

## CHILI

***Kuykendall Café,*** 220 Fredericksburg Road (732-0406). Louis Kuykendall opened this place 40 years ago and he is still known for the best chili recipe in town. New owners took over the tiny café on the west side of town a couple of years ago, but the food remains the same. It's a favorite of the courthouse crowd. Customers consume as much as 90 pounds of chili a week. In addition to chili, there are chili burgers, homemade tamales, enchiladas, chili and beans and other dishes. Lunch only. Closed Sunday. A bowl of chili is $1.55. No credit cards.

## MENUDO

***Los Arcos Café,*** 502 S. Zarzamora (432-9035). For a restaurant on the south side of town, this place isn't really that small; but by most standards it would be a hole in the wall. Either way, it is difficult to find a seat, even at two or three in the morning. The menu offers a wide variety of Tex-Mex food, but the specialties of the restaurant aren't even listed because everyone knows about them: *menudo* and *caldo de rez* (a beef vegetable soup). Customers here consume as much as 400 pounds of beef a week in *menudo* alone. Corn and flour tortillas are made here. Domestic and Mexican beer. Open from 6 A.M. to 3 A.M. Closed Tuesday. *Menudo* and *caldo,* $1.50 a bowl. *Menudo* served all the time, *caldo* from 11 A.M. to 1 P.M., or until the vegetables become mushy. Daily luncheon special of out-of-the-ordinary Tex-Mex food, $2.25. No credit cards.

## MEXICAN PASTRY

***Mi Tierra Café and Bakery,*** 218 Produce Row, El Mercado (225-1262). One of the landmark Mexican restaurants in San Antonio, frequented by local gringos and Chicanos as well as tourists. This 24-hour operation offers a wide variety of Mexican pastries and candies in addition to a large Tex-Mex menu. Average prices of pastries and candy is 25 cents each, and many of the pastries are larger than large American doughnuts. Buy them to go, or have them with a cup of coffee or hot chocolate. Open seven days a week. No credit cards.

## TACOS

***Texas Hot Stuff,*** 8719 Botts, one block east of Broadway, off Cee Gee, north of Loop 410 (824-0354). Joe Martinez was grossing more than $1 million a year with four taco locations on the west side of town until he decided he was going to wear himself out (two were 24-hour operations). So he sold them all and opened this place, located in a warehouse on the north side. The take-out service is a necessity because it is impossible to find a seat during peak breakfast and lunch hours. More than a dozen types of tacos, ranging from bacon and egg to sausage to *carne guisada.* Flour tortillas made in the restaurant. *Barbecoa* (Mexican barbecue) served on Saturday. A calf's head is wrapped in a sack and cooked in a barbecue pit until tender. Served in a taco, 55 cents. Though it may sound less than delicious, it is one of the most popular items in cafés throughout the city. Breakfast and lunch only. Open at 7 A.M. Closed Sunday. Taco prices range from 45 to 65 cents. No credit cards.

# FOR INDIVIDUAL NEEDS

## IF YOU HAVE TIME FOR ONLY ONE MEAL

***Fig Tree Restaurant,*** 515 Villita Street, 733 River Walk (224-1976). Located on the River Walk, it has a pleasant ambience, especially in the outdoor dining area, which only its nextdoor neighbor, Little Rhein, can come close to matching. The Continental dishes are flawless. The riverside terrace or the intimate dining room, along with the attentiveness of the handsome waiters, create a mood that literally lulls the customer. Wine list, full bar. Reservations necessary. Dinner only. Open seven days a week. Fixed-price dinner $16.50. AE, DC, MC, V.

# BEST HOTEL MEAL

***St. Anthony Hotel,*** 300 E. Travis, downtown (227-4392). One of the oldest major hotels in Texas, a tour of the building alone makes a stop worthwhile. Major changes in the dining rooms have been made in the last few years, though the service remains less than perfect. The **Garden Room** offers breakfast, lunch and dinner, with a wide variety of menu items ranging from unusual sandwiches and scrumptious salads to Mexican food and steaks. The **St. Anthony Room** offers one of the most extensive Continental menus in the city. Garden Room: open seven days a week. Entrées from $1.15 (B), $2.75 (L & D). St. Anthony Room: wine list, full bar. Reservations recommended. Dinner only. Closed Sunday. Entrées from $11.95. Both: AE, CB, DC, MC, V.

# RESTAURANT NEAR AIRPORT

***Old San Francisco Steak House,*** 10223 Sahara (342-2321). (See description under LATE-NIGHT SERVICE.)

# BUSINESS BREAKFAST

***El Mirador,*** 722 S. St. Mary's (225-9444). Located next to the restored downtown German district, the King William area, this tiny Mexican restaurant is considered by many the best Tex-Mex restaurant in the city. The food is simple, good and cheap. Finding a seat at lunch is impossible without waiting a few or many minutes, but breakfast is rarely so crowded one cannot find a place. Service could be better at times, though. Try the traditional Tex-Mex breakfast: *huevos rancheros* (eggs, fried or scrambled and prepared with a spicy tomato sauce) served with *chilaquiles,* refried beans and two tortillas, all for $1.25. American bacon and eggs served with toast or tortillas are also offered, as well as several Mexican breakfast dishes. Opens at 6:30 A.M. Closed Sunday. No credit cards.

# BUSINESS LUNCH

***Little Hipp's Gimmiedraw Parlour,*** 1423 McCullough (223-0416) and ***Hipp's Bubble Room,*** 1411 McCullough (222-8114). These twin restaurant-pubs located in the heart of the city are popular for evening get-togethers over a pitcher of beer. But lunchtime is a business crowd, and professionals and businessmen in suits and ties are to be found crowding the two places. Little Hipp's has a traditional Texana-San Antonio-style décor and then some. The

Bubble Room features Christmas tree lights year round and a special miniature train. Little Hipp's draws a younger, looser crowd while the clientele in the Bubble Room is older and more subdued. Both places specialize in Texas-sized hamburgers and other traditional Texas food. Try the shypoke eggs or nachos made with two colors of cheese and jalapeño pepper. Hearty eaters will have a heyday here but the less greedy may want to share a plate with a partner. Beer, wine. Little Hipp's open seven days a week. Bubble Room closed Sunday and Tuesday. Entrées from $1.25 (and that's for a huge plate of food!). No credit cards.

## LATE-NIGHT SERVICE

***Old San Francisco Steak House,*** 10223 Sahara (342-2321). Located just five minutes from the airport, on the north side of town, this superb steakhouse officially closes at 11 P.M., but you can walk in the door at 11, or later, if you call. Service and quality of food is reliable. The décor is Gay '90's in this huge restaurant. You can opt for quiet dining, or join in the fun at the piano bar. Some of the best steaks and the best baked potato in the city. Hot country bread and aged Swiss cheese served at each table. Lobster tail. Great desserts. Atmosphere is elegant without being formal. Extensive wine collection. Full bar. Dinner only. Open seven days a week. Entées from $5.50. AE, CB, DC, MC, V.

# MARKETS

***El Mercado,*** 612 W. Commerce Street. Otherwise known as Farmer's Market, this place offers a huge semi-outdoor market of fresh fruits and vegetables trucked in daily, plus dozens of shops offering everything from Mexican to Oriental and American goods, from furniture and clothes to food and jewelry. One of the major tourist stops in town, many locals shop here as well, especially for gifts and fresh food. Most places are closed Sunday.

# San Diego

Only twenty years ago, it was almost impossible for San Diegans and visitors to dine out on anything other than Mexican food, seafood, poultry and beef—or occasionally fresh game poached from the nearby coastal plains and foothills in this huge 4,261-square-mile county.

San Diego was Middle America on the Pacific and people ate what was convenient and abundant, rarely with fuss or any form of pomp or circumstance. Life, in short, was a barbecue in this place where fewer than ten inches of rain fall each year, and the average daytime temperatures are in the seventies.

As with any city in its pre-cuisine era, more formal dining was limited to a few hotels, such as the stately old Hotel del Coronado on the island of the same name, or the sturdy but drab U.S. Grant on Broadway, in the middle of downtown San Diego. Other than the numerous Mexican restaurants, ethnic eating places were in short supply and usually run by families in the small Italian, Filipino, Chinese or Portuguese neighborhoods. The only great dining in San Diego was seafood, always fresh and cheap with abundant dockside supplies of abalone, swordfish, perch, halibut, yellowtail, sea bass, red snapper, albacore, lobster, mussels and shark.

Even in the 1960's, when the county was one of the fastest growing in the nation, expansion of gastronomical horizons was limited. **Lubach's** flourished as a harborside Continental restaurant catering to an expense-account crowd and student couples out for the big dinner. The **Grant Grill** in the U.S. Grant was a male-only bastion of business talk and American food, complete with wood and leather trappings. **Mr. A's,** atop the Fifth Avenue Financial

Centre, became a favorite for wealthy tourists because of its plush furnishings and commanding view of the city, the bay, the airport, parts of Mexico and the nearby offshore islands in the Pacific. The Marine Room, next to La Jolla Beach and Tennis Club, attracted the leisure rich to sample its view of the breaking surf.

The lone French restaurant of interest was La Favorite in the Bird Rock area of La Jolla. It struggled along for several years before the emerging sybarites discovered that it was indeed possible to find an excellent béarnaise sauce, a *saucisson en brioche* and *canard à l'orange* this far south of Los Angeles. As the local population grew more mobile, people began finding dining excitement in steak and lobster houses such as the Chart House in Point Loma and Chuck's in La Jolla. Nothing fancy, but it was a start.

In this decade a new generation of active, well-traveled, involved San Diegans began demanding more from dining out than a sirloin steak and a trip to the salad bar—and more in the way of culture than occasional rock and folk concerts. The opera began selling out each season, the symphony flourished, and French chefs began arriving by way of San Francisco, New York and Montreal to find newly appreciative audiences for their cuisine. San Diego is now the ninth largest city in the United States and there are restaurants of consequence in almost every category, although the more predominant continue to be Mexican and seafood.

The best areas for dining in San Diego are all close to the ocean: in the north county in a narrow strip from near the Del Mar Race Track up to Carlsbad, in La Jolla Village around Prospect Street, in Pacific Beach, Mission Beach, Mission Bay, downtown and Coronado. The hotel strip in Mission Valley, off Interstate 8, has something for every taste in food and every style in dining—formal, casual or cross-legged on the floor. Four of the best Mexican restaurants and cafés in the county—Fidel's, The Blue Bird, The Market and Tony's Jacal—are within a hundred yards of one another on Valley Avenue just north of the Del Mar Race Track off Interstate 5.

Coming after Mexican and seafood restaurants in terms of local importance would be French, Italian, Continental (usually a combination of French, Italian and Californian) and Chinese. The cuisines of Germany, Yugoslavia, the Philippines, Vietnam, Japan and Lebanon are also available, but the selection is narrow and the quality rarely above average. However, the ethnic mix of San Diego County offers good shopping to anyone interested in buying the ingredients to use at home. **Woo Chee Chong's,** near downtown, is a delight to visit. It has something for almost every Oriental recipe, its prices are fair and there is a dedication to freshness. **Zolezzi's** and **Filippi's,** in the 1700 Block of India Street, have the Italian ingredients necessary for most meals. The Athens Market (414 E Street) is a decent Greek deli. Sausage and other meats are found in abundance at The Sausage King (811 W. Washington). At **Blumer's** (5379 El Cajon Boulevard), everything is kosher.

Good wine shops are scattered throughout the county and most have staffs well versed in European as well as California products. The best selections can be found at **Big Bear** in Del Mar, Crest in Pacific Beach, Riviera near Point Loma, Zolezzi's near downtown, Del Cerro by San Diego State University in East San Diego, Glenn's Market in Chula Vista and The Bottle Shop in La Jolla.

Despite a burgeoning interest in French cuisine and an increase in the number of top restaurants, dining out in San Diego still features the casual approach, with only a few places requiring coat and tie for the gentlemen. Dinner reservations are a must at the better restaurants, sometimes three days to a week in advance, although luncheon reservations can usually be made the same day. Most of the Mexican restaurants and the popular seafood restaurants, such as **Anthony's Fish Grottos,** do not accept reservations, but the wait rarely exceeds thirty minutes. Visitors with time who are interested in a dining adventure may take an afternoon drive along one of the county's many scenic routes to try small restaurants located in such places as Bonsall, Bankhead Springs, Rancho Bernardo, Carlsbad, Ramona or Alpine. In terms of local specialties, the visiting gastronome or food freak would be derelict if he or she didn't try at least one *chile relleno;* a shredded-beef taco with *guacamole;* abalone; and a sea-bass filet. Not to do so is almost like not visiting the world-famous zoo.

# Restaurants and Food Sources

**(Area code: 714)**

## BIG DEAL

### WORTH IT

***Anthony's Star of the Sea Room,*** Harbor Drive and Ash (232-7408). Elegant, formal dining on the waterfront, with excellent service, a good wine list and some of the best seafood in California, including the Gourmet Abalone. Coats and ties for the men. Reservations required several days in advance. Dinner only. Open seven days a week, except for major holidays. Entrées from $7. MC, V.

### NOT WORTH IT

***Lubach's,*** Hawthorn and Harbor Drive (232-5129). An expense-account favorite for businessmen, with high prices, an inadequate wine list, and Continental food that is mediocre. Closed Sunday. Entrées from $3.95 (L), $5.95 (D). MC, V.

## INTERNATIONAL

### BASQUE

***Château Basque,*** Old Highway 80, in Boulevard, near Jacumba (766-4663). This is a place for a far-out dinner, literally and figuratively. A fixed-price menu of $8.75 changes daily, offering sirloin, chicken and other, less standard items. Excellent preparation and friendly people as your hosts in this cozy spot. But it's over an hour's drive from the city, so make this one of your sightseeing tours. Tuesday through Saturday, dinner only. Open 1 P.M. to 9 P.M. Sunday. Closed Monday. Entrées from $3.25 (L), $8.75 (D). MC, V.

## CHINESE

***Mandarin House,*** 6765 La Jolla Boulevard, La Jolla (454-2555). Offering Peking cuisine, with a few Szechuan dishes. Busy, festive and usually crowded. Quality ingredients and consistency of preparation, particularly with the Mongolian beef, broccoli beef and their incredible *chow san shein,* a combination of shrimp, beef, chicken and vegetables in brown sauce. Entrées from $2 (L), $4 (D). AE, MC, V.

## CONTINENTAL

***Casina Valadier,*** 4445 Lamont, Pacific Beach (270-8650). The name is a combination of Italian and French and so is the food, prepared in this exquisite little converted house with its carefully coordinated interior design. Some of the best homemade fettuccine in town. A warm and hospitable place, where a tie is acceptable but not required. Dinner only. Closed Sunday and Monday. Entrées from $9.25. AE, CB, DC, MC, V.

## FRENCH

***La Chaumine,*** 1466 Garnet Street, Pacific Beach (272-8540). Tucked away in a commercial shopping area near the beach, La Chaumine is comfortable, casual and festive, with excellent sauces and generally superb food from the tiny kitchen. Reminiscent of a café one might find on the Île St.-Louis or on the Left Bank in Paris. Dinner only. Open seven days a week. Entrées from $7.75. AE, CB, DC, MC, V.

## ITALIAN

***Nino's,*** 4501 Mission Bay Drive, Mission Bay (274-3141). Small, quiet and undeniably outstanding for veal. The fried zucchini makes for great munching as an appetizer. Another casual place where you can enjoy an unhurried meal and, if you care to, chat with the chef who comes around to ask how you like the dinner. Saturday and Sunday, dinner only. Monday and Tuesday, lunch only. Open seven days a week. Complete meals from $3.50 (L), $9.50 (D). AE, CB, DC, MC, V.

***Taste of Rome,*** 639 Pearl Street, La Jolla (459-9360). As the name implies, it specializes in the cuisine of Northern Italy in general and Rome in particular. Great *saltimbocca, cannelloni,* and *fettuccine,* served *al burro.* Family-run. Comfortable, subdued lighting, good service. Just 10 tables. Dinner only. Closed Monday. Entrées from $5.50. MC, V.

## LEBANESE

***Antoine's Sheik,*** 2664 Fifth Avenue (234-5888). Lavishly decorated with rugs, brass lanterns, intricate tapestries. Dimly lit for a feeling of intimacy. The stuffed grape leaves are of vintage quality. Also good: baked *kibbe* and other lamb dishes. Saturday and Sunday, dinner only. Open seven days a week. Entrées from $2.50 (L), $4.95 (D). AE, CB, DC, MC, V.

## MEXICAN

***Alfonso's Hideaway,*** 1251 Prospect Street, La Jolla (454-2232). Crowded, festive, casual, with consistency all the way across the menu, that includes the best *carne asada* taco in town. Chile Colorado and the steak ranchero with the family "secret sauce" also are highly recommended. Open seven days a week. Dinners start at about $5 and come with salads, Mexican rolls and butter. Lunches from $2.50. AE, MC, V.

***El Indio,*** 3695 India Street (299-0333).Super take-out food, starting at 28 cents for the famous *taquitos,* small rolled tacos that border on being addictive. Beans, rice, tamales, or just about anything Mexican you are in the mood for. It is a favorite for lunch and closes at 6 P.M. daily. Open seven days a week. No credit cards.

## SERBIAN

***Restaurant Serbia,*** Highway 76 and Olive Hill Road, Bonsall (758-0310). This is inland from Oceanside in the north county, but is well worth the trip for the splendid shish kebab, *sarma* or moussaka. Another dinner you should plan around a scenic trip. Dinner only. Closed Monday through Wednesday. Entrées from $1.99 (L), $3.95 (D). AE, MC, V.

# SPECIALTY COOKING

## HAMBURGER

***The Boll Weevil,*** 10 locations throughout the county. Hamburgers start at $1.29. And they make them BIG, with top-grade beef. Each one a meal by itself. Open until 2 A.M., seven days a week. No credit cards.

## PIZZA

***Filippi's,*** 1747 India Street (232-5094). Also a good Italian deli. Open seven days a week. Pizzas from $3.70 (L & D). MC, V.

***Besta Wan,*** 148 Aberdeen, Cardiff-by-the-Sea (753-6707). The best in the north county. Closed Sunday. Pizzas from $2.95 (L & D). No credit cards.

## PRIME RIB

***The Rib Cage,*** Sand's Hotel, Kearny Mesa Road off Interstate 163 at Clairemont Mesa Boulevard (277-7937). Good cuts of meat, properly prepared, with tons of goodies at the salad bar and a lively band in the cocktail lounge. Casual and festive. Open seven days a week. Entrées from $2.95 (L), $5.45 (D). AE, DC, MC, V.

## SEAFOOD

***Anthony's Fish Grottos,*** Harbor Drive and Ash, and other locations. Top-quality fish, quick and efficient service, and a chance to try a variety of items at reasonable prices. Very popular family restaurants, so be prepared to wait during lunches or on Sundays. Closed Tuesday. Entrées from $2.75 (L & D). MC, V.

***La Maison des Pescadoux*** (The Fisherman's Bungalow), 2265 Bacon Street at West Point Loma (225-9579), across from The Bungalow. For the gourmet, La Maison offers some of the best seafood sauces this side of France. Excellent preparation. Try the lobster, no matter what style, or the scampi. A very good wine list, featuring fine California and Burgundy vintages. Dinner only. Closed Sunday. Entrées from $8.50. MC, V.

## STEAK

***Café La Rue,*** at La Valencia, 1132 Prospect Street, La Jolla (454-0771). Offers some of the best cuts of meat in town, plus old-world service that makes you feel pampered. The adjacent Whaling Bar is a popular watering hole for the local who's who. (See description under FOR DRINKS.) Open seven days a week. Entrées from $2.50 (L), $6.50 (D). AE, MC, V.

## VEGETARIAN

***The Gatekeeper,*** Interstate 8 and Waring Road, San Diego (282-2700) and Via de la Valle, just east of Interstate 5, Del Mar (481-

8861). Fresh ingredients, prepared with great care and served in a subdued, relaxing atmosphere. The Del Mar Gatekeeper is an architectural wonder; it is built half underground to better fit in with the surrounding countryside, and its roof is covered with sod. The search for serenity can end here. Open seven days a week. Entrées from $3 (L), $5 (D). AE, MC, V.

# FOR INDIVIDUAL NEEDS

## IF YOU HAVE TIME FOR ONLY ONE MEAL

***Anthony's Star of the Sea Room,*** Harbor Drive and Ash (232-7408). (See description under BIG DEAL/WORTH IT.)

## BEST HOTEL MEAL

***Fontainebleau Room,*** Westgate Hotel, 1055 Second Avenue, downtown (238-1818). This is one of the most elegant restaurants in the county, with Louis XIV and XV antiques, luxurious carpeting, imported chandeliers, sculptured moldings and white-gloved service. The rack of lamb is usually outstanding, and other entrées range from good to excellent. The hotel itself is worth visiting even just for a drink. Saturday, dinner only. Sunday, brunch and dinner. Open seven days a week. Entrées from $3.95 (L), $9.95 (D). AE, MC, V.

## RESTAURANT NEAR AIRPORT

***Tom Ham's Lighthouse,*** 2150 Harbor Island Drive, on the west end of the island (291-9110). A super view across the bay to the city from this Spanish-motif restaurant that is also an official lighthouse. Great *asada,* representative wine list and good service. Entrées from $2.50 (L), $4.75 (D). AE, CB, DC, MC, V.

## BUSINESS BREAKFAST

***The Gourmet Room,*** Town and Country Hotel, 500 Hotel Circle, Mission Valley (291-7131). This cozy, well-furnished dining room is a favorite of local businessmen for their breakfast meetings. Fastest coffee pourers in town, excellent service and out-sized omelets. Open seven days a week. Breakfast from $1.50. AE, CB, DC, MC, V.

## BUSINESS LUNCH

***Grant Grill,*** Fourth and Broadway, downtown (232-3121). Only in the past few years have women been allowed into this once sacred shrine of high finance, with its low lights, paneled walls and leather booths. Excellent beef dishes, including the ground top sirloin. Very efficient service. Saturday and Sunday, dinner only. Entrées from $3.25 (L), $10 (D). AE, CB, DC, MC, V.

## FAST, GOOD FOOD/BREAKFAST

***Hob Nob Hill,*** 2271 First Avenue (239-8176). Favorite hangout for lawyers and businessmen preparing for meetings or trials the same morning. Open from 7 A.M. Closed Saturday and Sunday. Broad menu, starting at $1.75, with great omelets. AE, CB, MC, V.

## FAST, GOOD FOOD/LUNCH

***Zolezzi's,*** 1703 India Street (239-9777). Hot and cold Italian food in a cafeteria line. Eggplant *parmigiana, frittatas, cannelloni* and lasagne are local favorites. Good wine selection at very reasonable prices. Sunday, dinner only. Daily specials at $1.99. Entrées from $1.95 (L), $4.25 (D). MC, V.

## FAST, GOOD FOOD/DINNER

***Old Spaghetti Factory,*** 275 Fifth Avenue (233-4323). Large helpings of spaghetti with salads, desserts and beverages. Full bar. Dinner only. Open seven days a week. Entrées from $2.85. No credit cards.

## BEST WINE LIST

***The Debauchery,*** 3714 Mission Boulevard, Mission Beach (270-6600). The interior is dark and comfortable—"sybaritic" is how some locals describe it. The wine list is extensive and includes some rare wines from small California wineries. Ask the waiter if they have anything that isn't on the list. Sometimes you will be rewarded. It features a Continental food menu at the set price of $13.50. Dinner only. Closed Sunday and Monday. MC, V.

## FOR DRINKS

***Old Ox,*** 881 Camino del Rio South, Mission Valley (291-1823), and Garnet and Mission Boulevard, Pacific Beach (275-3790). Lively place for under 40's, particularly singles. Young, attractive waiting staff provides as many diversions as the hustling clientele. Decent drinks. Food is available, though not a feature. Open seven days a week. AE, CB, DC, MC, V.

***Whaling Bar,*** La Valencia Hotel, 1132 Prospect Street, La Jolla (454-0771). The older, more sophisticated La Jolla set or pretenders to the various thrones of local commerce hang out in this woody, clubby, tweedy pub in the heart of La Jolla. Open seven days a week. AE, CB, DC, MC, V.

***Cargo Bar,*** San Diego Hilton Hotel, 1775 E. Mission Bay Drive, Mission Bay (276-4010). Popular at sunsets for a relaxing cocktail before the drive home, or after 9 P.M., when the live music starts and the dance floor fills. Equal mix of conventioneers from the resort hotel, locals who dance their socks off, and visiting California commuters. Open seven days a week. AE, CB, DC, MC, V.

***Mr. A's,*** 2550 Fifth Avenue, San Diego (230-1377). The best and plushest bar in town for a view. Sit high atop the Fifth Avenue Financial Centre near Balboa Park. Enjoy the good wine list, good service, good drinks and a view that wraps around from Balboa Park, to Mexico, to the Pacific and across some of San Diego's prettiest night scenery. Jets landing at San Diego International Airport pass by at eye level a mile away. Open seven days a week. AE, CB, DC, MC, V.

## ROMANTIC

***Prince of Wales Room,*** Hotel del Coronado, on Coronado, across the toll bridge (435-6611). Warm leather, wood, subdued lighting, quiet but thorough waiters, a feeling of intimacy although formal. It's worth visiting just for a drink, if you have the time, so you can drive across the Bay bridge and see the city on one side and look south to Mexico on the other. Dinner only. Open seven days a week. Dinners begin at $9.50. AE, CB, DC, MC, V.

## LATE SERVICE, FULL MEAL

***Saska's,*** 3768 Mission Boulevard, Mission Beach (488-7311). Good selection of steaks. Lively beach crowd uses this for a gathering place after hours. Open until 1 A.M., Sunday through Wednesday; until 3 A.M., Thursday through Saturday. Entrées from $4.25. AE, DC, MC, V.

## SUNDAY BRUNCH

***Versailles Room,*** Westgate Hotel, 1055 Second Avenue (232-5011). Buffet-style, fresh fruit, breads, four hot entrées, and omelets made to order at one of several "omelet stations." Fixed-price brunch ($6.95) from 10 A.M. to 2 P.M. AE, CB, DC, MC, V.

## SUNDAY-EVENING MEAL

***L'escargot,*** 5662 La Jolla Boulevard, "Bird Rock," La Jolla (459-6066). A winner any night of the week, this comfortable, stylish little French restaurant offers the perfect combination for your day of rest: eight separate escargot appetizers; an ambitious à la carte menu with 24 entrées; desserts made fresh on the premises by Chef Pierre Lustrat; and a good wine list. Reservations required. Entrées from $9.75. AE, MC, V.

## FOR FAMILIES WITH CHILDREN

***Anchor Inn,*** 7260 Clairemont Mesa Boulevard (571-1532). Part of a chain, the Anchor Inn offers good, wholesome food in an all-you-can-eat format for the main dishes as well as the side dishes. Woodsy, homey interior with plenty of motion from the fast-working staff. Dinner only. Open seven days a week. Fixed-price dinner $5.95. No credit cards.

## COUNTRY INN

***Thee Bungalow,*** 4996 West Point Loma Boulevard at Bacon, Ocean Beach (224-2884). Ocean Beach is not exactly country, but Thee Bungalow qualifies as a country inn because of its building (a converted house), its interior (rustic) and its food and wine (good to excellent). Very popular. Informal, unhurried and comfortable, with small vases of flowers on each table, subdued lighting and efficient service. Good veal and duckling, but always inquire about the chef's special, which may be venison, pheasant, salmon or other items as they come into season or supply. Reservations are required. Dinner only. Closed Monday. Entrées from $7.25. AE, MC, V.

# MARKETS

***Blumer's,*** 5379 El Cajon Boulevard, East San Diego (582-2791). They have it at Blumer's. Everything. Closed Monday. No credit cards.

***Woo Chee Chong,*** 633 16th Street (233-6311). Open daily 9 A.M. until 8 P.M. with everything the Oriental cook needs to create a masterpiece. You can browse there for hours. No credit cards.

# GIFT WINES

***Big Bear Market,*** Interstate 5 and Via de la Valle, Del Mar (481-8178). This supermarket has one of the best selections of wine in the county, plus a knowledgeable wine merchant and a decent delicatessen. In a supermarket? Yes, indeed. Open seven days a week. No credit cards. Also try the **Bottle Shop** in La Jolla (454-6115) or **Del Cerro Liquor** in Del Cerro (286-0321).

# San Francisco

San Francisco's reputation for great restaurant eating goes back to the 1840's, when the city was changed almost overnight from a sleepy frontier town called Yerba Buena (Spanish for "good herb" after a wild mint that grew everywhere) to a metropolis bustling with gold-seekers.

In the early days the population consisted almost entirely of men who were forced to eat in hotels and boardinghouses because there weren't many private residences. The habit of eating out continued, even when women began arriving later in the decade. Most of the early hotels and guesthouses provided inexpensive meals where guests ate family style at large communal tables. The tradition still exists. There are many Italian and French-Basque family-style restaurants in the North Beach section of the city where generous multicourse dinners are still served at communal tables—a nice experience especially for single diners who don't enjoy eating alone.

With the discovery of gold in 1849, fortune hunters came from almost every country of the world. Many immigrants were skilled chefs from France and the young city soon had a surprisingly large number of good, small French restaurants. (In recent years there's been a resurgence of cozy Gallic eateries.)

The French weren't the only ones who influenced local cuisine. German, Italian, Swiss, Austrian, Russian and Spanish cooks, waiters and hotel operators were also among the early newcomers. And droves of Chinese came to labor on the transcontinental railroad. With the immigrants came fruits, vegetables and specialty foods of their native countries to embellish what was—and still is—a rich agricultural area.

The opening of the grand Palace Hotel in 1875 brought elegance and some of the world's most famous culinary personalities to San Francisco. Jules Harder, a chef at the renowned Delmonico's in New York City, was lured to the opulent hotel. Several years later Victor Hirtzler, the colorful character who had once been the official "taster" for Czar Nicholas of Russia, took over as *chef de cuisine* at the Hotel St. Francis. (See description under "Business Breakfast" in listings.)

Many well-known dishes were invented at these two hotels. Spaghetti Tetrazzini, oysters Kirkpatrick, Green Goddess salad dressing and Palace Court salad were created at the Palace. (The most famous, probably, is the creamy salad dressing, which was invented in honor of actor George Arliss for the first-night party of the play *Green Goddess*. There are many recipes for the dressing floating around, but the hotel management claims all are inaccurate.) Hirtzler is famous for celery Victor, for his rendition of *filet de sole Marguery* and for orange soufflé St. Francis.

Even the most destructive earthquake and fire in North American history didn't stop San Francisco from becoming a culinary capital. As soon as the ground stopped rumbling and the fires died, restaurants began springing up—in makeshift shacks, burned-out buildings and tents. Food was even served from street vendors' carts.

Today San Francisco is considered one of the best-endowed restaurant cities in the nation. There are almost 3,000 eating places in a city of only 671,000 residents. There's a restaurant specializing in the cuisine of almost every country in the world.

The largest Chinese community outside of Asia lives in San Francisco and runs the greatest concentration of Chinese restaurants in America. Grant Avenue used to be the center of Asian life in the city. A stroll down this famous, narrow, crowded avenue will still bring you past dozens of restaurants, noodle bars, *dim-sum* tearooms, Asian delicatessens and bakeries; but you're apt to see more tourists than Chinese. A large portion of the Chinese community has moved out to the Richmond and Sunset districts of the city. Numerous Chinese restaurants now line Geary and Clement streets. The latest trend is toward restaurants specializing in the hotly spiced dishes of the Hunan and Szechuan regions. Chinatown, however, is still the place to go for the most diversified selection of *dim-sum* or for shopping for fresh produce, fish, seafood, poultry and exotic imported ingredients and cooking utensils. Chinatown also continues to spread. The area now is roughly bounded by California, Powell, Broadway and Columbus streets.

Just north of Chinatown is North Beach, the center of the city's night life. Numerous theaters, strip clubs, places with comedy and live music, coffeehouses and restaurants serving way past midnight are located between Broadway and Union streets. North Beach is the Italian section of the city and, in general, the best Italian food is found here. You'll also find Italian sausage companies, bakeries, pasta factories, delicatessens, family-style restaurants and coffeehouses.

A cluster of Japanese restaurants and *sushi* bars are located in Nihon Machi (Japan Town) at Post and Buchanan streets. Many are in the Japanese Cultural and Trade Center.

Dozens of Spanish, Mexican, Central and South American and South Pacific eateries are scattered throughout the Mission district, especially along Mission and Twenty-fourth streets.

Geary Avenue, past Arguello, and Clement Street both offer an international potpourri—Russian, Indonesian, Thai, Chinese, Japanese, Mexican, Armenian, Scandinavian and French restaurants plus many bars. Another cluster of eating places (mostly beef, sandwiches and Japanese food) with an emphasis on discotheques and night life can be found on Union Street between Gough and Fillmore streets. Both the Cannery (which once was the Del Monte cannery) and Ghirardelli Square (an old chocolate factory) are eating and entertainment centers. There's also a new development on the Embarcadero, Pier 39, with almost two dozen restaurants.

There are a number of restaurants—Alexis, Blue Fox, La Bourgogne, Canlis, Ernie's, Orsi's among them—with far-reaching reputations. Long-time regulars are very loyal of course, but they are costly and there is controversy over whether the value matches the price. Don't turn down dinner at Alexis if you're invited out, but if you're by yourself, less well-known places may prove more rewarding eating experiences.

For a flavor of what San Francisco used to be like, try Jack's, **Tadich Grill,** John's Grill (Dashiell Hammett's hangout), Hoffman Grill or Bardelli's.

About the only cluster of restaurants to avoid are the touristy places along Fisherman's Wharf, where the food is expensive and tastes mass-produced. Stop at the wharf, if you like, for a walk-away crab or shrimp cocktail; but for serious seafood eating (and that's what San Francisco is known for) head downtown to **Sam's**

**Grill** or the **Tadich Grill** or try out one of the Italian restaurants in North Beach. The Chinese also do wonderful things with crab, abalone and whole rock cod. Whatever the ethnic bent, seafood restaurants remain the rage here.

If you're new to San Francisco, be sure to sample sourdough bread, local Dungeness crab, abalone, sand dabs, cioppino (a seafood stew invented by Italian fishermen in the city. It is best when it's long on seafood and short on everything else), local fresh caviar (many aficionados claim it's as good as Iranian at one-fifth the price) and the local cheeses—Teleme, dry Monterey Jack and Rouge et Noir Camembert. Many restaurants pride themselves on their selections of California wines and have knowledgeable serving personnel to provide guidance.

The majority of San Francisco restaurants are moderately priced with the exception of the hotels and the well-known expense-account places downtown. The best buys are usually found in the small family-run Asian and Italian restaurants where it's not unusual to pay less than $7 for a meal.

If you'd like to do some marketing, **Jurgensen's** (2190 Union Street) has excellent produce, meats, poultry, cheese and imported foods. And the Normandy Lane at the Liberty House is a branch of Fortnum and Mason from London. **The French Pantry** (1570 California Street) stocks the ultimate picnic fare: unusual homemade pâtés, salads, sausages, scrumptious tortes, cheeses, bread and wine.

San Francisco has a number of fine wine shops that specialize in limited-production wines from the smaller California wineries. Shops with extensive selections of wine include: The Wine Shop (2175 Chestnut Street), Harris Liquors (443 Clement Street), John Walker & Co. (111 Montgomery Street) and Draper & Esquin (655 Sutter Street). Two other shops with huge selections and facilities for tasting include: London Wine Bar (415 Sansome Street) and the **Wine & Cheese Center** (205 Jackson Street).

Dining customs are fairly standard in the city. Generally the downtown restaurants are more crowded at lunch than in the evening, although reservations are recommended at either time. Many have higher prices in the evening, although portions are also larger. Very few places require formal dress. Pants suits for women are common. Jackets without ties, or turtlenecks are fine for men. One tip will suffice for the meal; multitiered tipping hasn't caught on.

Restaurant growth in the Bay Area is still focused on San Francisco. Only a few outside the city are outstanding.

# Restaurants and Food Sources

(Area code: 415)

## BIG DEAL

### WORTH IT

***Le Club,*** 1250 Jones Street (771-5400). An elegant, sophisticated, intimate French restaurant tucked away in a ritzy Nob Hill apartment building. Try the saddle of lamb, which is served with a perfectly seasoned purée of chestnuts in an artichoke bottom, or the *émincé de veau aux chanterelles.* Well-prepared salads (especially the wilted spinach) and imaginative desserts. Careful, attentive service. Reservations are essential and best made days in advance. Coats and ties are required. Dinner only. Closed Sunday. Entrées from $10. AE, DC, MC, V.

***Trader Vic's,*** 20 Cosmo Place (776-2232). This is the flagship of Vic Bergeron's chain, still the "in" place of the city's social elite. The service is outstanding, the food excellent. You can order from the Chinese or South Pacific section of the menu, from the Continental side or construct your own menu. Some of the outstanding dishes are the grilled sweetbreads on Canadian bacon with caper sauce, the triple-thick lamb chop cooked in the Chinese oven, barbecued double pork loin luau-style and kidneys Martinique flambé. Unfortunately, there is a "Siberia" at Trader Vic's. Unless you go with a regular or try to reserve a table in the intimate Captain's Cabin, you'll probably end up in one of the gaudy Polynesian-decorated rooms. Reservations are essential. So are coats and ties. Saturday and Sunday, dinner only. Open seven days a week. Entrées from $4.95 (L), $5.75 (D). AE, CB, DC, MC, V.

## NOT WORTH IT

***In general,*** the seafood restaurants on Fisherman's Wharf.

# INTERNATIONAL

## AMERICAN

***Mama's,*** 1177 California Street (928-1004). (A smaller Mama's is located at 1701 Stockton Steet, overlooking Washington Square; other branches are located in Macy's Department Store, Stockton and O'Farrell, and Macy's in San Mateo.) Large, bright, airy dining room with glass cases displaying luscious pastries (the chocolate cheesecake is sublime), fresh fruit and salad fixings. Breakfast and lunch are served all day. Omelets, seafood salads, quiche, large hamburgers on long *baguettes,* complete dinners (specializing in fresh, locally-caught seafood) in the evening. Open seven days a week. Dinners from $8.35. MC, V.

## CHINESE

***Yet Wah,*** 2140 Clement Street (387-8040), 1801 Clement Street (751-1231), 1829 Clement Street (387-8056). There are now nine Yet Wah restaurants in the Bay Area. The extensive menu reads like the Chinese yellow pages. Mostly Northern Chinese cuisine. *Moo shu* pork, Mongolian lamb and sweet-and-sour whole fish are specialties. Prices are still unbelievably low. There may be a wait, but once you're seated the service is fast. One caution—be as specific as possible when ordering, even if it means pointing to another diner's plate. Dinner only. Open seven days a week. (The Yet Wah at 1801 Clement Street is also open for lunch.) Entrées from $3.30. AE, MC, V.

***Hunan Restaurant,*** 924 Sansome Street (956-7727). Owner Henry Chung has a restaurant phenomenon in the Hunan. It was almost impossible to get a table at his original restaurant, a tiny hole-in-the-wall place. His new location seats way over 100 and it's still a feat to get a table. The capacity may have quadrupled, but the food is as exciting as ever. Some special recommendations: spicy bean curd with meat sauce, cold chicken salad, braised fishballs and chicken, ham or duck (which Chung smokes himself). Be sure to try the deep-fried onion cakes. Devotees are hoping Chung will reopen the original Hunan on Kearny Street. Currently the Sansome Street restaurant is closed Saturday and Sunday. Entrées from $4 (L & D). No credit cards.

***Szechwan,*** 2209 Polk Street (474-8282). A small, nicely decorated dining room serving hot peppery dishes. Try the wonderful shredded dry sautéed beef Szechwan style, sliced leg of lamb and spicy Szechwan-style bean curd. The menu also includes a number of milder dishes. The Szechwan is a very good buy at luncheon. The luncheon special ($2.35) offers a choice of Szechwan sliced pork, hot spicy shredded beef, sweet-and-sour pork, shrimp with peas, beef with green pepper or chicken with hot pepper, plus soup, spring roll, rice and tea. Sunday, dinner only. Open seven days a week. Complete dinners from $6. MC, V.

***Sun Hung Heung,*** 744 Washington Street (982-2319). This is one of the best all-around Chinese restaurants in the city. It's neither posh nor a hole in the wall. The mostly Cantonese menu is extensive. Try the fried, stuffed chicken wings; whole cracked crab in curry sauce (in season); boneless squab with cashews; and beef under snow. Open until midnight. Closed Tuesday. Entrées from $4 (L & D). MC, V.

***Hong Kong Teahouse,*** 835 Pacific Avenue (391-6365). A huge madhouse with many more Asians than Caucasians. Aficionados swear that this is the best *dim-sum* place in the Bay Area. Some hints on getting served: go early and be sure to take three or more people with you. There are only a few tables for two. If you get tired of waiting, buy *dim sum* at the carry-out counter and take it over to Portsmouth Plaza (Washington near Kearny) and picnic. The *dim-sum* selection seems endless. Be sure to try the egg rolls and steamed pork-filled buns. Lunch only. Open seven days a week. *Dim sum* from 85 cents, entrées from $2.65. No credit cards.

***The Mandarin,*** Ghirardelli Square (673-8812). An elegant, seductive atmosphere with brick walls, thick-beamed ceilings, a beautiful view of San Francisco Bay, the Golden Gate Bridge and Sausalito. Partitions divide the restaurant into many small rooms. To really experience the best the kitchen can offer, call in advance and place yourself in Madame Cecilia Chiang's hands. Many of the special dishes need to be ordered ahead including Peking duck, beggar's chicken and the Mongolian fire pot. Try the spicy minced squab, which is eaten in lettuce leaves, or the smoked tea duck. Reservations are advised, especially for window tables. Open seven days a week. Entrées from $4.95 (L), $6.50 (D), complete dinners from $10. AE, CB, DC, MC, V.

# FRENCH

***Le Central,*** 453 Bush Street (391-2233). In contrast to most of the city's dimly lit French restaurants, Le Central is more in the brasserie style—close banquette seating, bright lighting, brick walls hung with French art, and menus painted on mirrors and written on small blackboards. A beautiful copper bar. The food is brasserie style, too. Daily specials and a regular menu including *cassoulet* (white beans simmered with sausages, duck, pork and lamb), *choucroute alsacienne* (sauerkraut cooked in wine with bacon, pork and sausage) and *saucisson chaud* (thinly sliced, garlicky sausage served with hot potato salad). Reservations are needed at both lunch and dinner. Saturday, dinner only. Closed Sunday. Entrées from $5.25 (L), $5.95 (D). MC, V.

***Le Rhone,*** 3614 Balboa Street (387-4559). You're never rushed in this cozy candlelit restaurant because only one reservation per table is accepted each evening. The service is rather informal, the cuisine exemplary. Entrées to try: the light, delicate lobster soufflé, succulent rabbit with prunes, sweet scallops in Gratin de Saint Jacques au Safran. The owners' 19-year-old son is the baker. He produces wonderful tarts, pastries and homemade ices and ice creams. Dinner only. Closed Monday. Dinners from $9.95. MC, V.

***Le Trianon,*** 242 O'Farrell Street (982-9353). René Verdon was the White House chef when Kennedy was President. Now he's the chef-owner of Le Trianon, one of the city's most exclusive French restaurants. Nothing is inexpensive here, but the food is superb, especially the *filet d'agneau en croûte,* the *médaillon de veau lorrain* and the fresh salmon and scallop mousse appetizer. Delectable desserts including rich tarte tatin and fresh fruit soufflés. Dinner only. Closed Sunday. Entrées from $9.75. AE, CB, DC, MC, V.

# HUNGARIAN

***Paprikas Fono,*** Ghirardelli Square (441-1223). Decorated in the manner of a Hungarian country inn with whitewashed walls, brightly colored, hand-painted hutches, embroidered cloths. A sweeping view of San Francisco Bay comes as a bonus. The specialty is *gulyás*—a hearty beef-and-vegetable soup. Also try *langos,* a fried yeast bread you rub with garlic. Homemade strudel and *palacsintas* (crêpes). Reservations are advised. Open seven days a week. Entrées from $4.95 (L), $5.50 (D). MC, V.

# INDIAN

***Tandoori Restaurant,*** 2550 Van Ness Avenue (776-1455). A former motel coffee shop has been converted into a Northern Indian restaurant. A glass wall separates the deep *tandoor* ovens from the dining room. The extensive menu reflects the varied cuisine of Delhi. Try the *samosas* (pastries filled with a spicy mixture of potatoes, peas and cumin seeds), *bara kebab* (leg of lamb roasted in the *tandoor* oven) and *roghan josh* (a fiery, well-sauced lamb stew). Vegetable dishes are excellent, as are the homemade Indian breads and pastries. Open seven days a week. Entrées from $2.95 (L), $4.95 (D). AE, MC, V.

# INDONESIAN

***Sari's Indonesian Restaurant,*** 2459 Lombard Street (567-8715). At last count there were seven Indonesian restaurants in the Bay Area. This may be the best. It features Sumatran fare served in a cozy setting decorated with Indonesian artifacts and batik fabrics. Try the appetizer *pangsit goreng* (pastry puffs filled with beef and vegetables) followed by the *sate kambing* (skewered lamb), *ayam goreng* (Indonesian fried chicken). Dinner only. Closed Monday. Dinners from $3.50. There's also an extensive *rijsttafel* costing $16 for two. MC, V.

# ITALIAN

***Basta Pasta,*** 1268 Grant Avenue (434-2248). The atmosphere is pleasantly casual, the food fresh and ample, the price very reasonable. Homemade pasta is perfectly sauced. The catch of the day is a best buy at $4.50—a whole fish broiled until just done and served on a large platter with "al dente" vegetables. No reservations are taken, but Basta Pasta isn't as small as it looks. Open seven days a week, until 2 A.M. Entrées from $3.95 (L & D). MC, V.

***Little Joe's,*** 325 Columbus Avenue (982-7639). There's nothing fancy about Little Joe's. It's a long, narrow place with counter seating and just a few tables in the adjacent **Baby Joe's**. But superb pasta *al pesto, calamari* and minestrone are made in the small space behind that counter. All the cooking is done right there so dining is a visual as well as gustatory experience. Best of all is the *cacciucco alla livornese* (fish stew), which is served on Fridays and occasionally on Saturdays. The place is always crowded, but waiting in line here can be fun: Little Joe's fans are friendly folks. Open only until 7:30 P.M. Closed Sunday. Entrées from $4.75 (L & D). No credit cards.

***Tommaso's Neapolitan Restaurant,*** 1042 Kearny Street (398-9696). Unsurpassed pizza baked in an oak-burning oven and served in a small, romantic "Greenwich Village-type" cellar *trattoria*. The menu contains numerous veal dishes of which the piccata (with herbs and lemon) is recommended. But the real specialty is Tommaso's marinated salads. If several people are having dinner, order the broccoli, toasted peppers and zucchini salads and share. Dinner only. Closed Monday and Tuesday. Entrées from $4.50. MC, V.

***Modesto Lanzone,*** Ghirardelli Square (771-2880). A romantic setting, especially the small room overlooking the Ghirardelli Square fountain. Modesto's serves a fine selection of pastas including *cannelloni alla Rossini* (stuffed with veal, cheese and vegetables), *panzotti alla crema di noci* (layers of pasta with spinach and ricotta and a cream sauce studded with minced nuts) and exemplary fettuccine Alfredo. The extensive menu has some unusual offerings: *cima di vitello fredda* (cold stuffed breast of veal), *insalata di mare* (marinated salad of squid and shrimp) and *petto di cappone farcito Valdostana* (breast of capon with Italian ham and cheese). Scrumptious pastries and wonderful fresh-fruit desserts. Saturday and Sunday, dinner only. Closed Monday. Entrées from $5.25 (L), $6.95 (D). AE, CB, DC, MC, V.

## JAPANESE

***Sanppo Restaurant,*** 1702 Post Street (346-3486). Located across from the Japanese Cultural and Trade Center, this simply decorated restaurant has an astonishingly complete menu. Everything from *sashimi*, *gyoza* (dumplings that are steamed and then fried), to tempura, and casseroled noodle dishes. Efficient, friendly service. No reservations are taken, so it's best to go early or plan to browse through Japan Town should you have to wait. Dinner only. Closed Monday. Entrées from $3. No credit cards. A newer Sanppo Restaurant has opened in the tourist complex, Pier 39, that has longer hours (11:30 A.M. to 11 P.M. seven days a week), but a less authentic menu. MC, V.

## MEXICAN

***La Rondalla,*** 901 Valencia Street (647-7474). The menu offers the standards (tacos, enchiladas, *flautas, burritos, chiles rellenos*) plus chicken *mole,* barbecued goat and a spicy beef tongue. The place is always decorated as though Christmas were about to arrive. And it's always busy. You'll hear more Spanish spoken here than English. Open 11 A.M. to 4 A.M. seven days a week. Entrées from $3.50 (L & D). No credit cards.

## MIDDLE EASTERN

***Caravansary,*** 2263 Chestnut Street (921-3466), 310 Sutter Street (362-4640). The Chestnut Street restaurant is a tiny, dimly lit spot tucked behind a specialty cookware and food shop. The downtown Caravansary has a retail shop on the first floor and a large, airy, bright country restaurant on the second. A luncheon specialty is the Aram's sandwich (roast beef, cream cheese, tomatoes and lettuce rolled in Armenian *lavash* bread). Outstanding quiche. For dinner, a variety of Middle Eastern hors d'oeuvre, chicken breast baked in pomegranate juice and braised lamb shanks are good choices. Sutter Street: closed Sunday. Chestnut Street: open seven days a week. Sunday, brunch only. Both: entrées from $4.25 (L), $5.95 (D). AE, DC, MC, V.

## MOROCCAN

***Agadir,*** 746 Broadway (397-6305). Currently there are four Moroccan restaurants in San Francisco. The newest, and the one with the most varied menu, is Agadir. The lavish feast is served in a luxurious setting with seating on ottomans and pillows; thick rugs, intricately patterned tapestries on the walls and ceilings. The low tables are inlaid with wood in detailed floral and geometric designs. The dinner starts with soup, then a *mezza* with several salads, homemade Moroccan bread, *b'stilla* (pigeon, eggs, nuts and spices layered in buttered *filo* pastry) and a wide choice of entrées. Especially recommended are the whole squab stuffed with *couscous* and a lamb *tajine* with prunes. For dessert you have a selection of pastries and fresh-mint tea. There's also North African background music. Dinner only. Open seven days a week, until midnight. Complete dinners from $13.75. AE, MC, V.

## VIETNAMESE

***Thanh Long,*** 4101 Judah Street (665-1146). An unpretentious restaurant in the midst of a residential neighborhood near the Pacific Ocean. Thanh Long serves what may be the best whole roast fresh crab in the country. Delicious *cha gio* (the Vietnamese version of egg rolls) and sublime banana fritters. Dinner only. Closed Monday. Entrées from $3.55. MC, V.

# SPECIALTY COOKING

## DELI

***The Deli,*** 1980 Union Street (563-7274). Colorful, leaded and stained-glass windows and curved ceiling in the bar; hardwood floors, huge plants—in general, an air of congeniality. There's also a patio and porch for al fresco dining. Large heaping sandwiches, hearty soups and marvelous meat blintzes. Complete dinners too. Baked short ribs with potato pancakes and fresh vegetables are excellent. Open seven days a week. Bar open until 2 A.M. daily. Entrées from $5.95. AE, CB, DC, MC, V.

## HAMBURGER

***Perry's,*** 1944 Union Street (922-9022). In front there is a large, active bar with people crowded shoulder-to-shoulder. In the back you'll find a quiet dining room. Dark wood paneling hung with old photographs and posters, blue-and-white checkered tablecloths, fresh flowers and hanging plants. Thick, juicy hamburgers and cheeseburgers are served with homemade potato chips. Or try a crock of savory onion soup under a blanket of melted cheese, lovely fresh salads. Weekend brunches feature eggs Benedict and eggs Blackstone (crumbled bacon and sliced tomato). Open seven days a week, until midnight for food, until 2 A.M. for drinks. Sandwiches from $3.95 (L & D). AE, MC, V.

## HOT DOG

***The Noble Frankfurter,*** 3159 Fillmore Street (922-2520) and 1900 Polk Street (441-5307). Spicy Calabrese-style Italian sausage, plump kosher-style frankfurters, Sicilian-, German- and Swiss-style sausages served on large rolls. Also potato salad and cole slaw. Hours and days vary from store to store. Sandwiches from $1.05. No credit cards.

## SEAFOOD

***Sam's Grill,*** 374 Bush Street (421-0594). Sam's isn't fancy, but it's friendly, comfortable and serves some of the best seafood in town. The menu changes daily. Ask what the day's catch was. There's also an extensive selection of grilled items. To avoid the noontime crowd or to get one of the small, private dining rooms, go before 11:30 A.M. or after 2 P.M. Closed Saturday and Sunday. Entrées from $4 (L & D). MC, V.

***Scott's Seafood Bar and Grill,*** 2400 Lombard Street (563-8988), Embarcadero 3, Financial District (981-0622). It's been standing room only since Scott's opened its doors a few years ago at 2400 Lombard Street. There's still a lot of body contact each night as people wait, sometimes hours, for a table. All this hoopla, because many people believe Scott's serves the freshest seafood in town. The newer Scott's in the Embarcadero Center complex is three times larger than the original restaurant, not nearly as frenzied and the waits aren't too long. What to order? Because the selection varies with the day's catch, it's best to go to Scott's with an open mind and see what is featured that day. Lovely salads and delectable desserts too. Lombard Street: open seven days a week. Embarcadero: closed Sunday. Both: entrées from $5.50 (L & D). AE, MC, V.

***Tadich Grill,*** 240 California Street (391-2373). Tadich's is the oldest restaurant in San Francisco. From 1912 to 1967 it was located on Clay Street across from what is now the Transamerica Pyramid. Then it was moved board by board to the present address. Décor is uncomplicated but elegant. A long wood bar, intimate walnut booths, crisp white tablecloths and bentwood chairs. Exceptional seafood. Try the Rex sole, fresh salmon or sea bass. Tadich's is always crowded and doesn't take reservations. Service can be gruff. Open until 8:30 P.M. Closed Sunday. Entrées from $3.75 (L & D). No credit cards.

## VEGETARIAN

***Shandygaff Café Restaurant,*** 1760 Polk Street (441-1760). Everything here is made from scratch. Nothing is ordinary or predictable. The new owners, two French brothers, both accomplished chefs, have brought more than a new décor to this well-known vegetarian restaurant. The entrées are inspired. Examples: *tarte à l'oignon gratinée* (cheese and onion pie), *les chaussons de choux rouge au yogurt* (a turnover filled with braised cabbage, apple, cheese and served with a yogurt sauce), *scampi soufflé Bretonne* (scampi with mousseline of scallops garnished with julienne of fresh vegetables in white wine sauce). The platters of fruit and cheeses are beautiful. You'll not miss sugar, white flour or meat. Open seven days a week. Entrées from $5 (L), $6.50 (D). MC, V.

# FOR INDIVIDUAL NEEDS

## IF YOU HAVE TIME FOR ONLY ONE MEAL

***Carnelian Room,*** Bank of America Center, 555 California Street (433-7500). Not just another rooftop restaurant, although the view is breath-taking. The prestigious, and private, Bankers Club during the day becomes the elegant Carnelian Room in the evening and is open to the public. In addition to fine cuisine and impeccable service, the Carnelian Room has an outstanding wine list. (Even the sumptuous restrooms are memorable.) Some culinary high-points: scampi Chablisienne (scampi with lobster mousse in Chablis sauce), médaillons of venison with chanterelles, creamed Madeira sauce, wild rice, baked apple filled with chestnuts, carrots and lingonberries. The Carnelian Room is known for desserts—delectable pastries, homemade ice creams, sorbets, baked Alaska, raspberry soufflé, crêpes Suzette. Chaîne des Rotisseurs. Open to the public for dinner from 6 to 10:30 P.M. seven days a week and for brunch on Sunday. Entrées from $12.75. Brunch $11 adults, $6.75 children under 10. AE, CB, DC, MC, V.

## BEST HOTEL MEAL

***French Room,*** Clift Hotel at Geary and Taylor (775-4700). The luxurious setting, fine service and hushed atmosphere make this restaurant the perfect place to go for lunch, after a hectic day or before the theater. The specialty is roast prime rib of beef, carved and served to order from the Clift's silver London Simpson Cart, with Yorkshire pudding and creamed horseradish sauce. The fresh seafood, crisp roast duckling with lemon sauce and veal dishes are also recommended. Open seven days a week. Entrées from $5.50 (L), $10.25 (D). AE, CB, DC, MC, V.

***Fournou's Ovens,*** 905 California Street (989-1910). (See description under SUNDAY-EVENING MEAL.)

## RESTAURANT NEAR AIRPORT

***Kee Joon's,*** 433 Airport Boulevard, Burlingame (348-1122). An elegant, peaceful restaurant on the top floor of an office building south of San Francisco International Airport. A glass wall allows diners to watch the planes landing. The large restaurant is decorated in the manner of the Sung Dynasty (960-1279 A.D.), with hand-carved wood panels, a marble fountain, impressive jade collection. Dishes from Peking (north China), Yanchow (central China), Szechuan (western China) and Canton (south China) are served in the formal manner. Most dishes are mildly spiced. If you like your food strongly seasoned, be sure to mention this to the waiter. Some good choices include the Mongolian lamb served with homemade onion bread, prawns in lobster sauce and the *moo shu* pork. The chef will also do special dishes, such as smoked goose, on request. Complete dinners are the best buy. À la carte entrées are more expensive. Open seven days a week. Complete dinners from $7.95, Chinese lunch buffet $4.75. AE, MC, V.

## BUSINESS BREAKFAST

***Garden Court,*** Sheraton-Palace Hotel, Market and New Montgomery streets (392-8600). Originally the Palace was the most opulent, elegant hotel in the city. Then came the great earthquake and fire of 1906, which destroyed the old hotel. The rebuilt Palace Hotel may not be as impressive as it once was, but the Garden Court is still extraordinary—almost four stories high with a graceful, curved glass roof that softens the sunlight. Huge palm trees line the walls. Very quiet atmosphere, conducive to conducting business. There's the usual breakfast fare during the week, a groaning board buffet brunch on Sunday. Reservations are necessary for the brunch. Open seven days a week. Entrées from $2.25 (B). Complete buffet breakfast $5.95. Complete brunch $10.50. AE, CB, DC, MC, V.

## BUSINESS LUNCH

***Doro's,*** 714 Montgomery Street (397-6822). Some of the biggest deals in town are consummated here daily over cold poached salmon and *cannelloni.* Doro's is well-known for its elegant but unfussy décor; attentive, but unobtrusive service; consistently fine cuisine; spacious, uncrowded banquette seating. Continental menu with some emphasis on Italian specialties. Chaîne des Rotisseurs. Saturday, dinner only. Closed Sunday. Sandwiches from $4.25, entrées from $5.50 (L), $6.50 (D). AE, CB, DC, MC, V.

## FAST, GOOD FOOD/BREAKFAST

***Sears' Fine Foods,*** 439 Powell Street, just off Union Square (986-1160). Nothing fancy. A bustling coffee shop known for miniature Swedish pancakes (18 for $1.65), homemade coffee cakes, quick breads, apple dumplings. Larger breakfasts, salads, sandwiches and a few entrées (avoid the eggs Benedict). There's usually a line, but it moves rapidly. Open 7 A.M. to 3 P.M., seven days a week. No credit cards.

## FAST, GOOD FOOD/LUNCH

***Anxious Grape,*** in the Liberty House, O'Farrell and Stockton streets (772-2121). A fast cafeteria line offering hearty soups, large salads, some unusual sandwiches such as tuna salad with water chestnuts or chicken salad with fresh pineapple stuffed into *pita* bread. Daily luncheon specials. Good pastries. Closed Sunday. Sandwiches from $2.60. AE, MC, V.

## FAST, GOOD FOOD/DINNER

***Salmagundi,*** 442 Geary Street (441-0894) 355 Bush Street (397-5463), Embarcadero 2 (982-5603), 1236 Market Street (431-7337). Creative soups, bibb lettuce-romaine salads, rolls and butter for $3.10. If you're still hungry, go back for another bowl of soup at no additional charge. Also, quiche, yummy desserts, good coffee. Right across the street from San Francisco's largest professional theaters. Geary Street: open seven days a week, until midnight. Bush Street: lunch only. Closed Sunday. Embarcadero: closed Sunday. Market Street: open seven days a week. All: no credit cards.

## BEST WINE LIST

***Narsai's,*** 385 Colusa Avenue, Kensington, in the East Bay, just north of Berkeley (527-7900). A dramatic dining room with stark white walls, contemporary art and one wall that is fashioned from a gigantic redwood wine-storage tank. Owner Narsai David is a wine writer and collector. Inventive cuisine. Elaborate five-course dinners and formal service. On Monday nights the kitchen experiments with various international cuisines. The menus for the special Monday-night dinners (fixed price of $18) are available a month in advance. Fabulous desserts. Reservations are necessary. Dinner only. Open seven days a week. Complete dinner from $14. AE, CB, DC, MC, V.

## FOR DRINKS

***Henry Africa's,*** 2269 Van Ness Avenue (928-7044). The ultimate "fern bar." It's bright and busy, a model railroad runs overhead, piano music, Tiffany lamps, antique oak furniture, premium bar liquors (excellent "bar" wines, too), freshly squeezed juices, superb daiquiris. Hors d'oeuvre and Sunday brunch in the adjacent **Waterfront Restaurant**. A popular singles spot. Open seven days a week until 2 A.M. No credit cards in the bar.

***Redwood Room,*** Clift Hotel, at Geary and Taylor (775-4700). A dark, inlaid redwood-paneled room dominated by a long, convivial bar. Well-heeled crowd. Larry St. Regis is at the piano. In the early evening, *gravlax* is the bar appetizer. Open seven days a week. AE, CB, DC, MC, V.

## RESTAURANT WITH MUSIC

***Washington Square Bar and Grill,*** 1707 Powell Street (982-8123). A basically Italian and Continental menu served in an uncluttered environment. Unadorned walls are "iron oxide" color. White linens. Still one of the "in" spots in town, so it's usually crowded and noisy. Try the *osso buco,* chicken sauté sec, baked fresh salmon in shrimp sauce. Menu changes daily. Music starts around 8:30, mostly jazz. Open seven days a week until midnight. Complete dinners from $5.25. AE, CB, MC, V.

## ROMANTIC

***Le Vivoir,*** Casa Madrone Hotel, 156 Bulkley Avenue, Sausalito (332-1850). On the hill overlooking Sausalito is this small, cozy restaurant. Seductive, almost clandestine feeling. French menu, well-prepared food, unrushed service. For the ultimate romantic evening, take the ferry to Sausalito, have a long, leisurely meal at Le Vivoir, spend the night at the Casa Madrone (the most "European" of Bay Area hotels) and ferry back to the city the next morning. Dinner only. Open seven days a week. Entrées from $9. AE, CB, DC, MC, V.

## LATE-NIGHT SERVICE

***Vanessi's,*** 498 Broadway (421-0890). A favorite haunt of financial-district types and the Broadway-strip theatrical crowd. The restaurant sometimes seems like a madhouse—practically all the cooking is done behind the long, open counter and you can watch chefs tossing pasta and whipping up *zabaglione.* The extensive menu is predominately Italian. The pasta is wonderful, charcoal-broiled meat and veal dishes excellent, salads beautiful. You can't go wrong with any of the luncheon specials. Reservations are recommended. Sunday, dinner only. Open seven days a week: until 1:30 A.M. Monday through Saturday, until 12:30 A.M. Sunday. Entrées from $3.95 (L), $4.75 (D). AE, CB, DC, MC, V.

***Enrico's Sidewalk Café,*** 504 Broadway (392-6220). The original and still the most popular sidewalk café in the city is located in the midst of the Broadway strip of theaters and nightclubs. Good salads (especially the spinach and shrimp salad with bits of crumbled bacon), light entrées and nice desserts including wonderful homemade ice cream. A large selection of fancy coffee drinks. Open seven days a week, until 3 A.M. Entrées from $4.50 (L & D). AE, CB, MC, V for bills over $5.

## SUNDAY BRUNCH

***Cliff House Seafood & Beverage Co.,*** 1090 Point Lobos Avenue (386-3330). A beautiful setting overlooking the Pacific Ocean and Seal Rocks. (In summer, the early morning coastal fog often obscures the view.) Bright, cheerful décor with brass railings, hanging plants, stuffed couches in the lounge. Good Ramos fizzes, Bloody Marys, eggs Benedict, eggs San Francisco (poached eggs, sautéed King crab meat topped with a brandied cream sauce), crisp popovers and fresh fruit garnish. Sunday brunch from 9:30 A.M. to 2 P.M. Brunch entrées from $3.75. AE, MC, V.

## SUNDAY-EVENING MEAL

***Fournou's Ovens,*** 905 California Street (989-1910). A bright, new conservatory has been added to this tiled and terraced restaurant in the Stanford Court Hotel. Some of the loveliest tables are those in the room with the great tiled ovens. A French-inspired menu. Respected cuisine. Some superbly prepared meats are available under the menu section "From the Ovens." Excellent choices include: roast rack of lamb, roast boned duckling with green peppercorn and kumquat sauce, roast glazed filet of pork. Outstanding desserts. Save room for the dacquoise at dessert. Chaîne des Rotisseurs. Monday through Saturday, dinner only. Sunday, brunch and dinner. Entrées from $10.50. AE, DC, MC, V.

## FOR FAMILIES WITH CHILDREN

***Café de Young,*** de Young Museum, Golden Gate Park (752-0116). After spending the morning in the Japanese Tea Gardens, at the California Academy of Sciences (home of the Morrison Planetarium, Laserium and Steinhart Aquarium) or at the children's playground, wander over to the Café de Young for lunch. Well-prepared foods served in a bright, cheerful setting. During the warm weather, you can eat outside in the courtyard garden. Children will like the hamburgers, adults may enjoy the more unusual entrées such as cold salmon salad with artichoke hearts and green sauce or the chicken salad served on melon. Good desserts. Lunch only. Open seven days a week. Sandwiches from $1.45. No credit cards.

# IN THE SUBURBS

## BELMONT

***Pine Brook Inn,*** 1015 Alameda de las Pulgas at Ralston Avenue (591-1735). The setting is much like that of an Alpine inn perched above a bubbling brook and gardens. Full dinners of salad, variety of breads, soup, entrée (of which Wiener schnitzel and roulades of beef are excellent.) Chaîne des Rotisseurs. Monday, lunch only. Sunday, brunch and dinner only. Open seven days a week. Entrées from $3.50 (L), $6.50 (D), complete brunch $7.50. MC, V.

## BERKELEY

***Chez Panisse,*** 1517 Shattuck Avenue (548-5525). The menu changes daily at this country-inn-like restaurant. Creative cuisine. A full dinner may include poached baby artichokes, fresh crawfish bisque, leg of lamb with white beans, salad or cheese, fresh fruit. Only fresh in-season food is served and great care is given to the cheese and fruit selections. Also memorable à la carte desserts. Reservations are recommended and essential on weekends. Closed Sunday and Monday. Entrées from $3.50 (L); full five-course dinners $15. No credit cards.

## LARKSPUR

***464 Magnolia,*** 464 Magnolia Street (924-6831 or 924-0606). A beautiful, high-ceilinged dining room with plants hanging from the skylights and walls hung with quilts, tapestries, Oriental rugs and paintings. Continental cuisine. Imaginative cooking. Menu changes monthly. Full dinners including salad, entrée (such as roast loin of pork marinated in red wine or Sonoma duck with green peppercorns) with a variety of fresh vegetables. One of the best Saturday and Sunday brunches in the Bay Area. Pan-fried fresh trout is a popular choice. Saturday and Sunday, brunch and dinner only. Open seven days a week. Entrées from $2.75 (L), dinners from $9, brunch entrées from $3.50. AE, MC, V.

## PALO ALTO

***The Good Earth,*** 185 University Avenue (321-9449). A popular restaurant with the Stanford University crowd. Always packed. Décor isn't fancy, but the food is well prepared and in gigantic portions. Nothing on the menu costs more than $6. Inspired omelets, large fruit salads, vegetarian and meat entrées, homemade desserts and pastries. You can buy pastries and 10-grain bread to take home. Open seven days a week. No credit cards.

## SAN RAFAEL

***Maurice et Charles' Bistrot,*** 901 Lincoln Avenue (456-2010). Elegant, but not formal. There's graffiti on one of the walls. Owner Maurice Anzallag oversees the dining room. Outstanding food. For a starter, split an order of the quenelles, as light a fish mousse as you'll taste anywhere. Specialties include: young, fresh pheasant served with fresh juniper berries, chestnut purée and braised red cabbage; tender white veal with poached turnips and mirabelle brandy; lightly poached salmon served with a silken light cream sauce flavored with Pernod and poached oysters. Homemade ice cream and sorbets. Reservations are necessary. Dinner only, from 6:30 P.M. to 10:30 P.M. Closed Sunday. Entrées from $8.50. MC, V.

## SAUSALITO

***Seven Seas,*** 682 Bridgeway (332-1304) Instead of making the tourists' pilgrimage to overrated Ondine's, try this popular seafood restaurant. Active bar in front, garden dining room with a sliding glass roof in the back. Bouillabaisse and cioppino are specialties. Open seven days a week. Entrées from $4.95 (L & D). AE, DC, MC, V.

# MARKETS

## GIFT FOODS

***French Pantry,*** 1570 California Street (776-2585). A large selection of homemade pâtés, sausages, salads, main dish entrées, fine desserts, cheese, imported foods, wines. Open seven days a week. AE, CB, DC, MC, V.

***Jurgensen's Grocery Co.,*** 2190 Union Street (931-0100). Closed Sunday. MC, V.

## GIFT WINES

***Wine & Cheese Center,*** 205 Jackson Street (956-2518). An unbelievably broad selection of wines; also tasting facilities. Closed Sunday. MC, V.

# SPECIAL EVENTS

***Chinese New Year.*** During the lengthy New Year celebration, which generally takes place in late January, early February, most of the Chinatown restaurants put on special banquets. Also street vendors sell fresh Mandarin oranges, candied fruit, nuts and other traditional New Year's foods.

# San Juan

Before the Caribe Hilton Hotel opened in December 1949, the only night-time dining places in San Juan were the 100-year-old Mallorquina; a restaurant in the Condado Beach Hotel; La Estrella de Italia, a Puerto Rican-Italian restaurant in Old San Juan; Cecilia's Place, a seafood shack of a restaurant near the beach where the San Juan elite met to eat because the food was so good; and El Nilo and El Chevere, two side-by-side eateries in Santurce.

Most San Juaneros ate their large meals at home. They stopped for mid-morning snacks of *pastelillos* (meat- or cheese-filled pastries) washed down gingerly with steaming cups of *café con leche,* generally at counter restaurants. They went back for mid-afternoon pick-me-ups of *bocadillos* (narrow toasted buns filled with sliced ham and cheese) and *leche batidas* (milk shakes) or soda pop. If out for the evening, they would sometimes wind up at one of the few places still open, for a late-night repast of sweet guava-layered pastry or a portion of rich egg or coconut flan accompanied by *champolas* (fresh fruit shakes—an early Puerto Rican version of health-food drinks).

And there were the public market *fondas* (simple hole-in-the-wall eateries) where working people who couldn't get home and roamers who didn't want to go home could eat tasty rice and beans and stewed meat and *mondongo* (tripe stew) 24 hours a day. But on the whole, precious little was eaten outside the home.

The Caribe Hilton changed everything. The tourists came and clamored to be fed. **La Rotisserie,** the Caribe's main dining room, opened new horizons for local food buffs. La Rotisserie also brought in Swiss-French chefs and sous-chefs and butchers and pastry-

Spanish owners double as cook and maître d' and keep four very sharp eyes on things. Cristobal looks like Woody Allen and cooks like an angel. For starters try light-as-air brain fritters or garlicky sweetbreads or crisp fingertips of ham and chicken croquettes. Don't miss the *capitan al corto caldo* (fresh hog-fish filets in a *court bouillon* with a crisp julienne of carrots and celery). Call ahead to be sure it's available before making the necessary reservations. Skip desserts, prepared off the premises except for the chocolate, unbearably sweet Tatianoff. But do try any dessert that Cristobal prepares—generally the flan and *natilla* (a soft Spanish cream custard). Service is excellent. Closed Monday. Entrées from $5 (L & D). AE, DC, MC, V.

## SWISS

***The Swiss Chalet,*** Calle de Diego 105, Santurce (724-1200.) A bit of old Switzerland in San Juan. The bells don't tinkle and the cuckoo clocks don't announce the time, but the décor is decidedly alpine rather than tropical. So are the house specialties. *Viande des Grisons* is an unusual appetizer. The escargots (described as "the best west of Paris") should not be missed and crusty *pan de agua,* which mops up the herb butter beautifully, is the best in town. Veal sausage with onion sauce is delicious and the piccata Milanese is good. Broiled lamb chops are outstanding, as is the fondue, which properly is laced with kirsch. Desserts are good. There is a creamy bavarois au kirsch with raspberry sauce and French pastries are baked on the premises. Jackets required for men at dinner time. Open seven days a week, until 1 A.M. Entrées from $5.50 (L), $7 (D). The **Café Pierre,** an offshoot in the same building, has a similar but more limited and less expensive menu. It is open from 7 A.M. until midnight. No special dress is required. **El Bombon** sells pastries, cakes, cookies and European chocolates and sweets of all kinds. AE, CB, DC, MC, V.

# SPECIALTY COOKING

## COFFEE

***La Bombonera,*** Calle San Francisco 259, Old San Juan (722-0658). Go for *pan de agua*—split, buttered, toasted and served with native guava jelly—or *pan de Mallorca,* which is one of the great, light sweet breads of all time—split, buttered, toasted and drenched with powdered sugar. The Puerto Rican coffee is only one more of the reasons you should stop in at this favorite spot. The décor is strictly 1930's Coffee Shoppe—booths, counter seats and a few tables. The service is Puerto Rican Lindy casual: sassy and good. Breakfasts on Sunday are enormously popular. A cup of strong native coffee, plain or laced with hot milk, costs 35 cents. The *Mallorca* costs 45 cents. So does the bread. Open seven days a week, from 7:30 A.M. until 10 P.M. No credit cards.

## EGGS

***Palm Court Café and Restaurant,*** Calle Fortaleza 152, Old San Juan (723-1799). This is the loveliest restaurant in San Juan. Everything is done in good taste. The gay, floral pillows; tablecloths; napkins; and bentwood and cane chairs complement one of San Juan's early buildings. It provides a proper setting for fine, light omelets, crêpes and quiche that are whipped up in the kitchen and brought to the table piping hot and good enough to eat. Drinks and coffee are also good. Lunch only. Closed Sunday. Drinks until 6 P.M. Entrées from $4.50. AE

## SANDWICHES

***El Kiosko,*** Avenida Ponce de Leon 320, corner Avenida Franklin Delano Roosevelt, Hato Rey (753-6126). Sandwiches of every conceivable kind and nationality are served in a lovely setting of lush green plants and light, pleasant surroundings. Dinner plates are also available at very modest prices. A popular Sunday brunch includes a glass of Champagne and eight or nine different hot dishes. Open seven days a week. Sandwiches start at $1.55, dinner entrées from $3.95. AE, MC, V.

## SEAFOOD

***La Gallega,*** Calle Fortaleza 309, Old San Juan (725-8018). A warm, friendly, home-style seafood restaurant with Spanish décor—the usual bullfight posters. The owner, Doña Celia de Rio, stays in the kitchen and helps prepare the food. The *asopao de mariscos* is chock-a-block with well-seasoned shrimps, clams, scallops, rice and everything nice. Fresh *merluza en salsa verde* (hake in a green parsley sauce) is first rate. An excellent *paella marinera*—with lobster, shrimp, squid, scallops and clams—takes 35 to 40 minutes to prepare, but you can call ahead to order it. The lobster thermidor—surprisingly served on a bed of mashed potatoes—is as good as it is unusual. Desserts are homemade and sometimes heavy. Closed Monday. Entrées from $5 (L), $7 (D). AE, DC, MC, V.

## STEAK

***Scotch and Sirloin,*** 1020 Avenida Ashford in the Condado, Santurce (722-3640). An informal and pleasant steak and seafood restaurant with a spotty salad bar (when it is good, it's very good) and good, strong drinks. Inside-outside tables. Sit outside on the terrace as close to the lagoon as you can get. The steaks are fine. Also chicken teriyaki and broiled scallops, broiled lobster and crab. Two homemade desserts—cheesecake and mocha cake—are nothing to write home about. Reservations accepted . Dinner only. Open seven days a week. Entrées from $6.25. Salad bar $4.25. AE, CB, DC, MC, V.

# FOR INDIVIDUAL NEEDS

## IF YOU HAVE TIME FOR ONLY ONE MEAL

***La Fragua,*** Capitol Hotel, Ponce de Leon 800, entrance on Calle Cuevillas, Miramar, Santurce (722-4699). (See description under SPANISH.)

## BEST HOTEL MEAL

***La Rotisserie,*** Caribe Hilton Hotel, San Juan (725-0303). (See description under BIG DEAL/WORTH IT.)

## BUSINESS BREAKFAST

***Condado Plaza,*** in the Condado Convention Center, Avenida Ashford, Santurce (723-6090). (See description under AMERICAN.)

## BUSINESS LUNCH

***The Swiss Chalet,*** Calle de Diego 105, Santurce (724-1200). (See description under SWISS.)

## LATE-NIGHT SERVICE

***Café Valencia,*** Avenida Muñoz Rivera 994, Rio Piedras (764-6949). Near University of Puerto Rico campus. Take a taxi from San Juan or Santurce. An unpretentious Spanish restaurant, staffed by skilled waiters, that specializes in seafood. Try the excellent, thick Spanish soup of beans, cabbage and potatoes with bits of smoked pork called *caldo gallego.* The shrimps Malagueña are sizzlingly good and the paella Valencia is passable, although you must allow 40 minutes for it to be prepared. Open seven days a week: until 1:30 A.M. Sunday and Monday, until 2:30 A.M. Tuesday through Thursday, until 4 A.M. Friday and Saturday. Entrées from $2.50 (L & D). AE, CB, MC, V.

# MARKETS

***Santurce Public Market,*** Calle Canals between Ponce de Leon and Baldorioty de Castro. Native fruits, vegetables, honey and sweetmeats. Stall 46 won a prize in 1978 for the best fruits and vegetables. Open Monday through Saturday from 6 A.M. to 6 P.M. Sunday from 6 A.M. to noon.

***Rio Piedras Public Market,*** Calle de Diego, Rio Piedras. An enormous, bustling place full of produce and live fowl and rabbits and local handiwork and people. Not a place for the fastidious or the fainthearted, but a must for serious food buffs. Open Monday through Saturday from 6 A.M. to 6 P.M., Sunday from 6 A.M. to noon.

## GIFT FOODS

***Gourmet International,*** Calle San Francisco 153, Plaza de Armas, Old San Juan (723-4590). Select food and wine from all over the world. Gift baskets prepared to order. Closed Sunday and Monday. AE, MC, V.

# Seattle

Seattle traces its history back to 1851, when the first settlers arrived by ship at Alki Point. During the intervening years, the face of the land and the character of the residents have changed dramatically.

Forests that once covered the seven hills of the city area are no more. The giant Douglas fir trees that once palisaded the skyline have been replaced by man-made skyscrapers that range from the tourist-attracting Space Needle to fifty-floor-plus commercial buildings. Elliott Bay, bordering the city on the west, has become serrated with miles of piers and wharves. Lake Washington on the east is a mecca for boatmen and their moorings.

Styles of living have also changed in Seattle. World travel is now commonplace. And home dwellers with backyard barbecues who used to make only infrequent visits to restaurants have become supporters of eating establishments of a variety undreamed of only two decades ago.

The greatest transformation of Seattle's restaurant community has taken place since 1962, the year of the city's Century 21 Exposition, known more generally as the World's Fair. Since that time, the city has experienced a quiet revolution in its roster of restaurants, a proliferation of new eating places accompanied by an impressive diversity of cuisines that encompasses a decision-slowing wealth of choices for the diner.

Seattle's earlier restaurants didn't venture far from the foods familiar to the majority of the residents. The Scandinavians, for example, who poured into the city in record numbers during the half-century or so prior to World War I, established the smorgasbord as one of Seattle's favorite dining-out experiences. It has become virtually a culinary curiosity, however, since the closing of King Oscar's, the long-reigning monarch of local smorgasbord houses.

Seafood, available in abundance from nearby waters, has long been a keystone of Seattle's cuisine. Among the great variety of fish and shellfish are many of wide reputation, including the famed Olympia oyster of Lilliputian size, the full-flavored Dungeness crab, king salmon, North Pacific halibut, razor clams and butter clams, abalone, and the giant clam known as geoduck (pronounced gooey duck).

Much of the seafood bonanza is kitchen-prepared in the home, or used for clambakes, salmon barbecues and the like on outings. The majority of restaurants that drew upon this wealth of food from the sea treated the sea gold like dross, usually batter-dipping and deep-frying it in monotonous repetition. The use of crab and shrimp in salads was virtually the only departure from deep-frying.

But times have changed. In recent years the city's chefs have been using seafood more imaginatively, creating house specialties with it, even utilizing formerly ignored seafood such as local mussels.

The spirit of upgrading menus with more variety, greater imagination and classic kitchen techniques can be found throughout Seattle's dining-out industry.

Chinese restaurant fare has long been here, but slow to move away from the "chop suey" approach; menus have only recently become more extensive, representing the various regional Chinese cuisines.

Of all the cuisines in Seattle's restaurant world, none has received more impressive emphasis than that of the French. The local colony of French chefs and restaurateurs has mushroomed notably, and rather suddenly. Seattle has become the home of numerous chefs born and trained in France. With remarkable success, these chefs have, in a very few years, gone from kitchen service in some of the city's earlier French restaurants, to operation of their own restaurants.

Restaurateurs are showing strong optimism for the future. Local diners are developing greater interest in the culinary specialties of other lands. Together, they are building a restaurant community that holds much promise for visitors and residents alike.

Dining customs in Seattle are much like those in other metropolitan areas of the nation. Dress requirements have become less stringent, but men generally wear jackets and ties when dining in downtown restaurants. A one-tip system is usual, though it's not unheard of for a wine steward, headwaiter or maître d'hôtel to receive a separate emolument when special or exceptional service has been provided.

Pioneer Square, the "old town" at the southern edge of downtown Seattle, is an area rich with buildings that date back to the 1890's, among them the new and renovated structures that followed in the wake of recent upgrading and preservation of the area. There's a variety of attractions for the visitor—architecture that spans the city's past eight decades; competent restaurants and nightlife activity; shops with offerings that range from leather goods, pottery and jewelry to cookware and rare books.

Seattle is a spread-out city, cinched in at the central downtown area between Elliott Bay and Lake Washington. The many districts that dot the northern and southern areas swelling out from the city's hourglass waistline also have views of mountains and water, shops of wide variety, and restaurants worthy of patronage. Some of the latter are listed under the "In the Suburbs" category.

Seattle Center, the city's site of and legacy from the 1962 World's Fair, is served by quick monorail transport from downtown. It has many attractions, among them the Space Needle (with its revolving restaurant and an observation deck, both with commanding views of Mt. Rainier, the Olympic Mountains, the Cascade Mountain Range, Puget Sound and its islands, and downtown Seattle); the famed Pacific Science Center; the Repertory Theater and Seattle Opera House; Seattle Art Museum Pavilion; import shops in the International Bazaar; the Food Circus with its Belgian Waffle House, Burger Bar, Chinn's Tea House, El Taco, House of Japan, Mongolian Steak, Pie Pantry, and other fast-food operations.

Tourist magnets also include the **Pike Place Market,** the central waterfront with its shops and unrestricted views, the government locks at Ballard, Fishermen's Terminal with its moorage for hundreds of commerical fishing boats, harbor tours and golf courses.

Like most seaport cities, Seattle is hospitable and open-handed with visitors. Her leading restaurants display the same friendly traits.

# Restaurants and Food Sources

**(Area code: 206)**

## BIG DEAL

### WORTH IT

***Mirabeau,*** 4th and Madison (624-4550). As you enter this excellent restaurant with its understated décor, your first impression is that it's afloat on a sea of scenic views. Seated at one of the uncrowded tables in this dining room on the 46th floor of the Seattle-First National Bank Building, you find, repeated in rows of mirrored window enclosures, views of Puget Sound, Mt. Rainier, the Olympic Mountains, and downtown Seattle. The listing of French dishes on the menu is extensive, and house specialties include sole stuffed with salmon mousse. Lunch is especially attractive, with new items daily. Good wine list. Handsome bar. Chaîne des Rotisseurs. Saturday, dinner only. Closed Sunday. Entrées from $3.75 (L), $8.25 (D). AE, MC, V.

## INTERNATIONAL

### AMERICAN

***Jake O'Shaughnessey's,*** 100 Mercer Street (285-1897). In keeping with its name, this excellent restaurant has Irish décor, makes peerless Irish coffee and displays a plaque certifying that it's the world's largest seller of Murphy's Irish Whisky. The limited, well-considered menu offers American specialties that include sourdough bread, stews, beef roasted in a coating of salt, barbecued salmon (considered by some the best in town), rich ice cream and good coffee served in heated cups. No reservations. Dinner only. Open seven days a week. Entrées from $5.85. AE, MC, V.

# CHINESE

***Atlas Café,*** 424 Maynard Avenue S. (623-0913). Chinese account for most of its diners, which in itself is a testimonial to the competence of the kitchen. The menu is an extensive listing of Cantonese dishes. No alcoholic beverages. No reservations. Dinner only. Closed Monday. Entrées from $3.50. No credit cards.

***Tien Tsin,*** 1401 N. 45th Street (634-0223). Banquet area plus a café-like dining room in the front make this restaurant fairly capacious but its menu is even more impressive—a diner's (and reader's) delight with more than 160 listings. Mandarin-Peking cuisine ranging from chicken and prawns and dumplings to not-commonly-found-in-Seattle items such as sea cucumbers. Beer and wine. Closed Monday. Complete meals from $3.85 (L), $6.60 (D). MC, V.

# FRENCH

***The Other Place,*** 319 Union Street (623-7340). Robert Rosellini, son of long-time restaurateur Victor Rosellini, is the owner-proprietor. Young Rosellini spares no effort to offer the freshest, best possible foodstuffs, prepared with French finesse in an excellent kitchen. Live trout are kept in a *vivier,* ready for *au bleu* and other treatments. Fresh game from his own farms. Wild boar from a California ranch. A very fine cellar stocked by the wine-knowledgeable Rosellini. Closed Sunday. Entrées $2.95 (L), $14.50 (D). AE, DC, MC, V.

***Annique's,*** 2037 6th Avenue (624-2296). Fine French dining in a high-ceilinged room with Louis XVI décor. A competent kitchen backs up a well-planned menu, which includes house specialties such as abalone amandine, roast tarragon chicken, pepper steak Rodolphe; and with French-menu regulars ranging from quiche Lorraine to veal scallops *à la Normande* and duck *à l'orange.* Good wine list. Monday, lunch only. Saturday, dinner only. Closed Sunday. Entrées from $3.75 (L), $8.50 (D). AE, DC, MC, V.

***Brasserie Pittsbourg,*** 602 1st Avenue (623-4167). Butcher-paper "cloths" on the tables, travel posters on the walls, handsome copperware on display, and flowers in abundance. Classic French cuisine, rather than brasserie fare, is the mark of the fine dishes that emerge from the kitchen of chef-owner François Kissel. The name of the place is a tongue-in-cheek Frenchification of Pittsburgh Lunch, which once occupied the premises. Good wines, good service. Chaîne des Rotisseurs. Closed Sunday. Complete meals from $4.15 (L), $7 (D). AE, MC, V.

## ITALIAN

***Rosellini's Four-10,*** 4th and Wall (624-5464). Victor Rosellini, the genial dean of restaurateurs in Washington State and recent president of the National Restaurant Association, is doing his usual superlative job in this new home of the Four-10, opened after the original one became the victim of downtown demolition crews clearing ground for new construction. The menu is Continental, with emphasis on Italian pasta dishes and classic sauces prepared in palate-charming style. Good bar, good kitchen, good service, good wine list. Closed Sunday. Entrées from $3.85 (L), $8.25 (D). AE, MC, V.

## JAPANESE

***The Mikado,*** 514 S. Jackson Street (622-5206). A restaurant distinguished for its food preparation, service and atmosphere. Dining areas range from a counter with comfortable high-backed chairs to a Western-style dining room to handsome *tatami* rooms. Extremely competent kitchen, with seafood its forte, although almost all the culinary productions should thoroughly please the diner. Full bar. Dinner only. Closed Sunday. Dinners from $8. AE, MC, V.

## MEXICAN

***La Fiesta,*** 715 Pike Street (223-9280). For more than 20 years this no-nonsense restaurant has been serving authentic Mexican foods to Seattleites. The emphasis is on well-prepared dishes, not on atmosphere, so prices are moderate and trade is brisk. This veteran establishment is popular with the after-theater, after-hours crowd. Beer and wine. Open seven days a week until 3 A.M., except Sunday. Entrées from $2.50 (L), $3.50 (D).

## MIDDLE EUROPEAN

***Labuznik,*** 1924 1st Avenue (682-1624). The handsome two-level dining area has low-key décor "to avoid conflict with the food," in the words of Czech-born chef-owner Peter Cipra. The basically Continental menu is highlighted by Czech and Hungarian specialties, artfully prepared by the perfectionist proprietor. Full bar. Closed Sunday and Monday. Reservations recommended. Entrées from $3.85 (L), $7 (D). AE, MC, V.

# SPECIALTY COOKING

## CHARCOAL BROILER

***Canlis' Restaurant,*** 2576 Aurora Avenue N. (283-3313). A charming restaurant overlooking Lake Union, the interior highlighted with stone, wood and glass. Carefully selected steaks excellently cooked to order, local salmon and *mahi-mahi* from Hawaii, Canlis Special Salad with a Caesar accent. Kimono-clad waitresses. Good wine list. Attractive bar. Dinner only. Closed Sunday. Entrées from $8. AE, CB, DC, MC, V.

## CRÊPES

***Crêpe de Paris,*** Rainier Square (623-4111). This excellent crêperie, forced to move from its former location only a few blocks away, is a warm and friendly place with oak parquet flooring, leather-and-chrome chairs, handwoven carpeting in the bar, a wraparound map of Paris. It now offers a full French menu in addition to the customary 30 varieties of main-dish and dessert crêpes that start at $4.50. Full bar. Closed Sunday. Entrées from $4.50 (L), $8.50 (D). AE, MC, V.

## DANISH PASTRY

***John Nielsen Pastry,*** 1329 3rd Avenue (622-1570). A bit of Denmark in Seattle in this scrupulously clean shop selling typical Danish pastries. It was founded by John Nielsen, formerly a baker in Copenhagen, and is across the street from the main post office. It's a convenient stop for coffee and pastry while shopping—or buy a bagful to take out, to eat while sightseeing. Pastries 40 to 55 cents. Coffee 35 cents. Closed Sunday.

## DELI

***Rosellini's Gourmet Kitchen,*** 4th and Vine (622-1970). Attractive eat-it-there or take-it-out operation with cheerful, fast, short-order service for sandwiches, salads, chili, pastas and pastries. Closed Sunday. Sandwiches from $2 to a top of $4.10 for the Deli Raider with three kinds of meat and two cheeses. AE, DC, MC, V.

## OYSTERS

Oysters in great variety abound in local waters. Following are oysters bars that feature them in cooked preparations and on the half shell, with shuckers in attendance. All have full bars and restaurants and all are open seven days a week. Oysters on the half shell range from $2.40 to $4.50 per half dozen.

***Henry's Off Broadway,*** 1705 E. Olive Way (329-8063). AE, MC, V.

***McRory's,*** Occidental S. and S. King (623-4800). AE, MC, V.

***Shucker's,*** Olympic Hotel, 4th and Seneca (682-7700). AE, DC, MC, V.

***Oyster Grotto,*** 5414 Sand Point Way N.E. (525-3230). AE, MC, V.

***Olympia Oyster House,*** 2701 1st Avenue (682-0221). Not equipped with an oyster bar, but they serve local oysters on the half shell and in a variety of prepared dishes, as well as many other seafoods. AE, MC, V.

## SANDWICHES

***The Earl of Sandwich,*** 100 Mercer Street (284-8382). This mecca for sandwich fanciers, across the street from the Seattle Center, is so popular you can expect at least a short wait, especially at lunchtime. A dizzying variety of fillings, and cheerful service are keystones of its success. Also available are soups, salads, fruit, cider and other sandwich accompaniments, plus desserts. Beer and wine. Open seven days a week. Sandwiches from $2.20 to $3.25 (L & D). No credit cards.

## SEAFOOD

***Ivar's Salmon House,*** 401 N.E. Northlake Way (632-0767). The striking building presents an authentic re-creation of a Northwest Indian long house, complete with faithful renditions of Indian carving and design. Broad view of Lake Union. House specialty is salmon, Makah Indian style, smoke-barbecued over an alderwood fire. Full bar. Reservations for 8 or more only. Saturday and Sunday, dinner only. Open seven days a week. Entrées from $3.65 (L), $5.25 (D). AE, MC, V.

## STEAK

***El Gaucho,*** 624 Olive Way (682-3202). An efficiently operated restaurant with comfortable chairs, dim lighting, good service and competent kitchen. Excellent steaks are the stars on a menu that includes seafood, barbecued ribs, lamb chops. Popular specialty is the "hunt breakfast" available midnight to 2:30 A.M. Monday through Thursday, with a fruit starter, three kinds of meat (steak,

Italian sausage and one that changes daily), omelet, country-fried potatoes, muffins, priced at $8.95. Full bar. Saturday, dinner only. Closed Sunday. Steaks from $4.75 (L), $13.50 (D). AE, DC, MC, V.

# FOR INDIVIDUAL NEEDS

## IF YOU HAVE TIME FOR ONLY ONE MEAL

***Mirabeau,*** 4th and Madison (624-4550). (See description under BIG DEAL/WORTH IT.)

## BEST HOTEL MEAL

***The Golden Lion,*** Olympic Hotel, 5th and University (682-7700). Go there for the "Champagne Dinner à la Chef," which includes champagne throughout the meal, along with *quenelles de sole,* consommé, filet of beef with mushrooms and béarnaise sauce (or chicken breast in calvados and cream), spinach salad, dessert crêpes, coffee, petits fours, all for $19.95. This elegant room offers knowledgeable wine service by Frank Ferguson, who has been the wine steward since the restaurant opened in 1960. Excellent bar with music by Tubby Clark, veteran pianist at the Olympic. Chaîne des Rotisseurs. Open seven days a week. Continental menus for lunch and dinner, with entrées from $4.95 (L), $10.50 (D). AE, CB, DC, MC, V.

## RESTAURANT NEAR AIRPORT

***Top of the Inn,*** Holiday Inn, 17338 Pacific Highway S. (248-1000). Convenient for overnight stops between flights. Well-prepared specialties at this revolving restaurant with spectacular views include standards such as *Chateaubriand bouquetière,* steak Diane, roast duckling, veal Marsala. Full bar. Dinner only. Open seven days a week. Entrées from $5.95. AE, DC, MC, V.

## BUSINESS BREAKFAST

***Beef Room,*** Washington Plaza Hotel, 5th and Westlake (624-7400). Complete breakfasts with eggs, meat, fruit and beverage range from $3.50 to a top of $6.25 for the special Western Steak Breakfast. Service begins at 6 A.M. Open seven days a week. AE, CB, DC, MC, V.

## BUSINESS LUNCH

***Mirabeau,*** 4th and Madison (624-4550). (See description under BIG DEAL/WORTH IT.) Both the dining room and the pleasant bar are usually crowded for lunch, so reservations are recommended. A fine lunch menu with three new specialties (meat, fish, egg) offered each day. Entrées from $3.75. AE, MC, V.

## BEST WINE LIST

***Le Tastevin,*** 501 Queen Anne Avenue N. (283-0991). Broad and well-selected stock of bottlings that range from $5.95 up. Included are rare vintages from France, Germany and California, plus good representation of ports and sherries. Restaurant features French culinary specialties. Closed Sunday. Entrées from $4.50 (L), complete dinners from $12. MC, V.

## FOR DRINKS

***Annique's,*** 2037 6th Avenue (624-2296). (See description under FRENCH.) The Unicorn Bar in this fine French restaurant is a green and white, summery room with rattan chairs. It attracts a fairly mature crowd, drawn in partly by excellent complimentary hors d'oeuvre that are served from 5 to 7 P.M. Tuesday through Friday. Prepared on the premises with a definite French touch, the hors d'oeuvre are savory rather than highly seasoned and go well with white wine or champagne as well as with cocktails. Closed Sunday. AE, DC, MC, V.

***Jake O'Shaughnessey's,*** 100 Mercer Street (285-1897). (See description under AMERICAN.) Beams and small-pane windows give the feeling of an Irish pub. A popular spot for young adults, usually jam-packed. A singing bartender shares the spotlight with an impressive array of bottles filling long shelf upon long shelf behind the bar. Open seven days a week. AE, MC, V.

## RESTAURANT WITH MUSIC

***Edgewater Inn,*** 2411 Alaskan Way (624-7000). On the water end of a pier over Elliott Bay, with striking panoramic view. Continental menu. Music, dancing and entertainment Tuesday through Saturday. Full bar. Open seven days a week. Entrées from $3.50 (L), $8.50 (D). AE, CB, DC, MC, V.

## ROMANTIC

***Trader Vic's,*** Washington Plaza Hotel, 5th and Westlake (624-8520). Quiet, dimly lit restaurant that offers good Polynesian and Chinese foods as well as a sense of seclusion. Excellent meats from the wood-fire Chinese ovens, seafood specialties, and curried dishes. Full bar. Open seven days a week. Entrées from $5 (L), complete dinners from $9.95. AE, CB, DC, MC, V.

## LATE-NIGHT SERVICE

***Thirteen Coins,*** 125 Boren Avenue N. (682-2513). High-backed chairs at the counter provide comfort and a ringside view of food preparation. Table seating also available. An extensive menu offers a variety of sustenance for any meal, snack or time. Full bar. Open 24 hours a day, seven days a week. Entrées from $4.25 (L), $5.25 (D). AE, DC, MC, V.

***El Gaucho,*** 624 Olive Way (682-3202). (See description under STEAK.)

***La Fiesta,*** 715 Pike Street (223-9280). (See description under MEXICAN.)

## SUNDAY BRUNCH

***King Café,*** 723 S. King Street (622-6373). Specializing in superb Chinese tea pastries. Limited capacity, so usually crowded. Inexpensive. No reservations. Open from 11 A.M. to 5 P.M. *Dim sum* plate from 80 cents. No credit cards.

***Henry's Off Broadway,*** 1705 E. Olive Way (329-8063). A very attractive restaurant, perhaps the handsomest in Seattle, built with curving lines that delight the eye, tall windows giving onto plantings of trees and other greenery. Special children's plates. Table service, rather than buffet style, 10 A.M. to 2 P.M. Brunch entrées from $4.95. AE, MC, V.

## SUNDAY-EVENING MEAL

***Henry's Off Broadway,*** 1705 E. Olive Way (329-8063). (See description above.) The menu is rich with seafood dishes, but beef and veal and lamb are well represented. Full bar. Open seven days a week. Entrées from $7.50. AE, MC, V.

## FOR FAMILIES WITH CHILDREN

***Ivar's Acres of Clams,*** Pier 54 at the foot of Madison Street (624-6852). A large-capacity restaurant next to the terminal where ferries come and go on runs across Puget Sound. It's a good vantage point for viewing the city's harbor traffic. Close by are harborside attractions such as the city's aquarium and waterfront park, gift shops, busy piers where foreign cargo is loaded and unloaded.

Seafood specialties. Full bar. Open seven days a week. Entrées from $2.50 (L), $6.25 (D). No credit cards.

***Space Needle Restaurant,*** Seattle Center (682-5656). A 360-degree panoramic view from this revolving restaurant at the 500-foot level of the Space Needle, landmark of the city's 1962 World's Fair. Open seven days a week. Full bar. Entrées from $5.50 (L), $11.95 (D). AE, DC, MC, V.

# IN THE SUBURBS

## BALLARD

***Ray's Boathouse,*** 6049 Seaview Avenue N.W. (789-3770). Pleasant décor with fabric-covered walls, hanging greenery and grainy wood. Offers a broad view of water and mountains. Seafood a specialty. Full bar. Open seven days a week. Complete meals from $4 (L), $9 (D). AE, MC, V.

## BELLEVUE

***Yangtze,*** 1320 156th Avenue N.E. (747-2404). The dining area offers a pleasant and tasteful décor. The menu encompasses many Szechuan and Mandarin dishes. Competent kitchen and attentive service. Full bar. Closed Monday. Entrées from $2.95 (L), $4.50 (D). AE, MC, V.

## BOTHELL

***Gerard's Relais de Lyon,*** 17121 Bothell Way N.E. (485-7600). A former private residence remodeled into an attractive dining house in a country-like setting surrounded by trees. Fine French fare prepared by the chef-owner, Gerard Parrat. Good wine list. Chaîne des Rotisseurs. Dinner only. Closed Monday. Entrées from $9. DC, MC, V.

## DES MOINES

***Michel's,*** 21630 7th Place S. (878-4412). Charming, elegantly restrained restaurant. French cuisine highlighted by dishes such as bouillabaisse, *terrine de lapin.* Good wine list. Chaîne des Rotisseurs. Dinner only. Closed Monday. Complete dinners from $7.95. DC, MC, V.

## EDMONDS

***Chez Claude,*** 417 Main Street (778-9888). Plants, paintings and copperware add charm to this pleasant restaurant. Competent preparation of French dishes by the chef-owner, with strikingly fine vegetables never steamed to death. Full bar. Chaîne des Rotisseurs. Dinner only. Closed Monday. Entrées from $7. AE, DC, MC, V.

## HOLLY PARK

***Casa Romana,*** 6318 S. 38th Street (722-0449). Homey, cheerful place with conversation level often in the high-decibel bracket. Italian regulars on the menu include *fettuccine, saltimbocca, cannelloni, gnocchi, lasagne,* and *zabaglione,* plus *calzone,* the stuffed version of a pizza. Full bar. Open seven days a week. Entrées from $2.95 (L), $6 (D). MC, V.

## KIRKLAND

***Le Provençal,*** 212 Central Way (827-3300). Two smallish rooms with a see-through fireplace tying them together. French rustic style, with simplicity and charm reflected in the excellent dishes that issue from the kitchen. Specializing in foods of Southern France such as the *daube de boeuf* prepared just as the proprietor's father does it (the beef braised slowly with wine and stock) in his restaurant in Avignon. Full bar. Chaîne des Rotisseurs. Dinner only. Closed Sunday. Complete dinners from $6.25. AE, DC, MC, V.

## REDMOND

***Le Toulousain,*** 16701 N.E. 80th Street (883-1934). Two charming rooms with white-stuccoed walls, beamed ceilings and wood-burning fireplaces greet the diner at this warm and friendly restaurant devoted to French cookery. Dishes listed on the restrained menu are prepared by the chef-owner, Toulouse-born Leon Auriol, a maître d'armes who put down his fencing foils to "en garde" the kitchen "batterie." His American wife supervises the dining rooms. Wine and beer. Dinner only. Closed Monday and Tuesday. Entrées from $7. MC, V.

# MARKETS

***Pike Place Market,*** Pike Street and First Avenue. This "farmers' market" established more than 70 years ago is the object of active conservation efforts. Through the years it has changed from its original function as a marketplace for local farmers, though local farmers still sell their produce there. Now, in addition to striking views of the city's harbor, it offers a wealth of diversity with its vegetable and fruit stands, food stores, bakeries, fish and meat markets, cookware shops, cafés, lunch counters, and **Maximilien Bis,** a popular moderate-price French restaurant with two floors of sweeping vistas that include Puget Sound and the Olympic Mountain Range to the west. The entire market is closed Sunday.

## GIFT FOODS

***Delicacy Shop,*** Frederick & Nelson Department Store, 5th and Pine (682-5500). Broad range of delicatessen items, imported and domestic, including cheeses, specialty meats and wines. Open seven days a week. No credit cards.

***The Cheese Shoppe,*** 4760 University Village Place N.E. (523-2560). Scores of cheeses from dozens of countries. Also sausages and specialty delicatessen items. Open seven days a week. No credit cards.

***Port Chatham Packing Co.,*** 632 N.W. 46th Street (783-8200). Gift packages of salmon, sugar-cured and smoked over hardwood fire, in filet form or sliced and vacuum-packed; hand-packed sockeye salmon; North Pacific shrimp. Closed Sunday. No credit cards.

***Pure Food Fish Market,*** 1511 Pike Place (622-5765). Complete supply of seafoods, shipped anywhere in the United States. Closed Sunday. No credit cards.

## GIFT WINES

***Champion Cellars,*** 108 Denny Way (284-8306). More than 400 different bottlings from throughout the world. Glasses, books, and other wine-oriented items. Free parking. Closed Sunday. MC, V.

# Toronto

"Toronto the Good"—where "decent" people used to refuse to eat or drink anything outside of their homes—now considers itself a sophisticated city, a veritable North American gastronomic mecca. Happily it's the little ethnic restaurants, peppered along most streets, that are partially responsible for much of this transition. Before the large influx of immigrants to Toronto, shortly after World War II, most restaurants tried to match the Victorian opulence and impeccable white-glove service of the King Edward Hotel. The Victoria Room, long considered the finest dining room in the country, served the upper crust of Toronto the best Canadian beef, lobster thermidor and water sherbets from its opening in 1903.

Shortly thereafter, the T. Eaton Company opened The Grill Room in their department store, where it was acceptable for women to dine alone. That was 1910. It took until 1947 before a liquor license was granted to the Silver Rail cocktail lounge, allowing it to serve food along with drinks at their long bar.

By the mid-1950's, the immigrants had broken the mold, but the city's "gourmets" still sought out the best roast beef with Yorkshire pudding and sole Bonne Femme. Then **Troy's,** a charming restaurant with French overtones, took over a small renovated home near the heart of the city. For the first time, Torontonians found it difficult to get reservations for a relatively unknown, small restaurant. Chef Troy did fish and "en croûte" dishes well, assuring the restaurant of an audience. He and his partner, Leslie Stibinger, went on to teach Torontonians what innovative, good cooking was all about.

Soon after, aspiring restaurateurs followed suit, converting downtown homes into charming Continental restaurants—although none could touch Troy's standards.

Around the same time, John Arena was turning **Winston's** into the city's poshest eating establishment and building up an excellent wine cellar. The Westbury Hotel, under award-winning chef Tony Roldan, became a restaurant frequented by politicians and sports figures. Roldan is now keeping up his reputation at the helm of the restaurants, in the Sutton Place **(Royal Hunt Dining Room)** and Bristol Place **(Zackary's Dining Room)** hotels, as well as Peel County Feed House.

The most recent restaurant to make a mark on Toronto's dining is **Fenton's.** It has achieved a balance of beauty and casualness, coupled with quality food, that would be considered exciting in any city in the world.

At the same time, ethnic restaurants were becoming better and more numerous. Torontonians were traveling and actually dining on Caribbean or Mexican specialties. Supermarkets were stocking everything from sugar cane and mangoes to different types of paprika. Then **Metro International Caravan** (an international food fair that takes place each June) opened for the first time, and the whole city seemed to take part. Pavilions, run by different ethnic groups in the city, served up native specialties.

Toronto the Good now supports thousands of restaurants; but with a failure rate of 80 percent, it's clear that only the best survive. Today, a true restaurant find usually means a tiny Russian or Indian place, far from the heart of town, where food is cheap, spicy and good.

In addition to restaurants, Toronto offers fine specialty food shops scattered throughout the downtown area. A concentration of excellent food stores is at Summerhill and Yonge streets, where there is a very good greengrocer, the best fish shop in town, a natural-food bakery that turns out wonderful breads and cookies, an excellent cheese shop and a French *pâtisserie.* Just one example of what Toronto offers a tourist interested in good eating.

# Restaurants and Food Sources

**(Area code: 416)**

**Note:** Prices given are in Canadian dollars

## BIG DEAL

### WORTH IT

***Winston's,*** 104 Adelaide Street W. (363-1627). Winston's is Toronto's grand restaurant, where the financial barons of Bay Street plot Canada's future. Its success is due to owner John Arena, who refurbished the present Winston's with velvet banquettes, mirrored walls, Tiffany lamps and stained glass to create the opulence of Art Nouveau. The ever-present Arena oversees the kitchens and the service, and creates new dishes such as artichoke and oyster soup, hot avocado and seafood appetizer, and a filet of sole stuffed with a light salmon mousse wrapped in lettuce. Winston's preparation of Dover sole Bonne Femme is unequaled in Canada and the smoked salmon is superb. Rack of lamb is marinated in walnut oil, tarragon and mustard sauce before roasting. Hot soufflés are currently very prominent on the menu—from lobster to strawberry or Harlequin. Don't hesitate to ask Arena to plan a menu for you. Prices are not expensive for this caliber of dining, although a fine rare wine from the excellent cellar can cause the price to soar. Reservations necessary. Closed Sunday. Entrées from $5.75 (L), $13 (D). AE, DC, MC, V.

***Fenton's,*** 12 Gloucester Street (961-8485). Fenton's opening changed the course of Toronto dining. It's necessary to make reservations days, even weeks, in advance. Fenton's is casual, yet beautiful. It has expanded to three main rooms: The Restaurant, the original room in the basement; a Front Room with a long mahogany bar, a fireplace and lace curtains; and The Garden, a light, airy room with a glass roof, giant, colorful parasols and plants cascading from the balcony. There are fresh country-grown flowers and brightly colored vegetables everywhere. Waiters in white, with oversized bow ties, are most efficient. The menu is innovative. First courses include leek and Stilton soup; among the sweets are bitter-chocolate/orange ice cream. The menus change twice a year, but some dishes are always available. Curried mussels with celeriac, cream of scallop soup, a three-fish *terrine* or rabbit *rillettes* will not be disappointing as first courses. For an entrée, consider Fenton's lamb chops (stuffed with minced lamb, fresh rosemary and basil and served with a deviled sauce). Or try chicken breasts with a veal, nut and ginger stuffing, sautéed with orange and grapes. Veal and partridge pie is superb. They keep the portions small and each dish arrives looking as if care were taken in its arrangement. Even their special blend of coffee and flavored teas are excellent. The wine list is short but filled with good value. Reservations are a must. Open seven days a week. Entrées from $4.50 (L), $8.50 (D). AE, MC, V.

## NOT WORTH IT

***Le Provençal,*** 23 St. Thomas Street (924-3722). Provençal has all the earmarks of a fine French restaurant with its French-provincial décor and classic French menu. Alas, although it can serve superlative dishes, the chances seem to be just as high that your coquilles St.-Jacques will be gritty, the beef tough and cold, and the service haughty. At their prices, you deserve more. Closed Sunday. Entrées from $4.00 (L), $10.75 (D). AE, CB, DC, MC, V.

# INTERNATIONAL

## BALKAN

***The Balkan,*** 12 Elm (597-0424). Located very close to Toronto's two largest department stores, The Balkan offers a convenient location and dependably good food. The ceiling is draped like a tent and the lights are dim, creating a quiet, secluded atmosphere. You can have a complete Balkan or Middle Eastern dinner, or order à la carte. The Serbian bean and smoked-meat soup is recommended, as are marinated peppers, fried mushrooms and veal kebabs. Reservations advised. Dinner only. Closed Sunday. Entrées from $4.00 (D). AE, MC, V.

# CHINESE

***Pink Pearl,*** 142 Dundas Street W. (363-9339). One of the consistently best Chinese restaurants in town. Smack in the center of Chinatown, it stands out with a polished décor and extremely efficient service. While most dishes are Cantonese, some Szechuan are served. Try their array of sizzling dishes and any dish with snow peas. Surprisingly enough, rainbow trout is high on the requested list. Reservations recommended. Open seven days a week. Entrées from $4.50 (L), $6.00 (D). AE, DC, MC, V.

***Chinese Village,*** 581 Markham Street (532-9111). Toronto's most formal Chinese restaurant consistently serves up excellent Cantonese dishes. In a renovated home, far from Toronto's Chinatown, it's surrounded by bargain warehouses, classy dress shops and art galleries. Entrées range from "Rainbow chopped in crystal fold" (a Chinese taco) to chicken cubes in phoenix (a chicken shrimp and vegetable combination served in a fried potato nest). It's expensive by Chinese restaurant standards. Reservations required. Dinner only. Open seven days a week. Entrées from $4.25. AE, DC, MC, V.

# CONTINENTAL

***Troy's,*** 31 Marborough Avenue (921-1957). This charming restaurant was the first to bring excellent, innovative cooking to Toronto. Lace curtains, armoires and port-neuf pottery in the tiny renovated house make one think more of the Quebec countryside than of Toronto. The menu changes monthly, ranging from sweetbreads in calvados to a superb *couscous.* Lamb with *fines herbes,* rum *pot de crème* and chestnut torte are good choices, too. In warm weather ask for a table in the canopied garden. The wine list is short but excellent value. With only 30 seats, reservations are a must. Dinner only. Closed Sunday and Monday. Fixed-price dinner (5 courses) $14.50. No credit cards.

***The Corner House,*** 501 Davenport Road (923-2604). Reminiscent of a charming French country restaurant, this renovated small home with four dining rooms provides fine Continental cuisine and excellent service. The chef comes from a classic French background so sauces can be rich. Pâtés and cream soups are excellent, rack of lamb can always be counted on and desserts—from trifles to sherbets—should not be overlooked. Reservations necessary. Closed Monday and Tuesday. Entrées from $5 (L); fixed-price dinner $13.75. AE, MC, V.

***The Grill,*** Windsor Arms Hotel, 22 St. Thomas Street (979-2212). This room has the best maître d' in town, and some of the best food, if you enjoy a meal without a lot of sauces or fancy fixin's. All entrées are gilled—from Arctic char to tender liver and steaks. Chicken is wonderfully tender and the mixed grill has remained deservedly popular. The dessert ices are magnificent and there's a Continental touch in the appetizers and desserts. For lunch order shrimp salad or avocado and crab. Reservations recommended. Sunday, dinner only. Open seven days a week. Entrées from $5 (L), $6 (D). AE, DC, MC, V.

## DANISH

***The Copenhagen Room,*** 101 Bloor Street W. (920-3287). This well-appointed restaurant, in the basement of the Danish Food Centre, presents an authentic glimpse of fine Danish cooking and efficient service. There's an excellent selection of open-faced sandwiches at lunch, as well as seafood salads, egg dishes, and deep-fried Camembert accompanied by black currant jam. For dinner, go light with cheese soup and a selection of sandwiches or begin with superb *gravlax* (marinated salmon), proceed to stuffed pork tenderloin or any of their well-executed fish dishes, and finish with pastries. Closed Sunday. Entrées from $1.85 (L), $6 (D). AE, MC, V.

## EAST INDIAN

***Samina's Tiffin Room,*** 326 Dundas Street W. (362-0350). Despite brown tablecloths and Oriental rugs on the walls, this small room is airy and charming. In summer months you can opt for the garden. Flavors range from delicate to full-bodied, but are never overpowering. Try *karhai gosht* (veal cooked in the Indian version of a wok with green chilies, coriander and fresh tomatoes), or shrimp marinated in turmeric with tomatoes. Indian sherbet, filled with chopped almonds and pistachios, is a delightful dessert. Reservations necessary. Dinner only. Closed Sunday. Entrées from $3.25. AE, MC, V.

## FRENCH

***Napoleon,*** 79 Grenville Street (929-5938). Napoleon's is the crème-de-la-crème of French restaurants and, not surprisingly, expensive. Chef-owner Christian Vinassac expertly prepares each dish, and in true French fashion, his wife, Elizabeth, oversees its passage to the table. The dining room is small and very elegant and the menu is French classic and primarily *haute cuisine.* Reservations are a must. Dinner only. Closed Sunday. Entrées from $9. AE, DC, V.

***Glossops,*** 39 Prince Arthur Street (964-2440). The décor is sparse but elegant. Service is efficient and the imaginative entrées are beautifully presented. Start with saffron or frogs' legs soup. Proceed to a superlative filet mignon in green peppercorn sauce, encased in delicate crêpe; roast duckling with almond sauce; or rack of lamb with mushrooms and ham wrapped in filo. Baby pheasant is wrapped in vine leaves and cooked with green grapes. Veal scallops are served in champagne sauce with snails. Desserts are a weak point. Reservations essential. Saturday and Sunday, dinner only. Entrées from $3.50 (L), fixed-price dinner (5 courses) $18.75. AE, MC, V.

***The Restaurant,*** Windsor Arms Hotel, 22 St. Thomas Street (979-2212). Very formal, with a French menu. French service and a healthy respect for vegetables. When the kitchen and staff are up to par, the result is a flawless, most memorable meal. A notable wine list. Expensive and can be worth it. Closed Monday. Entrées from $5 (L), $12 (D). AE, DC, MC, V.

## ITALIAN

***Noodles,*** 60 Bloor Street W. (921-3171). Despite the glare of chrome and bright pink and orange colors in this ever-so-modern midtown restaurant, the kitchen delivers up some of the best freshly made pasta in town. Linguini with scallops and satiny fettuccine can always be counted on. Beyond pasta, the trout or sole with brandied lobster sauce and truffle garnish should be considered. The service can be devil-may-care and some people find the seats uncomfortable. Reservations recommended. Sunday, dinner only. Open seven days a week. Entrées from $4.50 (L), $6 (D). AE, DC, MC, V.

## JAPANESE

***Michi,*** 459 Church Street (924-1303). The dark interior, carpeted booths and attentive service has a very calming effect. All the traditional Japanese items are available, and they're consistently very good. Reservations needed for the weekends. Closed Sunday. Entrées from $2.50 (L), $8 (D). AE, DC, V.

# MEXICAN

***Viva Zapata,*** 2468 Yonge Street (489-8482). Viva Zapata's bar and inexpensive entrées provide an enjoyable evening that's easy on the pocketbook. Try their version of *chalupa* chicken in a mildly seasoned sauce with diced sweet red pepper and chunks of avocado. Topped with sour cream, it's served on a deep-fried tortilla. Service is cheerful and relaxed. A substantial dinner for two with sangría averages $18. Sunday, dinner only. Open seven days a week. Entrées from $2.25 (L), $4.75 (D). AE, MC, V.

# MIDDLE EASTERN

***The Jerusalem,*** 995 Eglinton Avenue W. (783-6494). In a city that boasts of first-rate ethnic restaurants, the Jerusalem shines. Victor Matiya is carrying on the tradition begun in his father's restaurant close to Jerusalem. Don't miss the fried tomatoes, sautéed with finely chopped hot green peppers and served in warm *pita* bread, but control the urge to dine on appetizers alone. Outstanding entrées are charcoal-broiled chicken, marinated in lemon and cinnamon and other mild spices; fried cubes of liver with hot green pepper and garlic; and fresh sea bass with lemon sauce served with *tahini.* For dessert, the pistachio pastries are worth every calorie. No reservations required but there are always lines on the weekends. Open seven days a week. Entrées from $4.50 (L & D). AE, DC, V.

# MOROCCAN

***La Mamounia,*** upstairs at 1280 Bay Street (961-0601). A truly relaxing culinary evening awaits diners in this small restaurant. It's draped to give the appearance of the inside of a tent. You curl up on low banquettes and lean on soft cushions while a costumed waiter brings the menu and explains the selections on a five-course, fixed-price menu. The soups are superbly spicy. The marinated vegetable salad is beautiful and pleasingly tangy. Lamb with honey and almonds or chicken with lemons are excellent choices for entrées. The pastries, redolent with anisette, or honey-dipped and filled with almonds, are perfect with Turkish coffee or sweet peppermint tea. Friday and Saturday evenings there's belly dancing. Reservations recommended. Saturday, dinner only. Closed Sunday. Entrées from $2.75 (L), fixed-priced dinner $11.75 (after 8:30 P.M. on Friday and Saturday, the price increases to $16.75). AE, DC, V.

## RUSSIAN

***Barmaley,*** 994 St. Clair West (651-5415). The décor is overdone with Russian artifacts and be sure your seat isn't arm-to-arm with the Russian singers. Then relax and enjoy the peasant-style food. Borscht with fresh dill is perfection itself. Proceed to the marinated grilled chicken or charcoal-grilled fish. Finish with a Russian "potato" (chocolate with a marinated prune and walnut center). Reservations recommended. Sunday, dinner only. Open seven days a week. Entrées from $3.75 (L), $4.25 (D). V.

# SPECIALTY COOKING

## DELI

***Switzer's Delicatessen,*** 322 Spadina Avenue (364-2309). The hot dogs taste as if they came from Coney Island, the French fries are freshly cut and the latkes are terrific, although some other items are wanting in flavor. The staff is friendly, even to newcomers. Open seven days a week, from breakfast to midnight. Hot dogs from 95 cents. MC, V.

***Pancer Delicatessen,*** 4130 Bathurst (633-1230). If you're a pastrami lover, Pancer's is worth a trip. Full-flavored and peppery, it's served lean if that's your preference. The other outstanding dish is cabbage borscht. Open seven days a week until midnight. Sandwiches from $1.90. No credit cards.

## FISH AND CHIPS

***Penrose Fish & Chips,*** 600 Mt. Pleasant (483-6800). In the English tradition, this small, family-run shop dishes out the best of crispy, coated halibut and freshly cut, non-greasy chips. It's always scrupulously clean. Saturday, dinner only. Closed Sunday. An order of fish and chips is $1.90. No credit cards.

## HAMBURGER

***Toby's Good Eats,*** 91 Bloor Street W. (925-2171). Smack in the center of Toronto's ritziest shopping area, this is the spot where the beautiful people satisfy their hamburger cravings. Hamburgers are thick and juicy, the chips are great, and the spinach salad is excellent. No liquor. Open seven days a week, until 3 A.M. Monday through Saturday, until 11:30 P.M. Sunday. Hamburgers from $2.55. No credit cards.

## HOT DOG

***Mr. Frankfurt,*** 908 Queen Street E. (461-1053). If you love frankfurters, don't miss your chance to have a Canadian Frank. A jumbo all-beef hot dog, smothered with Canada's prize-winning old Cheddar, is served in a poppyseed bun. It's but one of the specialties of this neighborhood restaurant. All sauces are homemade and excellent. Try a Franco-Italian (with a spicy sauce and mozzarella cheese) or pull out all stops and go for the Sub Frank (relish, mustard, coleslaw, hot peppers and melted mozzarella). Open seven days a week. Jumbo hot dogs from 99 cents. No credit cards.

## JEWISH

***The Bagel,*** 285 College Street (923-0171). If you're dieting, stay away. If not, the noisy Bagel is for you. Try the barley soup, chopped liver or main-course platters. But if you don't finish, chances are you'll be yelled at, and the whole place will know it. Open seven days a week, breakfast through dinner. Sandwiches from $1.90. No credit cards.

## SANDWICHES

***The Danish Food Centre,*** 101 Bloor Street W. (920-5505). It's impossible to imagine sandwiches tasting better than these offered by the Danish Food Centre. All are made by young Danes, trained in sandwich-making in their homeland. There's often a lineup at the small counters for sandwiches as well as salads such as shrimp and cucumber, and hot pastries. Among the sandwiches, shrimp and egg with homemade mayonnaise, liver paste with bacon and mushroom, breaded sole with rémoulade, and smoked pork loin are very popular. Fine coffee, too. Closed Sunday. Sandwiches from $1.25. AE, MC, V.

## SEAFOOD

***Mermaid Seafood House,*** 724 Bay Street (597-0077). There's nothing exciting about this restaurant, but over the years consistently high-quality food has made it difficult to get reservations. The seafood ranges from Arctic char to Canadian salmon. Try smoked eel with scrambled eggs for lunch and be sure to start with chowder at dinner. Closed Sunday. Entrées from $2.75 (L), $7.75 (D). AE, CB, MC, V.

***Round Window Seafood House,*** 729 Danforth Avenue (465-3892). The family that runs this operation tries very hard and they are succeeding. Word-of-mouth alone has made it the choice of fish-lovers seeking reasonable prices. The fish preparation is nearly faultless and there's a fine house sauce with a hint of garlic. Choices range from seafood platters to escargot, scampi, octopus and rainbow trout and everything is done well. Reservations necessary. Dinner only. Closed Monday. Entrées from $5.95. AE, DC, MC, V.

## SOUL

***Underground Railroad,*** 225 King Street E. (869-1400). The underground railroad movement spirited thousands of slaves to Canadian freedom. Memorabilia of anti-slavery heroes, barnwood, lanterns swinging from huge beams and waiters in railroad overalls add to the casual, warm atmosphere. Fare is the stick-to-the-ribs variety and plenty of it—from pigs' feet and mushroom appetizers to superb fried chicken, excellent ribs, baked ham and chitlins, and excellent fish dishes. Don't pass up the corn bread. Sunday brunch means ham or steak and eggs, Sadie's quiche (a soul-food version with ham and macaroni), chicken livers—all served with hot biscuits. Reservations recommended. Open seven days a week. Entrées from $5.85 (L & D), $3.60 for brunch. AE, DC, MC, V.

## STEAK

***Hy's,*** 133 Yorkville Avenue (961-7000). The city doesn't boast an outstanding steakhouse. While Hy's is one of the best and the choice of many businessmen, its weak points include ho-hum service, sauces and salads. Stick to plain steaks or ribs. Suprisingly enough, you can usually count on the lobster. Reservations recommended. Saturday, dinner only. Closed Sunday. Entrées from $6 (L), $12 (D). AE, MC, V.

## VEGETARIAN

***The Parrot,*** 325 Queen Street W. (366-4147). Few restaurants, vegetarian or otherwise, present as innovative a menu as the Parrot. It changes every few weeks, taking on a different international flavor—heavy on Mediterranean. Fettuccine with walnut cream, hot African salad, antipasto with hot garlic dressing, prune and orange salad, are but a sampling. No reservations. Sunday, brunch only. Closed Monday. Entrées from $3.50 (L & D). No credit cards.

# FOR INDIVIDUAL NEEDS

## IF YOU HAVE TIME FOR ONLY ONE MEAL

***Fenton's,*** 12 Gloucester Street (961-8485). (See description under BIG DEAL/WORTH IT.)

## BEST HOTEL MEAL

***The Windsor Arms Hotel,*** 22 St. Thomas Street (979-2212). (See description under FRENCH and CONTINENTAL.)

***Royal Hunt Dining Room,*** Sutton Place Hotel, 955 Bay Street (924-9221). With Tony Roldan, Canada's most renowned chef, at the helm, dining can be a lovely experience in this elegant room. Roldan has a wonderful touch with seafood, as some of the appetizers prove. Entrées include veal with calvados and partridge with green peppercorns and raisins. Service is very polished. Reservations recommended. Open seven days a week. Entrées from $4 (L), $11 (D). AE, CB, DC, MC, V.

## RESTAURANT NEAR AIRPORT

***Zackary's Dining Room,*** Bristol Place Hotel, very close to Toronto International Airport, 950 Dixon Road (675-9444). Travelers to Toronto are very fortunate to have a *haute-cuisine* dining room so close to the airport. For lunch there's a choice among 12 different fillings for omelets that are prepared at the table, or try crab meat *en coquille Roscoff*—a cold crab-meat and egg creation. Dinner listing includes *trois noisettes aux herbes* (a fish, chicken and veal noisette with fresh herbs), or scampi *Amoureux Petite Folie* (scampi and baby shrimp flambéed with Cognac and Pernod, served in a light cream sauce). Reservations recommended. Saturday and Monday, dinner only. Open seven days a week. Entrées from $3.50 (L), $9.50 (D). AE, CB, DC, MC, V.

## BUSINESS BREAKFAST

***Courtyard Café,*** Windsor Arms Hotel, 22 St. Thomas Street (979-2212). A beautiful room filled with plants and sun-brightened through the glass roof. It's quiet, the service is prompt and you may start the day with fresh orange juice or perhaps black currant juice. Food choices range from a hot croissant with preserves or marmalade to kippers or eggs, bacon and the works. Open seven days a week from 7 A.M. Complete breakfast from $3.95. AE, DC, MC, V.

## BUSINESS LUNCH

***Hazelton Café,*** in Hazelton Lanes, 55 Avenue Road (923-6944). A charming restaurant, all glass, greens and fresh flowers. The menu is imaginative and the omelets are the best in town, especially the chive version with smoked salmon. Servings are small and beautifully presented. The lemon cheesecake is very creamy and tangy, and the ice creams and ices are wonderful. Reservations are needed. Sunday, brunch only. Entrées from $4.50 (L), $7.00 (D). AE, MC, V.

***Winston's,*** 104 Adelaide Street W. (363-1627). (See description under BIG DEAL/WORTH IT.)

## FAST, GOOD FOOD

***The Cake Master,*** 128½ Cumberland Street (925-2879). Cumberland Street is lined with some of Toronto's finest boutiques, and the wee Cake Master shop stands conveniently among them. Plan a break in shopping to sample their Sacher Torte or one of the superlative pastries. Or for a quick lunch include a sandwich or light salad. The coffee is first-rate as well. Closed Sunday. Pastries from $1.00. No credit cards.

## FAST, GOOD FOOD/LUNCH

***Strawberry Patch,*** Toronto Eaton Centre, 2 Below (979-3208). Would that every shopping complex could have a snack bar as good as this one. Every item on the limited menu is excellent—from salads composed in full view, with lots of fresh mushrooms, real bacon bits and bean sprouts—to 2-inch-high shrimp sandwiches. The shrimp come with a homemade tomato-horseradish sauce served on the side. Frozen yogurt shakes and sundaes are superb. Closed Sunday. Sandwiches from $2.50. No credit cards.

## BEST WINE LIST

***The Windsor Arms Hotel,*** 22 St. Thomas Street (979-2212). (See description under FRENCH, CONTINENTAL and RESTAURANT WITH MUSIC). Over 150 wines, including a good mix of rare, and the best of Canadian. Prices range from $7.50 a bottle for Canadian. Happily the list is available in each of the four restaurants in this small hotel where there's food to match the quality of the wines.

## FOR DRINKS

***The Duke of York,*** 39 Prince Arthur Avenue (964-2441). A spiffy English pub—resplendent with warm mahogany, flock paper and red upholstery—that attracts a friendly crowd of all ages. As might be expected, lunches served at sit-down tables include steak and kidney pies, authentic Scotch eggs, fried oysters and gammon steaks. There are over 35 different kinds of beer and 8 drafts to choose from. Open seven days a week: until 1:30 A.M. Monday through Saturday, until 10 P.M. Sunday. Entrées from $2.50 (L). AE, MC, V.

## RESTAURANT WITH MUSIC

***Courtyard Café,*** Windsor Arms Hotel, 22 St. Thomas Street (979-2212). (See description under BUSINESS BREAKFAST.) Classical music is played Monday to Friday evening. The musicians change every week, so it might be a soloist or a three-piece group. Food is fairly good in the evenings, but for some reason it can't compare to that served in the other three rooms in the hotel. Open seven days a week. Dinner entrées from $6. AE, DC, MC, V.

## ROMANTIC

***The Grill,*** Windsor Arms Hotel, 22 St. Thomas Street (979-2212). (See description under CONTINENTAL.)

## LATE-NIGHT SERVICE

***Just Desserts,*** 306 Davenport (922-6824). Decadent desserts are culinary kingpins in this small restaurant, not far from the main drag. The chocolate bomber cake is a wonderous mountain of marzipan and chocolate, with layers of cream and chocolate cake. Praline cream cake and "good old" sour-cream apple pie are favorites. For cheesecake freaks there are over a dozen to indulge in, including a creation with a chocolate crust flecked with chocolate chips. There are a few savories such as quiche and a broccoli soufflé. Open seven days a week, until 3 A.M. Monday through Thursday. From Friday morning to Monday morning, it's open 24 hours a day. Desserts from $2. No credit cards.

## SUNDAY BRUNCH

***Royal Hunt Room,*** Sutton Place Hotel, 955 Bay Street (924-9221). In a city where going out for brunch is as popular as going out for dinner, the Royal Hunt Room remains a family favorite. Many linger for three or four hours enjoying both the hot and cold entrées. Breads and pastries come in a variety of shapes and sizes. There's smoked fish, cold meats, fruit and vegetable salads, kippers, chicken livers, eggs Mousseline, hot crêpes, pastries and on and on. Sunday from 9:30 A.M. to 1:30 P.M. Fixed price is $8.95 for adults, $4 for children under 12. AE, CB, DC, MC, V.

***Prince Arthur Room,*** Park Plaza Hotel, Avenue Road and Bloor (924-5471). Way past its heyday but elegant still, it serves a lovely brunch and draws the upper crust of Toronto, with their families, or alone, to read the Sunday paper. Begin with the fresh-fruit cocktail and proceed to eggs Benedict or one of the omelets or meat dishes. Open from 11 A.M. to 3 P.M. Entrées from $6. AE, CB, DC, MC, V.

## SUNDAY-EVENING MEAL

***Ed's Warehouse Restaurant,*** 270 King Street W. (593-6676). This one-time storage warehouse, converted into a 1,300-seat restaurant, is filled with antiques and artifacts. The size seems to have no detrimental effect on the cheerful service or quality of the limited steak and roast beef menu. It does enable owner Ed Mirvish to keep prices down and still serve good roast beef. Males over 12 must wear jackets and ties, and no jeans are allowed. Saturday and Sunday, dinner only. Open seven days a week. Entrées from $3.95 (L), $5.95 (D). AE, DC, MC, V.

## FOR FAMILIES WITH CHILDREN

***The Old Spaghetti Factory,*** 54 the Esplanade (864-9761). Be prepared to stand in line for this popular, child-pleasing restaurant. Early arrivals have the option of dining in a trolley car, smack in the center of this converted factory. Spaghetti with a multitude of sauces, chicken cacciatore and meatballs are part of a limited menu. Be prepared for a lot of noise. No reservations. Summer and winter hours are different but count on it being open from noon to at least 10 P.M., seven days a week. Entrées from $2.95 (L & D). AE, MC, V.

***The Grange Court Restaurant,*** in the Art Gallery of Ontario, 317 Dundas Street W. (361-0414). Nestled in the heart of the art gallery, this chic, small restaurant has glass doors leading to a patio for summer dining. A light menu with French overtones includes fresh mushroom soup and a reasonably good quiche. Service is slow.

Reservations recommended. Friday through Tuesday, lunch only. Open seven days a week. Entrées from $2.50 (L & D). AE, MC, V.

## COUNTRY INN

***The Doctor's House and Livery,*** Kleinburg (893-1615). Not far from the MacMichael Gallery, filled with the best of Canadian art, is a home built in the 1860's that was subsequently inhabited by several doctors. Now it houses a gift shop, and a livery at the back has been expanded for a quaint restaurant filled with rustic charm. There's an herb garden at the side. Costumed waitresses bring forth hearty homemade soups, steak and kidney pies, and good roast beef. Roast duck comes with rhubarb sauce, then there are veal sweetbreads Florentine and baked hare. Finish the meal with hot apple pie, peach and sour-cream pie or a more delicate Kahlúa soufflé. Reservations required on weekends. Closed Monday. Entrées from $4.25 (L), $10.50 (D). AE, CB, DC, V.

# MARKETS

***St. Lawrence Market,*** Front and Jarvis Streets (362-4766). Once a true "Farmers' Market," the south building has recently undergone a facelift. Now produce is "safely" displayed behind glass. Fortunately the vendors, most of whom have spent their working lives selling in the market, are unchanged. The north market still comes alive in the early hours of Saturday morning when farmers arrive with fresh meats, cheese, produce and plants. Open from 7 A.M. to 5 P.M. Closed Sunday and Monday.

***Kensington Market,*** in the Spadina, College Street area. This permanent market has all the flavor of a European market. There are stalls on the streets, and various ethnic groups are represented by a bakery, fish or cheese shop. Live chickens are displayed in cages and you're sure to find seasonal Caribbean fruits and vegetables. Open during regular business hours. Closed Sunday.

## GIFT FOODS

***Mullen & Cie.,*** 2615 Yonge Street (481-8889). Features an extensive line of pâtés, including salmon and pistachio, and *fines herbes.* Innovative salads such as pecan, apple and celery or hearts of palm, melon and shrimp are always available, as well as imported cheeses, French breads and pastries, and imported delicacies. Closed Sunday. Pâtés from $4.80 a pound. MC, V.

***The Cheese Wheel,*** 1097 Yonge Street (961-1641). In addition to the best of Cheddars, try Bavarian Baby Blue, St. André or Explorateur. The shelves are overflowing with imported mustards and other specialty items. Also available: coffee beans and home-made pâtés, quiches and breads. Closed Sunday. AE, MC, V.

***Dinah's Cupboard,*** 50 Cumberland Street (921-8112). Dinah Koo stocks a wide selection of fresh coffees, beans and spices. Teas include Sakura cherry, apricot, black currant and Estate Darjeeling. Along with a full range of imported French products there are Dinah's pâtés, home-baked goodies and pesto sauce. Closed Sunday. V.

# SPECIAL EVENTS

***Metro International Caravan.*** Each year during the last nine days of June, about 60 different pavilions are set up in church basements and community halls across the city. Each one represents, and is run by, an ethnic group. They display crafts, provide nightly entertainment and staff a large restaurant area where nothing but the finest homemade specialties are good enough. Passports, costing about $6 and necessary for admittance to the pavilions, are sold to thousands of Torontonians and tourists. Many cover four or five countries in an evening. It's an inexpensive way to make a culinary tour of many countries.

# Washington, D.C.

There has been a great transformation in Washington during the past two decades. Interest in and appreciation of food has been on the upswing, and the city, as befits a nation's capital, has become determinedly international in its restaurants. The tall white toques of French chefs are as familiar nowadays as were coonskin caps in the 1830's.

Thomas Jefferson, the first President to take office in the Federal City, had a French-trained chef in the White House. Jefferson went shopping for food himself in nearby Alexandria and Georgetown, and introduced his guests to such delicacies as French wine and ice cream. From that time until the Kennedy Administration (which brought another French-trained chef into the White House), dining in Washington was a source of limited pleasures. Entertaining was done in private homes and it was in these homes or in embassies that the great meals were served. Gastronomically, the city was akin to a Southern town; a good deal of public eating was done in boardinghouses. This style of living gave way to massive apartment buildings in this century; even during the 1950's, residents would frequent dowdy restaurants in their buildings. Perhaps because the elegance of embassy row and the homespun atmosphere on Capitol Hill were in such contrast, the city failed to develop a dining style of its own.

Then, as today, there was no shortage of fine raw materials. The Chesapeake Bay, only twenty-five miles away, provided fresh crabs, oysters and fin fish. In spring there was a grand supply of shad and roe. Soft-shell crabs followed, and boiled hard-shell crabs and crab cakes kept one going until fall. All year round, striped bass (called rockfish on the Chesapeake) was available, as were the fine hams of Virginia. Southern cooks did chicken and vegetables in the distinctive style of that region. But there was little relief. Diplomats and visitors complained. Local gastronomes looked to New York or to Europe for their pleasures. First-rate bakeries were as scarce as ethnic neighborhoods in a town that lacked industry and whose population changed significantly every four years.

Not all was bleak. The Willard Hotel, now closed, was something of an eaters' paradise in the time of the Civil War and after. **Harvey's**—along with seafood restaurants such as Hogate's and O'Donnells—became famous between the wars. Hammel's, a German-inspired restaurant, was popular, and The Occidental—its walls lined with photographs of political personalities—became nationally known in the 1940's and 1950's. The Occidental has closed. The others survive, although only Harvey's is in the first rank today. The Carlton's restaurant was in the first rank of hotel dining rooms before World War II, but declined during the postwar boom. Only recently has it begun to offer a fine luncheon buffet and Sunday brunch.

In the late 1950's, Washington had only one good French restaurant, **La Rive Gauche,** which stood in lonely isolation in Georgetown. In the 1960's, drinking hours and regulations were liberalized, and government business—and business expense accounts—grew. A restaurant explosion began. It has not yet stopped. There are literally a hundred or more eating places within a few blocks of La Rive Gauche, which has a talented chef and is still a place to go—with a credit card. A visitor who wants to browse before selecting a restaurant will find the blocks of M Street between 28th and 34th (Key Bridge to Virginia) crammed with restaurants and fast-food operations. More than a dozen nationalities are represented. One can find food served well after midnight.

Another cluster of eating places, with an emphasis on discotheques and nightlife, is to be found in an area bordered by L, M, 18th and 20th streets N.W. Enlarge the area to touch K Street, and Connecticut and Massachusetts avenues, and it will encompass most of the top-rated, expense-account restaurants.

Recently there has been a mini-boom of small, personalized restaurants. **Germaine's,** 209½, The Broker, **Le Gaulois,** Nora's—all are chef-directed. **The Bread Oven** produces the best French bread this city has seen. There are even signs of vitality on and near Capitol Hill, where ambitious restaurants have failed as regularly as closure votes fail to halt Senate filibusters.

Washington has attracted restaurateurs from as far away as Europe. The direction of the Italian **Tiberio** came from London; **Palm** from New York. Romeo and Juliet on K Street is a stepchild of New York's Romeo Salta; its next-door neighbor, **The Prime Rib,** was copyrighted in Baltimore. Chefs from France by way of New York have brought the pastel colors of *nouvelle cuisine* to two new restaurants, Le Pavillon and La Maison Blanche. Time is needed to learn if either or both will mature gracefully.

Chefs have come from Asia as well. Chinese chefs are repeating the French pattern here by playing musical chairs. Several with talent have left downtown restaurants for the suburbs, only to discover there is little demand there for adventuresome cooking.

Northern Italian and most French restaurants are popular and costly, but the city lacks moderately priced, family-run restaurants of Italian and other European ethnic persuasions. The visitor is advised to avoid the restaurants at the Kennedy Center for the Performing Arts, most hotel restaurants (expensive and undistinguished) and the mass-produced food at giant waterfront restaurants such as the Flagship and Hogate's.

The city's two most pretentious hotels are the Watergate and the Madison. The Watergate's restaurant fails to surmount culinary mediocrity. The Madison can do so on occasion, but prices are so steep that only high rollers indifferent to what they spend will want to risk the uneven performance of the kitchen. As for the wine list, Alexis Lichine once threw it to the floor, reacting in disgust to the unreasonable markups of wines readily available elsewhere. Food and service for private parties catered by the banquet department often are excellent, however.

For the visitor who wants to do some marketing, excellent produce, cheese, poultry and meats are sold at the Georgetown Market on Grace Street. Nearby, on Wisconsin Avenue, the Georgetown Wine and Cheese Company is making a worthy effort to find and promote regional food specialities from all across America. And Cannon's, also in Georgetown, is a fine seafood market. **The French Market** (on Wisconsin Avenue at the north end of Georgetown) imports from the mother country and makes its own pâtés. Near the Capitol, the Eastern Market (at North Carolina and 7th Street S.E.) and the Capitol Hill Wine and Cheese Shop (on Pennsylvania S.E. between 6th and 7th streets) attract food fanciers.

Washington has a number of wine shops with wide selections and prices generally lower than those found elsewhere in the nation. Among the volume leaders are: Central (518 9th Street

N.W.), MacArthur (4877 MacArthur Boulevard), Calvert (2312 Wisconsin Avenue), Woodley (3423 Connecticut Avenue) and Eagle (3345 M Street N.W.). For fanciers of American wines, Morris Miller Liquors (7804 Alaska Avenue N.W., where the city line touches Silver Spring) and Harry's (401 M Street S.W.) offer selections that rank with the best on the East Coast for depth and reasonable prices.

Dining customs in the city are fairly standard. The top restaurants downtown are more accessible in the evening than at lunch. Reservations are recommended at either time. Prices will be higher in the evening. The practice of multitiered tipping has never caught on in Washington: one tip for the meal will suffice. Dress codes have softened in all but a few places. Pants suits for women are common. Jackets with ties or turtlenecks are worn by men in downtown restaurants; sports shirts without jackets are not.

Restaurant growth in the past few years has focused on the Maryland and Virginia suburbs. There are only a handful, however, that would tempt one away from the District of Columbia.

# Restaurants and Food Sources

(Area code: 202)

## BIG DEAL

### WORTH IT

***Le Lion d'Or,*** 1150 Connecticut Avenue N.W. (entrance on 18th Street) (296-7972). Owner/chef Pierre Goyenvalle and his wife, Colette, have blended innovative cooking and elegance of setting in this striking below-ground restaurant. Half-a-dozen or more daily specials, including game and game birds in season, will be recited by the captain. Choose between modern dishes (navarin of lobster, rockfish in a pastry crust, filet of lamb with vegetables) and classics—*quenelles,* veal in several fashions. In addition to the expected fine French selections, the wine list offers an impressively broad and deep representation of prestigious California vineyards. More elaborate meals in the evening; can be noisy. Reservations essential. Saturday, dinner only. Closed Sunday. Entrées from $7.50 (L), $12 (D). AE, CB, DC, MC, V.

### NOT WORTH IT

***Montpelier Room,*** The Madison Hotel, 15th and M streets N.W. (862-1712). It's quiet in the comfortable dining room of what is arguably the city's best hotel. Certainly, you'll never hear the clink of change. Here prestige equals price, and quiet seems to equal boredom, at least when the maître d' and staff face unknown guests. Some preparations show the kitchen's capabilities, but inconsistency abounds, and any sense of excitement or adventure is totally lacking. The prices on the wine list and its paltry American selection show a careless disregard for value. Saturday and Sunday, dinner only. Open seven days a week. Entrées from $6.50 (L), $12.95 (D). AE, CB, DC, MC, V.

# INTERNATIONAL

## AFGHANI

***Khyber Pass,*** 2309 Calvert Street N.W. (234-4632). The opening of this attractive, second-floor dining room near the Shoreham and Sheraton-Park Hotels doubled the number of Washington's Afghani restaurants. The food is an inspired compromise between that of the Indian subcontinent and the Middle East, with yogurt as a catalyst. Vegetable-filled pastries, flavorful soups, lamb on skewers, tasty breads. The spicing is milder than in Indian restaurants. Dinner only. Open seven days a week. Entrées from $5.45. MC, V.

***Bamiyan Restaurant,*** 3320 M Street N.W. (338-1896). Older sister to the Khyber Pass, equally attractive, but with slightly higher prices to suit the Georgetown address. Dinner only. Open seven days a week. Entrées from $5.95. MC, V.

## AMERICAN

***Duke Zeibert's,*** 1722 L Street N.W. (296-5030). Sports figures and politicians mingle here for stiff drinks, loud conversation and hearty fare including steaks, chops, fine fresh fish, chicken or beef in the pot, sandwich platters. Favored customers sit in the more spacious front room. Sunday, dinner only. Open seven days a week. Entrées from $4.95 (L), $7.50 (D). AE, CB, DC, MC, V.

***The Prime Rib,*** 2020 K Street N.W. (466-8811). Imported from Baltimore, it is polyester among the conservative, 3-piece décor that typifies most local expense-account haunts. But, as they say on Broadway, you don't eat the sets. A lively crowd packs the bar, or sits down in padded chairs for prime rib, steak or crab imperial. The commendable wine list features quality California producers. Piano music. Saturday, dinner only. Closed Sunday. Entrées from $5.50 (L), $8.75 (D). AE, MC, V.

***The American Café,*** 1211 Wisconsin Avenue N.W. (337-3600). A trio of young men has turned a Georgetown submarine sandwich shop into a smart, modern café that successfully melds brick, neon and plant life. Their object is to illustrate contemporary taste, which they do with homemade soups, a superb chili, healthful salads and a lineup of sandwiches—some classic and some esoteric. Have a meal or stop for dessert and coffee. Open until 3 A.M., Sunday through Thursday; until 4 A.M., Friday and Saturday. Closed Monday. Sandwiches from $2.50 (L & D). MC, V. A Capitol Hill branch has opened recently at 227 Massachusetts Avenue N.E. (547-8200). Open seven days a week, until 3 A.M. MC, V.

***Old Ebbitt Grill,*** 1427 F Street N.W. (347-5560). This is an oasis in an area of generally dismal dining downtown to the east of the White House. It is one of Washington's oldest bars, given an infusion of modern menu and management by the people who brought you Clyde's. (See description under HAMBURGER.) Order nothing fancy here; stick to hamburgers, sandwiches, steak and eggs or maybe a stew. The atmosphere and service are agreeable. In addition, they serve ample drinks and on occasion a White House personage drops by. Open until 2 A.M. Monday through Friday, until 3 A.M. Saturday. Open Sunday, 10 A.M. to 2 A.M.; brunch to 4 P.M. Entrées from $1.75 (L), $3.95 (D). AE, MC, V.

## ASIAN

***Germaine's,*** 2400 Wisconsin Avenue (965-1185). The city's most stylish Asian restaurant offers comfortable, contemporary chairs and décor. Look through a long picture window out over Washington from a third-floor location a few blocks north of Georgetown. Germaine Swanson, a skillful cook and gracious hostess, has created a menu of specialties from her native Vietnam and other Southeast Asian countries. Spring rolls and saté, stuffed chicken breast, "squirrel" fish, firecracker shrimps, beef with basil and a dozen or more other dishes should please you. Some Chinese preparations can be mundane, however. A broad selection of imported beers and a hand-tooled, value-accented wine list are bonuses. Saturday and Sunday, dinner only. Open seven days a week. Entrées from $2.95 (L), $5.95 (D). AE, MC, V.

## CHINESE

***Szechuan,*** 615 Eye Street N.W. (393-0130). An outpost of northern Chinese cooking on the fringe of tiny, Canton-oriented Chinatown. The second-floor dining room isn't fancy, the service is often haphazard, but the chefs here have been producing the city's best and most authentic Chinese fare ever since Tony Cheng opened his doors in 1977. Crispy fried beef, tripe and casseroles in addition to exquisite pork, chicken and vegetable entrées. An excellent Chinese grocery is located on the ground floor. *Dim sum* served at luncheon Saturday and Sunday. Open seven days a week. Entrées from $2 (L), $3.75 (D). AE, V.

***Szechuan East,*** 1805 H Street N.W. (296-3588). No relative of the

Szechuan, but both illustrate how the cult of Chinese regional food has grown. Directly across Pennsylvania Avenue from the World Bank and International Monetary Fund, the Szechuan East draws crowds for lunch. A lively Northern Chinese menu, featuring a "traditional chicken" in chili-and-ginger sauce, duck with ginger and snow peas, and a variety of shrimp and vegetable dishes. The tables are too small and too close together. Closed Sunday. Entrées from $3.75 (L), $4.95 (D). AE, DC, V.

***Yenching Palace,*** 3524 Connecticut Avenue N.W. (362-8200). The management here supported the People's Republic of China before recognition, so its status has grown with the swing of the political weather vane. The food preparation seems improved, too. From a relatively short menu, you can be confident of the Peking duck, fried meat two-kinds, and most Mandarin-style preparations. Open seven days a week. Entrées from $2.95 (L), $5.25 (D). MC, V.

***China Inn,*** 631 H Street N.W. (628-9282). Décor distinguishes the Cantonese restaurants clustered in the 600 block of H Street from one another more than culinary skill. With selective ordering you can do well in any of them. Here good bets are steamed chicken with Chinese sausage, boiled whole fish with spices, broccoli with oyster sauce and, if available, smoked crabs. Like its neighbors, China Inn is open late, until 3 A.M. Monday through Thursday, until 4 A.M. Friday and Saturday, until 2 A.M. Sunday. Entrées from $4.25 (L), $5.25 (D). AE, MC, V.

## EASTERN EUROPEAN

***Serbian Crown,*** 4529 Wisconsin Avenue N.W. (966-6787). A list of two dozen vodkas, more or less, ensures a warm, lively atmosphere. Don't slight the food, though. Borscht, mushrooms, chicken Kiev, remarkable beef Stroganoff. An evening here can be costly. Closed Monday. Entrées from $4.50 (L), $7.95 (D). AE, CB, DC, MC, V.

## FRENCH

***Le Lion d'Or,*** 1150 Connecticut Avenue (296-7972). (See description under BIG DEAL/WORTH IT.)

***Jean Pierre,*** 1835 K Street N.W. (466-2022). A fixture on K Street's "restaurant row," Jean Pierre (actually under the capable direction of Jean Michel Farret, who also acts as maître d') has been undergoing a renaissance. The décor has been spruced up and the kitchen is producing several new and exciting dishes, including beef with Roquefort sauce, trout soufflé with lobster sauce and a combination of salmon and rockfish filets called *arlequin.* Daily specials are recited by the captain in the language of your choice. Saturday, dinner only. Closed Sunday. Entrées from $7 (L), $9.50 (D). AE, CB, DC, MC, V.

***Le Bagatelle,*** 2000 K Street N.W. (872-8677). A relaxing, garden-inspired setting for what can be one of the best meals in Washington. The chef, Robert Greault, once won a competition called the Crab Olympics. His crab is good, his rockfish flambéed in Pernod with *beurre blanc* is even better. Irish coffee after dinner here is a performance worth viewing. Too many tables and unaccountable lapses in service and food preparation are flaws that make a dinner here something of a gamble. Chaîne des Rotisseurs. Saturday, dinner only. Closed Sunday. Entrées from $6.50 (L), $10.50 (D). AE, CB, DC, MC, V.

***Le Gaulois,*** 2133 Pennsylvania Avenue N.W. (466-3232). This is no place for creature comforts. Narrow and overcrowded, with a modicum of décor, the attraction is a singular one: consistently well-prepared French food at modest prices. Pot-au-feu and other *cuisine bourgeoise* dishes are featured, but the young chef has a talent for cooking and saucing fish as well. Reserve and be prepared to wait anyway. Tables for two turn over faster than those for larger groups. Saturday, dinner only. Closed Sunday. Open Friday and Saturday until midnight, weekdays until 11 P.M. Entrées from $3 (L & D). AE, MC, V.

***Dominique's,*** 1900 Pennsylvania Avenue (452-1126). There's a lot of charm here, in the décor and in the greeting; no Gallic cold shoulder for strangers. The most dependable choices on the menu are smoked fish (trout and often salmon) and the simple dishes of *cuisine bourgeoise* origin. Otherwise the kitchen swings as unpredictably as a compass in the Bermuda Triangle. Located not far from the Kennedy Center, it's open late and draws an after-theater crowd. Closed Sunday. Entrées from $4.95 (L), $6.95 (D). AE, CB, MC, V.

***Le Provençal,*** 1234 20th Street N.W. (223-2420). A popular gathering place for diplomats and broadcast journalists along with a smattering of political and radio types. Not many frills. Owner-chef Jacques Blanc is from Provence and is thought to make the best bouillabaisse in town. While there are standard French items on the menu, the cooking accent is southern; outstanding dishes include mussels, soups, and broiled fish, Chaîne des Rotisseurs. Closed Sunday. Entrées from $5.75 (L), $10 (D). AE, CB, DC, MC, V.

***The Bread Oven,*** 1220 19th Street N.W. (466-4264). In this contemporary bakery-restaurant, the floor show is provided by the French baker, his oven and his wares, all on display behind a sit-down counter for customers. There are tables, too, where a limited menu is offered at attractively limited prices, Monday through Friday. Fancier dishes and higher prices Saturday night. Service is unpredictable—slow at lunch, faster in the evening. The French bread is Washington's best. Pastries are fine, too. Very popular in the mornings for exotic coffees, croissants, pastries. Eat in or take out. Continental breakfast weekdays, brunch Saturday. Closed Sunday. Entrées from $4.75 (L & D). No credit cards.

## GERMAN

***Old Europe,*** 2434 Wisconsin Avenue N.W. (333-7600). (See description under BEST WINE LIST.)

## INDIAN

***Apana,*** 3066 M Street N.W. (965-3040). No mere curry house, this airy and beautiful small restaurant features "classic" Indian dishes. *Samosas,* lamb dishes, breads and chutneys. Dinner only. Open seven days a week. Entrées from $6. AE, CB, DC, MC, V.

***Tandoor Restaurant,*** 3316 M Street N.W. (333-3376). Jack Katyal, a scholar of Indian cuisine, has brought Georgetown the one thing it may have lacked—a *tandoor* oven. As a result, "real" *tandoori* chicken, freshly-baked breads and oven-roasted lamb are yours for the asking, along with Indian beer in outsized bottles. Ask ahead for "butter chicken" and don't by-pass the rice dishes. The place is bigger than it looks; it has a second-floor dining room. Open seven days a week. Saturday and Sunday an Indian brunch is served from noon until 3 P.M. Entrées from $2.75 (L), $4.50 (D). DC, MC, V.

***Maharaja,*** 1639 Wisconsin Avenue, N.W. (338-4692). Also owned by Jack Katyal. No *tandoor* oven, but a fine representation of Indian cuisine nonetheless. Open seven days a week. Entrées from $1.50 (L), $3.25 (D). AE, DC, MC, V.

## ITALIAN

***Cantina d'Italia,*** 1214A 18th Street N.W. (659-1830). Small, cozy basement room with outsized portions of special dishes, and unusual wines described at tableside by the owner. Joseph Muran de Asserto (who answers with pleasure to Joseph) was the first to introduce Washington to Northern Italian cuisine. His favorite region is Piemonte, though the recipes are as likely to be Joseph originals. Distinctive pastas and salads. Closed Saturday and Sunday. Entrées from $5.95 (L), $7.50 (D). AE, CB, V.

***Tiberio,*** 1915 K Street N.W. (452-1915). Imaginative Italian menu (mostly Northern) and wine list presented in a stylish, modern room. Elegant surroundings and service. Giulio Santillo, who came from Italy via Tiberio of London, runs the show. The roses in the dining room are fresh, so is nearly everything in the kitchen. Try *agnolotti* in cream, daily fish or veal specials, desserts. Saturday, dinner only. Closed Sunday. Entrées from $6.50 (L), $10.50 (D), AE, CB, DC, MC, V.

***A.V. Ristorante,*** 607 New York Avenue N.W. (737-0550). The city's closest approach to New York's Little Italy type of restaurant is in a run-down but still very much alive section between midtown and Union Station. What to eat? "White" pizza or red, linguine with clams, any fresh vegetable. What to drink? The house wine. Service can be slow and surly. The best way to dine successfully is to go in a group and order family-style. Regular customers just walk into the kitchen and consult with the chef. Menu is the same for lunch and dinner. Open until 2 A.M. Closed Monday. Entrées from $2.25 (L), $3 (D). AE, CB, DC.

## JAPANESE

***Japan Inn,*** 1715 Wisconsin Avenue N.W. (337-3400). Not part of a chain, this is a locally owned version of the popular Japanese dining formula: tabletop steak and chicken cookery at a high table, or traditional poached-in-broth meals at a low table. The setting is restrained and handsome. Food quality and showmanship are first rate. A *tempura* bar, too. Closed Sunday. Entrées from $4.50 (L), $8.50 (D). AE, DC, V.

***Samurai Sushi-ko,*** 2309 Wisconsin Avenue N.W. (333-4187). Authentic in its small size and minimal décor, this narrow *sushi* house on Wisconsin Avenue north of Georgetown draws customers from the Japanese Embassy. Quality varies but usually the fish is attractively prepared and quite good. Saturday and Sunday, dinner only. Closed Monday. Entrées from $2.50 (L & D). No credit cards.

## LATIN

***El Caribe,*** 1828 Columbia Road N.W. (234-6969), 3288 M Street N.W. (338-3121). The Columbia Road original is small and cozy. The Georgetown branch is larger and more expensive, with a Spanish influence on the menu. At both places you will find dishes of various Latin American countries. Preparations involving squid, tripe and tongue are worthy of consideration. For the less adventuresome, roast pork, chicken and the indispensable rice and black beans are available. Both El Caribes are open seven days a week until 11 P.M. Entrées from $3.50 (L), $4.50 (D). M Street from $5.25 (L & D). AE, CB, DC, MC.

***Omega,*** 1856 Columbia Road N.W. (667-9600). The success of Omega is as easy to explain as rice and beans. Rice and black beans and other native Cuban foods are available in generous quantity for little money. Pork and chicken entrées are the logical choices along with beer from Mexico. Nothing about the décor will distract you from your meal. At night there probably will be a line waiting. Don't stroll in the surrounding area. Take a taxi. Closed Monday. Entrées from $3.50 (L & D). AE, CB, DC, MC.

## MIDDLE EASTERN

***Calvert Café,*** 1967 Calvert Street N.W. (232-5431). Here one finds *couscous, kibbe,* stuffed eggplant and other culinary wonders from the Middle East, compliments of a gifted woman known as Mama Ayesha. Not even redecoration and the exotic tones of Arabic music on a juke box can erase the impression of a down-at-the-heels, very informal neighborhood bar. Every few years, though, Mama's is rediscovered by the Georgetown cocktail party crowd and enjoys a brief season as an "in" place. Near the Shoreham and Sheraton-Park hotels. Open seven days a week. Entrées from $4 (L & D). No credit cards.

## THAI

***Thai Room,*** 5037 Connecticut Avenue N.W. (244-5933), 527 13th Street N.W. (638-2444). One of the liveliest Asian cuisines has found a receptive audience on upper Connecticut Avenue, not far from Maryland. The 13th Street branch, awkwardly superimposed on what was a gaudy Italian restaurant, is convenient to the Treasury and Justice Departments. Begin your exploration of the menu with lemon-grass soup, taste some *saté* or spiced fish patties and perhaps a curry. Eat the beef with green chilis—a good dish—with care. Those little green strands aren't scallion tops, they're dynamite! Service can be painfully slow. Closed Sunday. Entrées from $2.95 (L & D). DC, MC, V.

## VIETNAMESE

***Vietnam Georgetown,*** 2934 M Street N.W. (337-4536). At the Eastern gateway to Georgetown, in what once was a Greek pizza parlor, this tidy café does a good job of pleasing State Department Asia hands with dependable food at moderate prices. The spring rolls are a treat; so are beef or pork on a skewer, or any pork dish for that matter, and marinated chicken. If it suits your mood, and if you like the flavor of fresh coriander, try a soup. Open seven days a week. Entrées from $2.75 (L), $3.15 (D). No credit cards.

# SPECIALTY COOKING

## HAMBURGER

***Clyde's,*** 3236 M Street N.W. (333-0294). Draft beer, checkered tablecloths, lots of people trying to discover what constitutes a "Georgetown type." Ask that the burger be cooked from scratch. Multiple toppings. An omelet room, too. Open until 2 A.M., five days a week, until 3 A.M. Friday and Saturday. Jacket and tie required. Entrées from $3.50 (L), $4.25 (D). AE, MC, V.

## SEAFOOD

***Harvey's,*** 1001 18th Street N.W. (833-1858). Red and black décor and dim lighting are minuses, but there is she-crab soup, panned oysters, rockfish (Chesapeake Bay striped bass), red snapper, crab and beer in frosted mugs. Open seven days a week. Closed Sunday, July through August. Entrées from $4.50 (L), $8.75 (D). AE, CB, DC, MC, V.

## SOUL

***Florida Avenue Grill,*** 11th and Florida N.W. Near Howard University. Counter and booth service. Enormous portions of assertively seasoned food, including scrapple on the breakfast menu, ham hocks, smothered chicken and ribs, greens. Corn muffins and peanut pie. No telephone. Take a taxi. Breakfast all day. Open 6 A.M. to 8 P.M., seven days a week. Entrées from $1.75 (B, L & D). No credit cards.

## STEAK

***Palm,*** 1225 19th Street N.W. (293-9091). The successful New York formula of steak and lobster, both large and good, has worked here, too. Salads, potatoes, and creamed spinach are worthwhile. Some Southern Italian-style dishes as well. Divide orders to offset gargantuan portions. Closed Sunday. Entrées from $6 (L), $8.25 (D). AE, CB, DC, MC, V.

***The Golden Ox,*** 1615 L Street N.W. (347-0010). This is a barnlike place, dimly lighted and short on charm. But steak-lovers should know it is a sister to the famed Kansas City Golden Ox and serves steaks of comparable quality. At $10.45, the Kansas City strip is the best steak buy in town. Open seven days a week. Entrées from $3.25 (L), $4.15 (D). AE, DC, MC, V.

## VEGETARIAN

***Golden Temple of Conscious Cookery,*** 1521 Connecticut Avenue N.W. (234-6134). A wide variety of vegetarian dishes and fruit-based beverages. Service, by white-garbed men and women, is vague but cheerful. Pristine surroundings. Music sometimes. Closed Sunday. Soup and sandwich ($3.50), entrées around $5.95 (L & D). No credit cards.

# FOR INDIVIDUAL NEEDS

## IF YOU HAVE TIME FOR ONLY ONE MEAL

***Le Lion d'Or,*** 1150 Connecticut Avenue N.W. (296-7972). (See description under BIG DEAL/WORTH IT.)

## BEST HOTEL MEAL

***Sheraton-Carlton,*** 16th and K Street N.W. (ME 8-2626). Go there for the luncheon buffet, Monday through Friday. Open seven days a week. Buffet $8.25 Monday to Friday; buffet Sunday, $12.50. AE, CB, DC, MC, V.

## RESTAURANT NEAR AIRPORT

***Chez Froggie,*** 509 23rd Street, Arlington, Va. (979-7676). It's a pleasantly low-key spot, only five minutes from National Airport with the reasonable prices adding to the charm. Seafood and grilled meats are consistently good. Menu is more restricted, less ambitious at lunch. While Chez Froggie is often crowded, the 500 block of 23rd Street is a miniature restaurant row. (The Hungarian **Chardas,** among others, is at hand for the time-pressed traveler.) Saturday, dinner only. Closed Sunday. Entrées from $3.50 (L), $6.50 (D). MC, V.

## BUSINESS BREAKFAST

***The Carvery,*** Mayflower Hotel, 1127 Connecticut Avenue (347-3000). J. Edgar Hoover lunched here regularly, so you know it's safe to talk. The room has been renovated, but some vestiges of a classic hotel breakfast remain, including hot oatmeal, waffles, corned beef hash, blueberry muffins. Open seven days a week, from 7 A.M. Entrées from $2.45 (B). AE, DC, MC, V.

***Twig's,*** Capital Hilton, 16th Street between K and L streets, N.W. (393-1000). This dining room is light, bright and modern, with comfortable chairs and good-sized tables, a change of pace for hotels in the nation's capital. You can watch traffic flow toward—if not into—the White House as you dine on a three-egg omelet, creamed chipped beef or—a Twig's twist—pancakes wrapped around maple butter. Open seven days a week, from 7 A.M. Entrées from $2 (B). AE, CB, DC, MC, V.

## BUSINESS LUNCH

***Paul Young's,*** 1120 Connecticut Avenue N.W. (331-7000). Elaborate décor and service in an ornate dining room. American and Continental dishes. Crab-claw cocktail, cold seafood platter, dessert cart. Closed Sunday. Entrées from $3.95. AE, CB, DC, MC, V.

## FAST, GOOD FOOD/BREAKFAST

***U.S. Senate Cafeteria.*** Closed Saturday and Sunday. From 7:30 A.M. No credit cards.

## FAST, GOOD FOOD/LUNCH

***Le Souperb,*** 1221 Connecticut Avenue N.W. (347-7600). Four main-dish soups, sandwiches, beer and wine by the glass. Closed Saturday and Sunday. From $2.65. No credit cards.

## FAST, GOOD FOOD/DINNER

***The American Café,*** 1211 Wisconsin Avenue N.W. (337-3600) and 227 Massachusetts Avenue N.E. (547-8200). (See description under AMERICAN.)

***The Bread Oven,*** 1220 19th Street N.W. (466-4264). (See description under FRENCH.)

## BEST WINE LIST

***Old Europe,*** 2434 Wisconsin Avenue N.W. (333-7600). A wide range of German wines to match the cuisine, with some good French and American bottles as well as a choice of beers. Paintings and beer steins decorate the walls. Piano music, friendly waitress service. An emphasis on seasonal foods, including game. Moderate prices make it popular with families. Open seven days a week. Entrées from $2.75 (L), $4.95 (D). AE, CB, DC, MC, V.

***Le Lion d'Or,*** 1150 Connecticut Avenue N.W. (296-7972). (See description under BIG DEAL/WORTH IT.)

***La Chaumière,*** 2813 M Street N.W. (338-1784). A dreamer's vision of a French country restaurant, with an open fireplace that glows in season. The list created for a wine bar on the second floor has a fine European selection divided into low-, medium- and high-price groups. The menu is a combination of bistro and bourgeoise cuisines with pâtés, stews and once-a-week *couscous* its strongest points. Saturday, dinner only. Closed Sunday. Entrées from $3.50 (L), $7.25 (D). AE, MC, V.

## BEER

***Brickskeller,*** Marfax Hotel, 1523 22nd Street N.W. (293-1885). An emporium dedicated to beer and darts that occupies two floors in an old hotel just east of Rock Creek Park and Georgetown. There are more than 400 brands of domestic and foreign beers available. The owners claim it is the nation's largest selection. The bar is downstairs. Upstairs one finds a series of well-used, well-lighted dart boards. There is league competition some weekday nights. Food is incidental, but burgers and French fries are available. Open until 2 A.M., seven days a week. AE, CB, DC, MC, V.

## FOR DRINKS

***The Foundry,*** 1050 30th Street N.W. (337-1500). Almost everything but the setting—beside the historic C&O Canal in Georgetown—appears to have come from California. Light wood and suntans abound, year round. The ground level is for drinking and "light" dining (full meals on the second level). For nibblers: oysters and clams, a selection of vegetables with dip, cheese board, seven variations on the hamburger theme, salads, homemade desserts.

Food served from 11:30 A.M. till midnight, seven days a week. Sandwiches from $2.75, entrées from $6.95 (D). AE, MC, V.

## RESTAURANT WITH MUSIC

***Blues Alley,*** rear of 1073 Wisconsin Avenue N.W. (337-4141). The menu is on a record and the music comes from live performers with a jazz bent. Half a dozen entrées including steak and a daily fish special for a fixed price of $15.95. Shows begin at 9 P.M. Cover charge without dinner is $7. Dinner only. Open seven days a week. AE, DC, MC, V.

***F. Scott's,*** 1232 36th Street N.W. (965-1789). Just off the campus of Georgetown University, this beautiful, superbly camp, multilevel club provides vintage 1930's and '40's recorded music and draws patrons whose undergraduate days are well behind them. The French-accented menu is strongest in its desserts, spotty elsewhere. There's a dance floor, but conversation is the favored activity most nights. Open from 6 P.M. until midnight for dinner and until 2 A.M. for drinks Sunday through Thursday; 6 P.M. to 2 A.M. Friday and Saturday for dinner, drinks until 3 A.M. Good for after-theater. Entrées from $4.25. AE, CB, DC, MC, V.

## ROMANTIC

***Torremolinos,*** 2014 P Street N.W. (659-4382). Near Dupont Circle. Brick walls, working fireplace in season. Guitar and flamenco music. Mostly Spanish food, seafood the best bet. Closed Sunday. Entrées from $3.75 (L), $5.25 (D). AE, MC, V.

## LATE-NIGHT SERVICE

***Au Pied de Cochon,*** 1335 Wisconsin Avenue N.W. (333-5440). Authentic bistro feeling, mixed bag of customers. *Rillettes,* pigs' feet cold or hot, casserole dishes. Friday and Saturday until 3 A.M.; until 2 A.M. rest of week. Entrées from $3.45. No credit cards.

***The American Café,*** 1211 Wisconsin Avenue N.W. (337-3600) and 227 Massachusetts Avenue N.E. (547-8200). (See description under AMERICAN.)

## SUNDAY BRUNCH

***Szechuan,*** 615 Eye Street N.W. (393-0130). (See description under CHINESE.) *Dim sum* (a variety of filled dumplings) is offered here from 11 A.M. and you will find lots of Chinese have arrived before you. *Dim sum* from $1.50. AE, V.

***Sheraton-Carlton,*** 16th and K streets N.W. (638-2626). Quite simply, they try harder. Skip the "champagne"—unless you mix it with orange juice; instead search out the homemade breads, most cold-buffet items, the fresh vegetables and the pastry chef's dessert creations. Fresh flowers on the tables and piano music accompany the $14 champagne brunch. Service from 10 A.M. until 2:30 P.M. AE, CB, DC, MC, V.

## SUNDAY-EVENING MEAL

***La Rive Gauche,*** Wisconsin Avenue and M Street (333-6440). This elegant French restaurant serves Sunday evenings at two seatings, 6 P.M. and 9 P.M. Chef Michel Laudier is a classicist: lobster, sweetbreads and beef are foods he fashions well, and he spins superb sorbets. Service is very correct, but not always in proper syncopation. Open seven days a week. Entrées from $8.50 (L), $13.50 (D). AE, CB, DC, MC, V.

***Germaine's,*** 2400 Wisconsin Avenue (965-1185). (See description under ASIAN.)

## FOR TEA

***Palm Court,*** Sheraton-Carlton, 16th and K streets N.W. (638-2626). A beautifully refurbished lobby setting, plus a fine selection of hand-crafted pastries, "down the street" from the White House. From 3 until 5 P.M. every day of the week, tea, including cakes and strawberries with cream, is served for $5.50. AE, CB, DC, MC, V.

## FOR FAMILIES WITH CHILDREN

***Sholl's Cafeteria,*** 1433 K Street N.W. (783-4133) and ***Sholl's Colonial Cafeteria,*** 1990 K Street N.W. (296-3065). Happily, nostalgia repopularized old-fashioned cafeterias—the ones that actually make the food they sell—while Sholl's is still around. Among the high points are the crab cakes at the 1433 K branch served at Friday lunch and the homemade cakes and pies served anytime. Open for breakfast from 7 until 10 A.M., lunch from 11 A.M. to 2:30 P.M., and dinner from 4 to 8 P.M. The 1433 K branch is closed Sunday. Breakfast begins at 20 cents an egg, lunch and dinner entrées from 90 cents (for liver). No credit cards.

## COUNTRY INN

***Auberge Chez François,*** 332 Springvale Road, Great Falls, Virginia (703/759-3800). Near the Potomac River, 30 minutes' drive from downtown. A lovely country restaurant with décor and menu reflecting the Alsatian heritage of the owner. Food choices range from the rich and hearty (pâté and a splendid *choucroute*) to the light and delicate (crab mousse and salmon soufflé). Reservations essential. Dinner only, Saturday and Sunday. Closed Monday. Complete lunch from $5.50; complete dinner from $11.50. AE, MC, V.

# IN THE SUBURBS

## ALEXANDRIA

***Taverna Cretekou,*** 818 King Street (548-8688). Agreeable Greek food in an equally agreeable setting. Closed Monday. Entrées from $4 (L), $6.25 (D). AE, V.

## ARLINGTON

***Chalet de la Paix,*** 4506 Lee Highway (522-6777). Part Swiss, part French with classic dishes. The cooking is often the equal of that in the fine restaurants across the river. Due in part to Virginia regulations, the wine list is skimpy. Closed Monday. Entrées from $6.50 (L), $8.50 (D). AE, CB, MC, V.

## BETHESDA

***The Pines of Rome,*** 4709 Hampden Lane (657-8775). Southern Italian food, highly original cooking. White pizza, fried zucchini, fresh fish. Closed Monday. Entrées from $3.50 (L & D). AE, CB, DC, V.

***China Garden,*** 4711 Montgomery Lane (657-4665). The menu jumps from province to province, but the kitchen's heart is in Canton. Whole fish in black bean sauce is recommended, along with lemon chicken and Chinese broccoli. Saturday and Sunday they serve excellent *dim sum.* Open seven days a week. Entrées from $4.50 (L), $5.50 (D). AE, MC, V.

## SILVER SPRING

***Crisfield's,*** 8012 George Avenue (JU 9-1306). An old-fashioned, no-frills seafood house with a top-flight raw bar. Beer. No admission after 9:15 P.M. weekdays, 10:15 P.M. Friday and Saturday. Closed Monday. Entrées from $6.50 (L & D). No credit cards.

## WHEATON

***Tung Bor,*** 11154 Georgia Avenue (933-3687). The décor of plastic Polynesian—inherited from a previous occupant—lingers on, but this sizable restaurant is real Chinese during the week and real Hong Kong on Saturday and Sunday. Then the area's most extensive and best *dim sum* selection is wheeled about from 11:30 A.M. until the carts finally disappear in mid-afternoon. Open seven days a week. Entrées from $2.95 (L & D). MC, V.

***Siam Inn,*** 11407 Amherst Avenue (942-0075). A tiny storefront on a side street holds the key to understanding what's behind the flame-thrower in Thai cuisine. Lemon grass, fresh coriander, chiles and other spices and herbs are used with rare sophistication. Order satés, fish puffs, noodle dishes, chicken or pork, or whatever the friendly, helpful staff guides you toward. Open seven days a week. Entrées from $3.50 (L & D). MC, V.

# MARKETS

## GIFT FOODS

***Georgetown Coffee Tea & Spice,*** 1330 Wisconsin Avenue N.W. (338-3801). Coffees from around the world and other imports as well. Closed Sunday. AE, MC, V.

***The French Market,*** 1632 Wisconsin Avenue N.W. (FE 8-4828). Pâtés, sandwiches and imported French products. Closed Wednesday afternoon. No credit cards.

## GIFT WINES

***Mayflower Wines & Spirits,*** 1733 DeSales Street N.W. (628-5670). Full range of French wines, brandies; some rare Chiantis and vintage olive oil. Closed Sunday. No credit cards.

# Hungry for News?

Restaurants are living things. Almost a third of the listings in this edition of *Where to Eat in America* have changed since our original volume was published.

Our next edition, like this one, will be based on a total resurvey of each city. In the meantime, if you would like to know the latest restaurant news, or if you want to learn about the great restaurant that just lost its chef or about the new toast of the town, or if you want to learn of some exceptional restaurants in the countryside or in towns not surveyed in this volume, there's an exciting new publication just for you.

We are offering our readers three issues of *Restaurant Update,* a newsletter supplement to *Where to Eat in America*. It will be published in April 1980, November 1980 and April 1981, and it will be sold exclusively to subscribers. Send your name and address, along with the names and addresses of those for whom you wish gift subscriptions, to *Restaurant Update,* c/o WHERE TO EAT IN AMERICA, P.O. Box 1121, Ansonia Station, New York, N.Y. 10023. Each subscription is $7. Make checks payable to Cooks' Catalogue, Inc.

# WHERE I ATE IN AMERICA

Use this space to let us know your reaction to restaurants and food shops in this guide, or to make nominations for inspections for future editions. Feel free to include selections in any major city (or its environs) that is not covered in this guide. More detailed communications by letter will be welcome as well.

***Mail to:*** WHERE TO EAT IN AMERICA, P.O. Box 1121, Ansonia Station, New York, N.Y. 10023

CITY: ______________________________

RESTAURANT OR SHOP: ______________________________

RATING (please circle the number that best applies):

1 – No longer belongs in the guide
2 – Satisfactory, but food quality now lags
3 – Food quality high, but service was lacking
4 – Outstanding food and service
5 – Best of its kind in the city
6 – Not to be missed
7 – One of the best I've been to

COMMENTS: ______________________________

# ABOUT THE EDITORS

## WILLIAM RICE

WILLIAM RICE has written about food and wine in this country and in Europe as Executive Food Editor of the *Washington Post.* Raised in upstate New York, he holds degrees from the University of Virginia, Columbia University's Graduate School of Journalism and Le Cordon Bleu in Paris.

## BURTON WOLF

BURTON WOLF is one of the world's leading authorities on the selection and care of cooking equipment. He was the principal architect for the original *Cooks' Catalogue* and was co-editor of *The Garden-to-Table Cookbook.* Mr. Wolf is a regular contributor to numerous newspapers, magazines and television shows throughout the United States.